THE TRAGIC CONFLICT
The Civil War and Reconstruction

By William B. Hesseltine

THE TRAGIC CONFLICT

The Civil War and Reconstruction

SELECTED AND EDITED WITH INTRODUCTION
AND NOTES BY

William B. Hesseltine

GEORGE BRAZILLER

NEW YORK 1962

Copyright © 1962, by William B. Hesseltine

Published simultaneously in Canada by Ambassador Books, Ltd., Toronto

All rights reserved.
For information, address the publisher,
George Braziller, Inc.
215 Park Avenue South, New York 3

Library of Congress Catalog Card Number: 62-9693

First Printing

Printed in the United States of America

44078

Grateful acknowledgment is made to the
Louisiana State University Press for permission
to reprint Chapter 5, which appeared in THREE AGAINST LINCOLN
edited by William B. Hesseltine. Copyright © 1960 by Louisiana State University Press

Preface

The Civil War and Reconstruction, asserts William B. Hesseltine, "consti-tute the central epoch in American history." A full century afterwards, the titanic struggle between the Blue and the Gray has grown rather than diminished in its grip on the popular imagination, and the drama of Recon-struction has lost none of its romantic appeal. In the myths and realities of the old plantation South, of the brothers' war, and of the villainies of Recon-struction there are inexhaustible stores of lore for literature and history. The heroes and villains and their exciting deeds have long since assumed the legendary proportions of an *Iliad* for Americans.

The Civil War was indeed the last of the romantic wars, but to view it only in terms of Pickett's charge at Gettysburg or Morgan's sweeping cavalry forays is to indulge in escapism and to miss its vital significance for the present generation. It was the first of the modern wars as well, "the first of the industrial wars, the first of the total wars," and it offers serious mili-tary lessons. Further, it was, as Hesseltine says, a fiery crucible in which the old nation was melted down, and out of which modern America was poured. Out of this foundry came a new nationalistic United States. Out of it came an end to slavery, but also an unwillingness to grant full equality to the former slaves. Out of it came bitterness and animus so slow to evapo-rate that they still motivate some men's actions a hundred years later.

If one would understand the United States in the latter half of the twentieth century, one must study the larger aspects of the Civil War and Reconstruction. It is in these dimensions that Hesseltine has assembled this volume. In his lucid introduction—the distillate of decades of brilliant lecturing—he sets forth and weighs conflicting theories concerning the causes of the war, its nature, and its effect. These are theories that historians debate vigorously and are likely to continue to debate for generations to come. Hesseltine himself is the originator of one of the most widely accepted of these theories, that Northern businessmen, failing to realize anticipated profits in the South, helped to bring an end to Reconstruction.

The anthology, a fascinating assemblage of contemporary accounts covering economic, social, and intellectual history, as well as military events, should lead readers to a better understanding of that epoch and their own. They will find, too, that there was as much excitement behind the lines and after the war as there was on the battlefields. This is a vital survey of one of the greatest of American adventures.

FRANK FREIDEL

Contents

8

PART VII   RECONSTRUCTION 437

Introduction

William B. Hesseltine

From 1861 to 1865, the people of the United States were engaged in a Civil War. The years of the conflict and the dozen years of reconstruction which followed constitute the central epoch in American history. In terms of human lives uprooted, in casualties suffered, in economic costs, and in its consequences, it was the greatest war in which the American people have ever been involved.

In numbers alone, in proportion to the population, it was America's most costly war. During its four years—in a total population of less than 35,000,000 and a military population of 5,665,000—over 3,000,000 men were under arms. Of the 35,000,000 total, 26 were in the North, and 9—including 4,000,000 slaves—were in the South. The military populations were, respectively, 4,600,000 and 1,065,000. More impressive still was the casualty list. Out of the 2,750,000 soldiers in the North, 360,000 were killed or died of wounds and disease, while the Southerners lost 358,000. Adding the estimated total wounded, and dying of disease in the South, the figure for the United States as a whole was over 1,000,000—1,000,000 out of a total army of little more than 3,000,000.

The financial cost of the war was tremendous. Its direct costs were $4,475,000,000, while pensions and interest on the debt added other millions, reaching a grand total of $17,000,000,000. And these were but the cash figures. The extent of losses of earning power, of services diverted from production to destruction, of loss of material equipment, was beyond estimate. And certainly to be included were those social costs which can best be described as the consequences.

The consequences were far-reaching. From the ashes of the Civil War arose a new social order and a new economic regime. The dominance of the American economy passed from the hands of the agricultural class to the rising industrialists, and the institution of slavery disappeared while the new problem of the Negro took its place. Along with the economic and the social consequences came a constitutional change, an alteration of the nature of the American political and constitutional structure. In the crucible of war a new nation was formed.

In the light of the consequences, men have attempted to search the years before the war to find its causes. Hindsight is the peculiar gift of the historian, and historians have been prone to find the causes of the war in the consequences. Since a new nation emerged from the conflict, they have attempted to find the drive toward the nation as the cause.

Hindsight, indeed, reveals that the *results* of the Civil War were foreshadowed in many facets of American life. There was little in the America of 1880 that had not been foreshadowed in 1850. After the Civil War, the United States became an industrial nation; the institution of slavery gave way to other forms of labor. A new nation took the place of the Old Federal Union—and yet not one of these results was solely attributable to the war itself.

Perhaps, indeed, the Civil War was a desperate effort to stave off the inevitable. Certainly the Southern States, seceding from the Union, predicted a set of dire consequences to follow from the tendencies of the time, and sought to avoid the consequences which they foresaw. In seceding, the Southern States lost much and sacrificed much—the values of the Union, the South's share in the western territories of the United States, its share in the national offices. It lost them all in an effort to evade the trend of the age.

On the other hand, the war, even if it did not cause some of the things that happened later, hastened their occurrence and diverted the methods of social evolution from peaceful means to a reliance on force. It left a legacy of hate and suspicion which other solutions might not have brought about.

All this—the size of the conflict, the numbers, the casualty lists, the costs, and the consequences—may add up only to confusion. Repeatedly, for almost a century, Americans have been reviewing the background of the war, sometimes in scholarship, and sometimes in controversy, in an attempt to resolve the problem, and to offer an explanation. The confusion is illustrated by the various names which have been applied to, or suggested for, the conflict.

It has been described as a Brothers' War, as a War for Southern Independence, as a Second American Revolution involving a clash between agriculture and industry, and as a struggle between the forces of freedom and aristocracy. Each definition has had its devotees; each has its defects; and each is, in some measure, true.

Most popular of the modern explanations of the Civil War is that it was a mighty conflict between the forces of a rising industrialism and a declining agricultural system. The eleven states that seceded from the Union and established the Southern Confederacy were dominated by agriculture, and the secession was led by the cotton-growing states of the lower South. In a sense, the Civil War was the first great industrial war, the first war in which the industrial potential of the victor determined the outcome.

For a long time, there had been conflicts over policy between the representatives of agriculture and of industry. The industrial sections of the country wanted special legislation from the Government, legislation which was opposed by the representatives of the agricultural interests. The industrialists wanted a tariff to protect infant industries. The Southerners, selling their cotton in the markets of Europe and buying goods in Europe, opposed a tariff. The industrialists wanted favorable grants to railroads. The Southerners, who floated their cotton to the sea along the rivers, were not interested in taxing themselves for internal improvements. The Northerners wanted stable credit and banking laws, and the concentration of financial power in Northern cities. Southerners, dependent on a European market, saw no need for financial concentration. The areas of their disagreement were enormous, and had run through the course of American history. And in the end, when the war came, the industrialists seized their opportunity. While representatives of the South were absent, Congress enacted legislation favoring industry—a higher tariff, a national banking act, special subsidy to agricultural education, and grants in aid of railroad construction.

Perhaps the best statement of the industry *vs.* agriculture theme is that of Charles and Mary Beard. After the war, say the Beards, and after the fighting men had left their records,

> ... it was then that the economist and the lawyer, looking more closely on the scene, discovered that the armed conflict had been only one phase, that at the bottom the so-called Civil War, or the War Between the States, in the light of the Roman analogy, was a social war, ending in the unquestioned establishment of a new power in the government, making vast changes in the arrangement of classes, in the accumulation and distribution of wealth, in the course of industrial development, and in the constitution inherited from the fathers. Merely by the accident of climate, soil, and geography was it a sectional struggle. If the planting interests had been scattered evenly throughout the industrial region, had there been a horizontal rather than a perpendicular cleavage, the irrepressible conflict would have been resolved by other methods, and accompanied by other logical defense mechanisms . . .

Further, the Beards continue, it should be called a revolution like the French Revolution.

> Accuracy compels us to characterize by the same term the social cataclysm in which the capitalists, laborers and farmers of the North and West, drove from power in the national government the planting aristocracy of the South.[1]

This, indeed, reflects one approach to the Civil War. It was not one foreign to the thinking of the generation which fought the war. Nothing angered the Southerners more than the fact that the rapidly growing Northern section was outstripping them in all aspects of economic endeavor.

Captain Albert Pike told the New Orleans Commercial Convention of 1855:

From the rattle with which the nurse tickles the ear of the child born in the South to the shroud that covers the cold form of the dead, everything comes to us from the North. We rise from between sheets made in Northern looms, and pillows of Northern feathers, to wash in basins made in the North, dry our beards on Northern towels, and dress ourselves in garments woven on Northern looms; we eat from Northern plates and dishes; our rooms are swept with Northern brooms, our gardens dug with Northern spades, and our bread kneaded in trays or dishes of Northern wood or tin; and the very wood which feeds our fires is cut with Northern axes, helved with hickory brought from Connecticut and New York.[2]

Another Southerner remarked of a Southern funeral that the only thing the South furnished was the corpse.

T. P. Kettell estimated the amounts, running through many millions, that the North took from the South each year. Robert Barnwell Rhett said the South was the best colony to the North that any country ever had. Southern commercial conventions resolved, and re-resolved—and almost came to the point of acting—on the necessity for breaking the economic fetters which bound the South to the North.

But, although the concept that this was a war between agriculture and industry throws light upon the issues involved, it does not answer all of the questions. There were paradoxes: Why did the agricultural sections of the West not support the South? Southern agitators, advocating secession before the war, promised that the agricultural states of the West would follow the South into secession. And during the war, there were Northern opponents of the war who proposed that the Union be broken up into several confederacies—leaving the industrial states, New York and the New England states—in a separate confederation. But the Northern states resisted the agitation within their own ranks and the blandishments of the South, and remained the supporters of the Union.

Still another concept of the Civil War is that it was fought over psychological conflicts. One writer described it as a Brothers' War, a family affair, a difference between members of the same family.

In contrast, and dealing with the same theme, was the idea that the two sections of the country had grown so far apart that they had become, in fact, two separate nations. This is a concept that Southerners found particularly satisfying—but Northerners, too, have insisted that the psychology of the two peoples had effectively separated them. Southern society was, according to these arguments, based on the production of staple crops by slave labor. Northern society was sustained by industrial and commercial employments. Two such forms of society, say the proponents of the theory, could not live under the same government; one or the other must perish, or they must separate.

There was, it is true, much agitation about nationalism. Southern and Northern pundits eagerly developed entirely opposite philosophies of society. While Southerners were boasting of their aristocracy, Northerners were proclaiming their democracy. Southerners read the novels of Sir Walter Scott, and identified themselves with the noble knights and ladies who peopled the novelist's pages. Yet Northerners took Scott's "Covenanters" volumes to their hearts, and pictured themselves as stern and stalwart defenders of righteousness. Southerners developed a philosophy of racial supremacy which served to perpetuate the control of a class. Northerners found that the Puritan dogmas of a society ruled by the elect of God justified controlling society in the interests of men of virtue. Southerners proclaimed themselves the descendants of the Cavaliers who fought for Charles the First. They denounced the Roundhead Puritans of the New England area. As Tennessee's Dr. J. G. M. Ramsey said:

> I conceal from no one my deep conviction that the days of our present Union are nearly numbered. Our people will never again be a unit. The antagonism is too strong, the estrangement is too deep-seated to be reconciled or healed. We are essentially two people—we are not only not homogeneous but we have become radically heterogeneous. The high-toned New England spirit has degenerated into a clannish feeling of profound Yankeeism. Our passions, our tastes, our character, our vices even, are different and dissimilar. Our interests conflict. We are no longer one family. The masses of the North are venal, corrupt, covetous, mean, and selfish. The proud Cavalier spirit of the Huguenot, the probity and honor of the Presbyterian not only remain but have grown and become intensified . . . We are essentially two people . . .[3]

Each section, in fact, attempted to dramatize itself and to vilify the other. To the Northerner, the Northerner was a man of ability, a hardy democrat, partaking of the spiritual heritage of the Puritan and of the pioneer, a man of cunning and of shrewdness in business dealings, of ability in all situations. To the Southerner, the Northerner was a scheming, crooked Yankee, unworthy of trust, prating of democracy, uncouth in manners, corrupt in morals—the product of the intermixture of the scum of Europe. To the Southerner, the Southerner was a man of honor, God-fearing, proud of his family and of his possessions, devoted to his duty, to his subordinates and his slaves. He was gentle in manner, pure in morals, sane and conservative in his philosophy. To the Northerner, the Southerner was a Simon Legree.

But, once again, however much light these contentions throw on the issues, there are defects in the theory. Perhaps the best illustration came in the war itself. The two sides operated under the same constitution, the same laws, the same administrative system. They reacted in the same way to similar situations. They demonstrated that instead of being two nations, they were all Americans. It was, indeed, a Brothers' War.

Closely connected with the concept of the separate nationalities was the concept that the North stood for freedom and democracy. This theme ran through the propaganda of the war, permeated the speeches of the politicians, and found voice in the popular songs. Slavery, the plantation system by which slave labor produced the staple crops of the South—cotton, rice, sugar, and tobacco—was the characteristic institution of the South. Opposition to slavery on humanitarian grounds—and even sometimes on economic grounds—was as old as the institution itself.

In defense of slavery, Southern slaveholders and their apologists had erected an elaborate argument. They contended that slavery was justified by the Bible, approved by God, by the prophets, by Jewish history, by Jesus, and by St. Paul. They argued that they had taken Africans from heathenism and converted them to Christianity. They argued from history that all the great civilizations of the world had been founded on slavery. They contended that, from a sociological point of view, the Negro was better off in slavery than were the factory operatives in the Northern mills. They asserted the inferiority of the Negro to the white and insisted that he was incapable of freedom. They compiled statistics to show that slavery was economically desirable, and that the entire nation profited from it.

Despite the arguments, opposition continued, and early in the 1830's the opponents, demanding abolition, organized to carry on agitation against the moral evil of slavery. The organization passed into the hands of political agitators. Politicians, bidding for the votes of the abolitionists and using attacks on slavery to strike at the interests of the South, took up the cry for the limitation of slavery, for freeing the slaves, and for forbidding the extension of slavery into the western territories.

Southern politicians also found the agitation profitable, and they, in turn, called for Southerners to rally in defense of the peculiar institution. The agitation dominated the politics of the forties and the fifties, bringing about the dissolution of one political party and serious rifts in the ranks of the other. Southerners affected to believe that the election of Lincoln in 1860 presaged the destruction of their property rights in slaves, and that it justified the secession of the Southern States. During the war, the abolitionists brought pressure on Lincoln until he yielded to their demands and used his Constitutional power as commander-in-chief to declare the slaves of rebels emancipated. The abolition of slavery became one of the purposes of the war, changing the nature of the war, but giving emphasis, for the purposes of propaganda, to the allegation that the war was fought between the forces of democracy and those of a slaveholding aristocracy. It was, said New York's Governor William H. Seward, who became Secretary of State in Lincoln's cabinet, an "irrepressible conflict" between slavery and freedom. And Lincoln, in the finest speech in his career, and one of the greatest speeches of all times, declared that the war was a contest to insure that government of the people, by the people, and for the people should not perish from the earth.

But, for all of the moral content, and the high purposes which seemed to be involved in the concept of the Civil War as a struggle of freedom *versus* aristocracy and slavery, the explanation was neither adequate nor

sufficient. The abolitionists, with a few exceptions, were not in favor of the
Negro, and their professed humanitarianism was political and economic
more often than it was emotional. Abraham Lincoln, acclaimed as the Great
Emancipator, was reluctant over freeing the slaves. On the other hand,
despite the propaganda pictures, the South was not a land of great plantations of large slaveholders. The overwhelming majority of the Southerners
were small farmers with no direct interest in slavery. The differences between chattel slavery in the South and wage slavery in the North were more
apparent than real. The capitalists of the Northern counting-houses were
as much aristocrats as the cotton capitalists of the Southern plantations.
Both sides were waging a fight in the name of liberty—and Lincoln's Gettysburg Address might have been delivered just as appropriately by Jefferson
Davis, President of the Confederate States of America. And, too, in the
course of the war, the traditional bases and practices of human liberties
were violated as much in the democratic North as in the aristocratic South.
Whatever its propaganda value before, during, and after the war, the concept of the Civil War as a conflict between aristocracy and democracy,
liberty and slavery, was both unrealistic and inadequate.

There remains one other interpretation of the American Civil War—a
concept which involves a constitutional interpretation. This, too, has been
formalized into titles. Oldest of the names of the American Civil War is the
official title, "The War of the Rebellion." In contrast, Southerners have
often insisted upon the name, first used by Vice-President Alexander
Stephens of the C.S.A., "The War Between the States." Each of these titles
involves an interpretation of both the Constitution of the United States and
the nature of the American Union.

Equally significant with the issues of industry against agriculture, of
freedom against slavery, and of the psychology of contending nations, was
the question of the nature of the American system. The constitutional issue
involved the argument whether the Southern States had the right to secede
from the Union. It involved the doctrine of States' Rights, and stemmed
from the compact theory of the Constitution. By the time of the Alien and
Sedition Acts, in 1798, Thomas Jefferson had applied the compact theory
to the Constitution of the United States. The Union, said Jefferson, was a
compact between the states. The Constitution was the body of instructions
which the states gave to the federal Government. The federal Government
was the creature of the states, and bound to obey the instructions. The
secession of the South, by this theory, was merely the withdrawal of the
states from the compact.

The opposing view was that the Union was older than the states. The
Union had begun before the Revolution, the Congress of the Union had
called the states into being, and the people of the United States, not the
states, were the ultimate sovereigns. From time to time, as circumstances
warranted, each state had asserted the rights of the states as opposed to

the national Government. The states, under the theories of States' Rights, had an obligation to protect the people against the aggressions of the federal Government. It was Alexander Hamilton, in the *Federalist Papers*, who asserted that the state legislatures:

> . . . will always be not only vigilant but suspicious and jealous guardians of the rights of the citizens against encroachments from the federal government, will constantly have their attention awake to the conduct of the national rulers, and will be ready enough, if anything improper appears, to sound the alarm to the people, and not only to be the voice, but, if necessary, the ARM of discontent.[4]

And, a few years later, when Hamilton was one of the national rulers, the Virginia House of Delegates, protesting against one of Hamilton's measures, announced the Doctrine of Sentinelship:

> As the guardians then of the rights and interests of their constituents, as sentinels placed by them over the ministers of the federal government, to shield it from their encroachments, or at least to sound the alarm when it is threatened with invasion, they can never reconcile it to their consciences, silently to acquiesce.[5]

Out of the theory that the states were to guard the liberties of the people, Thomas Jefferson elaborated the constitutional theory of the compact nature of the Union. Jefferson knew that democracy was best served by local governments, and believed firmly in keeping power close to the people. And John C. Calhoun, too, used the doctrine of States' Rights to defend the rights of minorities against the aggressive tendencies of the national government. Although Calhoun's minority was that of the opulent and the conservative, States' Rights was still, in its essentials, a program of the liberals against national concentration and the national Government's threats to liberty. Even when the South seceded, men used the name of liberty to justify their acts. The Missouri *Republican*, on the day that Lincoln called for troops to suppress the rebellion, declared that it was becoming "alas, a question . . . whether our liberties are secured by laws, or whether they are subject to the mere will of despotism."[6]

But the doctrine of States' Rights was not confined to the South. Northerners, too, in 1860, were devotees of States' Rights, and there was no clearcut division in constitutional theory between the sides in the war. In the North States' Rights had been used to protect liberty from national aggression. The personal liberty laws of the Northern states—against which Southerners bitterly protested—were States'-Rights devices to protect the liberty of fugitive slaves and free Negroes in the Northern states. And the Republican Party of 1860, to make the paradox greater, declared that "The Rights of the States . . . must and shall be preserved," and added, "the maintenance inviolate of the rights of the states, and especially the right of each state to order and control its own domestic institutions according to its own judgement exclusively is essential to that balance of powers on which the perfection and endurance of our political fabric depends."[7]

Many Democrats, who had learned their constitutional principles from Jefferson and Calhoun, were in the Republican Party, and Northerners did not want, any more than Southerners did, to surrender the rights of the states. Yet it was in the name of the Union that Abraham Lincoln called for the militia after the Confederates had fired on Fort Sumter. And steadily, throughout the war, the forces of nationalism battled the doctrines of States' Rights in the North. Among the forces of nationalism were the advocates of a high protective tariff, of a national banking system, of government subsidies to a Pacific Railroad, whose interests could be better served by a strong national government. Steadily, throughout the war, the President, the swollen bureaucracy, and the representatives of these business interests, battled against States' Rights. In the process they called upon the doctrines of democracy, appealed to a hatred of aristocracy, wept bitter tears over the plight of Southern slaves, and formulated new dogmas to national supremacy. In the end they created a new nation, destroying the Old Federal Union, and with it the rights of the states.

In the process and in the end they destroyed one of the ancient bulwarks of human liberty—the power of the states to protect the people. Perhaps, in the end, there was less liberty in the land than before. It was not, therefore, a War Between the States. It was rather, in its larger aspects, a War Against the States, waged by the national Government on two fronts: against the armed embodiment of States' Rights in the Southern Confederacy, and against the political embodiment of the rights of the states in the North. It ended with the unquestioned supremacy of the Nation over the States.

The American Civil War is not only the greatest war that the United States ever fought, but it is also the central theme of American development. It is, as well, the most popular war in American annals. More books are written about it than about any other event in America. Novels and nonfiction works about the Civil War frequently appear—more frequently perhaps than those on any other subject—in the best-seller lists. There are more public parks, more monuments, more place-names commemorating personalities of the Civil War. There are 150 Civil War Round Tables, from Chicago, New York, and Atlanta, to Wiesbaden and London, where hobbyists assemble monthly to discuss the Civil War.

To some extent, the widespread interest in the Civil War has become a form of escapism—for the Civil War was the last war of the modern world about which men could afford to be romantic. It was the last—as it was the greatest—of the old-fashioned wars. It was the last war in which cavalry played an important part, in which the chevalier rode furiously upon his charger after the manner of romantic knights of old. It was the last war in which personal heroism was expected of every man, and in which personal heroics abounded. It was a war of great and fascinating personalities, of men who had not yet been molded into automatons, a war in which generals and soldiers gave free play to their imaginations.

There were personalities like Robert E. Lee, a supreme tactician sadly deficient in the concepts of strategy, who led, rather than commanded, the Army of Northern Virginia. There was Stonewall Jackson, a Presbyterian elder straight from the England of Oliver Cromwell, who prayed without ceasing, hesitated to march his men on the Sabbath, and who would not eat pepper because it made his left leg stiff. There was Phil Sheridan, bandy-legged little Irishman who was a genius as a cavalry leader; and Nathan Bedford Forrest, illiterate slavetrader, who really understood the problems of logistics better than any man on either side, and who once captured a gunboat with a troop of cavalry. There was Ulysses S. Grant, silent, taciturn, stubborn, and decisive, who came back into the army with a reputation for drunkenness, and who grew in an understanding of the strategy of the war. There were George McClellan, the Little Napoleon; John Pope, the braggart; "Fighting Joe" Hooker; gallant, one-legged John B. Hood of Texas. They were colorful characters, romantic figures, and the lore of their deeds has enriched American memory.

Yet the Civil War was more than the last of the old wars, the last of the romantic wars. It was, as well, the first of the modern wars—the first war in which the industrial potential of the victor counted more than the tactics of the generals or the man-power of the armies in determining the outcome. It was the first of the industrial wars, the first of the total wars, and its lessons have been gravely studied by military men and militarists. Out of the Civil War came such innovations as the iron-clad ship, the land mine, the first experiments in aeronautics, the repeating rifle, the scorched-earth policy. But, most of all, out of the Civil War there came to America a new nationalism, a nationalism which rested ultimately upon military force.

In four of its aspects—the raising of the national armies, the control of the armies and the direction of the war, the utilization of geography, and the development of national spirit—the military problems of the Civil War contributed to the making of the centralized American nation.

The first aspect of the military problem which contributed to the growing nationalism was the creation of a national army. At the beginning of the war, the United States had only 18,000 troops in the regular army, scattered over the frontier in small detachments as guards against the Indians. The Americans had been traditionally opposed to standing armies. These were, as the Revolutionary fathers knew, the instruments by which the liberties of a people were overthrown. Americans had been horrified by the European practice of using conscripts, and many an American citizen had come to the new world to escape conscription and army service in European countries. The American relied on the state militias, in which every able-bodied citizen was legally obliged to serve. But the militias had, in most of the states, fallen into disuse until only skeleton establishments existed.

From the beginning it was apparent that the regular army would be useless. Its personnel was not good. Many of the officers—among them the more reliable and capable—resigned in order to go with their states. But the Government solved the problem of the regular army. It ignored it, kept it on garrison duty, and called on the states for the militias. Lincoln's first call for troops was upon the governors of the states. The governors were the commanders-in-chief of the militias. They responded, for the most part, with enthusiasm and sent their troops. But the militia could only be called out for ninety days, and before three months had passed it became evident that the war would last longer, and that no reliance could be placed on successive calls for militia.

In addition, Lincoln called upon the governors for volunteers to serve in the Volunteer Army for three-year enlistments. Answering the call, the governors recruited three-year regiments, assembled them into state-operated camps, drilled them until they were mustered into the federal service. The system worked well. The troops were state troops, raised in the state, commanded by officers appointed by the governors, and bearing state designations. But after a time, as the war demanded more and more men, the governors found their tasks more difficult. The casualty lists mounted—the Confederates were firing real bullets—and the first enthusiasm for the war declined. Governors began to protest at the quotas assigned them, began making excuses for not being able to raise men, began complaining about the failure of the Government to pay the states for their expenses.

By 1863 the governors were having so much difficulty that Lincoln ordered them once more to call out the militia. When this failed, he ordered the governors to draft men into the militia. And, at the same time, Congress passed a conscription law. There were riots in Northern communities, and especially in New York City, but Lincoln suspended the writ of *habeas corpus,* enforced the draft under martial law, and gathered men. In actual fact, conscription did not get men, though it forced the governors to make efforts to raise troops. And, with the threat of the draft hanging over them, and the threat of a federal enforcement of the law, the governors became mere recruiting agents of a national army. Long before, the governors had lost the right to choose officers. The end result was that the army was a national army. The units still bore state designations, still were raised in the states, but they were a national army; and their dead were laid to rest in neat rows in *national* cemeteries.

Along with the decline of the governors' power over the troops went a consolidation of command in the hands of the national Government. In the beginning it seemed as though the governors were going to conduct the war. They raised the troops and then demanded that they be used as they directed. In May, 1861, governors of western states met and demanded that troops be used to protect the Ohio and Mississippi Rivers. The governor of Ohio sent Ohio troops into western Virgina to aid discontented Southerners in their rebellion against Virginia. In 1862, a number of New England governors seriously considered furnishing no more troops to the national army but placing their forces under the command of General Fremont and sending him on an independent campaign against the South. There were times when the Civil War might indeed have turned into, as the Southerners miscalled it, a "War Between the States." But Lincoln took command.

This was only one phase of the nationalization of command. In the beginning the armies were almost independent of the national Government and completely independent of each other. A series of departments confronted the Confederacy along the line between North and South, and each department commander planned and executed movements within his area with only a minimum of mutual co-operation or co-ordination. The war was almost a year old before General Henry W. Halleck was called to Washington to assume command and to co-ordinate action. Even then, Halleck acted for the most part as an information center rather than as the chief of staff. In the meantime, and after Halleck arrived, Lincoln attempted to co-ordinate and to direct the movements of the armies. In the process he displayed a politician's insight but no military genius.

In the early months of the war, as the militia assembled in Washington, Northern newspapers and politicians cried for a movement "On to Richmond." In July, 1861, Lincoln ordered the advance. The army got twenty miles beyond the Potomac, and at Bull Run suffered defeat and panic. Thereafter, realizing the need of discipline and planning, the advance was slowed while George B. McClellan undertook to drill the men, obtain supplies, and plan a campaign. His plans called for an approach against Richmond along the "Peninsula" between the Rappahannock and the James and York rivers. Just as the campaign got under way, Lincoln, fearing that Washington would be left defenseless, withheld some of the troops—enough, so McClellan claimed, to defeat his plans. Perhaps McClellan was right. At any rate, two years later, when the war was won, it was won on the same terrain and by substantially the methods that McClellan had planned.

But Lincoln had no patience with the slow methods of siege. He insisted that Lee's army was the objective of the war, and that the Union armies should destroy the Confederate armies. After the failure of McClellan in the Peninsula, Lincoln placed the command of the Army of the Potomac under John Pope, a braggart and an incompetent. Following Lincoln's idea, Pope advanced again across Virginia, and met defeat on the same battlefield as the First Bull Run. Then—it was the summer of 1862—Lee moved into the North, and Lincoln hurriedly placed McClellan again in command of the armies. McClellan met Lee at Antietam, and after an indecisive battle, Lee turned back. McClellan, having tested Lee's fighting power, and over Lincoln's protest, permitted him to recross the river without striking another blow. Then Lincoln put Ambrose E. Burnside in command. Burnside crossed the river, and Lee defeated him. Then Hooker tried, and failed. And Lee turned north again. This time he got to Gettysburg, where he met defeat by an army under George G. Meade. But Meade, too, permitted him to recross the river. It was, perhaps, the turning point in the war, but Lee's army was not destroyed and remained intact.

Early in 1864, Ulysses S. Grant, already successful in the west, was made lieutenant general, and came to Washington. With his arrival, came co-ordination in all the theaters of the war—and the national armies had a national commander. But Lincoln's idea that the Confederate armies should be destroyed was never of benefit. The war was not a war against the armies—Lee's army was never destroyed. The war was, in fact, a war against places; considerations of geography, of strategy, and of logistics, determined the outcome.

Perhaps, in the sense of the growth of the nation, it was the war which gave proof that the United States was a geographical unit. The Confederacy had no natural frontiers—it was a geographical part of the United States. The Confederate Government attempted to defend a geometrical line. It might have won the war if it had seized the Ohio; pushed up the rivers that flowed into the Ohio and up the Mississippi; effected a hold on the Great Lakes; cut the seaboard off from the West; pushed up the Appalachian highlands; and moved on across to Philadelphia and New York. Instead, it lacked aggressiveness and a sense of strategy. Lee never understood the significance of the West. The one who understood was Ulysses S. Grant, and before him, Winfield Scott. Scott was an able soldier. He was too old and too fat to take the field, but he understood the problem of the war. He proposed to use joint military and naval forces to seize the ports of the South, move up the rivers, use the water-lines as means of transportation, communication and supply. Ridiculed as the "Anaconda Plan," which would squeeze the South as the Anaconda snake squeezes the life from its victims, the plan was rejected. But, after the fumbling of command, and after experience, it was the basic outline of the Anaconda Plan which won the war.

Ulysses S. Grant came slowly to an understanding of the basic strategy of the war. From Cairo, in February, 1862, he attacked Fort Henry on the Tennessee River and Fort Donelson on the Cumberland River. Then Nashville fell. Then Memphis. Meantime, Farragut took New Orleans, and a campaign began against the Mississippi stronghold at Vicksburg, which was taken by the summer of 1863—and the Confederacy was cut in two. Grant prepared to move on Mobile, Pensacola, and Savannah, but the

Chattanooga campaign interfered. He then went to Washington, and for a year, from the spring of 1864 to the end of the war, he directed all activities. He crossed over into the Wilderness, fought Lee successively at the Wilderness, Spottsylvania, and Cold Harbor; then moved his army to the Peninsula and approached Richmond over the ground where McClellan had fought. Meantime, Sherman advanced on Atlanta, stretching his lines of communication, took Atlanta, cut loose from base, marched across Georgia to the sea, and turned northward across the Carolinas. Grant stretched Lee's army to the crucial point and broke through. Lee abandoned Richmond, fell back, was cut off from reaching supplies at Lynchburg or effecting a meeting with J. E. Johnston's army—and surrendered. Johnston surrendered to Sherman.

In all the campaigns, the rivers and the railroads—which were supplementary to the rivers—were important. The blockade and the destruction of the Southern potential in cities, factories, munitions and agricultural production—the sum of total war—brought victory. And with victory came the realization that the nation was a geographical and industrial unit. The military campaigns, on all fronts, served to intensify the nationalization which was going on on economic and political fronts.

And the war had increased the spirit of nationalism. The American people had been engaged in a great national undertaking. The armies were American, and their task was a national task. People looked for the direction of the war to the national Government, followed the national commanders, and shared in a national aim. There was an emotional unity which broke the bonds of particularism.

For a dozen years after Appomattox, the United States faced problems of readjustment. The period has been called the Period of Reconstruction and the word was generally used. But it was not reconstruction; it was in fact a new construction. During those dozen years and for many years following the formal ending of the Reconstruction, a new nation was being reconstituted, shaped, and molded. Out of the Civil War, a new nation had been born.

The period has, like the Civil War itself, been given many names. Allan Nevins has written about these years under the title *The Emergence of Modern America;* G. F. Milton called it the *Age of Hate;* Claude Bowers wrote of it as *The Tragic Era.* It was, perhaps, all of these. Certainly there was tragedy in it, and certainly there was hate—a long and lasting legacy of hate—but there were also the pains of birth, and the eventual emergence of the new nation.

It was, indeed, the whole nation which was "reconstructed." The Civil War was a war against the states in the North as well as in the South, and reconstruction involved both the formerly contending sections.

Many things were involved in Reconstruction. There had been many issues at stake in the Civil War. There was the conflict between the concepts of freedom and slavery, of democracy and aristocracy, and between industrialism and agriculture. There was humanitarianism, and there was also the phony humanitarianism which used high moral sentiments to catch votes for politicians. All were woven into the fabric, intertwined, tangled. There is no clear-cut, simple explanation of the forces involved.

Early writers on Reconstruction saw the picture in plain black and white. They were, for the most part, participants in reconstruction and defenders of the national policies. They found all Southerners black; they found all Northerners—that is, Northern Republicans—pure white. Negroes were, in their picture, black men with white hearts. About the turn of the century, Southerners began to write about Reconstruction. They, too, found the colors black and white. The blacks were the Black Republicans; their Negro allies were black inside as well as out. The Southerners were white.

But the black-and-white pictures do not tell all of the story. There were other colors. There was the gray of men who were good and evil, and of men of varying shades of evil on both sides. There were browns, even after the manner of the brown-shirted legions of Europe decades later. There was red; the red of those who would reform by force, promising a brighter social order—Russian red. And there was much green—the verdant hue of ignorance—the color of those who would make social experiments without benefit of experience. It was altogether a complex, multi-colored picture. There were in all of it various considerations, some political, some economic and social, and many psychological.

One of the first considerations was the question of who would reconstruct the South, the President or Congress. The war had resulted in the unquestioned supremacy of the national Government, but the location of power in the national Government was still open to controversy. During the war, Lincoln had ignored Congress, or bent Congress to his will. When the war was over Congress determined to assert its control. It opposed Lincoln's plans of reconstruction, and after Lincoln's assassination, it turned to fight his successor, Andrew Johnson. In the end Congress defeated Johnson. His enemies won a two-thirds majority to enable them to pass measures over his veto. They impeached him, and only failed by one vote in an effort to remove him from office. Presidential power declined, and Congress dominated the Government for decades.

In the midst of this fight there was a chance that the powers of the states might be revived. Johnson attempted to appeal to the states, and his victory could have resulted in the restoration of the rights of the states. Working against this possibility were the agitations of Johnson's opponents—the radicals in Congress. Thad Stevens, leader in the House of Representatives, contended that the Southern States were conquered provinces. They had seceded; they had established a separate nation; they had been conquered;

and their disposal was subject to the will of the conqueror. Charles Sumner, in the Senate, contended that the states had forfeited their rights and were reduced to the status of territories. The federal Government should govern them, make their laws, appoint their officers, and determine whether they might ever be readmitted to the Union.

Behind these theories lay the hard facts of economics. If the Southern States were restored to political power, they might endanger the economic results of the war. Faced with these considerations, the politicians of the congressional opposition set about to create a new electorate in the South; to disfranchise the Southerners; to enfranchise the Negroes.

But as they did so, they came to confront problems of a social nature. The Negroes were Africans, lacking a background for government. They had been slaves, and slavery was a poor training-ground for freedom. The slave system had secured the Negro laborers; the plantation system has disciplined and marshaled them. If these workers were to return to productivity, new devices of control were needed.

But this involved differences in psychology. Northerners were convinced that Negroes were white men with black skins. All that was needed was to educate them, train them, and they would be exactly like whites. Southerners, on the other hand, believed the Negroes were of a lower order of creation, fit only for labor under discipline, and incapable of education and culture and independent judgment. The conflict was deep-seated. Northerners were too far removed from the problem, Southerners were too close to it. Each lacked perspective; each misinterpreted the other's acts. Neither understood the other. It was not a situation likely to lead to harmony. It was, however, saved in the long run by the American capacity for compromise, for adjustment, for reconciling irreconcilable differences.

There was, however, one other consideration. As a system, the attempt to reconstruct the South in accordance with any of the theories did not succeed. The process that was tried brought serious consequences to its promoters, and failed to achieve its objectives. In the end, the conquerors abandoned it for a system which, if it had been tried in the beginning, might have brought fewer heartaches and headaches, and would have produced more profits.

For the desire for profits, the economic considerations, lay at the base of the attempt, after the war, to make the South over on the Northern model. From the beginning of the Civil War, two elements in the Republican Party struggled with each other over post-war plans for the conquered area. One was the Radicals, who planned to use the war to seize or destroy Southern weath. Economic issues may not have been the cause of the Civil War, but during the war, the economic benefits of victory became apparent and determined the course of reconstruction. The Radicals excoriated slavery, and loudly proclaimed their own devotion to freedom—but at no time did they lose sight of the South's agricultural and mineral resources. A "Free" South would mean better markets for Yankee factories, new investment opportunities, a cheap labor supply for Northern capital. Inspired by the hope of exploiting the South, the Radicals—who were Radicals only in their opposition to a moderate program for the South—insisted upon the unconditional subjugation of the seceded states. Congressman Owen Lovejoy of Illinois wanted to "make a solitude, and call it peace." A senator from Oregon proposed to reduce the states "to the condition of territories, and send from Massachusetts or from Illinois, governors to control them." Michigan's Senator Zach Chandler—who had eagerly welcomed the war because "without a little blood-letting the Union will not be worth a rush"—declared that "A rebel has sacrificed all his rights. He has no right to life, liberty, property or the pursuit of happiness." Venomous old Thad Stevens wanted the South to "be laid waste and made a desert" and "re-peopled by a band of freemen." Senator Lyman Trumbull of Illinois, announced with unctuous piety that "War means desolation, and they who have brought it on must be made to feel all its horrors."[8]

The hate-mongering Radicals, intent upon destroying the South and prating about freedom, established and controlled the Committee on the Conduct of the War, and made it an agency for advancing their predatory cause. The Radicals had no desire for an early peace. A negotiated peace would have defeated their purposes. Their committee set itself to promoting the war, "firing the Northern heart" and fostering the more extreme forms of war psychosis.

Against the Radicals were the moderates who supported Abraham Lincoln. Lincoln had no intention of destroying the South's social and economic system. Essentially a politician, Lincoln's own solution for the problem was political and almost completely devoid of economic details. As a politician interested in a politician's objectives, Lincoln struck a high moral tone which was almost completely devoid of the hate-psychosis of the Radicals. At the beginning, he declared that he only wanted the restoration of the Union. At the end, he was talking about going on without hate, "with malice toward none, with charity for all . . . let us strive on to finish the work we are in . . . to do all which may achieve and cherish a just and lasting peace among ourselves. . . ."[9] In this spirit, he first hit upon the device of using governments-in-exile to bring the states back into the fold. He supported a "loyal" government in Virginia, which was torn with dissensions. And after part of Virginia was made into the new Union state of West Virginia, Lincoln supported the remaining rump government in the hopes that it might be the nucleus about which Virginia could reorganize. When Nashville fell, Lincoln sent Andrew Johnson, a native of Tennessee and a former governor, as military governor. Then in December, 1863, Lincoln announced a program of Amnesty and Reconstruction. He offered to recognize the Southern States whenever ten per cent of the voting population of 1860 took an oath of allegiance. As an expert in the art of manipulating people, Lincoln knew that he could control the states. The patronage and the army could control ten per cent of the voters. Lincoln had already tested his ability to use them.

Three weeks before his Amnesty Proclamation, Lincoln had stood at Gettysburg and announced that the war was a war for democracy . . . that government of the people, by the people, and for the people should not perish from the earth. But at the moment he was speaking, November 19, 1863, there was an election in Delaware, seventy-five miles away, and there, by Lincoln's orders, were troops patrolling the polls, keeping Democrats from voting, and insuring a Republican victory. Less than a month before that, Lincoln had used the army and the patronage to insure that Ohio stay in the Republican column. He knew that he could control the South with his ten per cent plan. And so did the Radicals. And they knew, moreover, that Lincoln's plan would not permit their industrial and financial backers to penetrate the South. It would not even insure the continuance of the national bank system, guarantee payment in gold of bonds bought with greenbacks, keep the protective tariff, or give insurance of further protection and largess to industry. So knowing, the Radicals denounced Lincoln, complained when he vetoed the congressional Wade-Davis Bill for Reconstruction, and marshaled their forces to prevent senators from Lincoln-sponsored state governments from taking seats. And they mourned little when Lincoln was assassinated.

As Lincoln passed from the scene, and the war came to an end, many more Northerners saw opportunities in the South. Cotton speculators followed the advancing federal armies. Treasury agents moved in to seize cotton, horses, rice, sugar. They took over plantations and worked them for the benefit of the Government, and themselves. As the war closed, Yankee businessmen regarded the South as a colony into which they might expand. The New York *Commercial and Financial Chronicle* reported that Northern men "accustomed to business" were hurrying south to promote industrial development.[10] Northerners formed corporations to exploit the South's resources, minerals, coal. Young officers from the federal army, spotting likely opportunities on their military expeditions, rushed back as soon as they were out of uniform, bought plantations or built iron furnaces. The businessmen were not alone in their trek. Their ranks were swollen by missionaries and educators. Northern humanitarian groups sent teachers to open schools for the poor whites and the Negroes, to teach the principles of the victorious democracy. Northern churches hurried to possess themselves of Southern church property. "The true policy," said one religious paper, "is to be on the ground while society is in its chaotic state" in order to free the South from "utter barbarism" and to infuse a "purer, liberty-loving Christianity."[11]

As these people rushed south, the Radicals rejoiced that Abraham Lincoln with his narrow ideas of political reconstruction was not in the White

House. Andrew Johnson was President, and Johnson had none of Lincoln's humanitarianism or moderation. At various times, then and since, Andrew Johnson has been pictured as a drunken dictator or as a plebian knight in armor. Actually, Johnson was thoroughly misunderstood. He was a representative of the artisan and yeoman traditions of America. As such, he had long hated the South's cotton aristocracy and he had refused to follow Tennessee into secession. During the war, he had served on the radical Committee on the Conduct of the War; and he had been as loud and as vulgar as any of his colleagues in his castigation of the South. Treason, he had proclaimed, "must be made odious," and Southern traitors should be "punished and impoverished." No one noticed that he added "their great estates must be seized, and divided into small farms, and sold to honest, industrious men."[12] The Radicals were delighted. The Committee on the Conduct of the War called on the new President. "By the Gods," exclaimed chairman Ben Wade, "we will have no trouble now in running the country."[13]

But the Radicals were soon to learn that there was a fundamental cleavage between them and Johnson. The Radicals represented the industrial classes, the interests of the national banks, the protective tariff, and the subsidized railroads. Their cohorts wanted to exploit the South for the benefit of bankers, investors, and manufacturers. But to Andrew Johnson, on the other hand, the exploiting interests of Northern finance and industry had little appeal. His interests lay with the South's yeoman farmers. He began to organize governments in the South, and the Radicals perceived that he was not of them. They were not interested in reconstructing the South, or for that matter the nation, in the interests and for the benefit of small farmers, laborers, and poor whites. Moreover, these groups would stop the acquisitive activities of the southbound Northern businessmen and, as representatives of agricultural communities, might oppose congressional legislation for the benefit of industrialists. Promptly the Radicals began a campaign against Johnson and proclaimed, with tear-stained hypocrisy, their devotion to democracy and the Negro. "*Our* safety and the peace of the country . . ." said one Radical, "requires us to disfranchise the rebels and enfranchise the colored citizens."[14]

In the fight that ensued between Johnson and Congress, there was a gigantic struggle between the legislative and the executive branches of the government, between Johnson's efforts to re-establish the rights of the states and the forces of national consolidation. But, in the end, the fundamental struggle was over the economic control of the South, and eventually the forces of national consolidation defeated States' Rights, the Radicals wrenched control of reconstruction from the President and established governments under the national authority in the Southern States.

In the midst of the fight, the Radicals created another committee: the Joint Committee on Reconstruction, a fit successor to the Committee on the

Conduct of the War. It held hearings and published reports to prove that the Southerners were still rebels at heart, that they were secretly organizing, that they would re-enslave the Negroes. "The only way for this Government to make these people its friends, is just to keep them down," said the collector at Pensacola. "I would pin them down at the point of a bayonet so close they would not have room to wriggle."[15] And this method they adopted. Military governments took the place of the state governments that Johnson had started. General Phil Sheridan went to New Orleans, removed officers and fired the governor, and replaced them with carpetbaggers. In Virginia, Mississippi, and Texas, the generals turned out the elected governors. Thousands of local officers were replaced by Union men, by carpetbaggers from the North, and by army officers. Military authorities made law through army orders, levied and collected taxes, suppressed newspapers, censored speakers, licensed public meetings, and in one place, made applicants for marriage licenses swear to love, honor, and obey the United States.

This was an assertion of national power. But, in America, such power must rest on the consent of the electorate. In consequence, the Radicals set about to create a new electorate. The military governors disfranchised the white, enfranchised the Negroes, and eventually established governments controlled by scalawags and carpetbaggers, who were elected by Negroes herded to the polls by the army. There followed a carpetbag regime which, for a decade, was an era of unprecedented corruption. In collusion with state officers, Northern corporations looted the South's resources. And this, in time, brought its change. Fundamentally, the defect in the system was that it did not produce profits. The system of pinning the people down with the bayonet until they could not wriggle brought no friends. But it was profits, not friends, they were seeking.

Originally, the Northern people had had a humanitarian interest in the Negro and had regarded the South as a land fit for economic development. But, as the Southern reconstruction system developed, the Northern people began to realize a fundamental conflict between economic and political control. So long as corruption, supported by federal troops, held sway in the South, the conquered region gave no security for Northern investments. Moreover, Northerners began to see that the South was corrupting the nation. Federal troops in the South kept the Republicans in control of the nation, and the national Government was becoming as corrupt as the state governments in the South. In 1868, Grant was elected with a popular majority of 300,000 votes. But 402,000 controlled Negro votes went for him while whites were kept from the polls. In 1872, Grant was re-elected by the Negro votes. In addition, the Southern States sent representatives to Congress who became tools in the hands of big business. The Republican Party, freed from responsibility to the electorate, became rotten. A series of scandals broke on the nation—a "back-pay steal," Credit Mobilier, and a whiskey ring. Eventually the Northern people came to realize that the Southern system was costing more than it was worth.

And big business, too, began to realize that it was playing with fire. So long as the newly freed Negroes in the South remained placid and grateful, they elected, under the military, the right kind of state officers and sent compliant representatives to Congress. But the Negroes of the South began to learn the lessons of politics. Slavery had been a poor school of citizenship, but the freed Negro learned rapidly. Before many years, the Negroes had become dissatisfied with their new guardians. The carpetbaggers, as any Negro could see, took all the better offices. Moreover, economic conditions in the South were rapidly transforming the masses of Negroes into sharecroppers. The black voters compared the return to virtual servitude with the roseate promises that the carpetbaggers had made. Disillusioned, they became dangerous.

One alarmed observer reported on the situation. There were, he estimated, 9,000 illiterate whites in Georgia. If these were added to the Negroes, "so vast a mass of ignorance would be found that, if combined for any political purpose, it would sweep away all opposition the intelligent class could make. Many thoughtful men are apprehensive that the ignorant voters will, in the future, form a political party by themselves as dangerous to the interests of society as the communists of France. . . ."[16] Big business, the intelligent class, might well have been alarmed at the prospect. At the moment, the National Labor Union was organizing a Labor Reform Party among Eastern workers and the Patrons of Husbandry were organizing Granges among Western farmers. If these "ignorant voters" united with the Southern Negroes and poor whites, they might indeed have been "dangerous to the interests of society." This, after all, was the danger that resulted from national centralization. The destruction of the states' powers of resistance removed a bulwark of stability in society. The danger in the nation was that some group might control the national machinery and use its power against the interests of other groups. It was in the face of such a danger that the Northerners abandoned Reconstruction. The solution came by the revival of an old American device: compromise.

The final act of the Reconstruction came in 1877. The disputed election of 1876 was settled with a bargain, a compromise. As part of the bargain, President Rutherford B. Hayes withdrew the federal troops from the South, and with them went the carpetbag governors. The act symbolized the complete failure of the system used to reconstruct the South. It left its heritage—a Bourbon-dominated Solid South in politics, and intensified racial prejudice. The system failed to achieve either its noble humanitarian promises or its hidden predatory purposes. It did, however, mark the return of the United States to an ancient principle: The result of the election of 1876 was compromise.

Compromise was the traditional way in which Americans had settled their differences. There had been many compromises in the sectional struggle: in 1820, in 1833, and again in 1850. It was the failure of a compromise, the refusal to use it, the disappearance of the spirit of compromise that had produced the Civil War.

The Compromise of 1877 was more basic than the others and it has lasted longer. It was both an economic and a political compromise involving a division of power and function in the South. In the New South, the Republicans abandoned the Negro to his Southern master. The Southern Bourbon took control of Southern politics, returned the Negro "to his place" politically and economically. The masters of capital of the North retained control of the South's transportation system, of its credit arrangements, and of its natural resources. But the new settlement had one especial virtue: the Southerners were allowed to manage the property. Southern-born men, with the traditions of the slave system behind them, became the presidents of subsidiary corporations, superintendents of factories, and supervisors of branch offices: vassal owners of heavily mortgaged businesses. The masters of capital were no longer interested in the details of management; they were interested only in profits. In politics the Southerners could be counted upon to keep the Democratic Party conservative. In economics the Southerners kept race antagonism alive, and thereby kept wage levels down. And in return for their services, the Southerners received the rewards of management: the control of their localities, the semblance of power, and the social prestige inherent in being invited to the banquet tables of the mighty.

This was the settlement of Reconstruction. In different terms, it was nation-wide. In the agricultural West, there were local Bourbons to do the bidding and look after the interests of the Eastern owners. The national bank system kept control over the economy of the nation, and directed its profits into the right hands.

The Reconstruction period had completed the work of the Civil War. It had insured that the United States was, as a nation, unified and consolidated economically, and devoted to industrial production. There were problems left and new problems to arise. But they were no longer to be dealt with by states or by communities. The Civil War had made a nation, and the problems were national. War and Reconstruction had forged a nation.

NOTES

1. Charles A. and Mary R. Beard, *Rise of American Civilization,* 2 vols. in 1 (New York, 1930), Vol. 2, pp. 53-54.
2. *DeBow's* Review, Vol. XVIII (1855), p. 524.
3. Dr. J. G. M. Ramsey to L. W. Spratt, April 29, 1858, in William B. Hesseltine, ed., *Dr. J. G. M. Ramsey, Autobiography and Letters* (Nashville, Tenn., Historical Commission, 1954), pp. 94-95.
4. Henry Cabot Lodge, ed., *The Federalist* (New York, 1889), p. 157.
5. Herman V. Ames, *State Documents on Federal Relations, 1789-1861* (Philadelphia, 1900), p. 6.
6. *The Missouri Republican* (St. Louis), April 15, 1861.
7. William B. Hesseltine, ed., *Three Against Lincoln; Murat Halstead Reports the Caucuses of 1860* (Baton Rouge, La., 1960), p. 156.
8. *Congressional Globe,* 37th Congress, 1st Session, pp. 45, 75, 415; *Ibid.* 37th Congress, 3rd Session, p. 1338; Horace White, *Life of Lyman Trumbull* (New York, 1913), p. 171.
9. James D. Richardson, *Messages And Papers of the Presidents, 1789-1897,* 10 vols. (Washington, 1896-1899), Vol. 6, p. 277.
10. *New York Commercial and Financial Chronicle* (New York, August 26, 1865).
11. *The Ladies' Repository,* Vol. XXIV (January, 1864), p. 64.
12. Speech at Nashville, June 9, 1864, quoted in Edward McPherson, ed., *The Political History of the United States of America During the Period of Reconstruction* (Washington, 1871), p. 47
13. Quoted in Claude G. Bowers, *The Tragic Era* (Cambridge, Mass., 1929), p. 7.
14. Benjamin F. Loan to Charles Sumner, June 1, 1865, quoted in George Fort Milton, *Age of Hate* (New York, 1930), p. 215.
15. *Report of Joint Committee on Reconstruction* (Washington, 1866), pt. IV, p. 6.
16. *New York Tribune* (New York, June 21, 1871).

44078

PART I

DISUNION

In the bitter partisan writings of the Civil War epoch, one thing stood out clearly: each side believed itself the victim of a dark and deep-set conspiracy. Thomas Hart Benton, old Jacksonian and ardent expansionist, had little reason to love John C. Calhoun and his Southern cohorts. They had given his idol, Andrew Jackson, consistent opposition, and they had rallied the forces of contention in Benton's own Missouri. The Senator ended his personal reminiscences, Thirty Years View, *with a solemn warning that the slaveholders' conspiracy was on the verge of destroying the Union.*

Like Senator Benton, Edward A. Pollard, a Richmond editor, saw the events of the decade before secession as the culmination of a plot of evil Abolitionists who would destroy not only the rights of the states but the lives and property of Southerners. The true enemies of the Union, thought Pollard, were Northern fanatics and all events of the eighteen-fifties—the compromise of 1850, the struggle for Kansas, the continued agitation of the slavery issue, John Brown's raid, the publication and circulation of Hinton R. Helper's Impending Crisis of the South *and the nomination of Abraham Lincoln—were but the "unveiling of the designs of the Black Republican party." Pollard was, indeed, a severe critic of Jefferson Davis and the conduct of the Confederate Government during the war, but his criticism rested on the belief that the Southern officials did not see the issues clearly, and did not press the Confederate cause with sufficient efficiency and intensity.*

Of the notable events of the decade before the Civil War, two in particular seemed to bring the contending views into sharp focus. The Lincoln-Douglas debates of 1858 and John Brown's raid on Harper's Ferry in 1859 both illustrated the willingness of partisans to attribute only sinister motives to their opponents. Horace White, reporter for the Chicago Tribune, accompanied Lincoln on the campaign which the Springfield

37

lawyer, nominee of the fledgling Republican Party, waged for the Senate seat of Stephen A. Douglas. Lincoln contended that "Stephen and Franklin and Roger and James"—thus throwing together such disparate rivals as Douglas, presidents Pierce and Buchanan, and Chief Justice Taney—had conspired together to create and further the plot to make Kansas a slave state and to expand the area of slavery. White's Press and Tribune *reiterated the charges day after day.*

Another editor, Horace Greeley of the New York Tribune, *had spent twenty years before the war elaborating the details of "the slaveholders' conspiracy." After the war he pieced together in a badly designed but widely read book his version of* The American Conflict. *In it he told at length the story of the martyr John Brown and traced the evolution of Brown's strange actions, from Kansas to his execution at Charlestown. Brave but rash, said Greeley, were Brown's endeavors to "rescue" a race "from a hideous and debasing thraldom."*

By 1860 the insistence of each side that the other was conspiring against it brought a succession of results. Internal quarrels produced a split in the Democratic Party and cleared the way for Republican success. The Republicans assembled in Chicago, rejected the obvious leader of the party, and nominated Lincoln for the presidency. Murat Halstead, young Cincinnati journalist, "covered" all the conventions of that year, and published his accounts in a book, The Caucuses of 1860, *which for a century stood as a model of political reporting. His animadversions on the convention system —"a system of swindling, by which the people are defrauded out of the effective exercise of the right of sufferage"*—called attention to a different order of conspiracy, but one which was lost from sight in the more dramatic events of sectional struggle and the rush to war.*

Events moved swiftly after Lincoln's election. South Carolina and the Gulf States seceded, and before Lincoln's inauguration they had formed the Confederate States of America. In the view of Alexander H. Stephens, Vice-President of the Confederacy, the Southerners were not only exercising their constitutional rights, but were defending the constitution of the Founding Fathers from the victorious conspirators who had seized the apparatus of the federal government. So, too, thought Jefferson Davis, President of the Confederate States. In the years after the war both the President and the Vice-President reviewed the events and the thoughts of 1860-1861. Stephens used the device of Plato's Republic *to set forth his* Constitutional View of the War Between the States, *thereby giving not only a rationalization to succeeding generations of Southerners but donat-*

---

* WILLIAM B. HESSELTINE, ed., *Three Against Lincoln* (Baton Rouge, La., 1960), p. 279.

ing a name which ardent pro-Southerners adopted for the war. Davis told of The Rise and Fall of the Confederate Government *largely to vindicate himself against the charges of such critics as editor Pollard.*

Through the years of the Civil war, from the mounting intensities of the eighteen-fifties to the settlement of the disputed election of 1876, American social thought was dominated by the humanitarian arguments in relation to slavery and the question of the nature of the American constitution. Sectional controversy and war engulfed all aspects of American life and infused each question that was placed before the people. And basic to all thinking about sectional questions, about slavery, freedom, the powers and functions of government, there ran the charges and counter-charges of conspiratorial plots. It was not an atmosphere conducive to objective thinking or balanced judgments.

1

Disunion Movements

Thomas Hart Benton

When the future historian shall address himself to the task of portraying the rise, progress, and decline of the American Union, the year 1850 will arrest his attention, as denoting and presenting the first marshalling and arraying of those hostile forces and opposing elements which resulted in dissolution; and the world will have another illustration of the great truth, that forms and modes of government, however correct in theory, are only valuable as they conduce to the great ends of all government—the peace, quiet, and conscious security of the governed.

So wrote a leading South Carolina paper on the first day of January, 1850 —and not without a knowledge of what it was saying. All that was said was attempted, and the catastrophe alone was wanting to complete the task assigned to the future historian.

The manifesto of the forty-two members from the slave States, issued in 1849, was not a *brutum fulmen,* nor intended to be so. It was intended for action, and was the commencement of action; and regular steps for the separation of the slave from the free States immediately began under it. An organ of disunion, entitled "The Southern Press," was set up at Washington, established upon a contribution of $30,000 from the signers of the Southern manifesto and their ardent adherents—its daily occupation to inculcate the advantages of disunion, to promote it by inflaming the South against the North, and to prepare it by organizing a Southern concert of action. Southern cities were to recover their colonial superiority in a state of sectional independence; the ships of all nations were to crowd their ports, to carry off their rich staples and bring back ample returns; Great Britain was to be the ally of the new "United States South"; all the slave States were expected to join, but the new confederacy to begin with the South Atlantic States, or even a part of them; and military preparation was to be made to maintain by force what a Southern convention should decree. That convention was called—the same which had been designated in the first manifesto, entitled "The Crisis," published in the Charleston *Mercury* in 1835;

THOMAS HART BENTON, *Thirty Years View* . . . 1820-1850, Vol. II (New York, 1957), pp. 780-788.

and the same which had been repulsed from Nashville in 1844. Fifteen years of assiduous labor produced what could not be started in 1835, and what had been repulsed in 1844. A disunion convention met at Nashville, met at the home of Jackson, but after the grave had become his home.

This convention (assuming to represent seven States) took the decisive step, so far as it depended upon itself, towards a separation of the States. It invited the assembling of a "Southern Congress." Two States alone responded to that appeal—South Carolina and Mississippi; and the legislatures of these two passed solemn acts to carry it into effect—South Carolina absolutely, by electing her quota of representatives to the proposed congress; Mississippi provisionally, by subjecting her law to the approval of the people. Of course, each State gave a reason, or motive for its action. South Carolina simply asserted the "aggressions" of the slave-holding States to be the cause, without stating what these aggressions were; and, in fact, there were none to be stated. For even the repeal of the slave sojournment law in some of them, and the refusal to permit the State prisons to be used for the detention of fugitives from service or State officers to assist in their arrest, though acts of unfriendly import and a breach of the comity due to sister States and inconsistent with the spirit of the constitution, were still acts which the States, as sovereign within their limits upon the subjects to which they refer, had a right to pass. Besides, Congress had readily passed the fugitive slave recovery bill just as these Southern members wished it; and left them without complaint against the national legislature on that score. All other matters of complaint which had successively appeared against the free States were gone—Wilmot Proviso, and all. The act of Mississippi gave two reasons for its action:

> *First.* That the legislation of Congress, at the last session, was controlled by a dominant majority regardless of the constitutional rights of the slaveholding States: and,
> *Secondly.* That the legislation of Congress, such as it was, affords alarming evidence of a settled purpose on the part of said majority to destroy the institution of slavery, not only in the State of Mississippi, but in her sister States, and to subvert the sovereign power of that and other slaveholding States.

Waiving the question whether these reasons, if true, would be sufficient to justify this abrupt attempt to break up the Union, an issue of fact can well be taken on their truth: and first, of the dominant majority of the last session, ending September 1850: that majority, in every instance, was helped out by votes from the slaves States, and generally by a majority of them. The admission of California, which was the act of the session most complained of, most resisted, and declared to be a "test" question, was supported by a majority of the members from the slave States: so that reason falls upon the trial of an issue of fact. The second set of reasons have for their point, an assertion that the majority in Congress have a settled purpose to destroy the institution of slavery in the State of Mississippi, and in the other slave States, and to subvert the sovereignty of all the slave States. It is the duty of history to deal with this assertion, thus solemnly put in a legislative act as a cause for the secession of a State from the Union—and to say that it was an assertion without evidence, and contrary to the evidence, and contrary to the fact. There was no such settled purpose in the majority of Congress, nor in a minority of Congress, nor in any half-dozen members of Congress—if in anyone at all. It was a most deplorable assertion of a most alarming design, calculated to mislead and inflame the ignorant, and make them fly to disunion as the refuge against such an appalling catastrophe. But it was not a new declaration. It was part and parcel of the original agitation of slavery commenced in 1835, and continued ever since. To destroy slavery in the States has been the design attributed to the Northern States from that day to this, and is necessary to be kept up in order to keep alive the slavery agitation in the slave States. It has received its constant and authoritative contradiction in the conduct of those States at home, and in the acts of their representatives in Congress, year in and year out; and continues to receive that contradiction, continually; but without having the least effect upon its repetition and incessant reiteration. In the meantime there is a fact visible in all the slave States, which shows that, notwithstanding these twenty years' repetition of the same assertion, there is no danger to slavery in any slave State. Property is timid, and slave property above all: and the market is the test of safety and danger to all property. Nobody gives full price for anything that is insecure, either in title or possession. All property, in danger from either cause, sinks in price when brought to that infallible test. Now, how is it with slave property, tried by this unerring standard? Has it been sinking in price since the year 1835? Since the year of the first alarm manifesto in South Carolina, and the first of Mr. Calhoun's twenty years' alarm speeches in the Senate? On the contrary, the price has been constantly rising the whole time—and is still rising, although it has attained a height incredible to have been predicted twenty years ago.

But, although the slavery alarm does not act on property, yet it acts on the feelings and passions of the people, and excites sectional animosity, hatred for the Union, and desire for separation. The Nashville Convention, and the call for the Southern Congress, were natural occasions to call out these feelings; and most copiously did they flow. Some specimens, taken from the considered language of men in high authority, and speaking advisedly, and for action, will show the temper of the whole—the names withheld, because the design is to show a danger, and not to expose individuals.

In the South Carolina Legislature, a speaker declared:

We must secede from a Union perverted from its original purpose, and which has now become an engine of oppression to the South. He thought our proper course was for this legislature to proceed directly to the election of delegates to a Southern Congress. He thought we should not await the action of all the Southern States; but it is prudent for us to await the action of such States as Alabama, Georgia, Mississippi, and Florida; because these States have requested us to wait. If we can get but one State to unite with us, then we must act. Once being independent, we would have a strong ally in England. But we must prepare for secession.

2

The Road to Disunion

Edward A. Pollard

The American people of the present generation were born in the belief that the Union of the States was destined to be perpetual. A few minds rose superior to this natal delusion; the early history of the Union itself was not without premonitions of decay and weakness; and yet it may be said that the belief in its permanency was, in the early part of the present generation, a popular and obstinate delusion that embraced the masses of the country.

The foundations of this delusion had been deeply laid in the early history of the country, and had been sustained by a false but ingenious prejudice. It was busily represented, especially by demagogues in the North, that the Union was the fruit of the Revolution of 1776 and had been purchased by the blood of our forefathers. No fallacy would have been more erroneous in fact, more insidious in its display, or more effective in addressing the passions of the multitude. The Revolution achieved our national independence, and the Union had no connection with it other than consequence in point of time. It was founded, as any other civil institution, in the exigencies and necessities of a certain condition of society, and had no other claim to popular reverence and attachment than what might be found in its own virtues.

But it was not only the captivating fallacy that the Union was hallowed by the blood of a revolution, and this false inspiration of reverence for it, that gave the popular idea of its power and permanency. Its political character was misunderstood by a large portion of the American people. The idea predominated in the North, and found toleration in the South, that the Revolution of '76, instead of securing the independence of thirteen States, had resulted in the establishment of a grand consolidated government to be under the absolute control of a numerical majority. The doctrine was successfully inculcated; it had some plausibility, and brought to its support an array of revolutionary names; but it was, nevertheless, in direct opposition to the terms of the Constitution—the bond of the Union—which

EDWARD A. POLLARD, "The First Year of the War," *Southern History of the War*, reprinted from the Richmond Corrected Edition (New York, 1863), pp. 11-40.

defined the rights of the States and the limited powers of the General Government.

The first President from the North, John Adams, asserted and essayed to put in practice the supremacy of the "National" power over the States and the citizens thereof. He was sustained in his attempted usurpations by all the New England States and by a powerful public sentiment in each of the Middle States. The "strict constructionists" of the Constitution were not slow in raising the standard of opposition against a pernicious error. With numbers and the most conspicuous talents in the country they soon effected the organization of a party; and, under the leadership of Jefferson and Madison, they rallied their forces and succeeded in overthrowing the Yankee Administration, but only after a tremendous struggle.

From the inauguration of Mr. Jefferson, in 1801, the Federal Government continued uninterruptedly in Southern hands for the space of twenty-four years. A large proportion of the active politicians of the North pretended to give in their adhesion to the States'-Rights school of politics; but, like all the alliances of Northern politicians with the South—selfish, cunning, extravagant of professions, carefully avoiding trials of its fidelity, unhealthy, founded on a sentiment of treachery to its own section, and educated in perfidy—it was a deceitful union, and could not withstand the test of a practical question.

While acting with the South on empty or accidental issues, the "States'-Rights" men of the North were, for all practical purposes, the faithful allies of the open and avowed consolidationists on the question that most seriously divided the country—that of Negro slavery. Their course on the admission of Missouri afforded early and conclusive evidence of the secret disposition of all parties in the North. With very few exceptions, in and out of Congress, the North united in the original demand of the prohibition of slavery in the new State as the indispensable condition of the admission of Missouri into the Union; although the people of Missouri, previous to their application to Congress, had decided to admit within its jurisdiction the domestic institution of the South. The result of the contest was equally unfavorable to the rights of the South and to the doctrine of the constitutional equality of the States in the Union. The only approach that the North was willing to make to this fundamental doctrine was to support a "compromise," by which slavery was to be tolerated in one part of the Missouri Territory and to be forever excluded from the remaining portion. The issue of the controversy was not only important to the slave interest, but afforded a new development of the Northern political ideas of consolidation and the absolutism of numerical majorities. The North had acted on the Missouri matter as though the South had no rights guaranteed in the bond of the Union, and as though the question at issue was one merely of numerical strength, where the defeated party had no alternative but submission. "The majority must govern" was the *decantatum* on the lips of every demagogue, and passed into a favorite phrase of Northern politics.

The results of the acquiescence of the South in the wrong of the Missouri Restriction could not fail to strengthen the idea in the North of the security of the Union, and to embolden its people to the essay of new aggressions. Many of their politicians did not hesitate to believe that the South was prepared to pledge herself to the perpetuity of the Union upon Northern terms. The fact was, that she had made a clear concession of principle for the sake of the Union; and the inference was plain and logical, that her devotion to it exceeded almost every other political trust, and that she would be likely to prefer any sacrifice rather than the irreverent one of the Union of the States.

The events of succeeding years confirmed the Northern opinion that the Union was to be perpetuated as a consolidated government. It is not to be denied that the consolidationists derived much comfort from the course of President Jackson, in the controversy between the General Government and the State of South Carolina that ensued during the second term of his administration. But they were hasty and unfair in the interpretation of the speeches of a choleric and immoderate politician. They seized upon a sentiment offered by the President at the Jefferson anniversary dinner, in the second year of his first term—*"The Federal Union—it must be preserved"*— to represent him as a *"coercionist"* in principle; and, indeed, they found reason to contend that their construction of these words was fully sustained in General Jackson's famous proclamation and official course against Nullification.

General Jackson subsequently explained away, in a great measure, the objectionable doctrines of his proclamation; and his emphatic declaration that the Union could *not* be preserved by force was one of the practical testimonies of his wisdom that he left to posterity. But the immediate moral and political effects of his policy in relation to South Carolina were, upon the whole, decidedly unfavorable to the States'-Rights cause. His approval of the Force Bill gave to the consolidationists the benefit of his great name and influence at a most important juncture. The names of "Jackson and the Union" became inseparable in the public estimation; and the idea was strongly and vividly impressed upon the public mind, that the great Democrat was "a Union man" at all hazards and to the last extremity.

The result of the contest between South Carolina and the General Government is well known. The Palmetto State came out of it with an enviable reputation for spirit and chivalry; but the settlement of the question contributed to the previous popular impressions of the power and permanency of the Union. The idea of the Union became what it continued to be for a quarter of a century thereafter—extravagant and sentimental. The people were unwilling to stop to analyze an idea after it had once become the subject of enthusiasm; and the mere name of the "Union," illustrating, as it did, the power of words over the passions of the multitude, remained for years a signal of the country's glory and of course the motto of ambitious politicians and the favorite theme of demagogues. This unnatural tumor was not peculiar to any party or any portion of the country. It was deeply planted in the Northern mind, but prevailed also, to a considerable extent, in the South. Many of the Southern politicians came to the conclusion that they could best succeed in their designs as advocates and eulogists of what was paraphrased as "'the glorious Union"; and for a long time the popular voice of the South seemed to justify their conclusion.

The settlement of the sectional difficulties of 1850, which grew out of the admission of the territory acquired by the Mexican War, was but a repetition of the "Compromise" of 1820, as far as it implied a surrender of the rights of the South and of the principle of constitutional equality. The appeals urged in behalf of the Union had the usual effect of reconciling the South to the sacrifice required of her, and embarrassed anything like resistance on the part of her representatives in Congress to the "compromise measures" of 1850. South Carolina was the only one of the Southern States ready at this time to take the bold and adventurous initiative of Southern independence. In justice, however, to the other States of the South, it must be stated, that in agreeing to what was called, in severe irony or in wretched ignorance, the "Compromise" of 1850, they declared that it was the last concession they would make to the North; that they took it as a "finality," and that they would resist any further aggression on their rights, even to the extremity of the rupture of the Union.

This declaration of spirit was derided by the North. The anti-slavery sentiment became bolder with success. Stimulated by secret jealousies and qualified for success by the low and narrow cunning of fanaticism, it had grown up by indirection, and aspired to the complete overthrow of the peculiar institution that had distinguished the people of the South from those of the North, by a larger happiness, greater ease of life, and a superior tone of character. Hypocrisy, secretiveness, a rapid and unhealthy growth, and at last the unmasked spirit of defiance, were the incidents of the history of the anti-slavery sentiment in the North, from the beginning of its organization to the last and fatal strain of its insolence and power.

Until a comparatively recent period, the Northern majority disavowed all purpose of abolishing or interfering in any way with the institution of slavery in any State, Territory, or District where it existed. On the contrary, they declared their readiness to give their "Southern brethren" the most satisfactory guaranties for the security of their slave property. They cloaked their designs under the disguise of the Right of Petition and other concealments equally demagogical. From the organization of the Government, petitions for the abolition of slavery, signed in every instance by but a few persons, and most of them women, had at intervals been sent into Congress; but they were of such apparent insignificance that they failed to excite any serious apprehensions on the part of the South. In the year 1836, these petitions were multiplied, and many were sent into both Houses of Congress from all parts of the North. An excitement began. On motion of Mr. H. L. Pinckney of South Carolina a resolution was adopted by the House of Representatives, to refer to a select committee all anti-slavery memorials then before that body, or that might thereafter be sent in, with instructions to report against the prayers of the petitioners and the reasons for such conclusion.

On the 18th of May, 1836, the committee made a unanimous report, through Mr. Pinckney, its chairman, concluding with a series of resolutions, the last of which was as follows:

    Resolved,   That all petitions, memorials, resolutions, propositions, or papers relating, in any way, or to any extent whatever, to the subject of slavery, or the abolition of slavery, shall, without being either printed or referred, be laid upon the table, and that no further action whatever shall be had thereon.

The resolutions were carried by a vote of 117 yeas to 68 nays. A majority of the Northern members voted against the resolution, although there was then scarcely an avowed Abolitionist among them. They professed to be in favor of protecting the slaveholder in his right of property, and yet declared by their votes, as well as by their speeches, that the right of petition to rob him of his property was too sacred to be called in question.

The passage of the "Pinckney Resolutions," as they were called, did not silence the anti-slavery agitation in the House. In the month of December, 1837, a remarkable scene was enacted in that body, during the proceedings on a motion of Mr. Slade of Vermont to refer two memorials praying the abolition of slavery in the District of Columbia to a select committee. Mr. Slade, in urging his motion, was violent in his denunciations of slavery, and he spoke for a considerable time amid constant interruptions and calls to order. At length, Mr. Rhett of South Carolina called upon the entire delegation from all the slaveholding States to retire from the hall, and to meet in the room of the Committee on the District of Columbia. A large number of them did meet for consultation in the room designated. The meeting, however, resulted in nothing but an agreement upon the following resolution to be presented to the House:

    Resolved,   That all petitions, memorials, and papers touching the abolition of slavery, or the buying, selling, or transferring of slaves in any State, District, or Territory of the United States, be laid on the table without being debated, printed, read, or referred, and that no further action whatever shall be had thereon.

This resolution was presented to the House by Mr. Patton of Virginia and was adopted by a vote of 122 to 74.

In the month of January, 1840, the House of Representatives, on motion of Mr. W. Cost Johnson of Maryland adopted what was known as the "Twenty-first Rule," which prohibited the reception of all Abolition petitions, memorials, and resolutions.

The Twenty-first Rule was rescinded in December, 1844, on motion of John Quincy Adams, by a vote of 108 to 80. Several efforts were afterwards made to restore it, but without success. The Northern people would not relinquish what they termed a "sacred right"—that of petitioning the Government, through their representatives in Congress, to deprive the Southern people of their property.

During the agitation in Congress upon the right of petition, there was, as before stated, but very few open and avowed Abolitionists in either House, and the declaration was repeatedly made by members that the party was contemptibly small in every free State in the Union. Mr. Pierce of New Hampshire (afterwards President of the United States) declared, in 1837, in his place in Congress, that there were not two hundred Abolitionists in his State; and Mr. Webster, about the same time, represented their numbers in Massachusetts as quite insignificant. Mr. Calhoun of South Carolina, with characteristic sagacity, replied to these representations, and predicted that "Mr. Webster and all Northern statesmen would, in a few years, yield to the storm of Abolition fanaticism and be overwhelmed by it." The prophecy was not more remarkable than the searching analysis of Northern "conservatism" with which the great South Carolinian accompanied his prediction. He argued that such a consequence was inevitable from the way in which the professed "conservatives" of the North had invited the aggressions of the Abolitionists, by courteously granting them the right of petition, which was indeed all they asked; that the fanaticism of the North was a disease which required a *remedy,* and that palliatives would not answer, as Mr. Webster and men like him would find to their cost.

In the Thirtieth Congress, that assembled in December, 1849, the professed Abolitionists numbered about a dozen members. They held the balance of power between the Democratic and Whig parties in the House, and delayed its organization for about a month. Both the Whig and Democratic parties then claimed to be conservative, and of course, the opponents of the anti-slavery agitation.

In the presidential canvass of 1852, both Pierce and Scott were brought out by professed national parties, and were supported in each section of the Union. John P. Hale, who ran upon what was called the "straight-out" Abolition ticket, did not receive the vote of a single State, and but 175,296 of the popular vote of the Union. The triumphant election of Pierce, who was a favorite of the States'-Rights Democracy of the South, was hailed by the sanguine friends of the Union as a fair indication of the purpose of the North to abide, in good faith, by the Compromise of 1850. But in this they were deceived, as the sequel demonstrated.

During the first session of the first Congress under Mr. Pierce's administration, the bill introduced to establish a territorial government for Nebraska led to an agitation in Congress and the country, the consequences of which extended to the last period of the existence of the Union. The Committee on Territories in the Senate, of which Mr. Douglas of Illinois was chairman, reported the bill, which made two territories—Nebraska and Kansas—instead of one, and which declared that the Missouri Compromise Act was superseded by the Compromise measures of 1850, and had thus become inoperative. The phraseology of the clause repealing the Missouri Compromise was drawn up by Mr. Douglas, and was not supposed at the time to be liable to misconstruction. It held that the Missouri Compromise Act

> being inconsistent with the principles of non-intervention by Congress with slavery in the States and Territories, as recognized by the legislation of 1850, commonly called the Compromise Measures, is hereby declared inoperative and void; it being the true intent and meaning of this act not to legislate slavery into any Territory or State, nor to exclude it therefrom, but to leave the people thereof perfectly free to form and regulate their domestic institutions in their own way, subject only to the Constitution of the United States.

The clause here quoted, as drawn up by Mr. Douglas, was incorporated into the Kansas-Nebraska Bill in the Senate on the 15th of February, 1854. The bill passed the House at the same session.

The repeal of the Missouri Compromise caused the deepest excitement throughout the North. The Abolitionists were wild with fury. Douglas was hung in effigy at different places, and was threatened with personal violence in case of his persistence in his non-intervention policy. The rapid development of a fanatical feeling in every free State startled many who had but recently indulged dreams of the perpetuity of the Constitutional Union. Abolitionism, in the guise of "*Republicanism,*" swept almost every thing before it in the North and Northwest in the elections of 1854 and 1855. But few professed conservatives were returned to the Thirty-first Congress; not enough to prevent the election of Nathaniel Banks, an objectionable Abolitionist of the Massachusetts school, to the Speakership of the House.

The South had supported the repeal of the Missouri Compromise because it restored her to her rightful position of equality in the Union. It is true that her representatives in Congress were well aware that under the operations of the new act their constituents could expect to obtain but little if any new accessions of slave territory, while the North would necessarily, from the force of circumstances, secure a number of new States in the Northwest, then the present direction of our new settlements. But viewed as an act of proscription against her, the Missouri Compromise was justly offensive to the South; and its abrogation, in this respect, strongly recommended itself to her support.

The ruling party of the North, calling themselves "Republicans," had violently opposed the repeal of the act of 1820, in the same sentiment with which it was fiercely encountered by the Abolitionists. The two parties were practically identical; both shared the same sentiment of hostility to slavery; and they differed only as to the degree of indirection by which their purposes might best be accomplished.

The election of Mr. Buchanan to the Presidency, in 1856, raised, for a time, the spirits of many of the true friends of the Constitutional Union. But there was very little in an analysis of the vote to give hope or encouragement to the patriot. Fremont, who ran as the anti-slavery candidate received 1,341,812 votes of the people, and it is believed would have been elected by the electoral college, if the anti-Buchanan party in Pennsylvania had united upon him.

The connection of events which we have sought to trace brings us to the celebrated Kansas controversy, and at once to the threshold of the dissensions which demoralized the only conservative party in the country, and in less than four years culminated in the rupture of the Federal Union. A severe summary of the facts of this controversy introduces us to the contest of 1860, in which the Republican Party, swollen with its triumphs in Kansas, and infecting the Democratic leaders in the North with the disposition to pander to the lusts of a growing power, obtained the control of the Government, and seized the sceptre of absolute authority.

When Mr. Buchanan came into office, in March, 1857, he flattered himself with the hope that his administration would settle the disputes that had so long agitated and distracted the country; trusting that such a result might be accomplished by the speedy admission of Kansas into the Union, upon the principles which had governed in his election. Such, at least, were his declarations to his friends. But before the meeting of Congress in December he had abundant evidence that his favorite measure would be opposed by a number of senators and representatives who had actively supported him in his canvass; among them the distinguished author of the Kansas-Nebraska Bill, Mr. Douglas.

In the month of July, 1855, the Legislature of the Territory of Kansas had passed an act to take the sense of the people on the subject of forming a State government, preparatory to admission into the Union. The election took place, and a large majority of the people voted in favor of holding a Convention for the purpose of adopting a Constitution. In pursuance of this vote, the Territorial Legislature, on the 19th of February, 1857, passed a law to take a census of the people, for the purpose of making a registry of the voters, and to elect delegates to the Convention. Mr. Geary, then Governor of Kansas, vetoed the bill for calling the Convention, for the reason that it did not require the Constitution, when framed, to be submitted to a vote of the people for adoption or rejection. The bill, however, was reconsidered in each house, and passed by a two-thirds vote, and thus became a binding law in the Territory, despite the veto of the Governor.

On the 20th of May, 1857, Mr. F. P. Stanton, Secretary and Acting Governor of Kansas Territory, published his proclamation, commanding the proper officers to hold an election on the third Monday of June, 1857, as directed by the act referred to.

The election was held on the day appointed, and the Convention assembled, according to law, on the first Monday of September, 1857. They proceeded to form a Constitution, and having finished their work, adjourned on the 7th of November. The entire Constitution was not submitted to the popular vote; but the Convention took care to submit to the vote of the people, for ratification or rejection, the clause respecting slavery. The official vote resulted: For the Constitution, with slavery, 6,226; for the Constitution, without slavery, 509.

The Abolitionists, or "Free State" men, as they called themselves did not generally vote in this or any other election held under the regular government of the Territory. They defied the authority of this government and that of the United States, and acted under the direction of Emigrant Aid Societies, organized by the fanatical Abolitionists of the North, to colonize the new territory with voters. The proceedings of this evil and bastard population occasioned the greatest excitement, and speedily inaugurated an era of disorder and rebellion in this distant portion of the federal territory.

The Free State Party assembled at Topeka, in September, 1855, and adopted what they called a "Constitution" for Kansas. This so-called Constitution was submitted to the people, and was ratified, of course, by a large majority of those who voted; scarcely any but Abolitionists going to the polls. Under their Topeka Constitution, the Free State Party elected a Governor and Legislature, and organized for the purpose of petitioning Congress for the admission of Kansas into the Union. The memorial of the Topeka insurgents was presented to the Thirty-fourth Congress. It met with a favorable response in the House of Representatives, a majority of that body being anti-slavery men of the New England school; but found but a poor reception in the Senate, where there was still a majority of conservative and law-abiding men.

On the 2d of February, 1858, Mr. Buchanan, at the request of the president of the Lecompton Convention, transmitted to Congress an authentic copy of the Constitution framed by that body, with a view to the admission of Kansas into the Union. The message of the President took strong and urgent position for the admission of Kansas under this Constitution; he defended the action of the Convention in not submitting the entire result of their labors to a vote of the people; he explained that, when he instructed Governor Walker, in general terms, in favor of submitting the Constitution to the people, he had no other object in view beyond the all-absorbing topic of slavery; he considered that, under the organic act, the Convention was bound to submit the all-important question of slavery to the people; he added, that it was never his opinion, however, that independently of this act the Convention would be bound to submit any portion of the Constitution to a popular vote, in order to give it validity; and he argued the fallacy and unreasonableness of such an opinion, by insisting that it was in opposition to the principle which pervaded our institutions, and which was every day carried into practice, to the effect that the people had the right to delegate to representatives, chosen by themselves, sovereign power to frame Constitutions, enact laws, and perform many other important acts, without the necessity of testing the validity of their work by popular approbation. The Topeka Constitution Mr. Buchanan denounced as the work of treason and insurrection.

It is certain that Mr. Buchanan would have succeeded in effecting the admission of Kansas under the Lecompton Constitution, if he could have secured to the measure the support of all the Northern Democrats who had contributed to his election. These, however, had become disaffected; they opposed and assailed the measure of the Administration, acting under the lead of Mr. Douglas; and the long-continued and bitter discussion which ensued, perfectly accomplished the division of the Democratic Party into two great factions, mustered under the names of "Lecompton" and "Anti-Lecompton."

The latter faction founded their opposition to the Administration on the grounds that the Lecompton Constitution was not the act of the people of Kansas and did not express their will; that only half of the counties of the Territory were represented in the Convention that framed it, the other half being disfranchised, for no fault of their own, but from failure of the officers to register the voters and entitle them to vote for delegates; and that the mode of submitting the Constitution to the people for "ratification or rejection" was unfair, embarrassing, and proscriptive.

In reply, the friends of the Administration urged that twenty-one of the thirty-four organized counties of Kansas were embraced in the apportionment of representation; that, of the thirteen counties not embraced, nine had but a small population, as shown by the fact that in a succeeding election, to which the anti-Lecomptonites had referred as an indication of public sentiment in Kansas, they polled but ninety votes in the aggregate; that, in the remaining four counties, the failure to register the voters and the consequent loss of their representation were due to the Abolitionists themselves, who refused to recognize all legal authority in the Territory; and that the submission of the Constitution as provided by the Lecompton Convention afforded a complete expression of the popular will, as the slavery question was the only one about which there was any controversy in Kansas.

The bill for the admission of Kansas under the Lecompton Constitution was passed by the Senate. In the House an amendment offered by Mr. Montgomery of Pennsylvania was adopted, to the effect that as it was a disputed point whether the Constitution framed at Lecompton was fairly made or expressed the will of the people of Kansas her admission into the Union as a State was declared to be upon the fundamental condition precedent, that the said constitutional instrument should first be submitted to a vote of the people of Kansas, and assented to by them, or by a majority of the voters, at an election to be held for the purpose of determining the question of the ratification or rejection of the instrument.

The Senate insisted upon its bill; the House adhered to its amendment; and a committee of conference was appointed. The result of the conference was the report of a bill for the admission of Kansas, which became a law in June, 1858, and substantially secured nearly all that the North had claimed in the controversy.

The bill, as passed, rejected the Land Ordinance contained in the Lecompton Constitution and proposed a substitute. Kansas was to be admitted into the Union on an equal footing in all respects with the original States, but upon the fundamental condition precedent, that the question of admission, along with that of the Land substitute, be submitted to a vote of the people; that, if a majority of the vote should be against the proposition tendered by Congress, it should be concluded that Kansas did not desire admission under the Lecompton Constitution, with the condition attached to it; and that, in such event, the people were authorized to form for themselves a Constitution and State government, and might elect delegates for that purpose, after a census taken to demonstrate the fact that the population of the Territory equalled or exceeded the ratio of representation for a member of the House of Representatives.

Thus ended the six months' discussion of the Kansas question in Congress in 1858. The substitute to the Land Ordinance was rejected by the voters of the Territory; and Kansas did not come into the Union until nearly three years afterwards—just as the Southern States were going out of it. She came in under an anti-slavery Constitution, and Mr. Buchanan signed the bill of admission.

The discussions of the Kansas question, as summed in the preceding pages, had materially weakened the Union. The spirit of those discussions, and the result itself of the controversy, fairly indicated that the South could hardly expect under any circumstances the addition of another slave State to the Union. The Southern mind was awakened; the sentimental reverences of more than half a century were decried; and men began to calculate the precise value of a Union which by its mere name and the paraphrases of demagogues had long governed their affections.

Some of these calculations, as they appeared in the newspaper presses of the times, were curious, and soon commenced to interest the Southern people. It was demonstrated to them that their section had been used to contribute the bulk of the revenues of the Government; that the North derived forty to fifty millions of annual revenue from the South, through the operations of the tariff; and that the aggregate of the trade of the South in Northern markets was four hundred millions of dollars a year. It was calculated by a Northern writer that the harvest of gain reaped by the North from the Union, from unequal taxations and the courses of trade as between the two sections, exceeded two hundred millions of dollars per year.

These calculations of the commercial cost of the "glorious Union" to the South, only presented the question in a single aspect, however striking that was. There were other aspects, no less important and no less painful, in which it was to be regarded. The swollen and insolent power of Abolitionism threatened to carry everything before it; it had already broken the vital principle of the Constitution—that of the equality of its parts; and to injuries already accomplished, it added the bitterest threats and the most insufferable insolence.

While the anti-slavery power threatened never to relax its efforts until, in the language of Mr. Seward, a senator from New York, the "irrepressible conflict" between slavery and freedom was accomplished and the soil of the Carolinas dedicated to the institutions of New England, it affected the insolent impertinence of regarding the Union as a concession on the part of the North and of taunting the South with the disgrace which her association in the Union inflicted upon the superior and more virtuous people of the Northern States. The excesses of this conceit are ridiculous seen in the light of subsequent events. It was said that the South was an inferior part of the country; that she was a spotted and degraded section; that the national fame abroad was compromised by the association of the South in the Union; and that a New England traveller in Europe blushed to confess himself an American because half of the nation of that name were slaveholders. Many of the Abolitionists made a pretence of praying that the Union might be dissolved, that they might be cleared by the separation of North and South of any implication in the crime of slavery. Even that portion of the party calling themselves "Republicans" affected that the Union stood in the way of the North. Mr. Banks, of Massachusetts, who had been elected Speaker of the House in the Thirty-first Congress, had declared that the designs of his party were not to be baffled, and was the author of the coarse jeer—"*Let the Union slide.*" The New York *Tribune* had complained that the South "could not be *kicked* out of the Union." Mr. Seward, the great Republican leader, had spread the evangely of a natural, essential, and irrepressible hostility between the two sections; and the North prepared to act on a suggestion, the only practical result of which could be to cleave the Union apart and to inaugurate the horrors of civil war.

The raid into Virginia of John Brown, a notorious Abolitionist, whose occupations in Kansas had been those of a horse-thief and assassin, and his murder of peaceful and unsuspecting citizens at Harper's Ferry in the month of October, 1859, was a practical illustration of the lessons of the Northern Republicans, and of their inevitable and, in fact, logical conclusion in civil war. Professed conservatives in the North predicted that this outrage would be productive of real good in their section, in opening the eyes of the people to what were well characterized as "*Black* Republican" doctrines. This prediction was not verified by succeeding events. The Northern elections of the next month showed no diminution in the Black Republican vote. The manifestations of sympathy for John Brown, who had expiated his crime on a gallows in Virginia, were unequivocal in all parts of the North, though comparatively few openly justified the outrage. Bells were tolled in various towns of New England on the day of his execution, with the knowledge of the local authorities, and in some instances, through their co-operation; and not a few preachers from the pulpit allotted him an apotheosis, and consigned his example to emulation, as one not only of public virtue, but of particular service to God.

The attachment of the South to the Union was steadily weakening in the historical succession of events. The nomination in December, 1859, to the Speakership of the House of Representatives of Mr. Sherman of Ohio, who had made himself especially odious to the South by publicly recommending, in connection with sixty-eight other Republican members, a fanatical document popularly known as *Helper's Book*,* from the name of the author, and which openly defended and sought itself to excite servile insurrections in the South, and produced a marked effect in Congress, and was encountered by the Southern members with a determined spirit of opposition. The entire Southern delegation gave warning that they would regard the election of Mr. Sherman, or of any man with his record, as an open declaration of war upon the institutions of the South; as much so, some of the members declared, as if the Brown raid were openly approved by a majority of the House of Representatives. The Black Republican Party defiantly nominated Sherman, and continued to vote for him for near two

---

*The tone of this book was violent in the extreme. We add a few extracts, which will enable the reader to form a correct opinion of the character and object of the work—

"Slavery is a great moral, social, civil, and political evil, to be got rid of at the earliest practical period."—(p. 168.)

"Three-quarters of a century hence, if the South retains slavery, which God forbid! she will be to the North what Poland is to Russia, Cuba to Spain, and Ireland to England."—(p. 163.)

"Our own banner is inscribed—No co-operation with slaveholders in politics; no fellowship with them in religion; no affiliation with them in society; no recognition of pro-slavery men, except as ruffians, outlaws, and criminals."—(p. 156.)

"We believe it is as it ought to be, the desire, the determination, and the destiny of the Republican Party to give the death-blow to slavery."—(p. 234.)

"In any event, come what will, transpire what may, the institution of slavery must be abolished."—(p. 180.)

"We are determined to abolish slavery at all hazards—in defiance of all the opposition, of whatever nature, it is possible for the slaveocrats to bring against us. Of this they may take due notice, and govern themselves accordingly."—(p. 149.)

"It is our honest conviction that all the pro-slavery slaveholders deserve at once to be reduced to a parallel with the basest criminals that lie fettered within the cells of our public prisons."—(p. 158.)

"Shall we pat the bloodhounds of slavery? Shall we fee the curs of slavery? Shall we pay the whelps of slavery? No, never."—(p. 329.)

"Our purpose is as firmly fixed as the eternal pillars of heaven; we have determined to abolish slavery, and, so help us God! abolish it we will."—(p. 187.)

months, giving him within four votes of a majority upon every trial of his strength. Although he was finally withdrawn, and one of his party, not a subscriber to the *Helper's Book*, was elected, yet the fact that more than three-fourths of the entire Northern delegation had adhered to Mr. Sherman for nearly two months in a factious and fanatical spirit produced a deep impression on the minds of Southern members and of their constituents. The early dissolution of the Union had come to be a subject freely canvassed among members of Congress.

With the unveiling of the depth of the designs of the Black Republican Party, another danger was becoming manifest to the South. It was the demoralization of the Northern Democratic Party on the slavery question. This whole party had been an unhealthy product; its very foundation was a principle of untruth, and false to its own section, it could not be expected to adhere to friends whom it had made from interest and who had fallen into adverse circumstances. It had united with the South for political power. In the depression of that power, and the rapid growth of the anti-slavery party in the North, it had no hesitation in courting and conciliating the ruling element. This disposition was happily accommodated by the controversy which had taken place between Mr. Douglas and the administration of Mr. Buchanan. The anti-slavery sentiment in the North was conciliated by the partisans of the Illinois demagogue, in adopting a new principle for the government of the Territories, which was to allow the people to determine the question of slavery in their territorial capacity, without awaiting their organization as a State, and thus to risk the decision of the rights of the South on the verdict of a few settlers on the public domain. This pander to the anti-slavery sentiment of the North was concealed under the demagogical name of "popular sovereignty," and was imposed upon the minds of not a few of the Southern people by the artfulness of its appeals to the name of a principle, which had none of the substance of justice or equality. The concealment, however, was but imperfectly availing. The doctrine of Mr. Douglas was early denounced by one of the most vigilant statesman of the South as "a short cut to all the ends of Black Republicanism"; and later in time, while the *Helper's Book* controversy was agitating the country, and other questions developing the union of all the anti-slavery elements for war upon the South, a senator from Georgia was found bold enough to denounce, in his place in Congress, the entire Democratic Party of the North as unreliable and *"rotten."*

The States'-Rights Party of the South had co-operated with the Democracy of the North in the Presidential canvass of 1856, upon the principles of the platform adopted by the National Democratic Convention, assembled in Cincinnati in June of that year. They expressed a willingness to continue this co-operation in the election of 1860, upon the principles of the Cincinnati platform; but demanded, as a condition precedent to this, that the question of the *construction* of this platform should be satisfactorily

settled. To this end, the States'-Rights Democratic Party in several of the
Southern States defined the conditions upon which their delegates should
hold seats in the National Convention, appointed to meet at Charleston on
the 23d of April, 1860. The Democracy in Alabama moved first. On the 11th
of January, 1860, they met in convention at Montgomery and adopted a
series of resolutions, from which the following are extracted as presenting
a summary declaration of the rights of the South, a recapitulation of the
territorial question, and a definition of those issues on which the contest of
1860 was to be conducted:

Resolved, by the Democracy of the State of Alabama in Convention assembled, That holding all issues and principles upon which they have heretofore affiliated and acted with the National Democratic party to be inferior
in dignity and importance to the great question of slavery, they content themselves with a general reaffirmation of the Cincinnati platform as to such issues,
and also endorse said platform as to slavery, together with the following
resolutions:

Resolved, That the Constitution of the United States, is a compact between
sovereign and co-equal States, united upon the basis of perfect equality of
rights and privileges.

Resolved, further, That the Territories of the United States are common
property, in which the States have equal rights, and to which the citizens of any
State may rightfully emigrate, with their slaves or other property recognized
as such in any of the States of the Union, or by the Constitution of the United
States.

Resolved, further, That the Congress of the United States has no power to
abolish slavery in the Territories, or to prohibit its introduction into any of
them.

Resolved, further, That the Territorial Legislatures, created by the legislation
of Congress, have no power to abolish slavery, or to prohibit the introduction of
the same, or to impair by unfriendly legislation the security and full enjoyment
of the same within the Territories; and such constitutional power certainly does
not belong to the people of the Territories in any capacity, before, in the exercise of a lawful authority, they form a Constitution, preparatory to admission
as a State into the Union; and their action in the exercise of such lawful authority certainly cannot operate or take effect before their actual admission as
a State into the Union.

Resolved, further, That the principles enunciated by Chief Justice Taney, in
his opinion in the Dred Scott case, deny to the Territorial Legislature the power
to destroy or impair, by any legislation whatever, the right of property in slaves,
and maintain it to be the duty of the Federal Government, in *all* of its departments, to protect the rights of the owner of such property in the Territories;
and the principles so declared are hereby asserted to be the rights of the South,
and the South should maintain them.

Resolved, further, That we hold all of the foregoing propositions to contain
"cardinal principles"—true in themselves—and just and proper and necessary
for the safety of all that is dear to us; and we do hereby instruct our delegates

to the Charleston Convention to present them for the calm consideration and approval of that body—from whose justice and patriotism we anticipate their adoption.

Resolved, further, That our delegates to the Charleston Convention are hereby expressly instructed to insist that said Convention shall adopt a platform of principles, recognizing distinctly the rights of the South as asserted in the foregoing resolutions; and if the said National Convention shall refuse to adopt, in substance, the propositions embraced in the preceding resolutions, prior to nominating candidates, our delegates to said Convention are hereby positively instructed to withdraw therefrom.

Under these resolutions the delegates from Alabama received their appointment to the Charleston Convention. The delegates from some of the other Cotton States were appointed under instructions equally binding. Anxious as were the Southern delegates to continue their connection with the Convention, and thus to maintain the nationality of the Democratic Party, they agreed to accept, as the substance of the Alabama platform, either of the two following reports which had been submitted to the Charleston Convention by the majority of the Committee on Resolutions— this majority not only representing that of the States of the Union, but the only States at all likely to be carried by the Democratic Party in the presidential election:

I

Resolved, That the platform at Cincinnati be reaffirmed with the following resolutions:

Resolved, That the Democracy of the United States hold these cardinal principles on the subject of slavery in the Territories: First, that Congress has no power to abolish slavery in the Territories. Second, that the Territorial Legislature has no power to abolish slavery in any Territory, nor to prohibit the introduction of slaves therein, nor any power to exclude slavery therefrom, nor any power to destroy and impair the right of property in slaves by any legislation whatever.

II

Resolved, That the platform adopted by the Democratic Party at Cincinnati be affirmed, with the following explanatory resolutions.

First.   That the government of a Territory, organized by an act of Congress, is provisional and temporary; and, during its existence, all citizens of the United States have an equal right to settle with their property in the Territory, without their rights, either of person or property, being destroyed or impaired by congressional or territorial legislation.

Second.   That it is the duty of the Federal Government, in all its departments, to protect, when necessary, the rights of persons and property in the Territories and wherever else its constitutional authority extends.

Third.   That when the settlers in a Territory having an adequate population form a State Constitution, the right of sovereignty commences, and, being consummated by admission into the Union, they stand on an equal footing with the people of other States; and the State thus organized, ought to be admitted into the Federal Union, whether its Constitution prohibits or recognizes the institution of slavery .

The Convention refused to accept either of the foregoing resolutions and adopted, by a vote of 165 to 138, the following as its platform on the slavery question:

1. *Resolved,* That we, the Democracy of the Union, in Convention assembled, hereby declare our affirmance of the resolutions unanimously adopted and declared as a platform of principles by the Democratic Convention at Cincinnati, in the year 1856, believing that Democratic principles are unchangeable in their nature, when applied to the same subject-matters; and we recommend as the only further resolutions the following:

Inasmuch as differences of opinion exist in the Democratic Party as to the nature and extent of the powers of a Territorial Legislature, and as to the powers and duties of Congress under the Constitution of the United States, over the institution of slavery within the Territories:

2. *Resolved,* That the Democratic Party will abide by the decisions of the Supreme Court of the United States on the questions of constitutional law.

The substitution of these resolutions for those which were satisfactory to the South, occasioned the disruption of the Convention, after a session of more than three weeks, and its adjournment to Baltimore, on the 18th of June. The Cotton States, all, withdrew from the Convention; but the Border Slave States remained in it, with the hope of effecting some ultimate settlement of the difficulty. The breach, however, widened. The reassembling of the Convention at Baltimore resulted in a final and embittered separation of the opposing delegations. The majority exhibited a more uncompromising spirit than ever; and Virginia and all the Border Slave States, with the exception of Missouri, withdrew from the Convention, and united with the representatives of the Cotton States, then assembled in Baltimore, in the nomination of candidates representing the views of the South. Their nominees were John C. Breckinridge of Kentucky for President, and Joseph Lane of Oregon for Vice-President.

The old convention, or what remained of it, nominated Stephen A. Douglas of Illinois for President, and Benjamin Fitzpatrick of Alabama for Vice-President. The latter declining, Herschel V. Johnson of Georgia was substituted on the ticket.

The Southern Democracy and the Southern people of all parties, with but few exceptions, sustained the platform demanded by the Southern delegates in the Convention, and justified the course they had pursued. They recognized in the platform a legitimate and fair assertion of Southern rights. In view, however, of the conservative professions and glozed speeches of a portion of the Northern Democracy, a respectable number of Southern Democrats were induced to support their ticket. Mr. Douglas proclaimed his views to be in favor of non-intervention; he avowed his continued and unalterable opposition to Black Republicanism; his principles were professed to be "held subject to the decisions of the Supreme Court"— the distinction between judicial questions and political questions being purposely clouded; and his friends, with an ingenious sophistry that had imposed upon the South for thirty years with success, insisted that the support of Stephen A. Douglas was a support of the party in the North which had stood by the South amid persecution and defamation. In consequence of these and other protestations, tickets were got up for Mr. Douglas in most of the Southern States. The great majority, however, of the Democracy of the slaveholding States, except Missouri, supported Breckinridge.

A Convention of what is called the "Constitutional Union" Party met in Baltimore on the 9th of May, 1860, and nominated for President and Vice-President, John Bell of Tennessee and Edward Everett of Massachusetts. Their platform consisted of a vague and undefined enumeration of their political principles; as, "The Constitution of the Country, the Union of the States, and Enforcement of the Laws."

The National Convention of the Black Republican Party was held at Chicago, in the month of June. It adopted a platform declaring freedom to be the "normal condition" of the Territories; but ingeniously complicating its position on the slavery question by a number of vague but plausible articles, such as the maintenance of the principles of the Constitution, and especial attachment to the Union of the States.

The Presidential ticket nominated by the Convention was Abraham Lincoln of Illinois for President, and Hannibal Hamlin of Maine for Vice-President. Governed by the narrow considerations of party expediency, the Convention had adopted as their candidate for President a man of scanty political record, a Western lawyer, with the characteristics of that profession—acuteness, slang, and a large stock of jokes—and who had peculiar claims to vulgar and demagogical popularity, in the circumstances that he was once a captain of volunteers in one of the Indian wars, and at some anterior period of his life had been employed, as report differently said, in splitting rails or in rowing a flat-boat.

The great majority of the Southern Democracy supported the Breckinridge ticket; it was the leading ticket in all the slave States, except Missouri; but in the North but a small and feeble minority of the Democratic Party gave it their support. In several States, the friends of Douglas, of Breckinridge, and of Bell coalesced, to a certain extent, with a view to the defeat of Lincoln, but without success, except in New Jersey, where they partially succeeded.

The result of the contest was that Abraham Lincoln received the entire electoral vote of every free State, except New Jersey, and was, of course, elected President of the United States, according to the forms of the Constitution.

The entire popular vote for Lincoln was 1,858,200; that for Douglas, giving him his share of the fusion vote, 1,276,780; that for Breckinridge, giving him his share of the fusion vote, 812,500; and that for Bell, including his proportion of the fusion vote, 735,504. The whole vote against Lincoln was thus 2,824,784, showing a clear aggregate majority against him of nearly a million votes.

During the canvass, the North had been distinctly warned by the conservative parties of the country that the election of Lincoln by a strictly sectional vote would be taken as a declaration of war against the South. This position was assumed on the part of the South, not so much on account of the declaration of the anti-slavery principles in the Chicago platform, as from the notorious *animus* of the party supporting Lincoln. The Chicago Convention had attempted to conceal the worst designs of Abolitionism under professions of advancing the cause of freedom in strict accordance with the Constitution and the laws. The South, however, could not be ignorant of the fact, or wanting in appreciation of it, that Lincoln had been supported by the sympathizers of John Brown, the indorsers of the *Helper's Book*, the founders of the Kansas Emigrant Aid Societies, and their desperate abetters and agents, "Jim" Lane and others, and by the opponents of the Fugitive Slave law. It was known, in a word, that Lincoln owed his election to the worst enemies of the South, and that he would naturally and necessarily select his counsellors from among them, and consult their views in his administration of the Government.

Threats of resistance were proclaimed in the South. It is true that a few sanguine persons in that section, indulging narrow and temporizing views of the crisis, derived no little comfort and confidence from the large preponderance of the popular vote in the presidential contest in favor of the conservative candidates; and viewed it as an augury of the speedy overthrow of the first sectional administration. But those whose observations were larger and comprehended the progress of events took quite a different view of the matter. They could find no consolation or encouragement from the face of the record. The anti-slavery party had organized in 1840, with about seven thousand voters; and in 1860 had succeeded in electing the President of the United States. The conservative party in the North had been thoroughly corrupted. They were beaten in every Northern State in 1860, with a single exception, by the avowed enemies of the South, who but a few years ago had been powerless in their midst. The leaders of the Northern Democratic Party had in 1856 and in 1860 openly taken the position that freedom would be more certainly secured in the Territories by the rule of non-intervention than by any other policy or expedient. This interpretation of their policy alone saved the Democratic Party from entire annihilation. The overwhelming pressure of the anti-slavery sentiment had prevented their acceding to the Southern platform in the presidential canvass. Nothing in the present or in the future could be looked for from the so-called conservatives of the North; and the South prepared to go out of a Union which no longer afforded any guaranty for her rights or any permanent sense of security, and which had brought her under the domination of a growing fanaticism in the North, the sentiments of which, if carried into legislation, would destroy her institutions, confiscate the property of her people, and even involve their lives.

The State of South Carolina acted promptly and vigorously, with no delay for argument and but little for preparation. Considering the argument as fully exhausted, she determined, by the exercise of her rights as a sovereign State, to separate herself from the Union. Her Legislature called a Convention immediately after the result of the presidential election had been ascertained. The Convention met a few weeks thereafter, and on the 20th day of December, 1860, formally dissolved the connection of South Carolina with the Union by an ordinance of Secession which was passed by a unanimous vote.

On the same day Major Anderson, who was in command of the federal forces in Charleston harbor, evacuated Fort Moultrie, spiking the guns and burning the gun-carriages, and occupied Fort Sumter, with a view of strengthening his position. On the 30th of December, John B. Floyd, Secretary of War, resigned his office because President Buchanan refused to order Major Anderson back to Fort Moultrie—Mr. Floyd alleging that he and the President had pledged the authorities of South Carolina that the existing military *status* of the United States in that State should not be changed during the expiring term of the Democratic Administration.

The withdrawal of South Carolina from the Union produced some sensation in the North, but the dominant party treated it lightly. Many of these jeered at it; their leaders derided the "right of secession"; and their newspapers prophesied that the "rebellion" in South Carolina would be reduced to the most ignominious extremity the moment the "paternal government" of the United States should resolve to have recourse from peaceful persuasions to the chastisement of "a spoilt child." The events, however, which rapidly succeeded the withdrawal of South Carolina produced a deep impression upon all reflecting minds and startled, to some extent, the masses of the North, who would have been much more alarmed but for their vain and long-continued assurance that the South had no means or resources for making a serious resistance to the federal authority; and that a rebellion which could at any time be crushed on short notice might be pleasantly humored or wisely tolerated to any extent short of the actual commencement of hostilities.

On the 9th day of January, 1861, the State of Mississippi seceded from the Union. Alabama and Florida followed on the 11th day of the same month; Georgia on the 20th; Louisiana on the 26th; and Texas on the 1st of February. Thus, in less than three months after the announcement of Lincoln's election, all the Cotton States, with the exception of Alabama, had seceded from the Union, and had, besides, secured every federal fort within their limits, except the forts in Charleston harbor, and Fort Pickens, below Pensacola, which were retained by United States troops.

The United States Congress had, at the beginning of its session in December, 1860, appointed committees in both houses to consider the state of the Union. Neither committee was able to agree upon any mode of settlement of the pending issue between the North and the South. The Republican members in both committees rejected propositions acknowledging the right of property in slaves, or recommending the division of the territories between the slaveholding and non-slaveholding States by a geographical line. In the Senate, the propositions, commonly known as Mr. Crittenden's, were voted against by *every Republican senator;* and the House, on a vote of yeas and nays, refused to consider certain propositions, moved by Mr. Etheridge, which were even less favorable to the South than Mr. Crittenden's.

A resolution, giving a pledge to sustain the President in the use of force against seceding States, was adopted in the House of Representatives by a large majority; and, in the Senate, every Republican voted to substitute for Mr. Crittenden's propositions, resolutions offered by Mr. Clarke of New Hampshire, declaring that no new concessions, guaranties, or amendments to the Constitution were necessary; that the demands of the South were unreasonable, and that the remedy for the present dangers was simply to enforce the laws—in other words, *coercion and war.*

On the 19th day of January, the Legislature of the State of Virginia had passed resolutions having in view a peaceful settlement of the questions which threatened the Union, and suggesting that a National Peace Conference should be held in Washington on the 4th of February. This suggestion met with a favorable response from the Border Slave States and from professed conservatives in the North. The Conference met on the day designated, and ex-President Tyler, of Virginia, was called to preside over its deliberations. It remained in session several days and adjourned without agreeing upon any satisfactory plan of adjustment.

Most of the delegates from the Border Slave States indicated a willingness to accept the few and feeble guaranties contained in the resolutions offered, a short time before, in the Senate by Mr. Crittenden. These guaranties, paltry and ineffectual as they were, would not be conceded by the representatives of the Northern States. The Peace Conference finally adopted what was called the Franklin Substitute in lieu of the propositions offered by Mr. Guthrie of Kentucky—a settlement less favorable to the South than that proposed by Mr. Crittenden. It is useless to recount the details of these measures. Neither the Crittenden propositions, the Franklin Substitute, nor any plan that pretended to look for the guaranty of Southern rights, received a respectful notice from the Republican majority in Congress.

Shortly after its assemblage in January, the Virginia Legislature had called a Convention of the people to decide upon the course proper to be pursued by the State, with reference to her present relations to the Union and the future exigencies of her situation. The election was held on the 4th of February, and resulted in the choice of a majority of members opposed to unconditional secession. Subsequently, Tennessee and North Carolina decided against calling a Convention—the former by a large, the latter by a very small majority. These events greatly encouraged the enemies of the South, but without cause, as they really indicated nothing more than the purpose of the Border Slave States to await the results of the peace propositions, to which they had committed themselves.

In the meantime, the seceding States were erecting the structure of a government on the foundation of a new Confederation of States. A convention of delegates from the six seceding States assembled in congress at Montgomery, Alabama, on the 4th of February, 1861, for the purpose of organizing a provisional government. This body adopted a Constitution for the Confederate States on the 8th of February. On the 9th of February, Congress proceeded to the election of a President and Vice-President and unanimously agreed upon Jefferson Davis of Mississippi for President, and Alexander H. Stephens of Georgia for Vice-President. Mr. Davis was inaugurated Provisional President on the 18th of February and delivered an address explaining the revolution as a change of the constituent parts, but not the system, of the Government, and referring to the not unreasonable expectation that with a Constitution differing only from that of their fathers in so far as it was explanatory of their well-known intent, freed from sectional conflicts, the States from which they had recently parted might seek to unite their fortunes to those of the new Confederacy.

President Buchanan had, in his message to Congress, denounced Secession as revolutionary, but had hesitated at the logical conclusion of the right of "coercion," on the part of the Federal Government, as not warranted by the text of the Constitution. Timid, secretive, cold, and with no other policy than that of selfish expediency, the remnant of his administration was marked by embarrassment, double-dealing, and weak and contemptible querulousness. He had not hesitated, under the pressure of Northern clamor, to refuse to order Major Anderson back to Fort Moultrie, thus violating the pledge that he had given to the South Carolina authorities that the military status of the United States in Charleston harbor should not be disturbed during his administration. He added to the infamy of this perfidy by a covert attempt to reinforce Fort Sumter under the specious plea of provisioning a "starving garrison"; and when the federal steamship, the *Star of the West*, which was sent on this mission, was, on the 9th of January, driven off Charleston harbor by the South Carolina batteries on Morris Island, he had the hardihood to affect surprise and indignation at the reception given the federal reinforcements, and to insist that the expedition had been ordered with the concurrence of his Cabinet, including Mr. Thompson of Mississippi, then Secretary of the Interior, who repelled the slander, denounced the movement as underhanded, and as a breach not only of good faith towards South Carolina, but of personal confidence between the President and his advisers, and left the Cabinet in disgust.

On the incoming of the Administration of Abraham Lincoln, on the 4th of March, the rival government of the South had perfected its organization; the separation had been widened and cavenomed by the ambidexterity and perfidy of President Buchanan; the Southern people, however, still hoped for a peaceful accomplishment of their independence, and deplored war between the two sections, as "a policy detrimental to the civilized world." The revolution in the meantime had rapidly gathered, not only in moral power, but in the means of war and the muniments of defence. Fort Moultrie and Castle Pinckney had been captured by the South Carolina troops; Fort Pulaski, the defence of the Savannah, had been taken; the arsenal at Mount Vernon, Alabama, with 20,000 stand of arms, had been seized by the Alabama troops; Fort Morgan, in Mobile Bay, had been taken; Forts Jackson, St. Phillip, and Pike, near New Orleans, had been captured by the Louisiana troops; the Pensacola Navy-yard and Forts Barrancas and McRae had been taken, and the siege of Fort Pickens commenced; the Baton Rouge Arsenal had been surrendered to the Louisiana troops; the New Orleans Mint and Custom-House had been taken; the Little Rock Arsenal had been seized by the Arkansas troops; and, on the 16th of February, General Twiggs had transferred the public property in Texas to the State authorities. All of these events had been accomplished without bloodshed. Abolitionism and Fanaticism had not yet lapped blood. But reflecting men saw that the peace was deceitful and temporizing; that the temper of the North was impatient and dark; and that, if all history was not a lie, the first incident of bloodshed would be the prelude to a war of monstrous proportions.

3

Lincoln Campaigns Against Douglas

Horace White

It was my good fortune to accompany Mr. Lincoln during his political campaign against Senator Douglas in 1858, not only at the joint debates but also at most of the smaller meetings where his competitor was not present. We travelled together many thousands of miles. I was in the employ of the Chicago *Tribune*, then called the *Press and Tribune*. . . . My acquaintance with Mr. Lincoln began four years before the campaign of which I am writing, in October, 1854. I was then in the employ of the Chicago *Evening Journal*. I had been sent to Springfield to report the political doings of State Fair week for that newspaper. Thus it came about that I occupied a front seat in the Representatives' Hall, in the old State House, when Mr. Lincoln delivered a speech. . . . The impression made upon me by the orator was quite overpowering. I had not heard much political speaking up to that time. I have heard a great deal since. I have never heard anything since, either by Mr. Lincoln or by anybody, that I would put on a higher plane of oratory. All the strings that play upon the human heart and understanding were touched with masterly skill and force, while beyond and above all skill was the overwhelming conviction pressed upon the audience that the speaker himself was charged with an irresistible and inspiring duty to his fellow-men. This conscientious impulse drove his arguments through the hearers down into their bosoms, where they made everlasting lodgment. I had been nurtured in the Abolitionist faith, and was much more radical than Mr. Lincoln himself on any point where slavery was concerned, yet it seemed to me, when this speech was finished, as though I had had a very feeble conception of the wickedness of the Kansas-Nebraska Bill. I was filled, as never before, with a sense of my own duty and responsibility as a citizen toward the aggressions of the slave power.

Having, since then, heard all the great public speakers of this country subsequent to the period of Clay and Webster, I award the palm to Mr. Lincoln as the one who, although not first in all respects, would bring more

WILLIAM H. HERNDON and JESSE W. WEIK, eds., *Abraham Lincoln: The True Story of a Great Life*, 2 vols. (New York, 1888), Vol. II, Ch. 4.

men, of doubtful or hostile leanings, around to his way of thinking by talking to them on a platform, than any other.

Although I heard him many times afterwards I shall longest remember him as I then saw the tall, angular form with the long, angular arms, at times bent nearly double with excitement, like a large flail animating two smaller ones, the mobile face wet with perspiration which he discharged in drops as he threw his head this way and that like a projectile—not a graceful figure, yet not an ungraceful one. After listening to him a few minutes, when he had got well warmed with his subject, nobody would mind whether he was graceful or not. All thought of grace or form would be lost in the exceeding attractiveness of what he was saying.

Returning to the campaigns of 1858—I was sent by my employers to Springfield to attend the Republican State Convention of that year. Again I sat a short distance from Mr. Lincoln when he delivered the "house-divided-against-itself" speech, on the 17th of June. This was delivered from manuscript, and was the only one I ever heard him deliver in that way. When it was concluded, he put the manuscript in my hands and asked me to go to the *State Journal* office and read the proof of it. I think it had already been set in type. Before I had finished this task Mr. Lincoln himself came into the composing room of the *State Journal* and looked over the revised proofs. He said to me that he had taken a great deal of pains with this speech, and that he wanted it to go before the people just as he had prepared it. He added that some of his friends had scolded him a good deal about the opening paragraph and "the house divided against itself," and wanted him to change it or leave it out altogether, but that he believed he had studied this subject more deeply than they had, and that he was going to stick to that text whatever happened.

On the 9th of July, Senator Douglas returned to Chicago from Washington City. He had stopped a few days at Cleveland, Ohio, to allow his friends to arrange a grand *entrée* for him. It was arranged that he should arrive about eight o'clock in the evening by the Michigan Central Railway, whose station was at the foot of Lake Street, in which street the principal hotel, the Tremont House, was situated, and that he should be driven in a carriage drawn by six horses to the hotel, where he should make his first speech of the campaign. To carry out this arrangement it was necessary that he should leave the Michigan Southern Railway at Laporte and go to Michigan City, at which place the Chicago committee of reception took him in charge. It was noted by the Chicago *Times* that some malicious person at Michigan City had secretly spiked the only cannon in the town, so that the Douglas men were obliged to use an anvil on the occasion.

When Mr. Douglas and his train arrived at the Lake Street station, the crowd along the street to the hotel, four or five blocks distant, was dense, and for the Chicago of that day, tremendous. It was with great difficulty that the six-horse team got through it at all. Banners, bands of music, cannon and fireworks added their various inspiration to the scene. About nine o'clock Mr. Douglas made his appearance on a balcony on the Lake Street side of the hotel and made his speech. Mr. Lincoln sat in a chair just inside the house, very near the speaker, and was an attentive listener.

Mr. Douglas's manner on this occasion was courtly and conciliatory. His argument was plausible but worthless—being, for the most part, a rehash of his "popular sovereignty" dogma; nevertheless, he made a good impression. He could make more out of a bad case, I think, than any other man this country has ever produced, and I hope the country will never produce his like again in this particular. If his fate had been cast in the French Revolution, he would have out-demagogued the whole lot of them. I consider the use he made of this chip called popular sovereignty, riding upon it safely through some of the stormiest years in our history, and having nothing else to ride upon, a feat of dexterity akin to genius. But mere dexterity would not alone have borne him along his pathway in life. He had dauntless courage, unwearied energy, engaging manners, boundless ambition, unsurpassed powers of debate, and strong personal magnetism. Among the Democrats of the North his ascendency was unquestioned and his power almost absolute. He was exactly fitted to hew his way to the Presidency, and he would have done so infallibly if he had not made the mistake of coquetting with slavery. This was a mistake due to the absence of moral principle. If he had been as true to freedom as Lincoln was he would have distanced Lincoln in the race. It was, in fact, no easy task to prevent the Republicans from flocking after him in 1858, when he had, for once only, sided with them, in reference to the Lecompton Constitution. There are some reasons for believing that Douglas would have separated himself from the slaveholders entirely after the Lecompton fight, if he had thought that the Republicans would join in re-electing him to the Senate. Yet the position taken by the party in Illinois was perfectly sound. Douglas was too slippery to make a bargain with. He afterwards redeemed himself in the eyes of his opponents by an immense service to the Union, which no other man could have rendered; but, up to this time, there was nothing for anti-slavery men to do but to beat him if they could.

I will add here that I had no personal acquaintance with Mr. Douglas, although my opportunities for meeting him were frequent. I regarded him as the most dangerous enemy of liberty, and, therefore, as my enemy. I did not want to know him. Accordingly, one day when Mr. Sheridan courteously offered to present me to his chief, I declined without giving any reason. Of course, this was a mistake; but, at the age of twenty-four, I took my politics very seriously. I thought that all the work of saving the country had to be done then and there. I have since learned to leave something to time and Providence.

Mr. Lincoln's individual campaign began at Beardstown, Cass County, August 12th. Douglas had been there the previous day, and I had heard him. His speech had consisted mainly of tedious repetitions of "popular sovereignty," but he had taken occasion to notice Lincoln's conspiracy charge, and had called it "an infamous lie." He had also alluded to Senator Trumbull's charge that he (Douglas) had, two years earlier, been engaged in a plot to force a bogus Constitution on the people of Kansas without giving them an opportunity to vote upon it. "The miserable, craven-hearted wretch," said Douglas, "he would rather have both ears cut off than to use that language in my presence, where I could call him to account." Before entering upon this subject, Douglas turned to his reporters and said, "Take this down." They did so and it was published a few days later in the St. Louis *Republican*. This incident furnished the text of the Charleston joint debate on the 18th of September.

Mr. Douglas's meeting at Beardstown was large and enthusiastic, but was composed of a lower social stratum than the Republican meeting of the following day. Mr. Lincoln came up the Illinois River from the town of Naples in the steamer *Sam Gaty*. Cass County and the surrounding region was by no means hopeful Republican ground. Yet Mr. Lincoln's friends mustered forty horsemen and two bands of music, besides a long procession on foot to meet him at the landing. Schuyler County sent a delegation of three hundred, and Morgan County was well represented. These were mostly Old Line Whigs who had followed Lincoln in earlier days. Mr. Lincoln's speech at Beardstown was one of the best he ever made in my hearing, and was not a repetition of any other. In fact, he never repeated himself except when some remark or question from the audience led him back upon a subject that he had already discussed. Many times did I marvel to see him get on a platform at some out-of-the-way place and begin an entirely new speech, equal, in all respects, to any of the joint debates, and continue for two hours in a high strain of argumentative power and eloquence, without saying anything that I had heard before. After the Edwardsville meeting I said to him that it was wonderful to me that he could find new things to say everywhere, while Douglas was parroting his popular sovereignty speech at every place. He replied that Douglas was not lacking in versatility, but that he had a theory that the popular sovereignty speech was the one to win on, and that the audiences whom he addressed would hear it only once and would never know whether he made the same speech elsewhere or not, and would never care. Most likely, if their attention were called to the subject, they would think that was the proper thing to do. As for himself, he said that he could not repeat today what he had said yesterday. The subject kept enlarging and widening in his mind as he went on, and it was much easier to make a new speech than to repeat an old one.

It was at Beardstown that Mr. Lincoln uttered the glowing words that have come to be known as the apostrophe to the Declaration of Independence, the circumstances attending which are narrated in another part of this book. Probably the apostrophe, as printed, is a trifle more florid than as delivered, and, therefore, less forcible.

The following passage, from the Beardstown speech, was taken down by me on the platform by long-hand notes and written out immediately after-wards.

THE CONSPIRACY CHARGE

"I made a speech in June last in which I pointed out briefly and consecu-tively, a series of public measures leading directly to the nationalization of slavery—the spreading of that institution over all the Territories and all the States, old as well as new, North as well as South. I enumerated the repeal of the Missouri Compromise, which, every candid man must acknowledge, conferred upon emigrants to Kansas and Nebraska the right to carry slaves there and hold them in bondage, whereas formerly they had no such right; I alluded to the events which followed that repeal, events in which Judge Douglas's name figures quite prominently; I referred to the Dred Scott de-cision and the extraordinary means taken to prepare the public mind for that decision; the efforts put forth by President Pierce to make the people believe that, in the election of James Buchanan, they had endorsed the doc-trine that slavery may exist in the free Territories of the Union—the earnest exhortation put forth by President Buchanan to the people to stick to that decision whatever it might be—the close-fitting niche in the Nebraska Bill, wherein the right of the people to govern themselves is made "subject to the constitution of the United States"—the extraordinary haste made by Judge Douglas to give this decision an endorsement at the capitol of Illinois. I alluded to other concurring circumstances, which I need not repeat now, and I said that, though I could not open the bosoms of men and find out their secret motives, yet, when I found the framework of a barn, or a bridge, or any other structure, built by a number of carpenters—Stephen and Franklin and Roger and James—and so built that each tenon had its proper mortice, and the whole forming a symmetrical piece of workmanship, I should say that those carpenters all worked on an intelligible plan, and understood each other from the beginning. This embraced the main argu-ment in my speech before the Republican State Convention in June. Judge Douglas received a copy of my speech some two weeks before his return to Illinois. He had ample time to examine and reply to it if he chose to do so. He did examine and he did reply to it, but he wholly overlooked the body of my argument, and said nothing about the 'conspiracy charge,' as he terms it. He made his speech up of complaints against our tendencies to Negro equality and amalgamation. Well, seeing that Douglas had had the process served on him, that he had taken notice of the process, that he had come into court and pleaded to a part of the complaint, but had ignored the main issue, I took a default on him. I held that he had no plea to make to the general charge. So when I was called on to reply to him, twenty-four hours afterwards, I renewed the charge as explicitly as I could. My speech was reported and published on the following morning, and, of course, Judge Douglas saw it. He went from Chicago to Bloomington and there made another and longer speech, and yet took no notice of the 'conspiracy charge.' He then went to Springfield and made another elaborate argument, but was not prevailed upon to know anything about the outstanding indictment. I made another speech at Springfield, this time taking it for granted that Judge Douglas was satisfied to take his chances in the campaign with the imputation of the conspiracy hanging over him. It was not until he went into a small town, Clinton, in De Witt County, where he delivered his fourth or fifth regular speech, that he found it convenient to notice this matter at all. At that place (I was standing in the crowd when he made his speech), he bethought himself that he was charged with something, and his reply was that his 'self-respect alone prevented him from calling it a falsehood.' Well, my friends, perhaps he so far lost his self-respect in Beardstown as to actually call it a falsehood.

"But now I have this reply to make: that while the Nebraska Bill was pending, Judge Douglas helped to vote down a clause giving the people of the Territories the right to exclude slavery if they chose; that neither while the bill was pending, nor at any other time, would he give his opinion whether the people had the right to exclude slavery, though respectfully asked; that he made a report, which I hold in my hand, from the Committee on Territories, in which he said the rights of the people of the Territories, in this regard, are 'held in abeyance,' and cannot be immediately exercised; that the Dred Scott decision expressly denies any such right, but declares that neither Congress nor the Territorial Legislature can keep slavery out of Kansas and that Judge Douglas endorses that decision. All these charges are new; that is, I did not make them in my original speech. They are additional and cumulative testimony. I bring them forward now and dare Judge Douglas to deny one of them. Let him do so and I will prove them by such testimony as shall confound him forever. I say to you, that it would be more to the purpose for Judge Douglas to say that he did not repeal the Missouri Compromise; that he did not make slavery possible where it was impossible before; that he did not leave a niche in the Nebraska Bill for the Dred Scott decision to rest in; that he did not vote down a clause giving the people the right to exclude slavery if they wanted to; that he did not refuse to give his individual opinion whether a Territorial Legislature could exclude slavery; that he did not make a report to the Senate, in which he said that the rights of the people, in this regard, were held in abeyance and could not be immediately exercised; that he did not make a hasty endorsement of the Dred Scott decision over at Springfield;* that he does not now endorse that decision; that that decision does not take away from the Territorial Legislature the right to exclude slavery; and that he did not, in the original Ne-

* This refers to Douglas' speech of June 12, 1857.

braska Bill, so couple the words State and Territory together that what the Supreme Court has done in forcing open all the Territories to slavery it may yet do in forcing open all the States. I say it would be vastly more to the point for Judge Douglas to say that he did not do some of these things; that he did not forge some of these links of testimony, than to go vociferating about the country that possibly he may hint that somebody is a liar."

The next morning, August 13th, we boarded the steamer *Editor* and went to Havana, Mason County. Mr. Lincoln was in excellent spirits. Several of his old Whig friends were on board, and the journey was filled up with politics and story-telling. In the latter branch of human affairs, Mr. Lincoln was most highly gifted. From the beginning to the end of our travels the fund of anecdotes never failed, and, wherever we happened to be, all the people within ear-shot would begin to work their way up to this inimitable story-teller. His stories were always *apropos* of something going on, and oftenest related to things that had happened in his own neighborhood. He was constantly being reminded of one, and, when, he told it, his facial expression was so irresistibly comic that the bystanders generally exploded in laughter before he reached what he called the "nub" of it. Although the intervals between the meetings were filled up brimful with mirth in this way, Mr. Lincoln indulged very sparingly in humor in his speeches. I asked him one day why he did not oftener turn the laugh on Douglas. He replied that he was too much in earnest, and that it was doubtful whether turning the laugh on anybody really gained any votes.

We arrived at Havana while Douglas was still speaking. The deputation that met Mr. Lincoln at the landing suggested that he should go up to the grove where the Democratic meeting was going on and hear what Douglas was saying. But he declined to do so, saying: "The Judge was so put out by my listening to him at Bloomington and Clinton that I promised to leave him alone at his own meetings for the rest of the campaign. I understand that he is calling Trumbull and myself liars, and if he should see me in the crowd he might be so ashamed of himself as to omit the most telling part of his argument." I strolled up to the Douglas meeting just before its conclusion, and there met a friend who had heard the whole. He was in a state of high indignation. He said that Douglas must certainly have been drinking before he came on the platform, because he had called Lincoln "a liar, a coward, a wretch and a sneak."

When Mr. Lincoln replied, on the following day, he took notice of Douglas's hard words in this way:

"I am informed that my distinguished friend yesterday became a little excited, nervous (?) perhaps, and that he said something about fighting, as though looking to a personal encounter between himself and me. Did anybody in this audience hear him use such language? (Yes, Yes.) I am informed, further, that somebody in his audience, rather more excited or nervous than himself, took off his coat and offered to take the job off Judge Douglas's hands and fight Lincoln himself. Did anybody here witness that warlike proceeding? (Laughter and cries of "yes.") Well, I merely desire to say that I shall fight neither Judge Douglas nor his second. I shall not do this for two reasons, which I will explain. In the first place a fight would prove nothing which is in issue in this election. It might establish that Judge Douglas is a more muscular man than myself, or it might show that I am a more muscular man than Judge Douglas. But this subject is not referred to in the Cincinnati platform, nor in either of the Springfield platforms. Neither result would prove him right or me wrong. And so of the gentleman who offered to do his fighting for him. If my fighting Judge Douglas would not prove anything, it would certainly prove nothing for me to fight his bottle-holder. My second reason for not having a personal encounter with Judge Douglas is that I don't believe he wants it himself. He and I are about the best friends in the world, and when we get together he would no more think of fighting me than of fighting his wife. Therefore, when the Judge talked about fighting he was not giving vent to any ill-feeling of his own, but was merely trying to excite—well, let us say enthusiasm against me on the part of his audience. And, as I find he was tolerably successful in this, we will call it quits."

At Havana I saw Mrs. Douglas (*née* Cutts) standing with a group of ladies a short distance from the platform on which her husband was speaking, and I thought I had never seen a more queenly face and figure. I saw her frequently afterwards in this campaign, but never personally met her till many years later, when she had become the wife of General Williams of the regular army, and the mother of children who promised to be as beautiful as herself. There is no doubt in my mind that this attractive presence was very helpful to Judge Douglas in the campaign. It is certain that the Republicans considered her a dangerous element. . . .

The next stage brought us to Ottawa, the first joint debate, August 21st. Here the crowd was enormous. The weather had been very dry and the town was shrouded in dust raised by the moving populace. Crowds were pouring into town from sunrise till noon in all sorts of conveyances, teams, railroad trains, canal boats, cavalcades, and processions on foot, with banners and inscriptions, stirring up such clouds of dust that it was hard to make out what was underneath them. The town was covered with bunting, and bands of music were tooting around every corner, drowned now and then by the roar of cannon. Mr. Lincoln came by railroad and Mr. Douglas by carriage from La Salle. A train of seventeen passenger cars from Chicago attested the interest felt in that city in the first meeting of the champions. The great processions escorted them to the platform in the public square. But the eagerness to hear the speaking was so great that the crowd had taken possession of the square and the platform, and had climbed on the wooden awning overhead, to such an extent that the speakers and the committees and reporters could not get to their places. Half an hour was consumed in a rough-and-tumble skirmish to make way for them, and, when finally this was accomplished, a section of the awning gave way with its load of men and boys, and came down on the heads of the Douglas committee of reception. But, fortunately, nobody was hurt.

Here I was joined by Mr. Hitt and also by Mr. Chester P. Dewey of the New York *Evening Post,* who remained with us until the end of the campaign. Hither, also, came quite an army of young newspaper men, among whom was Henry Villard, in behalf of Forney's Philadelphia *Press.*

I have preserved Mr. Dewey's sketch of the two orators as they appeared on the Ottawa platform, and I introduce it here as a graphic description by a new hand:

"Two men presenting wider contrasts could hardly be found, as the representatives of the two great parties. Everybody knows Douglas, a short, thick-set, burly man, with large, round head, heavy hair, dark complexion, and fierce, bull-dog look. Strong in his own real power, and skilled by a thousand conflicts in all the strategy of a hand-to-hand or a general fight; of towering ambition, restless in his determined desire for notoriety, proud, defiant, arrogant, audacious, unscrupulous, "Little Dug" ascended the platform and looked out impudently and carelessly on the immense throng which surged and struggled before him. A native of Vermont, reared on a soil where no slave stood, he came to Illinois a teacher, and from one post to another had risen to his present eminence. Forgetful of the ancestral hatred of slavery to which he was the heir, he had come to be a holder of slaves, and to owe much of his fame to continued subservience to Southern influence.

"The other—Lincoln—is a native of Kentucky, of poor white parentage, and, from his cradle, has felt the blighting influence of the dark and cruel shadow which rendered labor dishonorable and kept the poor in poverty, while it advanced the rich in their possessions. Reared in poverty, and to the humblest aspirations, he left his native State, crossed the line into Illinois, and began his career of honorable toil. At first a laborer, splitting rails for a living—deficient in education, and applying himself even to the rudiments of knowledge—he, too, felt the expanding power of his American manhood, and began to achieve the greatness to which he has succeeded. With great difficulty, struggling through the tedious formularies of legal lore, he was admitted to the bar, and rapidly made his way to the front ranks of his profession. Honored by the people with office, he is still the same honest and reliable man. He volunteers in the Black Hawk War, and does the State good service in its sorest need. In every relation of life, socially and to the State, Mr. Lincoln has been always the pure and honest man. In physique he is the opposite to Douglas. Built on the Kentucky type, he is very tall, slender and angular, awkward even in gait and attitude. His face is sharp, large-featured and unprepossessing. His eyes are deep-set under heavy brows, his forehead is high and retreating, and his hair is dark and heavy. In repose, I must confess that 'Long Abe's' appearance is *not* comely. But stir him up and the fire of his genius plays on every feature. His eye glows and sparkles; every lineament, now so ill-formed, grows brilliant and expressive, and you have before you a man of rare power and of strong magnetic influence. He *takes* the people every time, and there is no getting away from his sturdy good sense, his unaffected sincerity and the unceasing play of his good humor, which accompanies his close logic and smoothes the way to conviction. Listening to him on Saturday, calmly and unprejudiced, I was convinced that he had no superior as a stump-speaker. He is clear, concise and logical, his language is eloquent and at perfect command. He is altogether a more fluent speaker than Douglas, and in all the arts of debate fully his equal. The Republicans of Illinois have chosen a champion worthy of their heartiest support, and fully equipped for the conflict with the great Squatter Sovereign."

One trifling error of fact will be noticed by the readers of these volumes in Mr. Dewey's sketch. It relates to Douglas, and it is proper to correct it here. Mr. Douglas was never a slaveholder. As a trustee or guardian, he held a plantation in Louisiana with the slaves thereon, which had belonged to Colonel Robert Martin of North Carolina, the maternal grandfather of his two sons by his first marriage. It is a fact that Douglas refused to accept this plantation and its belongings as a gift to himself from Colonel Martin in the life-time of the latter. It was characteristic of him that he declined to be an owner of slaves, not because he sympathized with the Abolitionists, but because, as he said once in a debate with Senator Wade, "being a Northern man by birth, by education and residence, and intending always to remain such, it was impossible for me to know, understand, and provide for the happiness of those people. . . ."

The Ottawa debate gave great satisfaction to our side. Mr. Lincoln, we thought, had the better of the argument, and we all came away encouraged. But the Douglas men were encouraged also. In his concluding half hour, Douglas spoke with great rapidity and animation, and yet with perfect distinctness, and his supporters cheered him wildly.

The next joint debate was to take place at Freeport, six days later. In the interval, Mr. Lincoln addressed meetings at Henry, Marshall County; Augusta, Hancock County, and Macomb, McDonough County. During this interval he prepared the answers to the seven questions put to him by Douglas at Ottawa, and wrote the four questions which he propounded to Douglas at Freeport. The second of these, *viz.:* "Can the people of a United States Territory, in any lawful way, against the wish of any citizen of the United States, exclude slavery from its limits prior to the formation of a

State Constitution?" was made the subject of a conference between Mr. Lincoln and a number of his friends from Chicago, among whom were Norman B. Judd and Dr. C. H. Ray, the latter the chief editor of the *Tribune*. This conference took place at the town of Dixon. I was not present, but Dr. Ray told me that all who were there counselled Mr. Lincoln not to put that question to Douglas, because he would answer it in the affirmative and thus probably secure his re-election. It was their opinion that Lincoln should argue strongly from the Dred Scott decision, which Douglas endorsed, that the people of the Territories could not lawfully exclude slavery prior to the formation of a State Constitution, but that he should not force Douglas to say yes or no. They believed that the latter would let that subject alone as much as possible in order not to offend the South, unless he should be driven into a corner. Mr. Lincoln replied that to draw an affirmative answer from Douglas on this question was exactly what he wanted, and that his object was to make it impossible for Douglas to get the vote of the Southern States in the next presidential election. He considered that fight much more important than the present one and he would be willing to lose this in order to win that.

The result justified Mr. Lincoln's prevision. Douglas did answer in the affirmative. If he had answered in the negative he would have lost the Senatorial election, and that would have ended his political career. He took the chance of being able to make satisfactory explanations to the slaveholders, but they would have nothing to do with him afterwards.

The crowd that assembled at Freeport on the 27th of August was even larger than that at Ottawa. Hundreds of people came from Chicago and many from the neighboring State of Wisconsin. Douglas came from Galena the night before the debate, and was greeted with a great torch-light procession. Lincoln came the following morning from Dixon, and was received at the railway station by a dense crowd, filling up all the adjacent streets, who shouted themselves hoarse when his tall form was seen emerging from the train. Here, again, the people had seized upon the platform, and all the approaches to it, an hour before the speaking began, and a hand-to-hand fight took place to secure possession.

After the debate was finished, we Republicans did not feel very happy. We held the same opinion that Mr. Judd and Dr. Ray had—that Douglas's answer had probably saved him from defeat. We did not look forward, and we did not look south, and even if we had done so, we were too much enlisted in this campaign to swap it for another one which was two years distant. Mr. Lincoln's wisdom was soon vindicated by his antagonist, one of whose earliest acts, after he returned to Washington City, was to make a speech (February 23, 1859) defending himself against attacks upon the "Freeport heresy," as the Southerners called it. In that debate Jefferson Davis was particularly aggravating, and Douglas did not reply to him with his usual spirit.

It would draw this chapter out to unreasonable length, if I were to give details of all the small meetings of this campaign. After the Freeport joint debate, we went to Carlinville, Macoupin County, where John M. Palmer divided the time with Mr. Lincoln. From this place we went to Clinton, De Witt County, via Springfield and Decatur. . . . Our course took us next to Bloomington, McLean County; Monticello, Piatt County, and Paris, Edgar County. . . .

My notes of the Paris meeting embrace the following passage from Mr. Lincoln's speech.

WHAT IS POPULAR SOVEREIGNTY?

"Let us inquire what Judge Douglas really invented when he introduced the Nebraska Bill? He called it Popular Sovereignty. What does that mean? It means the sovereignty of the people over their own affairs—in other words, the right of the people to govern themselves. Did Judge Douglas invent this? Not quite. The idea of Popular Sovereignty was floating about several ages before the author of the Nebraska Bill was born—indeed, before Columbus set foot on this continent. In the year 1776 it took form in the noble words which you are all familiar with: 'We hold these truths to be self-evident, that all men are created equal,' etc. Was not this the origin of Popular Sovereignty as applied to the American people? Here we are told that governments are instituted among men deriving their just powers from the consent of the governed. If that is not Popular Sovereignty, then I have no conception of the meaning of words. If Judge Douglas did not invent this kind of Popular Sovereignty, let us pursue the inquiry and find out what kind he did invent. Was it the right of emigrants to Kansas and Nebraska to govern themselves, and a lot of 'niggers,' too, if they wanted them? Clearly this was no invention of his, because General Cass put forth the same doctrine in 1848 in his so-called Nicholson letter, six years before Douglas thought of such a thing. Then what was it that the 'Little Giant' invented? It never occurred to General Cass to call his discovery by the odd name of Popular Sovereignty. He had not the face to say that the right of the people to govern 'niggers' was the right of the people to govern themselves. His notions of the fitness of things were not moulded to the brazenness of calling the right to put a hundred 'niggers' through under the lash in Nebraska a 'sacred right of self-government.' And here, I submit to you, was Judge Douglas's discovery, and the whole of it. He discovered that the right to breed and flog Negroes in Nebraska was Popular Sovereignty."

The next meetings in their order were Hillsboro, Montgomery County; Greenville, Bond County, and Edwardsville, Madison County. At Edwardsville (September 13th) I was greatly impressed with Mr. Lincoln's speech, so much so that I took down the following passages, which, as I read them now after the lapse of thirty-one years, bring back the whole scene with vividness before me—the quite autumn day in the quaint old town; the serious people clustered around the platform; Joseph Gillespie officiating as chairman, and the tall, gaunt, earnest man, whose high destiny and tragic death were veiled from our eyes, appealing to his old Whig friends, and seeking to lift them up to his own level.

"I have been requested," he said, "to give a concise statement of the difference, as I understand it, between the Democratic and the Republican parties on the leading issues of the campaign. This question has been put to me by a gentleman whom I do not know. I do not even know whether he is a friend of mine or a supporter of Judge Douglas in this contest, nor does that make any difference. His question is a proper one. Lest I should forget it, I will give you my answer before proceeding with the line of argument I have marked out for this discussion.

"The difference between the Republican and the Democratic parties on the leading issues of this contest, as I understand it, is that the former consider slavery a moral, social and political wrong, while the latter do not consider it either a moral, a social or a political wrong; and the action of each, as respects the growth of the country and the expansion of our population, is squared to meet these views. I will not affirm that the Democratic Party consider slavery morally, socially and politically right, though their tendency to that view has, in my opinion, been constant and unmistakable for the past five years. I prefer to take, as the accepted maxim of the party, the idea put forth by Judge Douglas, that he 'don't care whether slavery is voted down or voted up.' I am quite willing to believe that many Democrats would prefer that slavery should be always voted down, and I know that some prefer that it be always 'voted up'; but I have a right to insist that their action, especially if it be their constant action, shall determine their ideas and preferences on this subject. Every measure of the Democratic Party of late years, bearing directly or indirectly on the slavery question, has corresponded with this notion of utter indifference, whether slavery or freedom shall outrun in the race of empire across to the Pacific— every measure, I say, up to the Dred Scott decision, where, it seems to me, the idea is boldly suggested that slavery is better than freedom. The Republican Party, on the contrary, hold that this government was instituted to secure the blessings of freedom, and that slavery is an unqualified evil to the Negro, to the white man, to the soil, and to the State. Regarding it as an evil, they will not molest it in the States where it exists, they will not overlook the constitutional guards which our fathers placed around it; they will do nothing that can give proper offence to those who hold slaves by legal sanction; but they will use every constitutional method to prevent the evil from becoming larger and involving more Negroes, more white men, more soil, and more States in its deplorable consequences. They will, if possible, place it where the public mind shall rest in the belief that it is in course of ultimate peaceable extinction in God's own good time. And to this end they will, if possible, restore the Government to the policy of the fathers—the policy of preserving the new Territories from the baneful influence of human bondage, as the Northwestern Territories were sought to be preserved by the Ordinance of 1787, and the Compromise Act of 1820. They will oppose, in all its length and breadth, the modern Democratic idea that slavery is as good as freedom, and ought to have room for expansion all over the continent, if people can be found to carry it. All, or nearly all, of Judge Douglas's arguments are logical, if you admit that slavery is as good and as right as freedom, and not one of them is worth a rush if you deny it. This is the difference, as I understand it, between the Republican and Democratic parties."

I think that this was the most important intellectual wrestle that has ever taken place in this country, and that it will bear comparison with any which history mentions. Its consequences we all know. It gave Mr. Lincoln such prominence in the public eye that his nomination to the Presidency became possible and almost inevitable. It put an apple of discord in the Democratic Party which hopelessly divided it at Charleston, thus making Republican success in 1860 morally certain. This was one of Mr. Lincoln's designs, as has been already shown. Perhaps the Charleston schism would have taken place even if Douglas had not been driven into a corner at Freeport, and compelled to proclaim the doctrine of "unfriendly legislation," but it is more likely that the break would have been postponed a few years longer.

Everything stated in this chapter is taken from memoranda made at the time of occurrence. I need not say that I conceived an ardent attachment to Mr. Lincoln. Nobody could be much in his society without being strongly drawn to him.

4

John Brown:
Kansas and Harper's Ferry

Horace Greeley

On the 17th of October, 1859, this country was bewildered and astounded, while the fifteen slave States were convulsed with fear, rage, and hate, by telegraphic dispatches from Baltimore and Washington, announcing the outbreak, at Harper's Ferry, of a conspiracy of Abolitionists and Negroes, having for its object the devastation and ruin of the South, and the massacre of her white inhabitants. A report that President Buchanan had been proclaimed Emperor and Autocrat of the North American continent, and had quietly arrested and imprisoned all the members of Congress and Judges of the Supreme Court, by way of strengthening his usurpation, would not have seemed more essentially incredible, nor have aroused a more intense excitement. Here follow the dispatches which gave the first tidings of this audacious and amazing demonstration.

INSURRECTION AT HARPER'S FERRY!

To the Associated Press:

Baltimore, Monday, Oct. 17, 1859

A dispatch just received here from Frederick, and dated this morning, states that an insurrection has broken out at Harper's Ferry, where an armed band of Abolitionists have full possession of the Government Arsenal. The express train going east was twice fired into, and one of the railroad hands and a negro killed, while they were endeavoring to get the train through the town. The insurrectionists stopped and arrested two men, who had come to town with a load of wheat, and, seizing their wagon, loaded it with rifles and sent them into Maryland. The insurrectionists number about 250 whites, and are aided by a gang of negroes. At last accounts, fighting was going on. . . .

Probably the more prevalent sensation at first excited by this intelligence was that of blank incredulity. Harper's Ferry being the seat of a National Armory, at which a large number of mechanics and artisans were usually employed by the Government, it was supposed by many that some collision respecting wages or hours of labor had occurred between the officers and

HORACE GREELEY, *The American Conflict,* 2 vols. (Chicago, 1864-66), Ch. 20.

the workmen, which had provoked a popular tumult, and perhaps a stop-
page of the trains passing through that village on the Baltimore and Ohio
Railroad; and that this, magnified by rumor and alarm, had afforded a basis
for these monstrous exaggerations. Yet, as time wore on, further advices,
with particulars and circumstances, left no room to doubt the substantial
truth of the original report. An attempt had actually been made to excite
a slave insurrection in Northern Virginia, and the one man in America to
whom such an enterprise would not seem utter insanity and suicide was at
the head of it.

John Brown was sixth in descent from Peter Brown, a carpenter by trade,
and a Puritan by intense conviction, who was one of the glorious company
who came over in the Mayflower, and landed at Plymouth Rock, on that
memorable 22d of December, 1620. The fourth in descent from Peter the
pilgrim, was John Brown, born in 1728, who was captain of the West Sims-
bury (Connecticut) train-band, and in that capacity joined the Continental
Army at New York in the Spring of 1776, and, after two months' service, fell
a victim to camp-fever, dying in a barn a few miles north of the city. His
grandson, John Brown, of Osawatomie, son of Owen and Ruth Brown, was
born in Torrington, Connecticut, May 9, 1800. On his mother's side, he was
descended from Peter Miles, an emigrant from Holland, who settled at
Bloomfield, Connecticut, about 1700; and his grandfather on this side,
Gideon Mills, also served in the Revolutionary War, and attained the rank
of lieutenant.

When John was but five years old, his father migrated to Hudson, Ohio,
where he died a few years since, aged eighty-seven. He was engaged, during the last war, in furnishing beef cattle to our forces on the northern
frontier; and his son, John, then twelve to fourteen years of age, accompanied him as a cattle-driver, and, in that capacity, witnessed Hull's surrender at Detroit, in 1812. He was so disgusted with what he saw of military
life that he utterly refused, when of suitable age, to train or drill in the
militia, but paid fines or evaded service during his entire liability to military
duty. In an autobiographical fragment, written by him in 1857, for a child
who had evinced a deep interest in his Kansas efforts, speaking of himself
in the third person, he says:

> During the war with England, a circumstance occurred that in the end
> made him a most determined Abolitionist, and led him to declare, or swear,
> eternal war with slavery. He was staying, for a short time, with a very gentle-
> manly landlord, once a United States Marshal, who held a slave-boy near his
> own age, active, intelligent, and good-feeling, and to whom John was under
> considerable obligation for numerous little acts of kindness. The master made
> a great pet of John, brought him to table with his first company and friends—
> called their attention to every little smart thing he said or did, and to the fact
> of his being more than a hundred miles from home with a drove of cattle alone;
> while the Negro boy (who was fully, if not more than, his equal,) was badly

clothed, poorly fed and lodged in cold weather, and beaten before his eyes with iron shovels or any other thing that came first to hand. This brought John to reflect on the wretched, hopeless condition of fatherless and motherless slave children; for such children have neither fathers nor mothers to protect and provide for them. He sometimes would raise the question, Is God their Father?

Young John had very little of what is called education; poverty and hard work being his principal teachers. At sixteen years of age, he joined the Congregational Church in Hudson; and from fifteen to twenty he learned the trade of tanner and currier. He returned to New England while still a minor, and commenced, at Plainfield, Massachusetts, a course of study with a view to the Christian ministry; but, being attacked with inflammation of the eyes, which ultimately became chronic, he relinquished this pursuit and returned to Ohio, where he married his first wife, Dianthe Lusk, when a little more than twenty years of age. By her, he had seven children; the last of whom, born in 1832, was buried with her three days after its birth. He next year married Mary A. Day (who survives him), by whom he had thirteen children, of whom three sons were with him at Harper's Ferry, two of whom lost their lives there, and the third escaped. Eight of his children were living at the time of his death.

Brown worked for himself as a tanner and farmer five or six years in northern Ohio, and, for nine or ten years thereafter, in Crawford County, Pennsylvania, enjoying general respect as a sincere, earnest, upright, pious man. One who knew him in those days remembers that the wrong of slavery was a favorite topic with him, and that, though stern in manner, he was often affected to tears when depicting the unmerited sufferings of slaves. So early as 1839, the idea of becoming himself a liberator of the unhappy race was cherished by him. From 1835 to 1846, he lived once more in northern Ohio, removing thence to Springfield, Massachusetts, where he engaged in wool-dealing under the firm of Perkins & Brown, selling wool extensively on commission for growers along the southern shore of Lake Erie, and undertaking to dictate prices and a system of grading wools to the manufacturers of New England, with whom he came to an open rupture, which induced him at length to ship two hundred thousand pounds of wool to London, and go thither to sell it. This bold experiment proved a failure, wool bringing far higher prices in this country than in any other. He finally sold at a fearful loss and came home a bankrupt. But, meantime, he had traveled considerably over Europe, and learned something of the ways of the world.

In 1849, he removed with his family to North Elba, Essex County, New York, to some land given him by Gerrit Smith. He went thither expressly to counsel and benefit the Negroes settled in that vicinity, on lands likewise bestowed upon them by our noblest philanthropist. The location was a hard one, high up among the glens of the Adirondack Mountains, rugged, cold, and bleak. The Negroes generally became discouraged, in view of the incessant toil, privation, and hardships, involved in hewing a farm and a habitation out of the primitive wilderness, in a secluded, sterile region, and gave over in despair after a brief trial; but John Brown and his sons persevered, ultimately making homes for themselves, which, though not luxurious nor inviting, their families retain. In 1851, the father returned with his family to Akron, Ohio, where he once more carried on the wool business and managed the farm of a friend; but, in 1855, on starting for Kansas, he moved his family back to their own home at North Elba, where they remain, with his grave in the midst of them.

In 1854, his four elder sons—all by his first wife, and all living in Ohio—determined to migrate to Kansas. They went thither, primarily, to make that a free State; secondly, to make homes for themselves and their families. They went unarmed, having a very inadequate idea of the nature and spirit of the fiend they were defying. They settled in Lykins County, southern Kansas, about eight miles distant from the present village of Osawatomie, and not far from the Missouri border. Here they were soon so harassed, threatened, insulted, and plundered, by gangs of marauding ruffians from Missouri, that they found it impossible to remain without arms, and they wrote to their father to procure such as they needed. He obtained them; and, to make sure work of it, went with them. Nearly all others went to Kansas in the hope of thereby improving their worldly condition, or, at least, of making homes there. John Brown went there for the sole purpose of fighting, if need were, for liberty. He left his family behind him, for he had no intention of making Kansas his home. He was no politician, in the current acceptation of the term, having taken little or no interest in party contests for many years. . . .

Of course, he was not pleased with what he found and saw in Kansas. There were too much policy, too much politics, and too general a regard for personal safety and comfort. He would have preferred a good deal less riding about, especially at night, with more solid fighting. . . .

In the August following, a new invasion, on an extensive scale, of Kansas, from the Missouri border, was planned and executed. Inflammatory proclamations were issued, which affirmed that the pro-slavery settlers either had been or were about to be all killed or driven out of the Territory by the Abolitionists, and the Missourians were exhorted to rally all their forces for the conflict. Lexington, Missouri, was assigned as the place, and August 20th as the time, of assemblage for La Fayette County, and New Santa Fe, Jackson County, as the general rendezvous. "Bring your guns, your horses, and your clothing, all ready to go on to Kansas: our motto will be this time, 'No Quarter!' Let no one stay away!" A similar appeal was issued from Westport, signed by Atchison, Stringfellow, and others. A force of two thousand men was, by virtue of these appeals, collected at the petty village of Santa Fe, directly on the border; but soon divided into two expeditions, one of which, led by Senator Atchison, was confronted at Bull's Creek by not more than half its number under General J. H. Lane, and turned back without a fight—first halting, and refusing to advance against the determined front of the Free-State men, and finally disappearing in the course of the ensuing night. The other and smaller party, led by General Reid, consisted of four to five hundred men, well armed with United States cannon, muskets, bayonets, and revolvers, and liberally supplied with ammunition. They pursued a more southerly course, and, at daylight on the morning of August 30th, approached the little village of Osawatomie, which was defended by barely thirty Free-State men; but their leader was old John Brown. His son Frederick was shot dead, about a mile and a half from the village, by the Reverend Martin White, who led the pro-slavery advance or scouting party, before young Brown was aware of their hostile character. Two other Free-State men were likewise surprised and killed early in the morning.

John Brown, with his thirty compatriots, took position in great haste in the timber on the southern bank of the little river Osage, here known as the Marais-des-Cygnes, a little to the northwest of the village, and here fought the advance of the foe as they approached, until thirty-one or two of them were killed and from forty to fifty wounded. The Free-State men, fighting generally under cover against an undisciplined and badly managed force, lost but five or six in all; but the disproportion was too great, and, their ammunition becoming exhausted, they were forced to retreat, leaving Osawatomie to be sacked and burned again. Brown himself continued steadily firing, as well as directing his men, throughout the conflict, amid an incessant shower of grapeshot and bullets. Not until he saw the whites of his enemy's eyes did he give the order to his little band to retreat. The Ruffians killed the only wounded prisoner whom they took, as also a Mr. Williams, whom they found in Osawatomie, and who had taken no part in the conflict. The Missourians returned to their homes in triumph, boasting that they had killed old Brown and dispersed his band; but their wagon-loads of dead and wounded created a salutary awe, which was very efficient in preventing future invasions, or rendering them comparatively infrequent.

The Reverend Martin White, for his services in this expedition, was chosen a member of the next Lecompton (pro-slavery) Legislature, which he attended; and, in the course of its deliberations, he entertained his fellow-members with a graphic and humorous account of his killing of Frederick Brown. When the session was finished, he started for home, but never reached it. His body was found cold and stiff on the prairie, with a rifle-ball through his vitals.

Six weeks after the Osawatomie fight, Captain Brown was in Lawrence, stopping over Sunday on his way home from Topeka, when the startling announcement was made that 2,800 Missourians, under Atchison and Reid, were advancing upon that town. Not more than two hundred men in all could be rallied for its defense. Brown was unanimously chosen their leader. . . .

He proceeded to post his men so admirably as to conceal entirely their paucity of numbers, taking advantage of a gentle ridge running east and west, at some distance south of the town. The hostile forces remained through the night about half a mile from each other, with a corn-field between, each man covered by the grass and the inequalities of the ground, their positions only revealed by the flashes and reports of their guns. When the sun rose next morning, the Missourians had decamped.

Captain Brown left soon after for the East by the circuitous land route through Nebraska and Iowa; that through Missouri being closed against Free-State men. He took a fugitive slave in his wagon, and saw him safely on his way to freedom. He made two or three visits to the East in quest of aid and of funds, returning for the last time to southern Kansas in the autumn of 1858. Peace had finally been secured in all that part of the Territory lying north of the Kansas River, by the greatly increased numbers and immense preponderance of the Free-State settlers, rendering raids from Missouri, whether to carry elections or devastate settlements, too perilous to be lightly undertaken. When the Missourians still rallied, in obedience to habit, at Kansas elections, they did so at Oxford, Santa Fe, and other polls held just along the border, where they could suddenly concentrate force enough to make the operation a tolerably safe one. But southern Kansas was still very thinly settled, in part by Missourians; while Fort Scott, a military post and land-office in the heart of that section, afforded a nucleus and a rallying-point for pro-slavery terrorism. The Missourians, recognizing and acting under the Territorial Legislature and local officers created by the Border Ruffian irruptions and fraudulent elections, claimed to be the party of Law and Order, and often, if not usually, committed their outrages under the lead of a marshal or a sheriff. The Free-State men, repudiating and scouting those elections and their fruits, were regarded and treated, not only by the pro-slavery party on either side of the border, but by the Federal Administration and its instruments in Kansas, as outlaws and criminals. At length, Fort Scott itself was captured by Montgomery, one of the boldest of the Free-State leaders, who, with 150 men, entered it by night, made temporary prisoners of its dignitaries, and liberated a Free-State man imprisoned there. Montgomery soon after surrendered himself to the Federal Governor of the Territory, when a treaty or understanding was had between them, under which the region gradually settled into comparative peace.

But, while the ferment was at its height, and forces were gathering on both sides for the conflict, a slave named Jim came secretly across the border to Captain Brown's cabin, and told him that himself and his family had been sold, and were to be sent off to Texas next day. Brown, with twenty men, divided into two parties, crossed the border in the night, liberated Jim and his family, and, proceeding to the house of another slave-holder, gave deliverance to five more slaves. The other party, under Kagi, called at several houses in search of slaves, but found none until they reached the residence of David Cruse, who, learning their object, seized his rifle and raised it to fire, but was instantly shot dead. He had but one slave, who accompanied his liberators on their retreat. One of the captured slaveholders was carried several miles into the Territory to prevent his raising a hue-and-cry for rescue.

A furious excitement throughout western Missouri inevitably followed. The Governor offered a reward of three thousand dollars for the arrest of Brown, on his part; to which President Buchanan added two hundred and fifty dollars. It was reported that the slave population of the two adjacent Missouri counties was diminished from five hundred to fifty within a few weeks, mainly by removal for sale. The more moderate Free-State men earnestly disavowed all sympathy with Brown's doings over the border, or any acts of violence by Free-State men on their adversaries, not committed in necessary self-defense. Brown soon learned that he must leave Kansas, or remain there denounced and condemned by those who had hitherto been his friends. He resolved to leave, and started early in January, 1859, passing through Lawrence on his northward route. He had four white companions, three of whom afterward fought under him at Harper's Ferry, and three Negroes, beside women and children. He was pursued by thirty pro-slavery men from Lecompton so sharply that he was compelled to halt and prepare for a defense. He took possession of two deserted log-cabins in the wilderness, which his pursuers surrounded, at a respectful distance, and sent to Atchison and Lecompton for re-enforcements. From Atchison, twelve men arrived, making their force forty-two to his eight. As they were preparing to attack, Brown and his seven companions suddenly issued from the wood, in order of battle, when the valorous *posse* turned and fled. Not a shot was fired, as they, putting spurs to their horses, galloped headlong across the prairie, and were soon lost to the view. . . .

Brown was joined, soon after this "Battle of the Spurs," by Kagi, with forty mounted men from Topeka, of whom seventeen escorted him safely to Nebraska City. He there crossed the Mississippi into Iowa, and traveled slowly through that State, Illinois, and Michigan, to Detroit, where he arrived on the 12th of March, crossing immediately into Canada, where his twelve blacks—one of them born since he left Missouri—were legally, as well as practically, free. All of them were industrious, prosperous, and happy, when last heard from, many months thereafter.

A secret convention, called by Brown, and attended only by such whites and blacks as he believed in thorough sympathy with his views, had assembled in a Negro church at Chatham, Canada West, May 8, 1858; at which Convention a "Provisional Constitution and Ordinances for the People of the United States" had been adopted. It was, of course, drafted by Brown, and was essentially an embodiment of his political views. The nature of this Constitution is sufficiently exhibited in the following extracts:

"PREAMBLE.—*Whereas,* Slavery, throughout its entire existence in the United States, is none other than the most barbarous, unprovoked, and unjustifiable war of one portion of its citizens against another portion, the only conditions of which are perpetual imprisonment and hopeless servitude, or absolute extermination, in utter disregard and violation of those eternal and self-evident truths set forth in our Declaration of Independence:

"Therefore, We, the citizens of the United States, and the oppressed people, who, by a recent decision of the Supreme Court, are declared to have no rights which the white man is bound to respect, together with all the other people degraded by the laws thereof, do, for the time being, ordain and establish for ourselves the following Provisional Constitution and ordinances, the better to protect our people, property, lives, and liberties, and to govern our actions.

"ARTICLE I. *Qualifications of Membership.*—All persons of mature age whether proscribed, oppressed, and enslaved citizens, or of proscribed and oppressed races of the United States, who shall agree to sustain and enforce the Provisional Constitution and ordinances of organization, together with all minor children of such persons, shall be held to be fully entitled to protection under the same."

"ART. XXVIII. *Property.*—All captured or confiscated property, and all property the product of the labor of those belonging to this organization, and of their families, shall be held as the property of the whole equally, without distinction, and may be used for the common benefit, or disposed of for the same object. . . .

"ART. XXXVI. *Property Confiscated.*—The entire personal and real property of all persons known to be acting, either directly or indirectly, with or for the enemy, or found in arms with them, or found willfully holding slaves, shall be confiscated and taken whenever and wherever it may be found, in either Free or Slave States."

"ART. XLVI. *These Articles not for the Overthrow of Government.*—The foregoing articles shall not be construed so as in any way to encourage the overthrow of any State Government, or of the General Government of the United States, and look to no dissolution of the Union, but simply to amendment and repeal; and our flag shall be the same as that our fathers fought under in the Revolution."

Under this Constitution, the offices of President and Commander-in-Chief were to be separate, and in all cases to be held by different persons. John Brown was chosen Commander-in-Chief; J. H. Kagi, Secretary of War; Owen Brown (son of John), Treasurer; Richard Realf, Secretary of State.

Brown returned to the States soon after his triumphal entry into Canada as a liberator, and was at Cleveland from the 20th to the 30th of March. He entered his name on the hotel-book, as "John Brown, of Kansas," advertised two horses for sale at auction; and, at the time of the sale, stood in front of the auctioneer's stand, notifying all bidders that the title might be defective, since he had taken the horses with the slaves whom he liberated in western Missouri, finding it necessary to his success that the slaves have horses, and that the masters should not. "But," he added, when telling the story afterward, "they brought a very excellent price."

Early in April following, he was in Ashtabula County, Ohio, sick of the ague. He visited his family in Essex County, New York, toward the end of that month. In May, he was in New York City, Rochester, and Boston, where he learned to manufacture crackers. On the 3d of June, he was at Collinsville, Connecticut, where he closed a contract for a thousand pikes, that he had ordered some time before.

He was soon afterward again in northern Ohio, and in western Pennsylvania, proceeding by Pittsburgh and Bedford to Chambersburg, where he remained several days. He was in Hagerstown, Maryland, on the 30th, where he registered his name as "Smith, and two sons, from western New York." He told his landlord that they had been farming in western New York, but had been discouraged by losing two or three years' crops by frost, and they were now looking for a milder climate, in a location adapted to wool-growing, etc. After looking about Harper's Ferry for several days, they found, five or six miles from that village, a large farm, with three unoccupied houses, the owner, Dr. Booth Kennedy, having died the last spring. These houses they rented for a trifle until the next March, paying the rent in advance, purchasing for cash a lot of hogs from the family, and agreeing to take care of the stock on the farm until it could be sold, which they faithfully did. After they had lived there a few weeks, attracting no observation, others joined them from time to time, including two of Brown's young daughters; and one would go and another come, without exciting any particular remark. They paid cash for everything, were sociable and friendly with their neighbors, and seemed to pass their time mainly hunting in the mountains; though it was afterward remembered that they never brought home any game. On one occasion, a neighbor remarked to the elder Mr. Smith (as old Brown was called), that he had observed twigs and branches bent down in a peculiar manner; which Smith explained by stating that it was the habit of Indians, in traveling through a strange country, to mark their path thus, so as to be able to find their way back. He had no doubt, he said, that Indians passed over these mountains, unknown to the inhabitants.

Meantime, the greater number of the men kept out of sight during the day, so as not to attract attention, while their arms, munitions, etc., were being gradually brought from Chambersburg, in well-secured boxes. No meal was eaten on the farm, while old Brown was there, until a blessing had been asked upon it; and his Bible was in daily requisition.

The night of the 24th of October was originally fixed upon by Brown for the first blow against slavery in Virginia, by the capture of the Federal Arsenal at Harper's Ferry; and his biographer, Redpath, alleges that many

were on their way to be with him on that occasion, when they were paralyzed by the intelligence that the blow had already been struck, and had
failed. The reason given for this, by one who was in his confidence, is, that
Brown, who had been absent on a secret journey to the North, suspected
that one of his party was a traitor, and that he must strike prematurely, or
not at all. But the women who had been with them at the Kennedy farm—
the wives or daughters of one or another of the party—had already been
quietly sent away; and the singular complexion of their household had
undoubtedly begun to excite curiosity, if not alarm, among their neighbors.
On Saturday, the 15th, a council was held, and a plan of operations discussed. On Sunday evening, another council was held, and the programme
of the chief unanimously approved. He closed it with these words:

> And now, gentlemen, let me press this one thing on your minds. You all
> know how dear life is to you, and how dear your lives are to your friends; and,
> in remembering that, consider that the lives of others are as dear to them as
> yours is to you. Do not, therefore, take the life of any one if you can possibly
> avoid it; but if it is necessary to take a life in order to save your own, then make
> sure the work of it."

Harper's Ferry was then a village of some five thousand inhabitants,
lying on the Virginia side of the Potomac, and on either side of its principal
tributary, the Shenandoah, which here enters it from the south. Its site is
a mere nest or cup among high, steep mountains; the passage of the united
rivers through the Blue Ridge at this point having been pronounced by
Jefferson a spectacle which one might well cross the Atlantic to witness and
enjoy. Here the Baltimore and Ohio Railroad crosses the Potomac; and the
rich valley of the Shenandoah is traversed, for a considerable distance
hence, by the Winchester and Harper's Ferry Railroad. Washington is
fifty-seven miles distant by turnpike, Baltimore eighty miles by railroad.
Modest as the village then was, space had been with difficulty found for
its habitations, some of which were perched upon ground four hundred feet
above the surface of the streams. One of its very few streets was entirely
occupied by the work-shops and offices of the National Armory, and had an
iron railing across its entrance. In the old arsenal building, there were
usually stored from 100,000 to 200,000 stand of arms. The knowledge of
this had doubtless determined the point at which the first blow of the
liberators was to be struck.

The forces with which Brown made his attack consisted of seventeen
white and five colored men, though it is said that others who escaped
assisted outside, by cutting the telegraph wires and tearing up the railroad
track. The entrance of this petty army into Harper's Ferry on Sunday
evening, October 17th, seems to have been effected without creating alarm.
They first rapidly extinguished the lights of the town; then took possession
of the Armory buildings, which were only guarded by three watchmen,
whom, without meeting resistance or exciting alarm, they seized and

locked up in the guard-house. It is probable that they were aided, or, at least, guided, by friendly Negroes belonging in the village. At half-past ten, the watchman at the Potomac bridge was seized and secured. At midnight, his successor, arriving, was hailed by Brown's sentinels, but ran, one shot being fired at him from the bridge. He gave the alarm, but still nothing stirred. At a quarter-past one, the western train arrived, and its conductor found the bridge guarded by armed men. He and others attempted to walk across, but were turned back by presented rifles. One man, a Negro, was shot in the back, and died next morning. The passengers took refuge in the hotel, and remained there several hours; the conductor properly refusing to pass the train over, though permitted, at three o'clock, to do so.

A little after midnight, the house of Colonel Washington was visited by six of Brown's men under Captain Stevens, who captured the Colonel, seized his arms, horses, etc., and liberated his slaves. On their return, Stevens and party visited the house of Mr. Alstadt and his son, whom they captured, and freed their slaves. These, with each male citizen as he appeared in the street, were confined in the Armory until they numbered between forty and fifty. Brown informed his prisoners that they could be liberated on condition of writing to their friends to send a Negro apiece as ransom. At daylight, the train proceeded, Brown walking over the bridge with the conductor. Whenever anyone asked the object of their captors, the uniform answer was, "To free the slaves"; and when one of the workmen, seeing an armed guard at the Arsenal gate, asked by what authority they had taken possession of the public property, he was answered, "By the authority of God Almighty!"

The passenger train that sped eastward from Harper's Ferry, by Brown's permission, in the early morning of Monday, October 17th, left that place completely in the military possession of the insurrectionists. They held, without dispute, the Arsenal, with its offices, work-shops, and grounds. Their sentinels stood on guard at the bridges and principal corners, and were seen walking up and down the streets. Every workman, who ignorantly approached the Armory, as day dawned, was seized and imprisoned, with all other white males who seemed capable of making any trouble. By eight o'clock, the number of prisoners had been swelled to sixty-odd, and the work was still proceeding.

But it was no longer entirely one-sided. The white Virginians, who had arms, and who remained unmolested in their houses, prepared to use them. Soon after daybreak, as Brown's guards were bringing two citizens to a halt, they were fired on by a man named Turner, and, directly afterward, by a grocer named Boerly, who was instantly killed by the return fire. Several Virginians soon obtained possession of a room overlooking the Armory gates, and fired thence at the sentinels who guarded them, one of whom fell dead, and another—Brown's son Watson—was mortally wounded. Still, throughout the forenoon, the liberators remained masters of the

town. There were shots fired from one side or the other at intervals, but no
more casualties reported. The prisoners were by turns permitted to visit
their families under guard, to give assurance that they still lived and were
kindly treated. Had Brown chosen to fly to the mountains with his few
followers, he might still have done so, though with a much slenderer chance
of impunity than if he had, according to his original plan, decamped at midnight, with such arms and ammunition as he could bear away. Why he
lingered, to brave inevitable destruction, is not certain; but it may fairly
be presumed that he had private assurances that the Negroes of the surrounding country would rise at the first tidings of his movement, and come
flocking to his standard; and he chose to court the desperate chances of
remaining where arms and ammunition for all could abundantly be had.
True, he afterward said that he had arms enough already, either on or
about his premises; but, if so, why seize Harper's Ferry at all?

At all events, if his doom was already sealed, his delay at least hastened
it. Half an hour after noon, a militia force, one hundred strong, arrived
from Charlestown, the county seat, and were rapidly disposed so as to
command every available exit from the place. In taking the Shenandoah
bridge, they killed one of the insurgents, and captured William Thompson,
a neighbor of Brown at Elba, unwounded. The rifle-works were next
attacked, and speedily carried, being defended by five insurgents only.
These attempted to cross the river, and four of them succeeded in reaching
a rock in the middle of it, whence they fought with two hundred Virginians,
who lined either bank, until two of them were dead, and a third mortally
wounded, when the fourth surrendered. Kagi, Brown's Secretary of War,
was one of the killed. William H. Leeman, one of Brown's captains, being
pursued by scores, plunged into the river, a Virginian wading after him.
Leeman turned round, threw up his empty hands, and cried, "Don't shoot!"
The Virginia fired his pistol directly in the youth's face—he was but twenty-
two—and shattered his head into fragments.

By this time, all the houses around the Armory buildings were held by
the Virginians. Captain Turner, who had fired the first shot in the morning,
was killed by the sentinel at the Arsenal gate, as he was raising his rifle to
fire. Here Dangerfield Newby, a Virginia slave, and Jim, one of Colonel
Washington's Negroes, with a free Negro, who had lived on Washington's
estate, were shot dead; and Oliver Brown, another of the old man's sons,
being hit by a ball, came inside of the gate, as his brother Watson had done,
lay quietly down without a word, and in a few moments was dead. Mr.
Beckham, mayor of the town, who came within range of insurgents' rifles
as they were exchanging volleys with the Virginians, was likewise killed.

At the suggestion of Mr. Kitzmiller, one of Brown's prisoners, Aaron D.
Stevens, one of his most trusted followers from Kansas, was sent out with
a flag of truce to call a parley, but was instantly shot down by the Virginians, receiving six balls in his person. Thompson, their prisoner, was

attacked by scores of them in the parlor where he was confined, but saved for the moment by a young lady throwing herself between him and their presented rifles, because, as she afterward explained, she "did not want the carpet spoiled." He was dragged out to the bridge, there shot in cold blood, and his body riddled with balls at the base of the pier, whither he had fallen forty feet from the bridge.

By this time, more militia had arrived from every quarter, and a party from Martinsburgh, led by a railroad conductor, attacked the Armory buildings in the rear, while a detachment of the same force assailed them in front. Brown, seeing that his assailants were in overwhelming force, retreated to the engine-house, where he repulsed his assailants, who lost two killed and six wounded.

Still, militia continued to pour in; the telegraph and railroad having been completely repaired, so that the Government at Washington, Governor Wise at Richmond, and the authorities at Baltimore, were in immediate communication with Harper's Ferry, and hurrying forward troops from all quarters to overwhelm the remaining handful of insurgents, whom terror and rumor had multiplied to twenty times their actual number. At five P.M., Captain Simms arrived, with militia from Maryland, and completed the investment of the Armory buildings, whence eighteen prisoners had already been liberated upon the retreat of Brown to the engine-house. Colonel Baylor commanded in chief. The firing ceased at nightfall. Brown offered to liberate his prisoners, upon condition that his men should be permitted to cross the bridge in safety, which was refused. Night found Brown's forces reduced to three unwounded whites beside himself, with perhaps half a dozen Negroes from the vicinity. Eight of the insurgents were already dead; another lay dying beside the survivors; two were captives mortally wounded, and one other unhurt. Around the few survivors were fifteen hundred armed, infuriated foes. Half a dozen of the party, who had been sent out at early morning by Brown to capture slaveholders, and liberate slaves, were absent, and unable, even if willing, to rejoin their chief. They fled during the night to Maryland and Pennsylvania; but most of them were ultimately captured. During that night, Colonel Lee, with ninety United States Marines and two pieces of artillery, arrived, and took possession of the Armory guard, very close to the engine-house.

Brown, of course, remained awake and alert through the night, discomfited and beyond earthly hope, but perfectly cool and calm. Said Governor Wise, in a speech at Richmond soon after:

> Col. Washington said that Brown was the coolest man he ever saw in defying death and danger. With one son dead by his side, and another shot through, he felt the pulse of his dying son with one hand, held his rifle with the other, and commanded his men with the utmost composure, encouraging them to be firm, and to sell their lives as dearly as possible."

Conversing with Colonel Washington during that solemn night, he said he had not pressed his sons to join him in this expedition, but did not regret their loss—they had died in a good cause.

At seven in the morning, after a parley which resulted in nothing, the Marines advanced to the assault, broke in the door of the engine-house by using a ladder as a battering-ram, and rushed into the building. One of the defenders was shot and two Marines wounded; but the odds were too great; in an instant, all resistance was over. Brown was struck in the face with a saber and knocked down, after which the blow was several times repeated, while a soldier ran a bayonet twice into the old man's body. All the insurgents, it was said, would have been killed on the spot, had the Virginians been able to distinguish them with certainty from their prisoners.

Of course, all Virginia, including her Governor, rushed to Harper's Ferry upon learning that all was over, and the insurrection completely suppressed. The bleeding survivors were subjected to an alternation of queries and execrations, which they met bravely, as they had confronted the bullets of their numerous and ever-increasing foes. They answered frankly, save where their replies might possibly compromise persons still at liberty; and none of them sought to conceal the fact that they had struck for Universal Freedom at all hazards. The bearing of Brown was especially praised by his enemies (many of whom have since won notoriety in the ranks of the Rebellion), as remarkably simple and noble. Among others, Mr. C. L. Vallandigham of Ohio hastened to visit and catechise Brown, in the hope of making political capital out of his confessions, and was answered frankly and fully. On his return to Ohio, he said:

> It is in vain to underrate either the man or the conspiracy. Captain John Brown is as brave and resolute a man as ever headed an insurrection; and, in good cause, and with a sufficient force, would have been a consummate partisan commander. He has coolness, daring, persistency, the stoic faith and patience, and a firmness of will and purpose unconquerable. He is the farthest possible remove from the ordinary ruffian, fanatic, or madman. Certainly, it was one of the best planned and best executed conspiracies that ever failed.

On Wednesday evening, October 19th, after thirty hours of this discipline, the four surviving prisoners were conveyed to the jail at Charlestown under an escort of marines. Brown and Stevens, badly wounded, were taken in a wagon; Green and Coppoc, unhurt, walked between files of soldiers, followed by hundreds, who at first cried, "Lynch them!" but were very properly shamed into silence by Governor Wise.

It is not necessary to linger here over the legal proceedings in this case; nor do the complaints, so freely made at the time, of indecent haste and unfair dealing, on the part of the Virginia authorities, seem fully justified. That the conviction and death of Brown and his associates were predetermined, is quite probable; but the facts and the nature of the case were notorious, beyond dispute; and Virginia had but this alternative—to hang John Brown, or to abolish slavery. She did not choose to abolish slavery;

and she had no remaining choice but to hang John Brown. And as to trying him and Stevens while still weak and suffering severely from their wounds—neither able at times to stand up—it must be considered that the whole State had been terror-stricken by the first news of their attempt, and that fears of insurrection and of an armed rescue were still widely prevalent. That the lawyers of the vicinage who were assigned to the defense of the prisoners did their duty timidly and feebly, is certain; but they shared, of course, not only the prejudices but the terrors of their neighbors, and knew that the case, at any rate, was hopeless.

Brown's conduct throughout commanded the admiration of his bitterest enemies. When his papers were brought into court to be identified, he said: "I will identify any of my handwriting, and save all trouble. I am ready to face the music." When a defense of insanity was suggested rather than interposed, he repelled it with indignation. When, after his conviction, he was suddenly brought into court, on the 1st of November, to listen to the judgment, and directed to stand up, and say why sentence should not be passed upon him, though taken by surprise and somewhat confused, he spoke gently and tenderly as follows:

In the first place, I deny everything but what I have all along admitted—the design on my part to free the slaves. I intended certainly to have made a clear thing of that matter, as I did last winter, when I went into Missouri, and there took slaves without the snapping of a gun on either side, moved them through the country, and finally left them in Canada. I designed to have done the same thing again, on a larger scale. That was all I intended. I never did intend murder, or treason, or the destruction of property, or to excite slaves to rebellion, or to make insurrection.

I have another objection: and that is, it is unjust that I should suffer such a penalty. Had I interfered in the manner which I admit has been fairly proved (for I admire the truthfulness and candor of the witnesses who have testified in this case) had I so interfered in behalf of the rich, the powerful, the intelligent, the so-called great, or in behalf of any of their friends, either father, mother, brother, sister, wife, or children, or any of that class, and suffered and sacrificed what I have in this interference, it would have been all right, and every man in this Court would have deemed it an act worthy of reward rather than punishment

This Court acknowledges, as I suppose, the validity of the Law of God. I see a book kissed here which I supposed to be the Bible, or at least, the New Testament. That teaches me that all things "whatsoever I would that men should do unto me, I should do even so to them." It teaches me, further, to "remember those that are in bonds as bound with them." I endeavored to act upon that instruction. I say, I am yet too young to understand that God is any respecter of persons. I believe that to have interfered as I have done, as I have always freely admitted I have done, in behalf of His despised poor, was not wrong, but right. Now, if it is deemed necessary that I should forfeit my life for the furtherance of the ends of justice, and mingle my blood further with the blood of my children, and with the blood of millions in this slave country whose rights are disregarded by wicked, cruel, and unjust enactments—I submit: so let it be done.

Let me say one word further:

I feel entirely satisfied with the treatment I have received on my trial. Considering all the circumstances, it has been more generous than I expected. But I feel no consciousness of guilt. I have stated from the first what was my intention and what was not. I never had any design against the life of any person, nor any disposition to commit treason, or excite slaves to rebel, or make any general insurrection. I never encouraged any man to do so, but always discouraged any idea of that kind.

Let me say, also, a word in regard to the statements made by some of those connected with me. I hear it has been stated by some of them that I have induced them to join me. But the contrary is true. I do not say this to injure them, but as regretting their weakness. There is not one of them but joined me of his own accord, and the greater part at their own expense. A number of them I never saw, and never had a word of conversation with, till the day they came to me, and that was for the purpose I have stated.

Now I have done.

His letter to his family, written a week after his sentence to death, is as follows:

CHARLESTOWN, JEFFERSON CO., VA.,
8th Nov., 1859.

Dear Wife and Children—Everyone: I will begin by saying that I have in some degree recovered from my wounds, but that I am quite weak in my back, and sore about my left kidney. My appetite has been quite good for most of the time since I was hurt. I am supplied with almost everything I could desire to make me comfortable, and the little I do lack (some articles of clothing, which I lost), I may perhaps soon get again. I am, besides, quite cheerful, having (as I trust) the peace of God, which "passeth all understanding," to "rule in my heart," and the testimony (in some degree) of a good conscience that I have not lived altogether in vain. I can trust God with both the time and manner of my death, believing, as I now do, that for me at this time to seal my testimony (for God and humanity) with my blood, will do vastly more toward advancing the cause I have earnestly endeavored to promote, than all I have done in my life before. I beg of you all meekly and quietly to submit to this; not feeling yourselves in the least *degraded* on that account. Remember, dear wife and children all, that Jesus of Nazareth suffered a most excruciating death on the cross as a felon, under the most aggravating circumstances. Think, also, of the prophets, apostles, and Christians of former days, who went through greater tribulations than you or I; and (try to) be reconciled. May God Almighty comfort all your hearts, and soon wipe away all tears from your eyes. To Him be endless praise. Think, too, of the crushed millions who "have no comforter." I charge you all never (in your trials) to forget the griefs of "the poor that cry, and of those that have none to help them." I wrote most earnestly to my dear and afflicted wife not to come on, for the present at any rate. . . .

We must part; and I feel assured, for us to meet under such dreadful circumstances, would only add to our distress. . . .

"Finally, my beloved, be of good comfort." May all your names be "written in the Lamb's book of life"—may you all have the purifying and sustaining influence of the Christian religion—is the earnest prayer of your affectionate husband and father,

JOHN BROWN

During the forty-two days of his confinement at Charlestown, Brown received several visits from sympathizing Northern friends, many of whom had never before seen him. His wife, overcoming many obstacles, was finally permitted to spend a few hours in his cell, and to take supper with him a short time before his death. No Virginians, so far as is known, proffered him any words of kindness, unless it were the reverend clergy of the neighborhood, who tendered him the solace of religion after their fashion, which he civilly, but firmly, declined. He could not recognize anyone who justified or palliated slavery as a minister of the God he worshiped, or the Saviour in whom he trusted. He held arguments on several occasions with pro-slavery clergymen, but recognized them as men only, and not as invested with any peculiar sanctity. To one of them, who sought to reconcile slavery with Christianity, he said: "My dear Sir, you know nothing about Christianity; you will have to learn the A B C's in the lesson of Christianity, as I find you entirely ignorant of the meaning of the word. I, of course, respect you as a gentleman; but it is as a *heathen* gentleman." The argument here closed.

The 2d of December was the day appointed for his execution. Nearly three thousand militia were early on the ground. Fears of a forcible rescue or of a servile insurrection prevented a large attendance of citizens. Cannon were so planted as to sweep every approach to the jail, and to blow the prisoner into shreds upon the first intimation of tumult. Virginia held her breath until she heard that the old man was dead.

Brown rose at daybreak, and continued writing with energy until half-past ten, when he was told to prepare to die. He shook hands with the sheriff, visited the cell of Copeland and Green, to whom he handed a quarter of a dollar each, saying he had no more use for money, and bade them adieu. He next visited Cook and Coppoc, the former of whom had made a confession, which he pronounced false; saying he had never sent Cook to Harper's Ferry, as he had stated. He handed a quarter to Coppoc also, shook hands with him, and parted. He then visited and bade a kindly good-bye to his more especial comrade, Stevens, gave him a quarter, and charged him not to betray his friends. A sixth, named Hazlett, was confined in the same prison, but he did not visit him, denying all knowledge of him.

He walked out of the jail at 11 o'clock; an eye-witness said—"with a radiant countenance, and the step of a conqueror." His face was even joyous, and it has been remarked that probably his was the lightest heart in Charlestown that day. A black woman, with a little child in her arms, stood by the door. He stopped a moment, and, stooping, kissed the child affectionately. Another black woman, with a child, as he passed along, exclaimed: "God bless you, old man! I wish I could help you; but I can't." He looked at her with a tear in his eye. He mounted the wagon beside his jailer, Captain Avis, who had been one of the bravest of his captors, who had treated him very kindly, and to whom he was profoundly grateful. The wagon was instantly surrounded by six companies of militia. Being asked, on the way, if he felt any fear, he replied: "It has been a characteristic of me from infancy not to suffer from physical fear. I have suffered a thousand times more from bashfulness than from fear." The day was clear and bright, and he remarked, as he rode, that the country seemed very beautiful.

Arrived at the gallows, he said: "I see no citizens here; where are they?"

"None but the troops are allowed to be present," was the reply.

"That ought not to be," said he. "Citizens should be allowed to be present as well as others."

He bade adieu to some acquaintances at the foot of the gallows, and was first to mount the scaffold. His step was still firm, and his bearing calm, yet hopeful. The hour having come, he said to Captain Avis: "I have no words to thank you for all your kindness to me." His elbows and ankles being pinioned, the white cap drawn over his eyes, the hangman's rope adjusted around his neck, he stood waiting for death.

"Captain Brown," said the sheriff, "you are not standing on the drop. Will you come forward?"

"I can't see," was his firm answer. "You must lead me."

The sheriff led him forward to the center of the drop. "Shall I give you a handkerchief, and let you drop it as a signal?"

"No; I am ready at any time; but do not keep me needlessly waiting."

In defiance of this reasonable request, he was kept standing thus several minutes, while a military parade and display of readiness to repel an imaginary foe were enacted. The time seemed an hour to the impatient spectators; even the soldiers began to murmur—"Shame!" At last the order was given, the rope cut with a hatchet, and the trap fell; but so short a distance that the victim continued to struggle and to suffer for a considerable time. Being at length duly pronounced dead, he was cut down after thirty-eight minutes' suspension. His body was conveyed to Harper's Ferry, and delivered to his widow, by whom it was borne to her far northern home, among the mountains he so loved, and where he was so beloved.

There let it rest forever, while the path to it is worn deeper and deeper by the pilgrim feet of the race he so bravely though rashly endeavored to rescue from a hideous and debasing thraldom!

5

The Republicans
Nominate Lincoln

Murat Halstead

ENROUTE, May 15-16, 1860.

Leaving Baltimore in a flood we found the West afflicted with a drouth. At one end of the journey, there was a torrent tearing down every ravine; at the other there was a fog of dust all along the road.

The incidents of the trip were a land-slide on the Pennsylvania Central, and the unpleasantness of being behind time to the extent of six hours on the Pittsburgh, Fort Wayne and Chicago. The detention was occasioned by the fact of the train consisting of thirteen cars full of "Irrepressibles." I regret to say that most of the company were "unsound," and rather disposed to boast of the fact.

The difference between the country passed over between Baltimore and Chicago, and that between Louisville and Baltimore, by way of Charleston, is greatly in favor of the former. I have not had any disposition to speak in disparaging terms of the Southern country, but it is the plain truth that the country visible along the road from Baltimore to Harrisburg alone, is worth more by far than all that can be seen from Charleston to the Potomac. In the South few attempts have been made to cultivate any lands other than those most favorably situated, and most rich. But in Pennsylvania, free labor has made not only the valleys bloom, but the hill-tops are radiant with clover and wheat. And there are many other things that rush upon the sight in the North as contrasted with the South, that testify to the paramount glory of free labor.

And while pursuing the path of perfect candor in all these matters, it becomes necessary to say that the quantity of whiskey and other ardent beverages consumed on the train in which I reached this city was much greater than on any train that within my knowledge entered Charleston during Convention times. The number of private bottles on our train last night was something surprising. A portion of the Republicans are distressed by what they see and hear of the disposition to use ardent spirits which appears in members of their supposed to be painfully virtuous party. And

WILLIAM B. HESSELTINE, ed., *Three Against Lincoln* (Baton Rouge, La., 1960), Ch. 4.

our Western Reserve was thrown into prayers and perspiration last night by some New Yorkers who were singing songs not found in hymn-books. Others are glad to have the co-operation of Capt. Whiskey, and hail the fact of the enlistment of that distinguished partisan as an evidence that the Republicans are imbibing the spirit as well as the substance of the old Democratic Party. I do not wish, however, to convey the impression that drunkenness prevails here to an extent very unusual in National Conventions, for that would be doing an injustice. I do not feel competent to state the precise proportions of those who are drunk, and those who are sober. There are a large number of both classes; and the drunken are of course the most demonstrative, and according to the principle of the numerical force of the black sheep in a flock, are most multitudinous.

The crowd is this evening becoming prodigious. The Tremont House is so crammed that it is with much difficulty people get about in it from one room to another. Near fifteen hundred people will sleep in it tonight. The principal lions in this house are Horace Greeley and Frank P. Blair, Sr. The way Greeley is stared at as he shuffles about, looking as innocent as ever, is itself a sight. Whenever he appears there is a crowd gaping at him, and if he stops to talk a minute with someone who wishes to consult him as the oracle, the crowd becomes dense as possible, and there is the most eager desire to hear the words of wisdom that are supposed to fall on such occasions. . . .

The city of Chicago is attending to this Convention in magnificent style. It is a great place for large hotels, and all have their capacity for accommodation tested. The great feature is the Wigwam, erected within the past month expressly for the use of the Convention by the Republicans of Chicago, at a cost of seven thousand dollars. It is a small edition of the New York Crystal Palace, built of boards, and will hold ten thousand persons comfortably—and is admirable for its acoustic excellence. An ordinary voice can be heard through the whole structure with ease. . . .

May 16.

This is the morning of the first day of the Convention. The crowd is prodigious. The hotel-keepers say there are more people here now than during the National Fair last year, and then it was estimated that thirty thousand strangers were in the city. This figure was probably too high, but there are, beyond doubt, more than 25,000 persons here in attendance upon the Convention. This is a great place for hotels, and the multitude is fortunately distributed through them, all over the town. There are only a few points where the jam is painfully close. One of those places is the Tremont House, where about 1,500 persons are stowed away, and which is the focus of political excitement.

As in the case of all other Conventions, the amount of idle talking that is done is amazing. Men gather in little groups, and with their arms about each other, and chatter and whisper as if the fate of the country depended upon their immediate delivery of the mighty political secrets with which their imaginations are big. There are a thousand rumors afloat, and things of incalculable moment are communicated to you confidentially, at intervals of five minutes. There are now at least a thousand men packed together in the halls of the Tremont House, crushing each other's ribs, tramping each other's toes, and titillating each other with the gossip of the day; and the probability is, not one is possessed of a single political fact not known to the whole which is of the slightest consequence to any human being.

The current of the universal twaddle this morning is that "Old Abe" will be the nominee.

The Bates movement, the McLean movement, the Cameron movement, the Banks movement, are all nowhere. They have gone down like lead in the mighty waters. "Old Abe" and "Old Ben" are in the field against Seward. Abe and Ben are representatives of the conservatism, the respectability, the availability, and all that sort of thing. . . .

The badges of different candidates are making their appearance, and a good many of the dunces of the occasion go about duly labeled. I saw an old man this morning with a wood-cut of Edward Bates pasted outside his hat. The Seward men have badges of silk with his likeness and name, and some wag pinned one of them to Horace Greeley's back yesterday, and he created even an unusual sensation as he hitched about with the Seward mark upon him.

The hour for the meeting of the Convention approaches, and the agitation of the city is exceedingly great. Vast as the Wigwam is, not one-fifth of those who would be glad to get inside can be accommodated.

FIRST DAY, The Wigwam, May 16, 1860.

The Hon. Edward D. Morgan of New York, chairman of the National Republican Executive Committee, called the Convention to order, and read the call under which it had been summoned. He concluded by nominating the Hon. David Wilmot for temporary president. Mr. Wilmot, upon taking the Chair, made a very positive anti-slavery speech. . . .

Upon reassembling, the report of the Committee on Permanent Organization was in order and made. The Hon. George Ashmun, the presiding officer, was escorted to his chair by Preston King and Carl Schurz, the one short and round as a barrel and fat as butter, the other tall and slender. The contrast was a curious one, and so palpable that the whole multitude saw it, and gave a tremendous cheer. Mr. Ashmun was speedily discovered to be an excellent presiding officer. His clear, full-toned voice was one refreshing to hear amid the clamors of a Convention. He is cool, clear-headed and executive, and will despatch business. He is a treasure to the Convention, and will lessen and shorten its labors. His speech was very good for the occasion, delivered with just warmth enough. He was animated, and yet his emotions did not get the better of him. In conclusion he referred, as if it were an undoubted fact, to the "brotherly kindness" he had everywhere seen displayed. He had not heard a harsh word or unkind expression pass between delegates. Now, the gentleman must have kept very close, or his hearing is deplorably impaired. He certainly could not stay long among the Seward men at the Richmond House without hearing unkind and profane expressions used respecting brother delegates of conservative notions. He would very frequently hear Brother Greeley, for example, who is hated intensely by them, called a "d—d old ass." Indeed, that is a very mild specimen of the forms of expression used. Mr. Ashmun was, however, as nearly correct in his statement of the case as Caleb Cushing was at Charleston in adjourning the Convention, in praising it for unexampled decorum. It is worthy of remark that he had nothing directly to say of the "nigger." The Hon. David Wilmot had attended to that department sufficiently. . . .

The committee on Resolutions was appointed. When the roll was called on this committee, three names were received with great applause—Greeley of "Oregon," Carl Schurz, and Francis P. Blair, Sr. Greeley had the greatest ovation, and though there is an impression to the contrary, those who know him well know that nobody is more fond of the breath of popular favor than the philosophic Horace.

The Convention adjourned without transacting any further business. The question on which everything turns is whether Seward can be nominated. His individuality is the pivot here, just as that of Douglas was at Charleston.

The scenes, when the doors of that part of the Wigwam set apart for the masculine public in general are opened, are highly exciting and amusing. This afternoon the rush for places was tremendous. Three doors about twenty-feet wide each were simultaneously thrown open, and three torrents of men roared in, rushing headlong for front positions. The standing room, holding 4,500 persons, was packed in about five minutes. The galleries, where only gentlemen accompanied by ladies are admitted, and which contain nearly 3,000 persons, was already full. There was a great deal of fun, and some curious performances, in filling the galleries. Ladies to accompany gentlemen were in demand—school girls were found on the street and given a quarter each to see a gentleman safe in. Other girls, those of undoubted character (no doubt on the subject whatever), were much sought after as escorts. One of them, being asked to take a gentleman to the gallery and offered half a dollar for so doing, excused herself by saying she had already taken two men in at each of the three rooms and was afraid of arrest if she carried the enterprise any further. An Irish woman passing with a bundle of clothes under her arm was levied upon by an "irrepressible," and seeing him safely into the seats reserved for ladies and accompanying gentlemen, retired with her fee and bundle. Another "irrepressible" sought out an Indian woman who was selling moccasins, and attempted to escort her in. This was a little too severe however. He was informed that she was no lady—and the point argued with considerable vehemence. It was finally determined that a squaw was not a lady. The young Republican protested indignantly against the policeman's decision, claiming equal rights for all womankind.

The Republicans have all divided into two classes, the "Irrepressibles" and the "Conservatives."

The favorite word in the Convention is "solemn." Everything is solemn. In Charleston the favorite was "crisis." Here, there is something every ten minutes found to be solemn. In Charleston there was a *crisis* nearly as often. I observed as many as twenty-three in one day.

A new ticket is talked of here tonight, and an informal meeting held in this house since I have been writing this letter has given it an impetus. It is "Lincoln and Hickman." This is now the ticket as against Seward and Cash [Cassius] Clay. . . .

SECOND DAY, The Wigwam, May 17, 1860.

Masses of people poured into town last night and this morning, expecting the nomination to be made today and desiring to be present. All adjectives might be fairly exhausted in describing the crowd. It is mighty and overwhelming; it can only be numbered by tens of thousands. The press about the hotels this morning was crushing. Two thousand persons took breakfast at the Tremont House.

Many of the delegates kept up the excitement nearly all night. At two o'clock this morning part of the Missouri delegation were singing songs in their parlor. There were still a crowd of fellows caucusing—and the glasses were still clinking in the barrooms—and far down the street a brass band was making the night musical.

The Seward men made a demonstration this morning in the form of a procession. The scene at the Richmond House as they formed and marched away after their band of music—the band in splendid uniform and the Sewardites wearing badges—was exceedingly animated and somewhat picturesque. The band was giving, with a vast volume of melody, *"O isn't he a darling?"*—the procession was four abreast, filing away in a cloud of dust—and one of their orators, mounted upon a door-step, with hat and cane in his hands, was haranguing them as a captain might address his soldiers marching to battle. The Seward procession was heedless of the dust as regular soldiers, and strode on with gay elasticity and jaunty bearing.

As they passed the Tremont House, where the many masses of the opponents of "Old Irrepressible" were congregated, they gave three throat-tearing cheers for Seward. It will be a clear case, if he is not nominated, that the failure cannot be charged to his friends. Few men have had friends who would cleave unto them as the Sewardites to their great man here.

The Pennsylvanians declare if Seward were nominated they would be immediately ruined. They could do nothing. The majority against them would be counted by tens of thousands. New Jerseyites say the same thing. The Indianians are of the same opinion. They look heart-broken at the suggestion that Seward has the inside track, and throw up their hands in despair. They say Henry S. Lane will be beaten, the legislature pass utterly into the hands of the Democracy, and the two Republican Senators hoped for, be heard of no more. Illinois agonizes at the mention of the name of Seward, and says he is to them the sting of political death. His nomination would kill off Lyman Trumbull and give the legislature into the hands of Democrats to make the next Congressional apportionment. Amid all these cries of distress, the Sewardites are true as steel to their champion, and they will cling to "Old Irrepressible," as they call him, until the last gun is fired and the big bell rings.

The crowd in the Wigwam this morning is more dense than ever. The thing was full yesterday, but it is crammed today. . . .

The platform was now reported. The platform was received with immense enthusiasm. Several sections, at the demand of the audience, were read twice. Pennsylvania went into spasms of joy over the "Tariff Plank," her whole delegation rising and swinging hats and canes.

MR. CARTTER. Mr. Chairman: That report is so eminently unquestionable from beginning to end, and so eloquently carries through with it, its own vindication, that I do not believe the Convention will desire discussion upon it, and I therefore call the previous question upon it. [Applause, and mingled cries of "Good, good," and "No, no."]

MR. JOSHUA R. GIDDINGS. I arise, sir, solemnly to appeal to my friend. [Great confusion; cries of "Withdraw the previous question." A voice—"Nobody wants to speak, but we don't want to be choked off," etc.]

MR. CARTTER. I insist upon the previous question.

MR. GIDDINGS. I arise, and I believe I have the right, with the leave of my colleague, to offer a short amendment before the previous question is called.

MR. CARTTER. I did it to cut you off, and all other amendments, and all discussion. [Great confusion, and cries of "Giddings" by the audience.]

MR. GIDDINGS. Mr. President, I propose to offer, after the first resolution as it stands here, as a declaration of principles, the following:

That we solemnly reassert the self-evident truths that all men are endowed by their Creator with certain inalienable rights, among which are those of life, liberty and the pursuit of happiness [cheers]; that governments are instituted among men to secure the enjoyment of these rights.

Mr. Giddings made a short speech in favor of his amendment, concluding:

Now, I propose to maintain the doctrines of our fathers. I propose to maintain the fundamental and primal issues upon which the government was founded. I will detain this Convention no longer. I offer this because our party was formed upon it. It grew upon it. It has existed upon it—and when you leave out this truth you leave out the party.

Mr. Cartter called for the reading of the second section of the platform. It was read. Giddings' amendment was voted down. The old man quickly rose and made his way slowly toward the door. A dozen delegates begged him not to go. But he considered everything lost, even honor. His Philadelphia Platform has not been reaffirmed. The "twin relics" were not in the new creed. And now the Declaration of Independence had been voted down! He must go. He got along as far as the New York delegation, where he was comforted by assurances that the Declaration would be tried again; but he left the Convention—actually seceded in sorrow and anger. . . .

Mr. Curtis made a short speech. He said:

I have to ask this Convention whether they are prepared to go upon the record and before the country as voting down the words of the Declaration of Independence? [Cries of "No, no," and applause.] I ask gentlemen gravely to consider that in the amendment which I have proposed, I have done nothing that the soundest and safest man in all the land might not do; and I rise simply—for I am now sitting down—I rise simply to ask gentlemen to think well before, upon the free prairies of the West, in the summer of 1860, they dare to wince and quail before the men who in Philadelphia, in 1776—in Philadelphia, in the Arch-Keystone State, so amply, so nobly represented upon this platform today—before they dare to shrink from repeating the words that these great men enunciated. [Terrific applause.]

This was a strong appeal and took the Convention by storm. It was a great personal triumph for Curtis. His classical features, literary fame, pleasing style as a speaker, and the force of his case, called attention to him, and gave him the ear of the Convention, and gave him the triumph. And the Declaration again became part of the platform of the Republican Party.

THE PLATFORM

now stood:

Resolved, That we, the delegated representatives of the Republican electors of the United States, in Convention assembled, in discharge of the duty we owe to our constituents and our country, unite in the following declarations:

1. That the history of the nation during the last four years, has fully established the propriety and necessity of the organization and perpetuation of the Republican party, and that the causes which called it into existence are permanent in their nature, and now, more than ever before, demand its peaceful and constitutional triumph.

2. That the maintenance of the principles promulgated in the Declaration

of Independence and embodied in the Federal Constitution, "That all men are created equal; that they are endowed by their Creator with certain inalienable rights; that among these are life, liberty and the pursuit of happiness; that to secure these rights, governments are instituted among men, deriving their just powers from the consent of the governed," is essential to the preservation of our Republican institutions; and that the Federal Constitution, the Rights of the States, and the Union of the United States, must and shall be preserved.

3. That to the Union of the States this nation owes its unprecedented increase in population, its surprising developments of material resources, its rapid augmentation of wealth, its happiness at home, and its honor abroad; and we hold in abhorrence all schemes for disunion, come from whatever source they may: And we congratulate the country that no Republican member of Congress has uttered or countenanced the threats of disunion so often made by Democratic members....

4. That the maintenance inviolate of the Rights of the States, and especially the right of each State to order and control its own domestic institutions according to its own judgement exclusively, is essential to that balance of powers on which the perfection and endurance of our political fabric depends; and we denounce the lawless invasion by armed force of the soil of any State or Territory, no matter under what pretext, as among the gravest of crimes....

6. That the people justly view with alarm the reckless extravagance which pervades every department of the Federal Government....

7. That the new dogma that the Constitution, of its own force, carries slavery into any or all of the Territories of the United States, is a dangerous political heresy....

8. That the normal condition of all the Territory of the United States is that of freedom....

9. That we brand the recent re-opening of the African slave trade, under the cover of our national flag, aided by perversions of judicial power, as a crime against humanity and a burning shame to our country and age....

11. That Kansas should, of right, be immediately admitted as a State under the Constitution recently formed and adopted by her people, and accepted by the House of Representatives.

12. That, while providing revenue for the support of the General Government by duties upon imports, sound policy requires such an adjustment of these imports as to encourage the development of the industrial interests of the whole country; and we commend that policy of national exchanges, which secures to the working men liberal wages, to agriculture remunerating prices, to mechanics and manufactures an adequate reward for their skill, labor and enterprise, and to the nation commercial prosperity and independence.

13. That we protest against any sale or alienation to others of the Public Lands held by actual settlers....

14. That the Republican party is opposed to any change in our Naturalization Laws....

15. That appropriations by Congress for river and harbor improvements of a national character ... are ... justified by the obligation of government to protect the lives and property of its citizens.

16. That a railroad to the Pacific Ocean is imperatively demanded by the interests of the whole country; that the Federal Government ought to render immediate and efficient aid in its construction. . . .

So it was adopted. The vote was taken about six o'clock, and upon the announcement being made, a scene ensued of the most astounding character. All the thousands of men in that enormous Wigwam commenced swinging their hats, and cheering with intense enthusiasm; and the other thousands of ladies waved their handkerchiefs and clapped their hands. The roar that went up from that mass of ten thousand human beings under one roof was indescribable. Such a spectacle as was presented for some minutes has never before been witnessed at a Convention. A herd of buffaloes or lions could not have made a more tremendous roaring.

As the great assemblage poured through the streets after adjournment, it seemed to electrify the city. The agitation of the masses that pack the hotels and throng the streets, and are certainly forty thousand strong, was such as made the little excitement at Charleston seem insignificant.

The Convention adjourned without taking a ballot for President, as the tally sheets were not prepared.

The tactics of the Seward men in convention today were admirable. They made but one mistake, that of voting against the recommitment of the report of the Committee on Credentials. They made a beautiful fight against Wilmot's proposition to examine into the constituencies of slave State delegations, putting forward men to strike the necessary blows who were not suspected of Sewardism. There was also a splendid fight on the subject of the two-thirds rule (as it was in effect), which was sought to be used to slaughter Seward. So perfect were the Seward tactics that this rule, which his opponents had hoped to carry, was made odious, and defeated by a two-thirds vote. Then Giddings was anxious, beyond all description, to have the initial words of the Declaration of Independence in the platform. In attempting to get them in, he was snubbed by Seward's opponents most cruelly. He had been working against Seward, and was not without influence. Now a New York man took up and carried through his precious amendment. So confident were the Seward men, when the platform was adopted, of their ability to nominate their great leader, that they urged an immediate ballot, and would have had it if the clerks had not reported that they were unprovided with tally sheets. The cheering of the thousands of spectators during the day indicated that a very large share of the outside pressure was for Seward. There is something almost irresistible here in the prestige of his fame.

The New Yorkers here are of a class unknown to Western Republican politicians. They can drink as much whiskey, swear as loud and long, sing as bad songs, and "get up and howl" as ferociously as any crowd of Democrats you ever heard, or heard of. They are opposed, as they say, "to being too d—d virtuous." They hoot at the idea that Seward could not sweep all the Northern States, and swear that he would have a party in every slave State in less than a year that would clean out the disunionists from shore to shore. They slap each other on the back with the emphasis of delight when they meet, and rip out "How *are* you?" with a "How are you, hoss?" style that would do honor to Old Kaintuck on a bust. At night those of them who are not engaged at caucusing are doing that which ill-tutored youths call "raising h—l generally."

Wherever you find them, the New York politicians, of whatever party, are a peculiar people.

The Seward men have been in high feather. They entertain no particle of doubt of his nomination in the morning. They have a champagne supper in their rooms at the Richmond House tonight, and have bands of music serenading the various delegations at their quarters. Three hundred bottles of champagne are said to have been cracked at the Richmond. This may be an exaggeration, but I am not inclined to think the quantity overstated, for it flowed freely as water.

The delegation here is a queer compound. There is a party of tolerably rough fellows, of whom Tom Hyer is leader, and there is Thurlow Weed (called Lord Thurlow by his friends), Moses H. Grinnell, James Watson Webb, Governor Morgan, General Nye, George W. Curtis, and others of the strong men of the State, in commerce, political jobbing, and in literature—first-class men in their respective positions, and each with his work to do according to his ability. In the face of such "irrepressibles," the conservative expediency men—Greeley, the Blairs, the Republican candidates for governor in Pennsylvania, Indiana, and Illinois—are hard-pressed, sorely perplexed, and despondent.

THIRD DAY, The Wigwam, May 18, 1860.

. . . After adjournment on Thursday (the second day), there were few men in Chicago who believed it possible to prevent the nomination of Seward. His friends had played their game to admiration, and had been victorious on every preliminary skirmish. When the platform had been adopted, inclusive of the Declaration of Independence, they felt themselves already exalted upon the pinnacle of victory. They rejoiced exceedingly, and full of confidence, cried in triumphant tones, "Call the roll of States." But it was otherwise ordered. The Chair announced that the tally sheets had not been prepared, and that it would subject the clerks to great inconvenience to proceed to a ballot at that time. The Seward men expressed themselves greatly disgusted, and were still unwilling to adjourn. A motion was made to adjourn, however, and after an uncertain response, very little voting being done either way, the Chair pronounced the motion for adjournment carried. The Seward men were displeased but not disheartened.

They considered their hour of triumphing with brains and principle over presumptions of expediency as merely postponed. They did not fear the results of the caucusing that night, though they knew every hour would be employed against them. The opponents of Mr. Seward left the Wigwam that evening thoroughly disheartened. Greeley was, as has been widely reported, absolutely "terrified." The nomination of Seward in defiance of his influence would have been a cruel blow. He gave up the ship. . . . And every one of the forty thousand men in attendance upon the Chicago Convention will testify that at midnight of Thursday-Friday night, the universal impression was that Seward's success was certain.

The New Yorkers were exultant. Their bands were playing, and the champagne flowing at their headquarters as after a victory.

But there was much done after midnight and before the Convention assembled on Friday morning. There were hundreds of Pennsylvanians, Indianians and Illinoisans who never closed their eyes that night. I saw Henry S. Lane at one o'clock, pale and haggard, with cane under his arm, walking as if for a wager, from one caucus room to another, at the Tremont House. He had been toiling with desperation to bring the Indiana delegation to go as a unit for Lincoln. And then in connection with others, he had been operating to bring the Vermonters and Virginians to the point of deserting Seward. Vermont would certainly cast her electoral vote for any candidate who could be nominated, and Virginia as certainly against any candidate. The object was to bring the delegates of those States to consider success rather than Seward, and join with the battleground States—as Pennsylvania, New Jersey, Indiana, and Illinois insisted upon calling themselves. This was finally done, the fatal break in Seward's strength having been made in Vermont and Virginia, destroying at once, when it appeared, his power in the New England and the slave State delegations. But the work was not yet done.

The Pennsylvanians had been fed upon meat, such that they presented themselves at Chicago with the presumption that they had only to say what they wished, and receive the indorsement of the Convention. And they were for Cameron. He was the only man, they a thousand times said, who would certainly carry Pennsylvania. They were astonished, alarmed, and maddened to find public opinion settling down upon Seward and Lincoln, and that one or the other must be nominated. They saw that Lincoln was understood to be the only man to defeat Seward, and thinking themselves capable of holding that balance of power, so much depended upon, and so deceptive on those occasions, stood out against the Lincoln combination. Upon some of the delegation, Seward operations had been performed with perceptible effect. The Seward men had stated that the talk of not carrying Pennsylvania was all nonsense. Seward had a good tariff record, and his friends would spend money enough in the State to carry it against any Democratic candidate who was a possibility. The flood of Seward money promised for Pennsylvania was not without efficacy. The phrase used was, that Seward's friends "would *spend oceans of money.*"

The Wade movement died before this time. It had a brilliant and formidable appearance for a while; but the fact that it originated at Washington was against it, and the bitterness of those delegates from Ohio, who would not in any event go for any man from that State other than Chase, and who declared war to the knife against Benjamin F. Wade, and as a second choice were for Lincoln or Seward, stifled the Wade project.

It does not appear by the record that "Old Ben Wade" ever stood a chance for the place now occupied by "Old Abe Lincoln." If his friends in Ohio could have brought the friends of Mr. Chase to agree that the delegation should vote as a unit every time as the majority should direct, Wade might have been the nominee, and instead of hearing so much of some of the exploits of Mr. Lincoln in rail-splitting, when a farmer's boy, we should have information concerning the labors of Ben Wade on the Erie Canal, where he handled a spade. While touching the Wade movement as developed in the delegation from Ohio, it is proper to give as an explanatory note the fact that at least six gentlemen from Ohio who were engaged in it were understood to have aspirations for the Senate and to be regarding Mr. Wade's chair in the Senate chamber with covetous glances. These gentlemen were D. K. Cartter, Joshua R. Giddings, C. P. Wolcott, William Dennison, Jr., Tom Corwin, and Columbus Delano.

The cry of a want of availability, which was from the start raised against Seward, now took a more definite form than heretofore. It was reported, and with a well-understood purpose, that the Republican candidates for governor in Indiana, Illinois and Pennsylvania would resign if Seward were nominated. Whether they really meant it or not, the rumor was well circulated, and the effect produced was as if they had been earnest. Henry S. Lane, candidate in Indiana, did say something of the kind. He asserted hundreds of times that the nomination of Seward would be death to him, and that he might in that case just as well give up the canvass. He did not feel like expending his time and money in carrying on a hopeless campaign, and would be disposed to abandon the contest.

The Chicago *Press and Tribune* of Friday morning contained a last appeal to the Convention not to nominate Seward. It was evidently written in a despairing state of mind, and it simply begged that Seward should not be nominated. The Cameron men, discovering there was absolutely no hope for their man, but that either Seward or Lincoln would be nominated . . . and being a calculating company, were persuaded to throw their strength for Lincoln at such a time as to have credit of his nomination if it were made. There was much difficulty, however, in arriving at this conclusion, and the wheels of the machine did not at any time in Pennsylvania run smooth. On nearly every ballot Pennsylvania was not in readiness when her name was called, and her retirements for consultation became a joke.

The Seward men generally abounded in confidence Friday morning. The air was full of rumors of the caucusing the night before, but the opposition of the doubtful States to Seward was an old story; and after the distress of Pennsylvania, Indiana & Co., on the subject of Seward's availability had been so freely and ineffectually expressed from the start, it was not imagined their protests would suddenly become effective. The Sewardites marched as usual from their headquarters at the Richmond House after their magnificent band, which was brilliantly uniformed—epaulets shining on their shoulders, and white and scarlet feathers waving from their caps— marched under the orders of recognized leaders, in a style that would have done credit to many volunteer military companies. They were about a a thousand strong, and protracting their march a little too far, were not all able to get into the Wigwam. This was their first misfortune. They were not where they could scream with the best effect in responding to the mention of the name of William H. Seward.

When the Convention was called to order, breathless attention was given the proceedings. There was not a space a foot square in the Wigwam unoccupied. There were tens of thousands still outside, and torrents of men had rushed in at the three broad doors until not another one could squeeze in. . . .

Everybody was now impatient to begin the work. Mr. William M. Evarts of New York nominated Mr. Seward. Mr. Judd of Illinois nominated Mr. Lincoln. Mr. Thomas H. Dudley of New Jersey nominated Mr. Dayton. Mr. Andrew H. Reeder of Pennsylvania nominated Simon Cameron. Mr. Cartter of Ohio nominated Salmon P. Chase. Mr. Caleb Smith of Indiana seconded the nomination of Lincoln. Mr. Blair of Missouri nominated Edward Bates. Mr. Blair of Michigan seconded the nomination of William H. Seward. Mr. Thomas Corwin of Ohio nominated John McLean. Mr. Schurz of Wisconsin seconded the nomination of Seward. Mr. Delano of Ohio seconded the nomination of Lincoln. The only names that produced "tremendous applause" were those of Seward and Lincoln.

Everybody felt that the fight was between them, and yelled accordingly.

The applause when Mr. Evarts named Seward was enthusiastic. When Mr. Judd named Lincoln, the response was prodigious, rising and raging far beyond the Seward shriek. Presently, upon Caleb B. Smith seconding the nomination of Lincoln, the response was absolutely terrific. It now became the Seward men to make another effort, and when Austin Blair of Michigan seconded his nomination,

> At once there rose so wild a yell,
> Within that dark and narrow dell;
> As all the fiends from heaven that fell
> Had pealed the banner cry of hell.

The effect was startling. Hundreds of persons stopped their ears in pain.

The shouting was absolutely frantic, shrill and wild. No Comanches, no panthers ever struck a higher note, or gave screams with more infernal intensity. Looking from the stage over the vast amphitheatre, nothing was to be seen below but thousands of hats—a black, mighty swarm of hats—flying with the velocity of hornets over a mass of human heads, most of the mouths of which were open. Above, all around the galleries, hats and handkerchiefs were flying in the tempest together. The wonder of the thing was that the Seward outside pressure should, so far from New York, be so powerful.

Now the Lincoln men had to try it again, and as Mr. Delano of Ohio, on behalf "of a portion of the delegation of that State," seconded the nomination of Lincoln, the uproar was beyond description. Imagine all the hogs ever slaughtered in Cincinnati giving their death squeals together, a score of big steam whistles going (steam at 160 lbs. per inch), and you conceive something of the same nature. I thought the Seward yell could not be surpassed; but the Lincoln boys were clearly ahead, and feeling their victory as there was a lull in the storm, took deep breaths all around, and gave a concentrated shriek that was positively awful, accompanied it with stamping that made every plank and pillar in the building quiver.

Henry S. Lane of Indiana leaped upon a table, and swinging hat and cane, performed like an acrobat. The presumption is he shrieked with the rest, as his mouth was desperately wide open, but no one will ever be able to testify that he has positive knowledge of the fact that he made a particle of noise. His individual voice was lost in the aggregate hurricane.

The New York, Michigan and Wisconsin delegations sat together and were, in this tempest, very quiet. Many of their faces whitened as the Lincoln *yawp* swelled into a wild hozanna of victory.

The Convention now proceeded to business. The New England States were called first, and it was manifest that Seward had not the strength that had been claimed for him there. Maine gave nearly half her vote for Lincoln. New Hampshire gave seven out of her ten votes for Lincoln. Vermont gave her vote to her Senator Jacob Collamer, which was understood to be merely complimentary. It appeared, however, that her delegation was hostile or indifferent to Seward, otherwise there would have been no complimentary vote to another. Massachusetts was divided. Rhode Island and Connecticut did not give Seward a vote. So much for the caucusing the night before. Mr. Evarts of New York rose and gave the vote of that State calmly, but with a swelling tone of pride in his voice—"The State of *New York* casts her *seventy votes* for *William H. Seward!*" The seventy votes was a plumper, and there was slight applause, and that rustle and vibration in the audience indicating a sensation. The most significant vote was that of Virginia, which had been expected solid for Seward, and which now gave him but eight and Lincoln fourteen. The New Yorkers looked significantly at each other as this was announced. Then Indiana gave her twenty-six votes for Lincoln. This solid vote was a startler, and the keen little eyes of Henry S. Lane glittered as it was given. He was responsible for it. It was his opinion that the man of all the land to carry the State of Indiana was Judge John McLean. He also thought Edward Bates had eminent qualifications. But when he found that the contest was between Seward and Lincoln, he worked for the latter as if life itself depended upon success. The division of the first vote caused a fall in Seward stock. It was seen that Lincoln, Cameron and Bates had the strength to defeat Seward, and it was known that the greater part of the Chase vote would go for Lincoln.

The secretary announced the vote—

William S. Seward, New York	173½
Abraham Lincoln, Illinois	102
Edward Bates, Missouri	48
Simon Cameron, Pennsylvania	50½
John McLean, Ohio	12
Salmon P. Chase, Ohio	49
Benjamin F. Wade, Ohio	3
William L. Dayton, New Jersey	14
John M. Reed, Pennsylvania	1
Jacob Collamer, Vermont	10
Charles Sumner, Massachusetts	1
John C. Fremont, California	1

Whole number of votes cast, 465; necessary to a choice, 233.

The Convention proceeded to a second ballot. Every man was fiercely enlisted in the struggle. The partisans of the various candidates were strung up to such a pitch of excitement as to render them incapable of patience, and the cries of "Call the roll" were fairly hissed through their teeth. The first gain for Lincoln was in New Hampshire. The Chase and the Fremont vote from that State were given him. His next gain was the whole vote of Vermont. This was a blighting blow upon the Seward interest. The New Yorkers started as if an Orsini bomb had exploded. And presently the Cameron vote of Pennsylvania was thrown for Lincoln, increasing his strength forty-four votes. The fate of the day was now determined. New York saw "checkmate" next move, and sullenly proceeded with the game, assuming unconsciousness of her inevitable doom. On this ballot Lincoln gained seventy-nine votes! Seward had 184½ votes; Lincoln 181.

It now dawned upon the multitude that the presumption entertained the night before, that the Seward men would have everything their own way, was a mistake. Even persons unused to making the calculations and considering the combinations attendant upon such scenes, could not fail to observe that while the strength of Seward and Lincoln was almost even at the moment, the reserved votes, by which the contest must be decided, were inclined to the latter. There, for instance, was the Bates vote, thirty-

five; the McLean vote, eight; the Dayton vote, ten—all impending for Lincoln—and forty-two Chase votes, the greater part going the same way.

THIRD BALLOT. . . .

While this ballot was taken amid excitement that tested the nerves, the
fatal defection from Seward in New England still further appeared—four
votes going over from Seward to Lincoln in Massachusetts. The latter received four additional votes from Pennsylvania and fifteen additional votes
from Ohio. It was whispered about—"Lincoln's the coming man—will be
nominated this ballot." When the roll of States and Territories had been
called, I had ceased to give attention to any votes but those for Lincoln, and
had his vote added up as it was given. The number of votes necessary to a
choice were two hundred and thirty-three, and I saw under my pencil as
the Lincoln column was completed, the figures 231½—one vote and a half
to give him the nomination. In a moment the fact was whispered, about a
hundred pencils had told the same story. The news went over the house
wonderfully, and there was a pause. There are always men anxious to distinguish themselves on such occasions. There is nothing that politicians like
better than a crisis. I looked up to see who would be the man to give the
decisive vote. The man for the crisis in the Cincinnati Convention—all will
remember—was Colonel William Preston of Kentucky. He broke the Douglas line and precipitated the nomination of Buchanan, and was rewarded
with a foreign mission.

In about ten ticks of a watch, Cartter of Ohio was up. I had imagined
Ohio would be slippery enough for the crisis. And sure enough! Every eye
was on Cartter, and everybody who understood the matter at all knew
what he was about to do. He is a large man with rather striking features,
a shock of bristling black hair, large and shining eyes, and is terribly marked
with the smallpox. He has also an impediment in his speech, which amounts
to a stutter; and his selection as chairman of the Ohio delegation was, considering its condition, altogether appropriate. He had been quite noisy
during the sessions of the Convention, but had never commanded, when
mounting his chair, such attention as now. He said, "I rise (eh), Mr. Chairman (eh), to announce the change of four votes of Ohio from Mr. Chase to
Mr. Lincoln." The deed was done. There was a moment's silence. The
nerves of the thousands, which through the hours of suspense had been
subjected to terrible tension, relaxed, and as deep breaths of relief were
taken, there was a noise in the Wigwam like the rush of a great wind in
the van of a storm—and in another breath, the storm was there. There were
thousands cheering with the energy of insanity.

A man who had been on the roof and was engaged in communicating
the results of the ballotings to the mighty mass of outsiders, now demanded
by gestures at the skylight over the stage to know what had happened. One
of the secretaries, with a tally sheet in his hands, shouted—"Fire the Salute!

Abe Lincoln is nominated!" As the cheering inside the Wigwam subsided, we could hear that outside, where the news of the nomination had just been announced. And the roar, like the breaking up of the fountains of the great deep that was heard, gave a new impulse to the enthusiasm inside. Then the thunder of the salute rose above the din, and the shouting was repeated with such tremendous fury that some discharges of the cannon were absolutely not heard by those on the stage. Puffs of smoke, drifting by the open doors, and the smell of gunpowder, told what was going on.

The moment that half a dozen men who were on their chairs making motions at the president could be heard, they changed the votes of their States to Mr. Lincoln. This was a mere formality and was a cheap way for men to distinguish themselves. The proper and orderly proceeding would have been to announce the vote, and then for a motion to come from New York to make the nomination unanimous. New York was prepared to make this motion, but not out of order. Missouri, Iowa, Kentucky, Minnesota, Virginia, California, Texas, District of Columbia, Kansas, Nebraska and Oregon, insisted upon casting unanimous votes for Old Abe Lincoln before the vote was declared.

While these votes were being given, the applause continued, and a photograph of Abe Lincoln which had hung in one of the side rooms was brought in and held up before the surging and screaming masses. The places of the various delegations were indicated by staffs, to which were attached the names of the States, printed in large black letters on pasteboard. As the Lincoln enthusiasm increased, delegates tore these standards of the States from their places and swung them about their heads. A rush was made to get the New York standard and swing it with the rest, but the New Yorkers would not allow it to be moved, and were wrathful at the suggestion.

When the vote was declared, Mr. Evarts, the New York spokesman, mounted the secretaries' table and handsomely and impressively expressed his grief at the failure of the Convention to nominate Seward—and in melancholy tones moved that the nomination be made unanimous.

Mr. John A. Andrew of Massachusetts seconded the motion in a speech in which his vanity as a citizen of the commonwealth of Massachusetts was ventilated, and he said it had not been for old Massachusetts to strike down William Henry Seward, concluding by a promise to give the nominee of that Convention one hundred thousand majority.

Carl Schurz, on behalf of Wisconsin, again seconded the motion, but not so effectively in his speech as his reputation as an orator would have warranted us in expecting. There was a little clap-trap and something of anticlimax in shouting "Lincoln and victory," and talking of "defying the whole slave power and the whole vassalage of hell."

Austin Blair of Michigan made the speech of the hour. He said:

"Michigan, from first to last, has cast her vote for the great Statesman of New York. She has nothing to take back. She has not sent me forward to worship the rising sun, but she has put me forward to say that, at your behests here today, she lays down her first, best-loved candidate to take up yours, with some beating of the heart, with some quivering in the veins [much applause]; but she does not fear that the fame of Seward will suffer, for she knows that his fame is a portion of the history of the American Union; it will be written, and read, and beloved long after the temporary excitement of this day has passed away, and when Presidents themselves are forgotten in the oblivion which comes over all temporal things. We stand by him still. We have followed him with an eye single and with un-wavering faith in times past. We marshal now behind him in the grand column which shall go out to battle for Lincoln."

After a rather dull speech from Orvill H. Browning of Illinois, respond-ing in behalf of Lincoln, the nomination was made unanimous, and the Convention adjourned for dinner. The town was full of the news of Lin-coln's nomination, and could hardly contain itself. There were bands of music playing, and processions marching, and joyous cries heard on every hand, from the army of trumpeters for Lincoln of Illinois, and the thousands who are always enthusiastic on the winning side. But hundreds of men who had been in the Wigwam were so prostrated by the excitement they had endured, and their exertions in shrieking for Seward or Lincoln, that they were hardly able to walk to their hotels. There were men who had not tasted liquor who staggered about like drunkards, unable to manage themselves. The Seward men were terribly stricken down. They were mortified beyond all expression, and walked thoughtfully and silently away from the slaughterhouse, more ashamed than embittered. They acquiesced in the nomination, but did not pretend to be pleased with it; and the tone of their conversations, as to the prospect of electing the candidate, was not hopeful. It was their funeral, and they would not make merry.

A Lincoln man who could hardly believe that the "Old Abe" of his adora-tion was really the Republican nominee for the Presidency, took a chair at the dinner table at the Tremont House, and began talking to those around him, with none of whom he was acquainted, of the greatness of the events of the day. One of his expressions was, "Talk of your money and bring on your bullies with you!—the immortal principles of the everlasting people are with Abe Lincoln, of the people, by—." "Abe Lincoln has no money and no bullies, but he has the people, by —." A servant approached the eloquent patriot and asked what he would have to eat. Being thus recalled to tem-poral things he glared scornfully at the servant and roared out, "Go to the devil—what do I want to eat for? Abe Lincoln is nominated, G—d—d— it; and I'm going to live on air—the air of Liberty, by —." But in a moment he inquired for the bill of fare, and then ordered "a great deal of everything" —saying if he must eat he might as well eat "the whole bill." He swore he felt as if he could "devour and digest an Illinois prairie." And this was one of thousands.

During the dinner recess a caucus of the president of delegations was held, and New York, though requested to do so, would not name a candidate for the Vice-Presidency. After dinner we had the last act in the drama.

The nomination of Vice-President was not particularly exciting. Cassius M. Clay was the only competitor of Hannibal Hamlin, who made any show in the race; and the outside pressure was for him. At one time a thousand voices called "Clay! Clay!" to the Convention. If the multitude could have had their way, Mr. Clay would have been put on the ticket by acclamation. But it was stated that Mr. Hamlin was a good friend of Mr. Seward. He was geographically distant from Lincoln, and was once a Democrat. It was deemed judicious to pretend to patronize the Democratic element, and thus consolidate those who were calling the Convention an "old Whig concern." They need not have been afraid, however, of having it called an old Whig affair, for it was not "eminently respectable," nor distinguished for its "dignity and decorum." On the other hand, the satanic element was very strongly developed. . . .

The fact of the Convention was the defeat of Seward rather than the nomination of Lincoln. It was the triumph of a presumption of availability over pre-eminence in intellect and unrivaled fame—a success of the ruder qualities of manhood and the more homely attributes of popularity over the arts of a consummate politician and the splendor of accomplished statesmanship.

Now that the business of the Convention was transacted, we had the usual stump speeches, and complimentary resolutions, and the valedictory from the chairman, and the "three times three" upon adjournment for the candidates.

The city was wild with delight. The "Old Abe" men formed processions and bore rails through the streets. Torrents of liquor were poured down the hoarse throats of the multitude. A hundred guns were fired from the top of the Tremont House. The Chicago *Press and Tribune* office was illuminated. The paper says:

> On each side of the counting room door stood a *rail*—out of the three thousand split by "honest Old Abe" thirty years ago on the Sangamon River bottoms. On the inside were two more, brilliantly hung with tapers.

I left the city on the night train on the Fort Wayne and Chicago road. The train consisted of eleven cars, every seat full and people standing in the aisles and corners. I never before saw a company of persons so prostrated by continued excitement. The Lincoln men were not able to respond to the cheers which went up along the road for "Old Abe." They had not only done their duty in that respect but exhausted their capacity. At every station where there was a village, until after two o'clock, there were tar barrels burning, drums beating, boys carrying rails; and guns, great and small, banging away. The weary passengers were allowed no rest, but plagued by the thundering jar of cannon, the clamor of drums, the glare of bonfires, and the whooping of the boys, who were delighted with the idea of a candidate for the Presidency who thirty years ago split rails on the Sangamon River—classic stream now and forevermore—and whose neighbors named him "honest."

EPILOGUE, The Lesson.

The lesson to the Nation of the *Presidential Caucuses of 1860* is the necessity for the abolition of the Caucus System which, in whatever party organization operative, is a system of swindling, by which the people are defrauded out of the effective exercise of the right of suffrage. There is no honesty in caucuses, no sound principle or good policy, except by accident; and the accidents that furnish the exception are rare indeed.

The revenues of King Caucus are corruption funds—and his government costs the country at least fifty million dollars annually—his platforms of principles are elaborations of false pretenses—his nominees are his obsequious viceroys—and he is the power behind the chairs of our chief magistrates, and under the tables of our cabinets, far more potent than those who visibly assume authority.

If a Republican form of government is to be preserved in our confederacy, the people must make a bonfire of his throne.

6

Constitutional View of the War

Alexander H. Stephens

MR. STEPHENS. We have now, gentlemen, gone through with the preliminary questions; we have taken that historical review, which was necessary and essential for a correct understanding of the nature and character of the Government of the United States, from a violation of the organic principles of which, as I stated in the outset, the war had its origin. We have seen from this review that ours is a Federal Government. In other words, we have seen that it is a Government formed by a Convention, a *Fœdus*, or Compact between distinct, separate, and sovereign States. We have seen that this Federal or Conventional Government, so formed, possesses inherently no power whatever. All its powers are held by delegation only, and by delegation from separate States. These powers are all enumerated and all limited to specific objects in the Constitution. Even the highest sovereign power it is permitted to exercise—the war power, for instance—is held by it by delegation only. Sovereignty itself—the great source of all political power—under the system, still resides where it did before the Compact was entered into, that is, in the States severally, or with the people of the several States respectively. By the Compact, the sovereign powers to be exercised by the Federal Head were not surrendered by the States—were not alienated or parted with by them. They were delegated only. The States by voluntary engagements agreed only to abstain from their exercise themselves, and to confer this exercise by delegation upon common agents under the Convention, for the better security of the great objects aimed at by the formation of the Compact, which was the regulation of their external and inter-State affairs.

Our system, taken together, we have seen, is a peculiar one. The world never saw its like before. It has no prototype in any of all the previous Confederations, or Federal Republics, of which we have any account. It is neither a *Staaten-bund* exactly, nor a *Bundesstaat*, according to the classification of Federal Republics by the German Publicists. It differs from their

ALEXANDER H. STEPHENS, *A Constitutional View of the Late War Between the States . . .* , 2 vols. (Philadelphia, 1868), Vol. 2, *Colloquy*, xiii.

Staaten-bund in this, that the powers to be exercised by the Federal Head are divided into three departments, the Legislative, Judicial, and Executive, with a perfectly organized machinery for the execution of these powers within its limited sphere, and for the specific objects named, upon citizens of the several States without the intermediate act or sanction of the several States. In the *Staaten-bund*, or "States' Confederation," according to their classification, the Federal Government can enact no laws which will operate upon the citizens of the several States composing it, until the States severally give them their sanction. Such was our Federal Union under the first Articles. But our present system, as we have seen, went a step further, and introduced a new principle in Confederations. While, therefore, our system differs specifically in this particular from their *Staaten-bund*, or "States' Confederation," yet it agrees entirely with it in its essential *generic* difference from their *Bundesstaat*, in this, that the States collectively constitute an international unit as regards third parties, but do not cease to be international units as regards each other.

It differs further *generically* from their *bundesstaat*, or "Federative State," or what may properly be called "an incorporate union," in this, that no sovereign power whatever, under our system, is surrendered or alienated by the several States; it is only delegated. The difference between our system and their *Staaten-bund*, is, however, only *specific*, as we see. It is not *generic*. They are both essentially the same. Ours is a newly developed species of Government of their *genus Staaten-bund*. This specific difference is what struck De Tocqueville as "a wholly novel theory, which may be considered as a great discovery in modern political science," and for which there was as yet no specific name. His language, you recollect, is:

> This Constitution, which may at first be confounded with the Federal Constitutions which have preceded it, rests, in truth, upon a wholly novel theory, which may be considered as a great discovery in modern political science. In all the Confederations which preceded the American Constitution of 1789, the allied States, for a common object, agreed to obey the injunctions of a Federal Government; but they reserved to themselves the right of ordaining and enforcing the execution of the laws of the Union. The American States, which combined in 1789, agreed that the Federal Government should not only dictate, but should excecute its own enactments. In both cases, the right is the same, but the exercise of the right is different, and this difference produced the most momentous consequences.

Further on, he says:

> The new word, which ought to express this novel thing, does not yet exist. The human understanding more easily invents new things than new words, and we are hence constrained to employ many improper and inadequate expressions.

This new principle of so constituting a Federal Republic as to make us "one nation as to foreign concerns, and to keep us distinct as to domestic ones," with a division of the delegated powers into Legislative, Judiciary, and Executive Departments, and with an organization and machinery in the Conventional Government, thus formed, for the full exercise of all its delegated and limited powers, similar to those of the separate States creating it, we have seen, was indicated as early as December, 1786, by Mr. Jefferson in a letter to Mr. Madison. This was a grand step in progress in the science of Government. This was what so signalized our career for sixty years, and this is the peculiar *specific* difference between our Federal Republic and all others of similar general type, to which Lord Brougham alludes when he says:

> It is not at all a refinement that a Federal Union should be formed; this is the natural result of men's joint operations in a very rude state of society. But the regulation of such a Union upon pre-established principles, the formation of a system of Government and legislation in which the different *subjects* shall be *not individuals* but *States*, the application of legislative principles to such a *body of States*, and the devising means for keeping its *integrity* as a *federacy*, while the rights and powers of the individual States are *maintained entire*, is the very greatest refinement in social policy to which any state of circumstances has ever given rise, or to which any age has ever given birth.

From this exposition, we see clearly the proper solution of the vexed question, whether the United States constitute a Nation or not. We see clearly not only that they do constitute a Nation, but also what sort of a Nation it is. It is not a Nation of individuals, blended in a common mass, with a consolidated sovereignty over the whole; but a Nation with constituent elements or members of which are separate and distinct political organizations, States, or Sovereignties. It is a "Confederated Republic," as Washington styled our present Union. This is the same as if he had styled it a Confederated Nation. It is, in truth, a Confederated Nation. That is, it is a Nation of States, or in other words, a Nation of Nations. In this sense, these States, thus united, do constitute a Nation, and a Nation of the highest and grandest type the world ever saw! . . .

In our system, or united systems, sovereign powers are not only divided into the three great branches, as I have stated, both in the Federal Government and in the several State Governments; but they are also divided in like manner between these two systems of governments. Some of the sovereign powers are delegated to all the States to be exercised jointly by them in Congress assembled, as well as by special officers of the Federal Government; and some of them are delegated to the various officers of the several State Governments. Those delegated to each, being delegated by the sovereign power of the people of the several States separately; and divided similarly in each case. There is no alienation of any portion of sovereignty itself in either case. This continues to reside with the people of

the several States as separate, integral units. I have only further to add . . .
that by *ultimate* sovereignty in this argument, I mean that original, inherent, innate and continually existing rightful power, or *Will* of the several Bodies Politic, or States of our Union—that source and fountain of all
political power—which is unimpaired by voluntarily assumed obligations;
and which at any time, within the terms stated, can rightfully resume all
its delegated powers—those to the Federal Government as well as those
to the several State Governments.

Those great and essential truths of our history, therefore, being thus forever established beyond question or doubt, we will now, if agreeable to
you, proceed to consider the immediate and exciting question which
brought the organic principles of the Government into such terrible
physical conflict in the inauguration of the war. This was, as stated in the
outset, the question of Negro Slavery, or more properly speaking that
political and legal subordination of the black race to the white race, which
existed in the Seceding States.

I thus speak of Slavery as it existed with us, purposely. For, it is to be
remembered in all our discussions on this subject, that what was called
Slavery with us, was not Slavery in the usual sense of that word, as generally used and understood by the ancients, and as generally used and
understood in many countries in the present age. It was with us a political
Institution. It was, indeed, nothing but that legal subordination of an
Inferior race to a Superior one which was thought to be the best in the
organization of society for the welfare, politically, socially, morally and
intellectually of both races. The slave, so-called, was not in law regarded
entirely as a chattel, as has been erroneously represented. He was by no
means subject to the absolute dominion of his master. He had important
personal rights, secured by law. His service due according to law, it is true,
was considered property, and so in all countries is considered the service
of all persons who according to law are bound to another or others for a
term, however long or short. So is the legal right of parents to the service
of their minor children in all the States now considered as property. A
right or property that may be assigned, transferred or sold. Hamilton expressed the idea of this peculiar Institution, as it existed with us, clearly,
when he said: "The Federal Constitution, therefore, decides with great
propriety on the case of our slaves, when it views them in the mixed character of persons and property. This is in fact their true character. It is the
character bestowed on them by the laws under which they live." They
were so viewed and regarded by the Constitutions and laws of all the
States. The relation of master and slave under the Institution, as before
said, was but one of "reciprocal service and mutual bonds." The view of
them as property related to their services due according to law.

But not to digress. This matter of Negro subordination, I repeat, was the
exciting question in 1860. There were, it is true, many other questions in-

volving the same principles of the Government, which had agitated the public mind almost from the time it went into operation, still exciting the public mind to a greater or less degree: but this question of the *status* of the Black race in the Southern States, was by far the most exciting and all-absorbing one, at that time, on both sides, and was the main proximate cause which brought those principles of the Government into active play, resulting in the conflict of arms. This relation of political and legal subordination of the Inferior to the Superior race, as it existed in 1860, in all the Seceding States, had at one time, be it constantly kept in mind, existed in all the Union, and did so exist in all, save one, in 1787, when the present Articles of Union were entered into.

By these Articles this relation was fully recognized, as appears from the solemn covenant therein made, that fugitives from service, under this system, as it then thus existed, escaping from one State into another should upon claim be delivered up to the party to whom the service was due. This was one of the stipulations of the Compact upon which the Union was formed, as we have seen, and of which Judge Story said on an important occasion, in delivering an opinion from the Bench of the Supreme Court of the United States, "It cannot be doubted that it constituted a fundamental article, without the adoption of which the Union could not have been formed."

These are all great facts never to be lost sight of in this investigation of the rightfulness of this most terrible war, and in determining correctly and justly upon which side the huge responsibility of its inauguration, and of the enormous wrongs, and most disastrous consequences attending its subsequent conduct, must, in the judgment of mankind, forever rest.

It is not at all germane to our purpose in this investigation, at this time, to inquire into the Right, or Wrong, of the Institution of Slavery itself, as it thus existed in what were then known as the Slave States. Neither is it in the line of my argument now, to treat of the defects, or abuses of the system. Nor is it at all necessary, or pertinent to my present object, to trace from its inception to its culmination, the history or progress of that movement against it, which was organized for the purpose of bringing the questions it involved into the arena of Federal Councils, and within the range of Federal action. Suffice it here barely to say, and assume as a fact what is known to us all so well, that in 1860 a majority of the Northern States having long previously of their own accord abolished this Institution, within their own limits respectively, had also by the action of their Legislatures openly and avowedly violated that clause in the Constitution of the United States which provided for the rendition of fugitives of this class from service.

To give a history of that movement to which I allude, to trace its progress from its origin, would require a volume of itself. A volume both interesting and instructive might be devoted to it. This is what is known as the Abolition movement in this country, and this is what Mr. Greeley is pleased to style the "American Conflict." But from entering into an investigation of that sort, I now forbear. It is is in no way pertinent or essential to my purpose. Whoever feels an interest in the subject will see it treated fully, truthfully, and ably by the master hand of Mr. George Lunt of Boston, in his history of the "Origin of the War."

Suffice it, therefore, for me at present on this subject only to say generally that such a movement was started, such a conflict was begun at an early day after our present system of government went into operation. As early as the 12th day of February, 1790, within twelve months after Washington was inaugurated as President, a petition invoking the Federal authorities to take jurisdiction of this subject, with a view to the ultimate abolition of this Institution in the States respectively, was sent to Congress, headed by Dr. Franklin. This movement, in its first step thus taken so early, was partially checked by the Resolution to which the House of Representatives came, after the most mature consideration of the petition and its objects. That Resolution declared: "That Congress have no authority to interfere in the emancipation of slaves, or in the treatment of them within any of the States; it remaining with the several States alone to provide any regulations therein which humanity and true policy may require."

This clear exposition of the nature of the Federal Government, and its utter want of power to take any action upon the subject, as sought for by the petitioners, checked, I say, for a time, this movement, or conflict so started and commenced. The conflict, however, was only partially checked; it went on until in 1860, when those who so entered into this movement standing forth as the Abolition or Anti-Slavery Party under the name of Republican, but which in truth was the party of Centralism and Consolidation, organized upon the principle of bringing the Federal Powers to bear upon this Institution in a way to secure its ultimate Abolition in all the States, succeeded in the election of the two highest officers of the Government, pledged to carry out their principles, and to carry them out in open disregard of the decision of the Supreme Court, which highest Judicial Tribunal under the Constitution had by solemn adjudication denied the power of the Federal Government to take such action as this Party and its two highest officers stood pledged to carry out. With all these questions, I repeat, I have nothing now to do, except to say that the conflict from its rise to its culmination was not a conflict between the advocates and opponents of the Institution itself. It seems to have been Mr. Greeley's leading object, throughout his work, to give this idea of the nature of the conflict, as I stated in the beginning. This, however, was in no sense the fact of the case. The conflict, fierce and bitter as it was for seventy years, was a conflict between those who were for maintaining the Federal character of the Government and those who were for centralizing all power in the Federal Head. This was the conflict. It was a conflict between the true supporters of the Federal Union of States established by the Constitution and those whose object was to overthrow this Union of States, and by usurpations to erect a National Consolidation in its stead.

The same conflict arose upon divers other questions, also at an early day. It exhibited itself in the discussions of the first Judiciary Act. In the financial measures submitted by Mr. Hamilton, the then Secretary of the Treasury. In the assumption of the State debts. In the first Apportionment Bill, which was vetoed on these grounds by Washington, in 1792; and much more formidably it exhibited itself in the passage of the Alien and Sedition Acts, in 1798, under the elder Adams. This Party, as we have seen, then assumed the popular name of Federal, as it assumed the popular name of Republican in 1860. These latter measures of 1798 came near stirring up civil war, and would most probably have resulted in such a catastrophe if the Party so organized with such principles and objects had not been utterly overthrown and driven from power by the advocates of our true Federal system of Government, under the lead of Mr. Jefferson, in 1800. It was after this complete defeat on these other questions that the Centralists rallied upon this question of the *status* of the black race in the States, where it continued to exist, as the most promising one for them to agitate and unite the people of the Northern States upon, for the accomplishment of their sinister objects of National Centralization or Consolidation.

On this question, Mr. Greeley and other writers speak of only two Parties during the entire conflict. The Pro-Slavery Party, and the Anti-Slavery, or Liberty Party. The truth is there never was in the United States, or in any one of them, an organized Pro-Slavery Party. No such antagonism, as he represents, ever existed in the Federal Councils. The antagonism on this question, which was clearly exhibited in the beginning, as appears from the Resolution of the House of Representatives referred to, was an antagonism growing out of Constitutional principles, and not any sort of antagonism growing out of the principles involved in the right or wrong of Negro Slavery, as it then existed in the several States of the Union. It was an antagonism growing out of principles lying at the foundation of the common Government of the States. Of those men, for instance, who voted for the Resolution referred to, in 1790, how many can be supposed to have been Pro-Slavery in their sentiments, or in favor of the Institution? Let us look into it. Here is the record of the vote. Amongst the prominent supporters of the Resolution, and on the list of those who voted for it, is the name of Roger Sherman of Connecticut. Here is Benjamin Huntington, also of the same State. From Massachusetts, we see the names of Theodore Sedgwick, Elbridge Gerry, and Benjamin Goodhue. From New Hampshire, we see the name of Nicholas Gilman. From New Jersey, Elias Boudinot and Lambert Cadwallader. From Pennsylvania, Frederick A. Muhlenberg, Thomas Hartley, and Daniel Heister. These were all prominent men in the formation of the Constitution. All from the Northern States. The vote shows,

that not only a majority of the members from the Northern States voted
for the Resolution, but that a majority of those who did vote for it were
from the Northern States. Those from the South who voted against it, the
debate shows, so voted because they did not think the petition should be
considered or acted upon at all, as it related to subjects not within their
Constitutional jurisdiction.

But how many of this majority of the Northern members who voted for
it can be reasonably supposed to have been Pro-Slavery in sentiment? In
their action in entertaining the petition, they intended only to show what
they considered a due regard to the right of petition, and at the same time
prove themselves true to the Constitution of their country. This the debate
conclusively shows. So in all after times up to the election in 1860. Those
who resisted the action of the Abolitionists did so because it was based
upon revolutionary principles—principles utterly at war with those upon
which the Union was established. As a striking illustration of this, Mr.
Jefferson himself is well-known to have been as much opposed to the Institution of Slavery, as it then existed in the United States, as any man in
either of them; and yet he headed the great party in opposition to this
mode of effecting the object of those who desired its Abolition, as he led
the same party to success over the Centralists on other questions in 1800.
He utterly denied that the Federal Government could rightfully exercise
any power with the view to the change of any of the Institutions of the
States respectively.

The same is true of all the prominent leaders of this party, as well as the
great mass of the people composing it, from the days of Jefferson to those
of General Cass and Mr. Douglas, Mr. Pinckney and Mr. Clay, though
Southern men as Mr. Jefferson was, were decidedly Anti-Slavery in their
sentiments, and yet they ever acted with the party of Mr. Jefferson upon
this question. General Cass and Mr. Douglas were Northern men with
sentiments equally averse to Slavery, and for the same reasons opposed
the Abolition movement in the Federal Councils. Even Chief Justice Taney,
who delivered the opinion of the Supreme Court in the case referred to,
was by no means individually Pro-Slavery in his sentiments. His views upon
the Institution are understood to have been very similar to those of Mr.
Pinckney and Mr. Clay. Out of the million and half, and more, of men in
the Northern States who voted against Mr. Lincoln, in 1860, perhaps not
ten thousand could be said, with truth, to be in favor of the Institution, or
would have lived in a State where it existed. It was a subject with which
they were thoroughly convinced they had nothing to do, and could have
nothing to do under the terms of the Union by which the States were confederated, except to carry out and faithfully perform all the obligations
of the Constitutional Compact in regard to it. In opposing the "Liberty
Party," so-called, they enlisted under no banner of Slavery of any sort, but
only arrayed themselves against that organization which had virtually

hoisted the banner of Consolidation. The struggle or conflict, therefore, from its rise to its culmination was between those who, in whatever State they lived, were for maintaining our Federal system as it was established, and those who were for a consolidation of power in the Central Head.

But the great fact now to be considered in this investigation is that this Anti-Constitutional Party, in 1860, came into power upon this question in the Executive branch of the Federal Government.

This is the state of things which produced so much excitement and apprehension in the popular mind of the Southern States at that time. This Anti-Slavery Party had not only succeeded in getting a majority of the Northern States to openly violate their Constitutional faith in the avowed breach of the Compact, as stated; but had succeeded in electing a President and Vice-President pledged to principles which were not only at war with the domestic Institutions of the States of the South, but which must inevitably, if carried out, ultimately lead to the absorption of all power in the Central Government and end sooner or later in Absolutism or Despotism. These were the principles then brought into conflict which, as stated, resulted in the conflict of arms.

The Seceding States feeling no longer bound by a Compact which had been so openly violated, and a majority of their people being deeply impressed with the conviction that the whole frame-work of the Constitution would be overthrown by this Party which would soon have control of the Executive Department of the Government, determined to withdraw from the Union for the very reasons which had induced them to enter it in the beginning. Seven of these States—South Carolina, Georgia, Florida, Alabama, Mississippi, Louisiana, and Texas—did withdraw. Conventions of their people, regularly called by the proper authorities in each of these States respectively—Conventions representing the sovereignty of the States similar in all respects to those which by Ordinances had ratified the Constitution of the United States—passed Ordinances resuming the sovereign powers therein delegated. These were the Secession Ordinances, which we may hereafter have occasion to look into. These Conventions also appointed delegates, to meet in Montgomery, Alabama, on the 4th of February, 1861, with a view to form a new Confederation among themselves, upon the same essential basis of the Constitution of the United States.

It was not in opposition to the principles of that Government that they withdrew from it. They quit the Union to save the principles of the Constitution, and to perpetuate, on this continent, the liberties which it was intended to secure and establish. Mr. Buchanan was then President of the United States. He held that the Federal Government had no power to coerce a Seceding State to remain in the Union but, strangely enough, at the same time held that no State could rightfully withdraw from the Union. Mr. Lincoln came into power on the 4th of March, 1861. He held that the Federal Government did possess the Constitutional power to maintain the

Union of States by force, and it was in the maintenance of these views the war was inaugurated by him.

JUDGE BYNUM. Do you mean to say, Mr. Stephens, that the war was in-augurated by Mr. Lincoln?

MR. STEPHENS. Most assuredly I do.

JUDGE BYNUM. Why, how in the world, can you do that in the face of the well-known facts of the case? Did not General Beauregard in command of the Confederate forces, so-called, at Charleston, South Carolina, fire upon Fort Sumter in that harbor? Did he not compel Major Anderson, the United States officer in command of that Fort, to capitulate and surrender? Was it not this outrage upon the American flag that caused such deep and uni-versal excitement and indignation throughout the entire North? Was it not this that caused the great meetings in New York, Boston and every Northern city? Can you maintain in the face of these notorious facts, that the war was begun by Mr. Lincoln, or the Federal authorities? You rely mainly upon facts, as you say. Your whole argument professes to be based upon the facts of history. If there is any great fact that must go down to posterity forever, it is the fact that the Insurgents, or Confederates, if you please, began this war. This is a fact which, as you have said of other matters, "can never be erased or obliterated."

MR. STEPHENS. Not quite so fast, Judge. My whole argument is based upon fact, and upon facts that can never be erased or obliterated. It is a fact that the *first gun* was fired by the Confederates. It is a fact that General Beauregard did, on the 12th of April, 1861, bombard Fort Sumter before any blow had actually been struck by the Federal authorities. That is not disputed at all. That is a fact which I have no disposition to erase or oblit-erate in any way. That is a great truth which will live forever. But did the firing of the first gun, or the reduction of Fort Sumter inaugurate or begin the war; and in solving this question, you must allow me to say that in personal or national conflicts, it is not he who strikes the first blow or fires the first gun that inaugurates or begins the conflict. Hallam has well said that "the *aggressor* in a war (that is, he who begins it) is not the *first* who *uses force,* but the first who renders force *necessary.*"

Which side, according to this high authority (that only announces the common sentiments of mankind) was the *aggressor* in this instance? Which side was it that provoked and rendered the first blow necessary? The true answer to that question will settle the fact as to which side began the war.

I maintain that it was inaugurated and begun, though no blow had been struck, when the hostile fleet, styled the "Relief Squadron," with eleven ships carrying two hundred and eighty-five guns and two thousand four hundred men was sent out from New York and Norfolk, with orders from the authorities at Washington to re-enforce Fort Sumter peaceably—if per-mitted—"but forcibly if they must."

The war was then and there inaugurated and begun by the authorities at Washington. General Beauregard did not open fire upon Fort Sumter until this fleet was, to his knowledge, very near the harbor of Charleston, and until he had inquired of Major Anderson, in command of the Fort, whether he would engage to take no part in the expected blow then coming down upon him from the approaching fleet. Francis W. Pickens, Governor of South Carolina, and General Beauregard had both been notified that the fleet was coming, and of its objects, by a messenger from the authorities at Washington. This notice, however, was not given until it was near its destination. When Major Anderson, therefore, would make no such promise, it became necessary for General Beauregard to strike the first blow, as he did; otherwise the forces under his command might have been exposed to two fires at the same time—one in front and the other in the rear.

To understand this fully, let us see how matters stood in Charleston Harbor at the time.

The Confederate States, then seven in number, had, as stated, all passed Ordinances of Secession. All of them, in regularly constituted Conventions, had withdrawn all their sovereign powers previously delegated to the United States. They had formed a new Confederation, with a regularly constituted Government, at Montgomery, Alabama, as they had a perfect right to do if our past conclusions were correct, and these you have not been able to assail. This new Confederation had sent a commission to the authorities at Washington, as we shall see, to settle all matters amicably and peacefully. War was by no means the wish or desire of the authorities at Montgomery. Very few of the public men in the Seceding States even expected war. All of them, it is true, held themselves in readiness for it, if it should be forced upon them against their wishes and most earnest protestations.

This is abundantly and conclusively apparent from the speeches and addresses of their leading public men at the time. It is apparent from the resolutions of the State Legislatures, and the State Conventions, before and in their acts of Secession. It is apparent and manifest from their acts in their new Confederation at Montgomery. It is apparent from the inaugural address of President Davis. It is apparent from the appointment of commissioners to settle all matters involved in the separation from their former Confederates honorably, peaceably, amicably, and justly. It is apparent and manifest from every act that truly indicates the objects and motives of men, or from which their real aims can be justly arrived at. Peace not only with the States from which they had separated, but peace with all the world, was the strong desire of the Confederate States.

It was under these circumstances that the Confederate commissioners were given to understand that Fort Sumter would be peacefully evacuated. An assurance to this effect was given, though in an informal manner, by Mr. Seward, the Secretary of State under Mr. Lincoln. This pledge was most strangely violated by sending the armed squadron, as stated, to re-enforce and provision the Fort. The information that this fleet had put to sea with such orders reached General Beauregard when it was already near the offing, as I have stated. He immediately communicated the fact, by telegraph, to the authorities at Montgomery. In reply, he received this order from the Secretary of War of the Confederate States Government: "If you have no doubt of the authorized character of the agent who communicated to you the intention of the Washington Government to supply Fort Sumter by force, you will at once demand its evacuation; and if this is refused, proceed in such manner as you may determine, to reduce it."

Accordingly, on the 11th of April, General Beauregard made a demand on Major Anderson, in command of the Fort, for its evacuation.

In reply Major Anderson stated: "I have the honor to acknowledge the receipt of your communication demanding the evacuation of this Fort, and to say in reply thereto, that it is a demand with which I regret that my sense of honor and my obligation to my Government prevent my compliance."

To this he added, verbally, to the messenger: "I will await the first shot, and, if you do not batter us to pieces, we will be starved out in a few days."

This written reply, as well as the verbal remark, were forthwith sent by General Beauregard to the Secretary of War at Montgomery, who immediately returned the following response: "Do not desire needlessly to bombard Fort Sumter. If Major Anderson will state the time at which, as indicated by himself, he will evacuate, and agree that, in the meantime, he will not use his guns against us, unless ours should be employed against Fort Sumter, you are authorized thus to avoid the effusion of blood. If this or its equivalent be refused, reduce the Fort, as your judgment decides most practicable."

This was communicated to Major Anderson. He refused to comply with the terms. He would not consent to any such arrangement.

Whereupon, General Beauregard opened fire on the Fort at 4:30 on the morning of the 12th of April. The fire was returned. The bombardment lasted for thirty-two hours, when Major Anderson agreed to capitulate. General Beauregard exhibited no less of the magnanimity of the true soldier in the terms of the capitulation than he had of high military skill and genius in forming his plans, and in their execution, for the reduction of the Fort. The entire garrison numbering eighty in all, officers and men, was permitted to be marched out with their colors and music. They were permitted to salute their flag with fifty guns. All private as well as company property was also allowed to be taken by those to whom it belonged. These were the same terms that General Beauregard had offered on the 11th before he opened fire. As Providence ordered it, not a life was lost in this most memorable and frightful combat. The firing on both sides, at some times, particularly at night, was represented by those who witnessed it, as both "grand and terrific."

This was the first blow. It is true, the first gun was fired on the Confederate side. That is fully admitted. But all the facts show that if force was thus first used by them, it was so first used only because it was rendered necessary in self-defence on the part of those thus using it, and so rendered necessary by the opposite side. This first use of force, therefore, under the circumstances, cannot in fact be properly and justly considered as the beginning of the war.

What has been stated also shows how earnesly the authorities at Montgomery had in every possible way consistent with honor and safety endeavored to avoid a collision of forces. The whole question of the right or wrong, therefore, in striking this first blow, as well as the right or wrong of the war, depends upon the Constitutional points we have been discussing. If the Seceding States were right on these points, then this first blow was perfectly justifiable, even if it had not been given, as it was, to avert one then impending over them.

JUDGE BYNUM. Please allow me to interrupt you for a moment. The views you express seem to me not only novel, but altogether unsuited to the facts, even as you state them. Allow me to ask if the Fort did not belong to the United States? Was it not the property of the United States? Were not the officers and men in it attached to the service of the United States? What right, therefore, had General Beauregard, or anybody else, to attempt to prevent the United States Government from provisioning the garrison then holding it, and re-enforcing it, if they thought proper? Was it not the duty of Mr. Lincoln to do it, as well as his right?

MR. STEPHENS. Not if South Carolina had the sovereign right to demand the possession of the Fort. Rights, whether civil, moral, or political, never conflict. If South Carolina had this sovereign right to demand the possession of the place, which was within her jurisdiction, then Mr. Lincoln could have had no right to continue to hold it against this demand; nor was it his duty, in any sense, to attempt even to provision it by force, under the circumstances.

The Fort was within the jurisdiction of South Carolina. It was built specially for her protection and belonged to her in part as well as to the other States jointly. On the 11th of January, Governor Pickens, in behalf of the sovereign rights of the State, demanded its possession of Major Anderson for the use of the State. On his refusal to deliver it up, the Governor immediately sent I. W. Hayne, the Attorney General of the State, to Washington, and made a like demand for its possession of Mr. Buchanan, the President, alleging that the possession of this Fort was necessary for the safety of the State for whose protection it had been erected. In this letter, Governor Pickens also stated that a full valuation of the property would be accounted for, on settlement of the relations of South Carolina with the United States.

This whole question, relating to the right in this matter, and the side on which the right existed, depends, as I have said, upon the correctness

of our conclusions on the points discussed. If South Carolina, after the re-
sumption of her delegated powers, was a separate sovereign State (which
is one of our established truths), then, of course, she had a perfect right
to demand the possession of any landed property whatever lying within
the limits of her jurisdiction, if she deemed it of importance for her public
use and benefit. This perfect right so to do was subject to but one limitation,
and that was the moral obligation to pay a fair and just compensation for
the property so demanded for public use. There can be no question of the
correctness of this principle. It is the foundation of the great right of
Eminent Domain, which ever accompanies sovereignty. We have seen that
this right of Eminent Domain was never parted with by her, even under
the Constitution. South Carolina, then, even before Secession, and while
she held herself to be bound by the Constitution, had a perfect right to
demand of the United States Government the possession of this identical
property, on paying a just compensation for it, if she had deemed it essential for her public interests. This Fort never could have been erected on her
soil without her consent, as we have seen. The title, therefore, of the United
States to the land on which Fort Sumter was built, was in no essential respect different from the title of any other land-holder in the State. The
tenure by which the United States claimed and held this property differed
in no essential respect from the tenure by which every other land-owner
held similar property in the State; nor was this property of the United
States, so purchased and held under grant from South Carolina, any less
subject to the right of Eminent Domain on the part of the State than any
other lands lying within her limits. If this was so even before Secession
(and no one can successfully assail the position) then how much more
clearly this right (by virtue of the principle of Eminent Domain) to demand the possession of this property for public use, for *her own protection,*
appears after she had expressly resumed the exercise of all of her sovereign
powers? This right to demand the possession of this Fort, therefore, being
unquestionably perfect in her as a sovereign State after Secession, whether
it was before or not, she had transferred to the Confederate States. Hence,
their right to demand the evacuation of Fort Sumter was perfect, viewed
either morally, or politically.

The Confederate States had offered to come to a fair and just settlement
with the United States, as to the value of this property, as well as all other
public property belonging to all the States in common, at the time of their
separation. This Fort, as well as all else that belonged to the United States,
belonged in part to these seven Seceded States. They constituted seven of
the United States, to which all this joint property belonged. All the Forts
which lay within the limits of the Seceded States had been turned over by
these States, respectively, to the Confederacy, as we shall see. The Confederate States, therefore, through their authorities, had a right to demand
and take possession of all of these Forts, so lying within their limits, for

their own public use, upon paying a just compensation for them to their former associates of the United States, who still adhered to that Union. These principles cannot be assailed. The offer so to pay whatever should be found to be due upon a general and just account had been made. Mr. Lincoln, therefore, had no right under the circumstances to hold any of these forts by force, after the demand for the possession had been made; much less was it his duty either morally, or politically, when it was known that the attempt would inevitably lead to a war between the States. This is my answer to your property view.

Now, sir, I do stand upon facts, and these are the incontestable facts of this case, which will forever perpetuate the truth of my assertion that upon the head of the Federal Government will forever rest the inauguration of this most terrible war which did ensue.

No part of its responsibility rests upon the Southern States. They were the aggressors in no instance. They were ever true to their plighted faith under the Constitution. No instance of a breach of its mutual covenants can be ever laid to their charge. The open and palpable breach was committed by a number of their Northern Confederates. No one can deny this. Those States at the North, which were untrue to their Constitutional engagements, claimed powers not delegated and elected a Chief Magistrate pledged to carry out principles openly in defiance of the decision of the highest Judicial Tribunal known to the Constitution.

Their policy tended inevitably to a Centralized Despotism. It was under these circumstances that Secession was resorted to, as before stated; and, then, the war was begun and waged by the North to prevent the exercise of this right. All that the Southern States did was in defence, even in their firing the first gun.

MAJOR HEISTER. Do you say, Mr. Stephens, that the Southern States had never violated their Constitutional obligations, and that Northern States had openly repudiated theirs?

MR. STEPHENS. I do.

MAJOR HEISTER. How did they thus repudiate? What do you mean?

MR. STEPHENS. They did what I say by passing State laws—"Personal Liberty Bills," so-called—which effectively prevented the execution of that clause of the Constitution which provided for the rendition of fugitives from service. Several of these States also refused to deliver fugitives from justice, when the crime charged was that of stealing or enticing away any person owing service to another. For, besides their personal liberty acts, which nullified, in the language of Mr. Webster, that provision of the Constitution for the rendition of slaves, the governors of Maine, New York, and Ohio, had refused to deliver up fugitives from justice, who had been charged with a breach of the laws of the Southern States, in matters relating to the *status* of the black race.

MAJOR HEISTER. Where are those laws? Have you got them? I should like to see them.

MR. STEPHENS. I have some of them, perhaps not all. But as to the fact, there can be no doubt. Here, for instance, is the law of Vermont upon the subject.

> Every person who may have been held as a slave, who shall come or who may be brought into this State, with the consent of his or her alleged master or mistress, or who *shall come* or be brought, or *shall be* in this State, *shall be free.*
>
> Every person who shall hold, or *attempt to hold*, in this State, in slavery, as a slave, any free person, in any form or for any time, *however short*, under the *pretence* that such person *is* or *has been* a slave, shall, on conviction thereof, be imprisoned in the State prison for a term of not less than five years, nor more than twenty, and be fined not less than one thousand dollars, nor more than ten thousand dollars.

From this it clearly appears that that State utterly refused to comply with her Constitutional obligations. She did more. She made it penal for any person to attempt to carry out this provision within her limits.

The acts of Massachusetts were not dissimilar, as, I suppose, Judge Bynum will admit. But it is useless to go through with them. I have a document here which renders all that unnecessary. It is the speech of Judge Chase before the Peace Congress, so-called, in February, 1861.

So anxious were the people of the South to continue the Union under the Constitution, so desirous were they to stand by and perpetuate the principles of the Constitution, that even after South Carolina seceded, Virginia, the mother of States and Statesmen, she that took the lead in the separation from Great Britain and in the formation of our Federal Republic, as we have seen, made a great and strong effort still to save the Union by calling an informal Congress of the States to deliberate and see if no scheme could be devised to save the country from impending dangers and feuds. A number of States sent deputies to this Congress. Amongst these deputies was Judge Chase, then a distinguished leader of the Anti-Slavery Party, so-called, subsequently Mr. Lincoln's Secretary of Treasury, and now Chief Justice of the United States. In that Peace Congress, so assembled, Judge Chase, on the 6th of February, 1861, in all the candor of his nature, declared most emphatically to the Southern members that the Northern States never would fulfil that part of their Constitutional obligations. His whole speech is exceedingly interesting as one of the "footprints" of the momentous events of that day. Let me call your special attention to these parts:

> The result of the national canvass which recently terminated in the election of Mr. Lincoln, has been spoken of by some as the effect of a sudden impulse, or of some irregular excitement of the popular mind; and it has been somewhat confidently asserted that, upon reflection and consideration, the hastily formed opinions which brought about that election will be changed. It has been said,

also, that subordinate questions of local and temporary character have augmented the Republican vote, and secured a majority which could not have been obtained upon the national questions involved in the respective platforms of the parties which divide the country.

I cannot take this view of the result of the presidential election. I believe, and the belief amounts to absolute conviction, that the election must be regarded as a triumph of principles cherished in the hearts of the people of the Free States. These principles, it is true, were originally asserted by a small party only. But, after years of discussion, they have, by their own value, their own intrinsic soundness, obtained the deliberate and unalterable sanction of the people's judgment.

Chief among these principles is the Restriction of Slavery within State limits; *not* war upon Slavery within these limits, but fixed opposition to its extension beyond them. Mr. Lincoln was the candidate of the people opposed to the extension of Slavery. We have elected him. After many years of earnest advocacy and of severe trial, we have achieved the triumph of that principle. By a fair and unquestionable majority, we have secured that triumph. Do you think we, who represent this majority, will throw it away? Do you think the people would sustain us if we undertook to throw it away? I must speak to you plainly, gentlemen of the South. It is not in my heart to deceive you. I therefore tell you explicitly, that if we of the North and West consent to throw away all that has been gained in the recent triumph of our principles, the people would not sustain us, and so the consent would avail you nothing. And I must tell you further, that under no inducements, whatever, will we consent to surrender a principle which we believe to be so sound and so important as that of restricting Slavery within State limits.

This part of the speech was in reference to the claim of power on the part of the Federal Government to prevent the people of the Southern States from going into the common Territories with their slaves, and which power the Supreme Court had decided the General Government had no right to exercise. He here deliberately asserted that the Party which elected Mr. Lincoln would not regard this decision of the Supreme Court. But then he goes on to say:

Aside from the Territorial question—the question of Slavery outside the Slave States—I know of but one serious difficulty. I refer to the question concerning fugitives from service. The clause in the Constitution concerning this class of persons is regarded by almost all men, North and South, as a stipulation for the surrender to their masters of slaves escaping into Free States. The people of the Free States, however, who believe that Slave-holding is wrong, cannot and will not aid in the reclamation, and the stipulation becomes, therefore, a dead letter. You complain of bad faith, and the complaint is retorted by denunciations of the cruelty which would drag back to bondage the poor slave who has escaped from it. You, thinking Slavery right, claim the fulfilment of the stipulation; we, thinking Slavery wrong, cannot fulfil the stipulation without consciousness of participation in wrong. Here is a real difficulty, but it seems to me not insuperable. It will not do for us to say to you, in justification of non-performance, "the stipulation is immoral, and therefore we cannot execute it"; for you deny the immorality, and we cannot assume to judge for you. On the other hand, you ought not to exact from us the literal performance of the stipulation when you know that we cannot perform it without conscious culpability. A true solution of the difficulty seems to be attainable by regarding it as a simple case where a contract, from changed circumstances, cannot be fulfilled exactly as made. A court of equity in such a case decrees execution as near as may be. It requires the party who cannot perform to make compensation for non-performance. Why cannot the same principle be applied to the rendition of fugitives from service? We cannot surrender—but we can compensate. Why not then avoid all difficulties on all sides and show respectively good faith and good-will by providing and accepting compensation where masters reclaim escaping servants and prove their right of reclamation under the Constitution? Instead of a judgment for rendition, let there be a judgment for compensation, determined by the true value of the services, and let the same judgment assure freedom to the fugitive. The cost to the National Treasury would be as nothing in comparison with the evils of discord and strife. All parties would be gainers.

Whatever may be thought of this as a proposed *compromise* to induce the Parties to remain in the Union, no one can doubt its *unequivocal declaration* that the Non-Slave-holding States *would not* comply with their acknowledged *obligations* under the Constitution. It was a confession of one high in authority that that part of the Constitution was a *dead letter,* and, of course, if the Southern States would not agree to his offer, they were absolved from all further obligation to the Compact. This is conclusive upon well settled principles of public law.

This declaration that the Northern States would not comply with their Constitutional obligations, bear in mind, was made by the Chancellor of the Exchequer, under Mr. Lincoln. He spoke for the President and his Party. He spoke for that Party which, after the Southern States had seceded, in the House, passed this Resolution:

Resolved, That as our country, and the very existence of the best government ever instituted by man, are imperilled by the most causeless and wicked rebellion that the world has seen, and believing, as we do, that the only hope of saving this country and preserving this Government is by the power of the sword, we are for the most *vigorous prosecution of the war until the Constitution and laws shall be enforced and obeyed in all parts of the United States;* and to that end we oppose any armistice, or intervention, or mediation, or proposition for peace from any quarter, so long as there shall be found a Rebel in arms against the Government; and we ignore all party names, lines, and issues, and recognize but two parties in this war—patriots and traitors.

This Resolution passed the House, December 17, 1863, by a vote of ninety-four to sixty-five. The ninety-four votes all belonged to that party for which Judge Chase spoke.

Was there ever an instance in the history of the world of such inconsistency, or—no! I will withhold the word I was about to utter. But let me ask, if the Federal arms had been directed against those who *resisted* the *enforcement* of the *Constitution and the laws of the United States,* with the real purpose of preserving "the best Government ever instituted by man," was there a *single one* of those who voted for this Resolution, who would not justly have been the first subjects of slaughter? These are the men who still talk of *"loyal* States!" Who still have so much to say of *"loyal* men!" Was ever noble word, when properly applied, so prostituted as this is in its present use by this class of boasting patriots?

The Southern States were ever *loyal* and *true* to the Constitution. This I maintain as a great truth for history. The only *true loyalty* in this country is *fidelity* to the principles of the Constitution! The openly *"disloyal,"* or those *avowedly untrue* to the Constitution, were those who instigated, inaugurated, and waged this most unrighteous war against their Confederate neighbors! If I express myself with too much fervor on this point, you will please excuse me. I do, however, but express the thorough convictions of my judgment.

MAJOR HEISTER. Judge Bynum, how is this? Is it true, as stated, that any of the Northern States did thus openly and avowedly refuse to comply with their Constitutional engagements, while the Southern States were always true to theirs? Is this correct? I often heard of "Personal Liberty Bills" at the North, but I thought they were intended only to secure the liberty of our own free blacks against kidnappers. I never supposed it was true, that the Northern States deliberately refused to obey or enforce that clause of the Constitution in relation to actual fugitives from service. I am utterly astonished at what Mr. Stephens has read from the law of Vermont, and from Judge Chase's speech in the Peace Congress. You are better posted than I am on these matters, but I feel assured that the people at the North, generally, did not look upon the questions as he presents them; and it must be, that there is some answer to what he says and maintains with so much apparent confidence. Let us know how these things really are.

7

The Confederate States of America

Jefferson Davis

Mississippi was the second State to withdraw from the Union, her ordinance of secession being adopted on the 9th of January, 1861. She was quickly followed by Florida on the 10th, Alabama on the 11th, and, in the course of the same month, by Georgia on the 18th, and Louisiana on the 26th. The Conventions of these States (together with that of South Carolina) agreed in designating Montgomery, Alabama, as the place, and the 4th of February as the day, for the assembling of a congress of the seceding States, to which each State Convention, acting as the direct representative of the sovereignty of the people thereof, appointed delegates.

Telegraphic intelligence of the secession of Mississippi had reached Washington some considerable time before the fact was officially communicated to me. This official knowledge I considered it proper to await before taking formal leave of the Senate. My associates from Alabama and Florida concurred in this view. Accordingly, having received notification of the secession of these three States about the same time, on the 21st of January, Messrs. Yulee and Mallory, of Florida, Fitzpatrick and Clay, of Alabama, and myself, announced the withdrawal of the States from which we were respectively accredited, and took leave of the Senate at the same time.

In the action which she then took, Mississippi certainly had no purpose to levy war against the United States, or any of them. As her Senator, I endeavored plainly to state her position in the annexed remarks addressed to the Senate in taking leave of the body:

> I rise, Mr. President, for the purpose of announcing to the Senate that I have satisfactory evidence that the State of Mississippi, by a solemn ordinance of her people, in convention assembled, has declared her separation from the United States. Under these circumstances, of course, my functions are terminated here. It has seemed to me proper, however, that I should appear in the Senate to announce that fact to my associates, and I will say but very little more. The occasion does not invite me to go into argument; and my physical

JEFFERSON DAVIS, *The Rise and Fall of the Confederate Government*, 2 vols. (New York, 1881), Vol. 1, Pt. 3, Chs. 3-10.

condition would not permit me to do so, if it were otherwise; and yet it seems to become me to say something on the part of the State I here represent on an occasion so solemn as this.

It is known to Senators who have served with me here that I have for many years advocated, as an essential attribute of State sovereignty, the right of a State to secede from the Union. Therefore, if I had not believed there was justifiable cause, if I had thought that Mississippi was acting without sufficient provocation, or without an existing necessity, I should still, under my theory of the Government, because of my allegiance to the State of which I am a citizen, have been bound by her action. I, however, may be permitted to say that I do think she has justifiable cause, and I approve of her act. I conferred with her people before that act was taken, counseled them then that, if the state of things which they apprehended should exist when their Convention met, they should take the action which they have now adopted.

I hope none who hear me will confound this expression of mine with the advocacy of the right of a State to remain in the Union, and to disregard its constitutional obligations by the nullification of the law. Such is not my theory. Nullification and secession, so often confounded, are, indeed, antagonistic principles. Nullification is a remedy which it is sought to apply within the Union, and against the agent of the States. It is only to be justified when the agent has violated his constitutional obligations, and a State, assuming to judge for itself, denies the right of the agent thus to act, and appeals to the other States of the Union for a decision; but, when the States themselves and when the people of the States have so acted as to convince us that they will not regard our constitutional rights, then, and then for the first time, arises the doctrine of secession in its practical application.

A great man who now reposes with his fathers, and who has often been arraigned for a want of fealty to the Union, advocated the doctrine of nullification because it preserved the Union. It was because of his deep-seated attachment to the Union—his determination to find some remedy for existing ills short of a severance of the ties which bound South Carolina to the other States—that Mr. Calhoun advocated the doctrine of nullification, which he proclaimed to be peaceful, to be within the limits of State power, not to disturb the Union, but only to be a means of bringing the agent before the tribunal of the States for their judgment.

Secession belongs to a different class of remedies. It is to be justified upon the basis that the States are sovereign. There was a time when none denied it. I hope the time may come again when a better comprehension of the theory of our Government, and the inalienable rights of the people of the States, will prevent anyone from denying that each State is a sovereign, and thus may reclaim the grants which it has made to any agent whomsoever. . . .

It has been a conviction of pressing necessity—it has been a belief that we are to be deprived in the Union of the rights which our fathers bequeathed to us—which has brought Mississippi to her present decision. She has heard proclaimed the theory that all men are created free and equal, and this made the basis of an attack upon her social institutions; and the sacred Declaration of Independence has been invoked to maintain the position of the equality of the races. That Declaration of Independence is to be construed by the circumstances and purposes for which it was made. The communities were declaring their independence; the people of those communities were asserting that no man was born—to use the language of Mr. Jefferson—booted and spurred, to ride over the rest of mankind; that men were created equal—meaning the men of the political community; that there was no divine right to rule; that no man inherited the right to govern; that there were no classes by which power and place descended to families; but that all stations were equally within the grasp of each member of the body politic. These were the great principles they announced; these were the purposes for which they made their declaration; these were the ends to which their enunciation was directed. They have no reference to the slave. . . .

Then, Senators, we recur to the principles upon which our Government was founded; and when you deny them, and when you deny to us the right to withdraw from a Government which, thus perverted, threatens to be destructive of our rights, we but tread in the path of our fathers when we proclaim our independence and take the hazard. This is done, not in hostility to others, not to injure any section of the country, not even for our own pecuniary benefit, but from the high and solemn motive of defending and protecting the rights we inherited, and which it is our duty to transmit unshorne to our children. . . .

On my arrival at Jackson, the capital of Mississippi, I found that the Convention of the State had made provision for a State army, and had appointed me to the command, with the rank of major-general. Four brigadier-generals, appointed in like manner by the Convention, were awaiting my arrival for assignment to duty. After the preparation of the necessary rules and regulations, the division of the State into districts, the apportionment among them of the troops to be raised, and the appointment of officers of the general staff, as authorized by the ordinance of the Convention, such measures as were practicable were taken to obtain the necessary arms. The State had few serviceable weapons, and no establishment for their manufacture or repair. This fact (which is true of other Southern States as of Mississippi) is a clear proof of the absence of any desire or expectation of war. If the purpose of the Northern States to make war upon us because of secession had been foreseen, preparation to meet the consequences would have been contemporaneous with the adoption of a resort to that remedy—a remedy the possibility of which had for many years been contemplated. Had the Southern States possessed arsenals, and collected in them the requisite supplies of arms and munitions, such preparation would not only have placed them more nearly on an equality with the North in the beginning of the war, but might, perhaps, have been the best conservator of peace.

Let us, the survivors, however, not fail to do credit to the generous credulity which could not understand how, in violation of the compact of Union, a war could be waged against the States, or why they should be invaded because their people had deemed it necessary to withdraw from an association which had failed to fulfil the ends for which they had entered into it, and which, having been broken to their injury by the other parties, had ceased to be binding upon them. It is a satisfaction to know that the calamities which have befallen the Southern States were the result of their credulous reliance on the power of the Constitution, that, if it failed to protect their rights, it would at least suffice to prevent an attempt at coercion, if, in the last resort, they peacefully withdrew from the Union.

When, in after times, the passions of the day shall have subsided, and all the evidence shall have been collected and compared, the philosophical inquirer, who asks why the majority of the stronger section invaded the peaceful homes of their late associates, will be answered by History: "The lust of empire impelled them to wage against their weaker neighbors a war of subjugation."

The congress of delegates from the seceding States convened at Montgomery, Alabama, according to appointment, on the 4th of February, 1861. Their first work was to prepare a provisional Constitution for the new Confederacy, to be formed of the States which had withdrawn from the Union, for which the style "Confederate States of America" was adopted. The powers conferred upon them were adequate for the performance of this duty, the immediate necessity for which was obvious and urgent. This Constitution was adopted on the 8th of February, to continue in force for one year, unless superseded at an earlier date by a permanent organization. . . .

On the next day (9th of February) an election was held for the chief executive offices, resulting, as I afterward learned, in my election to the Presidency, with the Hon. Alexander H. Stephens of Georgia as Vice-President. Mr. Stephens was a delegate from Georgia to the Congress.

While these events were occurring, having completed the most urgent of my duties at the capital of Mississippi, I had gone to my home, Brierfield in Warren County, and had begun, in the homely but expressive language of Mr. Clay, "to repair my fences." While thus engaged, notice was received of my election to the Presidency of the Confederate States, with an urgent request to proceed immediately to Montgomery for inauguration.

As this had been suggested as a probable event, and what appeared to me adequate precautions had been taken to prevent it, I was surprised, and, still more, disappointed. For reasons which it is not now necessary to state, I had not believed myself as well suited to the office as some others. I thought myself better adapted to command in the field; and Mississippi had given me the position which I preferred to any other—the highest rank in her army. It was, therefore, that I afterward said, in an address delivered in the Capitol, before the Legislature of the State, with reference to my election to the Presidency of the Confederacy, that the duty to which I was thus called was temporary, and that I expected soon to be with the Army of Mississippi again. . . .

On my way to Montgomery, brief addresses were made at various places, at which there were temporary stoppages of the trains, in response to calls from the crowds assembled at such points. Some of these addresses were grossly misrepresented in sensational reports made by irresponsible persons, which were published in Northern newspapers, and were not considered worthy of correction under the pressure of the momentous duties then devolving upon me. These false reports, which represented me as invoking war and threatening devastation of the North, have since been adopted by partisan writers as authentic history. It is a sufficient answer to these accusations to refer to my farewell address to the Senate, already given, as reported for the press at the time, and, in connection therewith, to my inaugural address at Montgomery, on assuming the office of President of the Confederate States, on the 18th of February. These two addresses, delivered at an interval of a month, during which no material change of circumstances had occurred, being one before and the other after the date of the sensational reports referred to, are sufficient to stamp them as utterly untrue. The inaugural was deliberately prepared, and uttered as written, and, in connection with the farewell speech to the Senate, presents a clear and authentic statement of the principles and purposes which actuated me on assuming the duties of the high office to which I had been called.

INAUGURAL ADDRESS

Gentlemen of the Congress of the Confederate States of America, Friends, and Fellow-Citizens:

Called to the difficult and responsible station of Chief Magistrate of the Provisional Government which you have instituted, I approach the discharge of the duties assigned to me with humble distrust of my abilities, but with a sustaining confidence in the wisdom of those who are to guide and aid me in the administration of public affairs, and an abiding faith in the virtue and patriotism of the people. Looking forward to the speedy establishment of a permanent government to take the place of this, which by its greater moral and physical power will be better able to combat with many difficulties that arise from the conflicting interests of separate nations, I enter upon the duties of the office to which I have been chosen with the hope that the beginning of our career, as a Confederacy, may not be obstructed by hostile opposition to our enjoyment of the separate existence and independence we have asserted, and which, with the blessing of Providence, we intend to maintain.

Our present political position has been achieved in a manner unprecedented in the history of nations. It illustrates the American idea that governments rest on the consent of the governed, and that it is the right of the people to alter or abolish them at will whenever they become destructive of the ends for which they were established. The declared purpose of the compact of the

Union from which we have withdrawn was to "establish justice, insure domestic tranquility, provide for the common defense, promote the general welfare, and secure the blessings of liberty to ourselves and our posterity"; and when, in the judgment of the sovereign States composing this Confederacy, it has been perverted from the purposes for which it was ordained, and ceased to answer the ends for which it was established, a peaceful appeal to the ballot-box declared that, so far as they are concerned, the Government created by that compact should cease to exist. In this they merely asserted the right which the Declaration of Independence of July 4, 1776, defined to be "inalienable." Of the time and occasion of its exercise they as sovereigns were the final judges, each for itself. The impartial and enlightened verdict of mankind will vindicate the rectitude of our conduct; and He who knows the hearts of men will judge of the sincerity with which we have labored to preserve the Government of our fathers in its spirit. . . .

An agricultural people, whose chief interest is the export of commodities required in every manufacturing country, our true policy is peace, and the freest trade which our necessities will permit. It is alike our interest and that of all those to whom we would sell, and from whom we would buy, that there should be the fewest practicable restrictions upon the interchange of these commodities. There can, however, be but little rivalry between ours and any manufacturing or navigating community, such as the Northeastern States of the American Union. It must follow, therefore, that mutual interest will invite to good-will and kind offices on both parts. If, however, passion or lust of dominion should cloud the judgment or inflame the ambition of those States, we must prepare to meet the emergency and maintain, by the final arbitrament of the sword, the position which we have assumed among the nations of the earth.

We have entered upon the career of independence, and it must be inflexibly pursued. Through many years of controversy with our late associates of the Northern States, we have vainly endeavored to secure tranquillity and obtain respect for the rights to which we were entitled. As a necessity, not a choice, we have resorted to the remedy of separation, and henceforth our energies must be directed to the conduct of our own affairs, and the perpetuity of the Confederacy which we have formed. If a just perception of mutual interest shall permit us peaceably to pursue our separate political career, my most earnest desire will have been fulfilled. But if this be denied to us, and the integrity of our territory and jurisdiction be assailed, it will but remain for us with firm resolve to appeal to arms and invoke the blessing of Providence on a just cause. . . .

With a Constitution differing only from that of our fathers in so far as it is explanatory of their well-known intent, freed from sectional conflicts which have interfered with the pursuit of the general welfare, it is not unreasonable to expect that States from which we have recently parted may seek to unite their fortunes to ours under the Government which we have instituted. For this your Constitution makes adequate provision; but beyond this, if I mistake not the judgment and will of the people, a reunion with the States from which we have separated is neither practicable nor desirable. To increase the power, develop the resources, and promote the happiness of the Confederacy, it is requisite that there should be so much of homogeneity that the welfare of every portion shall be the aim of the whole. When this does not exist, antagonisms are engendered which must and should result in separation.

Actuated solely by the desire to preserve our own rights, and promote our own welfare, the separation by the Confederate States has been marked by no aggression upon others, and followed by no domestic convulsion. Our industrial pursuits have received no check, the cultivation of our fields has progressed as heretofore, and, even should we be involved in war, there would be no considerable diminution in the production of the staples which have constituted our exports, and in which the commercial world has an interest scarcely less than our own. This common interest of the producer and consumer can only be interrupted by exterior force which would obstruct the transmission of our staples to foreign markets—a course of conduct which would be as unjust, as it would be detrimental, to manufacturing and commercial interests abroad.

Should reason guide the action of the Government from which we have separated, a policy so detrimental to the civilized world, the Northern States included, could not be dictated by even the strongest desire to inflict injury upon us; but, if the contrary should prove true, a terrible responsibility will rest upon it, and the suffering of millions will bear testimony to the folly and wickedness of our aggressors. In the meantime there will remain to us, besides the ordinary means before suggested, the well-known resources for retaliation upon the commerce of an enemy.

We have changed the constituent parts, but not the system of government. The Constitution framed by our fathers is that of these Confederate States. In their exposition of it, and in the judicial construction it has received, we have a light which reveals its true meaning. . . .

After being inaugurated, I proceeded to the formation of my Cabinet, that is, the heads of the executive departments authorized by the laws of the Provisional Congress. The unanimity existing among our people made this a much easier and more agreeable task than where the rivalries in the party of an executive have to be consulted and accommodated, often at the expense of the highest capacity and fitness. Unencumbered by any other consideration than the public welfare, having no friends to reward or enemies to punish, it resulted that not one of those who formed my first Cabinet had borne to me the relation of close personal friendship, or had political claims upon me; indeed, with two of them I had no previous acquaintance.

It was my wish that the Hon. Robert W. Barnwell of South Carolina should be Secretary of State. I had known him intimately during a trying period of our joint service in the United States Senate, and he had won alike my esteem and regard. Before making known to him my wish in this connection, the delegation of South Carolina, of which he was a member, had resolved to recommend one of their number to be Secretary of the

Treasury, and Mr. Barnwell, with characteristic delicacy, declined to accept my offer to him.

I had intended to offer the Treasury Department to Mr. Toombs of Georgia, whose knowledge on subjects of finance had particularly attracted my notice when we served together in the United States Senate. Mr. Barnwell having declined the State Department, and a colleague of his said to be peculiarly qualified for the Treasury Department having been recommended for it, Mr. Toombs was offered the State Department, for which others believed him to be well qualified.

Mr. Mallory of Florida had been chairman of the Committee on Naval Affairs in the United States Senate, was extensively acquainted with the officers of the navy, and for a landsman had much knowledge of nautical affairs; therefore he was selected for Secretary of the Navy.

Mr. Benjamin of Louisiana had a very high reputation as a lawyer, and my acquaintance with him in the Senate had impressed me with the lucidity of his intellect, his systematic habits and capacity for labor. He was therefore invited to the post of Attorney-General.

Mr. Reagan of Texas I had known for a sturdy, honest Representative in the United States Congress, and his acquaintance with the territory included in the Confederate States was both extensive and accurate. These, together with his industry and ability to labor, indicated him as peculiarly fit for the office of Postmaster-General.

Mr. Memminger of South Carolina had a high reputation for knowledge of finance. He bore an unimpeachable character for integrity and close attention to duties, and, on the recommendation of the delegation from South Carolina, he was appointed Secretary of the Treasury, and proved himself entirely worthy of the trust.

Mr. Walker of Alabama was a distinguished member of the bar of north Alabama, and was eminent among the politicians of that section. He was earnestly recommended by gentlemen intimately and favorably known to me, and was therefore selected for the War Department. His was the only name presented from Alabama. . . .

The legislation of the Confederate Congress furnishes the best evidence of the temper and spirit which prevailed in the organization of the Confederate Government. The very first enactment made on February 9, 1861—the day after the adoption of the Provisional Constitution—was this:

> That all laws of the United States of America in force and in use in the Confederate States of America on the first day of November last, and not inconsistent with the Constitution of the Confederate States, be and the same are hereby continued in force until altered or repealed by the Congress.

The next act, adopted on February 14, was one continuing in office until April 1 next ensuing all officers connected with the collection of customs and the assistant treasurers entrusted with the keeping of the moneys arising therefrom, who were engaged in the performance of such duties within any of the Confederate States, with the same powers and functions which they had been exercising under the Government of the United States.

The Provisional Constitution itself, in the second section of its sixth article, had ordained as follows:

> The Government hereby instituted shall take immediate steps for the settlement of all matters between the States forming it and their other late confederates of the United States, in relation to the public property and public debt at the time of their withdrawal from them; these States hereby declaring it to be their wish and earnest desire to adjust everything pertaining to the common property, common liabilities, and common obligations of that Union, upon the principles of right, justices, equity, and good faith.

In accordance with this requirement of the Constitution, the Congress, on February 15—before my arrival at Montgomery—passed a resolution declaring "that it is the sense of this Congress that a commission of three persons be appointed by the President-elect, as early as may be convenient after his inauguration, and sent to the Government of the United States of America, for the purpose of negotiating friendly relations between the Government and the Confederate States of America, and for the settlement of all questions of disagreement between the two Governments, upon principles of right, justice, equity, and good faith.". . .

These acts and all other indications manifest the well-known wish of the people of the Confederacy to preserve the peace and encourage the most unrestricted commerce with all nations, surely not least with their late associates, the Northern States. Thus far, the hope that peace might be maintained was predominant; perhaps, the wish was father to the thought that there would be no war between the States lately united. Indeed, all the laws enacted during the first session of the Provisional Congress show how consistent were the purposes and actions of its members with their original avowal of a desire peacefully to separate from those with whom they could not live in tranquillity, albeit the Government had been established to promote the common welfare. Under this state of feeling the Government of the Confederacy was instituted. . . .

The conservative temper of the people of the Confederate States was conspicuously exhibited in the most important product of the early labors of their representatives in Congress assembled. The Provisional Constitution, although prepared only for temporary use, and necessarily in some haste, was so well adapted for the purposes which it was intended to serve, that many thought it would have been wise to continue it in force indefinitely, or at least until the independency of the Confederacy should be assured. The Congress, however, deeming it best that the system of Government should emanate from the people, accordingly, on the 11th of March, prepared the permanent Constitution, which was submitted to and ratified by the people of the respective States.

PART II

THE ARMIES

For all the widespread belief in conspiracy, and for all the horoscopes of disaster which politicians had cast, the beginning of armed conflict came as a shock. Men watched in disbelief as rival governments organized, and followed the moves which led to the firing on Fort Sumter, to the secession of the States of the upper South, and then to the gathering of untrained armies. Shortly after the war, Abraham Lincoln's friend and fellow-lawyer, Isaac N. Arnold, recalled the first days of the new and troubled Administration. Lincoln, thought Arnold, acted always on the defense, "while the rebels, from the first, assumed a bold, defiant tone." It was they who sought a collision, but when it came the North was ready to spring to arms. Arnold caught something of the feeling in the North, and against it he portrayed the confusion, even treason, in the Border States.

Not all the soldiers who eventually entered the armies were caught up in the first wave of enthusiasm. Charles Johnson, who later became a physician, lived in a quiet neighborhood in otherwise excited Illinois, and he waited months before he answered the call to arms. When he did, he noted carefully the prosaic details of assembling companies, drilling, and learning the routine of the camps. But intermittent with the prose of soldiering there was the poetry of rallies, of beautiful girls preparing and presenting flags to departing units, and of other women who greeted with cake and coffee the passing soldiers in railroad stations.

In the South, similar scenes took place in the early days—but a few Southerners, like John West, waited until the dark hour of need had descended upon the Confederacy before they went in search of a fight. Before John West got to the army, the Confederacy had full need of his fighting qualities. Richmond had often been threatened, and Gettysburg lay but short weeks ahead. In the Mississippi Valley, the phenomenal Ulysses S. Grant was approaching Vicksburg. As all the other soldiers had been doing

149

from the beginning, Grant was learning from experience. His application of the lessons he had learned from Donelson and Shiloh brought Vicksburg's fall.

Military experience and its lessons were not limited to service with the armed units. There were those—their number ran into thousands—who risked death, and even torture, to spy out the secrets of the enemy. Others, on both sides, found spiritual guidance and churchly consolations in the midst of war; while still others, like Mother Bickerdyke, rose from humble walks to lasting national prominence by caring for the sick and the wounded and the friendless.

With it all, the soldiers learned much. They learned military science— and by the end of the war they could pass military judgments on the conduct of campaigns and the competence of commanders. They became, as well, shrewd observers of men—both of those with whom they fought and of the populace, white and colored, whom they met in the countryside. George Pepper went with Sherman, and from Atlanta to the sea and up through the Carolinas he marked the scenery with a sharp eye, passed critical opinions on Georgia's inhabitants, and kept an ear tuned to the nuances of both dialect and social stratification. He recounted the devastation wrought by the armies, and assessed its possible consequences. In his judgment he was part sociologist, part avenging angel.

When the end came, the Confederates wandered home to take account of the devastation. Private Dyer made his way through Union camps and an occupying army. On the high seas, the cruiser Shenandoah *belatedly gave itself up in England. The old ship ended with an unseemly quarrel, but the Kentucky soldier rejoiced that the end had come, and that a new and strengthened Union had resulted from the war.*

Altogether the soldiers' experience, whether of North or South, gave to all those who fought a common background and a common basis for approaching many of the social and economic problems of post-war America.

8

The Opening Scenes

Isaac N. Arnold

On the 12th of March the Confederate authorities commissioned John Forsyth, M. J. Crawford and A. B. Roman, Commissioner to the United States, with a view, as they said, to a speedy adjustment of all questions growing out of the political separation.

Mr. Seward, Secretary of State, declined to receive them; denied that the Confederate States had, in law, or in fact, *withdrawn from the Union;* denied that they could do so, except through a National Convention assembled under the provisions of the Constitution. On the 9th of April the Commissioners withdrew from Washington, after addressing a letter to the Secretary of State, saying that they, on behalf of the rebel Government, *accepted* the gage of battle, etc. And yet, after the receipt of this letter, such was the unparalleled forbearance of the Government, that these Commissioners were not arrested, but permitted quietly to withdraw, with the open avowal of going home to wage war!

On the 18th of March, General Braxton Bragg, commanding insurgent forces in Florida, issued an order, forbidding the citizens of the Confederate States from furnshing supplies to the Navy of the United States.

At this period, in March, even Mr. Douglas had not fully made up his mind in favor of coercing the seceding States into submission. Prominent Democrats in the Free States openly advocated the joining of Northern States to the Confederacy. Such was the undecided condition of public sentiment in the Free States in March; and as yet the Government of Mr. Lincoln had taken no bold, decided action, clearly indicating his policy. Meanwhile the Confederate authorities had seized, as has been stated, with few exceptions, all the arsenals, forts, custom-houses, post-offices, ships, ordnance and material of war, belonging to the United States, and within the seceding States; and this, notwithstanding that General Dix, Secretary of the Treasury, had issued an order, directing that "If any man attempts to haul down the American flag, shoot him on the spot."

ISAAC N. ARNOLD, *History of Abraham Lincoln and the Overthrow of Slavery* (Chicago, 1866), Ch. 9.

No position of greater difficulty can be conceived than that of President Lincoln in the spring of 1861. Congress had adjourned, without making any provision for the approaching crisis. The office of Secretary of War, for eight years previous to Mr. Lincoln's Administration, had been conducted by Jefferson Davis and John B. Floyd, by whom a collision with the Federal Government had been anticipated. As we have already seen, they had strengthened the South by robbing the Northern national armories, and scattered beyond immediate recall our little army and navy. Besides this, they, and especially Davis, had driven out of the service of the army as far as possible, every man who was not a States'-Rights, pro-slavery man.

The North was politically divided; a powerful political party, from long association, was in sympathy with the seceding States. This party had just come out of a violent contest against the party which had elected Lincoln. The Border Slave States were nearly equally divided in numbers, and while the quiet, better educated and more conservative were for the Union, the young, reckless, and hot-headed were for secession.

While South Carolina and some of the other Cotton States were substantially a unit for secession, in other Slave States there was a strong majority opposed to it. To arouse sectional feeling and prejudice and secure co-operation and unanimity, it was deemed necessary to precipitate measures and bring on a conflict of arms. It was generally said that the first blood shed would bring all Slave States to the aid of the belligerent State. As before stated, there was a strong party in the North opposed to coercion. Had the President assumed the initiative, and commenced the war, while it would have united the Slave States against him, it is not at all clear but it would have alienated a large portion of the Democrats of the North. Mr. Lincoln fully appreciated these difficulties, and these facts explain much that he did, and omitted to do, for which many of his friends censured him in the earlier stages of the rebellion. He sought to hold Virginia, Maryland, Kentucky, Missouri and Tennessee. The rebel leaders made the most strenuous efforts to induce the above-named States to join the Slave Confederacy, but the discreet and judicious forbearance of the President, to some extent foiled their efforts, and he succeeded in holding Maryland, Kentucky and Missouri from joining the rebels.

As has been stated, the people of the Border States were divided in sentiment, and it was very doubtful, for a time, which way they would go. The House of Representatives of Kentucky, on the 22d of January, resolved by a vote of 87 to 6, to resist the invasion of the South at all hazards. The Legislature adopted a resolution directing Governor Magoffin, of that State, by proclamation, to order Confederate troops off Kentucky soil. Magoffin vetoed this, but it was passed over his veto.

In the beginning of Mr. Lincoln's Administration he acted on the defensive, while the rebels, from the first, assumed a bold, defiant tone. The Confederate Government immediately after it was established, raised troops, borrowed eight millions of money, and offered a letter of marque to all who might choose to prey upon the rich commerce of the United States. The rebel Secretary of War, Walker, in a grandiloquent speech, prophesied that, before the 1st of May, the Confederate flag should float over the dome of the old Capitol, and it might, eventually, float over Faneuil Hall itself!

It was determined to bring on a collision, by an attack on Fort Sumter. This was designed more especially and directly to carry the ordinance of secession through the convention of Virginia. To fire the Southern inflammable heart and raise a whirlwind of fury which would sweep everything before it was the reason Davis and his co-conspirators opened the war.

On the 11th of April, General Beauregard demanded of Major Anderson the surrender of Fort Sumter. The Major refused. On the night of the same day, Beauregard wrote to Anderson, under instructions from the authorities at Montgomery, that if he "would state the time at which he would evacuate Fort Sumter, and agree, that in the meantime he would not use his guns against the Confederates, unless theirs should be employed against Sumter, the Confederates would abstain from opening fire on him."

At half-past two, on the morning of the 12th, Anderson replied, he would evacuate the fort by noon of the 15th. At half-past three he was notified, in reply, that the rebels would open their batteries, in an *hour* from that time. Their batteries were opened, accordingly, and after a bombardment of thirty-three hours, which the little garrison endured and replied to with heroic courage (their provisions and ammunition having been exhausted), Anderson agreed to evacuate the Fort. He retired from it on Sunday morning.

It is clear the rebels sought a collision, in pursuance of their avowed policy of rousing and inciting the South. The attack on Sumter immediately precipitated the political elements, and the people ranged themselves for or against the Union.

The capital was in a most critical condition. Full of Secessionists, the roads leading to the North obstructed, and the city in a condition of siege. The mails, in every direction, were stopped, and the telegraph wires cut by the insurgents. The National forces, which were approaching Washington, were obstructed; the War and Navy departments were filled with spies, and probably, the White House itself. In this condition of things, it was not deemed safe to issue orders through the ordinary channels because everything sent in that way reached the enemy. Special and private messengers were sent North, who pursued a circuitous route to the Northern cities and governors of loyal States, calling on them to hasten troops to the rescue of the capital. A company of personal friends were organized, who guarded the White House, the Long Bridge crossing the Potomac, and the Arsenals, and probably saved the life of the President, and the Government from overthrow.

On the 15th of April, President Lincoln issued his proclamation, calling for 75,000 men.

This proclamation was prepared on Sunday. Before its issue, and while the President was considering the subject, he was visited by Senator Douglas, who expressed his full approval of this call, only regretting that it was not for 200,000 men instead of the number called for.

The following dispatch was written by Senator Douglas, and given to the agent of the Associated Press, and sent to every portion of the North:

> April 18, 1861, Senator Douglas called on the President, and had an interesting conversation, on the present condition of the country. The substance of it was, on the part of Mr. Douglas, that while he was unalterably opposed to the Administration in all its political issues, he was prepared to fully sustain the President, in the exercise of all his Constitutional functions, to preserve the Union, maintain the Government, and defend the Federal capital. A firm policy and prompt action was necessary. The capital was in danger, and must be defended at all hazards, and at any expense of men and money. He spoke of the present and future, without any reference to the past.

Thus Douglas lent the influence of his name, with his party and the country, in aid of this decisive step, towards suppressing the rebellion by force. He soon after returned to Illinois, and at Springfield and Chicago, made speeches sustaining the policy of the President, and declaring that now there could be but two parties, "patriots and traitors."

The speech of Douglas, at Chicago, was made in the immense building called the "Wigwam," built for and used by the National Convention which nominated Lincoln for the Presidency. Since the day of that nomination, no such crowd had gathered there as assembled to hear Douglas. He said we had gone to the very extreme of magnanimity. The return for all which had been done was *war*, armies marching on the capital—a movement to blot the United States from the map of the globe. "The election of Lincoln," said he, "is a mere pretext." The secession movement is the result of an enormous conspiracy formed by the leaders of the Southern Confederacy before the election of Lincoln. "There can be no neutrals in this war—only *patriots or traitors*."

There were those in the Border States who deprecated this call, and who expressed the belief that this act precipitated war, and that continued forbearance would have brought on a reaction at the South, which would have resulted in a restoration of the Union. They who indulged in such dreams little knew the spirit of the conspirators. Had this call been delayed, even a few hours, or had there been less promptness in responding to it, the President would have been assassinated, or he would have been a fugitive or a prisoner, and the rebel flag would have waved over the Capitol, and Jefferson Davis would have issued his Proclamations from the White House. Mr Lincoln pursued the policy of conciliation, in the vain hope of peace, to the very verge of National destruction.

The fall of Sumter and the President's call for troops were the signals for the rally to arms throughout the Loyal States. Twenty millions of people, forgetting party divisions, and all past differences, rose with one voice of patriotic enthusiasm, and laid their hearts and hands, their fortunes and their lives upon the altar of their country. The Proclamation of the President, calling for 75,000 men and convening an extra session of Congress to meet on the 4th of July, was followed, in every Free State, by the prompt action of the governors, calling for volunteers. In every city, town, village, and neighborhood, the people rushed to arms, and the strife was who should have the privilege of marching to the defense of the National capital. Forty-eight hours had not passed after the issue of the Proclamation at Washington before four regiments had reported to Governor Andrew, in Boston, ready for service. On the 17th, he commissioned B. F. Butler of Lowell, as their commander.

Governor Sprague of Rhode Island, calling the Legislature of that State together, on the 17th, tendered to the Government a thousand infantry and a battallion of artillery, and placing himself at the head of his troops, started for Washington.

The great State of New York, whose population was nearly four millions, through her Legislature, and the action of Governor Morgan, placed her immense resources in the hands of the National Executive. So did Pennsylvania, with its three millions of people, under the lead of Governor Curtin. And Pennsylvania has the honor of having furnished the troops, the first arrived for the defense of the capital, reaching there on the 18th just in time to prevent the seizure of the nearly defenseless city.

By the 20th of April, although the quota of Ohio under the President's call was only thirteen regiments, 71,000 men had offered their services through Governor Dennison, the Executive of that State. It was the same everywhere. Half a million of men, citizen volunteers, at this call, sprang to arms and begged permission to fight for their country. The enthusiasm pervaded all ranks and classes. Prayers for the Union and the integrity of the Nation were heard in every Church throughout the Free States. State Legislatures, municipalities, banks, corporations, and capitalists everywhere offered their money to the Government, and subscribed immense sums for the support of the volunteers and their families. Independent military organizations poured in their offers of service. Written pledges were widely circulated and signed, offering to the Government the lives and property of the signers, to maintain the Union. Great crowds marched through the principal cities, cheering the patriotic, singing National airs, and requiring all to show, from their residences and places of business, the stars and stripes, or "the red, white and blue." The people, through the press, by public meetings, and by resolutions, placed their property and lives at the disposal of the Government.

At this gloomy period, through the dark clouds of gathering war, up rose the mighty voice of the people to cheer the heart of the President. Onward it came, like the rush of many waters, shouting the words that became so familiar during the war—"We are coming, Father Abraham, six hundred thousand strong."

The Government was embarrassed by the number of men volunteering for its service. Hundreds of thousands more were offered than could be armed or received. Senators, members of Congress, and other prominent men, went to Washington to influence the Government to accept the service of the eager volunteers, everywhere imploring permission to serve.

The volunteer soldier was the popular idol. He was everywhere welcome. Fair hands wove the banners which he carried, and knit the socks and shirts which protected him from the cold; and everywhere they lavished upon him every luxury, and comfort, which could cheer and encourage him. Everyone scorned to take pay from the soldier. Colonel Stetson, proprietor of the "Astor House Hotel" in New York replied to General Butler's offer to pay—"The Astor House makes no charge for Massachusetts soldiers." And whether private or officer, the latch-string of the cabin and farm-house was never drawn in upon him who wore the National blue. Such was the universal enthusiasm of the people for their country's defenders.

The feeling of fierce indignation towards those seeking to destroy the Government was greatly increased by the attack of a mob in the streets of Baltimore, upon the Sixth Regiment of Massachusetts volunteers, while passing from one depot to the other, on their way to the capital. This attack on the 19th of April, in which several soldiers were shot down, roused the people to the highest pitch of excitement. The Secessionists were so strong in that State as to induce the Mayor of Baltimore, and Governor Hicks, a Union man, to protest against troops marching across the soil of Maryland, to the defense of the National capital. They burned the bridges on the railroads leading to Washington, and for a time, interrupted the passage of troops through Baltimore. The Governor so far humiliated himself, and forgot the dignity of his State and Nation, as to suggest that the differences between the Government and its rebellious citizens should be referred to Lord Lyons, the British Minister. The Secretary of State fittingly rebuked this unworthy suggestion; alluding to an incident, in the late war with Great Britain, he reminded the Governor of Maryland, "that there had been a time when a General of the American Union, with forces designed for the defense of its capital, was not unwelcome anywhere in Maryland"; and he added, "that if all the other noble sentiments of Maryland had been obliterated, one, at least, it was hoped would remain, and that was that no domestic contention should be referred to any foreign arbitrament, least of all to that of a European Monarchy."

While such was the universal feeling of loyal enthusiasm throughout the Free States, in the Border Slave States there was division and fierce conflict. Governor Magoffin of Kentucky in reply to the President's call, answered,

"I say, emphatically, Kentucky will furnish no troops for the wicked purpose of subduing her sister Southern States." Governor Harris of Tennessee
said, "Tennessee will not furnish a man for coercion, but 50,000 for the defense of our Southern brothers." Governor Jackson, of Missouri, refused,
saying, "not one man will Missouri furnish to carry on such an unholy
crusade"; and Virginia not only refused through her Governor to respond,
but her Convention then in session immediately passed an ordinance of
secession, by a vote of eighty-eight to fifty-five.

The Northwest, the home of the President and the home of Douglas, was,
if possible, more emphatic (it could scarcely be more unanimous than other
sections of the Free States) in the expression of its determination to maintain the Union at all hazards, and at any cost. The people of the vast
country between the Alleghanies and the Rocky Mountains, and north of
the Ohio, regarded the Mississippi as peculiarly *their* river, the great outlet
to the sea. Proud and confident in their hardy strength, familiar with the
use of arms, they never at any time, for any moment, hesitated in their
determination, in no event, to permit the erection of a foreign territory
between themselves and the Gulf of Mexico. Here were ten millions of the
most energetic, determined, self-reliant people on earth, who had overcome difficulties and surmounted obstacles; and the idea that anybody
should dare to set up a flag, other than theirs between them and the ocean,
was a degree of audacity they would never tolerate. "Our great river," exclaimed Douglas, indignantly, "has been closed to the commerce of the
Northwest." The seceding States, conscious of the strength of this feeling,
early passed a law providing for the free navigation of the Mississippi. But
the hardy Western pioneers were not disposed to accept paper guarantees
for permission to "possess, occupy and enjoy" their own. They would hold
the Mississippi, with their rifles. When closed upon them, they resolved
to open it, and did open it. They immediately seized upon the important
strategic point of Cairo, and from Belmont to Vicksburg and Fort Hudson,
round to Lookout Mountain, Chattanooga, and Atlanta, they never ceased
to press the enemy, until the great central artery of the Republic, and all
its vast tributaries, from its source to its mouth, were free; and then, marching to the sea, joined by their gallant brethren on the Atlantic coast, to aid
in the complete overthrow of the rebellion and the final triumph of liberty
and law.

It has been stated that the people of the Border States had been divided
in sentiment, and it was very doubtful for a time which way they would
go; but the attack upon Fort Sumter and the call by the President for
troops forced the issue, and the unscrupulous leaders were able to carry
Virginia, North Carolina, Tennessee, and Arkansas, into the Confederate
organization against the will of a majority of the people of those States.
Virginia, the leading State of the Revolution, the one which under the
leadership of Washington and Madison had been the most influential in

the formation of the National Government, the "Old Dominion," as she was usually called, the "Mother of States and Statesmen," had been for years descending from her high position. Her early and Revolutionary history had been of unequalled brilliancy; she had largely shaped the policy of the Nation, and furnished its leaders. Her early statesmen were anti-slavery men, and if she had relieved herself of the burden of slavery, she would have held her position as the leading State of the Union; but, with this heavy drag, the proud Old Commonwealth had seen her younger sisters of the Republic rapidly overtaking and passing her in the race of progress, and the elements of National greatness. Indeed she had fallen so low that her principal source of wealth was from the men, women, and children she raised and sent South to supply the slave markets of the Gulf States. Her leading men had been advocating extreme States'-Rights doctrines, fatal to National unity and thus sowing the seeds of secession. Her politicians had threatened disunion, again, and again. Still, when the crisis came, a majority of her people were true; a large majority of their convention was opposed to secession, and when afterwards, by violence and fraud, the ordinance was passed, the people of the northwest, the mountain region of Virginia, resisted and determined to stand by the Union. This portion of the State maintained its position with fidelity and heroism, and ultimately established the State of West Virginia.

Although Virginia, in January, 1861, voted a million dollars for defensive purposes, yet as late as April 4th, the convention, by a vote of eighty-nine to forty-five voted down an ordinance of secession. But the Union men in the convention, under various appliances—the promises, threats, and violence used—yielded one after another, until, under the excitement growing out of the attack upon Fort Sumter and the President's call to arms, the ordinance of secession was forced through. Before this could be done, however, a mob was raised at Richmond by the conspirators and a committee appointed to wait upon certain Union men in the convention, and advise them that they must either vote for secession, absent themselves, or be hung. The secession of Virginia added greatly to the danger of Washington, and a bold movement upon it, then, in its defenseless condition, would have been successful. Alexander H. Stephens, Vice-President of the Confederacy, came to Richmond, and everywhere raised the cry of "on to Washington!"

The State authorities of Virginia did not wait for the ratification of the secession ordinance by the people, to whom it was submitted for adoption or rejection, but immediately joined the Confederacy, commenced hostilities, and organized expeditions for the capture of Harper's Ferry and the Gosport Navy-yard. Senator Mason immediately issued an address to the people, declaring that those who could not vote for a separation of Virginia from the United States "*must leave the State!*" Submission, banishment, or death was proclaimed to all Union men of the Old Commonwealth. Nowhere, except in western Virginia, and some small localities, was there resistance to this decree. In the northwest, the mountain men rallied, organized, resolved to stand by the old flag and protect themselves under its folds.

The secession of Virginia gave to the Confederates a moral and physical power which imparted to the conflict the proportions of a tremendous civil war. She placed herself as a barrier between her weaker sisters and the Union, and she held her position, with heroic endurance and courage, worthy of a better cause and of her earlier days. Indeed, she kept the Union forces at bay for more than four long years, preserving her capital, and yielding only when the hardy soldiers of the North had marched from the Cumberland to the sea, cutting her off and making the struggle hopeless.

North Carolina naturally followed Virginia, and on the 21st of May, adopted by a unanimous vote an ordinance of secession, and her governor, Ellis, called for an enrollment of 30,000 men.

Tennessee was the daughter of North Carolina, yet her people were widely divided in sentiment and sympathy; east Tennessee, embracing the mountains of the Cumberland range and the western slopes of the Alleghanies, where there were few slaves, and peopled by a brave, hardy, and loyal race, were devoted to the Union. In the west, a majority of the people were in sympathy with those seeking to overthrow the Government. The governor, Isham G. Harris, was an active conspirator, and in full accord with the enemies of the Union. General Pillow, on the organization of the rebel Government, hastened to Montgomery, and tendered it 50,000 volunteers from Tennessee. On the 9th of February, the people voted down secession by 65,000 majority! The Union men of that State, under the lead of Andrew Johnson, Horace Maynard, Governor Brownlow, and their associates, determined to maintain the Union. But the loyal people of Tennessee were isolated from the free States, unapproachable from the east, except across Virginia, and over the Alleghanies; and from the north separated by the semi-rebellious State of Kentucky. Under these circumstances, it was difficult for Mr. Lincoln to furnish them aid and succor. The State was nearly surrounded by secession influences; the State Government was in the hands of traitors to the Union, and in June following, by means of fraud, violence, intimidation, and falsehood, an apparent majority was obtained in favor of secession. East Tennessee, however, still indignantly rejected secession, and her sons made a gallant fight for the Union.

Maryland, from her location between the Free States and the National capital, occupied a position of the utmost importance. Could she be induced to join the Confederates, their design of seizing the National capital and its archives would be made comparatively easy. Emissaries from the conspirators were busy in her borders during the winter of 1861. But while there were many rebel sympathizers and traitors among her slave-holders, and many leading families gave in their adhesion to the conspiracy, the mass of the people were loyal. The governor of the state, Thomas H. Hicks, though he yielded for a time to the apparent popular feeling in favor of the Confederates, and greatly embarrassed the Government by his protests against troops marching over Maryland soil to the defense of the capital, was, at heart, a loyal man, and in the end became a decided and efficient Union leader. He refused, against inducements and threats of personal violence, to call the Legislature of the State together, a majority of whom were known to be Secessionists, and who would have passed an ordinance of secession. But the man to whom the people of Maryland are most indebted, and who was the most influential in the maintenance of the Union cause at this crisis, and who proved the benefactor of the State in relieving her of the curse of slavery, was the bold, eloquent and talented Henry Winter Davis. He took his position from the start, for the unconditional maintenance of the Union.

The officials of the city of Baltimore were most of them Secessionists, and its chief of police was a traitor, and was implicated in the plot to assassinate Mr. Lincoln on his way to the capital.

On the 19th of April, a mob in the city of Baltimore had attacked the Massachusetts Sixth Regiment, while quietly passing through to the defense of the capital, and several soldiers and citizens were killed in the affray. The bridges connecting the railways from Pennsylvania and New York, with Baltimore, were burned, and for a time, communication by railroad was interrupted.

General B. F. Butler, leading the Massachusetts troops, together with the New York Seventh Regiment, were compelled to go around by Annapolis, and to rebuild the railway to Washington. But one dark, stormy night, General Butler marched into Baltimore, encamped on Federal Hill, and reopened communication with the North. The Union men of Maryland rallied; the leading Secessionists fled, or were arrested; and, from that time, Maryland was a Loyal State, lending to the Union the aid of her moral influence, and furnishing many gallant soldiers to fight its battles.

On the 18th of April, the day before the massacre of the Massachusetts soldiers by the Baltimore mob, intelligence reached Washington of a plot, on the part of the Secessionists in that city, aided by Virginia, to rise, fire the city, seize as prisoners the President and his Cabinet, and all officials present, take possession of the Government archives, and thus realize the prophecy of the rebel Secretary of War, Walker, that the flag of the Confederates should float over the dome of the Capitol before the first of May.

There were, at that time, but few troops in Washington, and the means of defense were very inadequate. Soldiers were hurrying to its defense from Pennsylvania, New York, and New England, but a part of the plan was the burning of the bridges of the railways, and the interruption of communication between Baltimore and the North, and this part was successfully executed.

When intelligence of this plot was received at Washington, there were several hundred gentlemen of high personal character and social position in the city. They immediately met, organized, took an oath of fidelity to to the Union, elected Cassius M. Clay of Kentucky, and General James H. Lane of Kansas their leaders, were armed by the War Department, and, for several days, acted as guards. The party under Lane took up their quarters in the East Room of the White House, and the others guarded the city. Arms were placed in the Capital, it was provisioned for a short siege, and it was prepared to be used in case of necessity as a citadel. Behind its massive marble walls it was believed that the President and the officials, and Government archives, might find safety, until the loyal people of the North, rallying to the rescue, should reach the capital.

But Butler soon opened communications; the New York Seventh reached the capital, and then there were troops enough to make the execution of the plot madness; and it was consequently abandoned. Meanwhile Fortress Monroe, Annapolis and Baltimore, were occupied by Federal troops, and all danger of an immediate attack of the insurgents disappeared.

What course would Missouri, the leading State west of the Mississippi take? With a population exceeding a million, she had only 115,000 slaves. Her interests were with the Free States, yet she had a governor in direct sympathy with the traitors, and so were the majority of her State officers. A State Convention was called, but an overwhelming majority of Union men had been elected. The truth is, that although the slave power had succeeded in destroying the political power of her great senator, Thomas H. Benton, yet the seeds of opposition to slavery had been scattered, were everywhere springing up in favor of Union and liberty. The city of St. Louis, the commercial metropolis of the State, had become a free-soil city; it had elected Francis P. Blair, Jr., a disciple of Benton, to Congress. The large German population, under the lead of Franz Siegel and others, were for the Union, to a man.

To the President's call for troops, the rebel governor, Claiburn F. Jackson returned an insulting refusal, but the people under the lead of Blair responded.

The United States Arsenal at St. Louis, was, at this time, under a guard commanded by Captain Nathaniel Lyon, one of the boldest and most energetic officers of the army. He, in connection with colonels Blair, Siegel, and others, organized volunteer regiments in St. Louis, preparing for a conflict which they early saw to be inevitable. The arms of the St. Louis Arsenal were, during the night of the 25th of April, under the direction of captains Stokes and Lyon, transferred to a steamer and taken to Alton, Illinois, for safety, and were soon placed in the hands of volunteers from that State.

Governor Jackson had gathered several hundred men whom he called a "*State Guard*" but whom he intended should be drilled and prepared as rebel soldiers, and with whom he intended to seize the United States arms and the arsenal. But his design was thwarted by captains Stokes and Lyon. Lyon then, on the 6th of May, followed up his success in saving the arms by marching with about six thousand men to Camp Jackson, where the "State Guards" were encamped, and surrounded and took them prisoners. He captured twenty cannon, 1,200 new rifles, several chests of muskets, and a large quantity of ammunition, most of which the "State Guard," under direction of Governor Jackson, had stolen from the United States arsenals.

On the 19th day of April, the President issued a proclamation blockading the ports of the Gulf States, and on the 27th of April, this was extended to North Carolina and Virginia, both of which States had been carried into the vortex of revolution. On the 3d of May, the President called into the service 42,034 volunteers, for three years, and provided for an addition of over 20,000 men to the regular army.

Meanwhile the insurgents had been active and enterprising. They had boldly seized Harper's Ferry, and the Gosport Navy-yard, near Norfolk, Virginia. Within twenty-four hours after the secession ordinance passed the Virginia Convention, they sent forces to capture those places where were very important arsenals of arms and ordnance. Harper's Ferry had long been a national armory, and commanded the Baltimore and Ohio Railroad, one of the most important connections of the capital with the great West. It was the gate to the beautiful valley of the Shenandoah, and of great importance as a military post. On the 18th of April it was abandoned by its small garrison, and taken possession of by the insurgents. At about the same time, the Gosport Navy-yard, with 2,000 pieces of heavy cannon and various material of war, and large ships, including the *Pennsylvania* of 120 guns, and the *Merrimac*, afterwards famous for its combat with the *Monitor*, fell into their hands. Owing to imbecility, or treachery, or both, this navy-yard, with its vast stores and property estimated to be worth from eight to ten millions was left exposed to seizure and destruction.

When it was too late, Commodore Paulding was sent to relieve the imbecile, if not treacherous, McCauley, and believing that he could not defend the yard and property, he set fire to the ships, attempted to destroy the ordnance, and commit to flames the yard and everything of value connected with it. The fire was only partially successful, and a very large amount of the property fell into the hands of the rebels.

Meanwhile troops gathered to the defense of the National capital. Among others, came Colonel Elmer E. Ellsworth, with a splendid regiment which he had raised, picked men from the New York firemen.

On the evening of the 23rd of May, the Union forces crossed the Potomac, took possession of Arlington Heights and the hills overlooking Washington and Alexandria.

As Colonel Ellsworth was returning from taking down a rebel flag from the Marshall House in Alexandria, he was instantly killed, by a shot fired by the keeper of the hotel over which the obnoxious symbol had floated.

This young man had accompanied Mr. Lincoln from Illinois to Washington and was a *protégé* of the President. He had introduced the zouave drill into the United States. He was among the first martyrs of the war, and his death was deeply mourned by the President. His body was taken to the executive mansion, and his funeral, being the first of those who died in defense of the flag, was very impressive, touching and solemn. He was, almost, the first soldier ever slain in the United States, in civil war. A gold medal was taken from his body after his death, stained with his heart's blood, with the inscription *"non solem nobis, sed pro patria"*—"Not for myself, but for my country."

The secession of Virginia had been followed by the removal of the rebel Government to Richmond. Virginia, North Carolina, Tennessee and Arkansas had joined the Confederacy. Thus eleven States, through State organizations, had withdrawn, and sought to divide the Republic.

At last freedom and slavery confronted each other, face to face, with arms in their hands. The Loyal States at this time had a population of 22,046,472; and the eleven seceding States had a population of 9,103,333, of which 3,521,110 were slaves.

9

To Arms! Out of
a Quiet Neighborhood

Charles Beneulyn Johnson

Not many weeks had the war been in progress when the "powers that be"
came to realize that the Southerners were terribly in earnest, that putting
down the Rebellion was no child's play, and that for its accomplishment
there would be needed a large number of well-trained soldiers and vast
sums of money.

Congress convened on July 4, 1861, in extra session, and in his message
to that body, President Lincoln recommended that four hundred thousand
men be enrolled and that four hundred million dollars be appropriated for
war purposes. In response Congress voted *five* hundred thousand men and
five hundred million dollars.

But while the Washington Government thus came to have some appreciation of the magnitude of the uprising in the South, the people at large
failed to do so till after the Battle of Bull Run. This battle, which at the
time seemed so disastrous to the Union cause, occurred July 21, 1861. Very
naturally the newspapers were filled with the details of this struggle, and
a little later some of them referred to it as "Bully Run," a facetious method
of speaking of the panic which seized the Union soldiers after the battle.

But Bull Run was really a blessing in disguise, for it roused the North
to a full appreciation of what it had to do in order to save the Union. This
battle occurred almost precisely seven months after the secession of South
Carolina, the event which first "fired the Southern heart"; and during the
whole of 1861 it is, perhaps, not too much to say that in all that pertains to
preparedness, the South was fully that many months in advance of the
North.

In conversation with a Southern sympathizer, late in the summer of 1861,

CHARLES BENEULYN JOHNSON, M.D., *Muskets and Medicine* (Philadelphia, 1917), Chs.
2, 3.

I remember urging in excuse for the recent Union defeat that our forces were greatly outnumbered.

"Yes," he replied, "just as they always have been and are always likely to be in the future."

During the first months of the Civil War the people of the West were greatly interested in the progress of events in Missouri. General Fremont had command of the Department of Missouri during most of the summer of 1861, and as he started in with considerable reputation, the people naturally believed he would accomplish much and develop into one of the great Civil War leaders. But while it was not perhaps wholly Fremont's fault, yet he fell short of achieving what was expected.

August 10, 1861 was fought the Battle of Wilson's Creek, near Springfield, Missouri, where our forces attacked and greatly demoralized the enemy, who outnumbered us three to one. But the Union cause that day sustained what, at the time, seemed an irreparable loss in the death of General Lyon, the Commander. After General Lyon's death the Federals fell back, first to Springfield and later to Rolla, Missouri. General Sigel, upon whom the command devolved, gained great reputation for the masterly manner in which he brought his little army from where it was so greatly outnumbered, and in danger of capture.

General Lyon's death was very much deplored all over the loyal North. In his person he seemed to combine qualities so much needed at that time, qualities that were clearly lacking in certain ones in high places. His energy, sagacity and promptness made him a great favorite in the West, where his deeds gave promise of a brilliant future, had his life been spared. He first came into the "lime-light" May 10, 1861 when, as Captain Lyon of the regular army, he promptly seized Camp Jackson at St. Louis, and thus early saved the contiguous country to the Union.

Emboldened by success at other points, secession in Missouri proposed to make its nest, so to speak, at Camp Jackson, within the corporate limits of St. Louis; and in this nest, early in May, 1861, whole broods of Confederate soldiers were going through the incubation process. But the Confederate commandant, General Frost, who possessed only the sagacity of a fledgling, made a sort of May-day merry-making of drilling, and here came the city nabobs in their coaches, ladies in carriages, others in buggies, men on horseback and hundreds afoot.

One day a fat lady in a buggy, unaccompanied, drove leisurely all about the camp apparently unconcerned, but from under "her" bonnet looked the eagle eyes of Captain Nathaniel Lyon of the United States Army, who carefully took in the whole situation.

Shortly afterwards, a body of armed soldiers was marched out to Camp Jackson, halted in front of it, when their commander, Captain Lyon, demanded and promptly received the surrender of the Confederate camp with its twelve hundred embryo soldiers.

This bold and sagacious act caused great rejoicing throughout the West, but especially in parts of Illinois as were tributary to St. Louis. The newspapers of the day were filled with accounts of the affair, and Captain Lyon at once came into prominence. But his career of glory was doomed to be short, as he fell precisely three months later at Wilson's Creek.

Our little county . . . furnished two companies of three months' men at the first call in April, 1861; these, before their time had fully expired, came home on furlough, preparatory to entering the three years' service for which period they had re-enlisted. Those from our community came walking in from the railroad station one bright June morning, dressed in their fresh, new uniforms: coats of dark or navy blue, with bright brass buttons, pants light blue, neat caps with long visors, and their blankets of gray woolen, neatly rolled and thrown gracefully over their shoulders. Thus seen, "soldiering" looked especially inviting to me, a boy not yet eighteen.

During the summer of 1861 a man came along and hired out upon the farm where I was working. He stated that he was from near Springfield, Missouri, where he had owned a well-stocked farm, but that the country being overrun by the contending armies everything had been "stripped off," and he was glad to get away. His family had gone to some relatives in Indiana, while he sought to earn a little money by hard work. He was the first Union refugee I had seen up to that time.

The Battle of Bull Run in the East, and Wilson's Creek in the West, were the principal engagements during the summer of 1861. I remember anxiously watching the papers during the summer and autumn of that year, instinctively hoping to read of the Confederates being overwhelmed by our forces. But my hopes were not gratified.

The winter of 1861-62 I spent in a remote and sparsely settled section, seven miles from a post office, where papers a week old were not considered stale. Not till General Thomas's first battle was I privileged to read an account of the whole matter. Here the Confederate forces were beaten and put to flight, General Zollicoffer killed, their lines penetrated and broken at Bowling Green.

Even in this early period every neighborhood had one or more representatives in the army, and during the winter, I remember serving upon several occasions as amanuensis to some of my friends, who were poor penmen, answering letters from soldiers at the front.

Towards night, one dreary, foggy day in February, 1862, the boom of cannon was heard away off to the southwest. Next day it was learned that a great victory had been won. That Fort Donelson, on the Tennessee River, had fallen. Fifteen thousand Confederates were reported captured, with all their arms and accoutrements. The cannonading heard proved to be the firing of a national salute at St. Louis, more than forty miles distant. Meeting a man next day who had seen the papers and read an account of the whole affair, I inquired the name of the Union commander.

The answer was: "General Grant."

"Grant? Grant?" said I. "Never heard of him. Who is he? What's his rank? Where's he from?"

"Don't know just who he is," was the reply, "except that he is a brigadier-general and is from Illinois."

I remember feeling a shade of disappointment at the time that an entirely new and unknown man should all at once come into such prominence and, so to speak, eclipse men with familiar names.

Fort Donelson surrendered February 14, 1862, and it must have been the evening of February 17 that the salute was heard. It is unusual for cannonading to be heard forty miles and more distant, but the damp, heavy atmosphere of the time, together with the level prairie, over which the sound wave traversed, had much to do with the long distance reached. . . .

In the autumn of 1861 the people began to be impatient with what was deemed the needless inactivity of the Army of the Potomac under McClellan, and concerning him and that organization, the phrase: "All quiet on the Potomac," first used as an expressive indication of no demonstration by either friend or foe in Virginia, came, as the period of inaction lengthened, to have a satirical meaning.

McClellan, soon after Bull Run, was called to the command of the Army of the Potomac, and for a time seemed very popular with the people, and was soon familiarly called "Little Mac," and a short time after, the Napoleon of the War. But as the winter drew near and the Army of the Potomac made no demonstration, many began to question McClellan's fitness for high command, and some even made the remark that he was the "biggest man never to have done anything on record." His most excellent service in western Virginia in July, 1861, was for the time forgotten or ignored, and his great ability as an organizer was not yet understood.

In April, 1862, in the West, all eyes were concentrated upon the Army of the Tennessee at Pittsburg Landing, on the Tennessee River. Here, on April 6, 1862, Grant came near being overwhelmed, and for a time passed under a shadow of public mistrust as dark and foreboding as the previous two months'—after the fall of Forts Henry and Donelson—sunshine of popular approval and confidence had been warm and cheering.

The 6th of April, 1862, made memorable to me by the death of a relative, is remembered as a typical April day—now a cloud, now a shower, now sunshine, a little wind, a little warm and a little mud, but pleasant withal and full of the promise of spring. Little did we of the North know when the sun went down that quiet Sabbath evening through what peril one of our great armies had passed.

In the same secluded, sparsely settled section, seven miles from a post office, where I spent the winter of 1861-62, I also spent the spring and summer of 1862 following the plow, contentedly farming and dreaming of the college life which I hoped was near at hand.

About this time, too, I first saw a national bank note. The man who had several five- and ten-dollar bills of this species said they were "legal-tenders." Their bright, crisp appearance and artistic workmanship were in striking contrast with the State bank—"wildcat"—currency, up to that period the only paper money in circulation. This State bank money was of such uncertain value that many of the old-fashioned, but sturdy, people refused to receive it in payment of dues, and insisted upon having only gold and silver. Consequently, paper money naturally held a lower place in the public esteem than *hard* money, the people's name for gold and silver coin.

The National currency soon banished from circulation the State currency. Gold and silver disappeared from circulation in 1862, and fractional paper money was issued by the Government of fifty-, twenty-five-, ten-, five- and even three-cents value.

In the region where I was, the daily newspaper was almost never seen, and even a good weekly but seldom. . . .

About the 1st of April, 1862, the Army of the Potomac, under General McClellan, began the Peninsular campaign, slowly approaching from Fortress Monroe towards Richmond. A month was consumed in the Siege of Yorktown; six weeks passed in the sickly swamps of the Chickahominy, after which McClellan changed his base to the James River, and then followed the Seven Days' Battles near Richmond, namely, Mechanicsville, June 26; Gaines' Mills, June 27 and 28; Savage's Station, June 29; Peach Orchard, June 29; White Oak Swamp, June 30; and Malvern Hill, July 1. July 2 the Army of the Potomac retreated to Harrison's Landing, on the James River, and thus had been accomplished the "change of base." This costly and humiliating repulse of McClellan was a sore disappointment to the North, but knowing the Nation's power, the President issued a call in the last days in July for 300,000 volunteers, which, a little later, was increased to 600,000.

Like most others I had all along been greatly interested in the war's progress, but fifteen months' continuance of the conflict had, in a degree, removed the keen edge of that interest, and I, all the while, consoled myself with the idea that there was no need for me to become identified with the conflict in any way personally. The previous winter I had been teaching and putting in leisure moments preparing for college. My studies I tried to prosecute, in a way, while farming during the spring and early summer of 1862, my zeal at times leading me in hot days, while my horse was resting, to use the freshly turned-up earth as a sort of make-shift board upon which, with a stick, I marked out for demonstration certain propositions in geometry.

From the foregoing it will be seen that my dreams were all of the Halls of Learning and not of the Temple of Mars, not of fields of strife and blood. These personal matters are mentioned because it is believed that many thousands of young men, up to this period, had aspirations like my own and bore a similar relation to the war, and most of these enlisted and thousands of them sacrificed their lives on their country's altar.

One day early in August, 1862, having followed the plow till noon, I came in from the field to dinner and found at the house a relative who had just arrived with the information that a war meeting was to be held the next day at Pocahontas, my home village, ten miles distant, and that the day previous a war meeting had been held at Greenville, Illinois, our county seat, and at which many of my old friends and schoolmates had enlisted.

Joining the army is not unlike measles, whooping-cough and even small-pox, for it's catching. Learning that A., B., C., and D. had volunteered, I henceforth saw "the light," and straightway resolved to enlist in my country's service, much as it would mar all my well-laid plans. With this intent uppermost in my mind I attended the war meeting at Pocahontas, August 9, 1862, which was held in the shade of a white oak grove.

There was a good attendance and much earnestness manifested. The exercises consisted of martial music, singing of patriotic songs and several eloquent speeches. One of the speakers was a ruddy-faced, good-looking Englishman, whose earnestness and eloquent words made a lasting impression on my mind. He began by reading in a most impressive manner a poem, then just published and beginning: "We are coming, Father Abraham, six hundred thousand more, from Alleghany's rugged heights, from Mississippi's winding shore . . ."

These lines are quoted from memory and may be inaccurate, but it is believed they are substantially correct. When through reading, the speaker said: "As most of you know, I am an Englishman; not a drop save English blood courses in my veins, and near to my heart is the memory of dear, merry old England. Her green, peaceful fields, her happy homes, her thrifty sons, her broad-chested, manly men; and her rosy-cheeked, healthy women; wives, sisters, mothers, sweethearts can never, never be forgotten. But much as I love old England, and proud as I am of the power and fair name of my native land, I am, today, an American citizen, and as such, should the English Government see fit to intervene and take up arms in favor of the South, I will shoulder a musket and fight against her as long as there is breath in my body."

The impassioned address of the eloquent Englishman was intently listened to and heartily cheered by the audience.

Amid these surroundings and under these patriotic influences I gave my name to an enrolling officer, and for three years thereafter saw service in the Union Army—service that, though humble, did not end till the last enemy had surrendered and our national flag was permitted to float in peace over every foot of the late eleven Seceded States—eleven Seceded States that comprised the Southern Confederacy, and whose people had desperately striven to take eleven stars from the flag of our common country, and with them form the "Stars and Bars," the emblem of a proposed new government, whose chief corner-stone was avowed to be human slavery, but

"Though the mills of God grind slowly, yet they grind exceeding small,
Though with patience He stands waiting, with exactness He grinds all."

At this period the war had been in progress a little less than sixteen months, and regarding the propriety and justness of the conflict, there were three classes, and of these the first included all members of the Republican Party who had elected Abraham Lincoln to the Presidency, and who, to a man, favored a vigorous prosecution of the war.

A second class was vacillating, now favoring the war and now hesitating, if not, indeed, objecting to its further prosecution.

A third class opposed President Lincoln in every move he made, and became so bitter and so obnoxious that they were not inaptly called "Copperheads," the name of a certain snake whose bite was especially poisonous, and whose method of attack was cowardly and vicious.

As time went by, the party favoring a vigorous prosecution of the war received a very large accession from certain patriotic men who came to be known as "War-Democrats," a *hyphenated* term that was especially popular with Union men in the early sixties.

As to the final outcome, a few people seemed, from the beginning, to have implicit faith in ultimate triumph, but the great majority were submerged in a sea of doubt and perplexity.

On July 4, 1861, I attended a Fourth of July celebration at Greenville, our county seat, and listened to a most eloquent and patriotic address from a prominent clergyman. Very naturally the theme of the speaker was the war, upon which the country was just entering. He handled his subject in a masterly manner, and I shall never forget his closing words: "Crowned with a halo of glory, the nation reunited will finally come out of this fiery ordeal, grander, nobler, stronger than ever before."

These words were, so to speak, burned into my memory, for they were wonderfully impressive and seemed to carry with them great weight and an indefinable sense of dignity and foreknowledge. Yet, in those trying days when everyone was at sea, and clarity of view was vouchsafed to few, if any, the prophetic words of the reverend speaker seemed all but impossible of fulfillment. However, those were stirring times, and men's minds underwent prompt and radical changes. . . .

The eloquent speaker referred to above was Reverend Thomas W. Hynes, of Greenville, Illinois, who was born in Kentucky and lived there till he was fifteen years of age, when he came north. He was a forceful speaker, with a rich, sonorous voice, and a suave, dignified gentleman, who, in his bearing and every-day life, represented the highest type of the true Christian gentleman.

Having been born and reared in a slave-environment he knew the wrongs and evils of the slave system, and when, in the fifties, the attempt was made to contaminate the free prairies of Kansas with slave labor, Reverend Mr. Hynes was a modest, but integral part of the great upheaval north of the Ohio River that finally engulfed the threatening movement on the part of the ultra-Southern leaders.

His three sons were in the Union Army, and one of them fell at Vicksburg, where he now fills a soldier's honored grave.

Among those who left their homes in the South on account of their dislike to slavery and came to the western wilderness in Illinois, while it was yet a territory, was my grandfather, Charles Johnson, who raised a large family; and when the Civil War came on not one of his descendants who was of suitable age and physically fit, failed to enlist, and one of them gave up his life at Chickamauga.

But what was true of these two patriots was true of thousands of Southern-born men in Illinois, Indiana and Ohio, among whom Abraham Lincoln was the great prototype, and who, when the terrible crisis came in the early sixties, stood like a wall of adamant for the integrity of the Federal Government. Indeed, the part borne by these stalwart Unionists of Southern birth and descent was so weighty that it really turned the scales and, in the final reckoning, made the preservation of the Union possible. What a theme for a volume would the work of these men afford! These stalwarts loved the sunny Southland, but they loved the Union more. Among the last-named were generals Scott, Thomas, Logan, Hurlburt, Commodore Farragut and scores of other great Civil War leaders.

Under Lincoln's call for 600,000 volunteers in July and August, 1862, two full companies were enlisted in my little native County of Bond, which came to be noted for its patriotism. During the month of August and early days of September these volunteers rendezvoused at Greenville, our county seat, a quiet old-time village of about fifteen hundred inhabitants and twenty miles distant from the nearest railway station. Here we were billeted, or quartered, at the two village taverns.

Very many of the two hundred young men composing these two companies were fine, stalwart fellows, whose bronzed faces showed the healthy traces of the sun's rays under which they had followed the plow during the cultivating season, then just over; though when I enlisted I let go the handles of the plow and left it sticking in the furrow. Most of us were under twenty-five years of age—a great many, indeed, under twenty—and a jolly, rollicking bunch we were, but, almost to a man, all were staunch, of sterling worth, and were members of the best families in the county. One night a number of us went out in the country two or three miles, if I remember correctly, in quest of watermelons, but whether or not we found them, I do not now recall. But one experience of that summer I shall never forget. We took with us a supply of cigars, for those who were already smokers and those who were not yet smokers alike. Those of us who had not before learned to smoke had become impressed with the idea that we never could become real, true soldiers till we added this last to our list of accomplishments. Once before I had tried to smoke, but my efforts ended in a severe attack of vomiting. This night, however, notwithstanding my former failure, I resolved to make one more heroic effort to acquire the smoking habit, but, much to my dismay and chagrin, soon after inhaling the smoke of about half a cigar I was seized with a violent attack of sick stomach and vomiting which made me so weak that I was hardly able to get back to our stopping place. This apparent failure of fifty-odd years ago I have long since come to regard as one of the decidedly fortunate occurrences of my life, for it kept me from acquiring a costly and questionable habit.

At the village taverns, beds for all could, of course, not be had. Consequently, we slept on lounges, benches, carpets, bare floors; indeed, on almost any smooth surface that was under shelter. It goes without saying that we all had fine appetites, the demands of which severely taxed the tavern larders.

So passed the remainder of August and the early days of September, when one day an order came for us to rendezvous at Belleville, Illinois, a small city forty miles away.

One moonless night in August, a little time before we left Greenville, our company was drawn up in front of the Court House to receive a beautiful flag, a present from the women whose husbands, brothers, sons, and sweethearts were soon to see service at the front. Two or three tallow candles furnished a flickering uncertain light, under whose dim rays a Miss Smith, a beautiful young woman, mounted the Court House steps, and in a few well chosen words, spoken in a sweet voice, presented the flag. John B. Reid, then the captain of the company in which I had enlisted, responded briefly and appropriately.

The flag was made of fine silk and most beautiful were its seven stripes of red, six of snowy white, and delicate field of blue, studded with thirty-four immaculate stars, representing as many States, although eleven of these were making war upon this flag and all it stood for.

After the fair young maiden had spoken her few words and the captain had responded, the flag was unfurled, three rousing cheers were given, and every man silently resolved, if need be, to give his life for the preservation of this noble emblem.

This flag we took with us when we went to the enemy's country, but unfortunately, during our various marches and transfers from one to another locality, it was misplaced and never afterward found. Thus it came about that not one of us was given opportunity to "die for its preservation."

In this same month of August, 1862, another beautiful Bond County flag, the handiwork of the wives, sisters, mothers, and sweethearts of the newly enlisted men, was made at Pocahontas, my native village, and by one of its fair maidens, Miss Sarah Green, presented to an organization that later became Company E, 130th Illinois Infantry Volunteers. In due time this

Pocahontas flag was carried to the enemy's country, and by his bullets its folds were more than once pierced during the Siege of Vicksburg. The war over, the flag was returned to the people from whence it came, and is today a highly cherished relic in the care of J. W. Miles, a Civil War veteran of Pocahontas.

Most certainly this shot-pierced, home-made flag, old and tattered by more than a half-century's history, is well and unquestionably entitled to be called "Old Glory."

The Pocahontas flag is only one of many, many thousands, that were given to outgoing volunteers by patriotic women whose prayers and hopes followed their loved ones wheresoever duty called them. But, sad to say, the great majority of the flags of this class are from one cause or another no longer in existence; hence, the possessors of the Pocahontas "Old Glory" have reason to congratulate themselves over their exceptional good fortune.

To the non-military reader it may be well to say that the State furnished every newly organized regiment a flag which became its recognized standard. In review, on parade, on all public occasions, and in battle, this flag was unfurled and borne at the head of the regiment by the color-bearer. In the event the flag was lost or destroyed, the State, as promptly as possible, furnished another one.

Finally, when the term of service ended and the regiment was mustered out, its flag reverted to the State, and was supposed to be ever after cared for.

Thus it will be seen that regimental flags are in a class to themselves, and, as such, cannot be claimed by individuals nor by communities.

In the latter part of August, 1862, while men all over the North were, in thousands, cheerfully responding to President Lincoln's latest and largest call for troops, General Pope was seriously defeated in Northern Virginia, and with his army had fallen back on the defenses of Washington.

A little later, about the middle of September, these reverses were, in part, retrieved by the same troops under McClellan at South Mountain and Antietam. All this occurred while the two companies from Bond County were yet in citizens' dress and eating the food of civil life. Already, however, each volunteer had taken an oath before a justice of the peace to support the Constitution and laws of the United States.

The round of routine at Greenville, eating, sleeping, drilling, etc.—the county seat of little Bond—was varied one evening by a social gathering in the audience room of the Court House, at which all the soldiers and many citizens and ladies were present. Some good vocal music was rendered, and one soloist, Miss Lucy White, daughter of President White of Almira College, sang with much effect a selection, then just published, in which are the words:

"Brave boys are they, gone at their country's call,
And yet, and yet, we cannot forget that many brave boys must fall."

If I remember correctly, these two lines were a sort of refrain at the end
of each verse, and the words "must fall" sounded to me especially doleful—
so doleful that I could not enter into the cheery character that it was intended the gathering should assume, and at its close, the words "must fall"
rang in my ears till I felt almost sure I was destined to die on some Southern
battlefield. However, next morning's sunshine dissipated all my gloomy
forebodings and my boyish vigor and innate optimism caused me to take a
cheerful view of the future—a view that time has justified, for, since that
social gathering in the Court House, fifty-four long years have run their
course, and of those assembled on that August night, I am one of the few
left to tell the story.

Miss White's solo, doleful as it seemed, was not without its good effect,
for even the most thoughtless among us was made to think seriously of the
new and dangerous duties upon which we were about to enter.

As elsewhere noted, an order had been received from the State capital
at Springfield, directing the two Bond County companies to rendezvous at
Belleville, Illinois, about forty miles away and not far from St. Louis.

As the time for departure drew near, every man visited his home, made
his final arrangements, said farewell to his friends, and then joined his comrades at Greenville.

But sad and tearful was this farewell, as father, mother, brother, sister,
wife, or sweetheart, took the parting one by the hand, none knowing how
soon he would fall in the frightful death-harvest a great devastating war
was every hour reaping.

At the appointed time friends, neighbors and relatives came with farm
wagons and, early one beautiful September morning, the vehicles were
loaded with hearty specimens of young manhood, all ideal "cannon-food,"
and the journey over a dusty road to the nearest railway station, twenty
miles away at Carlyle, was begun.

Three or four miles on the road was a hill where we, for some cause,
halted for a time. From here I remember taking a look at the Court House,
about which we had been drilling for several weeks and whose friendly
roof had sheltered us from rain and sun alike, and as its familiar outline
loomed up in the morning's sun I wondered if I should ever again look
upon it.

About noon we reached Carlyle, on what was then known as the Ohio &
Mississippi Railroad, now the Baltimore & Ohio Railway, and soon a west-
bound train came in and we all went aboard. And will the reader believe it,
to many of us this experience was absolutely new, for I, in common with
most of my comrades, had never before been inside a railway coach! To
satisfy any reader who may be in a wondering mood, let it be said that a
half century ago railways were very much fewer, and railway travel vastly
less, than now.

After going west on the train for about twenty-five miles we got off—

detrained as we say today—at O'Fallon and marched in a southwesterly direction till we came to Belleville, seven miles distant. This afternoon was hot, the roads dusty, and I remember suffering much discomfort from a pair of tight-fitting shoes I had bought the day previous. Before we reached Belleville my discomfort amounted to almost torture, and for this reason I look back upon this initial march of only seven miles as one of the hardest and most uncomfortable I was called upon to make during my whole three years' service.

Arrived at Belleville, we were directed to the Fair Grounds, where under the board roofs of horse and cattle stalls, we found quarters. An abundance of clean, bright straw had been provided, upon which the blankets and quilts were spread, which last we had brought from our homes. And thus we arranged for our first night's sleep in the new career before us. The grounds were enclosed with a high, tight fence, and within were groves of shade trees and green, thrifty grass. The September weather was delightful, and the novelty of the new situation and way of living was most enjoyable.

However, there was one drawback; meals were taken at the several boarding houses in the city, and as these were substantially all run by Germans, Belleville being largely populated with people of that nationality, the taste and fumes of garlic seemed to permeate every article of food on the table. It was, of course, in all the meats, in many of the vegetables; but every man would have taken oath that it was in the bread and butter if, indeed, not in the coffee and sugar as well.

Strange as it may seem to the more advanced sanitarians of today, we all suffered from severe colds not long after we began sleeping out, and the exposure incurred in this way was assigned as the cause.

At the end of about ten days we were ordered to Camp Butler, near Springfield. We boarded a train for St. Louis, and arriving there, went by steamboat to Alton, Illinois, and here, sometime after nightfall, we climbed on coal cars, entrained, and found seats on boards which were put across from side to side. We found the ride anything but pleasant. Those sitting near the outer edge seemed in constant danger of falling overboard, and the smoke, cinders and sparks were tormenting in the extreme.

Some time in the "wee-small" hours we arrived at Springfield and got off, detrained, at the Alton & Chicago Railway station. Meantime, a drizzling rain began to fall, and the men found shelter as best they could. With a companion I found this in the open vestibule of a church a little south of the station. Next morning we got breakfast at one of the cheaper hotels, and this was destined to be one of our very last meals eaten from dishes placed on a white tablecloth.

During the forenoon several of us visited the home of President Lincoln and picked some flowers from the front yard and sent them home in letters.

Near noon-time we boarded a train on the Wabash Railway for Camp Butler, seven miles east of Springfield. On this train was Major General

John C. Fremont, in full uniform, and we all took a good look at him, as he was the first officer of high rank we had seen. He was a man of medium stature, and wore rather light sandy whiskers. This last was a surprise to me, for when he was candidate for President in 1856 he was represented as heavily whiskered, so heavily, indeed, that he won the sobriquet of "Wooly Horse."

Arrived at Camp Butler we detrained and passed through a gate near the railway, guarded by a uniformed soldier with a gun in his hands, and entered an enclosure of about forty acres, surrounded by a high, tight board fence. Along two sides of this enclosure were rows of long, narrow buildings, which were known as barracks. At one end was the office of the post commandant, and nearby, the commissary and quartermaster's department. At the other end was the hospital, guard, house, sutler's store, etc. In the center was a large open space, used as a drill-ground. In the middle of the rear end, as at the front, was a large gate for teams to pass through, and beside it a smaller one, for the egress and ingress of the men; both were guarded by an armed soldier, and no one could go out without a pass signed by the post commandant.

A company was assigned to each of the long, narrow buildings, which we soon learned to familiarly call barracks. This had at one end a kitchen and store-rooms, and at the other end two or three small apartments for the officers. Through the center of the main room ran a long table made of rough boards, and from which all ate. At the sides of this main room were box-like structures, open in front, having tiers of boards upon which two men slept side by side. These we called bunks. Thus it was that our long, narrow barracks were not unlike a sleeping-car and dining-car combined. The barracks were made of rough boards put on "up-and-down," with no ceiling overhead save the shingle roof, and windows and doors were few, purposely, to save space.

Here began the crude, coarse fare of soldier life. Rations in abundance and of essential good quality were supplied, but their preparation lacked the skilled, delicate hand of woman; but of this more hereafter.

Not long after reaching Camp Butler I was attacked with ague, and for this the post surgeon very properly prescribed quinine. The hospital steward gave me six powders of that drug, put up in as many papers, and as the bitter taste of quinine was especially repugnant to me, I cast about for some means to overcome this, and in the end could think of no better plan than the one I had seen my mother put in use. In seeking to carry this out I called on the sutler and paid him five cents for an especially mellow apple, and some of the scrapings of this I placed in the bottom of an iron spoon which I borrowed from one of the cooks, thus forming layer No. 1. On this I put the contents of one paper, forming layer No. 2, then over all I put some more apple scraping, forming layer No. 3. So far all went well, but unfortunately all went *wrong* when I attempted to swallow the bolus;

for I got the upper layer of apple and about two-thirds of the quinine and all its horrid taste, as this was, no doubt, added to by the acid in the apple. Just how I managed to take the remainder of the powders I do not now recall, but, in any event, I made a prompt recovery from my ague.

Some weeks after this I was attacked with a terrible pain in the bowels, and, as it was in the middle of the night, one of my comrades went for the post surgeon, who prescribed paregoric, which finally brought relief after several doses had been taken. Unfortunately for my more speedy relief, the hypodermic syringe had not yet come into use; but fortunately, perhaps, for my permanent peace and comfort, appendicitis had not yet taken its place in the category of distinct disease entities, and consequently the operation of appendectomy had not yet been devised. Had there been recognized such a disease as appendicitis, or had there been such an operation as appendectomy, the outcome might have been altogether different. I was a vigorous youth, suffering with agonizing pain in the classic region of McBurney's Point. My medical adviser was recently out of school, and was possessed of an aggressive make-up. Had it been possible to project the situation a generation into the future, this story might have had a different ending, and I might not be here to tell it; or I might be wearing a certain cross-abdomen slash, so to speak, familiar to modern surgeons.

But as things were, in that autumn day in 1862, my case was diagnosed colic, or, in plain English, "belly-ache," an old-time, old-fashioned, honest disease that appendectomists have nearly, or quite, crowded out of the category of human ailments.

Doubtless, my trouble was due to an attack of acute indigestion, in turn due to too many amateur cooks (among whom I had been one) in our barrack kitchen.

As said before, we received an abundance of good rations, but we did not know how to cook them. Each day two men were detailed from the company to do duty in the kitchen. These, the first day, served as assistants to two other men who but the day previous were themselves assistants, and with the *ripe experience gained in one day's apprenticeship,* were now full-fledged cooks, and capable of instructing the uninitiated.

Little wonder is it that, with these constant changes in the kitchen, the food was at nearly all times ill prepared, and chance too often an important factor in the results obtained. For illustration, meat which was placed in the oven to roast, from the presence of too much fat turned out a *fry,* and beef put in the kettle to boil, from the absence of water at a critical stage, would be *baked* instead, if indeed it was not hopelessly burned.

Potatoes were almost never properly cooked, even when apparently well done, a raw core would frequently be found in the center. Coffee was, at times, only a little stronger than water, at others it was like lye.

But rice, white beans and dried apples gave the amateur cooks the most trouble. In cooking these the novice would invariably fill the camp kettle, a large sheet-iron vessel, holding two or more gallons, with one of these articles, and then pour in water and set it over the fire. In a little time the beans or dried apples would begin to swell and run over the sides of the vessel; meantime, the new cook would dip out the contents and put them in another vessel; the swelling process continued, the dipping proceeded, till a second vessel was as full as the first, and there seemed to be enough for two or three companies instead of only one.

Good cook stoves and serviceable utensils were furnished by the Government, in addition to rations in abundance and of exceptional quality. The lame factor was in the food's preparation. Had it been possible for the Government to have supplied newly enlisted companies with good cooks till others could have been trained, an untold amount of sickness would have been prevented, and many graves would have remained unfilled, not to speak of the many thousands who were discharged from the service by reason of ailments due to ill-prepared food.

10

A Texan in Search of a Fight

John C. West

Left Waco, Texas on the morning of April 11, 1863; bid adieu to my dear little Stark and Mary at home; said good-bye to my sweet wife at the ferry-boat landing (at the foot of Bridge Street). Nothing of interest occurred on the way to Springfield (about forty miles east of Waco); saw two or three prairie chickens and a green sportsman trying to kill one; saw at Springfield, as I had left at Waco, a good many stout, able-bodied patriots, who somehow kept out of the service; stopped at McCracken's, fifteen miles east of Springfield, for the night; found Mr. McCracken a strong Houston man and would vote for him for governor if he "had to be hauled to the polls in a wagon."

I fear there are too many of this kind, and others worse, who will elect Houston if he runs. His election will be an invitation to Yankee invasion. However honest he may be in his devotion to the South, the North would regard his election as an endorsement of his past action.

April 12th. Left McCracken's at 3 o'clock in the morning. It is my birthday. I am 20 years old today (Sunday). Reached Fairfield (70 miles east of Waco) . . .

Palestine, April 13th . . . We discovered here some defect in our transportation tickets, and will have to pay our way to Rusk. It will be just my luck to have to pay all the way to Richmond, Va. I have already paid out since the war commenced five times as much for the privilege of serving in the ranks as the government has paid me, but I am perfectly willing to give all I have if the sacrifice will aid my country in achieving its liberty.

April 14th. Left Palestine about 5 o'clock A.M., in a two-horse wagon;

JOHN C. WEST, *Texan in Search of a Fight* (Waco, Tex., 1901), pp. 1-60.
Like Charles B. Johnson of Illinois, John West waited until the first flush of enthusiasm for combat had passed and the war's seriousness had become apparent. Only when it was apparent that the Confederacy desperately needed his services did he volunteer. Extracts from his poorly printed diary furnish glimpses of the impact of war on Texas, and bear testimony to his determination to make his way to the battlefront.

same company, with the addition of Mr. Mathus of the First Texas. The ride to Rusk would have been insupportably dull but for good company; nothing but red clay hills and deep gullies, ornamented with pine and oak. It, however, brought up some pleasing reminiscences of old South Carolina and my boyhood days—the season when ambitious hopes burned in my breast and I determined I would be *a man*—little dreaming then that I would have the satisfaction of striking a blow in the holiest cause that ever fired the breast of man, and illustrating by action the feelings which glowed and burned in my little heart, on reading the stories of Wallace and Tell.

We reached Rusk about 4 o'clock in the afternoon without an incident of interest, and found W. G. Thomas to be the quartermaster there. He appears to be an accommodating and clever officer and refunded our transportation which we had paid out at Palestine.

Today is the fifth anniversary of my wedding day, and I have thought often of my dear wife and little ones and wished I could be with them, but I am resolved not to remain quietly at home another moment while a foe is on our soil.

April 15th. I went to the supper table last night too sick to eat anything; left the table and laid down on a lounge until the hotel-keeper could show me a room; I retired early and slept well; got up this morning all right; but did not go to the breakfast table; took a lunch from my own haversack; walked out in town; went to the ten-pin alley and spent an hour rolling; had not played a game before for eight years, and enjoyed it very much; smoked a cigar, a notable scarcity in these times, and returned to the hotel, where I wrote a letter to Judge Devine, and one to my dear wife; may Heaven's choicest blessings rest upon her and my sweet children; went to the dinner table and found the landlady apologizing for some defect and two young females discussing the merits of the Episcopal and Baptist faith; got through dinner somehow and walked down to the quartermaster's office; got the Vicksburg *Whig;* stretched myself out on the counter; read and took a nap; got up; went to the armory and would have enjoyed looking over the work very much but felt sick; it produces four Mississippi rifles per day at $30 apiece on contract with the state; I am now sitting at the foot of the hill below the armory.

April 17th. I left Rusk on the morning of the 16th on a six-passenger coach; there were *fourteen* aboard; the driver was skillful and the road good; I was suffering intensely from dysentery and had a high fever from breakfast time until sundown; oh, the long, long weary miles pent up in that crowded coach; I slept half an hour at Henderson; at the next stand I bathed in the horse bucket and my fever left me; I chewed a piece of salt ham; it was now dark; I laid down on top of the stage-coach and was very comfortable about half of the night, but suffered tortures during the latter part of the night; reached Marshall about 7 o'clock in the morning; sent for a physician and will remain here for a day or two, until I am able to travel; Lieutenant Selman had a cup of genuine coffee made for me which I enjoyed very much; Burwell Aycock is trying to get a soft-boiled egg for me; I think I will be well in a day or two; this attack was brought on by a check of perspiration after becoming overheated in the walk of four miles to Palestine.

April 18th. I spent a very uncomfortable night; a dull, steady pain all night; had taken twenty drops of laudanum; had no matches and did not wish to disturb my companions; I did not sleep more than an hour; my friends left this morning for Alexandria via Shreveport; I could have gone with them if my physician, Dr. Johnson, had kept his promise and given me medicine yesterday evening that would have insured a night's rest, but he was detained in the country by an urgent case; General Chambers thinks Texas ought to give three hundred and twenty acres of land for every new-born boy; the doctor came in about 8 o'clock in the morning, left three pills for me to take at intervals of two hours and a powder to be taken at bed time; I am getting on very well and will leave here on Monday, I think; I have just discovered that my pocketbook is lost, containing about sixty dollars; I am satisfied that I lost it off the top of the stage between here and the twelve-mile stand this side of Rusk; I have had advertisements struck off to this effect, headed, "Lost! Lost!! the Last Red!!!" and asked the stage driver to have them posted on the road every five or six miles; since my pocketbook is gone I feel bound to accept the kind invitation of Mrs. Brownnigg, formerly Octavia Calhoun, to take a room in her house; she has just sent me a nice breakfast, and I have sent her word that I will come down.

I am at Mrs. Brownnigg's in a comfortable room; do not feel as if I were in the way as there is plenty of house room; Mrs. Bacon, formerly Anne Haralson, is here; she arrived yesterday and started to Georgia with Mr. Bacon, but became disgusted with the trip; she and Mrs. Brownnigg both treat me as kindly as though I were a brother, and I know my precious wife would feel very well satisfied if I could receive such treatment every time I am away from her, but there is no attention that approaches the gentle and delicate touch of a wife's hand, and there is no wife whose tenderness and sympathy can equal that of *my Mary;* I must forego the pleasure of her gentle words and smiles for a season until the kindness of Providence brings us together again; I am located as well here as I could possibly be at home and may God and good Angels guard my benefactors.

April 19th. I rested well last night but had the most hideous dreams all night; Mrs. Brownnigg came in early this morning and asked me into her room; I went and found the fire very comfortable; the doctor came to see me and seems to think I am all right now, but must be careful about my diet; says some brandy is exactly what I need to recruit on; so I missed it by leaving mine at home. Major Holman called to see me this morning; says he will see my transportation fixed all right; offers relief from the loss of my pocketbook; the doctor does likewise; Mrs. Brownnigg offers me money also. I ate nice toast and drank genuine coffee for breakfast; had chicken soup for dinner. . . .

April 29th. Left Natchitoches at 9 o'clock P.M. on Tuesday and had a very disagreeable ride, taking all night to get to Dutchman Cumberlando to breakfast; ate a strip of bacon and a piece of corn bread for which he charged me a dollar, and that on the heels of an invective against extortions and speculators. I saw on the road today large numbers of negroes from the lower parishes of Louisiana whose masters were retreating from the Yankee vandals; saw the tracks of several severe whirlwinds, which have occurred in the last three weeks; was quite sick for a while this afternoon and was not improved by hearing that all stragglers and recruits belonging across the Mississippi were to be detained on this side of Red River; reached Mansfield about 4:30 this afternoon; saw two young ladies riding on horseback; they worked very hard and their arms seemed to be in their way, dangled about very ungracefully; they, however, appeared to enjoy the ride very much.

April 30th. Left Mansfield at 4 o'clock this morning; had a delightful ride partly through groves of magnolia and beech to the breakfast stand, Mrs. Gamble's. This is the same beautiful place of which I have spoken before; roses and honeysuckles clinging on oaks and hickory. One beautiful cluster of roses was high up among the branches of an old oak which had lately died, its withered leaves still clinging to their places. I thought of fair young maidens bedecking with wreathes the tomb of some powerful giant. Oh, for peace and such a home as this with my precious wife and little darlings, with $10,000 per annum *and an unwavering faith in the Bible;* this would be paradise enough for me. I got an elegant breakfast here and talked a good deal with a sprightly widow who could not understand how one Confederate dollar could redeem another and make the currency any better. Came to Mr. Allen's to dinner and had divers and sundry vegetables; the first I have had this season; enjoyed them hugely. Reached Shreveport at 5 o'clock; washed and put on some clean clothes; the first in three weeks; got shaved and passed for a gentleman; went to the quartermaster's office and protested against my transportation being paid to Alexandria as the stage company failed to carry me there; met Colonel Bagby, of Sibley's brigade. He was wounded in the Bisland fight; told me that Captain Brownnigg was killed by the bursting of a shell, which killed his horse also. Lieutenant Ochiltree is to introduce me after supper to Captain Rice of Houston, of the First Texas Regiment. I am to consult with him about getting across the river; trust I may not be delayed any longer. Must find a fight on this side if I cannot get across the river. While I am

writing this, my landlady, Mrs. ——— ————, is thundering in my
ears against the Baptists of Shreveport. She says they countenance thieving,
false-swearing, etc. It is now 10 o'clock P.M. I have been uptown; met Captain Walsh Hill and Captain Dave Rice. Hill is just from Richmond and
says it is impossible for me to get across the river. I will start, however,
with Captain Rice tomorrow morning, for Monroe, and see what can be
done. Attended a Baptist prayer meeting tonight; not spiritual enough;
too cold.

May 1st. After breakfast read the Marshall *Republican;* found a very
good speech from Horatio Seymour, Democratic candidate for governor of
New York. Walked about town until I met Captain Rick. Engaged my seat
on the stage for Monroe, Louisiana; found Bulwer's "Strange Story" in Captain Rice's room and read about twenty pages; spent the morning with
Captain Rick and with lieutenants Davis and Eastman; took dinner at the
restaurant; went back home; wrote letters to my dear wife and to Mr.
Carter; walked to the post office, and met Lieutenant Moore; went to the
Veranda and took supper with him; met Hall of El Paso, Myers of Corpus
Christi and Patrick of Leon County, Texas; spent the evening discussing
our prospects of getting across the river.

May 2nd. Got up this morning and wrote a letter to my dear wife before
breakfast; after breakfast walked down to see the *Anne,* the boat we expected to go down the river in, found her a dirty little craft; went to the
quartermaster's office to find out when the boat would leave; he could not
tell for two or three hours yet; returned to the hotel; met Ormsby; he is in
the post office department; he has a thousand pounds of postage stamps
and is on his way to Texas.

I saw a very interesting game of poker between Captain R——— and a
professional gambler; it was twenty dollars ante, and the pile grew fast
and soon reached twenty-five hundred dollars, and everybody went out of
the game except Captain R——— and the professional, who was a very
rough-looking customer, reminding me of the descriptions I have read of
pirates in yellow-covered novels; he was weather-beaten and fierce-looking;
Captain R——— was only about twenty years of age, with a beardless face
as smooth as a woman's. A dispute arose and each man seized the pile
(paper money) with his left hand and drew his pistol with his right; they
rose at arm's length and stood glaring at each other like tigers; one looked
like a black wolf, the other like a spotted leopard; the crowd retired from
the table; it was one of the most fearful and magnificent pictures I ever
saw. They were finally persuaded to lay their pistols and the money on the
table in charge of chosen friends. . . .

May 22nd. Left Raleigh about 9 o'clock yesterday morning. The road
from Raleigh to Weldon is the most crooked and through the most broken

country I ever saw. Every foot of it is over an embankment or through a deep cut. The land along the route is all poor and barren and yet there are some beautiful residences and the people seem to be doing well. How they live I cannot tell. There were occasionally fine apple orchards and clover fields. I had the good fortune to meet up with Mr. Carpenter, a member of the North Carolina Legislature. He was a pleasant companion and had some genuine whiskey, having married the heiress of a distiller. I made also the acquaintance of an old gentleman named Miller, who was on his way to Richmond to see two wounded nephews, one of whom had lost an arm; he also had some whiskey, which he said came from the drug store and must be good. He had also some cakes, good ham and fresh butter, which I enjoyed very much. He is a Baptist and is acquainted with Mr. Lemmond, of Waco, Texas. We reached Weldon about 5 o'clock in the afternoon, and as the cars were not to start until 9 o'clock, I concluded to take a stroll. . . .

May 24th. Left Richmond yesterday about 6:30 o'clock A.M. Found a number of the Texas Brigade and a few of my regiment on the cars and soon became acquainted with them. The trip was monotonous, as usual, until we reached Gordonsville, where the crowd was so great that twenty of us had to stand on the platform. General J. E. B. Stuart was aboard and appeared to be very fond of ladies and flowers. He is of medium size, well formed, fair complexion, blue eyes, whiskers and mustache of sun-burnt reddish color, usually accompanying fair skin. I had quite a pleasant time on the platform watching the attempts of the proscribed to get a seat in the cars and their repulse by the provost guard. The cars were for the accommodation of ladies and commissioned officers. I never knew soldiers of any grade to be put in the same category with women before. I happened, however, to meet Tom Lipscomb, my old college classmate, who is now a major, who managed to get me in under his wing. We had a long talk about Columbia and old college days. He informed me that Lamar Stark, my wife's brother, was a prisoner confined in the Old Capitol in Washington City. We reached Mitchell's Station at 4 o'clock P.M.; walked five miles, a hot walk, to camp on the Rapidan, near Raccoon Ford. My regiment, the Fourth Texas, has a delightful camping place in a grove of large chestnut trees, on a hillside. We have no tents and the ground is hard and rocky, but we are all satisfied, and one day's observation has led me to believe that no army on earth can whip these men. They may be cut to pieces and killed, but routed and whipped, never! I called on Colonel B. F. Carter this morning and had quite a pleasant interview. He is a calm, determined man, and one of the finest officers in the division. Today was the regular time for inspection and review. One barefooted and ragged hero came to Colonel Carter's tent with the inquiry, "Colonel, do you want the barefooted men to turn out today?" to which the Colonel replied negatively,

with a smile. I went out to the review which took place in an open field
about 600 yards from camp. There were some ladies on horseback on the
field. Their presence was cheering and grateful. They were all dressed in
black, as were more than *two-thirds* of the women in the Confederacy. On
returning to camp I called on Major Bass, of the First Texas, and gave him
$25, which I had received for him from Lieutenant Ochiltree, at Shreveport,
Louisiana, to be handed to Bass if I did not need it.

I received two haversacks today, miserably weak and sleazy, made of
thin cotton cloth. I have only taken a change of underwear, towel, soap and
Bible and Milton's "Paradise Lost.". . .

June 8th. We dragged along until 10 o'clock at night and were then
ordered to camp without fires. We slept on the wet ground in a perfect
heap; 10,000 or 12,000 men lying promiscuously on the side of a public
road, like so many tired hounds, was a novel sight, or rather sound, to me.
I slept soundly, except when waked up by the rain falling in my face. At
daylight on Sunday morning we were ordered to form and were marched
back over the same road to our camp near Culpeper, a distance of sixteen
miles. We remained there until morning, when we moved to this place,
about half a mile farther from Culpeper. This marching and counter-marching is what the military authorities call making a demonstration. It is a
tiresome and monotonous business, but if it accomplishes the purpose for
which I left home I will be satisfied.

June 9th. This morning about six o'clock there was a heavy cannonading
towards the Rappahannock. It is now after nine o'clock and the firing still
continues. We have just received orders to form and are now resting in
line ready to move at the word of command. Perhaps I may see my first
battle today or tomorrow—will it be the last?

11

The Fall of Vicksburg

Ulysses S. Grant

I now determined upon a regular siege—to "outcamp the enemy," as it were, and to incur no more losses. The experience of the 22d convinced officers and men that this was best, and they went to work on the defences and approaches with a will. With the navy holding the river, the investment of Vicksburg was complete. As long as we could hold our position the enemy was limited in supplies of food, men and munitions of war to what they had on hand. These could not last always.

The crossing of troops at Bruinsburg commenced April 30th. On the 18th of May the army was in rear of Vicksburg. On the 19th, just twenty days after the crossing, the city was completely invested and an assault had been made: five distinct battles (besides continuous skirmishing) had been fought and won by the Union forces; the capital of the State had fallen and its arsenals, military manufactories and everything useful for military pur-

ULYSSES S. GRANT, *Personal Memoirs*, 2 vols. (New York, 1885), Vol. 1, Chs. xxxvii-xxxix.

Late in October, 1862, Ulysses S. Grant was placed in command of the Department of the Tennessee. Since the early months of the year, he had been growing in stature, in military experience, and in public acclaim. In February he had moved from Cairo southward. He had taken Fort Henry on the Tennessee River with little trouble, and Fort Donelson on the Cumberland with little more. Nashville had fallen without a fight and he had occupied it and begun the work of clearing the rebels out of middle and western Tennessee. In April he had won a desperate victory at Shiloh. After Shiloh General Henry W. Halleck took command of Grant's army and advanced slowly upon Corinth. Late in May, the city fell to the Federal forces. During the summer Grant occupied Memphis and repelled a Confederate effort to retake Corinth. This accomplished, he suggested to Halleck, now in Washington as general-in-chief, that he advance upon Vicksburg, the last Confederate stronghold on the Mississippi River.

During the winter of 1862-63, Grant made a series of efforts to strike Vicksburg. He advanced to Holly Springs, Mississippi, and directed an effort to move toward Vicksburg from the north. He attempted to cut a canal across a peninsula caused by a bend in the river, hoping to divert the river from the city. Finally, he marched his men down the west side of the river to a point south of the city, while Admiral David D. Porter ran the batteries of Vicksburg with gunboats and transports. Then Grant moved eastward, taking Grand Gulf and Port Gibson, capturing Jackson, the capital of Mississippi, and defeating the Confederates at the Battle of Champion's Hill. The Confederate commander, John C. Pemberton, fell back into Vicksburg and prepared to defend the city. Twice, on May 18th and 22d, Grant assaulted Pemberton's works and was defeated.

poses had been destroyed; an average of about one hundred and eighty miles had been marched by the troops engaged; but five days' rations had been issued, and no forage; over six thousand prisoners had been captured, and as many more of the enemy had been killed or wounded; twenty-seven heavy cannon and sixty-one field pieces had fallen into our hands; and four hundred miles of the river, from Vicksburg to Port Hudson, had become ours. The Union force that had crossed the Mississippi River up to this time was less than forty-three thousand men. One division of these, Blair's, only arrived in time to take part in the battle of Champion's Hill, but was not engaged there; and one brigade, Ransom's of McPherson's corps, reached the field after the battle. The enemy had at Vicksburg, Grand Gulf, Jackson, and on the roads between these places, over sixty thousand men. They were in their own country, where no rear guards were necessary. The country is admirable for defence, but difficult for the conduct of an offensive campaign. All their troops had to be met. We were fortunate, to say the least, in meeting them in detail: at Port Gibson, seven or eight thousand; at Raymond, five thousand; at Jackson, from eight to eleven thousand; at Champion's Hill, twenty-five thousand; at the Big Black, four thousand. A part of those met at Jackson were all that was left of those encountered at Raymond. They were beaten in detail by a force smaller than their own, upon their own ground. Our loss up to this time was:

AT	KILLED	WOUNDED	MISSING
Port Gibson..	131	719	25
South Fork Bayou Pierre...............................	....	1	....
Skirmishes, May 3...	1	9	....
Fourteen Mile Creek......................................	6	24	....
Raymond..	66	339	37
Jackson...	42	251	7
Champion's Hill..	410	1,844	187
Big Black..	39	237	3
Bridgeport...	....	1	....
Total..	695	3,425	259

Of the wounded many were but slightly so, and continued on duty. Not half of them were disabled for any length of time.

After the unsuccessful assault of the 22d the work of the regular siege began. Sherman occupied the right starting from the river above Vicksburg, McPherson the centre (McArthur's division now with him) and McClernand the left, holding the road south to Warrenton. Lauman's division arrived at this time and was placed on the extreme left of the line.

In the interval between the assault of the 19th and 22d, roads had been completed from the Yazoo River and Chickasaw Bayou, around the rear of the army, to enable us to bring up supplies of food and ammunition; ground had been selected, and cleared, on which the troops were to be encamped, and tents and cooking utensils were brought up. The troops had been without these from the time of crossing the Mississippi up to this time. All was now ready for the pick and spade. Prentiss and Hurlbut were ordered to send forward every man that could be spared. Cavalry especially was wanted to watch the fords along the Big Black, and to observe Johnston. I knew that Johnston was receiving reinforcements from Bragg, who was confronting Rosecrans in Tennessee. Vicksburg was so important to the enemy that I believed he would make the most strenuous efforts to raise the siege, even at the risk of losing ground elsewhere.

My line was more than fifteen miles long, extending from Haines' Bluff to Vicksburg, thence to Warrenton. The line of the enemy was about seven. In addition to this, having an enemy at Canton and Jackson, in our rear, who was being constantly reinforced, we required a second line of defence facing the other way. I had not troops enough under my command to man these. General Halleck appreciated the situation and, without being asked, forwarded reinforcements with all possible dispatch.

The ground about Vicksburg is admirable for defence. On the north it is about two hundred feet above the Mississippi River at the highest point and very much cut up by the washing rains; the ravines were grown up with cane and underbrush, while the sides and tops were covered with a dense forest. Farther south the ground flattens out somewhat, and was in cultivation. But here, too, it was cut up by ravines and small streams. The enemy's line of defence followed the crest of a ridge from the river north of the city eastward, then southerly around to the Jackson road, full three miles back of the city; thence in a southwesterly direction to the river. Deep ravines of the description given lay in front of these defences. As there is a succession of gullies, cut out by rains along the side of the ridge, the line was necessarily very irregular. To follow each of these spurs with intrenchments, so as to command the slopes on either side, would have lengthened their line very much. Generally therefore, or in many places, their line would run from near the head of one gully nearly straight to the head of another, and an outer work triangular in shape, generally open in the rear, was thrown up on the point; with a few men in this outer work they commanded the approaches to the main line completely.

The work to be done, to make our position as strong against the enemy as his was against us, was very great. The problem was also complicated by our wanting our line as near that of the enemy as possible. We had but four engineer officers with us. Captain Prime, of the Engineer Corps, was the chief, and the work at the beginning was mainly directed by him. His health soon gave out, when he was succeeded by Captain Comstock, also of the Engineer Corps. To provide assistants on such a long line I directed that all officers who had graduated at West Point, where they had necessarily to study military engineering, should in addition to their other duties assist in the work.

The chief quartermaster and the chief commissary were graduates. The chief commissary, now the Commissary-General of the Army, begged off, however, saying that there was nothing in engineering that he was good for unless he would do for a sap-roller. As soldiers require rations while working in the ditches as well as when marching and fighting, and as we would be sure to lose him if he was used as a sap-roller, I let him off. The general is a large man; weighs two hundred and twenty pounds, and is not tall.

We had no siege guns except six thirty-two pounders, and there were none at the west to draw from. Admiral Porter, however, supplied us with a battery of navy-guns of large calibre, and with these, and the field artillery used in the campaign, the siege began. The first thing to do was to get the artillery in batteries where they would occupy commanding positions; then establish the camps, under cover from the fire of the enemy but as near up as possible; and then construct rifle-pits and covered ways, to connect the entire command by the shortest route. The enemy did not harass us much while we were constructing our batteries. Probably their artillery ammunition was short; and their infantry was kept down by our sharpshooters, who were always on the alert and ready to fire at a head whenever it showed itself above the rebel works.

In no place were our lines more than six hundred yards from the enemy. It was necessary, therefore, to cover our men by something more than the ordinary parapet. To give additional protection sand bags, bullet-proof, were placed along the tops of the parapets far enough apart to make loopholes for musketry. On top of these, logs were put. By these means the men were enabled to walk about erect when off duty, without fear of annoyance from sharpshooters. The enemy used in their defence explosive musket-balls, no doubt thinking that, bursting over our men in the trenches, they would do some execution; but I do not remember a single case where a man was injured by a piece of one of these shells. When they were hit and the ball exploded, the wound was terrible. In these cases a solid ball would have hit as well. Their use is barbarous, because they produce increased suffering without any corresponding advantage to those using them.

The enemy could not resort to our method to protect their men, because we had an inexhaustible supply of ammunition to draw upon and used it freely. Splinters from the timber would have made havoc among the men behind.

There were no mortars with the besiegers, except what the navy had in front of the city; but wooden ones were made by taking logs of the toughest wood that could be found, boring them out for six- or twelve-pound shells and binding them with strong iron bands. These answered as coehorns, and shells were successfully thrown from them into the trenches of the enemy.

The labor of building the batteries and intrenching was largely done by the pioneers, assisted by Negroes who came within our lines and who were paid for their work; but details from the troops had often to be made. The work was pushed forward as rapidly as possible, and when an advanced position was secured and covered from the fire of the enemy the batteries were advanced. By the 30th of June there were two hundred and twenty guns in position, mostly light field-pieces, besides a battery of heavy guns belonging to, manned and commanded by the navy. We were now as strong for defence against the garrison of Vicksburg as they were against us; but I knew that Johnston was in our rear, and was receiving constant reinforcements from the east. He had at this time a larger force than I had had at any time prior to the battle of Champion's Hill.

As soon as the news of the arrival of the Union army behind Vicksburg reached the North, floods of visitors began to pour in. Some came to gratify curiosity; some to see sons or brothers who had passed through the terrible ordeal; members of the Christian and Sanitary Associations came to minister to the wants of the sick and the wounded. Often those coming to see a son or brother would bring a dozen or two of poultry. They did not know how little the gift would be appreciated. Many of the soldiers had lived so much on chickens, ducks and turkeys without bread during the march, that the sight of poultry, if they could get bacon, almost took away their appetite. But the intention was good.

Among the earliest arrivals was the Governor of Illinois, with most of the State officers. I naturally wanted to show them what there was of most interest. In Sherman's front the ground was the most broken and most wooded, and more was to be seen without exposure. I therefore took them to Sherman's headquarters and presented them. Before starting out to look at the lines—possibly while Sherman's horse was being saddled—there were many questions asked about the late campaign, about which the North had been so imperfectly informed. There was a little knot around Sherman and another around me, and I heard Sherman repeating, in the most animated manner, what he had said to me when we first looked down from Walnut Hills upon the land below on the 18th of May, adding: "Grant is entitled to every bit of the credit for the campaign; I opposed it. I wrote him a letter about it." But for this speech it is not likely that Sherman's opposition would have ever been heard of. His untiring energy and great efficiency during the campaign entitle him to a full share of all the credit due for its success. He could not have done more if the plan had been his own.

On the 26th of May I sent Blair's division up the Yazoo to drive out a force of the enemy supposed to be between the Big Black and the Yazoo. The country was rich and full of supplies of both food and forage. Blair was instructed to take all of it. The cattle were to be driven in for the use of our army, and the food and forage to be consumed by our troops or destroyed by fire; all bridges were to be destroyed, and the roads rendered as nearly impassable as possible. Blair went forty-five miles and was gone almost a week. His work was effectually done. I requested Porter at this time to send the Marine brigade, a floating nondescript force which had been assigned to his command and which proved very useful, up to Haines' Bluff to hold it until reinforcements could be sent.

On the 26th I also received a letter from Banks, asking me to reinforce him with ten thousand men at Port Hudson. Of course I could not comply with his request, nor did I think he needed them. He was in no danger of an attack by the garrison in his front, and there was no army organizing in his rear to raise the siege.

On the 3d of June a brigade from Hurlbut's command arrived, General Kimball commanding. It was sent to Mechanicsburg, some miles northeast of Haines' Bluff and about midway between the Big Black and the Yazoo. A brigade of Blair's division and twelve hundred cavalry had already, on Blair's return from the Yazoo, been sent to the same place with instructions to watch the crossings of the Big Black River, to destroy the roads in his (Blair's) front, and to gather or destroy all supplies.

On the 7th of June our little force of colored and white troops across the Mississippi, at Milliken's Bend, were attacked by about 3,000 men from Richard Taylor's trans-Mississippi command. With the aid of the gunboats they were speedily repelled. I sent Mower's brigade over with instructions to drive the enemy beyond the Tensas Bayou; and we had no further trouble in that quarter during the siege. This was the first important engagement of the war in which colored troops were under fire. These men were very raw, having all been enlisted since the beginning of the siege, but they behaved well.

On the 8th of June a full division arrived from Hurlbut's command, under General Sooy Smith. It was sent immediately to Haines' Bluff, and General C. C. Washburn was assigned to the general command at that point.

On the 11th a strong division arrived from the Department of the Missouri under General Herron, which was placed on our left. This cut off the last possible chance of communication between Pemberton and Johnston, as it enabled Lauman to close up on McClernand's left while Herron intrenched from Lauman to the water's edge. At this point the water recedes a few hundred yards from the high land. Through this opening no doubt the Confederate commanders had been able to get messengers under the cover of night.

On the 14th General Parke arrived with two divisions of Burnside's corps, and was immediately dispatched to Haines' Bluff. These latter troops —Herron's and Parke's—were the reinforcements already spoken of sent by Halleck in anticipation of their being needed. They arrived none too soon.

I now had about seventy-one thousand men. More than half were disposed across the peninsula, between the Yazoo at Haines' Bluff and the Big Black, with the division of Osterhaus watching the crossings of the latter river farther south and west from the crossing of the Jackson road to Baldwin's ferry and below.

There were eight roads leading into Vicksburg, along which and their immediate sides, our work was specially pushed and batteries advanced; but no commanding point within range of the enemy was neglected.

On the 17th I received a letter from General Sherman and one on the 18th from General McPherson, saying that their respective commands had complained to them of a fulsome, congratulatory order published by General McClernand to the 13th corps, which did great injustice to the other troops engaged in the campaign. This order had been sent North and published, and now papers containing it had reached our camps. The order had not been heard of by me, and certainly not by troops outside of McClernand's command until brought in this way. I at once wrote to McClernand, directing him to send me a copy of this order. He did so, and I at once relieved him from the command of the 13th army corps and ordered him back to Springfield, Illinois. The publication of his order in the press was in violation of War Department orders and also of mine.

On the 22d of June positive information was received that Johnston had crossed the Big Black River for the purpose of attacking our rear, to raise the siege and release Pemberton. The correspondence between Johnston and Pemberton shows that all expectation of holding Vicksburg had by this time passed from Johnston's mind. I immediately ordered Sherman to the command of all the forces from Haines' Bluff to the Big Black River. This amounted now to quite half the troops about Vicksburg. Besides these, Herron and A. J. Smith's divisions were ordered to hold themselves in readiness to reinforce Sherman. Haines' Bluff had been strongly fortified on the land side, and on all commanding points from there to the Big Black at the railroad crossing, batteries had been constructed. The work of connecting by rifle-pits where this was not already done, was an easy task for the troops that were to defend them.

We were now looking west, besieging Pemberton, while we were also looking east to defend ourselves against an expected siege by Johnston. But as against the garrison of Vicksburg we were as substantially protected as they were against us. Where we were looking east and north we were strongly fortified, and on the defensive. Johnston evidently took in the situation and wisely, I think, abstained from making an assault on us because it would simply have inflicted loss on both sides without accomplishing any result. We were strong enough to have taken the offensive against him; but I did not feel disposed to take any risk of losing our hold upon

Pemberton's army, while I would have rejoiced at the opportunity of defending ourselves against an attack by Johnston.

From the 23d of May the work of fortifying and pushing forward our position nearer to the enemy had been steadily progressing. At three points on the Jackson road, in front of Ransom's brigade, a sap was run up to the enemy's parapet, and by the 25th of June we had it undermined and the mine charged. The enemy had countermined, but did not succeed in reaching our mine. At this particular point the hill on which the rebel work stands rises abruptly. Our sap ran close up to the outside of the enemy's parapet. In fact this parapet was also our protection. The soldiers of the two sides occasionally conversed pleasantly across this barrier; sometimes they exchanged the hard bread of the Union soldiers for the tobacco of the Confederates; at other times the enemy threw over hand-grenades, and often our men, catching them in their hands, returned them.

Our mine had been started some distance back down the hill; consequently when it had extended as far as the parapet it was many feet below it. This caused the failure of the enemy in his search to find and destroy it. On the 25th of June at three o'clock, all being ready, the mine was exploded. A heavy artillery fire all along the line had been ordered to open with the explosion. The effect was to blow the top of the hill off and make a crater where it stood. The breach was not sufficient to enable us to pass a column of attack through. In fact, the enemy having failed to reach our mine had thrown up a line farther back, where most of the men guarding that point were placed. There were a few men, however, left at the advance line, and others working in the countermine, which was still being pushed to find ours. All that were there were thrown into the air, some of them coming down on our side, still alive. I remember one colored man, who had been under ground at work when the explosion took place, who was thrown to our side. He was not much hurt, but terribly frightened. Some one asked him how high he had gone up. "Dun no, massa, but t'ink 'bout t'ree mile," was his reply. General Logan commanded at this point and took this colored man to his quarters, where he did service to the end of the siege.

As soon as the explosion took place the crater was seized by two regiments of our troops who were near-by, under cover, where they had been placed for the express purpose. The enemy made a desperate effort to expel them, but failed, and soon retired behind the new line. From here, however, they threw hand-grenades, which did some execution. The compliment was returned by our men, but not with so much effect. The enemy could lay their grenades on the parapet, which alone divided the contestants, and roll them down upon us; while from our side they had to be thrown over the parapet, which was at considerable elevation. During the night we made efforts to secure our position in the crater against the missiles of the enemy, so as to run trenches along the outer base of their parapet, right and left; but the enemy continued throwing their grenades, and brought boxes of field ammunition (shells), the fuses of which they would light with port-fires, and throw them by hand into our ranks. We found it impossible to continue this work. Another mine was consequently started which was exploded on the 1st of July, destroying an entire rebel redan, killing and wounding a considerable number of its occupants and leaving an immense chasm where it stood. No attempt to charge was made this time, the experience of the 25th admonishing us. Our loss in the first affair was about thirty killed and wounded. The enemy must have lost more in the two explosions than we did in the first. We lost none in the second.

From this time forward the work of mining and pushing our position nearer to the enemy was prosecuted with vigor, and I determined to explode no more mines until we were ready to explode a number at different points and assault immediately after. We were up now at three different points, one in front of each corps, to where only the parapet of the enemy divided us.

At this time an intercepted dispatch from Johnston to Pemberton informed me that Johnston intended to make a determined attack upon us in order to relieve the garrison at Vicksburg. I knew the garrison would make no formidable effort to relieve itself. The picket lines were so close to each other—where there was space enough between the lines to post pickets—that the men could converse. On the 21st of June I was informed, through this means, that Pemberton was preparing to escape, by crossing to the Louisiana side under cover of night; that he had employed workmen in making boats for that purpose; that the men had been canvassed to ascertain if they would make an assault on the "Yankees" to cut their way out; that they had refused, and almost mutinied, because their commander would not surrender and relieve their sufferings, and had only been pacified by the assurance that boats enough would be finished in a week to carry them all over. The rebel pickets also said that houses in the city had been pulled down to get material to build these boats with. Afterwards this story was verified: on entering the city we found a large number of very rudely constructed boats.

All necessary steps were at once taken to render such an attempt abortive. Our pickets were doubled; Admiral Porter was notified, so that the river might be more closely watched; material was collected on the west bank of the river to be set on fire and light up the river if the attempt was made; and batteries were established along the levee crossing the peninsula on the Louisiana side. Had the attempt been made, the garrison of Vicksburg would have been drowned, or made prisoners on the Louisiana side. General Richard Taylor was expected on the west bank to co-operate in this movement, I believe, but he did not come, nor could he have done so with a force sufficient to be of service. The Mississippi was now in our possession from its source to its mouth, except in the immediate front of Vicksburg and of Port Hudson. We had nearly exhausted the country, along a line drawn from Lake Providence to opposite Bruinsburg. The roads west were not of a character to draw supplies over for any considerable force.

By the 1st of July our approaches had reached the enemy's ditch at a number of places. At ten points we could move under cover to within from five to one hundred yards of the enemy. Orders were given to make all preparations for assault on the 6th of July. The debouches were ordered widened to afford easy egress, while the approaches were also to be widened to admit the troops to pass through four abreast. Plank, and bags filled with cotton packed in tightly, were ordered prepared, to enable the troops to cross the ditches.

On the night of the 1st of July Johnston was between Brownsville and the Big Black, and wrote Pemberton from there that about the 7th of the month an attempt would be made to create a diversion to enable him to cut his way out. Pemberton was a prisoner before this message reached him.

On July 1st Pemberton, seeing no hope of outside relief, addressed the following letter to each of his four division commanders:

> Unless the siege of Vicksburg is raised, or supplies are thrown in, it will become necessary very shortly to evacuate the place. I see no prospect of the former, and there are many great, if not insuperable obstacles in the way of the latter. You are, therefore, requested to inform me with as little delay as possible, as to the condition of your troops and their ability to make the marches and undergo the fatigues necessary to accomplish a successful evacuation.

Two of his generals suggested surrender, and the other two practically did the same. They expressed the opinion that an attempt to evacuate would fail. Pemberton had previously got a message to Johnston suggesting that he should try to negotiate with me for a release of the garrison with their arms. Johnston replied that it would be a confession of weakness for him to do so; but he authorized Pemberton to use his name in making such an arrangement.

On the 3d about ten o'clock A.M. white flags appeared on a portion of the rebel works. Hostilities along that part of the line ceased at once. Soon two persons were seen coming towards our lines bearing a white flag. They proved to be General Bowen, a division commander, and Colonel Montgomery, aide-de-camp to Pemberton, bearing the following letter to me:

> I have the honor to propose an armistice for —— hours, with the view to arranging terms for the capitulation of Vicksburg. To this end, if agreeable to you, I will appoint three commissioners, to meet a like number to be named by yourself, at such place and hour to-day as you may find convenient. I make this proposition to save the further effusion of blood, which must otherwise be shed to a frightful extent, feeling myself fully able to maintain my position for a yet indefinite period. This communication will be handed you under a flag of truce, by Major-General John S. Bowen.

It was a glorious sight to officers and soldiers on the line where these white flags were visible, and the news soon spread to all parts of the command. The troops felt that their long and weary marches, hard fighting, ceaseless watching by night and day, in a hot climate, exposure to all sorts of weather, to diseases and, worst of all, to the gibes of many Northern papers that came to them saying all their suffering was in vain, that Vicksburg would never be taken, were at last at an end and the Union sure to be saved.

Bowen was received by General A. J. Smith, and asked to see me. I had been a neighbor of Bowen's in Missouri, and knew him well and favorably before the war; but his request was refused. He then suggested that I should meet Pemberton. To this I sent a verbal message saying that, if Pemberton desired it, I would meet him in front of McPherson's corps at three o'clock that afternoon. I also sent the following written reply to Pemberton's letter:

> Your note of this date is just received, proposing an armistice for several hours, for the purpose of arranging terms of capitulation through commissioners, to be appointed, etc. The useless effusion of blood you propose stopping by this course can be ended at any time you may choose, by the unconditional surrender of the city and garrison. Men who have shown so much endurance and courage as those now in Vicksburg, will always challenge the respect of an adversary, and I can assure you will be treated with all the respect due to prisoners of war. I do not favor the proposition of appointing commissioners to arrange the terms of capitulation, because I have no terms other than those indicated above.

At three o'clock Pemberton appeared at the point suggested in my verbal message, accompanied by the same officers who had borne his letter of the morning. Generals Ord, McPherson, Logan and A. J. Smith, and several officers of my staff, accompanied me. Our place of meeting was on a hillside within a few hundred feet of the rebel lines. Near-by stood a stunted oak-tree, which was made historical by the event. It was but a short time before the last vestige of its body, root and limb had disappeared, the fragments taken as trophies. Since then the same tree has furnished as many cords of wood, in the shape of trophies, as "The True Cross."

Pemberton and I had served in the same division during part of the Mexican War. I knew him very well, therefore, and greeted him as an old acquaintance. He soon asked what terms I proposed to give his army if it surrendered. My answer was the same as proposed in my reply to his letter. Pemberton then said, rather snappishly, "The conference might as well end," and turned abruptly as if to leave. I said, "Very well." General Bowen, I saw, was very anxious that the surrender should be consummated. His manner and remarks, while Pemberton and I were talking, showed this. He now proposed that he and one of our generals should have a conference. I had no objection to this, as nothing could be made binding upon me that they might propose. Smith and Bowen accordingly had a conference, during which Pemberton and I, moving a short distance away towards the enemy's lines were in conversation. After a while Bowen suggested that the Confederate army should be allowed to march out with the honors of war, carrying their small arms and field artillery. This was promptly and unceremoniously rejected. The interview here ended, I agreeing, however, to send a letter giving final terms by ten o'clock that night.

Word was sent to Admiral Porter soon after the correspondence with Pemberton commenced, so that hostilities might be stopped on the part of both army and navy. It was agreed on my parting with Pemberton that they should not be renewed until our correspondence ceased.

When I returned to my headquarters I sent for all the corps and division commanders with the army immediately confronting Vicksburg. Half the army was from eight to twelve miles off, waiting for Johnston. I informed them on the contents of Pemberton's letters, of my reply and the substance of the interview, and that I was ready to hear any suggestion; but would hold the power of deciding entirely in my own hands. This was the nearest approach to a "council of war" I ever held. Against the general, and almost unanimous judgment of the council I sent the following letter:

> In conformity with agreement of this afternoon, I will submit the following proposition for the surrender of the City of Vicksburg, public stores, etc. On your accepting the terms proposed, I will march in one division as a guard, and take possession at eight A.M. to-morrow. As soon as rolls can be made out, and paroles be signed by officers and men, you will be allowed to march out of our lines, the officers taking with them their side-arms and clothing, and the field, staff and cavalry officers one horse each. The rank and file will be allowed all their clothing, but no other property. If these conditions are accepted, any amount of rations you may deem necessary can be taken from the stores you now have, and also the necessary cooking utensils for preparing them. Thirty wagons also, counting two two-horse or mule teams as one, will be allowed to transport such articles as cannot be carried along. The same conditions will be allowed to all sick and wounded officers and soldiers as fast as they become able to travel. The paroles for these latter must be signed, however, whilst officers present are authorized to sign the roll of prisoners.

By the terms of the cartel then in force, prisoners captured by either army were required to be forwarded as soon as possible to either Aiken's landing below Dutch Gap on the James River, or to Vicksburg, there to be exchanged, or paroled until they could be exchanged. There was a Confederate commissioner at Vicksburg, authorized to make the exchange. I did not propose to take him prisoner, but to leave him free to perform the functions of his office. Had I insisted upon an unconditional surrender there would have been over thirty thousand men to transport to Cairo, very much to the inconvenience of the army on the Mississippi. Thence the prisoners would have had to be transported by rail to Washington or Baltimore;

thence again by steamer to Aiken's—all at very great expense. At Aiken's they would have had to be paroled, because the Confederates did not have Union prisoners to give in exchange. Then again Pemberton's army was largely composed of men whose homes were in the southwest; I knew many of them were tired of the war and would get home just as soon as they could. A large number of them had voluntarily come into our lines during the siege, and requested to be sent north where they could get employment until the war was over and they could go to their homes.

Late at night I received the following reply to my last letter:

I have the honor to acknowledge the receipt of your communication of this date, proposing terms of capitulation for this garrison and post. In the main your terms are accepted; but, in justice both to the honor and spirit of my troops, manifested in the defence of Vicksburg, I have to submit the following amendments, which, if acceded to by you, will perfect the agreement between us. At ten o'clock A.M. to-morrow, I propose to evacuate the works in and around Vicksburg, and to surrender the city and garrison under my command, by marching out with my colors and arms, stacking them in front of my present lines. After which you will take possession. Officers to retain their side-arms and personal property, and the rights and property of citizens to be respected.

This was received after midnight. My reply was as follows:

I have the honor to acknowledge the receipt of your communication of 3d July. The amendment proposed by you cannot be acceded to in full. It will be necessary to furnish every officer and man with a parole signed by himself, which, with the completion of the roll of prisoners, will necessarily take some time. Again, I can make no stipulations with regard to the treatment of citizens and their private property. While I do not propose to cause them any undue annoyance or loss, I cannot consent to leave myself under any restraint by stipulations. The property which officers will be allowed to take with them will be as stated in my proposition of last evening; that is, officers will be allowed their private baggage and side-arms, and mounted officers one horse each. If you mean by your proposition for each brigade to march to the front of the lines now occupied by it, and stack arms at ten o'clock A.M., and then return to the inside and there remain as prisoners until properly paroled, I will make no objection to it. Should no notification be received of your acceptance of my terms by nine o'clock A.M. I shall regard them as having been rejected, and shall act accordingly. Should these terms be accepted, white flags should be displayed along your lines to prevent such of my troops as may not have been notified from firing upon your men.

Pemberton promptly accepted these terms.

During the siege there had been a good deal of friendly sparring between the soldiers of the two armies, on picket and where the lines were close together. All rebels were known as "Johnnies," all Union troops as "Yanks." Often "Johnny" would call: "Well, Yank, when are you coming into town?" The reply was sometimes: "We propose to celebrate the 4th of July there."

Sometimes it would be: "We always treat our prisoners with kindness and do not want to hurt them"; or, "We are holding you as prisoners of war while you are feeding yourselves." The garrison, from the commanding general down, undoubtedly expected an assault on the fourth. They knew from the temper of their men it would be successful when made; and that would be a greater humiliation than to surrender. Besides it would be attended with severe loss to them.

The Vicksburg paper, which we received regularly through the courtesy of the rebel pickets, said prior to the fourth, in speaking of the "Yankee" boast that they would take dinner in Vicksburg that day, that the best receipt for cooking a rabbit was "First ketch your rabbit." The paper at this time and for some time previous was printed on the plain side of wall paper. The last number was issued on the fourth and announced that we had "caught our rabbit."

I have no doubt that Pemberton commenced his correspondence on the third with a two-fold purpose: first, to avoid an assault, which he knew would be successful, and second, to prevent the capture taking place on the great national holiday, the anniversary of the Declaration of American Independence. Holding out for better terms as he did he defeated his aim in the latter particular.

At the appointed hour the garrison of Vicksburg marched out of their works and formed line in front, stacked arms and marched back in good order. Our whole army present witnessed this scene without cheering. Logan's division, which had approached nearest the rebel works, was the first to march in; and the flag of one of the regiments of his division was soon floating over the court-house. Our soldiers were no sooner inside the lines than the two armies began to fraternize. Our men had had full rations from the time the siege commenced, to the close. The enemy had been suffering, particularly towards the last. I myself saw our men taking bread from their haversacks and giving it to the enemy they had so recently been engaged in starving out. It was accepted with avidity and with thanks.

Pemberton says in his report:

If it should be asked why the 4th of July was selected as the day for surrender, the answer is obvious. I believed that upon that day I should obtain better terms. Well aware of the vanity of our foe, I knew they would attach vast importance to the entrance on the 4th of July into the stronghold of the great river, and that, to gratify their national vanity, they would yield then what could not be extorted from them at any other time.

This does not support my view of his reasons for selecting the day he did for surrendering. But it must be recollected that his first letter asking terms was received about 10 o'clock A.M., July 3d. It then could hardly be expected that it would take twenty-four hours to effect a surrender. He knew that Johnston was in our rear for the purpose of raising the siege, and he naturally would want to hold out as long as he could. He knew his men would not resist an assault, and one was expected on the fourth. In our interview he told me he had rations enough to hold out for some time—my recollection is two weeks. It was this statement that induced me to insert in the terms that he was to draw rations for his men from his own supplies.

On the 4th of July General Holmes, with an army of eight or nine thousand men belonging to the trans-Mississippi department, made an attack upon Helena, Arkansas. He was totally defeated by General Prentiss, who was holding Helena with less than forty-two hundred soldiers. Holmes reported his loss at 1,636, of which 173 were killed; but as Prentiss buried 400, Holmes evidently understated his losses. The Union loss was 57 killed, 127 wounded, and between 30 and 40 missing. This was the last effort on the part of the Confederacy to raise the siege of Vicksburg.

On the third, as soon as negotiations were commenced, I notified Sherman and directed him to be ready to take the offensive against Johnston, drive him out of the State and destroy his army if he could. Steele and Ord were directed at the same time to be in readiness to join Sherman as soon as the surrender took place. Of this Sherman was notified.

I rode into Vicksburg with the troops, and went to the river to exchange congratulations with the navy upon our joint victory. At that time I found that many of the citizens had been living under ground. The ridges upon which Vicksburg is built, and those back to the Big Black, are composed of a deep yellow clay of great tenacity. Where roads and streets are cut through, perpendicular banks are left and stand as well as if composed of stone. The magazines of the enemy were made by running passage-ways into this clay at places where there were deep cuts. Many citizens secured places of safety for their families by carving out rooms in these embankments. A door-way in these cases would be cut in a high bank, starting from the level of the road or street, and after running in a few feet a room of the size required was carved out of the clay, the dirt being removed by the door-way. In some instances I saw where two rooms were cut out, for a single family, with a door-way in the clay wall separating them. Some of these were carpeted and furnished with considerable elaboration. In these the occupants were fully secure from the shells of the navy, which were dropped into the city night and day without intermission.

I returned to my old headquarters outside in the afternoon, and did not move into the town until the sixth. On the afternoon of the fourth I sent Captain Wm. M. Dunn of my staff to Cairo, the nearest point where the telegraph could be reached, with a dispatch to the general-in-chief. It was as follows:

> The enemy surrendered this morning. The only terms allowed is their parole as prisoners of war. This I regard as a great advantage to us at this moment. It saves, probably, several days in the capture, and leaves troops and transports ready for immediate service. Sherman, with a large force, moves immediately

on Johnston, to drive him from the State. I will send troops to the relief of Banks, and return the 9th army corps to Burnside.

This news, with the victory at Gettysburg won the same day, lifted a great load of anxiety from the minds of the President, his Cabinet and the loyal people all over the North. The fate of the Confederacy was sealed when Vicksburg fell. Much hard fighting was to be done afterwards and many precious lives were to be sacrificed; but the *morale* was with the supporters of the Union ever after.

I at the same time wrote to General Banks informing him of the fall and sending him a copy of the terms; also saying I would send him all the troops he wanted to insure the capture of the only foothold the enemy now had on the Mississippi River. General Banks had a number of copies of this letter printed, or at least a synopsis of it, and very soon a copy fell into the hands of General Gardner, who was then in command of Port Hudson. Gardner at once sent a letter to the commander of the National forces saying that he had been informed of the surrender of Vicksburg and telling how the information reached him. He added that if this was true, it was useless for him to hold out longer. General Banks gave him assurances that Vicksburg had been surrendered, and General Gardner surrendered unconditionally on the 9th of July. Port Hudson with nearly 6,000 prisoners, 51 guns, 5,000 small-arms and other stores fell into the hands of the Union forces: from that day to the close of the rebellion the Mississippi River, from its source to its mouth, remained in the control of the National troops.

Pemberton and his army were kept in Vicksburg until the whole could be paroled. The paroles were in duplicate, by organization (one copy for each, Federals and Confederates), and signed by the commanding officers of the companies or regiments. Duplicates were also made for each soldier and signed by each individually, one to be retained by the soldier signing and one to be retained by us. Several hundred refused to sign their paroles, preferring to be sent to the North as prisoners to being sent back to fight again. Others again kept out of the way, hoping to escape either alternative.

Pemberton appealed to me in person to compel these men to sign their paroles, but I declined. It also leaked out that many of the men who had signed their paroles intended to desert and go to their homes as soon as they got out of our lines. Pemberton hearing this, again appealed to me to assist him. He wanted arms for a battalion, to act as guards in keeping his men together while being marched to a camp of instruction, where he expected to keep them until exchanged. This request was also declined. It was precisely what I expected and hoped that they would do. I told him, however, that I would see that they marched beyond our lines in good order. By the eleventh, just one week after the surrender, the paroles were completed and the Confederate garrison marched out. Many deserted, and fewer of them were ever returned to the ranks to fight again than would have been the case had the surrender been unconditional and the prisoners sent to the James River to be paroled.

As soon as our troops took possession of the city, guards were established along the whole line of parapet, from the river above to the river below. The prisoners were allowed to occupy their old camps behind the intrenchments. No restraint was put upon them, except by their own commanders. They were rationed about as our own men, and from our supplies. The men of the two armies fraternized as if they had been fighting for the same cause. When they passed out of the works they had so long and so gallantly defended, between lines of their late antagonists, not a cheer went up, not a remark was made that would give pain. Really, I believe there was a feeling of sadness just then in the breasts of most of the Union soldiers at seeing the dejection of their late antagonists.

The day before the departure the following order was issued:

> Paroled prisoners will be sent out of here to-morrow. They will be authorized to cross at the railroad bridge, and move from there to Edward's Ferry,* and on by way of Raymond. Instruct the commands to be orderly and quiet as these prisoners pass, to make no offensive remarks, and not to harbor any who fall out of ranks after they have passed.

The capture of Vicksburg, with its garrison, ordnance and ordnance stores, and the successful battles fought in reaching them, gave new spirit to the loyal people of the North. New hopes for the final success of the cause of the Union were inspired. The victory gained at Gettysburg, upon the same day, added to their hopes. Now the Mississippi River was entirely in the possession of the National troops; for the fall of Vicksburg gave us Port Hudson at once. The Army of northern Virginia was driven out of Pennsylvania and forced back to about the same ground it occupied in 1861. The Army of the Tennessee united with the Army of the Gulf, dividing the Confederate States completely.

The first dispatch I received from the government after the fall of Vicksburg was in these words:

> I fear your paroling the prisoners at Vicksburg, without actual delivery to a proper agent as required by the seventh article of the cartel, may be construed into an absolute release, and that the men will immediately be placed in the ranks of the enemy. Such has been the case elsewhere. If these prisoners have not been allowed to depart, you will detain them until further orders.

Halleck did not know that they had already been delivered into the hands of Major Watts, Confederate commissioner for the exchange of prisoners.

* Meant Edward's Station.

At Vicksburg 31,600 prisoners were surrendered, together with 172 cannon, about 60,000 muskets and a large amount of ammunition. The small-arms of the enemy were far superior to the bulk of ours. Up to this time our troops at the west had been limited to the old United States flint-lock muskets changed into percussion, or the Belgian musket imported early in the war—almost as dangerous to the person firing it as to the one aimed at—and a few new and improved arms. These were of many different calibres, a fact that caused much trouble in distributing ammunition during an engagement. The enemy had generally new arms which had run the blockade and were of uniform calibre. After the surrender I authorized all colonels whose regiments were armed with inferior muskets, to place them in the stack of captured arms and replace them with the latter. A large number of arms turned in to the Ordnance Department as captured, were thus arms that had really been used by the Union army in the capture of Vicksburg.

In this narrative I have not made the mention I should like of officers, dead and alive, whose services entitle them to special mention. Neither have I made that mention of the navy which its services deserve. Suffice it to say, the close of the siege of Vicksburg found us with an army unsurpassed, in proportion to its numbers, taken as a whole of officers and men. A military education was acquired which no other school could have given. Men who thought a company was quite enough for them to command at the beginning, would have made good regimental or brigade commanders; most of the brigade commanders were equal to the command of a division, and one, Ransom, would have been equal to the command of a corps at least. Logan and Crocker ended the campaign fitted to command independent armies.

General F. P. Blair joined me at Milliken's Bend a full-fledged general, without having served in a lower grade. He commanded a division in the campaign. I had known Blair in Missouri, where I had voted against him in 1858 when he ran for Congress. I knew him as a frank, positive and generous man, true to his friends even to a fault, but always a leader. I dreaded his coming; I knew from experience that it was more difficult to command two generals desiring to be leaders than it was to command one army officered intelligently and with subordination. It affords me the greatest pleasure to record now my agreeable disappointment in respect to his character. There was no man braver than he, nor was there any who obeyed all orders of his superior in rank with more unquestioning alacrity. He was one man as a soldier, another as a politician.

The navy under Porter was all it could be, during the entire campaign. Without its assistance the campaign could not have been successfully made with twice the number of men engaged. It could not have been made at all, in the way it was, with any number of men without such assistance. The most perfect harmony reigned between the two arms of the service.

There never was a request made, that I am aware of, either of the flag-officer or any of his subordinates, that was not promptly complied with.

The campaign of Vicksburg was suggested and developed by circumstances. The elections of 1862 had gone against the prosecution of the war. Voluntary enlistments had nearly ceased and the draft had been resorted to; this was resisted, and a defeat or backward movement would have made its execution impossible. A forward movement to a decisive victory was necessary. Accordingly I resolved to get below Vicksburg, unite with Banks against Port Hudson, make New Orleans a base and, with that base and Grand Gulf as a starting point, move our combined forces against Vicksburg. Upon reaching Grand Gulf, after running its batteries and fighting a battle, I received a letter from Banks informing me that he could not be at Port Hudson under ten days, and then with only fifteen thousand men. The time was worth more than the reinforcements; I therefore determined to push into the interior of the enemy's country.

With a large river behind us, held above and below by the enemy, rapid movements were essential to success. Jackson was captured the day after a new commander had arrived, and only a few days before large reinforcements were expected. A rapid movement west was made; the garrison of Vicksburg was met in two engagements and badly defeated, and driven back into its stronghold and there successfully besieged. It looks now as though Providence had directed the course of the campaign while the Army of the Tennessee executed the decree.

Upon the surrender of the garrison of Vicksburg there were three things that required immediate attention. The first was to send a force to drive the enemy from our rear, and out of the State. The second was to send reinforcements to Banks near Port Hudson, if necessary, to complete the triumph of opening the Mississippi from its source to its mouth to the free navigation of vessels bearing the Stars and Stripes. The third was to inform the authorities at Washington and the North of the good news, to relieve their long suspense and strengthen their confidence in the ultimate success of the cause they had so much at heart.

Soon after negotiations were opened with General Pemberton for the surrender of the city, I notified Sherman, whose troops extended from Haines' Bluff on the left to the crossing of the Vicksburg and Jackson road over the Big Black on the right, and directed him to hold his command in readiness to advance and drive the enemy from the State as soon as Vicksburg surrendered. Steele and Ord were directed to be in readiness to join Sherman in his move against General Johnston, and Sherman was advised of this also. Sherman moved promptly, crossing the Big Black at three different points with as many columns, all concentrating at Bolton, twenty miles west of Jackson.

Johnston heard of the surrender of Vicksburg almost as soon as it occurred, and immediately fell back on Jackson. On the 8th of July Sherman was within ten miles of Jackson and on the 11th was close up to the defences of the city and shelling the town. The siege was kept up until the morning of the 17th, when it was found that the enemy had evacuated during the night. The weather was very hot, the roads dusty and the water bad. Johnston destroyed the roads as he passed and had so much the start that pursuit was useless; but Sherman sent one division, Steele's, to Brandon, fourteen miles east of Jackson.

The National loss in the second capture of Jackson was less than one thousand men, killed, wounded and missing. The Confederate loss was probably less, except in captured. More than this number fell into our hands as prisoners.

Medicines and food were left for the Confederate wounded and sick who had to be left behind. A large amount of rations was issued to the families that remained in Jackson. Medicine and food were also sent to Raymond for the destitute families as well as the sick and wounded, as I thought it only fair that we should return to these people some of the articles we had taken while marching through the country. I wrote to Sherman: "Impress upon the men the importance of going through the State in an orderly manner, abstaining from taking anything not absolutely necessary for their subsistence while travelling. They should try to create as favorable an impression as possible upon the people." Provisions and forage, when called for by them, were issued to all the people, from Bruinsburg to Jackson and back to Vicksburg, whose resources had been taken for the supply of our army. Very large quantities of groceries and provisions were so issued.

Sherman was ordered back to Vicksburg, and his troops took much the same position they had occupied before—from the Big Black to Haines' Bluff.

Having cleaned up about Vicksburg and captured or routed all regular Confederate forces for more than a hundred miles in all directions, I felt that the troops that had done so much should be allowed to do more before the enemy could recover from the blow he had received, and while important points might be captured without bloodshed. I suggested to the general-in-chief the idea of a campaign against Mobile, starting from Lake Pontchartrain. Halleck preferred another course. The possession of the trans-Mississippi by the Union forces seemed to possess more importance in his mind than almost any campaign east of the Mississippi. I am well aware that the President was very anxious to have a foothold in Texas, to stop the clamor of some of the foreign governments which seemed to be seeking a pretext to interfere in the war, at least so far as to recognize belligerent rights to the Confederate States. This, however, could have been easily done without wasting troops in western Louisiana and eastern Texas, by sending a garrison at once to Brownsville on the Rio Grande.

Halleck disapproved of my proposition to go against Mobile, so that I was obliged to settle down and see myself put again on the defensive as

I had been a year before in west Tennessee. It would have been an easy thing to capture Mobile at the time I proposed to go there. Having that as a base of operations, troops could have been thrown into the interior to operate against General Bragg's army. This would necessarily have compelled Bragg to detach in order to meet this fire in his rear. If he had not done this the troops from Mobile could have inflicted inestimable damage upon much of the country from which his army and Lee's were yet receiving their supplies. I was so much impressed with this idea that I renewed my request later in July and again about the 1st of August, and proposed sending all the troops necessary, asking only the assistance of the navy to protect the debarkation of troops at or near Mobile. I also asked for a leave of absence to visit New Orleans, particularly if my suggestion to move against Mobile should be approved. Both requests were refused. So far as my experience with General Halleck went it was very much easier for him to refuse a favor than to grant one. But I did not regard this as a favor. It was simply in line of duty, though out of my department.

The general-in-chief having decided against me, the depletion of an army, which had won a succession of great victories, commenced, as had been the case the year before after the fall of Corinth when the army was sent where it would do the least good. By orders, I sent to Banks a force of 4,000 men; returned the 9th corps to Kentucky and, when transportation had been collected, started a division of 5,000 men to Schofield in Missouri, where Price was raiding the State. I also detached a brigade under Ransom to Natchez, to garrison that place permanently. This latter move was quite fortunate as to the time when Ransom arrived there. The enemy happened to have a large number, about 5,000 head, of beef cattle there on the way from Texas to feed the eastern armies, and also a large amount of munitions of war which had probably come through Texas from the Rio Grande and which were on the way to Lee's and other armies in the east.

The troops that were left with me around Vicksburg were very busily and unpleasantly employed in making expeditions against guerrilla bands and small detachments of cavalry which infested the interior, and in destroying mills, bridges and rolling stock on the railroads. The guerrillas and cavalry were not there to fight but to annoy, and therefore disappeared on the first approach of our troops.

The country back of Vicksburg was filled with deserters from Pemberton's army and, it was reported, many from Johnston's also. The men determined not to fight again while the war lasted. Those who lived beyond the reach of the Confederate army wanted to get to their homes. Those who did not, wanted to get North where they could work for their support till the war was over. Besides all this there was quite a peace feeling, for the time being, among the citizens of that part of Mississippi, but this feeling soon subsided. It is not probable that Pemberton got off with over

4,000 of his army to the camp where he proposed taking them, and these were in a demoralized condition.

On the 7th of August I further depleted my army by sending the 13th corps, General Ord commanding, to Banks. Besides this I received orders to co-operate with the latter general in movements west of the Mississippi. Having received this order I went to New Orleans to confer with Banks about the proposed movement. All these movements came to naught.

During this visit I reviewed Banks' army a short distance above Carroll-ton. The horse I rode was vicious and but little used, and on my return to New Orleans ran away and, shying at a locomotive in the street, fell, probably on me. I was rendered insensible, and when I regained conscious-ness I found myself in a hotel near-by with several doctors attending me. My leg was swollen from the knee to the thigh, and the swelling, almost to the point of bursting, extended along the body up to the arm-pit. The pain was almost beyond endurance. I lay at the hotel something over a week without being able to turn myself in bed. I had a steamer stop at the nearest point possible, and was carried to it on a litter. I was then taken to Vicks-burg, where I remained unable to move for some time afterwards.

While I was absent General Sherman declined to assume command because, he said, it would confuse the records; but he let all the orders be made in my name, and was glad to render any assistance he could. No orders were issued by my staff, certainly no important orders, except upon consultation with and approval of Sherman.

On the 13th of September, while I was still in New Orleans, Halleck telegraphed to me to send all available forces to Memphis and thence to Tuscumbia, to co-operate with Rosecrans for the relief of Chattanooga. On the 15th he telegraphed again for all available forces to go to Rosecrans. This was received on the 27th. I was still confined to my bed, unable to rise from it without assistance; but I at once ordered Sherman to send one division to Memphis as fast as transports could be provided. The division of McPherson's corps, which had got off and was on the way to join Steele in Arkansas, was recalled and sent, likewise, to report to Hurlbut at Memphis. Hurlbut was directed to forward these two divisions with two others from his own corps at once, and also to send any other troops that might be returning there. Halleck suggested that some good man, like Sherman or McPherson, should be sent to Memphis to take charge of the troops going east. On this I sent Sherman, as being, I thought, the most suitable person for an independent command, and besides he was entitled to it if it had to be given to anyone. He was directed to take with him another division of his corps. This left one back, but having one of McPher-son's divisions he had still the equivalent.

Before the receipt by me of these orders the battle of Chickamauga had been fought and Rosecrans forced back into Chattanooga. The Administration, as well as the general-in-chief, was nearly frantic at the situation of affairs there. Mr. Charles A. Dana, an officer of the War Department, was sent to Rosecrans' headquarters. I do not know what his instructions were, but he was still in Chattanooga when I arrived there at a later period.

It seems that Halleck suggested that I should go to Nashville as soon as able to move and take general direction of the troops moving from the west. I received the following dispatch dated October 3d: "It is the wish of the Secretary of War that as soon as General Grant is able he will come to Cairo and report by telegraph." I was still very lame, but started without delay.

12

A Glimpse at the Secret Service

Charles A. Dana

After Early's invaders had retired and quiet was restored, I went to Mr. Stanton for new orders. As there was no probability of an immediate change in the situation before Petersburg, the Secretary did not think it necessary for me to go back to Grant, but preferred that I remain in the department, helping with the routine work.

Much of my time at this period was spent in investigating charges against defaulting contractors and dishonest agents, and in ordering arrests of persons suspected of disloyalty to the Government. I assisted, too, in supervising the spies who were going back and forth between the lines. Among these I remember one, a sort of peddler—whose name I will call Morse—who traveled between Washington and Richmond. When he went down it was in the character of a man who had entirely hoodwinked the Washington authorities, and who, in spite of them, or by some corruption or other, always brought with him into the Confederate lines something that the people wanted—dresses for the ladies or some little luxury that they couldn't get otherwise. The things that he took with him were always supervised by one of our agents before he went away. When he came back he brought us in exchange a lot of valuable information. He was doubtless a spy on both sides; but as we got a great deal of information, which could be had in no other way, about the strength of the Confederate armies, and the preparations and movements of the enemy, we allowed the thing to go on. The man really did good service for us that summer, and, as we were frequently able to verify by other means the important information he brought, we had a great deal of confidence in him.

CHARLES A. DANA, *Recollections of the Civil War* (New York, 1898), Ch. xvii.
 Not all of military affairs consisted of camping and campaigning. Romantic deeds of daring attracted wide attention and filled the contemporary press and later reminiscences with wondrous tales. Equally daring and dangerous were the unsung and unheralded deeds of spies who gathered information upon which campaigns might be based. Charles A. Dana was an Assistant Secretary of War whose major assignments were those of a "troubleshooter"—hurrying to various theaters of war and gathering on-the-spot information and impressions for the War Department.

Early in October, 1864, he came back from Richmond, and, as usual, went to Baltimore to get his outfit for the return trip. When he presented himself again in Washington, the chief detective of the War Department, Colonel Baker, examined his goods carefully, but this time he found that Morse had many things that we could not allow him to take. Among his stuff were uniforms and other military goods, and all this, of course, was altogether contraband to be passed. We had all his bills, telling where he had bought these things in Baltimore. They amounted to perhaps twenty-five thousand dollars, or more. So we confiscated the contraband goods and put Morse in prison.

But the merchants in Baltimore were partners in his guilt, and Secretary Stanton declared he would arrest every one of them and put them in prison until the affair could be straightened up. He turned the matter over to me then, as he was going to Fort Monroe for a few days. I immediately sent

Assistant-Adjutant-General Lawrence to Baltimore with orders to see that all persons implicated were arrested. Lawrence telegraphed me, on October 16th, that the case would involve the arrest of two hundred citizens. I reported to the Secretary, but he was determined to go ahead. The next morning ninety-seven of the leading citizens of Baltimore were arrested, brought to Washington, and confined in Old Capitol Prison, principally in solitary cells. There was great satisfaction among the Union people of the town, but great indignation among Southern sympathizers. Presently a deputation from Baltimore came over to see President Lincoln. It was an outrage, they said; the gentlemen arrested were most respectable merchants and faultless citizens, and they demanded that they all be set instantly at liberty and damages paid them. Mr. Lincoln sent the deputation over to the War Department, and Mr. Stanton, who had returned by this time, sent for me. "All Baltimore is coming here," he said. "Sit down and hear the discussion."

They came in, the bank presidents and boss merchants of Baltimore—there must have been at least fifty million dollars represented in the deputation—and sat down around the fire in the Secretary's office. Presently they began to make their speeches, detailing the circumstances and the wickedness of this outrage. There was no ground for it, they said, no justification. After half a dozen of them had spoken, Mr. Stanton asked one after another if he had anything more to say, and they all said no. Then Stanton began, and delivered one of the most eloquent speeches that I ever heard. He described the beginning of the war, for which, he said, there was no justification; being beaten in an election was no reason for destroying the Government. Then he went on to the fact that half a million of our young men had been laid in untimely graves by this conspiracy of the slave interest. He outlined the whole conspiracy in the most solemn and impressive terms, and then he depicted the offense that this man Morse, aided by these several merchants, had committed. "Gentlemen," he said, "if you would like to examine the bills of what he was taking to the enemy, here they are."

When Stanton had finished, these gentlemen, without answering a word, got up and one by one went away. That was the only speech I ever listened to that cleared out the entire audience.

Early in the winter of 1863-64 a curious thing happened in the secret service of the War Department. Some time in the February or March before, a slender and prepossessing young fellow, between twenty-two and twenty-six apparently, had applied at the War Department for employment as a spy within the Confederate lines.

The main body of the Army of Northern Virginia was then lying at Gordonsville, and the headquarters of the Army of the Potomac were at Culpeper Courthouse. General Grant had not yet come from the West to take command of the momentous campaign which afterward opened with his movement into the Wilderness on the 5th of May.

The young man who sought this terrible service was well dressed and intelligent, and professed to be animated by motives purely patriotic. He was a clerk in one of the departments. All that he asked was that he should have a horse and an order which would carry him safely through the Federal lines, and, in return, he undertook to bring information from General Lee's army and from the Government of the Confederacy in Richmond. He understood perfectly the perilous nature of the enterprise he proposed.

Finding that the applicant bore a good character in the office where he was employed, it was determined to accept his proposal. He was furnished with a horse, an order that would pass him through the Union lines, and also, I believe, with a moderate sum of money, and then he departed. Two or three weeks later he reported at the War Department. He had been in Gordonsville and Richmond, had obtained the confidence of the Confederate authorities, and was the bearer of a letter from Mr. Jefferson Davis to Mr. Clement C. Clay, the agent of the Confederate Government in Canada, then known to be stationed at St. Catherine's, not far from Niagara Falls. Mr. Clay had as his official associate Jacob Thompson, of Mississippi, who had been Secretary of the Interior in the Cabinet of President Buchanan, and, like Mr. Clay, had been serving the Confederate Government ever since its organization.

The letter from Mr. Davis the young man exhibited, but only the outside of the envelope was examined. The address was in the handwriting of the Confederate chief, and the statement of our young adventurer that it was merely a letter of recommendation advising Messrs. Clay and Thompson that they might repose confidence in the bearer, since he was ardently devoted to the Confederate cause and anxious to serve the great purpose that it had in view, appeared entirely probable; so the young man was allowed to proceed to Niagara Falls and Canada. He made some general report on the condition of the rebel army at Gordonsville, but it was of no particular value, except that in its more interesting feature it agreed with our information from other sources.

Our spy was not long in returning from St. Catherine's with a dispatch which was also allowed to pass unopened, upon his assurance that it contained nothing of importance. In this way he went back and forward from Richmond to St. Catherine's once or twice. We supplied him with money to a limited extent, and also with one or two more horses. He said that he got some money from the Confederates, but had not thought it prudent to accept from them anything more than very small sums, since his professed zeal for the Confederate cause forbade his receiving anything for his traveling expenses beyond what was absolutely necessary.

During the summer of 1864 the activity of Grant's campaign, and the fighting which prevailed all along the line, somewhat impeded our young man's expeditions, but did not stop them. All his subsequent dispatches, however, whether coming from Richmond or from Canada, were regularly brought to the War Department, and were opened, and in every case a copy of them was kept. As it was necessary to break the seals and destroy the envelopes in opening them, there was some difficulty in sending them forward in what should appear to be their original wrappers. Coming from Canada, the paper employed was English, and there was a good deal of trouble in procuring paper of the same appearance. I remember also that one important dispatch, which was sealed with Mr. Clay's seal, had to be delayed somewhat while we had an imitation seal engraved. But these delays were easily accounted for at Richmond by the pretense that they had been caused by accidents upon the road and by the necessity of avoiding the Federal pickets. At any rate, the confidence of the Confederates in our agent and in theirs never seemed to be shaken by any of those occurrences. Finally our dispatch bearer reported one day at the War Department with a document which, he said, was of extraordinary consequence. It was found to contain an account of a scheme for setting fire to New York and Chicago by means of clock-work machines that were to be placed in several of the large hotels and places of amusement—particularly Barnum's Museum in New York—and to be set off simultaneously, so that the fire department in each place would be unable to attend to the great number of calls that would be made upon it on account of these Confederate conflagrations in so many different quarters, and thus these cities might be greatly damaged, or even destroyed.

This dispatch was duly sealed up again and was taken to Richmond, and a confidential officer was at once sent to New York to warn General Dix, who was in command there, of the Confederate project. The general was very unwilling to believe that any such design could be seriously entertained, and Mr. John A. Kennedy, then superintendent of the police, was equally incredulous. But the Secretary of War was peremptory in his orders, and when the day for the incendiary attempt arrived both the military and police made every preparation to prevent the threatened catastrophe. The officer who went from Washington was lodged in the St. Nicholas Hotel, one of the large establishments that were to be set on fire, and while he was washing his hands in the evening, preparatory to going to dinner, a fire began burning in the room next to his. It was promptly put out, and was found to be caused by a clock-work apparatus which had been left in that room by a lodger who had departed some hours before. Other fires likewise occurred. In every instance these fires were extinguished without much damage and without exciting any considerable public attention, thanks to the precautions that had been taken in consequence of the warning derived from Mr. Clay's dispatch to Mr. Benjamin in Richmond. The plan of setting fire to Chicago proved even more abortive; I do not remember that any report of actual burning was received from there.

Later in the fall, after the military operations had substantially terminated for the season, a dispatch was brought from Canada, signed by Mr. Clay, and addressed to Mr. Benjamin, as Secretary of State in the Confederate Government, conveying the information that a new and really formidable military expedition against northern Vermont—particularly against Burlington, if I am not mistaken—had been organized and fitted out in Canada, and would make its attack as soon as practicable. This was after the well-known attempt upon St. Albans and Lake Champlain, on October 19, 1864, and promised to be much more injurious. The dispatch reached Washington one Sunday morning, and was brought to the War Department as usual, but its importance in the eyes of the Confederate agents had led to its being prepared for transportation with uncommon care. It was placed between two thicknesses of the pair of re-enforced cavalry trousers which the messenger wore, and sewed up so that when he was mounted it was held between his thigh and the saddle.

Having been carefully ripped out and opened, it was immediately carried to Mr. Stanton, who was confined to his house by a cold. He read it. "This is serious," he said. "Go over to the White House and ask the President to come here." Mr. Lincoln was found dressing to go to church, and he was soon driven to Mr. Stanton's house. After discussing the subject in every aspect, and considering thoroughly the probability that to keep the dispatch would put an end to communications by this channel, they determined that it must be kept. The conclusive reason for this step was that it established beyond question the fact that the Confederates, while sheltering themselves behind the British Government in Canada, had organized and fitted out a military expedition against the United States. But while the dispatch afforded evidence that could not be gainsaid, the mere possession of it was not sufficient. It must be found in the possession of the Confederate dispatch bearer, and the circumstances attending its capture must be established in such a manner that the British Foreign Office would not be able to dispute the genuineness of the document. "We must have this paper for Seward," said Mr. Lincoln. "As for the young man, get him out of the scrape if you can."

Accordingly, the paper was taken back to the War Department and sewed up again in the trousers whence it had been taken three hours before. The bearer was instructed to start at dusk on the road which he usually took in passing through the lines, to be at a certain tavern outside of Alexandria at nine o'clock in the evening, and to stop there to water his horse. Then information was sent through Major-General Augur, commandant of Washington and the surrounding region, to Colonel Henry H. Wells, then provost-marshal-general of the defenses south of the Potomac, stationed at Alexandria, directing him to be at this tavern at nine o'clock in the evening, and to arrest a Confederate dispatch bearer, concerning whom authentic information had been received at the War Department, and whose description was furnished for his (Wells's) guidance. He was to do the messenger no injury, but to make sure of his person and of all papers that he might have upon him, and to bring him under a sufficient guard directly to the War Department. And General Augur was directed to be present there, in order to assist in the examination of the prisoner, and to verify any dispatches that might be found.

Just before midnight a carriage drove up to the door of the War Department with a soldier on the box and two soldiers on the front seat within, while the back seat was occupied by Colonel Wells and the prisoner. Of course, no one but the two or three who had been in the secret was aware that this gentleman had walked quietly out of the War Department only a few hours previously, and that the paper which was the cause of the entire ceremony had been sewed up in his clothes just before his departure. Colonel Wells reported that, while the prisoner had offered no resistance, he was very violent and outrageous in his language, and that he boasted fiercely of his devotion to the Confederacy and his detestation of the Union. During the examination which now followed he said nothing except to answer a few questions, but his bearing—patient, scornful, undaunted—was that of an incomparable actor. If Mr. Clay and Mr. Benjamin had been present, they would have been more than ever certain that he was one of their noblest young men. His hat, boots, and other articles of his clothing were taken off one by one. The hat and boots were first searched, and finally the dispatch was found in his trousers and taken out. Its nature and the method of its capture were stated in a memorandum which was drawn up on the spot and signed by General Augur and Colonel Wells and one or two other officers who were there for the purpose, and then the dispatch bearer himself was sent off to the Old Capitol Prison.

The dispatch, with the documents of verification, was handed over to Mr. Seward for use in London, and a day or two afterward the warden of

the Old Capitol Prison was directed to give the dispatch bearer an opportunity of escaping, with a proper show of attempted prevention. One afternoon the spy walked into my office. "Ah!" said I, "you have run away."

"Yes, sir," he answered.

"Did they shoot at you?"

"They did, and didn't hit me; but I didn't think that would answer the
purpose. So I shot myself through the arm."

He showed me the wound. It was through the fleshy part of the forearm,
and due care had been taken not to break any bones. A more deliberate and
less dangerous wound could not be, and yet it did not look trivial.

He was ordered to get away to Canada as promptly as possible, so that
he might explain the loss of his dispatch before it should become known
there by any other means. An advertisement offering two thousand dollars
for his recapture was at once inserted in the New York *Herald,* the Pittsburgh *Journal,* and the Chicago *Tribune.* No one ever appeared to claim
the reward, but in about a week the escaped prisoner returned from Canada
with new dispatches that had been intrusted to him. They contained
nothing of importance, however. The wound in his arm had borne testimony in his favor, and the fact that he had hurried through to St. Catherine's without having it dressed was thought to afford conclusive evidence
of his fidelity to the Confederate cause.

The war was ended soon after this adventure, and, as his services had
been of very great value, a new place, with the assurance of lasting employment, was found for the young man in one of the bureaus of the War
Department. He did not remain there very long, however, and I don't know
what became of him. He was one of the cleverest creatures I ever saw. His
style of patriotic lying was sublime; it amounted to genius.

13
Spiritual Welfare

IN THE NORTH
Horatio B. Hackett

Scattered over the battlefields and camping-grounds of the present war are consecrated spots, Bethels, every one of them sacred to some soul who there held sweet communion with God. A laborer in the work of the Christian Commission gives the following account of a prayer-meeting which was organized and held for a time, in the churchyard of a village, near Fredericksburg, in Virginia.

Prayer-meetings (he says) had been held previously every evening, and many souls, I trust, converted to God. In the Seventh Michigan, especially, a glorious work commenced erelong, and I trust that it has been carried on by the Holy Spirit of God, and that eternity will reveal glorious results which God wrought for the souls of these earnest, truth-seeking men. Before leaving them, I assisted in organizing a prayer-meeting of their own. Nine or ten, sometimes more, faithful young men, retired every evening after roll-call to their little retreat, and there they prayed together, and talked together to strengthen each other in faith and love. That retreat was the village churchyard. Around a broad, flat, old-fashioned tombstone, as an altar, this faithful little band met, and God met with them and blessed them. . . .

These faithful, Christian young men did not forget their prayer-meeting when the fortunes of war called them away from this chosen spot. They still met as often as the evening came. On one of the evenings during the battle of Gettysburg, when the hour arrived for the meeting, some of the wonted attendants were present, but it was found that some of the most devoted had that day fallen as sacrifices on the altar of their country. They

HORATIO B. HACKETT, *Christian Memorials of the War* (Boston, 1864), Ch. v.
The moral and religious life of the soldiers received full attention from churches who supplied chaplains, distributed Bibles and tracts, and sent evangelists to the armies. In the North the United States Christian Commission co-ordinated the work of Protestant denominations and often ministered to the physical needs of soldiers in hospitals. The South had no Christian Commission, but the spiritual welfare of the Confederate soldiers received full attention. A revival spread through the Southern armies.

had fallen, but they fell with their armor on, bright and polished. They died exemplifying the power of that faith which had sustained and supported them during the weeks they had lived as Christians.

A gratifying feature which religious effort in behalf of the soldiers assumed during the progress of the war, was the formation, in some of the regiments, of temporary churches. These churches (wrote one of the promoters of this measure) are designed to embrace those who are already professors of religion, as well as new converts. In these they find a spiritual home in which they can receive the benefits of church care and fellowship. As in the camp, the tent is the soldier's substitute for his ordinary dwelling, so this church is the soul's tabernacle, in the absence of his regular and permanent sanctuary.

A church in the camp! What a novelty! With it is connected the prayer-meeting, the Bible-class, the singing of God's praise, the preaching of the Word, the rite of baptism, the communion of the saints, and all those sacred services which bless communities at home. We hail the movement as a happy device of Christian enterprise. Faithful, efficient chaplains are needed; but, in the hands of such men, an institution like this must be a great blessing to those whom it is designed to benefit.

A minister of the gospel sits beside me (writes Mr. Alvord, in one of his letters), who has just related to me a scene that took place last Sunday under his own eye.

A young man who had been converted in their meetings was received to the camp church. The chaplain had been preaching to at least eight hundred of the regiment, and, at the close of the service, this young man was asked to give some account of his experience and hopes. He rose to his feet, and was stepping forward to a place where he could be heard. At that moment, most unexpectedly, a group of soldiers joined him, and all pressed forward together to the stand. They were Christian men, and they wished in this way to uphold their comrade, and show themselves on the side of Christ. The candidate was then admitted into the church in due form, while the regiment looked on, and showed by their earnest attention how deeply the scene had interested them.

"The major," said the chaplain, "though he did not profess to be a pious man, grasped me by the arm, after the service, saying with deep feeling, 'Never did I witness so impressive a scene as that!'"

The following narrative was written by the Reverend Dr. Marks, chaplain of the Sixty-third Pennsylvania Volunteers.

It must ever be a source of relief and hope to thousands of Christian parents, whose sons have gone into the army without any avowed interest in religion, and have been slain in battle, or have died in hospitals, that their lost ones had an opportunity to witness such scenes as this narrative describes; and that the symbol of the divine presence rested so visibly here and there on the tents in which they sojourned. We need not put away from us the consolation of thinking that many of those who have been thus cut off may have been reached by the silent operation of such influences, and fitted for their end, though they may not have left the recorded proof of their acceptance of the terms of mercy.

The Sixty-third Regiment of Pennsylvania Volunteers entered the service of the Government on the 25th of August, 1861, at Pittsburgh. We reached Washington about the first of September, and very soon entered General Heintzelman's division, and were stationed on the Mt. Vernon road, about three miles from Alexandria.

The first Sabbath after the chaplain arrived in camp, he noticed unusual solemnity, and on that day gave away more than three hundred Testaments to those who called at his tent. On the next Sabbath, he gave away, in the same manner, more than three hundred of your hymn-books; and from that time, has distributed every week from five hundred to a thousand religious papers, small books and tracts. These were uniformly read, and deep and permanent religious impressions were produced.

We were for three months without any shelter or tent for religious worship; but uniformly had two services on the Sabbath day, and one or more prayer-meetings during the week.

In the month of December, the heart of the chaplain was cheered by more than one soldier coming to him, confessing his sins, and asking prayers. Others came to the chaplain earnestly desiring religious instruction, and professing some interest in the question of salvation.

About the last of January, through the kindness of some Christian friends in Pittsburgh, I was enabled to purchase a tent for worship. This we immediately pitched, and on a rainy night, the mud fabulously deep in camp, we met in the new tent and, without fire and almost without light, stood up and dedicated it to God.

The following Sabbath was one of marked solemnity. Many of the soldiers were deeply moved. The chaplain announced, during the service, that he would that day take measures to organize a church in the regiment, and invited all Christians to unite with the new association, and thus aid to advance the cause of the gospel in the army. Many gave their names that day, and rejoiced greatly in the privilege of "standing up for Jesus." The evening was marked by still greater solemnity, and many requested the privilege of enrolling themselves with the people of God.

On Monday morning, I commenced going from tent to tent, talking to the soldiers and officers in each, and praying in several. I found that the Lord had gone before me, and that it was wholly his work. Many had been deeply impressed by recent letters from home. There had been excited in western Pennsylvania a great interest for the moral and spiritual welfare of the army. The papers abounded with appalling details descriptive of the crimes, vices, and impiety of the troops upon the Potomac. These accounts, when read, excited the deepest concern in many hearts, and led to letters of entreaty, warning, and earnest appeal. No doubt these letters were often wet with tears and sent with many prayers.

During the week, the religious solemnity increased. We held meetings every morning, and again visited from tent to tent. I was nowhere repulsed, but in many places received kindly, and often with gratitude. Often, the mess of a tent would confess their sins, and promise to each other a better life. While I was talking with one of these companies of soldiers, one of the mess, with tears in his eyes, lifted from under a pile of books and clothes a pack of cards, and put them, with the approbation of all, into the fire.

During this week, I was, for many hours each day, conversing and praying with those who came to seek advice and help. We celebrated the Lord's Supper on the morning of the 3rd of February. The day was most beautiful and balmy; never had there been such quiet and stillness in camp. It was like a Sabbath in one of the most orderly of our villages. We had a most delightful prayer-meeting at nine o'clock, and commenced more public services at half-past ten.

First, after singing and prayer, I read the Articles of Faith, which were the basis of union, then administered baptism to six young men, and read the names of those who desired to associate themselves as a church in the army. There were one hundred and fifty-nine names, among which forty-six were the names of those who had been recently converted, and confessed Christ for the first time.

There were, likewise, thirteen persons who placed themselves under the care and teaching of the church as catechumens or inquirers. Several of these, I have no doubt, will soon be confirmed in the love of God.

In the afternoon, I preached at the hospital, during which there was a most precious prayer-meeting held in the tent, and many spoke, and with the deepest emotion told of the new joys they felt. Sabbath night I preached on the words, "My Spirit shall not always strive with man." Five or six remained after preaching for religious conversation and prayer. Thus ended the most memorable day in the life of many, and one that must have a most important influence on our future in time and eternity.

IN THE SOUTH

William W. Bennett

The preparations on both sides in the early spring of 1864 gave promise of a year of great battles. After the repeated failures of six successive Federal generals to take Richmond, General Grant was appointed to the command of all the Federal armies, and he fixed his headquarters with the Army of the Potomac. General Lee confronted him with the Army of northern Virginia. At Dalton, Georgia, was General Johnston with an admirably equipped army, and opposed to him were the gathering thousands of Federals led against him by General Sherman in the memorable campaign that ended with the capture of Atlanta.

At other places the opposing powers brought smaller armies to confront each other. There were few in the South that did not feel that this year's work must decide the great question at issue. The Confederate Government made another call for men, embracing those between seventeen and eighteen and forty-five and fifty. The strictest measures were adopted for the purpose of securing the service of every available man. All absentees were recalled to the ranks, and the different armies brought up to the last degree of strength. The year 1864 was to witness the battles of the giants.

But in the midst of all this preparation for the hideous work of blood, the revival rather increased than decreased in power. The deep and solemn conviction that great events were impending turned the thoughts of the people to God. From the Confederate Congress came a call to humiliation, fasting, and prayer. The people in the armies and at home were urged to call upon God, "That He would so inspire our armies and their leaders with wisdom, courage, and perseverance, and so manifest Himself in the greatness of His goodness and the majesty of His power, that we may be safely and successfully led through the war to which we are being subjected, to the attainment of an honorable peace; so that while we enjoy the blessings of a free and happy government we may ascribe to Him the honor and the glory of our prosperity and independence."

The Southern people strove to maintain a calm trust in God in the presence of their great danger. Even in beleaguered Charleston, while shells were screaming in the air and falling in the streets and houses, the people met in the churches and devoutly worshiped. They had encouragement to pray. For it really seemed that the shield of God's protection was over the city. . . .

WILLIAM W. BENNETT, A Narrative of the Great Revival Which Prevailed in the Southern Armies (Philadelphia, 1877), Ch. xxii.

From the armies that knew how each passing day brought them nearer to death the reports were most cheering.

"It does one's heart good," writes a chaplain, "to be at some of our Chaplain and Missionary Associations and hear the reports come up from the various regiments and brigades of the wonderful revival in the army."

Another says: "The awakening has been very extensive. Strong men bow themselves, and the man hardened by three years of war and the corrupting influences of the camps comes to the altar of prayer and 'mourns his follies past,' praying God for pardon.". . .

The religion of the soldier was of the best type. Reverend C. W. Miller says:

> My observation is that the religion of the army approximates more nearly that of the primitive days of Christianity than anything which I have witnessed in the halcyon days of peace. The soldier's situation is peculiarly favorable to the growth of a benevolent, unselfish, and primitive piety. Political storms disturb not the calm of his soul. His musket is his platform. The "love of gain" finds no fostering facilities. Necessity has taught him to be "content with his wages"—eleven dollars per month. Sectarian strife and pulpit gladiators no longer warp and embitter the great current of his heart. And thus, freed from these former hindrances, he cultivates that religion which teaches the heart to love God with all the mind, soul, and body, and his neighbor as himself.

The work at Dalton while the army lay there was almost without a parallel. In the coldest and darkest nights of winter the rude chapels were crowded, and at the call for penitents hundreds would bow down in sorrow and tears.

Dr. McFerrin was a tower of strength. He won his way to the hearts of the soldiers by his candor and kindness, and had the blessed privilege of leading thousands to Christ. He was ably supported by other missionaries and by their chaplains, and under their combined efforts such a revival flame was kindled as is seldom seen in this sinful world. Dalton was the spiritual birthplace of thousands. Many are in heaven. Some still rejoice and labor on the earth. "Come to the army," shouted a missionary to his brethren, "for the harvest truly is great, but the laborers are few."

14

Mother Bickerdyke

Frank Moore

Among the many noble women whose names will be forever enshrined with those of the brave defenders of their country, that of Mrs. Bickerdyke of Illinois will be held in especial honor. From no merely romantic impulse, but acting from the dictates of her mature sense of duty, she entered the service of the country as a volunteer nurse for its soldiers early in the war, and continued her work of patriotic charity until the war closed. By all those who remain of the armies who conquered their way down the Mississippi, Mrs. Bickerdyke is affectionately and gratefully remembered, as one of the most constant, earnest, determined, and efficient laborers for their health and comfort in the hospital and in the field.

Mrs. Bickerdyke, who is a woman of middle age, commenced her labors for the soldiers in August, 1861, when—at her own solicitation, and because her judgment was confided in—she was sent from Galesburg, Illinois, to Cairo, to ascertain what was needed by the troops stationed there. After ascertaining the condition of affairs there and reporting, her Galesburg friends advised her to remain, which she did, exerting all her energies to remedy the many miseries attending the establishment of a large camp of soldiers, nearly all of whose officers were as ignorant of camp discipline as themselves. When the battle of Belmont sent a large number of the wounded to the brigade hospital at Mound City, she went there, and remained until the most of them were sent to their homes.

Returning herself to her home, she barely continued long enough to put her household in order for a more prolonged absence. She had enlisted for

FRANK MOORE, *Women of the War* (Chicago, 1867), pp. 466-472.
Hundreds of women, North and South, left their homes to serve in hospitals. Thousands more, at home, organized Sanitary Fairs and raised money for the Sanitary Commission. For Louisa May Alcott, hospital service was a chapter in her literary career. For Cordelia Harvey, widow of Wisconsin's governor, caring for the wounded grew into a lifetime employment caring for orphans. Most of the nurses, however, were conscientious and single-minded, in their services. Typical was Mary Ann Ball (Mrs. Robert) Bickerdyke, 1817-1901, a "botanic physician" before the war. After the war she devoted herself variously to veterans' affairs, to settlement-house work, and to caring for veteran's widows and orphans.

the war. At the bloody field of Donelson—where the sufferings of our wounded were most distressing, from the lack of medical attendance and the severity of the weather—she was untiring in her efforts for the poor fellows. She took a prominent part in shipping five boat-loads of wounded men, her kind and motherly care doing more than aught else to save the soldiers from neglect. Hardly through with this severe labor of love, she was in a few days called to Pittsburg Landing, to assist in the care of the immense numbers of wounded men for whom the provisions of the medical department were not half adequate. She stationed herself at Savannah, ten miles below Pittsburg Landing, where the most of our wounded were brought. An incident of her experience while there will illustrate her character better than anything we can say. It was told us by an officer who was at Savannah at the time.

Governor Harvey of Wisconsin had been visiting the field of battle, and the hospitals there and at Savannah to learn what was the condition and what were the wants of the soldiers from his State. He had a small but excellent staff of volunteer surgeons, and ten tons of the best sanitary supplies. He saw every sick and wounded Wisconsin soldier individually, and gave to all the medical attendance and sanitary supplies they needed. Our informant could not restrain the tears as he recalled the kind acts, the cordial and sympathetic greetings of this noble-hearted governor, whose life was so suddenly ended in its prime by a distressing casualty. After his work was through, Governor Harvey met our friend at the Savannah levee, perfectly satisfied that he had done all in his power, and happy that he had been permitted to do so much good. He had still five tons of sanitary stores left, and had been in great doubt as to what to do with them. He distrusted the surgeons in charge at Savannah, and finally concluded to turn over the stores to Mrs. Bickerdyke. He had known nothing of her antecedents, and had only seen her while at Savannah. Still, as he told our friend, he observed how efficient she was, with how much business-like regularity she was performing her work, and that honesty, decision, and judgment seemed written on her plain but good-looking face. He would trust her, and no one else.

After the governor's death, Mrs. Bickerdyke began to suspect that her supplies were diverted to the private uses of a certain surgeon's mess. She resolved to stop that, and did, in a very summary manner. Going into the tent of this surgeon just before dinner, she discovered on the table a great variety of the jellies, wines, and other comforts belonging to her stores. She at once made a clean sweep of these articles, went straight down to the levee, took a boat to Pittsburg Landing, saw General Grant, and within twenty-four hours had the guilty surgeon under arrest. The surgeons had little disposition to interfere with her or her stores after this example, and the sick and wounded men rejoiced to find that their faithful friend had won so complete a victory.

Occupied all the time of the Corinth campaign with the wounded in the rear of General Halleck's army, she was put in charge of the main hospital at Corinth, when our force entered that place. While there her indomitable force and determination to serve the soldiers had another trial and another victory. Learning that a brigade was to march through the hospital grounds, and knowing that the soldiers would be nearly exhausted from their long march under a burning sun, she got out her barrels of water which had been brought for the men in hospital, had a corps of her assistants ready with pails and dippers, and gave the soldiers water as they passed through. When the commanding officer came up, Mrs. Bickerdyke asked that the men be halted; but he refused, and, going ahead, ordered his men to march along. At the same time a voice in the rear—that of Mrs. Bickerdyke—was heard giving the reverse order—"Halt!"—in very clear tones. The woman's order was obeyed, and the "Tin Cup Brigade" worked energetically for a few minutes, rejoicing in the triumph of *their* commander.

At the siege of Vicksburg Mrs. Bickerdyke undertook the difficult task of correcting abuses in the use and distribution of sanitary supplies. The lasting gratitude of the sick and wounded, and the approval of the higher officers in command, attest the fidelity and efficiency with which she executed this trust. She was not at all times a welcome guest to the agents and officers having in charge of sanitary supplies. One of these latter applied to headquarters to have a woman removed from his hospital, on the complaint of improper influence. "Who is she?" inquired the general. "A Mrs. Bickerdyke," replied the major. "Oh, well," said the general, "she ranks me; you must apply to President Lincoln."

After the battles of Mission Ridge and Lookout Mountain she remained in the field thirty days, till the last of the wounded were removed to Northern hospitals, working with all her remarkable energy, and with her untiring determination, that the soldiers should be well cared for. On the Atlantic campaign she followed the army with a laundry, and had daily from fifteen hundred to two thousand pieces washed, besides the bandages and rags used in dressing wounds. In addition to this work, which was more than enough for one woman to perform, she superintended the cooking for the field hospitals, and, when the commissary stores failed, supplied the tables from those of the Christian and Sanitary Commissions. To meet emergencies, she has been known to take passage in an afternoon train, ride fifteen miles, get her supplies to the hospital, and have the bread baked and distributed to over a thousand patients the same day, and in proper season.

Perhaps a good idea of the nature and value of the labors of Mrs. Bickerdyke can best be given from an extract of a letter, written from Chattanooga by Mrs. Porter—another noble laborer for the soldiers—soon after the battle there. Mrs. Porter says:

"I reached this place on New Year's Eve, making the trip of the few miles from Bridgeport to Chattanooga in twenty-four hours. New Year's morning was very cold. I went immediately to the field hospital, about two miles out of town, where I found Mrs. Bickerdyke hard at work, as usual, endeavoring to comfort the cold and suffering sick and wounded. The work done on that day told most happily on the comfort of the poor wounded men.

"The wind came sweeping around Lookout Mountain, and uniting with the currents from the valleys of Missionary Ridge, pressed in upon the hospital tents, overturning some, and making the inmates of all tremble with cold and anxious fear. The cold had been preceded by a great rain, which added to the general discomfort. Mrs. Bickerdyke went from tent to tent in the gale, carrying hot bricks and hot drinks, to warm and to cheer the poor fellows. 'She is a power of good,' said one soldier. 'We fared mighty poor till she come here,' said another. 'God bless the Sanitary Commission,' said a third, 'for sending women among us!' The soldiers fully appreciate 'Mother Bickerdyke,'—as they call her—and her work.

"Mrs. Bickerdyke left Vicksburg at the request of General Sherman and other officers of his corps, as they wished to secure her services for the then approaching battle. The field hospital of the Fifteenth (Sherman's) army corps was situated on the north bank of the Genesee River, on a slope at the base of Missionary Ridge, where, after the battle was over, seventeen hundred of our wounded and exhausted soldiers were brought. Mrs. Bickerdyke reached there before the din and smoke of battle were well over, and before all were brought from the field of blood and carnage. There she remained the only female attendant for four weeks. Never has she rendered more valuable service. Dr. Newberry arrived in Chattanooga with sanitary goods, which Mrs. Bickerdyke had the pleasure of using, as she says, 'just when and where needed'; and never were sanitary goods more deeply felt to be *good goods*. 'What could we do without them?' is a question I often hear raised, and answered with a hearty 'God bless the Sanitary Commission,' which is now everywhere acknowledged as 'a great power for good.'

"The field hospital was in a forest about five miles from Chattanooga; wood was abundant, and the camp was warmed by immense burning 'log heaps,' which were the only fireplaces or cooking-stoves of the camp or hospitals. Men were detailed to fell the trees and pile the logs to heat the air, which was very wintry; and beside them Mrs. Bickerdyke made soup and toast, tea and coffee, and broiled mutton, without a gridiron, often blistering her fingers in the process. A house in due time was demolished to make bunks for the worst cases, and the brick from the chimney was converted into an oven, when Mrs. Bickerdyke made bread, yeast having been found in the Chicago boxes, and flour at a neighboring mill, which had furnished flour to secessionists through the war until now. Great multitudes were fed from these rude kitchens. Companies of hungry soldiers were refreshed before those open fireplaces and those ovens."

We will merely add a few words in conclusion. Mrs. Bickerdyke not only performed a great work in the field, but several times visited the leading cities of the northwest, and by her judicious advice did much to direct aright the enthusiastic patriotism and noble charity of the ladies of that region. They needed no stimulus to effort. Distinguished from the outset of her efforts by her practical good sense, firmness in maintaining the rights of the soldiers, and an unceasing energy, she was soon known among all the western soldiers as one of their best and most faithful friends. In addition to the consciousness of having performed her whole duty, Mrs. Bickerdyke has another reward in the undying gratitude of the thousands of gallant fellows who have received or witnessed her motherly ministrations. May she live long to enjoy both of these rewards for her good deeds.

15

With Sherman

George W. Pepper

Sherman's triumphal march to the sea is the most stupendous movement of this or any other age. Never, perhaps, did the name of any one of our great generals so widely and deeply stir the public mind. The wheels of commerce, hard to stay as the sun upon his march, stood still; the strifes of party, restless as the sea, and unmanageable as the winds, were calmed; people of all countries and tongues were drawn to one spot.

The spectacle was most inspiring, as the stream of the long, long procession came flowing out of the Gate City with their flags waving in the winds of Heaven, and swords and bayonets glistening in the sun. The splendid regiments of Slocum's column, moved as if on parade, with waving banners and strains of martial music. The whole programme comprised a magnificent pageant, beautiful to behold. The bronzed countenances of the men who carried muskets were suffused with one expression, and the thoughts and feelings were so much alike that it might be said the hearts of thousands were as the heart of one man.

The order for the expedition was issued on the 8th of November from Kingston, northwest from Atlanta, around which place the army was again concentrated. In this order Sherman says: "It is sufficient for you to know that it involves a departure from our present base, and a long and difficult march to a new one. All the chances of war have been considered and provided for as far as human sagacity can. . . ."

Sherman, starting out from Atlanta with his army at this season of the year, is an event of the largest suggestiveness. He proposed, after gathering sufficient supplies at Atlanta, to abandon the railroad from Chattanooga to Atlanta, and start with a movable column on a winter tour of the Cotton States. Two of his army corps will be left at Chattanooga to watch Hood's movements, while the rest of the corps will cut loose from all lines of supply and push across the States of Georgia and the Carolinas. He will take with him such supplies as can be carried conveniently, and when these are exhausted, will live upon the country. Of his destination nothing is known.

GEORGE W. PEPPER, *Personal Recollections of Sherman's Campaigns in Georgia and the Carolinas* (Zanesville, Ohio, 1866), Chs. xvii-xix.

Before him lies the broad expanse of the Gulf and Atlantic States, and he can shape his march to suit his own inclinations. To his right is Mobile, around which the Gulf forces are concentrating; to his left is Andersonville, a pen in which are rotting thousands of gallant soldiers; and not an immeasurable distance to the south, and east, are Savannah, Charleston, Wilmington, and Richmond. . . .

On the 15th, Atlanta was evacuated, and the campaign begins. The hills which had been white with tents were made desolate, and nothing save the smouldering fires of the doomed city remained to mark the course of the advancing hosts. It begins to be seen that Sherman means *business*. The two distinguishing qualities, Conception and Execution, are found to exist in an eminent degree in the great leader. The General commanding, the staff, and the private soldiers fare alike. The broad canopy of Heaven, the great blue tent which God first spread out over the Garden of Eden, is the only one they know by night, and the forward movement which strikes into the very vitals of the rebellion is the feature of the coming day. More action and less waiting, is the motto of their never wearied leader, and endeared to them from the fact that he participates in all their hardships. The soldiers go cheerfully to the accomplishment of their mission. This auspicious opening—the terrible castigation given the fierce legions of Hood, in and around Atlanta, maintains well the ever hopeful confidence of the army, and gives assurance of the glorious triumphs that await our arms in the coming struggles.

Stone Mountain, which we passed on the Decatur Road, has an adventurous interest from its extraordinary height. It is two thousand feet high, and seven miles in circumference. This being the greatest elevation, almost the entire surrounding country is brought under the eye. Far to the west, mountain rises beyond mountain until it presents an ocean-like appearance —a vast verdant sea frilled into ten thousand billows. . . .

It is said that an Irish colonel once clambered up to the top of this mountain, with a few boon companions, and after gazing for some time upon the fearfully grand and sublime scenery, he stretched himself to his utmost height and exclaimed at the top of his voice: "*Attention, the universe! by Empires, to the right about wheel.*"

I defy any mortal man to look on this scene without feeling the power of its grandeur. Each object in itself is rich in beauty, and not less full of individual interest; all conspire to form a panorama, unrivalled for the beauty and grouping and perfection of its elements.

On the third day we reached Madison, a very fine town, which in the days of peace and prosperity, must have been a delightful place for a residence. It is situated on the Augusta line, and is the capital of Morgan County. The extensive stores, public buildings, and plantations, which form its environs, give it the appearance of beauty, wealth and comfort. One is forcibly struck with the appearance and situation of this handsomely built, neat, and respectably inhabited town, and with the fine plantations surrounding it, all which contrast so strongly with the bleak tract just travelled through. There are several splendid churches in the place. The soil around Madison is rich, and the land well cultivated.

This region of country before the war was peopled with a numerous population, simple in their habits, industrious and active, and not less happy in their associations. There were a few Union men in this town. I cannot forbear mentioning the name of the good and tried Joshua H. Hill. He was once arrested by the rebels for his fealty to the Union. The devils incarnate told him they would sweat the Lincoln fever out of him. Hill was always an old line Whig, and continued a staunch Unionist, when it was dangerous to avow such sentiments. If we are not mistaken, he was among the two or three Representatives of the extreme South who still continued to linger in Washington, when the rest of their colleagues had packed off to Dixie, to serve in the cause of Jeff. Davis and his experimental Confederacy.

In the Georgia Convention, recently held at Milledgeville, Hill delivered a noble speech, in vindication of his Union sentiments and his conduct to the Davis *regime*, during the war. We insert the closing sentences of this magnificent speech: "In standing by the Union of the States, I risked more than the loss of goods or political preferment. For sooner than raise my hand against the Government, I would have thought it happiness to die. . . ."

Resuming the march towards the capital of the State, we pass through one of the richest and best farmed districts; and the appearance of many of the houses evidently shows that the occupants have had both skill and capital. The fine old plantations, prolific orchards, and the beauty, richness, and culture of the soil, have altogether a more respectable appearance than the generality of Southern territory. The citizens show their taste in their handsome dwelling-houses, splendid churches, and neat school-houses.

Hundreds of miserable-looking men and women, Negroes and the lower class of whites, would flock to our ranks, telling tales of distress, and uttering savage imprecations on the authors of the rebellion. It was enough to puzzle a saint, or to bother Job. As to my deductions, there will be a thousand different opinions. The country in this section is rough, the houses and the general appearance of the people, wretched, and only a small part of the soil seems to be under cultivation. The melancholy and terrible condition of the people was evinced by the large number of deserted mansions and cabins that we saw on the journey.

One of the most horrible effects of the war in the South is the sundering of family affections and social ties, which has taken place in all ages, in beleaguered cities and countries. In the course of our journey, we heard of many instances of this kind; and I saw many perpetrators of deeds of cruelty, which at ordinary times would have excited the universal horror of the community. At the present crises, our feelings called forth are rather those of compassion than indignation; for we in the North can form no idea of the disruption of family associations in the South. A noted Unionist, whom we met here, had two sons and all his male relatives in the rebel army. He has devoted himself with great energy and eloquence to the Union. His personal and pecuniary sacrifices have been enormous. He describes to us, in strong terms, the amount of tyranny displayed by the Davis *Regime*, and the difficulty of getting rid of it.

In accounting for this horrible condition of affairs, it is just and fair to ascribe it all to the mercenary slaveholders. They were haughty, improvident, intemperate and full of hate to the poor whites and blacks. One word as to the origin of this fell hate. Among the multitudes of profundities which distinguish the pages of Tacitus, there is not one more sagacious or pertinent to the present case than his declaration that *"men hate those whom they have injured."* This is the utmost stretch of philosophy on the point—it reaches the bottom at once. The quenchless hatred of the slaveholders to the blacks is founded solely in their boundless injuries toward them. The fires of their Pandemonium hate are always fed by the remembered cruelties they have perpetrated and do still perpetrate on millions of the helpless. Walking in so fierce an atmosphere of crime, the hearts of evil-doers are reduced to an alternative—they must either burn against themselves or their victims.

They resemble the images of a frightful dream, rather than living men, women and children. Their voice is peculiar. They speak in a low, puling, whining tone, that is most distressing to hear. In fact, the poor of this section are as ignorant, filthy and wretched as can be found anywhere in the world. They are the dirtiest people I ever saw. The hands and faces of many of them were positively loathsome and thick with dirt. This indifference to cleanliness may be ascribed in part to the war; but, I am persuaded that they never had great love for soap or water at any time. Throughout the whole route there seemed to be much destitution and misery.

The state of the habitations of the poor in many parts of Georgia, is a libel on the humanity of their more wealthy superiors. A fine dressed lawn, surrounded with miserable cabins and hovels of the poor, nothing can reflect more discredit on the character of the dominant class than such a contrast. The lordly mansion and park want their most beautiful appendages, when filthy and unwholesome huts are substituted for clean and comfortable cabins: and pleasure grounds are *nicknamed,* when at every step of your progress, and at each opening of the prospect, your eyes are pained by dwellings for laborers not half so convenient as the wigwam of the savages.

As we drew nigh to the first town, we were met by a party of the most miserable-looking beings I ever beheld. Bare-footed and bare-legged, with scarcely as many tatters hung round them as covered their naked limbs; some of them, in fact, *sans-culotte,* with misery and wretchedness pictured on their countenances, these "sons of the sod, poor white trash," deserters, many of them, from the rebel army, trudged along their weary way, having more the appearance of a set of malefactors going to execution than men returning to their wives and families.

THE CAPTURE OF MILLEDGEVILLE

Milledgeville, the capital of Georgia, was occupied on the 20th of November by a small detachment of the left wing under General Slocum. Milledgeville is a rather pleasant city and is situated on one of the numerous eminences which are scattered throughout this devious region of country. The capital is a picturesque edifice of stone—encircled by a ten-acre square, containing, in the more sheltered places, some handsome trees, together with two neat churches.

Governor Brown, after urging the citizens to seize muskets and defend their homes, fled to parts unknown. He was in such haste to run from the detested Yankees that the carpets were cut from the floors of his house.

In the hospitals we found over two hundred sick and wounded rebels. Five hundred stand of arms and scores of pikes were seized. The penitentiary was set on fire by some Negro or soldier, and twenty convicts, all in striped uniform, made their escape. Tuesday afternoon was employed by the working-men of the army, in preparing for a grand advance, but thousands of the troops pushed their investigations into the utmost recesses of the city; every house was liberally patronized. Pursuant to notice, four hundred citizens of Georgia, dressed in blue, met in the State House, for the purpose of reconstructing the sovereign State of Georgia. Committees were appointed to draft resolutions, and after an exciting discussion, Georgia was restored and reinstated in the Union.

SAVANNAH THE OBJECTIVE POINT

Savannah is the grand point in the present campaign. Other cities secure but a cursory glance, and the mind's eye turns almost instinctively toward this beautiful forest city. It is well known to the soldiers whither Sherman is leading them, for despite his well known reticence, his course has been too clearly marked out. It appears to have been General Sherman's plan when he set out, to strike effectively the most vital points in Georgia; and, as rapidly as possible, inflict the necessary damage and gain a place of safety. Permanent occupation of the country does not seem to have been a part of his plan. He proposed to do all the damage possible to the road over which he moved, and the cities and the towns through which he passed, and gain with his army, a point of the sea-board where it would be disembarked for future operations. His purpose, as indicated in his order of march, was to destroy all the public material which could be of use to the enemy; and to forage on the country, sparing only such property as he could have no military excuse for destroying. . . .

I have used the word "bummer" in my accounts, and it has been suggested that many of your readers do not know the meaning of the term. It has now a recognized position in the army lexicon. Any man who has seen the object that it applies to will acknowledge that it was admirably selected. Fancy a ragged man, blackened by the smoke of many a knot fire, mounted on a scrawny mule, without a saddle, with a gun, a knapsack, a butcher knife and a plug hat, stealing his way through the pine forests far out on the flanks of a column. Keen on the scent of rebels, or bacon, or silver spoons, or corn, or anything valuable, and you have him in your mind. Think how you would admire him if you were a lone woman, with a family of small children, far from help, when he blandly inquired where you kept your valuables. Think how you would smile when he pried open your chests with his bayonet or knocked to pieces your tables, pianos and chairs; tore your bed clothing in three-inch strips, and scattered the strips about the yard. The "bummers" say it takes too much time to use keys. Color is no protection from these rough-riders. They go through a Negro cabin in search of diamonds and gold watches with just as much freedom and vivacity as they "loot" the dwelling of a wealthy planter. They appear to be possessed of a spirit of "pure cussedness." One incident of many will illustrate. A "bummer" stepped into a house and inquired for sorghum. The lady of the house presented a jug, which he said was too heavy, so he merely filled his canteen. Then taking a huge wad of tobacco from his mouth he thrust it into the jug. The lady inquired in wonder why he spoiled that which he did not want. "Oh, some feller'll come along and taste that sorghum, think you've poisoned him; then he'll burn your damned old house." There are hundreds of these mounted men with the column, and they go everywhere. Some of them are loaded down with silverware, gold coin and other valuables. I hazard nothing in saying that three-fifths (in value) of the personal property of the country we passed through was taken. . . .

At one of the stations near Millen, we came across an old man named Wells, who was a most peculiar character. He was depot master in the days when there was a railroad here. He is a shrewd old man, and seemed to understand the merits of the war question perfectly.

He said: "They say you are retreating, but it is the strangest retreat I ever saw. Why, dog bite 'em, the newspapers have been lying in this way, all along. They are always whipping the Federal armies, and they always fall back after the battle is over. It was that 'ere idea that first opened my eyes. Our army always whipping the Federals, and we always fell back. I always told them that it was a d—d humbug, and now I know it, for here you are right in old John Wells' place; hogs, potatoes, corn, fences all gone. I don't find any fault. I expected it all. Jeff. Davis and the rest talk about splittin' the Union. Why, if South Carolina had gone out by herself, she would have been split in four pieces by this time. Splittin' the Union! Why the State of Georgia is being split through from end to end. It's these rich fellers who are making this war, and keeping their precious bodies out of harm's way. There's John Franklin went through here the other day, running from your army. I could have played dominoes on his coat-tail. There's my poor brother sick with the smallpox at Macon, working for eleven dollars a month and hasn't got a cent of the stuff for a year—'leven dollars a month, and 'leven thousand bullets a minute—I don't believe in it.

"I heard as how they cut down the trees across your road up country; and burnt the bridges! Why (dog bite their hides), one of you Yankees can take up a tree and carry it off, top and all; and there's that bridge you put across the river in less than two hours—they might as well try to stop the Ogeechee as you Yankees. The blasted rascals who burnt this 'ere bridge thought they did a big thing; a natural born fool cut in two has more sense in either end than any of them."

From Atlanta to Savannah there was presented to the eye one vast sheet of misery. The fugitives from ruined villages or desolated fields seek shelter in caves and dens. Cities sacked, towns burnt, population decimated are so many evidences of the desolations of war. I saw enough of this part of Georgia to get a vivid and painful impression of the horrors of civil strife. This is a beautiful country, exclaimed a friend. How beautiful in the brightness and warmth of summer, teeming with fruits and grain, and waving with groves that grow to forests in the distance. In every town the more public buildings and residences were destroyed. In some instances churches have not escaped, they have been stripped for fire wood. Fences were demolished, and here and there a lordly mansion stands an unsightly ruin. A beautiful country! but woe to it, when slavery brought upon it the curse of rebellion. A beautiful country it shall be, when re-peopled by manly, free labor.

There was something grand in the spirit and bearing of Sherman's army when the line of march was resumed for the State of South Carolina. There has been no grander sight seen since the sailing of the expeditions from the Greek Republic. The march of the British troops for the Crimea was a solemn spectacle; but this expedition of the western troops was sublime. Never did the country behold a finer spectacle. The march through Georgia was the key of this glorious consummation—the triumphant Sherman did not rest upon his laurels—the hosts of treason were confounded by the unprecedented movements in Georgia, and no time was allowed them to recover from the blow.

Never in the history of this war, has the mail gone north, freighted with news so grand, so startling, so suggestive of overwhelming emotions, of mingled hope and success to the Union cause.

It was much, that Sherman had, with the suddenness of thought, thrust forth his veteran hosts into the very heart of the South, and proclaimed the supremacy of law and order. The world was still gazing in wonder at the strange and unexpected march through Georgia, when another and grander movement burst forth.

There is scarce a corner in Europe where the hearts of people will not bound in response to the splendid deeds of the Union army. How soon these victories will end this horrid rebellion, Heaven only knows. But the voice of earnest patriot soldiers, demanding the restoration of loyalty in the revolted States, and with a fierce earnestness thundering at the very gates of rebellion, is grand beyond all sounds that have yet reached the ears of earthly listeners. It is almost a descent from the sublime to the ridiculous, to turn from the heroic battalions of the Union, to the people of the South, so panic-stricken, so without counsel, so confounded, and so despondent. The charm of slavery and secession have faded forever from the minds of even the aristocratic slave-owners. These prime patrons of rebellion have, at last, awakened to the knowledge that they have been merely enacting the delusion of the theatre.

The soldiers entered on this campaign with light hearts and exultant feelings. The very hope of treading the soil of the wretched State that inaugurated secession fired every heart and brightened every eye. They looked forward anxiously to the issues of an expedition which would materially affect the interests of the whole country. They felt, however, that through the superb skill of Sherman and his captains, the Confederacy would be shorn of its strength, and the rebel army so thoroughly broken that it would not be able again to regain its power. The absolute necessity of victory was so completely infused into our army that they must conquer—with what anxiety the brave boys awaited the blast that ordered them forward!

THE CHARACTER OF THE COUNTRY

The face of South Carolina is like a triangle, having the Atlantic coast for a base, and Georgia and North Carolina, along its southern and northern frontier. . . . Its natural advantages indicate that this State is capable, under the hands of honest labor, of supporting as dense a population as any State of equal size in the Union. Slavery, however, has left its blighting curse upon the State, and consequently it has as yet scarcely commenced developing its inexhaustible resources. The magnificent schemes of railroad enterprise which pervade the North have not, to any great extent, penetrated into the borders of the Palmetto State. Her progress in manufactures, mechanical, educational and other improvements, is behind any other State. The abolishment of slavery will, in a few years, add one hundred per cent to the population and wealth of South Carolina.

The inhabitants of South Carolina are classed as follows: planters, farmers, cottagers, and squatters. This fourfold division resembles the system of castes which exists in England, and other monarchical countries. The planters have large incomes, live easy, enjoy much, work little, are high-minded, imperious and domineering. They have the same pride of birth, the same high and haughty bearing, the same contempt of the masses, and the same aversion to labor and mechanical employments, that distinguish the aristocracies of Europe. Their manners are polished and courteous. Their morals are reckless and dissolute.

The virtues of the second class, the farmers, are less showy, but their vices are fewer than that of the planters. They are more active and industrious, depending on their own exertions, and are better able to bear the frowns of fortune. They own few slaves. This class is not very large, and since the war commenced, their numbers are getting fewer. They are generally intelligent and have tolerable experience in the politics of the country. The third class are called cottagers; they constitute a large number of the people. They are in a depressed state, having no slaves of their own; and unwilling to work with those of the more wealthy neighbors, and not being able to procure the position of overseers, many of them, having no resources left them, engaged in some slight business which did not afford suitable employment. The conscription, however, has swept them into the ranks.

The lowest grade are the squatters or the poor white trash. These are a lazy, thriftless, thoughtless set, unimproved in either mind or morals. . . .

Columbia, the capital of the State, is a very handsome place, situated near the river, in the midst of an undulating country. A splendid prospect meets the eye in every direction. It is regularly and tastefully laid off, and the wide streets are shaded by rows of trees. The private residences are elegantly fashioned and uniformly built. They indicate wealth and refinement. The gardens and public walks, for beauty and variety of flowers and ornamental trees, are unequaled by any that we have ever seen. The mansion of General Preston is a truly magnificent structure. It is a commodious and elegant dwelling, and is arranged with taste and display. When I visited it, it was grandly furnished, with splendid carpets, plate, mirrors, library, and sculptured paintings.

Our first attention was directed to the superb paintings, many of them yet remaining in the splendid rooms. These pictures rank decidedly among the most perfect and most choice. Some of them are truly fascinating. The owner of this princely dwelling is in the rebel army. He is a brother of the eloquent W. C. Preston, and is possessed of many of his brother's gifts. The next house of importance is that of the famous Wade Hampton. It is surrounded by a lofty wall, and an enclosure beautifully sprinkled with flowers and trees. In its construction it is very similar to the castles of the English lords. Several officers and soldiers were promenading in the grounds. General Hammond's mansion is of the gorgeous order, and is surrounded by a colonnade. The city of Columbia is sixty-five years old. Its population before the war was eight thousand.

The State House is a superb pile, and is justly celebrated in the South as one of the foremost of architectural beauties. Though incomplete, it cost over six millions of dollars. It was almost finished when the war broke out; the workmen, being from the North, left the city when the State seceded.

The lunatic aslyum, the Methodist Female College, the State College, and the churches are splendid gems of architecture. They are indications of the wealth, elegance, and fine taste of the people. The eloquent and violent divine, Dr. Palmer, preaches here. He fled at the approach of our troops. His house was burned. Three noted rebel generals have resided here—Gregg, Hampton, and Hood. The view of Columbia from the cupola of the asylum is enchanting. The morning was serene and lovely, and in the general aspect of the surrounding scenery, as well as in the brightness and purity of the heavens, the scenes became associated in my mind with the sacredness and quietude of the Sabbath.

THE BURNING OF COLUMBIA

In the evening of the 17th of February, before our troops entered the town, several bales of cotton were set on fire, it was supposed, by some rebel citizen. The wind blowing very heavily at the time, it spread with great rapidity, and in a few hours a whole block of large buildings, in Richardson Street, was in flames. From these it caught to the extensive rebel store-rooms, to the Episcopal Church, then to the Ursuline Convent, and thence to nearly every street in the city. Vast quantities of corn, flour, sugar, etc., were destroyed. The passenger depots, used as store-houses, and filled with blankets and various other articles, were burned. Had it not been for the activity and magnanimous conduct of our troops, there would not be one house as a shelter for those who fled from the smoking ruins of their burning dwellings.

I shall never forget the terrible scenes of that night. The sight was heart-rending; men, women and children rushed into the streets, from the showers of ashes and burning brands that were falling in all directions. The houses were soon emptied. Half-eaten suppers remained on splendid tables. The infuriated Negroes dashed four abreast through the deserted mansions, soon to be in flames. They glut their eyes on trunks and wardrobes. A few drunken soldiers push their bayonets into beds and tapestry. The cushioned carpets and splendidly gilt books are scattered everywhere. The mob spare nothing; ticks are ripped open, and rich laces lie in tatters. Chandeliers and crimson hangings are utterly destroyed. Silk dresses, just imported, costing ten thousand dollars, in long strips, stream out of the windows, and the Negroes below catch them, and make apron strings of them.

Among the many instances which took place during that dreadful night, this one is the most touching. A lady who had just removed her trunks to a place of safety suddenly remembered that one of her little children was missing from the family circle. She came up to the spot where the beautiful house once stood, sobbing as if her heart would break, and commenced searching for the lost one. In her frenzy, she thought the child to be burnt; she looked wildly agonizing. Perceiving a crowd of people, she rushed toward it, and beholding the sweet little fellow in the arms of a soldier, she cried: "It is my boy, it is my Charlie!" Then she paused, and drawing herself up to her full height, a prayer of gratitude breaks from her lips, and she beseeches the benediction of the God of Heaven on the gallant soldier, the savior of her child, and upon the holy cause in which we are engaged. Grasping the dear child, she called out, "Speak to me, Charlie." There was scarce an eye in the crowd that was not moistened with tears.

Down into cellars and vaults the sable mob rushes, and brings up mouldy-topped bottles of wine. Sitting on the fragments of pianos they drink confusion to their runaway masters. The scene beggars all description. Timid and frantic women, in all the corners of the streets—they have flung themselves from their burning dwellings, and with their frightened little ones are gazing at the smouldering remains of their former elegant homes. The storm increases. At eleven o'clock it begins to blow from the southwest, and the fire spreads over the city in the opposite direction. The next morning, at two o'clock, every street was burning, and the whole city was awfully and solemnly illuminated. The turn-out on the streets is immense, and the utmost excitement prevailed. Thousands of soldiers did their best endeavors to stop the terrible display of fire. In vain! The streets through which the fire raged were the principal ones of the place. Old men pronounced it the most terrible scene they had ever beheld. Think of twenty thousand, including all classes, suddenly turned out of doors. Scores who rose that morning with their thousands, are now penniless, homeless! Refined and cultivated ladies are seen, in beseeching attitudes, calling for help. They convulsively clasp their little ones to their bosoms, and then utter a piercing prayer to Heaven for deliverance. Few who were present were unmoved at these scenes, and tears could be seen on many a soldier's cheek.

Hark! What a tremendous crash! The very earth quakes. It is the explosion of a vast quantity of powder in the arsenal. What a gigantic fire—it blazes on all the adjacent squares! Thousands gather around it. The engines are dashing hither and thither.

The grand conflagration which destroyed the city commenced about dark. The fire started near the rear of the jail. A high wind prevailed, and in a short time the flames were in full and unconquerable progress. The sky was one broad sheet of flame, above which, amid the lurid smoke, drifted in eddying circles, a myriad of sparks. These falling, scattered the seeds of conflagration on every side. The monotone of the hissing, waving, leaping tongues of flame, as they careered on their wild course, alone filled hearts with dismay. The air was like that of a furnace. The arsenal was burned to the ground. This vast and magnificent building was wrapt in flame and smoke. As the wind swept the dense volumes away to the northeast, the southern slope of the roof appeared composed of molten gold, instinct with life and motion. It soon fell with a tremendous crash, and immediately, as if with fiendish joy, the destructive element in a hugh column of mingled fire and smoke leaped unto the very skies. Morning revealed to some extent the broad sweep of destruction. Eighty-five blocks in the city were burned, and Columbia is the Palmyra in the desert. Five thousand citizens were houseless. From the State House to Cottontown, nothing but blackened ruins remained. The beautiful city of Columbia no longer existed. It is a mass of charred ruins—Herculaneum buried in ashes. . . .

South Carolina is reaping at last the consequence of her treason. Though the chief instigator of the rebellion, her people have yet, until very recently, almost entirely escaped the evils which have fallen upon the sister States which she hurried into a participancy in her mad crime. While the war of her creation has depopulated other sections, ravaging the fields, obliterating towns and cities, and filling whole communities with suffering and death, disaster has not come near her doors; her fields have not been devastated; her people have only now and then felt the pressure of calamity. But at last, to her lips, also, the chalice is presented. The danger she has defied is upon her in fatal earnest. A hostile and irresistible army treads her soil, laying waste her luxuriant plantations, arresting her cultivation, breaking down her haughty pride, and inflicting upon her people, with fullest measure, the losses and pains which they have braved and scorned through all the years of conflict. Now, if never before, South Carolinians will learn what it is to have a great army, stirred and moved by memories of the part they have played in precipitating the nation into the bloody struggle, sweeping with unpitying purpose over peaceful fields, and through affrighted and defenceless towns. Now, following the desolate track of Sherman's majestic columns, and witnessing everywhere the wreck and ruin they have left as memorials of their presence, these rebel cavaliers who claim to be better stuff than Puritan mudsills, and boast a purer blood than flows in Northern veins, may see how fearful is the crime they have committed, how terrible the punishment it has invoked, and how false all their pretensions of superiority, and all their hopes of defense against aroused national law.

Nor will she find sympathy in her sufferings. She has sowed the wind; now when the whirlwind is come, prostrating all her vaunted strength and carrying desolation everywhere, she must be content to sit, unpitied, among the ruins. The thousands of homes she has filled with mourning, and unnumbered hearts she has wrung with anguish, are all witnesses of the justice of her punishment. Let her drink the cup she has brewed, and lie on the bed she has made. The law of compensations enforces inexorably its own fulfillment; and the projectors of this rebellion cannot escape its inevitable power. Some perception of this truth seems to have dawned even in the minds of the South Carolina conspirators, and now flashes out through all their frantic appeals for help.

The Negroes were the most fearful in their ravages. I do not speak of ordinary foraging in an enemy's country, for the purpose of living as you pass through it, nor of taking horses and mules to supply the place of those falling out by exhaustion; this is right, necessary, in the system of warfare we have been compelled to wage. Nor of the wholesale destruction of public property, railroads, mills, canals, etc.; this is also justified by the laws of civilized warfare. Nor of the burning of houses from which shots have been fired upon our advancing troops; this is perhaps a necessity. Nor even of the wholesale destruction of everything which could be destroyed in the Shenandoah valley by Sheridan, under command of a superior; this was an exceptional case, and may have been—from the peculiar location of that valley, as the gate of entrance to the North, and from the deceitful character of its people—a military necessity. Let these pass unquestioned.

But there is another class of devastations widely different from these, which has been perpetrated to an extent of which the North has little conception. These may be classified, as first, "deliberate and systematic robbery for the sake of gain." Thousands of soldiers have gathered by violence hundreds of dollars each, some of them thousands, by sheer robbery. When they come to a house where an old man may be found whom the most rigid conscription had not taken, they assume that he has gold and silver hidden, and demand it. If he gives up the treasure cheerfully he escapes personal violence. If he denies the possession of treasure and they believe him, he escapes. If they do not believe him they resort to violent means to compel its surrender. With a rope they will hang him until he is nearly gone, then let him down and demand the money—and this is repeated until he or they give up. Again, they will compel a man to "double-quick" for one, two or three miles, until he sinks from exhaustion, and then threaten him with death unless he reveals the hiding place of his riches. Again, they prepare the torch, and threaten to burn his house and all it contains, unless the money is forthcoming.

This robbery extends to other valuables in addition to money. Plate and silver spoons, silk dresses, elegant articles of the toilet, pistols, indeed whatever the soldier can take away and hopes to sell; these are gathered up and carried off to the extent sometimes of loading a wagon at one mansion. "What is done with these?" How many of them finally reach the North "by hook or crook," I will not affirm; some through the soldier's mail, some wrapped up in the baggage of furloughed officers, some passed through the hands of the regular official, having the permit of the Government.

A second form of devastation practiced by some of our soldiers consisted in the "wanton destruction of property which they could not use or carry away." Of this I have the evidence of sight, in some cases, of undoubted testimony in others.

Pianos cut to pieces with axes, elegant sofas broken and the fragments scattered about the grounds, paintings and engravings pierced with bayonets or slashed with swords, rosewood centre-tables, chairs, etc., broken to pieces and burned for fuel in cooking the food taken from the cellar or meat-house—these are the subjects of bitter complaint from hundreds of non-combatants, many of them undoubted, true, original, Union men.

"But would our soldiers wantonly destroy property of Union men?" Not surely because they were Union men. But the claim of being such was often made untruly, and was therefore generally disbelieved by the soldier. If the claim was well founded, then the boldness and persistency with which it would be urged was taken as an offence, and the weaker party generally lost his money and had his property destroyed. The amount of property thus destroyed during the last year of the rebellion no one can tell. I have heard it estimated at hundreds of millions.

This robbery and wanton waste were specially trying to the people, not only because contrary to right and the laws of war, but because it completed their utter and almost hopeless impoverishment. The depth of their losses and present want can hardly be overstated. In the proclamation of freedom to the slaves, their laborers, they lost what at the lowest figures they valued at two thousand millions of dollars. This might have been borne if the able-bodied men of the white families had been at home to take the place of the absent or idle freedmen, but they had been drawn into the war, many of them by a merciless conscription, and were now dead or hopelessly disabled for valuable labor on the farm. Further, four years of exhausting war had reduced the entire people to the barest necessities of life—ladies of former wealth declared to me that they had lived on bread and water for two months at a time—others that they had seen meat but once per week, no tea or coffee or sugar for months; the demands of the army, and the less efficient labor of the slaves during the war having cleaned out the granaries and meat-houses of the entire population. Still more, the people are absolutely without money. The gold and silver have gone to Europe or the North, the State banks have ceased, the Confederate money is worthless, and men of large wealth formerly—hundreds of thousands—have not had a dollar for months. Now add to this accumulation of deprivations, robbery and wanton destruction of what little is left them, and you can easily see how bitter their reproaches. I am persuaded that all other causes of estrangement will pass away and be forgotten long before this one is forgiven, and because it has neither justification nor palliation.

16

A Confederate Goes Home

John Will Dyer

Just now, General Lee surrendered at Appomattox and our cause was lost, but President Davis hoped to transfer headquarters west of the Mississippi River and there make another effort to save the day. Our brigade was complimented by being selected as the President's escort and met him and his cabinet at Greensboro, North Carolina. We made all the haste possible, but owing to circumstances, did not get along very fast. General McCook was trying to head us off on the north and General Stoneman on the south and we had to run the gauntlet. We skirmished right and left and kept the "dogs off," as it were, until we reached Savannah River, which we crossed about five miles from Washington, Georgia. Here the news reached us of Johnston's surrender, and that we were included.

We also found that General Wilson with his cavalry corps was in front of us and that we were completely surrounded by an overwhelming force.

Recognizing the futility of a further attempt to escape with any considerable number of men, President Davis decided to divide the contents of the Treasury with the men who were with him and make an attempt to get out of the country. He failed, as all know.

On the morning of May 7th, 1865, I was ordered to report to Secretary Trenholm, who was stopping at the house of the ferryman. On presenting myself and my credentials, I was handed a little cotton bag—sealed—which I was ordered to turn over to the captain of our company.

On breaking the seal, the captain found a pay-roll, allotting officers and men the same amount, without distinction of rank, and we were all handed $26.40 in gold and silver.

There has been much written about the buried "Confederate treasure," but this is all "moonshine." We got all the money there was in the Treasury and the only wonder is that we got to keep it. The Yankees didn't know we had it or they would have prowled us sure.

And then, I have read an article purporting to give an account of a night raid on the Confederate Treasury wagons near Abbeville, South Carolina,

JOHN WILL DYER, *Reminiscences; or Four Years in the Confederate Army* (Evansville, Ind., 1898), Chs. xix, xx.

and the looting of the same by a detachment of our cavalry. This is all a fabrication made out of whole cloth, as hundreds of our brigade can testify. We got all the money there was in these wagons and we got it "honest."

We knew it was there all the time and guarded it, and nobody ever got near it but we never stole any of it either—but we got it.

But to go back a little in this narrative, as before stated, we met President Davis and his cabinet officers at Greensboro, North Carolina, and escorted them as far as Washington, Georgia, passing through Salisbury, Charlotte, Abbeville and other towns of less note.

It was at Charlotte that Mr. Davis received the telegram announcing the assassination of Mr. Lincoln. Mr. Davis was just about to enter the hotel door, when a courier dashed up with the dispatch and it was passed to him over the heads of the crowd of men in the front yard.

I was standing just inside the hall door, and when the President opened and read the dispatch, I noticed that he was greatly affected by it. Turning to Mr. Reagan, who was by his side, he handed him the paper with the remark, "This is very unfortunate, read it to the men." When Mr. Reagan had read it aloud, a solemn stillness, approaching awe, settled over the crowd for several minutes, when the terrible deed was discussed in whispers among the men.

All looked on the deed as an outrage and a calamity. While we had fought against the ideas upheld by Mr. Lincoln, none held him personally responsible, and although we differed with him in principle we respected him as a patriot from his standpoint and honest in his convictions.

We had long since learned that he was not to blame for the horrors of the war, but the passive agent of a lot of ambitious and avaricious men who had gained control and used him as an instrument to further their ambition. The same men tried this on General Grant after the war, but found him made of sterner stuff.

Right here I did the only horse-trading I ever had or ever have done, and after they read of it, I will ask my readers, if they think I made it pay. I swapped my gray mule to an old citizen near Abbeville, for a mustang pony and the pony for a three-year-old roan colt with four white feet and glass eyes. I expected to ride home and as this kind of a horse was entitled to free ferriage and I had several rivers to cross, the saving would be considerable. But a young man, riding a very fine seventeen-hand mule, took a fancy to my horse and we traded. I sold out, mule, saddle and bridle to a Georgia farmer for fifteen dollars in gold, and started out to walk home with forty-one dollars and forty cents in my pocket. This was more money than I had seen for three years and I felt rich. Had I met Jay Gould, Vanderbilt or any of our big rich men at that time, I doubt if I should have spoken to them, except as a mere condescension. But I walked into Washington and into the provost marshal's office—there were two of them, both Jews, Asahel Mann and Lot Abraham. I went to Mann's office—and got my parole, went down to the depot, jumped on a freight train and rode to Atlanta. Got to Atlanta about midnight and went to the Kimball House, the only one left in town, got breakfast, paid a round silver (Mexican) dollar for it, and at ten o'clock, started out with six others, to walk to Dalton or home as necessity required.

You see, about this time we were not choice as to our accommodations and accommodated ourselves to circumstances. If we had a chance to ride we rode, if not, "bejabbers," we walked.

We had done all we could and had our heads turned towards home and nothing could stop or turn us. It was home or "bust" like the Pike's Peakers.

By the terms of surrender, cavalrymen were allowed to retain their horses and side-arms and all men without horses were to be furnished transportation to their respective States. To those traveling through the country, arms were indispensable for protection against bushwhackers who infested the route and it was also unsafe for us to travel except in sufficient numbers together to protect ourselves.

Organizing a party of six and eating our dollar breakfast, we started out to walk to Dalton (101 miles) the railroad having been destroyed to that point. We were unable to draw any rations and left Atlanta at ten A.M. to walk this hundred miles with nothing to depend on but our dollar breakfast under our belts and no prospect of adding to it before we reached the end of our tramp. This may seem a gloomy outlook, but we had practiced starving for so long that it did not discourage us. We depended on some streak of good luck to pull us through and it did. We were fresh and made the twenty-two miles to Marietta by 4 P.M.

There were only a few small cottages left of the once handsome town and they were occupied by some women and children who drew rations from Uncle Sam. I went prospecting for "grub" and made myself so agreeable to one of the women that she baked us a corn pone apiece out of the meal she had saved.

An idea of the character and size of this ration can be formed from a description. Made of kiln-dried army meal with cold water and no salt, baked in an eight-inch skillet or "spider," two to the spider, until the top of the pones cracked open in nice squares, resembling a diminutive map of the earth, showing the parallels of latitude and longitude and at which point the mass is supposed to be hot through and "done" and there you have it. Meat of any kind was out of the question, but we were glad to get the bread; such as it was, it "beat nothin'."

With a corn "pone" in each of our haversacks we proceeded on our journey and walked out to Big Shanty, where we camped and started out next morning by daybreak, eating our breakfast as we went. We had discovered the night before than we had been going the "pace that kills" and must move more slowly, if we expected to reach our destination. I was chosen leader and set the pace the rest of the way. I divided the march into relays of six miles and an hour and a half to each relay, giving a rest of fifteen minutes at the latter end of each. The boys all stood this arrangement well except Al Smith of the Ninth.

He was tall and heavy, his boots had high heels and fit him a little "too quick" and he was soon, after leaving Big Shanty, walking like a frost-bitten chicken.

I wore a pair of English army shoes, prowled at Greensboro—I didn't steal them, just prowled them—which were very comfortable. In order to help Al along I exchanged with him and an hour after I was as badly crippled as he. The boots were too short for me and on a down-hill pull inflicted indescribable torture. It seemed inevitable that our whole expedition was to be wrecked by Al Smith's boots and we stopped to hold a parley and devise ways and means to save at least enough of the party to carry the news home, when our usual good luck came to the rescue and we were saved.

An old citizen from near Chattonooga came driving up and we proceeded to interview him. We learned that he was returning from the sea coast, where he had been after salt.

He drove an old crooked-legged mule and a little "flea bitten" gray pony to a ramshackle wagon tied together with withes and bits of hoop iron, and his load consisted of himself, three bags of salt and about a dozen bundles of fodder. A less inviting conveyance for a long ride could hardly be imagined, but we were not in condition to be squeamish and made the best of circumstances. With the aid of our Kentucky eloquence, supplemented by a ten-dollar gold-piece, we at last prevailed on him to haul Al to Dalton on condition that Al should walk up all the bad hills. This was a necessary proviso as the team was very light and Al on the other extreme.

We five again took up our line of march, but had not gone very far before we began to grow uneasy about Al. The old "cit" had insisted on pay in advance and Smith had imprudently exposed his "pile" when paying him. This coupled with the fact that the old fellow told us he would take a different road from the one we were on—it being more level—made us suspicious and we feared foul play. But we finally concluded that Al had his two pistols and had been through so many close places he would look out for himself, and pushed on. But I need not tell you that we felt good when about ten o'clock the second night a wagon drew up near our camp, a mile out from Dalton, and Al Smith's voice hailed us with, "What command do you belong to?" We soon had him and the old man out of the wagon, the horses watered and fed, and in a few minutes were sitting around a bright fire reveling on broiled ham and hard-tack and enjoying a feast, from our standpoint, fit for the Gods.

"But where did you get these things?" says someone. "Now, we have caught you in a lie, because you have done said that you had nothing to eat but some cold corn bread."

Yes! But let me tell you something. We had walked along eating our corn "pone," a pinch now and then, followed by a refreshing drink of water from one of the delicious springs found all over north Georgia and east Tennessee, and when we felt hungry we buckled our belts a little tighter. The constant pinching on the "pone" and natural abrasion, by the end of the first day, reduced our bread to crumbs. This did not make much difference as it saved chewing and we got the nourishment. We only had to take out a handful of crumbs, open our mouths pretty wide, pour the crumbs down our throats and our stomachs did the rest. Of course we drank at the next branch, always. By this arrangement we used a large amount of water, which was not strictly in keeping with the Kentucky idea, but it was the thickest drink we could get and we had to take it.

Now, about that ham and E—crackers. When within about two miles of Dalton, our party met a Federal cavalry company. The captain halted us and asked whom we were.

Being spokesman for our party, I stepped forward and replied, "Members of Williams' Kentucky cavalry on our way home."

"Have you paroles?" asked the captain.

We exhibited our paroles and at the same time gave him to understand that we were hungry and would like to know if we could get something to eat when we got to town.

"No," said he, "rations are issued at nine in the morning, and your names will have to be reported, or you will be left out. But I think I can arrange it for you to have your supper anyway."

Turning to his men, he said, "Boys, these men are hungry. We have three days' rations with us for a two days' trip. Let's divide with them. Some of you give them bread and some meat. Open. Order. March."

They opened up the column, we mached down the ranks and received their contributions as long as we had any place to store them and declined the balance with thanks. The captain advised us to camp at a spring of water near-by, which we did, and went into town the next morning.

I am glad to record the kindness of this captain and his command. While numerous instances of this kind occurred during our war, they were always unexpected, and I am proud to believe would be impossible in any other country. All honor to this captain and his men. I am very sorry that I lost the memorandum I had of his name and command.

We went into Dalton next morning and found that the train would leave for Chattanooga in a half hour. Anxious to get home we made no attempt to draw "rations," but went to the provost marshal for transportation. Examining our paroles he kindly gave us a ticket to Chattanooga, which was the limit of his jurisdiction.

We took the train, arrived in Chattanooga about eleven A.M., and reported to the provost marshal, who acted like he was in control of the United States Government, and a very mean man. When we exhibited our paroles, he very promptly hung them on his file, called a squad of soldiers and ordered them to take us to prison. They very kindly relieved us of our pistols and in spite of our remonstrance marched us off to the "bull pen."

Our paroles were afterwards returned to us, but they kept our pistols as trophies of the great victory the provost marshal had won over our large force of six.

We had received universally kind treatment since our surrender until now and it was easy for us to decide that this P. M. had not done any duty on the field, but now, having the power, was determined to end the war. Grant and Sherman, from his point of view, were failures, and what they had failed to do in four years he would do in a day. If now living, I have no doubt he is claiming all the credit for having conquered the South and boasts of this capture of our squad as the culmination of his great feat.

When our mounted men arrived in Chattanooga, this same P. M. refused to respect the terms of surrender and dismounted and disarmed them. When General Williams arrived later and found this out, he went to headquarters and read "the riot act" to the P. M. with such effect as to get an order for the return of the horses and equipments. Going with the boys to the government lot where there was a large number of horses and mules, the general told them to go in and "If you come out worse mounted than you was before, it will be your own fault." Most of the boys stuck to their old horses that had shared their past trials and dangers, but many of them came out with better mounts than they had ever possessed. The general did not know that we were in prison or he would have had us out, too.

Our foot squad stayed in prison and reveled in good (?) grub for three days. Our rations consisted of three army crackers and a piece of raw codfish of the size of a cracker issued to us each morning. We had nothing to cook and no fire to cook it on, but there was a good well of water in the prison, and fortunately the supply was not limited, and by punching more holes in our belts and by drawing them tighter every day, we managed to hold out for three days, when they decided to send us on.

This was our most annoying experience. We had our "heads set" for home, had the right to go on, and to be detained by a little shoulder-strapped upstart who never smelt powder was very aggravating I can assure you; but we lived through it and after we got started on our way again soon forgot it.

Such is a soldier's life. He takes his chances and makes the most of his experiences. Enjoying his victories, he soon forgets defeat and is ready for another trial.

It may seem strange that General Williams could keep his men out of prison and I should fail with mine, as we were both subject to the same conditions under the terms of surrender, but I think I can explain.

General Williams was a general and "ranked" the provost marshal, who was a captain, and they both "ranked" me, who could only sport three "chevrons." The general weighed 320 pounds, while I only weighed 204, which gave him the weight over me. The P. M., backed by his bayonets, also outranked me. Then the general had a more effective way of "cussin'" than I. He had been in the Mexican war and practiced on the "greasers," while I had only four years' experimenting on Yankees, and you know experience counts in all business.

It would have afforded me immense satisfaction to have had that P. M. off to himself for about two minutes. I would have fixed him up in such a shape that his mother would not have known him, but discretion said "no," and I didn't invite him out. Perhaps it was best. He might have died and I would have always felt bad about it.

But, maybe, you think I didn't "cuss" him. Yes, I did. After we were turned into the pen and the gates closed, I turned loose on that P. M. and created a perfect blue sulphurous halo around him. Fortunately, he was in his office down-town and didn't hear it.

In the forenoon of the fourth day of our imprisonment, the gate was thrown open and we were requested to abandon the premises. As none of us were particularly attached to the place there was no "kicking," and we did not wait for the invitation to be repeated. As we were not encumbered with baggage, it did not take us long to get a move on us.

As we passed out of the gate each man was handed his parole and a transportation ticket to Nashville. To show the difference in men, I will relate our experience at the gate.

The officer in charge had an empty sleeve, showing that he had "been there," and he proved himself a good judge of human nature and a noble man.

He made us a little talk after we had assembled and I will endeavor to repeat his words, as I have never forgotten the impression he left on my mind, and he was the first man from the North to sound the keynote of reconciliation.

"Men," said he, "I have here the parole of every man who is entitled to one.

"There are some who have not been paroled and they will try to claim that belonging to another in order to escape. In order to do justice I shall require everyone claiming to identify himself by at least three of his comrades. Every man here is entitled to what he has honestly earned. While you were wrong from my standpoint, you have proven yourselves brave men and as such deserve the respect of all other brave men and whatever is your due.

"Exercise a little patience and I will try to do you all justice."

I noticed that a rough-looking gang—sporting extra long hair and big spurs—which had taken the head of the column, began to disperse and knew at once that the old Yankee captain had them "spotted" when he made his remarks.

As we passed out of the prison an orderly handed us our paroles and tickets and the captain shook hands with us and gave each a word of encouragement as we passed. Somehow, I can't help but like that kind of a man, if he was a Yankee soldier, and wherever he is now, living or dead, may he be enjoying the happiness due to a noble Christian manhood.

I ask pardon for this long digression, but the contrast was so great between the provost marshal and the "one arm" captain that I could not help it. Brave men respect bravery, even in a foe, while a coward—with authority —is a tyrant.

But we got out of prison and made our way to the railroad and "piled" into a lot of box and stock cars provided for our trip to Nashville and pulled out at 4 P.M. There were eight hundred of us and our train consisted of an engine and twelve cars. So it is easy to understand that we were loaded inside and out.

As the inside was crowded, I took a top berth. Soon after leaving Chattanooga a very angry cloud made its appearance over Waldron's Ridge and one of the worst rainstorms that I ever witnessed burst upon us. I was on top of a car and, of course, got wet, but cared nothing for it as I was accustomed to it and, then, I was going home. We were running down the Tennessee River valley between high mountains and the night was "pitch" dark only relieved by occasional flashes of lightning which added to the weirdness of the trip.

Just before daylight the engineer whistled "down brakes" and we came to a standstill. Investigation showed our engine standing with the cowcatcher hanging over an abyss of raging water, where a trestle a hundred feet long had been washed away. Fortunately, the Yankees still retained guards at all railroad bridges, or we would have gone into this washout and no one can tell what would have been the consequence. Lucky again.

We backed up a sidetrack, a wrecking train came down from the city, and by ten next morning we were again on our way. After crossing the Tennessee at Bridgeport, and when we started up the mountain, our engine gave out. We had no "Moguls" then, our train was heavy and the track was slick, so we dismounted and helped the train up to the tunnel, where we boarded it again and went on to Nashville, where we arrived about bedtime, were sidetracked and left to make ourselves as comfortable as circumstances would allow and slept until late the next morning. We were aroused by a colonel with a regiment of "blue coats," who marched us to headquarters. We supposed that we would be furnished "transportation" home and went along rather joyfully.

But a new surprise was in store for us. Arriving at headquarters, we were marched four at a time, into the august presence of the major-in-charge.

He informed us that we must take the oath of allegiance, "the first thing." Well, they had it on us and we couldn't help ourselves. So we stepped under their measuring machine and on their weighing machine. A cross-eyed clerk took the color of our eyes and hair (looking at somebody else out of his good eye all the time) and we signed the oath, because we were in a hurry to get home. But this did not satisfy the major. He wanted us to swear to it, and ordered his sergeant, who was a Dutchman, to take us out on the street and swear us. The Dutchman—or sergeant—knew how to form us in line, but he hadn't been long enough in this country to learn to read English as "she is writ," hence the Dutchman got a little confused.

Forming us in line, two ranks on the street, his first order was: "Addenchun, repels. Holt oup your hands unt pe schwordt."

To better convey the idea and show how ridiculous the farce was, I will give you the proceedings as they occurred.

"Now, you tam repels listen," said he, "I am goin' to schwar you. Hol't up your recht handt."

We all "held up" and he began to read the oath: "I—rebeat you names," said he. "Effery feller got to call his name oudt.—Vell, I—too—sollemnly—swear—dat—I—vill—defent—de—gonstitution—off . . ." About now we got tired and at the same time his reading ran out and he had to turn over a leaf. Lifting his eyes, he saw us with all hands down and it made him furious. Of course we couldn't hold our hands up until a Dutchman read that oath through and we wasn't going to do it.

After making three trials, our Dutch sergeant gave up the job and told us to go. He called up a company of infantry with fixed bayonets and swore he would have us run through if we didn't keep our hands "oup," but they had seen service in the field and appreciated our feelings. They joined in with us in a big laugh at the Dutchman's expense and this settled the business.

The irony of this affair was that a "flannel mouth" Dutchman, who could neither speak or read good "United States," was chosen to administer the oath of allegiance to American citizens.

On a vacant lot near headquarters, five or six Jews had set up lemonade stands, and as we passed they rushed out at us crying, "Ice lemonade; five cents a glass" and kept up a terrible din.

We all felt a little devilish and did not care much for consequences. One of our boys, a six-footer weighing over two hundred, who was in front of us, called a halt and made a little speech. "Boys," said he, "we are about to separate, perhaps, never to meet again. Thanks to Jeff Davis, I have the means to 'set 'em up' at the price. I want you all to join me in a pledge of eternal friendship and this is a good opportunity. Come up and call for what you want."

The Jews were happy, and we all took lemonade. The glasses being small, our leader ordered them refilled. After draining them we started off, our leader in the lead, and the Jews rushed at him demanding pay. He tried to reason with them, but only made them more importunate. They pulled at him and "cussed" him in Dutch until he could stand it no longer, and grabbing one of them by the shoulders, he gave him a swing, knocked down two of his companions and pitched him over onto his stand utterly demolishing it. You ought to have seen the Jews gather up their traps and run. We were near a regiment of Federal soldiers and they enjoyed the fun as much as we; and we had no trouble over it.

We went up to the Capitol grounds, where it was shady and quiet, and there had our leave-taking. The occasion was pathetic beyond description. Strong men, who but a few minutes before were full of fun and deviltry, wept as if their hearts would break; and each one registered a vow in heaven to be true to his comrade and his cause. How well that vow has been kept, let the history of the last thirty years bear witness.

We separated; each going his way. Never all to meet again until we assemble at the last "great tattoo."

Louis Wall had stuck to me like a brother since our night adventure with Sherman's army in South Carolina, and being unable to dispose of his mule at Washington, left him and came along with me. We were the only boys from Union County and at the separation were left to ourselves. We went up in the city and bought some clean clothes. Expecting to obtain transportation home, Louis invested all his money and if I had not had my "mule money" extra I would have been in the same fix.

We went to the provost marshal's office to get our ticket home, presented our credentials to a little upstart of a sergeant, who seemed to be in charge, and who examined them carefully, stepped over to a map hanging on the wall and after running his pen staff around over the map a few minutes, came over to us, handed us back our papers with the remark: "It ain't very far home, you fellows can walk."

"But," said I, "Sergeant, we are entitled to transportation by the terms of surrender."

"You can walk, I say," said he, "and you had better be at it—quick."

Whoop! But how I wanted to wring his neck! But he had a lot of soldiers with sharp-pointed guns around him, and we had to "walk," so we walked down to the river and found the steamer *Silver Spray* preparing to leave for Cincinnati and engaged passage to Caseyville at six dollars apiece. I paid for both and found that my bank account was nearly exhausted, but this caused but little trouble, as I was on my last relay for home.

Before we got away from Nashville there were six hundred men aboard and the little boat was crowded almost to suffocation. Owing to the obstructions in Cumberland River, our progress was very slow and our supplies ran a little short, but the captain did all he could to make us comfortable. About 9 o'clock on the second night out, we landed to take coal at Brown's landing on the Ohio River.

Old Dick McConnel had charge of the coal-yard. He came aboard and recognized me and began to tell me a most horrible yarn of six returned Confederates being shot down and that all Confederate soldiers coming back would be treated the same way. He offered to board Louis and me until things settled down. When he proposed this, I saw through his scheme and felt greatly relieved.

Dick was after a board bill and his tale was a lie made of whole cloth, as I suspected and afterwards learned to be true.

The captain heard Dick's story and put more faith in it that I and grew very uneasy. He wanted us to stay on the boat until it was safe for us to return home.

His words were: "I don't want you to be murdered, stay with me until you can go home in safety and it won't cost you a cent."

I thanked him and told him that I fully appreciated his kindness, but that I was in no danger with my neighbors and would go home. The river was very high and the boat could not land at Caseyville, so we got off at Battery Rock, Illinois. After landing us and backing out, the captain had the engines stopped when abreast of us and offered to land if we would come aboard, but we declined with thanks.

I saw the captain at Caseyville a few weeks after and when he saw me safe and sound, had I been his own son, I don't see how he could have shown more joy. I am sorry that I cannot recall his name, but he was a fine old Christian gentleman. One of the kind to show his faith by his work.

Climbing the hill at Battery Rock, Louis and I ran upon a cabin where the young folks were having a party.

As we neared the house I discovered a couple seated on a rustic seat outside, and, approaching, inquired for the ferryman.

The young man replied that he was half a mile away and asleep.

My late experience had made my ears pretty sharp and I detected something familiar in the man's voice. Calling him to "one side," I soon discovered that I was talking to Sam Penrod.

Now Sam had enlisted in the infantry at Camp Boone, was at Fort Donelson, and when he was exchanged concluded he had enough and quit, and was now working in the coal mine at Battery Rock. It did not take long to make myself known to Sam and enlist his sympathy. He took his girl to the house and came back with two pairs of oars and we were soon across the river.

I gave Sam all the money I had, except thirty-five cents, which I kept for luck, and Louis and I struck out for home. We walked out to Mrs. Metcalfe's woodland pasture, two miles out, being tired and sleepy, spread our blankets down under a large tree and slept the sweet sleep of content. Awakening the next morning, I discovered that we were surrounded by a circle of fox hounds, sitting solemnly around us like a coroner's jury over a "floater" and when I opened my eyes on the scene I wondered if this was a new world or had I only been dreaming. Four years before I had hunted the festive fox behind these same hounds and while I remembered them I asked myself the question, "Will they know me?"

Rising to a sitting posture, I called out "Dave, Kate, Rattler, Bill, Spanker!" Before I could get through the list, with a howl, they all rushed on me, over me, licking my face and hands and by every other means known to a dog expressing their delight. They knew me and were glad to see me and you know, my readers, that although their welcome was rough I enjoyed it because I knew it was genuine. Louis was asleep and not prepared for the demonstration. He jumped up and ran a few steps, but when he saw the dogs on me and thought that I was being torn to pieces he grabbed a fence stake and came to the rescue; and had I not been able to get up and stop him, some or probably all of my dog friends would have gotten hurt.

Rolling up our blankets we went up to the house followed by the hounds, and when I knocked the door was opened by Mrs. Metcalfe.

On recognizing me the good old lady threw up her hands and said, "Thank God, I see you once more." She flew around and soon had everything on the place in to see us—Negroes and all. So far we had found nothing to kill us, and took heart to go on. After eating a good breakfast, we struck out for home.

Except the danger, our trip was almost as slow as the Dalton-Atlanta campaign. Every one we met demanded a history of our experience. At last, in sheer desperation, we left the road—"took to the woods"—and I got home in time for dinner. By some means they had heard that I was coming and my old black "mammy"—God bless her—had "spread herself." Had I eaten to her satisfaction I would not be here now to tell of it.

But don't think I failed to do justice to the subject—Oh, no. I had lived on half rations, quarter rations, nothing and less until there was a good big storage room under my belt, and as this was the first chance I had had to fill it, I used it.

But the home-coming. How pleasant and yet how sad. Although Mother's greeting is as warm as heart could wish, we see the lines of care and anxiety pictured on the loved countenance and realize that we have caused it, and at the same time she says, "God bless you, my son, I am proud of you." The mothers of the world have been the sufferers while their sons have been the heroes. The one suffers in silence while the other wins his fame. And the stern old father whose honor is at stake, proud of his ancestry and yet too old to take active part. His welcome home to the wanderer is worth all the cost.

How many Kentuckians of the Confederate army there are who can realize the picture! Kentucky honor was involved, and a true Kentuckian holds honor above every other consideration. For this reason Kentucky troops have always been famous for their devotion to duty. In the late war Kentuckians, on both sides of the line, proved themselves the "true grit." This is the fault of their "raisin'" and they can't help it, you know.

We will soon all cross the dark river and the world will soon forget us (individually) in its great rush, but our deeds will be perpetuated in living fire. The heroic deeds of the American soldier will be a theme for history, romance and song as long as the world exists. Like the struggle of William Tell for freedom for Switzerland, and like Banquo's ghost, the gallant deeds of men and noble deeds of women in our late struggle "will not down."

What has been written in "Reminiscences" has been the truth so far as my memory serves me, and is endorsed by numbers now living who were present and participated in the occurrences recorded.

I have attempted to give events as they transpired and impressed me at the time.

I have, also, tried to be fair with my Yankee brother and give him all the credit he is entitled to. I have endeavored to "set down nought in malice, nor in aught to extenuate." I have tried (conscientiously) to record "things" just as they occurred and as I saw them, and as many of my comrades yet living can identify. If I have erred in any statement that I have made, I am unconscious of it and the error was not intentional. I believe that my experience, in the main, was that of thousands of other Confederate soldiers and will be readily recognized by numbers who read these chapters.

Young men gather around me of evenings and ask me to tell them of the war—they have learned how to draw me out—and one of them is sure to ask me if I would go to war again. My answer is, "There never will be cause for a civil war in this country, but should any foreign power undertake to 'bulldoze' us, no telling what might happen." Of course, I am too old now but I could stir the young fellows up and get them into it. As they have their "dad's" experience before them and everyone thinks he is bigger than his "dad," we would have the finest army in the world and whip the daylights out of anything that came before us.

But let us pray for peace. War brings so much suffering to the women and children, and is so costly in lives and money, that it is, taken all in all, an unprofitable investment.

A word now to the old soldiers: thirty-three years have passed—eventful for some of us—since the end of the greatest struggle recorded in any history. Looking backward to those stirring times we can see where mistakes were made; opportunities lost and foolish acts performed; yet we can point with pride to the heroic deeds of the American soldier of the late civil war, and coming on up to the present, to his still nobler acts in time of peace.

The men of the North and the South disagreed as to public policy, failed to settle their differences peaceably; took up arms and fought to a finish. After the war was over these same men came together to form a new nation out of the wreck of the old and how well they succeeded all can see.

The civil war cost us millions of treasure, oceans of blood and tears, untold suffering and misery and the lives of thousands of our best men; yet it has been worth to our country all its cost.

From a people divided on sectional lines as to policy, interest and ambition, we have emerged from the wreck of war and are now a united people, proud that we have the greatest country and grandest record of any nation on the globe. No contention exists among our people, "except that noble contention, or rather emulation as to who can best work and best agree" for the good and the honor of our common heritage.

Those who were the best soldiers have proven themselves the best citizens, and having fought for the honor of their country, have felt in duty bound to maintain it. But old age is creeping on us and it will be but a few short years till we shall all answer the last tattoo and be mustered out of service. Have we discharged our whole duty? Have we been as zealous as we should in inculcating the principles we have so faithfully held sacred, into the coming generations?

If we have not our work is not finished and our duty not done. We do not live for ourselves alone and all our work will have been for nought if we fail to instill those principles into the posterity for whom we are responsible.

One of the greatest pleasures of the old soldier is to meet a comrade and together fight over the old battles and live over the scenes of long ago. This is one object which impelled me to write these lines, and I commend them in unbounded love to my old comrades who wore the gray. You, my Yankee brother who have read these pages, I think I have found that those who faced you on so many bloody fields have nothing but the greatest regard and honest good will toward you; that the blue and gray have blended and stand shoulder to shoulder for the common good! One in pride, one in honor and one in love of country.

17

The Last Confederate Cruiser

Cornelius E. Hunt

The principal part of the duty assigned us had been discharged in the destruction and dispersing of the New England whaling fleet, and it was with feelings of profound relief that we at last saw these frozen seas, with their many perils seen and unseen, where for weeks we had been battling with ice or groping blindly in impenetrable fogs, fading in the distance.

All were in good spirits, as we had reason to be, after performing well a laborious and in many respects unpleasant duty, and as each day carried us nearer these genial seas where for a time we expected to cruise, the memory of many hardships faded from our minds. Thus we sped us on our way. . . .

We saw no sail after leaving the Straits on the 30th of June, until the 2d of August, when we sighted a barque. The wind was very light, so we got up steam, and stood toward her, flying the English ensign at our peak. As we approached, she showed the same colors, and although we had no reason to doubt from her general appearance but that she had a perfect right to carry the flag she flew, we stopped our engines and dispatched an officer on board, in the hope of obtaining some comparatively recent news from the world of which we had known so little for many weary months.

In the course of half an hour the boat returned, bringing intelligence of the gravest possible moment. The Southern cause was lost—hopelessly—irretrievably—and the war ended. Our gallant generals, one after another, had been forced to surrender the armies they had so often led to victory. State after State had been overrun and occupied by the countless myriads of our enemies, until star by star the galaxy of our flag had faded, and the Southern Confederacy had ceased to exist. . . .

CORNELIUS E. HUNT, *The* Shenandoah; *or the Last Confederate Cruiser* (New York, 1867), Chs. ix, x.
The *Shenandoah*, purchased by the Confederacy in England, was second only to the more famous *Alabama* in the amount of damage inflicted on United States commerce. Cruising mainly in the Arctic, it captured and destroyed or released on bond 38 ships of the New England whaling fleet in Northern Pacific waters. Cornelius Hunt was a minor officer, and his charges of Commander Waddell's peculations have been doubted. Yet Waddell, who lived until 1885, took no notice of the charges.

The news gathered from the *Barracouta* was as overwhelming as it was unexpected, and every man felt as though he had just learned of the death of a near and dear relative. Indeed, it is seldom that men find themselves so strongly circumstanced as we then were, and we might well feel serious apprehension.

It had been three months since hostilities ceased, leaving us without a flag or a country, and during that time we had been actively engaged in preying upon the commerce of a Government that not only claimed our allegiance, but had made good her claim by wager of battle.

It required no prophet to foretell what construction the people of the North would put upon our actions. We well knew the inveterate hatred with which they regarded the people of the seceded States. From the first they had stigmatized our cruisers as pirates, even when we were recognized as belligerents by the leading powers of the world, and they would not be likely to let slip such an opportunity as our last escapade had furnished them with to glut their vengeance with our blood should we fall into their hands.

True, it would have been apparent to any unprejudiced person that cruising as we had been in the Arctic Seas, entirely out of the track of news, we could not have become cognizant, except through the interposition of a miracle, of any event transpiring in the United States, short of three or four months; but the people, who without a shade of reason, could incarcerate Jefferson Davis, and accuse him of being implicated in a brutal murder, would not be very apt to see any extenuating circumstances in our case, and every man of us knew that if the *Shenandoah* was captured before she could reach an English port, his days were numbered.

The officers of the *Barracouta* deeply sympathized with us in our unpleasant dilemma, but they could do nothing save wish us God-speed and a safe deliverance from the hands of our enemies; but it was very evident they entertained small hopes of our eluding the many snares that were and would be set for our feet. Several United States cruisers and one English man-of-war, they knew, had been dispatched in search of us, and it was like running a very gauntlet of life to hope to escape all these dangers unscathed.

But there was no use in repining. What had been done in the past could not be helped; the record of our deeds was written in imperishable characters, and could not be gainsaid. And now that we had no longer a country to claim our services, self-preservation was the first thing to be considered.

As soon as the English vessel had proceeded on her way, Captain Waddell summoned his whole ship's company aft, and formally announced to them the startling intelligence he had just received. No man of them, he said, had any reason to blush for the service in which he had been engaged; our cruise had been projected and prosecuted in good faith; it had inflicted heavy blows upon the commerce of our late enemies, which would not soon be forgotten; but now there was nothing more to be done but to secure our personal safety by the readiest and most efficacious means at hand. As a cruiser we had no longer a right to sail the seas, for in that character we were liable to capture by the ship of any civilized nation, for we had no longer a flag to give a semblance of legality to our proceedings.

The address was listened to respectfully, and after a brief consultation among themselves, the crew presented a petition signed by nearly all of their number, requesting our captain to proceed at once to Sydney, Australia, the nearest English port, and there abandon the ship to Her Majesty's authorities, and let each man look out for his own personal safety.

Captain Waddell at once professed to accede to this request, and for twenty-four hours the vessel was actually headed for Sydney; but events proved that he had really no intention of ever going there, and at the expiration of the time I have mentioned, he altered the course of the ship without announcing the fact to anyone, and steered for Cape Horn en route for Liverpool.

From a letter of Captain Waddell's . . . it will be seen that he gives a somewhat different version of this affair, but I speak from my own personal knowledge when I say that he promised his crew to run the *Shenandoah* into Sydney, and then, without their cognizance, steered for another and more distant port, thus subjecting them to what they considered unnecessary peril, for the sake of securing a considerable sum of money which he knew to be lodged in the hands of one of our secret agents at Liverpool, and I further assert that nothing like a mutinous spirit even, unless a petition they subsequently submitted may be called so, was ever manifested by any officer from the time we left the English shores till we returned to them.

It will be remembered that when we first set sail from Madeira, the labor devolved upon us of transforming the merchantman *Sea King* into the cruiser *Shenandoah*, and now, so far as possible, that work was to be undone, and with sad hearts we betook ourselves to the task. The same tackles which had been used in transferring our armament from the *Laurel* to our decks, were again got aloft to assist in dismounting the heavy guns, and striking them below, beyond the reach of prying eyes—port-holes were closed up, our smoke-stack whitewashed, and in appearance our ship was a quiet merchantman, peacefully pursuing her way, with naught to apprehend from any vessel she might encounter on the high seas. . . .

We made a splendid run from the line to the Cape and nearly rounded it, well to the southward, without any incident worth recording, but we were not destined to get entirely clear of the Horn without a specimen of the tempestuous weather for which that locality is so widely celebrated.

We were just congratulating ourselves upon our fortunate passage round this dreaded Cape, when we encountered a gale which for a few hours was absolutely terrific, and lay to under close-reefed main-topsail, and fore-storm staysail, with a tarpaulin in the fore-rigging to ride it out. The sea ran mountains high, dashing its spray far up into the rigging, and more than one huge wave made a clean breach over us, leaving such a quantity of water on our decks as to engender at times grave fears for our safety. The ship was tossed about like a cockle-shell, but happily we sustained no serious injury, and when the tempest had finally blown itself out we got clear of "old Cape Misery," as it is sometimes aptly called by sailors, and were once more standing on our course to the eastward, but keeping much further to the south than is ordinarily done by vessels bound for the port that we were, to avoid falling in with any cruisers that might be looking for us. . . .

Of course long before this time the crew had discovered that whatever part of the world they might be steering for, they were certainly not heading for Australia, and some dissatisfaction was felt, not only by them, but by the officers, at Captain Waddell's open violation of his pledge.

Justice compels me to say that the captain's conduct was not free from censure. He had his own reasons, as I have intimated, for preferring to reach Liverpool and there surrender his ship, but he should have announced this fact in the first place instead of promising what he did not intend to perform, and thus leading many to apprehend that he was actuated by some motive that would not bear explanation.

About this time a petition was gotten up among the officers, and signed by all of them with the exception of five, requesting the captain to run for Cape Town, then to the eastward of us, and there surrender the ship to the proper authorities.

To this petition he vouchsafed no response direct or otherwise. With the quartermaster he held long, confidential interviews, and to him confided his plans, which he studiously concealed from one and all of his officers, and it was only through this subaltern that we could obtain any information as to where we were bound, though of course our destination was by many suspected.

Such conduct was as injudicious as it was unjust, and gave rise to grave suspicions touching our commander's integrity or purpose, which, I am sorry to say, the event did not prove to be altogether unfounded.

At length, after several days had passed without any notice being taken of his officers' petition, he called the five who had not signed it, upon the quarter-deck, and for the first time informed them that he intended taking the ship to Liverpool. . . .

But although I differed from my brother officers as to the expediency of their proposed measure, I fully agreed with them in regarding the conduct of Captain Waddell as unwarranted and ungentlemanly, and the letter he subsequently wrote denouncing them as mutineers was one of the most dastardly returns a commander ever made to officers who from first to last had faithfully discharged every duty assigned to them, and certainly never committed an act to sully their honor while on board the *Shenandoah*. . . .

On the 4th of November, our reckoning showed us to be near land, and all eyes were anxiously scanning the horizon, for a glimpse of old England. We knew not what reception was in store for us, for momentous changes had taken place since we set forth on that adventurous pilgrimage round the world, but we were weary of suspense and all were desirous of making port, and learning the worst as soon as possible.

Night, however, closed around us, with nothing but the heaving sea with which we had been so long familiar, in sight, and the following morning a dense fog was hanging over the water, effectually concealing everything from view at a ship's length distance.

Extreme caution was now necessary, as we had only our chronometers and the patent log towing astern to rely upon for showing us our position, but we steamed slowly ahead with all sails furled, laying our course for St. George's Channel.

Soon the fog lifted, revealing to our view the green shores of Ireland, on our port beam—the first land we had seen since we lost sight of the snow-clad bluffs of Northern American, one hundred and thirty-one days before.

Notwithstanding the uncertainty in which our fate was still enshrouded, there were many happy faces to be seen on the *Shenandoah's* decks that memorable morning, as we glided on toward Tuska Rock Light. Soon we had that abeam, and were steaming, at the rate of nine knots an hour, to the northward and eastward toward Holyhead.

Thirteen months before, we set sail from that point in the steamer *Laurel*, to join our ship at Madeira, little anticipating such a return. Shipwreck, capture, and disaster in many forms, we were prepared to look forward to as things possible, but the utter collapse of our Government, that had so long and so successfully stood upon the defensive, leaving our ship a veritable Ishmael of the sea, with none to claim or recognize her for other than a lawless freeboater, was such a culmination of misfortunes as none of us had counted upon. And while from full hearts more than one sincere thanksgiving, silent, but nonetheless acceptable, perhaps, went up to Almighty God for our almost miraculous escape from those who had gone forth to hunt us, like wild beasts, to death; there was many a sorrowful association connected with this spot, where began and ended our world-renowned cruise.

At midnight the pilot boat was seen approaching, and ere long that functionary was on board. As soon as this was known everyone was on the alert, anxious to see him and learn what news he had to tell, and perhaps gain some inkling as to the spirit in which the wanderers were to be received.

As he came over the side he was met by our first lieutenant, who bade him "Good morning."

"Good morning," the pilot responded; "what ship is this?"

"The late Confederate Steamer *Shenandoah*."

"The deuce it is! Where have you fellows come from last?"

"From the Artic Ocean."

"Haven't you stopped at any port since you left there?"

"No; nor been in sight of land either. What news from the war in America?"

"It has been over so long people have got through talking about it. Jeff Davis is in Fortress Monroe, and the Yankees have had a lot of cruisers out looking for you. Haven't you seen any of them?"

"Not unless a suspicious-looking craft we sighted off the Western Islands was one."

The pilot then took command of the ship, which would have been received in Liverpool with so much *éclat* had our cause triumphed in the late contest. In that event we should have been the heroes of the hour, sought after and feted as we had been in Melborne, and crowds of visitors would have besieged us from morning till night.

But we returned under no such auspices and our glory was departed. From no quarter did we receive a word of cordial welcome, and the journals once most clamorous for our cause were the first to bestow upon us the epithet of "pirates," and to querulously ask why we had come there to get them in trouble with the United States. So much for the disinterested friendship of Great Britain. As long as their workshops were busy turning out arms and munitions of war for our armies in the field, and blockade runners from Southern ports were arriving at Liverpool and London, laden with coveted cotton, they were loud in their protestations of sympathy and friendship; but when the hour of adversity came, when there was nothing more to be made out of us, these fair-weather friends coolly ignored our existence.

Before reaching the city, our pilot managed to run us aground on the bar, where we were obliged to remain until the following morning. During the night, the first lieutenant came around and warned the officers to keep their revolvers about them, as he had seen enough to make him apprehensive that a plot was on foot among the crew to secure what valuables there were on board, and decamp. The fear that their wages would not be forthcoming had suggested to them this desperate expedient.

It must be confessed that their prospects for payment were not brilliant; at least none but a very credulous man could feel much confidence in the feasibility of collecting a debt due him from a defunct Government.

The officers profited by the suggestion, kept their arms within reach, and maintained a vigilant watch. The crew made no demonstration, perhaps because they perceived that their plans were discovered, and that we were ready for any emergency, and possibly because sober second thought had led them to abandon a rashly formed determination.

Soon after daylight we got clear of the bar, and steamed up the river toward the city, with the flag that had accompanied us round the world flying at our peak for the last time. The fog shut out the town from our view, and we were not sorry for it, for we did not care to have the gaping crowd on shore witness the humiliation that was soon to befall our ship.

That afternoon we ranged astern of Her Britannic Majesty's Ship *Donegal,* and dropped anchor. . . .

About six o'clock in the evening, Captain Paynter of the *Donegal,* to whom the *Shenandoah* had surrendered, received a telegram ordering him at once to release such officers and crew of that ship as were not British subjects.

As soon as he received these instructions, Captain Paynter proceeded to the Rock Ferry slip and applied for a steamboat. Mr. Thwarts, who had charge of these boats, at once placed at his disposal the steamer *Bee,* in which he immediately went off to our cruiser. On gaining the deck he made known the object of his visit to Captain Waddell, who ordered his officers and crew to be summoned to the quarter-deck. The roll books were brought out, and the names called in regular order. As each man answered to his name he was asked to what country he belonged, but in no instance did any acknowledge himself a British subject. The majority claimed to be either native or adopted citizens of America; but several, who insisted that they had been born in some one of the Confederate States, had an unmistakably Scotch accent, and probably opened their eyes for the first time on this world a good deal nearer the Clyde than the Mississippi.

This formality having been gone through with, Captain Paynter informed them that they were at liberty to proceed on shore, and the intelligence was received with boisterous demonstrations of joy. Away they went forward and commenced packing up their bedding and such other articles of personal property as they possessed, which they conveyed on board the *Bee,* waiting to take them off to the landing stage.

When all were ready to bid a final adieu to the vessel, they collected forward and gave three lusty cheers for their late commander, and Captain Waddell acknowledged the compliment in a brief but appropriate address. The crew then went on board the little steamer, and the last Confederate force was disbanded.

Among the many excellent and high-minded gentlemen who, first and last, during the war, acted as Confederate Agents in England, Mr. J. D. B———— stands preëminent. For the many and valuable services he rendered to his native country during the hour of her trial, he steadfastly refused to receive any compensation. A short time prior to the final collapse, several thousand pounds of the public fund came into his hands, which he laid aside, not knowing how else to dispose of it, to provide for the immediate necessities of such naval officers of the Confederacy as the close of the war should leave homeless and proscribed in England. Two hundred pounds from this fund was appropriated to each of the officers of the

Shenandoah, as a just recompense for the long service they had rendered, and for which they could never hope to receive any other compensation.

At two different times, this fund, with directions for its disbursement, was privately conveyed to Captain Waddell after he landed in Liverpool, it being of course presumed that no more trusty custodian could be found for it.

The event proved that this confidence was shamefully abused, and a clue was at last furnished for our commander's singular anxiety to take his ship to Liverpool instead of to Sydney or Cape Town.

Before any of his officers had learned of this provision that kindness and forethought had made for them, he summoned them to his quarters— George's Hotel, Dale Street, Liverpool. One at a time they were admitted to his presence, and as the humor actuated him, he presented them from fifty to one hundred pounds apiece, out of the two hundred that was justly theirs. A few of his favorites, I believe, received their full bounty. The balance he coolly appropriated to himself, probably as a commission for transacting the business, nor was this the whole extent of his peculations.

The paymaster of the ship, Mr. W. Beadlove Smith, who had formerly been secretary to the captain of the *Alabama,* volunteered his services to settle with the crew, from the pay-roll in his possession, but the offer was declined, and he subsequently sent our old quartermaster Wiggins, as honest and straightforward an old sailor as ever walked a deck, to get them together and pay them from one-third to one-half of what was actually due them, and promise the remainder at some indefinite time in the future. For weeks after, his residence at Waterloo, a little way out of Liverpool, was besieged by these poor men clamoring for the hard-earned pittance out of which he had mercilessly defrauded them.

I may mention also, that after getting safely on shore, Captain Waddell became very solicitous to get possession of the old flag, upon which he set so little value when it was offered to him on board the *Shenandoah.* Its custodian declined to surrender it, whereupon the captain had the effrontry to threaten him with the loss of his pay and bounty if it was not given up, but the man who had taken that flag to his keeping valued it far higher than pounds and pence—the threat was indignantly disregarded, and for once, virtue was rewarded, for B———— got his money.

It is exceedingly painful for a sailor to write such things concerning a commander under whom he has served. Had Captain Waddell been contented with simply enriching himself at the expense of those who shared the toils and perils of that cruise, which has made his name famous, I should have been silent, for the credit of the service to which I had the honor to belong, but when, after all his officers had left England, and he therefore felt secure from personal chastisement, he ventured to publish that atrocious libel concerning their honor and courage, I could not in justice to myself and my associates do less than exhibit the man to the world in his true colors.

PART III

EMANCIPATION
AND THE NEGRO

Southerners contended, then and later, that slavery was but an incident in the conflict and not a cause of the Civil War. But whatever role slavery may have played in the thinking of men North and South, the Negro was a factor of no mean importance to both antagonists. From the beginning, Southerners claimed that the victory of Black Republicans constituted a threat to their property, and steadily the Abolitionists insisted that the war's purposes should include the extinction of slavery. Never was the problem of the Negro, whether slave or free, absent from the consideration of either side.

Fugitives from bondage sought asylum within the ranks of the Union armies. A few commanders, unwilling to be burdened with their care, returned the escaping slaves to their owners—citing the Federal Fugitive Slave Act as their warrant and excuse. Then General B. F. Butler, commanding at Fortress Monroe, concluded that slaves, being of military use to the Confederates, were "contrabands of war," and set them to work on his own fortifications. His words added a new phrase to the slang of war, and his acts furnished a precedent for experiments in using the South's labor force for Northern objectives.

Steadily the Abolitionists pressed Lincoln to change the purpose of the war. The President, mindful both of the political problems in the Border States still in the Union, and of the social problems of the freed Negro, yielded slowly. He recalled John C. Fremont's order freeing slaves of rebel sympathizers in Missouri, and forbade the enlistment of Negro soldiers on the captured Sea Islands of South Carolina. Yet the pressure grew, and gained added strength from the need of soldiers for the armies. Lincoln's Emancipation Proclamation, forced by the threat of the governors assembling to demand Negro soldiers, came prematurely and failed to rise to the dignified and exalted prose of his two inaugurals and his Gettysburg

Address. Nor did it furnish soldiers, or even free the slaves within the Union lines. Yet it changed the avowed purpose of the war, and gave new attention to the problems of the Negro.

A partial solution was found by Ulysses S. Grant in the Mississippi Valley. There, army agents turned abandoned lands over to Negroes, and permitted them to earn their own subsistence and to grow the cotton needed by Northern industry. Beyond the Union lines, Southerners, too, faced the problem of adapting slave labor to wartime conditions. By the close of the war the question of slavery had been solved, but yet to be resolved was the problem of organizing the Negro's productive capacities for the national benefit.

18

Lincoln's Road to Emancipation

John A. Logan

The rebels themselves . . . by the employment of their slaves in the construction at Bull Run and elsewhere, against the Union forces, brought the Thirty-seventh Congress, as well as the military commanders, and the President, to an early consideration of the slavery question. But it was nonetheless a question to be treated with the utmost delicacy.

The Union men, as well as the secession-sympathizers, of Kentucky and Tennessee and Missouri and Maryland, largely believed in slavery, or at least were averse to any interference with it. These, would not see that the right to destroy that unholy institution could pertain to any authority, or be justified by any exigency; much less that, as held by some authorities, its existence ceased at the moment when its hands, or those of the State in which it had existed, were used to assail the general Government.

They looked with especial suspicion and distrust upon the guarded utterances of the President upon all questions touching the future of the colored race.

They believed that when Fremont issued the general order . . . in which that general declared that "The property, real and personal, of all persons, in the State of Missouri, who shall take up arms against the United States, or who shall be directly proven to have taken an active part with their enemies in the field, is declared to be confiscated to the public use, and *their Slaves*, if any they have, *are hereby declared Free men*," it must have been with the concurrence, if not at the suggestion, of the President; and, when the President subsequently, September 11, 1861, made an open order directing that this clause of Fremont's general order, or proclamation,

JOHN A. LOGAN, *The Great Conspiracy: Its Origin and History* (New York, 1886), Ch. xx.

At the outbreak of the war, John A. Logan, an ardent supporter of Stephen A. Douglas, and Congressman from Illinois, seemed to waver, and his Republican opponents loudly proclaimed that he was preparing to join the Confederates. Logan became a General of Volunteers, and was one of the few "political" generals to come out of the war with an unblemished military reputation. After the war he returned to the House of Representatives, and then, to the Senate as an ardent Republican. His ill-done compilation, *The Great Conspiracy*, lacked literary or historical merit but embodied the full spirit of the Republicanism which he embraced ardently, almost compulsively.

should be "so modified, held, and construed, as to conform to, and not to transcend, the provisions on the same subject contained in the Act of Congress entitled 'An Act to Confiscate Property used for Insurrectionary Purposes,' approved August 6, 1861," they still were not satisfied.

It seemed as impossible to satisfy these Border-State men as it had been to satisfy the rebels themselves. . . .

Nothing satisfied them. It was indeed one of the most curious of the many phenomena of the War of the Rebellion, that when—as at the end of 1861— it had become evident, as Secretary Cameron held, that it "would be national suicide" to leave the rebels in "peaceful and secure possession of slave property, more valuable and efficient to them for war, than forage, cotton, and military stores," and that the slaves coming within our lines would not "be held by the Government as slaves," and should not be held as prisoners of war—still the loyal people of these Border States, could not bring themselves to save that Union, which they professed to love, by legislation on this tender subject.

On the contrary, they opposed all legislation looking to any interference with such slave property. Nothing that was proposed by Mr. Lincoln, or any other, on this subject, could satisfy them. . . .

Their opposition, however, to the march of events, was of little avail— even when backed, as was almost invariably the case, by the other Democratic votes from the Free States. The opposition was obstructive, but not effectual. For this reason it was perhaps the more irritating to the Republicans, who were anxious to put slavery where their great leader, Mr. Lincoln, had long before said it should be placed—"in the course of *ultimate extinction.*"

This very irritation, however, only served to press such anti-slavery measures more rapidly forward. By the 19th of June, 1862, a bill "to secure freedom to all persons within the territories of the United States"—after a more strenuous fight against it than ever, on the part of loyal and Copperhead Democrats, both from the Border and Free States—had passed Congress, and had been approved by President Lincoln. It provided, in just so many words, "That, from and after passage of this act, there shall be neither slavery nor involuntary servitude in any of the territories of the United States now existing, or which may at any time hereafter be formed or acquired by the United States, otherwise than in punishment of crime, whereof the party shall have been duly convicted."

Here, then, at last, was the great end and aim, with which Mr. Lincoln and the Republican Party started out, accomplished. To repeat his phrase, slavery was certainly now in the course of ultimate extinction.

But since that doctrine had been first enunciated by Mr. Lincoln, events had changed the aspect of things. War had broken out, and the slaves of those engaged in armed rebellion against the authority of the United States Government, had been actually employed, as we have seen, on rebel works and fortifications whose guns were trained upon the armies of the Union.

And now, the question of slavery had ceased to be simply whether it should be put in course of ultimate extinction, but whether, as a war measure—as a means of weakening the enemy and strengthening the Union —the time had not already come to extinguish it, so, far, at least, as the slaves of those participating in the rebellion, were concerned.

Congress ... had already long and heatedly debated various propositions referring to slavery and African colonization, and had enacted such of them as, in its wisdom, were considered necessary; and was now entering a further stormy period of contention upon various other projects touching the abolition of the fugitive slave laws, the confiscation of rebel property, and the emancipation of slaves—all of which, of course, had been, and would be, vehemently assailed by the loyal Border-State men and their Free-State Democratic allies.

This contention proceeded largely upon the lines of construction of that clause in the Constitution of the United States and its Amendments which provides that no person shall be deprived of life, liberty, or property, without due process of law, etc. The one side holding that, since the beginning of our government, slaves had been, under this clause, unconstitutionally deprived of their liberty; the other side holding that slaves being "property," it would be unconstitutional, under the same clause, to deprive the slave-owner of his slave *property*.

Mr. Crittenden, the leader of the loyal Border-State men in Congress, was at this time especially eloquent on this latter view of the Constitution. In his speech of April 23, 1862, in the House of Representatives, he even undertook to defend American slavery under the shield of English liberty!

Said he: "It is necessary for the prosperity of any government, for peace and harmony, that every man who acquires *property* shall feel that he shall be protected in the enjoyment of it, and in his right to hold it. It elevates the man; it gives him a feeling of dignity. It is the great old English doctrine of liberty. Said Lord Mansfield, the rain may beat against the cabin of an Englishman, the snow may penetrate it, but the King dare not enter it without the consent of its owner. That is the true English spirit. It is the source of England's power...."

There was at this time, a growing belief in the minds of these loyal Border-State men, that this question of slavery-abolition was reaching a crisis. They saw "the handwriting on the wall," but left no stone unturned to prevent, or at least to avert for a time, the coming catastrophe. They begged Congress, in the language of the distinguished Kentuckian, to "Let these unnecessary measures alone, *for the present*"; and, as to the President, they now, not only volunteered in his defense against the attacks of others, but strove also to capture him by their arch flatteries. ...

President Lincoln's duty, and inclination alike—no less than the earnest importunities of the Abolitionists—carried him in the opposite direction;

but carried him no farther than he thought it safe, and wise, to go. For, in whatever he might do on this burning question of emancipation, he was determined to secure that adequate support from the people without which even presidential proclamations are waste paper.

But now, May 9, 1862, was suddenly issued by General Hunter, commanding the "Department of the South," comprising Georgia, Florida and South Carolina, his celebrated order announcing martial law, in those States, as a military necessity, and—as "slavery and martial law in a free country are altogether incompatible"—declaring all slaves therein, "forever free."

This second edition, as it were, of Fremont's performance, at once threw the loyal Border-State men into terrible ferment. Again, they, and their Copperhead and other Democratic friends of the North, meanly professed belief that this was but a part of Mr. Lincoln's programme, and that his apparent backwardness was the cloak to hide his anti-slavery aggressiveness and insincerity.

How hurtful the insinuations, and even direct charges, of the day, made by these men against President Lincoln, must have been to his honest, sincere, and sensitive nature can scarcely be conceived by those who did not know him; while, on the other hand, the reckless impatience of some of his friends for "immediate and universal emancipation," and their complaints at his slow progress toward that goal of their hopes, must have been equally trying.

True to himself, however, and to the wise conservative course which he marked out, and thus far followed, President Lincoln hastened to disavow Hunter's action in the premises, by a proclamation . . . declaring that no person had been authorized by the United States Government to declare the slaves of any State, free; that Hunter's action in this respect was void; that, as Commander-in-Chief he reserved solely to himself, the questions, first, as to whether he had the power to declare the slaves of any State or States, free, and, second, whether the time and necessity for the exercise of such supposed power had arrived. And then . . . he proceeded to cite the adoption, by overwhelming majorities in Congress, of the joint resolution offering pecuniary aid from the national Government to "any State which may adopt a gradual abolishment of slavery"; and to make a most earnest appeal, for support, to the Border States and to their people, as being "the most interested in the subject matter."

In his special message to Congress, recommending the passage of that joint resolution, he had plainly and emphatically declared himself against sudden emancipation of slaves. He had therein distinctly said: "In my judgment, *gradual, and not immediate, emancipation,* is better for all." And now, in this second appeal of his to the Border-State men, to patriotically close with the proposal embraced in that resolution, he said: "The changes it contemplates would come gently as the dews of Heaven, not rending or wrecking anything. Will you not embrace it! So much good has not been done, by one effort, in all past time, as, in the providence of God, it is now your high privilege to do! *May the vast future not have to lament that you have neglected it!*"

But stones are not more deaf to entreaty than were the ears of the loyal Border State men and their allies to President Lincoln's renewed appeal. "Ephraim" was "wedded to his idols."

McClellan too—immediately after his retreat from the Chickahominy to the James River—seized the opportunity afforded by the disasters to our arms, for which he was responsible, to write to President Lincoln a letter (dated July 7, 1862) in which he admonished him that owing to the "critical" condition of the Army of the Potomac, and the danger of its being "overwhelmed" by the enemy in front, the President must now substantially assume and exercise the powers of a dictator, or all would be lost; that "neither confiscation of property . . . nor forcible abolition of slavery, should be contemplated for a moment"; and that "A declaration of radical views, especially upon slavery, will rapidly disintegrate our present armies."

Harried, and worried, on all sides—threatened even by the commander of the Army of the Potomac—it is not surprising, in view of the apparently irreconcilable attitude of the loyal Border-State men to gradual and compensated emancipation, that the tension of President Lincoln's mind began to feel a measure of relief in contemplating military emancipation in the teeth of all such threats.

He had long since made up his mind that the existence of slavery was not compatible with the preservation of the Union. The only question now was, how to get rid of it? If the worst should come to the worst—despite McClellan's threat—he would have to risk everything on the turn of the die—would have to "play his last card"; and that "last card" was military emancipation. Yet still he disliked to play it. The time and necessity for it had not yet arrived—although he thought he saw them coming.

Things were certainly, at this time, sufficiently unpromising to chill the sturdiest patriot's heart. It is true, we had scored some important victories in the west; but in the east our arms seemed fated to disaster after disaster. Belmont, Fort Henry, Fort Donelson, and Pittsburg Landing were names whose mention made the blood of the patriots surge in their veins; and Corinth, too, had fallen. But in the east, McClellan's profitless campaign against Richmond, and especially his disastrous "change of base" by a "masterly" seven days' retreat, involving as many bloody battles, had greatly dispirited all Union men, and encouraged the rebels and rebel-sympathizers to renewed hopes and efforts.

And, as reverses came to the Union arms, so seemed to grow proportionately the efforts, an all sides, to force forward, or to stave off, as the case might be, the great question of the liberation and arming of the slaves, as a war measure, under the war powers of the Constitution. It was about this time (July 12, 1862) that President Lincoln determined to make a third, and last, attempt to avert the necessity for thus emancipating and arming the slaves. He invited all the senators and representatives in Congress from the Border States, to an interview at the White House, and made to them . . . an earnest, eloquent, wise, kindly, patriotic, fatherly appeal in behalf of his old proposition, for a gradual, compensated emancipation, by the Slave States, aided by the resources of the national Government.

At the very time of making it, he probably had, in his drawer, the rough draft of the proclamation which was soon to give liberty to all the colored millions of the land. Be that as it may, however, sufficient evidences exist, to prove that he must have been fully aware, at the time of making that appeal to the supposed patriotism of these Border-State men, how much, how very much, depended on the manner of their reception of it.

To him, that meeting was a very solemn and portentous one. He had studied the question long and deeply—not from the standpoint of his own mere individual feelings and judgment, but from that of fair constitutional construction, as interpreted by the light of national or general law and right reason. What he sought to impress upon them was that an immediate decision by the Border States to adopt, and *in due time carry out,* with the financial help of the general Government, a policy of gradual emancipation, would simultaneously solve the two intimately blended problems of slavery-destruction and Union-preservation, in the best possible manner for the pockets and feelings of the Border-State slaveholder, and for the other interests of both Border-State slaveholder and slave.

His great anxiety was to "perpetuate," as well as to save, to the people of the world, the imperiled form of popular government, and assure to it a happy and grand future.

He begged these congressmen from the Border States, to help him carry out this, his beneficent plan, in the way that was best for all, and thus at the same time utterly deprive the rebel Confederacy of that hope, which still possessed them, of ultimately gathering these States into their rebellious fold. And he very plainly, at the same time, confessed that he desired this relief from the Abolition pressure upon him, which had been growing more intense ever since he had repudiated the Hunter proclamation.

But the President's earnest appeal to these loyal representatives in Congress from the Border States was . . . in vain. It might as well have been made to the actual rebels, for all the good it did. For, a few days afterward, they sent to him a reply signed by more than two-thirds of those present . . . in which—after loftily sneering at the proposition as "an interference by this Government with a question which peculiarly and exclusively belonged to" their "respective States, on which they had not sought advice or solicited aid," throwing doubts upon the constitutional power of the general Government to give the financial aid, and undertaking by statistics to prove that it would absolutely bankrupt the Government to give such aid—they insultingly declared, in substance, that they could not "trust anything to the contingencies of future legislation," and that Congress must "provide sufficient funds" and place those funds in the President's hands for the purpose, before the Border States or their people would condescend even to "take this proposition into careful consideration, for such decision as in their judgment is demanded by their interest, their honor, and their duty to the whole country."

Very different in tone, to be sure, was the minority reply, which after stating that "the leaders of the Southern rebellion have offered to abolish slavery among them as a condition to foreign intervention in favor of their independence as a nation," concluded with the terse and loyal deduction: "If they can give up slavery to destroy the Union, we can surely ask our people to consider the question of emancipation to save the Union."

But those who signed this latter reply were few, among the many. Practically, the Border-State men were a unit against Mr. Lincoln's proposition, and against its fair consideration by their people. He asked for meat, and they gave him a stone.

Only a few days before this interview, President Lincoln—alarmed by the report of McClellan, that the magnificent Army of the Potomac under his command, which only three months before had boasted 161,000 men, had dwindled down to not more than "50,000 men left with their colors"—had been to the front, at Harrison's Landing, on the James River, and, although he had not found things quite so disheartening as he had been led to believe, yet they were bad enough, for only 86,000 men were found by him on duty, while 75,000 were unaccounted for, of which number 34,472 were afterward reported as "absent by authority."

This condition of affairs, in connection with the fact that McClellan was always calling for more troops, undoubtedly had its influence in bringing Mr. Lincoln's mind to the conviction, hitherto mentioned, of the fast-approaching military necessity for freeing and arming the slaves.

It was to ward this off, if possible, that he had met and appealed to the Border-State representatives. They had answered him with sneers and insults; and nothing was left him but the extreme course of almost immediate emancipation.

Long and anxiously he had thought over the matter, but the time for action was at hand.

And now, it cannot be better told, than in President Lincoln's own words, as given to the portrait-painter Carpenter, and recorded in the latter's, *Six Months in the White House*, what followed:

"It had got to be," said he, "midsummer, 1862. Things had gone on from bad to worse, until I felt that we had reached the end of our rope on the plan of operations we had been pursuing; that we had about played our last card, and must change our tactics, or lose the game!

"I now determined upon the adoption of the emancipation policy; and, without consultation with, or the knowledge of, the Cabinet, I prepared the original draft of the proclamation, and, after much anxious thought, called a Cabinet meeting upon the subject. This was the last of July, or the first part of the month of August, 1862." (The exact date he did not remember.)

"This Cabinet meeting took place, I think, upon a Saturday. All were present, excepting Mr. Blair, the Postmaster-General, who was absent at the opening of the discussion, but came in subsequently. I said to the Cabinet, that I had resolved upon this step, and had not called them together to ask their advice, but to lay the subject-matter of a proclamation before them; suggestions as to which would be in order, after they had heard it read.

"Mr. Lovejoy was in error when he stated that it excited no comment, excepting on the part of Secretary Seward. Various suggestions were offered. Secretary Chase wished the language stronger, in reference to the arming of the blacks. Mr. Blair, after he came in, deprecated the policy, on the ground that it would cost the Administration the fall elections.

"Nothing, however, was offered, that I had not already fully anticipated and settled in my own mind, until Secretary Seward spoke. He said in substance: 'Mr. President, I approve of the proclamation, but I question the expediency of its issue at this juncture. The depression of the public mind, consequent upon our repeated reverses, is so great that I fear the effect of so important a step. It may be viewed as the last measure of an exhausted Government, a cry for help; the Government stretching forth its hands to Ethiopia, instead of Ethiopia stretching forth her hands to the Government.'

"His idea," said the President "was that it would be considered our last *shriek*, on the retreat." (This was his *precise* expression.) " 'Now,' continued Mr. Seward, 'while I approve the measure, I suggest, sir, that you postpone its issue, until you can give it to the country supported by military success, instead of issuing it, as would be the case now, upon the greatest disasters of the war!' "

Mr. Lincoln continued: "The wisdom of the view of the Secretary of State, struck me with very great force. It was an aspect of the case that, in all my thought upon the subject, I had entirely overlooked. The result was that I put the draft of the proclamation aside, as you do your sketch for a picture, waiting for a victory."

It may not be amiss to interrupt the President's narration to Mr. Carpenter, at this point, with a few words touching "the military situation."

Afer McClellan's inexplicable retreat from before the rebel capital—when, having gained a great victory at Malvern Hills, Richmond would undoubtedly have been ours had he but followed it up, instead of ordering his victorious troops to retreat like "a whipped army"—his recommendation, in the extraordinary letter (of July 7th) to the President, for the creation of the office of General-in-Chief, was adopted, and Halleck, then at Corinth, was ordered east, to fill it.

Pope had previously been called from the west, to take command of the troops covering Washington, comprising some 40,000 men, known as the Army of Virginia; and, finding cordial co-operation with McClellan impossible, had made a similar suggestion.

Soon after Halleck's arrival, that general ordered the transfer of the Army of the Patomac, from Harrison's Landing to Acquia Creek—on the Potomac—with a view to a new advance upon Richmond, from the Rappahannock River.

While this was being slowly accomplished, Lee, relieved from fears for Richmond, decided to advance upon Washington, and speedily commenced the movement.

On the 8th of August, 1862, Stonewall Jackson, leading the rebel advance, had crossed the Rapidan; on the 9th the bloody Battle of Cedar Mountain had been fought with part of Pope's army; and on the 11th Jackson had retreated across the Rapidan again.

Subsequently, Pope having retired across the Rappahannock, Lee's forces, by flanking Pope's army, again resumed their northern advance. August 28th and 29th witnessed the bloody battles of Groveton and Gainsville, Virginia; the 30th saw the defeat of Pope, by Lee, at the second great Battle of Bull Run, and the falling back of Pope's army toward Washington; and the succeeding Battle of Chantilly took place September 1, 1862.

It is not necessary at this time to even touch upon the causes and agencies which brought such misfortune to the Union arms, under Pope. It is sufficient to say here that the disaster of the second Bull Run was a dreadful blow to the Union cause, and correspondingly elated the rebels.

Jefferson Davis, in transmitting to the rebel Congress at Richmond, Lee's victorious announcements, said, in his message: "From these dispatches it will be seen that God has again extended His shield over our patriotic army, and has blessed the cause of the Confederacy with a second signal victory, on the field already memorable by the gallant achievement of our troops."

Flushed with victory, but wisely avoiding the fortifications of the national capital, Lee's forces now swept past Washington; crossed the Potomac, near Point of Rocks, at its rear; and menaced both the national capital and Baltimore.

Yielding to the apparent necessity of the moment, the President again placed McClellan in command of the armies about Washington, to wit: the Army of the Potomac; Burnside's troops that had come up from North Carolina; what remained of Pope's Army of Virginia; and the large reinforcements from fresh levies, constantly and rapidly pouring in.

Yet, it was not until the 17th of September that the Battle of Antietam was fought, and Lee defeated—and then only allowed to slip back, across the Potomac, on the 18th—McClellan leisurely following him, across that river, on the 2nd of November! On the 5th, McClellan was relieved—Burnside taking the command—and Union men breathed more freely again.

But to return to the subject of emancipation. President Lincoln's own words have already been given—in conversation with Carpenter—down to the reading of the proclamation to his Cabinet, and Seward's suggestion to "wait for a victory" before issuing it, and how, adopting that advice, he laid the proclamation aside, waiting for a victory.

"From time to time," said Mr. Lincoln, continuing his narration, "I added or changed a line, touching it up here and there, anxiously waiting the progress of events. Well, the next news we had was of Pope's disaster at Bull Run. Things looked darker than ever. Finally, came the week of the Battle of Antietam. I determined to wait no longer.

"The news came, I think, on Wednesday, that the advantage was on our side. I was then staying at the Soldiers' Home (three miles out of Washington). Here I finished writing the second draft of the preliminary proclamation; came up on Saturday; called the Cabinet together to hear it; and it was published the following Monday."

It is not uninteresting to note, in this connection, upon the same authority, that at the final meeting of the cabinet prior to this issue of the proclamation, when the third paragraph was read, and the words of the draft "will recognize the freedom of such persons," were reached, Mr. Seward suggested the insertion of the words "and *maintain*," after the word "recognize"; and upon his insistence, the President said, "the words finally went in."

At last, then, had gone forth the fiat—telegraphed and read throughout the land, on that memorable 22nd of September, 1862—which, with the supplemental proclamation of January 1, 1863, was to bring joy and freedom to the millions of black bondsmen of the South.

Just one month before its issue, in answer to Horace Greeley's open letter berating him for the "seeming subserviency" of his "policy to the slave-holding, slave-upholding interest," etc., President Lincoln had written his famous "Union letter," in which he had conservatively said: "My paramount object is to save the Union, and not either to save or destroy slavery. If I could save the Union without freeing any slave, I would do it—and if I could save it by freeing all the slaves, I would do it—and if I could save it by freeing some, and leaving others alone, I would also do that."

No one outside his cabinet dreamed, at the time he made that answer, that the Proclamation of Emancipation was already written, and simply awaited a turn in the tide of battle for its issue!

Still less could it have been supposed, when, on the 13th of September—only two days before Stonewall Jackson had invested, attacked, and captured Harper's Ferry with nearly 12,000 prisoners, 73 cannon, and 13,000 small-arms, besides other spoils of war—Mr. Lincoln received the deputation from the religious bodies of Chicago, bearing a memorial for the immediate issue of such a proclamation.

The very language of his reply—where he said to them: "It is my earnest desire to know the will of Providence in this matter. And if I can learn what it is, I will do it! These are not, however, the days of miracles, and I suppose it will be granted that I am not to expect a direct revelation. I must study the plain physical aspects of the case, ascertain what is possible, and learn what appears to be wise and right"—when taken in connection with the very strong argument with which he followed it up, against the policy of emancipation advocated in the memorial, and his intimation that a proclamation of emancipation issued by him "must necessarily be inoperative, *like the Pope's bull against the comet!*"—would almost seem to have been adopted with the very object of veiling his real purpose from the public eye, and leaving the public mind in doubt. At all events, it had that effect.

Arnold, in his *Life of Lincoln,* says of this time, when General Lee was marching northward toward Pennsylvania, that "now, the President, with that tinge of superstition which ran through his character, 'made,' as he said, 'a solemn vow to God, that, if Lee was driven back,' he 'would issue the proclamation'"; and, in the light of that statement, the concluding words of Mr. Lincoln's reply to the deputation aforesaid—"I can assure you that the subject is on my mind, by day and night, more than any other. *Whatever shall appear to be God's will, I will do*"—have a new meaning.

The Emancipation Proclamation, when issued, was a great surprise, but nonetheless generally well-received by the Union armies, and throughout the loyal States of the Union, while, in some of them, its reception was most enthusiastic.

It happened, too . . . that the convention of governors of the loyal States met in Altoona, Pennsylvania, on the very day of its promulgation, and in an address to the President adopted by these loyal governors, they publicly hailed it "with heartfelt gratitude and encouraged hope," and declared that "the decision of the President to strike at the root of the rebellion will lend new vigor to efforts, and new life and hope to the hearts, of the people."

On the other hand, the loyal Border-State men were dreadfully exercised on the subject; and those of them in the House of Representatives emphasized their disapproval by their votes, when, on the 11th and 15th of the following December, resolutions, respectively denouncing, and endorsing, "the policy of emancipation, as indicated in that proclamation," of September 22, 1862, were offered and voted on.

In spite of the loyal Border-State men's bitter opposition, however, the resolution endorsing that policy as a war measure, and declaring the proclamation to be "an exercise of power with proper regard for the rights of the States and the perpetuity of free government . . ." passed the House.

Of course, the rebels themselves, against whom it was aimed, gnashed their teeth in impotent rage over the proclamation. But they lost no time in declaring that it was only a proof of what they had always announced: that the war was *not* for the preservation of the American Union, but for the destruction of African slavery, and the spoliation of the Southern States.

Through their friends and emissaries, in the Border and other loyal States of the Union—the "Knights of the Golden Circle," the "Order of American Knights" or "Sons of Liberty," and other Copperhead organizations, tainted with more or less of treason—they stirred up all the old dregs of pro-slavery feeling that could possibly be reached; but while the venomous acts and utterances of such organizations, and the increased and vindictive energy of the armed rebels themselves, had a tendency to disquiet the public mind with apprehensions as to the result of the proclamation, and whether, indeed, Mr. Lincoln himself would be able to resist the pressure, and stand up to his promise of that supplemental proclamation which would give definiteness and practical effect to the preliminary one, the masses of the people of the loyal States had faith in him.

There was also another element, in chains, at the South, which at this time must have been trembling with that mysterious hope of coming emancipation for their race—conveyed so well in Whittier's lines, commencing: "We pray de Lord; he gib us signs, dat some day we be Free"—a hope which had long animated them, as something almost too good for them to live to enjoy, but which, as the war progressed, appeared to grow nearer and nearer, until now they seemed to see the promised land, flowing with milk and honey, its beautiful hills and vales smiling under the quickening beams of freedom's glorious sun. But ah! should they enter there?—or must they turn away again into the old wilderness of slavery, and this blessed liberty, almost within their grasp, mockingly elude them?

They had not long to wait for an answer. The 1st of January, 1863, arrived, and with it—as a precious New Year's gift—came the Supplemental Proclamation, bearing the sacred boon of liberty to the emancipated millions.

At last, at last, no American need blush to stand up and proclaim his land, indeed, and in truth, "the Land of Freedom."

19

The Governors and Emancipation

New York *Herald*

The treasonable developments at the Convention of State Governors, held on Wednesday at Altoona, in Pennsylvania, fully confirm the opinion we have long since expressed that a plot had been set on foot by the radicals at the North to abolish the Union, the Constitution and Negro slavery together, without regard to the legal, moral or social obstacles in the way, or any disastrous consequences that might ensue from the execution of their desperate programme. Even the President himself, if he should continue to stand in their path, must be swept away, and with him all the guarantees of law and public order.

That a revolutionary conspiracy has been organized for some time at the North, under the designation of the Roundheads, or the Puritans, is now placed beyond a doubt. The originators are the lineal descendants of the rebel Roundheads in England, who kept that country for forty years in hot water and civil war. This treasonable conspiracy began in New England; but it has its ramifications in New York and various other Northern States, and some of its ruling spirits are to be always found at the national capital.

The first intimation we had of the existence of this secret organization was the disloyal response of Governor Andrew of Massachusetts to the call of Secretary Stanton for troops, in May last, when he refused to send the desired regiments, intimating that the call was not a "real," but a sham one, but that if the President was in earnest, and would proclaim Negro fraternity and equality, and let the blacks fight side by side with white men, then "the roads would swarm with the multitudes that New England would pour out to obey the call" of the Secretary of War. In other words,

New York *Herald* (September 26, 28, 1862).

The official version of the origins of Lincoln's Emancipation Proclamation, which Logan borrowed from Carpenter, was seriously challenged at the time by the New York *Herald*. A *Herald* reporter attended the meeting of Northern governors at Altoona, and reported their astonishment at the news of the President's proclamation. The *Herald's* version was repeated by Kentucky's Senator Lazrous Powell in Congress, and called forth a vigorous denial by Lincoln.

Governor Andrew would deliberately let the government be overthrown by the rebels of the South unless it consented to submit to the dictation of the Roundheads, and agreed to a fanatical policy which, if successful, would make the South another St. Domingo, and inflict a blow upon the whole country, from which it could not recover in half a century.

The next evidence we have of the existence and objects of the Society of Roundheads is the meeting at Providence of the New England Governors with the New York Jacobin Club which goes by the misnomer of "The National War Committee." Then and there it was proposed, in view of the refusal of the Government to permit them to organize a revolutionary army of fifty thousand men, to be placed under the command of General Fremont, that the governors of the Northern States should be applied to for that number of men and arms, as a nucleus around which the elements of Northern fanaticism and revolution might gather for the destruction of the Government unless it fell in with their designs to abolish the Constitution of the United States by force and arms. The recent withholding of troops from the general Government in the hour of need, and the developments of the radical governors at Altoona, complete a chain of evidence as to the existence of a most dangerous conspiracy. Their object appears to be to prolong the war, in order to make fortunes for themselves or their friends by contracts, and at the same time to insure the final dismemberment of the United States, in order to (secure?) the permanent control of the Northern section by a fanatical faction which would compel all men to adopt their standard of morality and religion, like the tyrant Procrustes, who, if his victims were too long, cut off their legs in order to reduce them to the dimensions of the bed on which he tortured them, or, if they were too short, stretched them to the requisite length.

Upon one frivolous pretence or another the troops raised in several of the Northern States have not been sent forward by these governors to Washington. In a single State ten thousand are said to be retained. The fact of the troops having been held back at this particular crisis, when their presence in the field might have rendered the great battle in Maryland immediately decisive by preventing the escape of the rebel army into Virginia, is very significant, when coupled with another fact developed at Altoona, that the radicals proposed to call upon the President to remove General McClellan just after he had won the most brilliant victory of the war, and were only defeated in their attempt to carry this proposition by the threat of Governor Tod of Ohio that the people would rise up en masse against them, and by the conservative course of Governor Curtin of Pennsylvania, who supported General McClellan, and by the rebuke of Governor Morgan of New York, who declined attending the Convention because he disapproved of its object, and maintained that the loyal and patriotic way to serve the Government was to send it men, as he did, New York having contributed more troops in proportion to its population than any other

State, under the last two calls. The conspirators showed their teeth; but, with the representatives of the great States of New York, Pennsylvania and Ohio against the radicals of the New England States, what could they do? The population of the State of New York alone far exceeds their combined population.

Governor Morgan is right. There was no necessity for any convention. The President is made by the Constitution Commander-in-Chief of the army and navy, and it is the duty of the governors to obey, and not to dictate. The Constitution, moreover, expressly forbids any combinations or alliances of States. Article I, section 9, declares that "No State shall, without the consent of Congress, enter into any agreement or compact with another State." But this assemblage was worse than the Hartford Convention of half a century ago; and had the President sent a division of General McClellan's army to disperse the illegal gathering at the point of the bayonet, and sent the whole batch to the nearest fort, he would not have transcended his duty. But the President checkmated them in another way. He took the wind out of their sails by issuing his proclamation one day in advance of their meeting. Had he not done so they would have demanded immediate and unconditional emancipation, just as they demanded the dismissal of McClellan, and the appointment of foolish Fremont in his stead. But under the President's proclamation published yesterday these radical governors are all liable to be seized and sent to some fortress, as "discouraging volunteer enlistments, and resisting militia drafts, thus affording aid and comfort to the rebels." The volunteer troops have been held back by their interposition and the militia drafts have been delayed by their authority. We trust, therefore, that Mr. Lincoln will direct that these "disloyal persons" (men whose loyalty by their own showing is only conditional) will be arrested by the United States marshals, particularly Governor Andrew of Massachusetts and Governor Sprague of Rhode Island, who manifested the most treasonable spirit under the pretense of Negro philanthropy. Let a signal example be made. There is still room in Forts Lafayette and Warren.

It seems that the radical governors have become alarmed at their work at the Altoona Conference. They have discovered that their conspiracy against our generals is recoiling upon their own heads, and are endeavoring to clear their skirts and stay the storm they have raised about themselves, by denying our report, and asserting that the removal of McClellan was not broached in the Conference. The organs of the radicals in this city—the *Tribune* and *Times*—have also come out in their defence, and are doing their best to prove that the gubernatorial conspirators did not refer to our generals. Unfortunately for them, our report was made on too good authority for their denial to have any effect.

The main topic of conversation among the New England and a portion of the western governors in the morning, before the Conference assembled, was in reference to our generals. It was the current remark of outsiders who conversed with the radical governors that these officials are decidedly "down" on many of our generals, and are of the opinion that a radical change must be made. But, with this evidence of the views of the extremists, our correspondent did not believe that they would have the audacity to broach the subject in the Convention; but the evidence was so conclusive, and upon so reliable authority, that even the most skeptical could not doubt its truth. The statements made and the substance of the debate given by our representative were upon the authority of three persons who took part in the deliberations of the Convention. All of the three held official positions in their respective States, and one of the number is a governor. No person who has the least acquaintance with these officials would for a moment doubt any statement that they might make.

That the radical governors are endeavoring to wriggle themselves out of the real position taken at the convention only shows the desperate condition that our *exposé* of their conspiracy has placed them in before the country. No person could have watched the movements of the New England and a portion of the western governors at Altoona without becoming convinced that they assembled there for the sole purpose of endeavoring to force the President to make a change in our generals. Furthermore, there is not the least doubt but that if the Conference had been held prior to the battle of Antietam a proposition urging the President to remove McClellan would have received the endorsement of a majority of those present. But the skill exhibited by McClellan in that battle, and the decided victory won on that battlefield, were more than they could overcome, notwithstanding the efforts of Governor Sprague to disparage our generals and soldiers by endeavoring to prove that it was a rebel and not a Union victory. That the Convention was called by governors Curtin, Tod and Pierpoint for a good object, and for no other purpose than to devise means whereby they could all act in concert in strengthening the hands of the President, for the purpose of bringing the rebellion to a speedy end, no one can doubt. The position taken by these three officials in the Conference is a sufficient guarantee that none but the purest patriotic motives prompted them to invite the governors to consult together at Altoona. But that a majority of the radical governors consented to take part in its deliberations for a far different object is too self-evident to need any argument to sustain the assertion.

But their treasonable schemes were defeated. The noble defence of McClellan, and the manly stand taken by Governor Curtin of Pennsylvania, the eloquent endorsement by Governor Bradford of Maryland, and the decisive assertion of Governor Tod of Ohio, "that the people would rise up *en masse* and repudiate such a proposition," forced them to abandon their position. Thus foiled and defeated, with a decided manifestation of indignation by the public, it is not strange that they should pursue the course characteristic of the radical Jacobin faction ever since the war commenced, and attempt to get themselves out of their dilemma. But, as it was with Senator Wilson on stopping enlistments, the record is against them, and the proof is too strong to enable them to accomplish this last much coveted object. They stand before the public indicted, and all their assertions will not remove the dark and treasonable mark upon them. They stand before the world convicted.

20

Caring for the Freedmen

John Eaton

In order to place the work which we carried on in the Department of the Tennessee in its proper relation to the general subject of the Negro and the Government, it seems advisable to turn back at this point and review for a moment the policy of the Union toward the black refugees—in so far as the nation may be said to have had a policy at that time—and see how the question was treated by the commanders of the Union forces.

I have already alluded to Butler's use of the term "contraband" in reference to the slaves of those in rebellion against the Government. It will at once be recalled that during Butler's command of the forces at Fortress Monroe, three fugitive slaves were received into the Union lines. Upon learning that they were to have been employed by their masters in building rebel fortifications, Butler exclaimed, "These men are contraband of war; set them at work." The words were in a sense a forecast of the policy which later prevailed wherever the Union army exercised any supervision over the Negro. In fact, Butler worked out among the freedmen at Fortress Monroe a system which presented most of the essential features of the subsequent efforts in their behalf; that is to say, he gave them employment on a wage basis, caused army rations to be issued to the destitute, and provided for the needs of the non-laborers out of the earnings of the laborers. These efforts were inaugurated in May, 1861, and General Butler's policy was an honorable exception to that of many of the commanders. It was ably carried on by General Wood, who succeeded Butler in the Department of Virginia, and by General Banks, who carried out the work begun by General Butler at New Orleans.

The efforts of E. L. Pierce of the Treasury Department at Port Royal in the fall of 1861, and the yet more successful work carried on in South Carolina—especially on the Sea Islands, of which he was military governor—

JOHN EATON, *Grant, Lincoln and the Freedmen: Reminiscences of the Civil War* (New York, 1907), Chs. v, vi, viii.

Eaton, an army chaplain whom Grant assigned to care for freedmen and refugees in the Department of Tennessee, proved an excellent choice. He performed his duties with judgment, efficiency, and humanitarianism. He later became Commissioner of Education.

by General Rufus Saxton, Pierce's successor, under definite instructions from the Secretary of War, were, however, by far the most elaborate and the most productive of good results of any of these first efforts for the relief, employment, and education of the contrabands.

In the West, General Halleck, in his famous Order No. 3, issued November, 1861, expressly excluded fugitive slaves from the Union lines within his department. General Dix, on taking possession of Accomac and Northampton in Virginia, followed the same policy of denying the colored refugees the privilege of coming into his lines. Among those commanders who received the fugitives at all, the majority permitted Confederate "slave hunters" to enter the Union lines and carry off their slaves upon identification. General McCook and General Johnson were especially commended by a Confederate newspaper correspondent for courtesies extended to a slave hunter within their lines. The Confiscation Act of August, 1861, which provided for the confiscation of property used for insurrectionary purposes, was so little regarded by commanders in the field, that at least two officers were deprived of their commands for attempting to act in accordance with it. Colonel H. E. Paine of the 4th Wisconsin, Department of the Gulf, protested against orders to turn all fugitive slaves out of the lines, as "a violation of law for the purpose of returning fugitive slaves," and was relieved of his command in consequence. Lieutenant-Colonel D. R. Anthony, commanding the 7th Kansas in Tennessee, suffered the same fate for declaring the slave hunters a nuisance and taking measures to protect himself against them. Grant, on the other hand, in an order issued from Fort Donelson, February 26, 1862, while admitting the necessity for obedience to Halleck's Order No. 3, distinctly states that no permits will be granted citizens to pass through the camps in search of fugitive slaves, and provides further that all slaves within the Union lines at the time of the capture of Donelson who had been "used by the enemy in building fortifications, or in any manner hostile to the Government, will be employed by the quarter-master's department for the benefit of the Government, and will under no circumstances be permitted to return to their masters."

The Union was committed by the action of Congress and the official utterances of the Administration to a support of the policy of receiving within the Union lines and withholding from the enemy the slaves of those in rebellion against the Government. The Government had indeed committed itself yet further. As pointed out by Mr. T. D. Eliot in a speech on the Freedmen's Bureau, delivered February, 1864, in the House of Representatives, the Act of June, 1862, providing for the collection of taxes in insurrectionary districts, empowered the tax commissioners to lease abandoned lands on terms which should secure proper and reasonable employment and support at wages or on shares to persons and families residing on the lands. This, I believe, was the first notice taken by legislation of the freedmen, save such as referred to questions of military expediency, and it practically recognized the destitute Negro as in some sense a ward of the Government. It also brought the civil arm of the Government into unavoidable conflict with the military supervision of Negro affairs, and so led, as reported by General Saxton, to sad complications in his plans for the Negroes under him. This was but another illustration of the fatal error of introducing into the same field two agencies with imperfectly differentiated functions—an error from which our work in the Mississippi Valley likewise suffered.

To return from this digression to the question of the reception and detention of slaves within the Union lines. Early in the war Lincoln, while repudiating and suppressing the more unguarded and emotional statements made by Secretary of War Cameron in his annual report on December 1, 1861, inserted in the same report a brief sentence urging the military necessity of withholding fugitive slaves from the enemy, a course which in his wisdom he realized would have "no tendency to induce the horrors of insurrection even in the rebel communities." Even so early Cameron had advocated arming the Negroes for the defense of the Union. No vigorous enforcement, however, of the policy of treating slaves as contraband of war was attempted, owing without doubt to the extreme intricacy of the situation, and to the importance—ever present in Mr. Lincoln's mind—of preserving the sympathy of the Union slaveholders in the Border States. Butler's efforts in behalf of the Negro had been commended, but it depended upon the common sense of the individual commanders whether such efforts called forth commendation or rebuke.

A new Article of War, created by Act of Congress, and approved March 13, 1862, tended materially to protect the slaves against the claims of their pursuers. By the terms of this Article, all persons in the military service were prohibited, on pain of dismissal from the service, from employing the forces at their command to aid in returning slaves to those claiming to be their owners. Gradually, as events progressed, there was a change in the attitude of the Government, which is well expressed in an unofficial letter from Halleck to Grant dated March 31, 1863. Referring to the policy of the Government of withdrawing the Negro from the Confederate territory as a means of crippling the productive capacity of the enemy, and the further efforts that were to be undertaken to render him actively efficient as a soldier, Halleck wrote: "The character of the war has very much changed within the last year. There is now no possible hope of reconciliation with the rebels. . . . There can be no peace but that which is forced by the sword." Halleck then urged Grant as a "friend" to see to it that his officers exerted themselves in sympathetic co-operation with the efforts of the Government to use the Negro as a laborer (Halleck's letter was written six months after Grant's order issued to me at Grand Junction) and as a soldier.

This brings us to the consideration of how the policy of arming the Negro originated. Aside from an effort made by the Confederacy to arm the free

Negroes of Memphis, which in spite of its success was not followed up, the first Negro regiment to be organized in the Civil War was recruited under orders issued by General David Hunter, commanding the Department of the South at Port Royal, South Carolina, in May, 1862. It was known as the 1st South Carolina Volunteer Regiment. In a delightfully impertinent and ironical letter, nominally addressed to the adjutant-general of the army but intended for the enlightenment of his own fiercest critic, Representative Wickliffe of Kentucky, Hunter claimed to have acted under instructions empowering him to enlist all "loyal persons"; but his policy was untimely, the regiment was not sustained by the Government, and in default of funds with which to pay the men, it was necessarily disbanded. Early in August of the same year Governor Sprague of Rhode Island issued a call for colored troops to be issued at the North. Later in the month General Butler issued an appeal to the free Negroes of New Orleans, which resulted in the mustering of a full regiment on September 27. The first definite executive action to be taken by the United States Government was, however, an order, issued by the Secretary of War in August, 1862, to General Saxton, who succeeded Hunter at Port Royal in the control of Negro affairs, directing the enlistment of colored troops with the same pay, rations, and equipment allotted white volunteers. Congress had authorized the enlistment of colored troops only a month before. The order of the Secretary of War also directed General Saxton to occupy plantations, harvest crops, and otherwise administer affairs for the improvement of property. General Ullman's important work in the Department of the Gulf was begun under authority of the War Department early in January, 1863. He had previously been active in interesting President Lincoln in the question of recruiting Negro regiments.

From this very fragmentary outline of the early attempts to arm the blacks, it may be seen that the Union—especially after the Emancipation Proclamation had been issued—had entered upon the definite and acknowledged policy of making soldiers of ex-slaves; but the undertaking was everywhere considered experimental, and was most unpopular in many quarters, especially in the army. In fulfilment of the new policy, the War Department, on the 25th of March, 1863, issued an order to Brigadier-General Lorenzo Thomas, Adjutant-General, United States Army, directing him to make an inspection of the military situation in the west, with special reference to the condition of the freedmen and the enlistment of Negro troops. . . .

The attitude of the army toward the Negro as a soldier was gradually undergoing a change, although intense prejudice still existed against him. Not a few of the subordinate officers confessed no sympathy with the freedom assured the Negro by the President's proclamation, but even they for the most part, were attentive that no unnecessary suffering should exist. The commanding officers, with few exceptions, did what they could to insure the working out of the Government's policy, even though they may personally have been opposed to it. The Emancipation Proclamation had become more popular, however, with all classes and among all ranks of soldiers, so that the situation was more or less favorable to General Thomas's mission in the Valley.

In my capacity of Superintendent of Freedmen, it devolved upon me to see that General Thomas was given every facility for the pursuit of his task. I therefore went with him in person to the principal camps within my jurisdiction, following the route of the Memphis and Charleston Railroad as far as Corinth and returning to Memphis by way of Jackson (Tennessee), Grand Junction, and Colliersville. On May 18, after the completion of this tour, General Thomas reported to the War Department his return from Corinth to Memphis, having addressed the troops at twelve different points. About a month before this date he had addressed the troops immediately under General Grant at Grant's headquarters before Vicksburg, at Milliken's Bend. The adjutant-general of the army manifestly felt the importance of the change in policy which he was announcing, and his mission was fulfilled with no little ceremony. The command to which he was to address himself would be drawn up before him in single rank or in a hollow square, according to its size, and the order of the War Department would be read to officers and men. Sometimes the general would make a speech. When he had finished, he would ask those who were opposed to the order to move out one step from the ranks. A few would do so, impelled by the strength of their prejudice, and these General Thomas would promptly order to the guardhouse, there to revise the opinion he had invited them to express. The general's order, as we have seen, made it the urgent duty of everyone to further the plans of the Government in arming the Negro; he was further empowered "to dismiss and to commission officers according as they were for or against the new policy without referring their cases to Washington," so that his action in thus taking means to assure himself of the spectacle of a soldier invited to express his opinion, and forthwith disciplined for having an opinion to express, was not without a certain grim humor.

So great a change in policy had not been effected without much agitation and effort on the part of those convinced of the advisability of arming the blacks. All who had been termed "Abolitionists" were by no means agreed upon how much the Negro might be able to accomplish as a soldier; but there was a distinct element, led among others by Governor Andrew of Massachusetts, Wendell Phillips, Major Stearns, and the Shaws, father and son, that stanchly advocated the policy of arming him. That Mr. Lincoln withheld his consent in the face of the powerful advocacy of good men such as these, until he felt assured that the measure would prove a benefit and not a menace to the Union cause, and would not subject the people of the South to the horrors of an insurrection, is a manifestation of his poise and wisdom which is sometimes overlooked. With the announcement of the change of policy, efforts to create a sentiment on behalf of the Negro were not remitted.

In spite of the widespread distrust as to how the Negro would conduct himself in the field much evidence was circulated in his favor; his record in the Revolution was sent broadcast, and gradually the number of those in favor of arming him greatly increased. In this work of creating sentiment in the Negro's favor the Union League Club bore, of course, an active part, publishing pamphlets in connection with its efforts to raise Negro regiments, under national authority, in the State of New York. With some exceptions it was curious to see how the feeling against the Negro subsided when it became clear that he might figure as a useful factor in saving the Union. Our soldiers soon ceased to offer any objection to his replacing the white man on the firing line and receiving rebel bullets. Moreover, an officer of a colored regiment risen from the ranks had small cause to find fault with the policy which was responsible for his opportunity for such advancement. As for the Negro, himself, he very soon vindicated the action of the Government and won for himself the commendation of his officers and the respect of his companions in the service. . . .

When the first regiments were organized in the territory under my jurisdiction, a good deal of pressure was brought to bear upon me to induce me to take command of one of the regiments; but I was devoted to my profession and although General Grant's orders had detached me from my duties as chaplain, I was able still to devote myself to the alleviation of suffering.

As the months passed, our efforts in behalf of the Negroes in the Valley assumed more satisfactory shape, although before the year was done we were to encounter as great difficulties as any that had yet confronted or discouraged us. In order to convey to the reader some definite and reliable notion of the magnitude of a task which is all but forgotten by the present generation, but which at the time represented an important phase in the national policy, and one closely associated with the principles of the Union cause, I can do no better than to quote somewhat freely upon the report of the year 1864, prepared at the time by myself and my assistants and submitted officially to General Thomas. The report opens as follows:

General—This supervision has extended, during the year, over a territory from Cairo southward, in the Mississippi Valley, populated according to the census of 1860, by 770,000 blacks, and including the cities of Memphis, Vicksburg, Natchez, and Little Rock, and the military posts of Columbus, Island 10, Corinth, Helena, Du Vall's Bluff, Pine Bluff, Fort Smith, Goodrich Landing, Milliken's Bend, and Davis Bend.

The rebellion at the outset began to disturb this population. The frequent marching and counter-marching of loyal and disloyal armies, consuming or destroying the material comforts of life, such as food, shelter, and the implements of industry, the actual shock of arms, or the terror of their motion, left hardly an individual, white or black, unaffected. It was soon evident that the strength of these regions consisted in three distinct elements: masters, slaves, and the so-called poor whites. Of the last named, many were forced into the rebel armies. They were furnished with horses and better food and clothing, their families were supported, and they failed, therefore, to see so soon as some of the Negroes and the Southern unionists, that the interests of the three distinct elements already noted were not only diverse, but hostile, and that the war was the natural effort of the master to render irrevocably supreme the power of his own caste. The Negroes very soon felt that their interests were identical with the objects of our armies. This identity of interest came slowly but surely to be perceived by our officers and soldiers and by the loyal public. The blacks gave information for the guidance of campaigns; they became laborers for the various staff departments; they took upon themselves all the serving of the army; they were finally accepted as capable of the soldier's discipline and endurance in all arms of the service, and worthy of a soldier's pay and honor. Out of those who came within our lines, probably not less that 80,000 either died in the United States service or (in 1864) were still in it as laborers or soldiers.

It is not unworthy of note here, that the army, although engaged in active warfare, though embracing in itself all the instrumentalities for the destruction of its foe—at whatever cost of comfort, treasure, and life—though having in it the usual admixture of good and bad, and although looked upon by many benevolent people as only another master for the blacks, accomplished practically all that could be done to free, feed, shelter, and protect the Negro and to give him medical attendance. It formed the only safe channel for the benevolence that came from other sources to his aid. More than this, the army sought to evolve out of its forms for administering justice an adaptation of those forms, fitted to the peculiar condition of the freed people. . . .

Not a cent of money was ever drawn from Government for the freedmen on any account. For the support of the sick and those otherwise dependent, a tax was temporarily required (by Order No. 63) on the wages of the able-bodied. It was thought at first that the Negroes would submit with reluctance to the collection of such a tax. But in this we were mistaken. Being a tax on wages, it compelled the employer and the employed to appear, one or both, before the officer charged with its collection, and this officer allowed no wages to go unpaid. The Negro soon saw in the measure his first recognition by Government, and although the recognition appeared in the form of a burden, he responded to its with alacrity, finding in it the first assurance of any power protecting his right to make a bargain and hold the white man to its fulfilment. This comprehension of the affair argued a good sense of economic justice in a people entirely unused to such responsibilities. It was most interesting to watch the moral effect of taxing the ex-slaves. They freely acknowledged that they ought to assist in bearing the burden of the poor. They felt ennobled when they found that the Government was calling upon them as men to assist in the process by which their natural rights were to be secured. Thousands thus saw for the first time any money reward for their labor. . . . This tax, together with the funds accruing from the profits of labor in the Department, met all the incidental expenses of our widespread operations; paid $5,000 for hospitals; the salaries of all hospital stewards and medical assistants (as per Order No. 94), and enabled us to supply implements of industry to the people, in addition to abandoned property. The same funds secured to the benefit of the Negroes clothing, household utensils, and other articles essential to their comfort, to the amount of $103,000. The Negroes could not themselves have secured these commodities for less than $350,000. The management of these funds and supplies was regulated by the exigencies of the people's condition, and was adapted as far as necessary to army methods, requiring a rigid system of accounts, monthly reports covered by certificates and vouchers, followed by careful inspections, not only from my office, but from the generals commanding.

According to Order No. 9 issued by General L. Thomas, certain officers known as provost-marshals were selected from the men in the Freedmen's Department to discharge toward the Negroes scattered on plantations the duties of superintendents of freedmen. These officers were appointed by the commanding generals, and themselves appointed assistant provost-marshals, who patrolled the districts assigned to them, correcting abuses on plantations and acting as the representatives of the law as upheld by the military power. There was some difficulty in maintaining the incorruptibility of these officers, and the territory which had to be covered by each individual was too extended, but the system, nevertheless, worked extremely well.

In addition to the superintendents . . . H. B. Spelman, president of the Cleveland's Freedmen's Aid Commission, performed a particularly valuable service as agent for the sale of freedmen's crops. The trade regulations would not allow the freedmen to sell their cotton on the spot, and as they were without means of shipping it north they had to appoint attorneys to transact the business for them, and did not always succeed in getting honest men. Mr. Spelman, with the permission of the proper treasury official, arranged that the small lots of cotton produced at various points within our lines by different owners should all be shipped under one set of permit papers taken out by Mr. Spelman himself, thereby saving the freedmen. . . .

A rough classification of the freed people will serve to clarify the reader's appreciation of the various groups in whose interests we labored:

First, all new arrivals; with whom were grouped those employed as laborers in military service, as hospital attendants, officers' servants, employees in the commissary and quarter-master's departments, etc.

Second, those resident in cities. Freedmen supplied by far the larger share of industrial pursuits with laborers: They worked as barbers, hackmen, draymen, porters, carpenters, shoemakers, blacksmiths, tailors, seamstresses, nurses, laundresses, waiters in hotels and private families, cooks, etc. Not a few of this second class were well-to-do; many conducted enterprises of their own, either mechanical or commercial. Some were teachers. Properly connected, too, with those resident in cities, were the employees and waiters on steamboats, and stevedores.

A third and large class found employment as woodchoppers, on islands and at points of security along the river, rendering a service absolutely essential to our commercial and military operations.

Fourth, those who labored on plantations. These were subdivided as follows: first, those who were employed by the owners of the lands, or the whites or blacks who leased from the government; second, those who were independent planters or gardeners—either cultivating on shares, or leasing of the owners or of the Government.

Fifth, the sick and those otherwise incapacitated who were distributed among the hospitals or on the "home farms," where they contributed what labor they could toward their own support. With these should be classed the hundreds of orphaned or abandoned children for whom, with the help of private benevolence, orphanages were established as soon as practicable.

In the meanwhile another element had come into prominence. The suffering and destitution of the Negroes had been in part alleviated by the many aid societies . . . whose work can never be overestimated or adequately acknowledged. One of the most efficient of these was the Western Sanitary Commission. This society had been particularly active and helpful at Helena in the winter of 1862-63, where better hospital facilities had been established under its patronage, and in October of the latter year its efforts were directed to other points along the Mississippi River. James E. Yeatman, president of the Commission, made a personal tour of inspection of most of the cities and camps under my jurisdiction. . . .

Abuses connected with the leasing system and the general provisions for the employment of the Negroes were the most difficult and important of the questions confronting us, and on the strength of Yeatman's report and the representations made to the Government by the Western Sanitary Commission, Mr. Yeatman was invited to co-operate with the Supervising Special Agent of the Treasury Department, Mr. William P. Mellen, in the formation of the new regulations under which the treasury purposed to assume control of the plantation interests. These regulations were devised with a view to obviating the worst of the abuses under which we were suffering, and many of the provisions were extremely well considered.

For instance, in order to check if possible the employment of overseers, who were responsible for many of the freedmen's difficulties, no lessee was to be permitted to lease more than one plantation—two planters had previously been in possession of four plantations each, another of five—and preference was given to those wishing small tracts of land. This was a very wise provision which would have tended to increase the number of small homesteads owned by whites and blacks—a phase of social evolution which The Freedmen's Department always tried to foster. Unfortunately the money-making fever which afflicted the lessees led them to take on large properties, which in the disturbed conditions of the country it was often impossible to operate. A new minimum rate of wages was introduced—for men of the first grade twenty-five dollars per month; for the second grade, twenty dollars per month. For women of the first and second grades, eighteen and fourteen dollars respectively. Persons between twelve and fourteen and over fifty years of age were to constitute a third grade, of which the men and boys were to receive fifteen dollars a month, and the women and girls ten. The wages were to constitute a first lien upon the crops. . . .

A special effort was made to secure to the Negro the full amount of wages due him, except in cases of sickness or neglect to work. The freedmen had been woefully discouraged by the facility with which the planter contrived to evade paying them full wages in cases where he had himself failed to furnish them a full month's work. Cases were reported by Mr. Yeatman in which the laborer—through no fault of his own—received, for instance, but two dollars and seventy cents for his month's labor. . . .

Theoretically the Yeatman-Mellen plan was better than the system previously inaugurated by Adjutant-General Thomas, but in practice it must be confessed the new system was subject to quite as many complications.

In the first place, the question of giving the plantations protection from physical violence was full of difficulty, and this in turn reacted on the industrial conditions. While the use of the land was under military control, little attempt had been made to cultivate in sections where a reasonable defense against guerrillas could not be secured. The lessees, however, under the far more extensive system of agricultural operations encouraged by the Treasury, forsook all prudence in their eagerness to acquire wealth, and rented lands in districts where extreme exposure was inevitable. As a result of this, impossible demands were made upon the military forces, whose operations the planters came to feel should be especially directed to forwarding the personal interests of the individual planter. Mr. Mellen himself foresaw this difficulty and the threatened downfall of his whole system, and in his report to Secretary Chase, dated February 11, 1864—about one month after the promulgation of the new orders—urgently demanded that "adequate military protection to this planting interest . . . be afforded *at once,* or the hundreds of persons now there (i.e., on plantations) and of others going there will abandon their contemplated work." But such protection as Mr. Mellen received did not suffice.

The introduction into the Valley of a distinct class whose interests were primarily commercial and involved patriotism or humanity only as secondary and incidental considerations, had already complicated matters in the limited plantation activities with which we had been experimenting. That class was now alarmingly increased. The high price at which cotton was selling tempted many Northerners into the enterprise. Besides the out-and-out speculators there was a large number of men whose energies were not directly absorbed by the war, but who, feeling its disturbing influence, and drawn thereby away from their ordinary occupations, were ready for any venture that might improve their fortunes. These men availed themselves recklessly of the opportunity thus offered them. They came on the ground to make money, whether the Union cause—not to mention the Negro—suffered by their operations or not. Money and information, together with vast quantities of contraband articles, went into the Confederate lines; and incidentally the cotton within the Confederate lines came out. The army was powerless to assert its authority over affairs controlled by the Treasury; the Treasury had no vehicle at its command whereby to enforce its own authority in a district where martial law was the only law, and the result was that in too many cases no authority was exercised at all. No sweeping accusation of the Treasury Department or of the planters is to be inferred from this. The Treasury Department was trying to insure the benefits of trade to a territory barely delivered of the curse of war; but the small army of agents which it sent out failed, on the whole, even more lamentably than individuals in the military service, to withstand the peculiar temptations which the situation offered. As for the planters, with all their cupidity and selfishness, they were—like everyone else in those days—largely in the grip of circumstances that proved too much for them, and moreover there were among them, as among the officers of the Treasury, men of high standards who remained incorruptible throughout. Indeed, so numerous were the planters whose records were creditable, that Colonel Thomas was able at one time to report he believed the lessees in the neighborhood of Vicksburg—his district—would compare favorably with any body of businessmen. . . .

In our efforts to provide educational facilities for those so long in want of them, the white refugees were kept in mind as far as circumstances would permit. At Natchez, Vicksburg, and Memphis, schools were established by missionaries, chaplains, or aid societies, and were visited and aided by our officers. The General Superintendent of Refugee and Colored Schools, Chaplain Joseph Warren, says in this connection: "This unfortunate class of people is so unsettled that any permanent plan for the instruction of the children of it is impracticable. They generally, of course, hope to be able to return to their homes before a long time passes. . . . The best we can do now for the children is to seize such fleeting opportunities as may be found to awaken a desire for education, and to continue the process of instruction."

Owing to the fact that not all teachers co-operated with complete friendliness in the supervision of the Freedmen's Department over their work—though all claimed the benefits of its protection, and, in a measure, of its support—it was difficult to get statistics that were absolutely reliable. It may be said, however, with perfect assurance, that with the close of the year 1864 thousands had become able to read the simpler school-books, while hundreds were able to read well. Many learned to write, and began the study of arithmetic and geography. . . . The report from the colored schools under my jurisdiction for the quarter ending March 31, 1865, shows that in the following cities, towns, and camps, that is, Memphis, Vicksburg, Natchez, Helena, Vidalia, Little Rock, Pine Bluff, President's Island, Davis Bend, and camps around Vicksburg, there was a total of 51 schools, 105 teachers, an enrollment of 7,360 pupils, and an average attendance of 4,667. Irregular, cramped, partial, and necessarily rudimentary as was the best education we could give them, it unfitted these men, women, and children whom the Nation had freed, for being chattels. They were no longer creatures whom it would be safe to re-enslave. No one realized this fact better than some of the ex-slaves' former masters, and no one was more bitter in denunciation against the measures we inaugurated—unless, indeed, it was the poorest and most illiterate among the whites, who for years had hampered the progress of the South by their ignorance and fanaticism. There were honorable exceptions, however, among Southern men of judgment and humanity who foresaw, not without relief, the passing of the old system, and who felt, in their best moments, that no price was too great to have paid for redemption from that. To encourage these men in their efforts at readjustment was not the least important or valuable work of the Freedmen's Department or of its successor, the Freedman's Bureau. The systems of education and industry devised for the Negro were of the utmost value here, for nothing so completely demonstrated the ideal of free labor and of ultimately equal rights and opportunities for all. . . .

Before turning from the subject of the Freedmen's Department, it may be worth-while to present a brief summary of the characteristics of the Negro as they were revealed to my officers, and to mention at the same time certain general conditions of our work to which no reference has as yet been made.

One fact in connection with the Negro must ever be borne in mind. The testimony alike of my officers and of the visitors to the Valley is all but unanimously to the effect that in spite of the suffering to which the freedmen were subjected in their desperate passage from slavery to freedom—suffering which in many cases must have far exceeded that which they had experienced in bondage—scarcely a single instance could be quoted in which a Negro voluntarily returned as a slave to his master. Discouraged, panic-stricken, suspicious they were; but ready to exchange their hard-won and unhappy freedom for the sometime easier conditions of slavery, they were not. It was their terror of finding themselves tricked into some form of bondage that constituted one of our greatest difficulties in persuading the refugees to return to their old masters, or to the representatives of the master class, and labor for them on a wage basis. . . .

That the Negro was stirred with an immediate impulse to profit by his new opportunities is amply proved by the passion for education which was exhibited by old and young. It is true that, to the Negro, one form of book-learning was as good as another. Anyone devoted to his books was on the road to freedom; anyone ignorant of books was on his way back to slavery. But even this crude notion brought thousands of Negroes into line with those who have turned their backs forever on dumb ignorance and who face the opportunities and responsibilities of literate men and women. . . .

The adaptability of the Negro was a quality which stood him in good stead during the difficult time of which I write, and probably helped him more than any other single trait to enter the arena of business competition. . . .

I think the statement may safely be made that no single group of men ever observed the Negro under more discouraging circumstances than did my assistants in the Mississippi Valley. To them was revealed the Nation's freedman in all his ignorance, destitution, bewilderment, immorality, and emotional extravagance. The men who thus observed him had been chosen for their ability to comprehend large issues and enforce adequate means of achieving large results. It is not claimed that they were always successful—no human agency could have met and mastered the situation that confronted us—but they were devoted workers, intelligent, moderate in judgment, and courageous in the execution of what they deemed right. The testimony of these men should be considered in all estimates of the Negro's character and achievement. With full recognition of his shiftlessness, and the unsatisfactory condition of his industrial and family relations, the faith of the men who labored among the freedmen never wavered in its insistence upon the capacity of these people to develop themselves, as a race, into the self-supporting, self-respecting, and moral type of human being. This faith was based upon the large number of men and women who had already attained such a standard, and also upon the evidences of improvement in the general mass. . . .

Viewed broadly, the history of the Negro from that day to this has been to a somewhat remarkable extent what my officers, from the data before them, felt it must be. There have been legislative errors which have been productive of untold evil in both races. There has been displayed by the Negro himself a spirit of trifling with great opportunities; while those who have opposed or supported him have not done so without betraying both prejudice and sentimentality. But notwithstanding this, and the fearful difficulties which the colored race has had to surmount, it has continued to produce more and more remarkable instances of honest achievement among noteworthy individuals, together with a general uplift of the race itself. On the basis of that record we can afford to be hopeful and even confident.

21

Slaves and War Times

Susan Dabney Smedes

On the day after our mother's death one of the daughters went to the kitchen to attend to the housekeeping. She found the cook in a flood of tears. "I have lost the best friend that I had," she said. She spoke the truth, for few besides the mistress who was gone could have had patience with Alcey. She was the cook who had been bought from Mr. Dabney's mother's estate, and had been treated with marked kindness on account of her being a stranger; but she seemed to be vicious and heartless, and nothing but the untiring forebearance and kindness of this mistress had touched the hardened nature.

When one hires servants and they do not give some sort of satisfaction, redress is at hand. The servant is dismissed. But with slaves, at Burleigh, and with all the good masters and mistresses in the South—and I have known very few who were not good—there was no redress.

It may be thought that Southerners could punish their servants, and so have everything go on just as they pleased. But he who says this knows little of human nature. "I cannot punish people with whom I associate every day," Thomas Dabney said, and he expressed the sentiment of thousands of other slave-owners. It was true that discipline had sometimes to be used, but not often, in very many instances only once in a lifetime, and in many more, never. George Page, who in his youth, and in his middle age, was about his master's person and knew him well, said: "Marster is a heap more strict with his children than he is with his servants. He does not overlook things in his children like he does in his people."

Apart from the humane point of view, common sense, joined with that great instructor, responsibility, taught slave-owners that very little can be effected by fear of punishment.

SUSAN DABNEY SMEDES, *A Southern Planter; Social Life in the Old South* (New York, 1900), Ch. xvi.
Not all the slaves, even in the Mississippi Valley, fled to the Union lines to be cared for by John Eaton and the Freedmen's Department, which he created. Many remained at home. The adjustments to the war made in plantation life are simply stated in Susan Dabney's account of life at Burleigh in Mississippi.

Fear and punishment only tend to harden the rebellious heart. What, then, was to be done with a grown servant who was too lazy or too ill-tempered to do half work, with abundant and comfortable support insured whether the work was done or not? It is clear that unless the moral nature could be appealed to that servant had to be endured. It would not have answered to have set that one free; that would have made dissatisfaction among the others. Very many slave-owners looked on slavery as an incubus, and longed to be rid of it, but they were not able to give up their young and valuable Negroes, nor were they willing to set adrift the aged and helpless. To have provided for this class, without any compensation for the loss of the other, would have reduced them to penury.

Now that the institution is swept away, I venture to express the conviction that there is not an intelligent white man or woman in the South who would have it recalled, if a wish could do it. Those who suffered and lost most—those who were reduced from a life of affluence to one of grinding poverty—are content to pay the price.

Good masters saw the evil that bad masters could do. It is true, a bad master was universally execrated, and no vocation was held so debasing as the Negro trader's. Every conscientious proprietor felt that these were helpless creatures, whose life and limb were, in a certain sense, under his control. There were others who felt that slavery was a yoke upon the white man's neck almost as galling as on the slaves; and it was a saying that the mistress of a plantation was the most complete slave on it. I can testify to the truth of this in my mother's life and experience. There was no hour of the day that she was not called upon to minister to their real or imaginary wants. Who can wonder that we longed for a lifting of the incubus, and that in the family of Thomas Dabney the first feeling, when the war ended, was of joy that one dreadful responsibility, at least, was removed? Gradual emancipation had been a hope and a dream not to be realized.

It may not be out of place to give an illustration of how one of the Burleigh servants carried her point over the heads of the white family.

After the mistress had passed away, Alcey resolved that she would not cook any more, and she took her own way of getting assigned to field work. She systematically disobeyed orders and stole or destroyed the greater part of the provisions given to her from the table. No special notice was taken, so she resolved to show more plainly that she was tired of the kitchen. Instead of getting the chickens for dinner from the coop, as usual, she unearthed from some corner an old hen that had been sitting for six weeks, and served her up as a fricassee! We had company to dinner that day; that would have deterred most of the servants, but not Alcey. She achieved her object, for she was sent to the field the next day, without so much as a reprimand, if I remember rightly. We were very sorry, for she was the most accomplished cook whom we had had in Mississippi. But what was to be done? No master could have made her cook unless by making a brute of himself, and using such measures as would lower him in his own eyes. Her master merely said, "Choose anyone whom you like as your cook, and let Alcey go out to the field."

Those were days of trial and perplexity to the young mistresses. The old house-servants, though having at heart an affection for them, considered or pretended to consider them too young to know what they wanted.

Besides, had they not known these young ladies ever since they were born? And did not they call them mammy or aunt in consideration of superior age?

If complaint were made to the master, his answer was, "If you cannot get along with the servants, and they will not recognize your authority, choose any others that you think will do better." Several had to be sent to the fields before some of the old trained servants, who had never worked out of the "great house" in their lives, saw that there was to be a head to the house, even though that head was set on young shoulders.

In this time of change and discouragement Mammy Maria's strong, true love for the house showed itself, and was indeed a help and support. She had never in her life received what could be called an order from any younger member of the family. To her everything was put in the form of a request. She was too much beloved for any one of her "white children" to wish to alter this relationship now. But mammy decided herself on changing her manner to us. Instead of her independent way of letting us know her views, and expecting us to follow her advice, she addressed her young mistresses in a manner marked by the most studied deference. The slightest expressed wish, though couched as ever in the form of a request, was a command to mammy, and was obeyed with more punctilious exactness than if it had come from the father or mother. She and they had been *bons camarades* many a year together, and understood each other—there was no need to obey strictly, or to obey at all, if she saw a better way. But here was a different state of things—here was upheaval and rebellion. The servants hardly meant it so; most of it was thoughtlessness on their part, but the result was discomfort and perplexity to mammy's "white children." Her loyal heart showed her this way of giving comfort to us.

After the war actually began, Thomas Dabney espoused the side of the South with all the enthusiasm of his nature. As has been said, he did nothing by halves. He at once organized his household on a more economical footing that he might have the more to aid in carrying on the war. He said that we at home ought not to live more luxuriously than our soldiers in camp, and he himself set the example of giving up many luxuries which were yet abundant in the land. It was considered unpatriotic to plant cotton, and he urged his neighbors to turn all their energies towards sustaining the Southern soldiers. They planted half crops of cotton; but not a cottonseed was allowed to be put in the ground on the Burleigh plantation. Every acre was planted in corn, that the army should not lack food for man and beast.

He gave his money with both hands, and his sons as freely. He was most restive at not being in the army himself. He was on the point of enlisting many times, and did enlist once, when special troops were called for to go to Columbus, Kentucky, where heavy fighting was expected.

His daughters were in despair at seeing him at the age of sixty-two preparing to go into the trenches. No argument on the subject of his age could move him when this uncontrollable longing to go into the army got possession of him, as it did from time to time. His daughters came around him and reminded him that all their brothers who were old enough to handle a musket were at the front, and he ought not to run the risk of leaving them without a natural protector. Perhaps the strongest argument used was that he could best serve his country by remaining at home and giving his personal supervision to the fields which were to feed the armies. He finally yielded to their wishes and stayed at home.

His fourteen-year-old son, Benjamin, caught the war fever, and his father gave his consent for him to go into the ranks. He sent a trusted body-servant with his sons.

"William," he said, "I wish you to stand by your young masters, and to look after them as well as you can. And if they are killed, I want you to bring them home to me."

"Yes, Marster."

"And here is my sword, William. I give it to you to take to the war. You can fight with it, too, if you see a chance."

"Yes, Marster, I will show them the English of it."

And William, who was about six-feet-two-inches in height, threw his head back and looked proud of his trust.

William was armed with the master's own sword, which he had had sharpened before handing it to him. It had been his when, at the age of fourteen years, he had gone to Old Point Comfort, where the British were expected to land. The edge had been ground off when peace was declared after the War of 1812, and it had not been sharpened till the Confederate war broke out.

Thomas wrote much for the papers in these days, urging every Southerner to take care of the soldiers in the field. Five young men, who were guests at Burleigh in the first spring of the war, were fitted out by him and sent off with one hundred dollars apiece, and directions to have their bills charged to him. Gray cloth was ordered up from New Orleans, and uniforms cut out and made by the dozen in the house and sent to the camps. Blankets were not to be bought in any Southern market, and he decided to give every one that he owned, but his daughters begged to be allowed to keep some, and he compromised on giving away nineteen of the largest size, about half. He wished us to cut up the carpets to put on the beds. Great boxes of food and wine were sent off to the hospitals. He sent his carriage for sick soldiers, and took care of them as long as they were allowed to stay, treating each private as if he were the commander-in-chief of the army. . . .

The plantation life went on as usual. The servants went about their duties, we thought, more conscientiously than before. They seemed to do better when there was trouble in the white family, and they knew that there was trouble enough when all the young men in the family were off at the wars. They sewed on the soldiers' clothes and knit socks for the army, and packed the boxes with as much alacrity as the white people did. They were our greatest comfort during the war.

When hostilities began, the younger children were taught by a tutor who had been in the family for several years. Mr. Dabney had not thought of sending him away, though he was a Northern man, and, it was to be supposed, with Northern sympathies. He was so quiet that we at Burleigh rarely thought of his sympathies, for he never seemed to speak if he could avoid it. But the neighbors had a report that he was a spy, and Mr. Dabney was informed of it, with a request that Mr. T———— should be dismissed. This was communicated to the tutor in the kindest manner, and the man was moved to tears as Thomas talked with him.

Thomas Dabney originated the scheme for the Confederate Government to raise money by getting out bonds on the basis of the cotton then in the hands of the planters. The cotton bonds supplied the sinews of war during the early part of the struggle. . . .

The Episcopal Church of St. Mark's at Raymond had been built years before the war, and had been the parish church of Thomas and his family. The drive of ten miles did not seem inconvenient then. But it became impossible to get so far afterwards. The family fell into a way of reading the service at home, and the neighbors liked to attend, and the large household was frequently swelled to quite a congregation. Occasionally the bishop or one of the clergy were there, and were surprised to see the number that could be gathered together, almost without giving out any notice. In the afternoon the daughters held a service and Sunday-school for the Negroes, and the large library was well filled by them. They delighted in the chants and hymns, and knew much of the service and the catechism by heart.

Many years after they were all free, a brawny blacksmith sent a message to his teachers of these days, "Tell de ladies I ain't forgit what dey teach me in de Sunday-school." . . .

In the spring of 1863 Thomas Dabney began to feel that his children were in one of the worst places in the world for non-combatants, the neighborhood of a beleaguered city. He lamented that all his children were not sons. He longed more and more to go into the army as the fighting drew closer to us. He ordered an army uniform to be made for himself, and we feared that we should not be able to keep him with us. His intense sufferings from loneliness urged him, no less than his love for the military life, to plunge into the excitement now so near at hand. In his grief he said not

infrequently in these days that it would have been better for him if he had
had no children left him to take care of. All the men in the land who were
men indeed were off in the army; the whole country seemed forsaken,
except by the old men and the boys and the women and children. He envied
every soldier in the ranks, and felt like a chained lion. Not to go into the
army cost him, without a doubt, the greatest struggle of his life.

The rumor came that the whole country around Vicksburg was to be
abandoned to the enemy. Already General Grant's troops were moving on
Vicksburg, and that place would soon be in a state of siege. The citizens
were fleeing in every direction. Thomas Dabney, feeling that he had a home
and food to offer to these homeless ones, caused to be inserted in one of
the Vicksburg papers an invitation to any and all citizens desirous of leaving the city to take refuge at Burleigh.

One family of Louisiana refugees had come to us before this. This invitation brought out an Englishwoman, Mrs. Allen, and her two children, and
later on her husband.

At this juncture our hopes were raised by the arrival of an officer, sent
out by General Pemberton, with orders to seize every pleasure horse in the
country. A large body of men were to be mounted, we were told, and this
body of cavalry was to patrol the country lying around Vicksburg; and even
to relieve that place when the time came. The officer was astonished when
he was hailed as the bringer of joyful tidings. Many ladies, he said, had
shed tears when their carriage and other favorite horses had been carried
off by him. He had gotten nervous, and hated to come among the women
of the country with that dreadful order in his hand. Every horse in the
Burleigh stables was brought out freely. One riding horse was exempted
from the draft as a necessary part of the plantation equipment. My father
preferred to retain his buggy horse, Gold Dust, and he was allowed to do so.

Alas! in a few weeks Gold Dust was to be in the service of the enemy and
pitted against his own master's son, and against the Burleigh carriage horses
and other equine acquaintances of the stables and pastures. When last seen
our carriage horses, powerful young roans, were on the battlefield of Big
Black in the artillery service.

We now set to work to bury the money and silver. Some of our friends
had buried their watches, and so destroyed them. We sewed up our watches
and such valuables as would be spoiled by dampness in the form of a bustle,
and gave it to our trusted Aunt Abby to wear. Mammy Maria was too
nervous and cried too much to have any responsibility put on her. Large
hoops were in fashion at this time, and we tied our silver in bags and put
these under our hoops, and went out one May day a mile from the house
to a rock-quarry. Here we dug a hole with the dinner-knives that we had
secreted about our persons for the purpose, and in this hole we placed our
valuables. Then we put over them the largest stone that six or seven girls
could move.

As we were not in the habit of walking out in the hot sun, someone proposed that we should dig up a young holly, or something of the kind, and set it out on our return to the house. This would account, it was thought, to the servants for our walk. So we pulled up a shrub or two and set them out as soon as we got home.

Mammy Maria watched these proceedings in silence, and then said in her brusque way, and in her capacity of a privileged servant, "You needn't think you is foolin' me. I know you don't go out in de hot sun in May to set out trees and 'spect 'em to live."

The children buried their treasures too; Tom, a powder-can, as the most prized of his possessions. It was of a brilliant red, and a late acquisition, and might be coveted by the enemy. Little Lelia buried her dolls and their wardrobes securely in a hole dug in the greenhouse. Lelia's nurse, who helped at the frequent exhumings and re-interments, as rumors of the war were cheering or alarming—for we had a fresh rumor nearly every day—was true to her, but Tom was less fortunate in his confidant, and that red powder-can was near costing the thirteen-year-old boy his life. Ida buried her chief treasure, a pair of cheap china vases, a quarter of a mile from the house, down the spring hill.

In the midst of all this Mrs. Allen's baby died. One of the plantation carpenters made a coffin, and the Burleigh family buried the little child. No clergyman was to be had. Many of them were gone as chaplains in the army. Our pastor led his company into the first battle of Manassas.

The baby was buried in the park under a small oak-tree. The deer, seeing the procession of the family and the coffin borne by the Negro men come in, with the curiosity of their species drew near. The gentler ones mingled with the group around the open grave, one special pet licking the hands of her human friends and stretching out her beautiful neck to reach the flowers that the young children had brought to strew on the little coffin.

The rude coffin and the absence of the minister, and of any white man save one silvery-haired one, spoke of war. But it was a beautiful and peaceful scene. The setting sun threw its slanting rays on the deer as they stood in the background near the forest-trees, and on the little group gathered close to the grave.

A woman's voice was repeating the solemn ritual of the Episcopal Church for the burial of the dead.

PART IV

THE
CONFEDERATE EFFORT

*The interplay of morale and matériel has long interested students of the
Civil War. In the years after the war, it was customary for Confederate
veterans, often from the sounding-board of the United States Congress, to
proclaim that the South was "defeated" but never "beaten." It lost because
the overwhelming manpower and the massive industrial might of the
North crushed the feeble armies of Lee and Johnston, but the indomitable
spirit of the South survived.*

*The allegation, for all its consoling qualities, was not true. Eventually,
the will to fight went out of both the Southern people and the Confederate
soldiers. Eventually, the collapse of morale seemed to be a concomitant of
the economic consequences of an inflated, almost worthless, currency, the
exhaustion of the accumulated matériel for warfare, the effectiveness of
the Northern blockade, and the devastating war which Northern forces
made against the rivers and the railroads of the South. Economic collapse
was accompanied by—and may have been the cause of—the failure of
spirit.*

*Yet both the spirit and the resources held out better than Confederate
opponents predicted and later historians proclaimed. Early in 1861, an
English reporter found the South, as well as the North, filled with con-
fusing rumors, yet he predicted that the South could only be crushed by
overwhelming force. Two years later, an English officer found both spirit
and matériel holding up well. Critical Northern observers declared the
South not devoid of resources, nor of the capacity to use them effectively.*

*The maintenance of both spirit and matériel was, indeed, the product of
extraordinary exertions. In military supplies and in ordnance the concentrated Confederate effort surpassed all expectations. Agents bought arms
in Europe, while the ordnance bureau of the Confederacy, organized with
efficiency and managed with creative imagination, kept the armies ade-*

307

quately supplied. Had the same energy and ingenuity been devoted to other segments of the Southern economy, the Confederacy might indeed never have been "beaten."

22

Facts and Opinions in North and South

William H. Russell

Although I have written two letters since my arrival at Charleston, I have not been able to give an account of many things which have come under my notice, and which appeared to be noteworthy; and now that I am fairly on my travels once more, it seems only too probable that I shall be obliged to pass them over altogether. The roaring fire of the revolution is fast sweeping over the prairies, and one must fly before it or burn. I am obliged to see all that can be seen of the South at once, and then, armed with such safeguards as I can procure, to make an effort to recover my communications. Bridges broken, rails torn up, telegraphs pulled down—I am quite in the air, an air charged with powder and fire.

One of the most extraordinary books in the world could be made out of the cuttings and parings of the newspapers which have been published within the last few days. The judgments, statements, asseverations of the press, everywhere necessarily hasty, ill-sifted, and off-hand, do not aspire to even an ephemeral existence here. They are of use if they serve the purpose of the moment, and of the little boys who commence their childhood in deceit, and continue to adolescence in iniquity, by giving vocal utterance to the "sensation" headings in the journals they retail so sharply and curtly. Talk of the superstition of the Middle Ages, or of the credulity of the more advanced periods of rural life; laugh at the Holy Coat of Treves, or groan over the Lady of Salette; deplore the faith in winking pictures, or in a *communiqué* of the *Moniteur;* moralize on the superstition which discovers more in the liquefaction of the ichor of St. Gennaro than a chemical trick; but if you desire to understand how far faith can see and trust among the people who consider themselves the most civilized and intelligent in the world, you will study the American journals, and read the telegrams which appear in them. One day the 7th New York Regiment is

WILLIAM H. RUSSELL, *The Civil War in America* (Boston, 1861), Letter vii.
"Bull Run" Russell won fame and bitter Northern excoriation for his report, to the London *Times,* of the panic of the Federal troops fleeing from the Battle of Manassas. As a correspondent, he kept his English readers abreast of developments and aware of the virtues of the Confederate cause.

destroyed for the edification of the South, and is cut up into such small pieces that none of it is ever seen afterward. The next day it marches into Washington, or Annapolis, all the better for the process. Another, in order to encourage the North it is said that hecatombs of dead were carried out of Fort Moultrie, packed up, for easy travelling, in boxes. Again, to irritate both, it is credibly stated that Lord Lyons is going to interfere, or that an Anglo-French fleet is coming to watch the port, and so on through a wild play of fancy, inexact in line as though the batteries were charged with the aurora borealis or summer lightning, instead of the respectable, steady, manageable offspring of acid and metal, to whose staid deportment we are accustomed at a moderate price for entrance. As is usual in such periods, the contending parties accuse each other of inveterate falsehood, perfidy, oppression, and local tyranny and persecution. "Madness rules the hour."

It was only a day or two ago I took up a local journal of considerable influence, in which were two paragraphs which struck me as being inexpressibly absurd. In the first it was stated that a gentleman who had expressed strong Southern sentiments in a New York hotel had been mobbed and thrown into the street, and the writer indulged in some fitting reflections on the horrible persecution which prevailed in New York, and on the atrocity of such tyrannical mob-lawlessness in a civilized community. In another column there was a pleasant little narrative how citizens of Opelika, in Georgia, had waited on a certain person, who was "suspected" of entertaining Northern views, and had deported him on a rustic conveyance, known as a rail, which was considered by the journalist a very creditable exercise of public spirit. Nay, more; in a *naïve* paragraph relative to an attempt to burn the huge hotel of Willard, at Washington, in which some hundreds of people were residing, the paper, to account satisfactorily for the attempt, and to assign some intelligible and laudable motive for it, adds that he supposes it was intended to burn out the "Border ruffians" who were lodged there—a reproduction of the excuse of our Anglo-Irish lord, who apologized for setting fire to a cathedral on the ground that he imagined the Bishop was inside. The exultation of the South when the flag of the United States was lowered at Sumter has been answered by a shout of indignation and a battle-cry from the North, and the excitement at Charleston has produced a reflex action there, the energy of which cannot be described. The apathy which struck me at New York, when I landed, has been succeeded by violent popular enthusiasm, before which all Laodicean policy has melted into fervent activity. The truth must be that the New York population did not believe in the strength and unanimity of the South, and that they thought the Union safe, or did not care about it. I can put down the names of gentlemen who expressed the strongest opinions that the Government of the United States had no power to coerce the South, and who have since put down their names and their money to support the Government in the attempt to recover the forts which have been taken. As to the change of opinion in other quarters, which has been effected so rapidly and miraculously that it has the ludicrous air of a vulgar juggler's trick at a fair, the public regard it so little, that it would be unbecoming to waste a word about it.

I expressed a belief in my first letter, written a few days after my arrival, that the South would never go back into the Union. The North thinks that it can coerce the South, and I am not prepared to say they are right or wrong; but I am convinced that the South can only be forced back by such a conquest as that which laid Poland prostrate at the feet of Russia. It may be that such a conquest can be made by the North, but success must destroy the Union as it has been constituted in times past. A strong Government must be the logical consequence of victory, and the triumph of the South will be attended by a similar result, for which, indeed, many Southerners are very well disposed. To the people of the Confederate States there would be no terror in such an issue, for it appears to me they are pining for a strong Government exceedingly. The North must accept it, whether they like it or not. Neither party, if such a term can be applied to the rest of the United States and to those States which disdain the authority of the Federal Government, was prepared for the aggressive or resisting power of the other. Already the Confederate States perceive that they cannot carry all before them with a rush, while the North have learnt that they must put forth all their strength to make good a tithe of their lately uttered threats. But the Montgomery Government are now, they say, anxious to gain time, and to prepare a regular army. The North, distracted by apprehensions of vast disturbances in its complicated relations, is clamoring for instant action and speedy consummation. The counsels of the moderate men, as they were called, have been utterly overruled.

I am now, however, dealing with South Carolina, which has been the *fons et origo* of the Secession doctrines, and their development into the full life of the Confederate States. The whole foundation on which South Carolina rests is cotton and a certain amount of rice, or rather she bases her whole fabric on the necessity which exists in Europe for those products of her soil, believing and asserting, as she does, that England and France cannot and will not do without them. Cotton, without a market, is so much flocculent matter encumbering the ground. Rice, without demand for it, is unsalable grain in store and on the field. Cotton at ten cents a pound is boundless prosperity, empire, and superiority, and rice or grain need no longer be regarded. In the matter of slave labor, South Carolina argues pretty much in this way: England and France require our products. In order to meet their wants, we must cultivate our soil. There is only one way of doing so. The white man cannot live on our land at certain seasons of the year; he cannot work in the manner required by the crops. We must, therefore, employ a race suited to the labor, and that is a race which will only work when it is obliged to do so. That race was imported from Africa, under the sanction of the law, by our ancestors, when we were a British colony, and it has been fostered by us, so that its increase here has been as that of the most flourishing people in the world. In other places where its labor was not productive, or imperatively essential, that race has been made free, sometimes with disastrous consequences to itself and to industry. But we will not make it free. We cannot do so. We hold that slavery is essential to our existence as producers of what Europe requires; nay, more, we maintain it is in the abstract right in principle; and some of us go so far as to maintain that the only proper form of society, according to the law of God and the exigencies of man, is that which has slavery as its basis. As to the slave, he is happier far in his state of servitude, more civilized and religious than he is or could be if free or in his native Africa.

23

A Run Through the Southern States

An English Officer

Whilst at Mobile, I had the pleasure of being introduced to Admiral Buchanan, who commanded the *Merrimac* in her combat with the *Monitor*. He was formerly an officer of the United States Navy, but on the war breaking out he joined the Southern cause; and having done good service in the James River, received the naval command of Mobile. He was severely wounded in the battle between the *Merrimac* and *Monitor*. The failure of the *Merrimac* to run down the *Monitor* is accounted for by the fact that her ram was broken in her previous attack on the *Congress*.

Admiral Buchanan kindly invited me to form one in an expedition down the bay to visit the *Ovieto* or *Florida*, lying about fifteen miles from Mobile. It was a beautiful bright day when we left the quay, in a small river steamer, our party consisting of one of the generals in command, a few officers, and several of the ladies of Mobile. These, like their sisters elsewhere, are most zealous in the cause of the Confederacy, and their zeal is shown not only in words, for they sacrifice many of their comforts, and, without murmuring, willingly put up with the serious inconvenience caused by the blockade. Gloves and ladies' shoes are very scarce articles; and it was said that one ship, which was endeavoring to run the blockade laden with crinolines, was ruthlessly captured by the federal cruisers. Can such barbarity be true! Still, somehow or other, ladies always contrive to dress nicely and look well, and the ladies of Mobile were no exception to the rule. We steamed through the narrow and winding channel which affords the only access to the actual port of Mobile, passing two or three iron-clad river steamers, either lying off the quay, or else on the stocks. We left to our right a battery on the shore, and arrived at a boom thrown across the entrance of the fort, under fire of some newly constructed forts on small islands, and of the shore batteries, which are concealed from view by thick forest. Through this intricate navigation, and under fire of these formidable batteries, would the invading fleet have to approach Mobile after having passed the forts which guard the entrance to the harbor. The channel also, even at the

The Record of News, History, and Literature (Richmond, July 30, 1863).

deepest part, is but shallow, and only navigable for small vessels of war. There were only a very few fishing and coasting vessels to be seen. Sometimes small vessels contrive to run the blockade, or to make their way along the coast to New Orleans, running the risk of being captured by the cruisers off Ship Island, the rendezvous of the federal fleet. We found the *Ovieto,* under the command of Captain Maffit, lying at anchor about fifteen miles down the bay. She had been built at Glasgow, had run out unarmed and, trusting to her great speed, had, in broad daylight, passed through the whole blockading squadron, and so entered Mobile. She was pursued for thirty miles, and received an almost incredible number of shots, some of the blockading vessels having approached close enough to fire into her with shrapnel. At Mobile she had taken in her armament and recruited her crew. She is armed with Blakely rifled guns on the main deck, is not ironclad, and a large proportion of her crew are Englishmen. When we arrived, she was anxiously waiting an opportunity of again passing through the blockading squadron, and entering on her mission of destruction to federal merchantmen.

Every now and then, among all the changes which a new country, and especially this state of war, has produced among those who originally came from England, an Englishman still sees much that reminds him of home. This is especially the case on Sunday, when the church, identical in its architecture with the London churches of the last century, the service the same as that of the Church of England, excepting the change of a few words, and the numbers of well-dressed people flocking to church at eleven o'clock, almost make one fancy that one has suddenly returned to some pleasant country town in England. It was, however, melancholy to see in the church of Mobile the numbers of families in mourning, bespeaking the losses in the war! The people at Mobile were most hospitable. Many had visited Europe, and looked forward to again doing so after this war has terminated, and when a market is again open for their cotton. The British consul, an old inhabitant of the place, endeavored in every way to render my stay agreeable.

From Mobile I took the steamer across the bay to the railway station of the line leading to Montgomery and Richmond. A young fellow on board spoke to me. He was a private in the Confederate cavalry, but was, by birth, a Northerner; and his brother was serving on the opposite side; his cousin, also, was a general in the Northern armies. Frequently men of good family and wealth are found in the ranks of the Confederate armies: for instance, a rich planter will raise a company, even arming and clothing it, and then, feeling that he has no talent for military matters, will delegate the command of it to another, and take service in the ranks.

But the officers of the old army complain that there is but little military spirit among the troops. They do not seek or appear to care for glory; and a sort of neighborly feeling of each man to his comrade as coming from the same village is a species of substitute for the *esprits de corps* of regiments. They have the organization of armies; but it is difficult to carry out discipline without injuring the very feeling that insures them victory. If the details of discipline are too strictly insisted on, disgust ensues, and the men lose their keenness for the cause. There is no time to make them good regular troops; therefore, latitude in discipline must be allowed, in order to keep them as good volunteers. They are better supplied than formerly with arms and military stores, but they have the wastefulness of undisciplined troops; and it is very difficult to make them carry their proper supplies of rations on the march, and to prevent them from wasting or consuming those supplies too quickly.

It was a drizzling wet day when I left Mobile, and the great marshes and swamps looked very dreary: they afford shelter to alligators—who, however, only make their appearance in warm weather—and to other species of game with which Florida abounds. The line led us through dreary forests of the live oak, the ilex, and other trees, covered with long pendants of moss; and on leaving these we entered on almost endless forests of pines, now and then passing Confederate pickets, the horses tied, ready saddled and bridled, to the trees. At the culverts and bridges small parties of soldiers were usually stationed to guard them, and prevent any sudden raid from the neighboring federal post of Pensacola being made for the purpose of destroying the rail. Little amusement is there to be found in a Southern railway car, as the passengers are not much given to conversation; and, in, fact, the main portion of the travellers are usually soldiers, going to, or returning from their regiments. But it is rather amusing to sit for a short time in the car reserved for the niggers. They are a most ridiculous race of beings, and always appear to be caricaturing themselves. No representation of their manners can be too ridiculous or extravagant for the reality. A nigger in the South is almost always addressed by the whites as "uncle," especially if he be rather old. What this term has arisen from, I cannot say. As we approached Montgomery, the country became more cultivated, and the forest receded; and towards evening we reached the town, or rather the station, where omnibuses and flies were waiting to convey us to Montgomery.

Montgomery is a well-built, nice town, with, as usual, the courthouse containing room for the sittings of the Senate and Congress of the State. Large hotels, filled to overflowing, received the passengers; but as, for some reason, the morning train of that day had not left Montgomery, there was very little accommodation for the new arrivals. After waiting for a long time, a mattress on the floor of the hall was allotted to me, whilst around, on various mattresses, lay my fellow-travellers. Certainly the accommodations of Southern hotels is not at present first rate.

We started again early next morning, the train awfully crowded, as two days' passengers had to be accommodated. I have a dim recollection of passing through the towns of Atlanta and Augusta, some time during the next two days and night, but they have left no impression on my memory. The cotton crops converted into corn fields, the pine forests, and, as we approached Charleston, the rice fields, succeeded each other without leaving any mark on the mind. Sometimes the train stopped for refreshments, when, as before, we obtained hard-boiled eggs, corn bread, and sometimes pieces of chicken, from niggers who charged an enormous price for those delicacies.

On the third day after leaving Mobile I reached Charleston, an older-looking town than one generally sees in the States, and perhaps rather more cheerful than Mobile, for there is still a slight appearance of business about it. A large, and even at this time a well-conducted, hotel received me—and to appreciate a good hotel, a journey of two or three days in a Southern railway is no bad preparation. The fire which devastated Charleston about a year ago, has left terrible traces of its progress: it seems to have swept clean through one of the best parts of the city; and, owing to the war, which employed labor elsewhere, no steps to repair the damage have been taken. Still Charleston is a pleasant place, and the walk along the quays by the side of the bay is delightful; the houses, being built somewhat in the Italian style of architecture, and standing on the very edge of the waters of the bay, remind one of some of Claude Lorraine's sea pictures.

However, warlike preparations appeared on all sides. Batteries had been erected along the quay; a regiment was encamped in the public gardens; iron-clad vessels were in course of preparation; the forts at the entrance of the harbor were all armed; and people spoke of a desperate defence, and of burning the town rather than allowing it to fall into the enemy's hands. General Beauregard's head-quarters were in the town. I had the pleasure of passing the evening in his company, and a remarkably nice person and good officer he appeared to be. He is a small, very intelligent-looking man, with remarkably bright dark eyes and rather gray hair; in fact, his appearance bespeaks a more Southern descent than that of the Anglo-Saxon. He spoke confidently of being able successfully to defend the place. General Beauregard corroborated the curious facts one heard respecting the bombardment of Fort Sumter. It is perfectly true that after a most severe bombardment, the fort replying vigorously, it surrendered, because untenable, and not one man of the garrison was either killed or wounded; whilst on the attacking side the casualties only amounted to three men slightly wounded. The fact that such was the case is almost unaccountable.

The situation of Charleston, on the point of land between the Ashley and Cooper rivers, and surrounded with forests and marshy country, renders it very strong on the land side, whilst the forts at the entrance of the bay, it was hoped, would afford insurmountable obstacles to the federal navy. As usual, they (the federals) have lost their opportunity. At one time the town was scarcely defended, and a few resolute captains of ships might have forced a passage into the bay, and bombarded it. Now, however, deficiencies have been remedied, and an obstinate defence will be the result. Every day people expected the attack to take place; the large force which was under the command of General Banks threatened the whole southern coast, and each city supposed itself to be the object of menace.

The rail to Wilmington was open, and as that was the shortest way to Richmond, I took the train, and reached Wilmington about one A.M., where a steam ferry carried the passengers across the harbor. We were kept waiting in an awfully cold night, crowding round the doors of the railway cars; and as it was a case of first come, first served, those who got in first secured a seat, whilst those who did not were forced to stand.

The usual uncertainty attending Southern railway travelling prevented me from making any calculation as to the time of reaching Richmond. At Weldon we "missed connection," which means that the train had gone off without waiting for us, and we had the agreeable prospect of passing twenty-four hours at one of the most miserable places I ever saw. Even in peacetime it has a bad name, and during the present state of things it has become ten times worse than before. Two dreary houses, dignified by the name of hotels, received the passengers. I was fortunate enough to obtain a bed, two soldiers of the Confederate army occupying the other bed in my room. We even procured the luxury of a fire, and, whilst sitting round it, my two companions discussed their campaigns, and, in doing so, described two battles at which I had been present on the opposite side. It was very amusing to hear their descriptions, especially that of one man, who gave me an account of his charging squares and performing other prodigies of valor, no such squares, to my certain knowledge, having existed. I did not tell them that I had seen the battles from another point of war. At Weldon there is an important bridge across a river, on which a guard was stationed, as it was supposed to be an object of attack of the federals, who occupied parts of the country lying in the vicinity near the coast. After our twenty-four hours' delay, a train arrived and carried us on to Petersburg, a large well-built town, near the James River. Omnibuses, driven by niggers, conveyed us through the town to the Richmond railway station, and on my way I took the opportunity of asking the "intelligent contraband" who was driving me whether the Yankees had any gun-boats on the James River. "Oh, yeth, massa," was the answer, "them Yankees have got three thousand gun-boats down there." This awful piece of information ought, of course, to have been forwarded to President Davis, if he had been in the same habit of acquiring information from "intelligent contrabands" as the other President. The train conveyed me to Richmond, where I arrived about seven o'clock P.M., very glad to have accomplished the long journey from Mobile.

Of all the expeditions I have made, the ride I took out of Richmond to the scene of the old battlefields of the Chickahominy was to me the most curious. Six months previously, I had been encamped with the federal army for a month, within four and a half miles of the city, and now I was about to visit the same localities from the opposite side. To do this I hired a wretched horse—horses are scarce articles at Richmond—and started off alone to find my way to the Chickahominy, feeling sure when once there of knowing every inch of the ground. After leaving the town, I passed the redoubts which encircle it—earthworks thrown up hastily during the war— and found the guard stationed on the road: however, my pass ensured me every civility, and I was put in the right way of reaching Newbridge on the Chickahominy.

Very soon the country showed palpable signs of war—fences broken down and destroyed, houses burnt—in short, a fertile country had become a waste. I looked in vain for the lines of earthworks which I was led to believe had prevented the advance on Richmond of the federal army; they did not exist, a very small trench and breastworks being the only signs of any fortification. Still I rode on, expecting to meet some traces of field-works, until I found myself among the well-remembered places facing the heights, from which I had often watched the federal batteries play on the very ground I was riding over. There was the house which, I remembered, served as a mark for the federal artillery; there was the steep piece of road down which, through a telescope, I had watched the Confederate wagons hastening to avoid the fire. In fact, I almost seemed to have two separate existences, and imagined that I should see myself and former companions appear on the opposite heights. My ride was stopped by the bridge (called Newbridge) having been destroyed. Men were engaged in repairing it, the muddy stream of the Chickahominy flowing on, unconscious of having separated two vast armies and played so considerable a part in a great struggle.

Across the deserted fields, the former stations of the Confederate pickets, I made my way; then through the abandoned federal camps and entrench- ments, across the country, and through the woods, and among the numerous graves of those who fell at Fairoaks and the Seven Days' battles, until I reached the redoubt, the scene of Hooker's fight, where the last battle was fought with the object of advancing on Richmond. The battles which suc- ceeded it were for existence, not victory. The country was deserted; a soli- tary sportsman looking for partridges was the only person I encountered. Where were all those I had known so intimately six months before? Some were killed in those last disastrous battles; most had left the army in disgust, or been driven from it by the politicians at Washington.

I crossed the rail, and returned to Richmond by the road which passes the Seven Pines, from which the battle of that name is called. Richmond must be singularly changed from what it was two years ago—then a State capital, as little known to fame as any other of the numerous capitals of the various States—now the centre of the Confederacy, and the object for which vast armies are contending. It is a pleasant town on the left bank of the James River, whose winding course can be seen for many miles from one of the numerous hills on which it stands. There is still traffic in the streets; the theatres are open; ladies riding and driving (the latter usually in ambulances, instead of carriages) pass not unfrequently, and the whole town appears endeavoring under difficulties to keep up an appearance of peace and prosperity. When I was there but few soldiers were to be seen in the streets; they were concentrated in front of Fredericksburg, where a battle was daily expected. The crowded state of the hotels, filled with officers, the appearance every now and then of some rough-looking cavalry or artillery, the enormous hospitals which cover one of the hills overlooking the river, the iron-clads built and in course of building on that river—all told of war. Although great confidence was felt in General Lee and his army, yet a certain uneasiness existed as to the result of the approaching battle. In the event, however, of utter defeat and the occupation, by the federals, of Richmond, the resolution had been formed to leave nothing but its ashes to receive the enemy. Commodore Pegram, who formerly commanded the *Nashville*, was kind enough to show me the new *Merrimac*, to which he had been appointed. She differs slightly from her namesake, and is armed with very large rifled guns made at the foundry at Richmond. She is destined to co-operate with the fort at Drury's Bluff, in order to ensure the safety of Richmond from any attempt at attack which might be made from the James River. Two other iron-clads were in the course of construction, one built by contributions from the ladies of Richmond. On the land side, a circle of bastioned field-works guard the town; they are insignificant compared with the works round important European towns, but are as strong or stronger than the lines of Yorktown, which for so long a time held in check the federal troops.

It was an easy matter enough to get into Richmond, but quite the reverse to get out again, and so on to Washington. A flag-of-truce boat, for exchange of prisoners, frequently went down the James River, but no passengers were allowed on board; and in the present state of affairs, when any day might bring news of some great conflict, the authorities were chary about granting passes. Still they were very kind, and I was told I might make my way across the lines by what is called the underground railway. The officer in charge of the secret service furnished me with a pass in the event of my meeting any Confederate pickets, and directed me to make my way by rail to Culpeper Courthouse, and then as best I could to Alexandria or Leesburg, from which places the journey to Washington was easy enough. However, he asked me at the time to take charge of a lady and her two grandchildren, which, "pleasant as their company might be," would considerably add to my difficulties in traversing a country devastated by war.

We started on a cold bright winter's morning, driving to the station, where, to begin with, all the luggage, including the ladies' big boxes, were nearly left behind. We arrived late at the station; the train would not wait, and the desperate nigger in charge, after trying to drive after it, ended by jumping out of the cart, and with myself running along the rails, with the luggage on our shoulders, which we just managed to shove up behind the last carriage, the train being in motion at the time. We crossed the Chicka-hominy, and reached Hanover junction, the scene of a battle at which I had been present six months before.

Some persons in the train fancied they could hear guns in the distance. Little did we then think that the battle of Fredericksburg was being fought at that moment within a few miles of where we were. At Gordonsville, we passed a depot of military stores and a train full of niggers, or contrabands, as they are called, who were cheering lustily, and were, we were told, on their way to work on the fortifications at Richmond—poor fun, I should think, for them; but they are unaccountable beings, and always appear ready to laugh. I remember once seeing a lot of niggers sitting round a house which was being shelled, and on my remarking to their master, who was looking very mournful, that he was being shot at, they went into fits of laughter.

It was all plain sailing for us as far as Culpeper Courthouse; but there we came to a standstill. How were the ladies and their big boxes to be con-veyed through a country where there were no horses or carriages? For two days and a half I wandered through the town, looking over the palings and into the yards wherever there was the sign of a horse, mule, or even ox; running after any cart that might make its appearance in the town; routing up teamsters at all hours of the day or night; but to no purpose. We were regularly fixed. At length I espied a cart bringing a load of women and baggage to the railway station. I ran up to the driver, and at once concluded a bargain with him to take the ladies and baggage to Warrenton, I walking.

The following day we were to start; but during the night the rain fell in torrents, and my friend the driver did not make his appearance until some hours after the appointed time. When he did arrive and saw the big boxes, he tried to shirk his bargain, but we kept him to it. To vent his dis-pleasure at this result he drove his wagon, containing the unlucky ladies, for some distance over the sleepers of the broken-up railway.

Well, we started. The country showed many signs of recent battles. Over this very ground had General Pope advanced towards Richmond, and just beyond Culpeper he had met with his first repulse, ending in his disgraceful retreat to Washington. The fences were destroyed and burnt, the trees cut down, skeletons of dead horses were lying about, whilst pieces of uniform and remains of old encampments marked out the burial places of the dead, and the former residences of the living. These were the inevitable results of war. Much wanton damage did not appear to have been perpetrated, nor did the inhabitants of Culpeper accuse the federal soldiers of misbehavior.

Virginia roads are not the best in wet weather, and we progressed very slowly; sometimes we plunged through deep mud, then we were obliged to drag away a great trunk of a tree placed as an obstruction across the road; then we had to cross a river, where the water almost flowed into the cart. It was near one of these rivers that we encountered the Confederate pickets, a rough-looking set of horsemen. One, a Swiss, was disposed to make himself rather disagreeable, in order to obtain a bribe; but fortunately an officer passed, who ordered him back to his post. There was much that was pretty in the scenery: the country was thickly wooded and undulating, the fine range of the Blue Ridge Mountains bounding the view towards the northwest. We could only reach Jefferson, a small village, that evening, where a lady, residing in a comfortable house, was induced to receive us, and give us some supper and beds. A few of the neighboring gentlemen called in in the evening, including the schoolmaster and clergyman—very agreeable, pleasant people.

The next day we crossed the Rappahannock, where some houses showed, by their dilapidated appearance, signs of a bombardment. On the opposite bank, before the war, stood a large hotel and watering place; now only the bare walls mark the place where formerly the Virginia gentry used to flock in the summer season; it was said that the buildings had been wantonly destroyed by the retreating federals. Snow was falling as we entered Warrenton, twenty-five miles from Culpeper, and little prospect did there appear of our getting on. People would not let out their carts to go through the lines, for fear of being refused permission to return; and our driver had engaged to take another traveller from Warrenton, so he could not take the ladies and the big boxes any farther. I was hopelessly mooning through the streets, when a Confederate picket asked me for my pass. I gave it rather sulkily; but directly they knew who I was, and what I wanted, they could not be too civil. They busied themselves to find a conveyance, and soon discovered a gentleman who had brought in a load of pork, and who, for a consideration, was willing, having sold his pork, to carry us, big boxes and all, to another gentleman's house in the neighborhood. This was a great relief to our minds.

Several of the pickets were in the room where we dined, and were talking of the capture of a federal commissariat wagon, which I had seen standing in the street. One of them, a mere boy, was saying how he had shot and killed the driver, having been ordered to do so by his officer, as the driver had resisted after being captured. He was a quiet, good-humored country lad, but he talked of shooting the man in much the same terms as one talks of killing a dog, so great a change of feeling does war create. A few of the cavalry rode a portion of the way with us, and afterwards, we heard, roused up a federal cavalry picket near Bull's Run, capturing several horses and shooting one man. We drove up to the gentleman's house, and asked for food and shelter, saying we had come to stay with him. Although we were all perfect strangers, nothing could be kinder than our reception. Mr. ———— not only received us most hospitably, but used all his endeavors to procure conveyance for us to Alexandria. In fact, without his assistance, I believe we should never have been able to accomplish our journey. He lent me a horse, and a friend of his acted as my guide. The ladies and small boxes—the big ones had to be left behind—were put into a light cart, and off we started again. We had forty miles to make before reaching Alexandria. Our road lay through Gainesville, and over the old battle ground of Bull's Run. At the latter place, dead horses, fortunately frozen when we passed, were lying in great numbers; shot and shell were strewed about; the half-burnt chimney stacks marked where houses had formerly stood, and even, in some places, skeletons and bones of human beings appeared above the ground; in fact, there were all the signs of great battles having been fought on the ground over which we were passing.

Close to the stream of Bull's Run, on an eminence commanding a view of the surrounding country, we encountered the first federal picket. It was a party of cavalry, under charge of a sergeant, patrolling the country. As we approached they drew their revolvers and unslung their carbines; and I was rather anxious lest they might take me and my friend for Confederate cavalry, knowing how lately they had been roused up by them. It turned out, when we came up to them, that they had done so, and were only convinced of their mistake by our extremely peaceable appearance. They had been out during the night, were very cold, and had no desire of fighting that morning; and so were only too pleased to find we were quiet travellers, and not the black horse cavalry. In fact, they could not be too civil; they took us to the picket fire, reported our arrival to the officer in command, who forwarded us on, under escort, to his colonel. He (the colonel) was at Centreville, where the old field-works, thrown up by the Confederates after the battle of Bull's Run, were still standing. From thence an escort conducted us to Fairfax Courthouse, with orders to take us to the provost-marshal. Nothing could exceed the civility of everyone, from the colonel to the troopers of the escort; they, poor fellows, were heartily sick of the war, and wished they were back at their farms in Ohio. The provost-marshal, having seen my permit, by means of which I had passed the federal lines at Memphis, was perfectly satisfied, and gave both myself and the ladies permission to proceed. My friend took the horses back to Mr. ————'s house, and I luckily found a sutler's cart, in which I made the journey to Alexandria. Large bodies of troops were bivouacked and encamped along the road, and all appeared to be what the Americans call "on the stampede"—I suppose in consequence of the attack lately made by the Confederate cavalry. Little did they think that the only forces opposed to them in that part of the country were two or three troops of irregular cavalry.

About four o'clock I passed through the well-remembered forts round Alexandria, and the whole party arrived just in time to catch the steamer up the Potomac to Washington, which we reached about seven o'clock.

Thus terminated my rapid two months' travelling through the Confederate States; and from all I have seen and heard, I feel fully convinced that no danger will ever frighten, or bribes of power induce, the States of the Confederacy to join again the Northern Union. They are unanimous; there is no party feeling in the South; they have confidence in their President, their Government, and their generals; and in all these respects how great is the contrast they present to the States of the North! Their troops also have proved themselves victorious in almost every great action, and are fully capable of defensive warfare. What the future boundaries of the Confederates may be, no one can prophesy, or into how many distinct governments the Union may be split up; but never again will the Slave States consent to a reunion with the North, the hatred between the two countries (especially on the side of the South) is too intense, and is transmitted with increased bitterness from parents to children. It is a bitter pill for the Americans to swallow, and hard for them to admit that their Government has proved a failure, and that the extent of dominion which gave them so much power, is at an end.

24

Resources of the North and South

The Knickerbocker Magazine

One of the most frequent arguments with which the newspapers attempt to reconcile their readers to the continuance of a war which is desolating large tracts of the country, destroying the prosperity of the nation, and pouring out like water the blood and treasure of the people, is that the superior resources of the North will soon compel the South to succumb; and that the restoration of the Union will repay all our losses and expenditures, while it will secure for us forever both against future wars of North and South, and against the aggression of European Powers. If we admit the premises to be correct, the conclusion by no means follows. Superior resources do not always decide the contest, particularly in wars of subjugation and invasion. For example, Spain at the time that she was the greatest maritime nation of Europe, and the most powerful, waged a war of eighty years' duration to subjugate her seven revolted provinces of the Netherlands. With her vastly superior resources and population she utterly failed, and the United Netherlands became a great power on the earth. The British North-American colonies, with a poor population of about three millions, threw off the yoke of the mother country, and braved her fury for seven long years in a devastating war, in which the sufferings and wretched condition of the troops led by Washington far exceeded the wants and privations of the forces now under Lee. George Washington was denounced as a traitor by the British government, and the inhabitants of the revolted colonies were stigmatized as "rebels." Had they failed, they would have been always regarded as traitors and rebels by the self-complacent British nation.

> Rebellion! foul dishonoring word,
> Whose wrongful blight so oft hath stained
> The holiest cause that tongue or sword
> Of mortal ever lost or gained.

The Knickerbocker Magazine (New York, November, 1862).
The argument that economic superiority foreordained Northern victory, proclaimed by propagandists in the North and echoed by later historians, was subjected to skeptical analysis in *The Knickerbocker Magazine*. The *Knickerbocker's* early indifference to the war had grown to open "copperheadism" after the preliminary Emancipation Proclamation. Its arguments pleased the Confederates.

How many a spirit born to bless,
   Hath sunk beneath that withering name,
Whom but a day's or hour's success,
   Had wafted to eternal fame!

But the arms of the colonial rebels were triumphant at last, and they established their revolution upon the principle laid down in their Declaration of Independence, that "Governments derive their just powers from *the consent of the governed;* that whenever any form of government becomes destructive" (of the rights of the governed) "it is the right of the people to alter or to abolish it, and to institute a new government; laying its foundation on such principles, and organizing its powers in such form as *to them shall seem most likely to effect their safety and happiness.* . . . When a long train of abuses and usurpations, pursuing invariably the same object, evinces a design to reduce them under absolute despotism, it is their right, it is their duty to throw off such government, and *to provide new guards for their future security.*" If the three millions of colonists successful in their revolution, and therefore now always designated heroes, sages and patriots, could not be subdued by the superior resources of England, but established for themselves a new government on the principles indicated in the Declaration of Independence, what right have we to expect that our resources (supposing them to be superior) can prevent the success of a similar revolution on the part of some of these same colonies now that they are sovereign States, and that the disproportion in population is far less than it was in the war of the first Revolution? Again, it is well known that the Great Powers of Europe have only consented to abstain from interference in the strife for a limited period, such as would give the United States Government a fair opportunity to recover the revolted States, and to test the question whether any considerable portion of the people of the South really cherished a desire to be reunited to the North. The trial has been fairly made. After a year and a half of frightful war and carnage, the Southern Confederacy is relatively stronger to-day than it was at the start; and it is admitted on all hands that Unionism is utterly extinct at the South. If that were not the case before, undoubtedly the late Emancipation Proclamation of Mr. Lincoln will unite the South as one man, whilst it is evident that it has already become the entering-wedge to divide the North; and may, if not speedily withdrawn, result in scenes of the bloodiest character in the so-called Loyal States. The conservatives claim that they do not owe any allegiance to Abraham Lincoln, but to the Constitution of the United States which he himself has sworn to obey; that he has violated the Constitution by issuing a proclamation suspending the *habeas corpus*—a privilege that belongs only to Congress, and the suspension to be limited only to States in actual insurrection—that he has violated the Constitution in another fundamental point, by issuing a proclamation which alters the very organization of the Government—a proclamation which casts to the winds the pledge given in the Chicago platform upon which Mr. Lincoln was elected, that slavery within the limits of a State was beyond the control of the federal power, and that it was contrary to the principles and designs of the Republican Party to meddle with any State institution; that not-withstanding this pledge, he proceeds to lay violent hands on an institution which pervades fifteen Southern States and is recognized and protected by the Constitution, which provides for the return of fugitive slaves, gives representation in Congress for slave population in a certain ratio to the free, and commands the federal government to prevent servile or other insurrections against the authority of State governments; whereas the proc-lamation enjoins upon the generals and the troops not to interfere to pre-vent wholesale massacres even of white women and children, and pledges the whole military power of the United States Government to the sustain-ment of Negro insurrection if successful. The Southern Congress have adopted measures of retaliation, which if the war continues will result in shocking barbarities, and will certainly cause foreign nations to interfere in the interest of humanity—even if the time had not come for interposition in behalf of their own special interests which have suffered so severely by this fruitless war.

The Emperor of the French has said that, "France is the only nation that goes to war for an idea." With more truth it might be said that "The United States is the only nation that goes to destruction for an idea." There is nothing practical in such a war. If it be a war to really restore the Union and the authority of the Constitution, the existence of slavery must be recognized in every Southern State just as it was before the war began. We cannot change any State institution in the South except by revolutionary violence and usurpation. If it is a war of abolition and subjugation, and that we are ever successful—which no dispassionate sane man believes—then it will require as large a standing army to keep rebellion down in the future as it now requires to effect the conquest. Will that pay in any sense of the term? Then this war of emancipation and subjugation, or extermination, is a war to destroy the production of the South, and to impoverish ourselves by making her poor. Her prosperity was the greatest element of Northern wealth. The raw cotton sent from the South to the North in 1859 was seven hundred and sixty thousand bales, worth forty million dollars. Louisiana in the same year sent north two hundred and eighty thousand hogsheads of sugar, valued at nineteen million dollars. The city of Richmond sent north four million dollars' worth of tobacco. New England alone received from the South raw materials to the amount of fifty million dollars annually. In 1858 about one-third of all the flour sold in Boston was received from the commercial ports of the Southern States; and in the same year seven-fifths of all the corn sold in New York was received direct from the States of Delaware, Maryland and Virginia. By the census tables it is ascertained that two hundred and sixty-two million, five hundred and sixty thousand, three hundred and seventy-four dollars were annually remitted to the North, in the shape of sterling bills drawn against that portion sent directly in Northern ships to Europe, or in produce sent to the North. There are no census statistics for all the produce sent north from the South, and the data must be gathered from the statistics of Southern cities. The following figures will scarcely cover the whole amount:

Sent north in raw materials and bills $262,560,394
Sent north in other produce 200,000,000

Total to the annual credit of the South 462,560,394

This leads us to a comparison of the productions of North and South, in order to examine the soundness of the argument which predicates the success of our arms from the superiority of Northern resources. The ignorance and the wilful misrepresentation on this point are worthy of attention. For instance, we find frequently such statements as this: "The annual hay crop of the free States is worth more in dollars and cents than all the cotton, tobacco, rice, hay, hemp and cane-sugar, annually produced in the fifteen slave States." The absurdity of the argument founded on such premises as this, even if true, will appear to the reader from the fact that the South maintains three million head of cattle more than the North, without the immense expense of hay-making. The object of making hay is to cure the grass, so that it can be transported to subsist our feed-cattle through the rigorous Northern winter which prevents them from seeking their own food in its natural state. Where those winters do not exist, that necessity does not arise; but the cattle have not the less food. The making of hay, therefore, is not a valuable labor, but an expense in the keeping of cattle imposed by climate. There is no comparison between the nature of such productions as hay and cotton—the one is consumed by animals which might be fed upon other vegetable substances, the other is the food of manufactures which give employment and bread to millions of human beings. A favorite argument with the war organs in the beginning of the civil war was that the South must be absolutely starved by the blockade of the Mississippi at Cairo, and at its mouths, preventing a supply of food from the West or from foreign nations. Now what are the statistical facts as ascertained by authentic records in 1850? Let us compare the productions of South, West and North. "The North" consists of New England, New York, New Jersey and Pennsylvania. "The West," of Ohio, Michigan, Illinois, Indiana, Wisconsin, Iowa, California, Minnesota and the Territories. "The South" consists of Maryland, Delaware, District of Columbia, Virginia, North Carolina, South Carolina, Georgia, Alabama, Louisiana, Florida, Texas, Arkansas, Missouri, Mississippi, Tennessee and Kentucky.

According to the census, the whole population of the United States in 1860 was 31,641,981—that of the free States being 18,802,124; of the slave

States, 12,433,512, and of the Territories, 406,345. The white population of the Southern States is 8,434,159, the slaves being 3,999,353. For war purposes, in some respects, the slave population is just as valuable as the free; for instance, in raising food and digging intrenchments. The white population, therefore, of the South will stand as high in a military sense as the population of the North. And as the population of the North and West, together, only stand as three to two for the South, the disparity is certainly not such that any reliance can be placed on it in point of numbers. In the following table the population is from the census of 1850; but the relative proportions now are nearly the same:

	SOUTH	WEST	NORTH
Area in acres	871,458	1,417,991	160,747
Population	9,664,656	4,900,369	8,626,852
Live stock	40,823,748	19,967,176	16,441,953
Agricultural productions and slaughtered animals	$408,030,077	$246,097,028	$295,566,699
Per head of population	$42	$60.25	$34.26

In the foregoing table, under the head of agricultural productions, the grain or cereals amount for each section to the following figures:

	SOUTH	WEST	NORTH
Grain	$307,828,112	$173,744,236	$132,026,727

The South, therefore, produces as much as both the other sections together. The produce of the South is equal to about thirty dollars per head, including the slaves. The product of the North is equal to fifteen dollars per head. The product of the West is thirty-five and a half dollars per head. The average product of North and West together is about twenty-five dollars per head. Consequently, the South exceeds the two sections in its product per head. The following table will show the value per hand, with the number of men employed:

	No. employed in Agriculture	Value produced	Per hand
South	849,285	$409,030,079	$481
West	728,127	246,097,028	355
North	828,171	295,568,699	359

Here we have the fact that the South outstrips either of the two sections in the value per head of cereal productions. The crop of hay at the North, estimated at $94,736,000, ought to be deducted from its agricultural productions, as compared with the South, for the reasons already assigned. The danger of starvation in the South, is therefore, entirely unfounded, and the black population is a source of strength to it instead of weakness. That the blacks will not revolt against their masters is now well understood. The wants of the black man are fewer, and it takes less to support him than the the white. The climate suits him, and his health flourishes where the white laborer would sicken and die.

To show that property at the South is increasing more rapidly than at the North, we subjoin the following table:

	1850	1858
South	$2,947,781,366	$4,620,617,554
North	3,095,833,338	3,426,180,318
West	1,022,948,262	2,111,233,346

On the ground of comparative resources, therefore, it would be a great error to expect the subjugation of the South. The South has a far larger surplus of agricultural produce than any other section, in proportion to population; and then, when it is taken into account that this year the South has planted little or no cotton, and sown corn in the lands usually devoted to that plant, every man can determine for himself how little value is to be attached to statements depreciating the military resources of the South. The truth is, that the North is more likely to be starved than the South, in the event of great military success on the part of the Southern generals. The Eastern States now depend on the West for supplies of food. If the Confederates, about the time the navigation of the lakes closes, should occupy in strong force the country between the Ohio, at Wheeling in Virginia, and Cleveland on Lake Erie, which is only about one hundred miles, the communication between the East and the West would be cut off, and not only would our army be starved, but the whole population, unless that military line could be broken.

It is admitted that Southern men fight at least as well as ours, and one man defending his own soil is equal to two invaders. The Southern climate, too, is altogether in favor of the invaded, and so is the immense area of the country, and the difficulty of military operations. The principal Southern generals are greatly superior to ours, and are not likely to be soon or easily defeated.

All things considered, therefore, it would be better to make peace as soon as possible, so as to prevent the humiliation of foreign dictation in our affairs, or the necessity of going to war with half of Europe, with a domestic war on our hands at the same time. The currency is already depreciated thirty per cent below gold, the standard of value. What would it be if a foreign war were to be added to our calamities? The taxation is now terrible; the taxes on the State of New York alone will not fall short of $70,000,000 per annum, besides the revenue which it is paying in a high tariff, partly inflicted as a war-tax, and partly to benefit the manufacturers of New England.

The public corruption and plunder, and the incapacity of the Administration, are other reasons which might be added why a useless effusion of blood and treasure should not be continued till the nation is utterly prostrate, bankrupt, and disgraced, and none is so poor as to do her reverence.

25

Supplies for the Confederacy

Caleb Huse

We finally arrived and my ship was in sight at anchor. I confess to a feeling of relief when I stepped on board from the tug and that feeling was enhanced when we weighed anchor and the screw began pushing us out into the neutral territory of the broad Atlantic.

There were few passengers, and the voyage was without incident save one of no importance except as tending to confirm the theory of transmission of thought without language. My table-neighbor was a young sea-captain from Maine, who was returning to his vessel, which he had left in Liverpool some weeks before, to confer with the owners.

One day at dinner, without any previous conversation whatever to lead even indirectly to such a remark, he said, "I believe you are going to Europe to buy arms for Jeff. Davis."

I was in the act of taking a piece of potato on my fork, and, to gain time before answering, I passed the potato to my mouth and then made about as foolish a reply as was possible, saying, "If he wanted arms he would be likely to select a man who knew something about arms." The captain immediately remarked, "Sometimes those fellows that know the most say the least." I could think of nothing to say to advantage, and said nothing; the matter was never referred to again.

On arriving in London I went to what was then a favorite hotel for Americans, Morley's in Trafalgar Square. The remark of the ship-captain interested me, and I resolved to probe the matter a little by calling on a gentleman with whom I had conversed more freely than with any other passenger. He was a lawyer from Portland, who in his younger days had taught school in Mississippi. He was stopping at a near-by hotel on the Strand. On meeting him, I asked if he knew the object of my visit to Europe. He replied he had not the slightest idea why I was there. I then told him

CALEB HUSE, *The Supplies for the Confederacy . . . Personal Reminiscences and Unpublished History* (Boston, 1904), pp. 18-27.

Huse, a native of Massachusetts and a graduate of West Point, was commandant of cadets at the University of Alabama when the war began. Jefferson Davis, recognizing his competence as an ordnance expert, sent him to Europe to purchase arms for the Confederacy.

of the captain's remark, and that his surmise was correct. I am very sure that, during the voyage, I said nothing from which the nature of my business could be inferred; and as for papers, I had received none since leaving Montgomery.

My orders were to purchase 12,000 rifles and a battery of field artillery, and to procure one or two guns of larger calibre as models. A short time before the beginning of the war, the London Armory Company had purchased a plant of gun-stocking machinery from the Ames Manufacturing Company of Chicopee, Massachusetts. Knowing this, I went to the office of the Armory Company the day after my arrival in London, with the intention of securing, if possible, their entire output.

On entering the superintendent's office, I found there the American engineer who superintended the erection of the plant. I had known him in Chicopee. Suspecting he might be an agent for the purchase of arms for the United States Government, I asked him, bluntly, if he was, and added, "I am buying for the Confederate Government." Such a disclosure of my business may seem to have been indiscreet, but at that time I thought it my best plan, and the result proved that I was right. He made no reply to my inquiry, but I was satisfied my suspicion was correct and resolved on the spot to flank his movement if possible.

As he had entered the office first, it was in order for me to outstay him, which I did. On his leaving, I asked for a price for all the small-arms the company could manufacture.

The superintendent said he could not answer me, but would refer me to the chairman of the company—president, we should call him—and would accompany me to his office. There I repeated my inquiry for a price for all the arms the company could make for a year, with the privilege of renewing the order. The president was not prepared to give me a price, but would do so the next day. On calling at his office the following day, he told me that the company was under contract for all the arms it could turn out, and considering all the circumstances, the directors felt they ought to give their present customer the preference over all others.

Confirmed in my belief that my competitior was no other than the man whom I had encountered the day before, I was now more determined than ever to secure the London Armory as a Confederate States arms factory. The Atlantic cable was not then laid, and correspondence by mail required nearly a month—an unreasonable time for a commercial company to hold in abeyance a desirable opportunity for profit. Within a few days I succeeded in closing a contract under which I was to have all the arms the company could manufacture, after filling a comparatively small order for the United States agent. This company, during the remainder of the war, turned all its output of arms over to me for the Confederate army.

Baring Brothers were, at that time, the London financial agents for the United States Government, and they would unquestionably have been supported and gratefully thanked had they assumed the responsibility of contracting for all the arms in sight in England. Any army officer, fit for such a mission as that of buying arms for a great government at the outbreak of a war, would have acted, if necessary, without instructions, and secured everything that he could find in the line of essentials, especially arms, of which there were very few in the market. There were *muskets* enough to be had for almost any reasonable offer, but of modern Enfield or Springfield rifles—which were practically the same—there were only a few thousand in England, and none elsewhere except in Austria, where all were owned by the Government. And, according to Mr. Cushing, these would be available by the United States but impossible of purchase by "the South." Yet even so high an authority as ex-Attorney-General Cushing proved to be wrong in his assumption, as will be shown below.

Any young, intelligent West Point graduate holding an army commission and as fearless in assuming responsibility as the average "graduate," would not only have prevented my making this important contract, but would have blocked my efforts in every direction; for in all Europe the supply of arms ready for use or possible of manufacture was very limited. Such an officer would have secured everything worth having—in other words, all the best—and only inferior arms of antiquated model would have been left for the Confederacy. The effect would have been not only to give the United States good arms in profusion, but utterly to discourage their opponents by the inferiority of their weapons.

Mr. Davis did not make the great mistake of sending a civil agent to purchase supplies—a duty as thoroughly military as any that could be named—nor the still greater blunder of setting several men to do what one man, with uncontrolled authority, could do so much better. Doubtless he could have found men who would have performed the duty as well as did the young officer whom he selected, and some who would have done their part better: but, during the whole war, no change was made, although not to remove him often required that firmness, not to say obstinacy, which was a prominent trait of Mr. Davis's character, and which, right or wrong, but especially when he was right, he exercised to a remarkable degree.

When I arrived in England, the Confederate States Government was already represented by Hon. William L. Yancey, Commissioner to England; his secretary, Mr. Walker Fearn, afterwards United States Minister to Greece; Judge Rost of New Orleans, Commissioner to France, with his son as secretary; and Mr. Dudley Mann, commonly known as Colonel Mann, who held an appointment as Commissioner, but to what country I do not know. Later, Hon. L. Q. C. Lamar, afterwards United States Secretary of the Interior, and later still, Justice of the United States Supreme Court, was appointed Commissioner to Russia, but he went no further than Paris, and returned to Richmond before the end of the war. Commander James D. Bulloch, previously of the United States Navy, whose sister was the mother of President Roosevelt, was in charge of all naval matters. Messrs. Fraser, Trenholm & Co., of Liverpool, were the fiscal agents.

All these representatives worked in complete harmony, without jealousy or clashing of opinion; each was ready to assist the others in every way possible. They were all cultured men, of agreeable personality, and as far removed from the *genus homo* which has been designated as "hot-headed Southerner," as can well be imagined. They lived unostentatiously, in modest, but entirely respectable lodgings in the West End, London; except Judge Rost, who resided in Paris, and Commander Bulloch, who made his headquarters in Liverpool. None of the representatives of the Confederate Government required much money in the discharge of his duties, except Commander Bulloch and myself. We were both to look to Fraser, Trenholm & Co., for all the money we were to expend, as indeed were all the diplomatic agents.

The fiscal system was almost of necessity, of the most simple character. Fraser, Trenholm & Co., of Liverpool; John Fraser & Co., of Charleston, South Carolina; and Trenholm Brothers, of New York, were practically one concern; and the senior member of John Fraser & Co., Mr. William Trenholm, became Confederate States Secretary of the Treasury early in the war. Mr. Wellsman, senior member of Trenholm Brothers, in New York, joined the Liverpool house, the senior member and manager of which was Charles K. Prioleau, formerly of Charleston. There was no loan to negotiate; for the Confederacy—recognized only as belligerents—had no credit among nations, and no system of taxation by which it could hope to derive any revenue available for purchasing supplies abroad. But it possessed a latent purchasing power such as probably no other Government in history ever had.

The cotton crop of its people was a prime necessity for the manufacturing world outside, and, for want of machinery, was utterly valueless in all the Southern States except Georgia, where there were a few small factories. Almost immediately after the outbreak of hostilities the Confederate authorities began to buy cotton, paying in such "money" as it had; that is to say, its own promises to pay whenever it could. Some of these promises bore interest and were called *bonds;* some bore no interest, and these constituted the currency of the country. The cotton, as it lay on the plantations or in the warehouses, was for sale, and the Government was almost the only buyer. To all others there was a difficulty, amounting almost to impossibility, in getting cotton to market. Some, no doubt, was smuggled across the border, to the advantage of "patriots" of each side; but this outlet for a bulky article like cotton was altogether inadequate, and practically, everyone was compelled by the very condition of affairs, without the application of even moral force, to sell to the Government and receive in payment the best that the Government had to offer; namely, its own promises to pay, which, whether stated as a condition of the promise or not, could not be made good till after the favorable close of the war. If the South failed, the promises would be valueless; if it succeeded, the obligations would be met as promptly as possible. The situation was accepted by the people, and the Government acquired cotton and shipped it to Nassau, Bermuda, and Havana as fast as it could.

To get cotton through the blockading squadron called for daring and skill; but there seems to have been no lack of either, and it was not long before every steam vessel that could carry even a few bales, and was seaworthy enough to reach Nassau, was ready with a crew on board, eager to sneak out any dark night and run to a neutral point, generally Nassau.

For a long time this traffic went on almost without a capture, and the Confederate Government not only deposited in places of safety large quantities of a commodity in general demand throughout the world, but also had the satisfaction of seeing its property advance rapidly in value as the war went on, and its necessities increased. The cotton thus shipped was all consigned to Fraser, Trenholm & Co., Liverpool, and the consignments for the army, navy and diplomatic departments were carefully kept separate. There was, therefore, no clashing of interests between the army and navy, as to disposition of proceeds. The requirements for the diplomatic agents were trifling compared with those of the army for supplies and the navy for building, equipping and manning ships.

I had not been long in England before the sinews of war began to be available, and I found myself able to meet my engagements in a manner entirely satisfactory to my creditors. To buy supplies was simple enough; but to ship them was another matter. As was to be expected, detectives employed by the U. S. Government as well as volunteer spies were about me. Efforts were made to intercept telegrams and to tamper with employees, but few of these attempts at stopping Confederate army supplies were successful.

One success scored by the United States was the capture of the *Stephen Hart*, a schooner of American build, but purchased by an English house and put under the British flag for Confederate use. The proof that she was loaded with army supplies destined for the Confederate States was so complete that no expense was incurred in defending the rights of the quasi-British owners. It was a mistake to ship such supplies by sailing vessels, and there were other errors of judgement which were not repeated.

After the *Stephen Hart* episode, all army supplies were carried by steamer, either to a Confederate port direct, or to Nassau or Bermuda. There was little difficulty in chartering steamers to carry supplies to "The Islands." Generally, both ship and cargo belonged in good faith to British subjects; and, as the voyage was from one British port to another, the entire business was as lawful as a similar shipment would have been from London to Liverpool. But one of the most innocent shipments was not only captured, but the capture was confirmed, and there was not on board one penny's worth of property belonging to the Confederate States or to any American citizen. The ship *The Springbock,* was loaded by a firm from whom I had purchased many supplies; but in this instance, the cargo was to be sold in Nassau, and there was nothing of a suspicious character on board, excepting some brass buttons bearing the device "C.S.A.," and these buttons were put on board the last day against the wishes of one of the partners, who feared they would be considered as tainting the whole cargo. And so the United States Court decided. Everything else on board was likely to be wanted in any country whose ports had been blockaded for several months, but none of the articles were such as could be classified as *military* supplies.

To get the supplies from "The Islands" to the main-land required sea-worthy steamers of light draught and great speed. Many such vessels were purchased and sent out under captains who were equal to any emergency, among whom were several former U. S. Navy officers. Some of these steamers had been private yachts, as for example, the *Merrimac;* (there were two *Merrimacs*); some were engaged in trade between British ports, as the *Cornubia;* some were taken from the Channel service between England and France, as the *Eugenie;* and some were built for opium smuggling in China. Later in the war, steamers were built expressly for the service.

During the first two years, the captures were so infrequent that, it may be safely stated, never before was a government at war so well supplied with arms, munitions, clothing and medicines—everything in short, that an army requires—with so little money as was paid by the Confederacy. The shipment from England to "The Islands" in ordinary tramp steamers, the landing and storage there, and the running of the blockade, cost money; but all that was needed came from cotton practically given to the Confederate Government by its owners.

The supplies were, in every instance, bought at the lowest cash prices by men trained in the work as contractors for the British army. No credit was asked. Merchants having needed supplies were frankly told that our means were limited, and our payments would be made by cheques on Fraser, Trenholm & Co., Liverpool, an old established and conservative house. The effect of such buying was to create confidence on the part of the sellers, which made them more anxious to sell than were we to purchase. When the end came, and some of the largest sellers were ruined, I never heard a word of complaint of their being over-reached or in any manner treated unfairly.

As long as the system thus described continued, the South not only equipped an army able to cope with the colossal forces constantly advancing upon it, but it accomplished this without distressing its people with taxes. And thus, in part, was answered Mr. Cushing's apparently unanswerable exclamation: "What *possible* chance can the South have?"

But the supply of acceptable arms was not equal to the demand. The civilized powers had but recently been equipped with modern arms. The United States had the Springfield; England had the Enfield, which was practically the same as the Springfield; Austria had a rifle bearing a close resemblance to both, and of about the same calibre; Prussia had a breech-loader which no Government would now think of issuing to troops; France had an inferior muzzle-loader, and was experimenting with an imitation of the Prussian needle-gun, which finally proved ruinous to the Empire. There were few arms for sale, even in the arsenals of Europe, which Mr. Cushing had said would be open to the United States and closed to the South. Austria, however, had a considerable quantity on hand, and these an intermediary proposed I should buy.

I knew something of the armament of Austria, having visited Vienna in 1859, with a letter from the United States War Department, which gave me some facilities for observation. At first I considered the getting of anything from an Imperial Austrian Arsenal as chimerical. But my would-be intermediary was so persistent that finally I accompanied him to Vienna and, within a few days, closed a contract for 100,000 rifles of the latest Austrian pattern and ten batteries, of six pieces each, of field artillery, with harness complete, ready for service, and a quantity of ammunition, all to be delivered on ship at Hamburg. The United States Minister, Mr. Motley, protested in vain. He was told that the making of arms was an important industry of Austria; that the same arms had been offered to the United States Government and declined, and that, as belligerents, the Confederate States were, by the usage of nations, lawful buyers. However unsatisfactory this answer may have been to Washington, the arms were delivered, and in due time were shipped to Bermuda from Hamburg. Mr. Motley offered to buy the whole consignment, but was too late. The Austrian Government declined to break faith with the purchasers.

I confess to a glow of pride when I saw those sixty pieces of rifled artillery with caissons, field-forges, and battery-wagons, complete—some two hundred carriages in all—drawn up in array in the arsenal yard. It was pardonable for a moment to imagine myself in command of a magnificent park of artillery. The explanation of Austria's willingness to dispose of these batteries is that the authorities had decided on the use of gun-cotton in the place of powder; and the change involved new guns, although those sold to me were of the latest design for gunpowder. I believe gun-cotton was given up not long after.

Again Mr. Cushing's "What possible chance can the South now have?" was in part answered. At least *one* of the greatest arsenals of Europe had been opened to the South.

That the ports of the South were blockaded, as Mr. Cushing said they would be, was true; but never before had steam vessels been employed by a vigilant enemy to search out the weak intervals in the line and avail himself of darkness and even storm, to enter and leave blockaded harbors. In spite of large squadrons, under command of competent and zealous officers, enough war material was carried into ports of the Confederate States to enable them, for three years, to contend vigorously against all the armies the United States could collect, not only from its own population, but from all the countries of Europe.

Well may the people of the Northern portion of the reconstructed Union be proud of their fellows, who for four long years contended against such fearful odds.

26

The Work of the Ordnance Bureau

J. W. Mallett

President Jefferson Davis bluntly stated the truth when he wrote that "it soon became evident to all that the South had gone to war without counting the cost. Our chief difficulty was the want of arms and munitions of war."

In the interval between the election and the inauguration of President Lincoln, when one Southern State after another was withdrawing from the Union, men's minds were full of rapidly passing political events, and much doubt was felt as to whether there would be a war; certainly but few looked forward to war on so great a scale, or to be waged for so many years as actually took place.

As soon as it became clear to the authorities of the newly established Confederate States' Government that an armed conflict was inevitable, they must have been alarmed at the terrible lack of material preparation for it at the South. In the arsenals of the United States within Confederate limits there were 120,000 muskets (for the most part altered from flint-lock to percussion), besides some 12,000 or 13,000 rifles, and with some arms belonging to the individual States, it may be set down that about 150,000 serviceable fire-arms for infantry were available.

There were a considerable number of heavy sea-coast guns at the fortified sea-ports, and others were seized on board men-of-war at Norfolk and among the stores of the Norfolk Navy-yard. But there was no serviceable field artillery except a few old iron guns of 1812 and a few more modern pieces belonging to the States. There was scarcely any gun-powder save 60,000 pounds, mainly old cannon powder, at Norfolk. And there were practically no arms for cavalry, no fixed ammunition, nor percussion caps, no accoutrements—cartridge-boxes, knapsacks, haversacks, etc.—no saddles and bridles, no artillery harness, no adequate stores of shoes, nor of horse-shoes, nor provision of the many minor articles of equipment required by an army in the field. Of special machinery for ordnance use there was none

J. W. MALLET, "Work of the Ordnance Bureau," *Southern Historical Society Papers*, Vol. 37 (Richmond, 1909), pp. 1-20.

Lieutenant-Colonel Mallet was superintendent of the Confederate ordnance laboratories.

save that for the manufacture of small-arms at Harper's Ferry. This was saved, though somewhat damaged by fire, when the armory was abandoned by the U. S. officers in charge; this machinery was removed to Richmond, Virginia, and Fayetteville, North Carolina, where it was set up and operated. At first, all arms and ordnance supplies of the United States were claimed by the several seceding States in which they were found, and no little delay was caused by the necessity for negotiating their transfer to the custody of the Confederacy.

The first steps towards provision for ordnance needs were taken by the Confederate Government while it was still at Montgomery, Alabama. Colonel (afterwards General) Josiah Gorgas, who had been an ordnance officer in the U. S. Army, was commissioned as Chief of the Ordnance Bureau, and near the end of February, 1861, Captain (afterwards Admiral) Raphael Semmes was sent to New York and Major (afterwards Lieutenant-Colonel) Caleb Huse, to London, with instructions to buy arms, gun-powder and munitions. For a few weeks, the supplies bought by Captain Semmes came South through the as yet unbroken channels of commerce, but naturally this very soon ceased, before any important results had been attained. Major Huse found no very large supplies upon the European market, and for the most part, had to make contract for future delivery; but by December, 1861, he had sent over many thousand stand of modern rifled muskets, which, with other supplies, were got safely through the federal blockade, and thereafter he remained at his post up to the close of the war, his shipments being of incalculable value all through 1862, '63 and '64. Originally furnished with a credit of £10,000 only, he very soon made contracts to the extent of nearly fifty times that sum.

The seat of the Confederate Government having been moved to Richmond, Colonel Gorgas was, in the spring of 1861, busily engaged in organizing his work and arranging for the ordnance demands of the large forces which were being rapidly mustered into service. He had to look to three sources of supply: arms, etc., already on hand, importation from abroad and manufacture within the bounds of the Confederacy.

The arms already on hand came forward chiefly in the hands of the men who first volunteered and were equipped as far as possible by the States from which the regiment came. In response to a call for private arms, a good many thousand shot-guns and old sporting rifles were turned in, and served to some extent to satisfy the impatience of men eager to take the field until better provision could be made for them, or they provided for themselves, on some of the battlefields of the early part of the war.

The importation of arms and ordnance supplies of all kinds from Europe through the blockade soon assumed great importance. Major T. L. Bayne was put in special charge at Richmond of this branch of the service, agencies were established at Bermuda, Nassau and Havana to manage it, and gradually the purchase was made of a number of steamers specially suited to blockade-running, the *R. E. Lee, Lady Davis, Eugenie, Stag*, etc., which brought, chiefly to Wilmington and Charleston, stores for which there was the most urgent need, and took out cargoes of cotton in payment, which were almost as eagerly desired in Europe. Most of the mercury used in the early part of the war for making the fulminating mercury of percussion caps was obtained from Mexico, and after the "Trans-Mississippi" region had become isolated from the rest of the Confederacy and had in the main to look out for its own supplies, much material of various kinds was obtained from Mexican sources across the Rio Grande, though the long distances to be covered without railroads seriously limited this traffic. Until a short time before the fall of Fort Fisher (in January, 1865) which, under the gallant Colonel William Lamb, defended Wilmington, blockade-running continued to be of untold importance.

In arranging for the manufacture of arms and munitions at home, there were set on foot establishments of two different kinds: those which are intended to be permanent, built and equipped for their special purpose and intended to concentrate work on a large scale; and those of a more temporary character, capable of yielding results in the shortest time, and intended to meet the immediate demands of the war with such resources as the country then afforded.

The first of the permanent works undertaken was a first-class powder mill, the erection and equipment of which were placed in charge of Colonel G. W. Rains of North Carolina, who had been an officer of the U. S. regular army, and was a most accomplished and energetic man. The site selected was a large piece of land on the line of the canal at Augusta, Georgia, where work was begun in September, 1861. All of the massive machinery was constructed in the Confederate States, the largest parts, the heavy incorporating rollers and pans, being made at the Tredegar Works at Richmond. Powder began to be produced in April, 1862, and the works continued in successful operation up to the end of the war, furnishing all the gun-powder needed, and of the very best quality. The statement may seem startling in view of the difficulties under which this establishment was built up, but it is no exaggeration to say that it was amongst the finest and most efficient powder mills in the world at the time, if not the very best in existence. The erection of a central ordnance laboratory for the production of artillery and small-arms ammunition and the innumerable minor articles of ordnance equipment was decided upon in September, 1862, and placed in my charge, and work was begun a few weeks later. A tract of about 145 acres was purchased near Macon, Georgia, and enclosed, a branch track was run out from the Macon and Western Railroad, and the erection of buildings begun.

The third permanent establishment projected was a large central armory, which was to be equipped with a thoroughly modern plant of machinery for making small-arms, and to which would have been removed the machinery temporarily in operation at Richmond and Fayetteville. This was put in charge of Lieutenant-Colonel J. H. Burton, who had had experience at the government factory at Enfield, in England. It was determined to place this armory also at Macon, Georgia, where one of the temporary arsenals had already been established.

The work of preparing ordnance supplies for the immediate demands of the armies in the field had to be scattered at a number of different places throughout the South. The railroads were not very amply equipped at the outbreak of the war, and were grievously over-burdened in operation, so that it would have been impossible to transport material to any single point from great distances or to secure like transportation over long lines for finished products. It was, moreover, uncertain how far any particular place could be counted upon as secure from molestation by the enemy. And there was not time for the removal of machinery and appliances from the places at which they were to be found. Hence the various temporary ordnance works grew up about existing foundries, machine shops, railroad-repair shops, etc., and at the few small U. S. arsenals and ordnance depots. . . .

At these various places different lines of work were specially pushed as local facilities made feasible. Heavy artillery was at first turned out only at Richmond, though later it was produced handsomely at Selma, first in conjunction with the navy ordnance officers and afterwards by them alone. Field artillery was made and repaired chiefly at Richmond and Augusta, small-arms at Richmond and Fayetteville, and caps and friction primers at Richmond and Atlanta, accoutrements quite largely at Macon, while bullets (cast) and small-arms cartridges were prepared almost everywhere. In like manner the products of the different arsenals and work-shops naturally went in large measure to supply such armies and forts as were nearest, though demand from a distance often had to be met. Thus the Army of Northern Virginia was mainly supplied from Richmond, as was also Wilmington; the Army of Tennessee drew chiefly upon Atlanta and Augusta, on which places also Charleston and Vicksburg, to a large extent, counted; while all the armies and fortified sea-ports looked to Augusta for powder. It should be added that large supplies of such articles as saddlery, harness, accoutrements, etc., were obtained by contract with private persons widely scattered over the country. The Tredegar Works at Richmond, under the able management of General Joseph R. Anderson, were of overshadowing importance.

In 1861, the Southern States were almost wholly occupied with agricultural pursuits, and their resources immediately available in the way of manufacturing establishments were poor indeed. There were two small private powder mills in Tennessee, two in South Carolina, one in North Carolina, and a little stamping mill in New Orleans. There were but two first-class foundries and machine shops—the Tredegar Works at Richmond and the Leeds Foundry at New Orleans; the loss of the latter was one of the sorest consequences of the fall of that city. There were several fairly respectable machine shops of the second class. There were woolen mills in Virginia, notably the Crenshaw Mills at Richmond, and several cotton mills, turning out coarse cloth, which, however, proved of enormous value, two of the largest being at Augusta and Macon. There were twenty paper mills, for the most part small, of which eight were in North Carolina and five in South Carolina. There were small iron furnaces and forges in Virginia, North Carolina, Tennessee, Georgia and Alabama. But the production of iron by these was very meagre. There had been recently established at Ducktown, Tennessee, the smelting and rolling of copper, though upon no great scale, and some lead was being produced from the ore of Wytheville, Virginia. There were, of course, numerous carpenters' and blacksmiths' shops, and there were a very moderate number of tanneries. Coal was mined chiefly in Virginia, the Cumberland field of Tennessee, and in Alabama, and as yet upon no great scale. Skilled mechanics were scarce, and of those in the country a good many had come from Northern States and returned thither when actual hostilities began.

As the war went on the newly organized arsenals and ordnance shops, in addition to their task of producing new munitions of war, had to do an immense amount of work in repairing arms sent in from the field and utilizing material captured or gleaned from the battlefields. Arrangements were made with the field ordnance officers for the collection of such material, and very large lots of lead, shot and shell, infantry and artillery ammunition, etc., were thus secured. The small-arms from the fields of the Seven Days' battles below Richmond and the second battle of Manassas, and from the capture of Harper's Ferry by General Jackson, were, in 1862, of immense value.

In the scramble of the early part of the war to obtain at once arms of *some* kind, both at home and abroad, a most heterogeneous collection was gathered. There were in the hands of troops Springfield and Enfield muskets, Mississippi and Maynard rifles, Hall's and Sharp's carbines, and arms of English, German, Austrian and Belgian manufacture, of many different calibres. I had at one time samples of more than twenty patterns of infantry weapons alone. Much the same state of things existed as to artillery, both sea-coast and field guns. . . .

As a natural consequence there was serious trouble at the arsenals and in the field, from confusion in regard to ammunition—trouble which was made worse by the gauges in use in the ordnance shops, which were not very accurate and often did not agree among themselves.

During the Civil War of 1861, the armament and warlike munitions of the world were very different from, and much simpler than, those of the present day. Armor-clad vessels and torpedoes had been experimented with, gun-cotton and nitroglycerine were known, but not in practical use, rifled cannon were being rapidly improved and brought into service, but there were no "machine guns," and there was as yet very little use made of waterproof metallic cartridge cases for small-arms; the main reliance was on gun-powder as the only explosive, muzzle-loading artillery and hand rifles, paper cartridges and separate percussion caps.

To produce on a large scale even such equipment as this involved in the Southern States, shut out from free commerce with the rest of the world, most formidable difficulties arising from dearth of materials, machinery and skilled labor. As regards the materials for making gun-powder, search was made for nitre earth, and considerable quantities were obtained from caves in Tennessee, Georgia and north Alabama, as also from old buildings, cellars, plantation quarters and tobacco barns. Colonel I. M. St. John was, in 1862, given separate charge of this work, and developed it systematically on a large scale. He also established artificial "nitre beds" at Columbia and Charleston, South Carolina, Augusta and Savannah, Georgia, Selma and Mobile, Alabama, and elsewhere. The end of the war had come before these beds had become "ripe" enough to be leached, but it was estimated that by that time they already contained some three or four million pounds of salt-petre. In fact, much the larger part of the nitre used at the Augusta powder mill came in through the blockade. Sulphur was early secured, as there were found at New Orleans several hundred tons intended for use in sugar making. For the third ingredient of powder, namely charcoal, recourse was had chiefly to cottonwood (mainly *populus heterophylla*) from the banks of the Savannah River. It was abundant, and gave an excellent product. Lead was obtained from the ore of Wythe County, Virginia, from the gleanings of the battlefields, and quite largely from the collection throughout the country of window weights, lead pipe, cistern linings, etc. Small lead smelting works were set up at Petersburg, Virginia, and under the direction of Dr. Piggott, formerly of Baltimore, not only was the ore from Wythe County and a few other points reduced, but even some progress was made in desilverization by the Pattinson process, several tons of enriched lead being set aside, which, however, before cupellation, had to be sent as bullets to the field under one of the sudden urgent demands for ammunition. Much lead was also brought from abroad through the blockade. A moderate amount of sheet copper was found at Cleveland, Tennessee, produced from the Ducktown ore, but later recourse was had for making percussion caps and friction primers to the turpentine stills scattered through the pine forests of North and South Carolina.

Really important results were produced in 1862 and '63 in the development of the iron ores of the country, particularly in Alabama, unconsciously laying the foundation for this great industry as it now exists. The Nitre and Mining Bureau under Colonel St. John, partly by its own officers and partly through contractors, opened mines, erected furnaces and rolling mills, and turned out large quantities of iron of superior quality. But before this work had got well under way much care was taken in the collection of shot and shell, and of scrap iron of all kinds. During the bombardment of Charleston, as a heavy Parrott shell came down, the little street urchins were to be seen ready for a rush to claim it, or its fragments if it burst, in order to claim payment for the iron at the arsenal. Much ingenuity was shown by a few skilled mechanics in constructing with but poor appliances special machinery for ordnance purposes, such as the rolling, punching and forming of percussion caps, the drawing the tubes for friction primers, the "squirting" of lead rods, and making pressed bullets, etc. Much labor was spent, but success never achieved, in drawing the copper cylinders for small-arms cartridges. Careful search for trained mechanics was made throughout the country and among the army in the field, and details for ordnance service were made on proper evidence of the value of such service, great pains being often necessary to prevent any mere evasion of military duty. Some attempts were made to import mechanics from Europe, but with practically no success. Every effort was made to convert unskilled into skilled labor by the teaching of the few who were already themselves trained.

From time to time, under stress of necessity, some poor makeshift materials had to be substituted for better ones. At one time, for instance, the supply of nitric acid for making fulminate for caps had been exhausted, and two or three million caps had to be issued which were charged with a mixture of potassium chlorate and sulphur. These did fairly well if kept dry, but soon became untrustworthy in damp air, so that an extra number was issued with each packet of cartridges until the use of fulminate could be resumed. In view of the scarcity of leather, and almost absolute lack of india-rubber, extensive use was made of heavy cotton cloth, for some purposes in double or quadruple thicknesses heavily stitched together, treated with one or more coats of drying oil. Sheets of such cloth were issued to the men in the field for sleeping on damp ground, and belts, bridle reins and cartridge-boxes were made in whole or in part of the same material. Linseed oil answered best for making this cloth, and much was imported through the blockade, but it was eked out to some extent by fish oil, a fishery being established on the Cape Fear River to procure it, while the fish were in part utilized for the food of operatives.

In spite of the difficulties to be overcome and the constantly urgent pressure for immediate production of results, the work of the Confederate Ordnance Department was able to boast of some useful new experiments and some improvements. One of the most notable of these was the method of steaming the mixed materials for gun-powder just before incorporation in the cylinder mills, which was invented and brought into use by Colonel Rains, and which very greatly increased the capacity of the mills for work besides improving the quality of the powder. As other examples may be mentioned the casting of shells with polygonal cavities, securing the bursting into a determinate number of pieces, ingenious devices for the ignition of time fuses for the shells of rifled guns, etc. . . .

Beside the immediate work of the Ordnance Bureau, it had to undertake a great number of most onerous outside tasks rendered necessary by the disorganized condition of society. While indispensable help was obtained from the railroads, they had in turn to be helped, and largely, in making repairs to their rolling stock and tracks. In fact, a silent partnership grew up, and materials and labor had to be used almost in common for a common end. It is easy to see how vitally necessary it was that the railroads should be kept going; but few people now seem to be aware how nearly exhausted at the close of the war the railroad system of the South had become. Almost every yard or siding that could be spared had been taken up to patch the main lines, less important roads had been despoiled to help out the greater ones, fractional parts of wrecked locomotives had been built up into new ones of more or less feeble constitution, cars had been mended until they would hardly hold together, and it may not unreasonbly be doubted whether, aside from sources of weakness, this alone might not in a few months more at furthest have put an end to the maintenance of Confederate armies in the field.

To keep up the all-important importations through the blockade, the Ordnance Department purchased, as has been stated, its own blockade-running steamers, besides contracting largely with private adventurers. It also erected at Wilmington a steam compress for preparing cotton bales for shipment, and it arranged through its agents for the purchase of cotton in the interior, and for its transport by railroad to the ports whence it was to go abroad. And, not only had ordnance officers everywhere great difficulty in securing and keeping their workmen, but they had largely to concern themselves with feeding, clothing and housing them, both the men and not infrequently their wives and children, who were in many cases refugees from parts of the country in possession of the enemy.

On the whole it is perhaps remarkable that there were so few serious accidents and disasters in dealing with such dangerous explosive agents, but there were some such with sad consequences. Quite early in the war there was a destructive explosion in a building at Jackson, Mississippi, in which small-arms cartridges were being made, and some fifteen or twenty poor girls were killed, portions of their bodies and clothing thrown up among the branches of trees standing near. In the early days of April, 1865, a railroad train conveying ammunition on the road from Columbus to Macon, Georgia, was blown up, with small loss of life, but with serious loss of stores and the production of a craterlike depression in the ground where there had been a low embankment. The march of great events caused this to be scarcely noticed.

Among the trials and tribulations of ordnance officers some little account was to be taken of occasional desertions of workmen, and occasional reminders of the need for guarding against treachery. There was not much trouble of this sort, but it was now and then spoken of, and at one time, I remember, there was no small uneasiness felt as to the fidelity of a rather important mechanic at the Richmond arsenal.

In view of the general lack of previous experience in ordnance matters, the personnel of the corps, both at arsenals and in the field, honestly deserved praise for intelligence, zeal and efficiency. As a rule, the officers not only did their individual work well, but showed the most cordial readiness to confer with and to help each other. . . .

This is also true of our commanding officer, Colonel—in the latter part of the war, Brigadier-General—J. Gorgas, the Chief of Ordnance of the Confederate States, who well deserved to be held in honored and grateful remembrance by all who served under him. His difficult task was performed with great ability. Obstacles that could be overcome were resolutely faced with intelligent energy, and insuperable difficulties and hindrances were borne with uncomplaining patience. Out of confusion his organizing skill brought such order as was possible. He was firm and at the same time most kindly and encouraging in his relations with all his subordinate officers. Never buoyant, he never gave way to depression. By his personal example and by the tone of his orders and correspondence, he spread about him the spirit of hearty performance of present duty, regardless of self, but in ever present mindfulness that it *was* duty. It is pleasant to know that now, after nearly half a century since General Gorgas' service to the Confederate Government ended, his son, Colonel W. C. Gorgas, of the Medical Department of the United States Army, is conspicuously reproducing his father's organizing power as the Chief Sanitary Officer of the Panama Canal Works.

There remains to mention but one other phase of the work of ordnance officers in the troublous times of 1861-65—namely, the organizing and drilling of forces for local defense against the enemy, made up of the white workmen and other employees at several of the arsenals. There was quite a respectable force of this kind at Richmond; Augusta had a good strong battalion of infantry and a battery of field guns; and at Macon, the arsenal, laboratory and armory together furnished a small battalion of two companies, of which I held command, and a section of artillery commanded by Major Talliaferro. . . .

At the very end of the war a serious move upon Macon was made by the heavy column of cavalry commanded by General James Wilson. This force came down from north Alabama, had a heavy fight with Forrest at Selma, and then swept eastward through Montgomery and Columbus to Macon, destroying much property on the way. Large ordnance stores were sent out of his way, to Macon, but could not be got any further on account of the previous wrecking of the railroads by Sherman. General Howell Cobb, who was in command at Macon, determined to defend the place with its valuable ordnance works and accumulation of stores, though the prospect of success was not brilliant, there being but a few hunded men available with which to face a splendid body of five or six thousand cavalry. The ordnance battalion was again called out as a part of the defending force. As there was a practically unlimited supply of ammunition on hand, all of which would, of course, be lost if the place were captured, it was ordered that as brave a show as possible should be made by keeping up heavy fire all along the line as soon as the enemy should appear. We were on the afternoon of the 20th of April—eleven days after the surrender of General Lee's army and six days after President Lincoln had been assassinated—drawn up on the line of earth-work which had been prepared several months before, and were hourly expecting the arrival of Wilson's force, known to be near at hnad, when a joint telegram was received from Generals Johnston and Sherman in North Carolina, announcing negotiations for the close of hostilities, and ordering an immediate armistice between Wilson's command and the Confederate forces opposed to him. Our men were kept in position but ordered not to fire, and a flag of truce with the telegram was sent out to meet the head of the enemy's column. The officer commanding the leading regiment refused to halt, but sent on the flag to General Wilson, who was at some distance in the rear.

As soon as he received it he rode forward and halted his forces, but claimed that the place had been captured, as his leading troopers had penetrated our lines by literally a few yards when they were brought to a halt. General Cobb resisted this claim, saying that the armistice should have been enforced as soon as the flag of truce had reached the advance, and that even when it was put in force resistance was still possible. The Confederate troops were withdrawn from the earth-works, a single federal regiment only, the 17th Indiana Cavalry, was allowed to come into the city, and a long discussion of the question of the capture of the city took place, lasting up to a very late hour of the night, and finally it was agreed that the question should be left open for settlement by the higher military authorities, so that a few days later the paroles of all Confederate soldiers in Macon were made out in conditional form, it being stipulated that if the capture of the city should be declared by competent military authority to be valid, rendering the garrison prisoners of war, the parole should be binding, otherwise of no effect. So far as I know, that question has not to this day been settled! For myself, individually, the temporary recognition of a state of truce or armistice had the odd result that in the small hours of the night of the arrival of the enemy I found myself in command of a squad of cavalry of the Indiana regiment riding round to post these men as sentries at the various ordnance stores, by agreement with Major McBirney, Chief Ordnance Officer on General Wilson's staff, he and I acting under orders from Generals Wilson and Cobb, with a view to safe-guarding the city from possible disaster by fire or explosion.

PART V

POLITICAL
DEVELOPMENTS

As Confederate apologists, echoed by Northern Copperhead critics, pointed out, the Civil War made new adjustments in the relations between the States and the Federal Government. In the beginning, Abraham Lincoln talked much of "saving the Union." For that purpose he called for troops, and on that ground he justified his early acts. Even so late as August, 1863, he was asserting—in his famous reply to Horace Greeley's "Prayer of Twenty Million" for the abolition of slavery—that whatever he did was done solely to save the Union. Not until his Gettysburg Address in November, 1863, did a change in his vocabulary indicate that the President realized that he was, indeed, creating a unitary nation. Our fathers, he asserted at Gettysburg, had brought forth on this continent a new nation, and the struggle was to determine whether the nation should exist.

Critics of Lincoln carefully and indignantly recounted the steps by which the nation steadily won supremacy over the States. And, curiously enough, the same exigencies of war were producing the same results—and arousing the same criticism—in the Confederacy. Perhaps, indeed, as one Richmond lawyer phrased the prevailing Southern view, the old Union contained two "irreconcilably hostile systems." Yet the war itself changed the political nature of both South and North. Society in general underwent alterations, new concepts of government gained attention and adherents, and a new nation, with a new spirit of nationality, was born of a war which was a war against the States.

27

The Political Revolution
The (Columbus) *Crisis*

As in the progress of events and by the *consent* of Administration organs, we have at last drifted into some consideration of what shall be the end of war, if it is to ever end at all, and the question of "reconstruction," it is an opportune moment for all hands to think about what kind of a government we have had, and what kind of a government we want.

With an implicit confidence that an overwhelming majority of the American people neither desire nor expect any fundamental change in the character of the institutions under which we so long happily flourished, the conviction is a sequence that there can be no danger of such change but through the ignorance or inattention of the people as to the organic nature of those institutions. To assist in cultivating their intelligence up to the standard of their instinctive devotion to the characteristics of American freedom, no repetition can be too frequent, no illustration of those characteristics too varied.

It cannot escape the attention of the most strenuous disciple of the abnegation or abeyance of all questions of the policy of the Administration till "the rebellion is crushed," that the advocacy of this sentiment is consentaneous with a persistent depreciation of State power, and a concurrent exaggeration of Federal authority. This fact is patent to both the adherents and antagonists of the political organization in accordance with the views of which the Government is attempted to be guided. What bearing then the maintenance or overthrow of State importance has in our political system, it is of immense importance to elucidate and determine. If State identity—preponderating State sovereignty—has coexisted with our national prosperity and been an essential feature in its promotion, it is wise to appreciate the fact. If to Federal autocracy and State degradation, our past glory

The Crisis (Columbus, Ohio, August 26, 1863).

Samuel A. Medary, old "wheel-horse of the Ohio Democracy," had been briefly governor of Kansas Territory under Buchanan. Long an editor of the *Ohio Statesman,* he returned to Columbus at the outbreak of the war to publish the *Crisis*. His penetrating analyses of Republican plans and procedures gave him importance as an intellectual leader of the Copperhead faction of the Democratic Party. His editorials were widely copied in the Democratic press, and roundly denounced in the Republican.

is to be attributed, it is of prime importance that the misapprehension of millions and of generations should be decidedly corrected. In order to reach correct conclusions upon a matter of such grave import, it is absolutely necessary to appeal to history: as neither speculation nor passion can be safely relied upon for the development of a practical, prosperous operation of a political system; and no departure into a career of experiment can cope in the confidence of the people with the example of a successful experience.

Our governmental experience though comparatively brief, has been decisive. Its history is demonstrative of the prominent part sustained by State identities. No disparagement of State authority can drown the individual consciousness that State jurisdiction has provided all the safeguards of personal and family preservation. State institutions shelter and protect us from cradle to the grave. They define our rights to life, liberty and property, and provide the means of asserting our claim to them. They protect us on our hearthstone, at the altar of God, *and when we exercise a freeman's privilege of choosing public guardians.* —Our marriages are regulated and the graves of our fathers and kindred are protected by State enactments. Nearly everything that pertains to personal happiness is under the supervision and control of State legislation. With few exemptions, and these mostly very modern, every right, privilege and duty appertaining to us, our wives and children, are all directed by State statutes. This consciousness naturally attracts the minds of freemen to the philosophy, the cause, the history of their immediate obligations to State prerogatives. Their affections are warmed by the experience; their obligations strengthened by the history. In looking from beneath the folds of the State aegis which is over us is seen a Union of States and a Constitution which declares itself to be their supreme law. Whence originated that Union—that Constitution—and what entitles it to that reverence which it claims? It is found that it was conferred by State action! With the construction of the Constitution—*by representatives of States*—separately and individually—by name—declared to be *free and independent States* by the King of Great Britain—it was made binding only on the States which should adopt it; and it itself decreed that when *nine* States should accede to its existence, a Union should be considered as formed, *for which* it should be the supreme law to the extent of its provisions. The august act of State authority was all that bound citizens to obey that instrument. It appeals to the citizens of Pennsylvania, New York, or any of the original thirteen for obedience only by virtue of scraps of paper yet in the archives of the Government certifying that those States had, in solemn conventions of their citizens, *consented* to that Constitution. For two years after the Constitution was submitted for acceptance by the *States*, it had no more authority over Rhode Island than the abdicated power of Great Britain. She was entirely independent of that instrument after twelve States had associated under the jurisdiction of the Federal Government. The collective voice of those twelve States—the power of the instrument they had created by acceptance—were impotent in Rhode Island till the sovereign will of that community had also declared that it should be a law for them. The ordinance of a State Convention imposed the obligations of the Constitution upon the citizens of Rhode Island, as had been the case with all the States which preceded her into the Union; and no other power on earth short of subjugation could have submitted that free community to obedience to the Constitution. These considerations might be pursued much further. There is nothing in the Constitution to determine whether its jurisdiction includes nine States, thirteen or thirty-four. Its language was the same when it extended over nine, as it was when it included thirteen States; and there is nothing in its provisions to indicate *what States* are subject to its provisions. From acts emanating from thirteen different State Conventions did the Federal Government alone learn that its jurisdiction extended over them!

The features of the Government thus established lost none of their characteristics by the "admission of new States"—its acceptance of new States within its protecting fold out of territory it held in trust for the whole, or acquired by the resources of them all. The instrument provided that new States could only be received on *an equality in all respects* with those originally adopting it. Every State added to its authority took their place in the same relations as if they were of the original thirteen. Those thirteen conceded no powers to the "General Government" other than those embraced in the Constitution which was its whole existence. All other powers and rights were reserved to the respective States; and by virtue of the instrument, as much to new States as to old. As to the extent of those powers and rights it requires no inspiration to determine that they are all those not expressly delegated to the General Government. As to whether the preponderance of rights and powers were delegated or reserved, it requires but little honest and patriotic reflection to decide.

There can be no "restoration of the Union"—no continuance of the civil institutions which have vouchsafed to the citizens of this land all the privileges and blessings which have enabled them to achieve so much prosperity and glory, which is not specifically founded upon, and which does not include the marked characteristics which have heretofore distinguished it. If for the sake of standing by an Administration under its audacious claim to be "the Government"—if for the sake of inflicting chastisement upon offending members—if for the sake of demonstrating the power of our national resources—if for the sake of achieving a supremacy of importance to the section in which we live—if for the sake of abolishing the system of slavery in all parts of our broad domain—we are compelled to interpolate radically new features upon our governmental system, we are utterly without any security for the life of a single privilege which has heretofore distinguished an American citizen.

When such a complete and gigantic revolution as that enunciated in the letter of Mr. [William] Whiting—"the law officer of the Government"—drawing its inspiration distinctly from the spirit of the Administration in the hands of which are the destinies of the Republic—*subject only to the will of the people*—when such a fearful and immense departure from the paths which we have alone known from the time when our political life was spoken into existence is prepared for imposition on the people—it is enough to startle the most maddened and dreamy man in America to the altars of his country.

28

A Copperhead View
of Northern Consolidation

Alexander Harris

When the Thirty-seventh Congress met on December 1st, 1862, the Government had thrown aside all disguise that its future policy should embrace emancipation as a means of weakening the rebellion. President Lincoln had seemingly permitted himself to be dragooned, by his active abolition partisans, into fulminating the proclamation of September 22d, which, by the beginning of the new year, should set all the slaves in the rebellious States in absolute freedom; and yet a more unwise measure for the accomplishment of that object was scarcely conceivable, as the President himself expressed it, in his interview with the Chicago divines, a few days prior to its promulgation. It could scarcely be believed, even by the most enthusiastic champions of Negro liberation, that a paper proclamation, issued by the Executive of one of the contesting sections of the country, would be able to emancipate the slaves of the other more rapidly than the progress of arms warranted. But fanaticism reasons not, it sympathises, agitates, and runs counter to the rules of ratiocination! and in this instance, having engulfed philosophical forecast in clamor, it could do what at another time would have been utterly impossible.

The enactment of a few measures were still demanded of the American Congress, in addition to the numerous unconstitutional encroachments already made, in order that the consolidating programme of the revolutionary party might have a finished and symmetrical contour. The union of the purse and sword, a necessity of despotism, was the grand desideratum yet to be accomplished in the subversion of the rights of the States and of the immunities of the people. The traditionally recognized power of the States must be overthrown by every possible means, and no conceivable method

ALEXANDER HARRIS, *A Review of the Political Conflict in America* (New York, 1876), Chs. xviii, xxiii.

Harris, a Jeffersonian Democrat of Lancaster, Pennsylvania, had an especial aversion to his fellow-townsman, Congressman Thaddeus Stevens.

seemed to promise greater results in this direction than the establishment of a national banking system. A national bank was one of the darling projects of Alexander Hamilton, the idol of Federalism and its successors; and in the history of American politics it proved one of the onerous burdens that always weighed upon the shoulders of those who favored its establishment.

And although a national bank had ceased to be a question in American politics since the period of John Tyler's Administration, yet with the advent of Republicanism to power, the new brood soon betrayed their parentage in the advocacy of the old measures which Webster himself had declared obsolete. So thoroughly grounded, however, had become the opposition of Americans towards a bank of the United States, that the establishment of an institution of this character was deemed hazardous; and was only attempted after the leaders had discovered that the will of the people could with safety be defied, with large armies in the field, from which all information dangerous to party success could easily be excluded. And again, for the purpose of avoiding the popular objections which stood coined in the general mind against the establishment of a national bank, the scheme was varied by proposing a bill to incorporate banks in all sections of the country. A very captivating variation, indeed, was it, and one promising popular advantages to business circles. The danger of a national bank proving a political engine in the hands of whatever party might happen to control the Government, the main evil foreseen by President Jackson was equally great, whether one central establishment were created or thousands of banks with national privileges, because the latter, equally with the former, would be subordinate to federal control.

The establishment of a system of national banks was believed by the revolutionary leaders to be one of the most efficient means to subvert the rights of the States, and to draw all authority into the hands of the General Government. In this manner it was hoped that objects could be grasped by a species of monarchical encroachment, which otherwise were unattainable; and that a grand Central Government, nearly resembling that of Great Britain, could be established in the midst of the turbulence and excitement of the rebellion. Indeed, Alexander Hamilton himself had predicted that the Federal Government would prove a failure; and that it would only, after a time, be molded into consistency when it should have experienced the shock of war. That federal aspirations prompted the warm advocates of the national banking scheme, seems disclosed in the following extract from the speech of Elbridge G. Spaulding, a Republican Representative from New York, of February 19th, 1863. Mr. Spaulding said:

> It is now most apparent that the policy advocated by Alexander Hamilton, of a strong central government, was the true policy. A strong consolidated government would most likely have been able to avert the rebellion; but, if

not able to prevent it entirely, it would have been much better prepared to have met and put down the traitorous advocates of secession and State rights, who have forced upon us this unnatural and bloody war. A sound national bank upheld and supported by the combined credit of the Government, and rich men residing in all the States of the Union, would have been a strong bond of union before the rebellion broke out, and a still stronger support to the Government in maintaining the army and navy to put it down.

The national banking system deduced its whole genealogical descent from monarchical principles. Its successful inauguration depended upon the suppression of the State banks, which existed constitutionally, as the Supreme Court of the United States had authoritatively declared; and which the General Government had no delegated power, either directly or indirectly, to suppress. But, when men could be found that had the boldness openly to declare that Congress had the right to appoint a dictator, as Thaddeus Stevens had already done, it is not strange that any kind of bill could be enacted depriving the States of their clear and constitutional authority to establish banks with State charters. During the discussion on the National Bank Bill, the right of the States to create banks was not questioned; but a sufficient tax was imposed in the bill upon the circulation of the State banks, as would compel them to exchange their notes for the new ones to be issued by the General Government. It was, in brief, simply a new method of indirectly doing that which the Constitution, as interpreted by the highest judicial tribunal of the country, had forbidden to be done.

The National Banking Bill met the approval of the most revolutionary Republicans of both Houses of Congress; and received the sanction of President Lincoln February 25th, 1863. It encountered, however, the united opposition of the Democracy and of a considerable number of the more conservative Republican members of Congress, in the Senate and House of Representatives. In the Senate, such Republicans as Collamer, Cowan, Grimes, Howard and Trumbull, refused to support the measure.

The Democrats in general viewed the bill as one of the consolidating measures designed to wrest power from the States and strengthen the central authority. Senator Powell, in his speech of February 10th, 1863, said: "It is a grand scheme of consolidation; one that, in my judgement, will become dangerous to the public liberties, and I believe that it should not be forced upon the people of the States, particularly when it is forced there to destroy their banking institutions.". . .

The Federal Government, by the passage of the bank bill, had become the keeper of the people's purse; the sword must next be grasped, and then the power of the States and the citizens thereof could with impunity be defied. Men, as well as money, were in abundance for a period, after the inauguration of the war, in answer to the calls of the President; but time disclosing the great deception that had been practised, neither could any longer be had in such quantities as the exigency demanded. Congress, at its extra session in 1861, had given authority for raising vast armies; and all the soldiers whose services could be secured were enlisted under various proclamations of the President, but still more were in demand to end a rebellion whose resistance had far surpassed the popular expectation. . . .

By the middle of 1862, Northern patriotism was greatly flagging, because enlisting for the war was already discovered to be no holiday recreation, but a stern reality that few cared to encounter, save those whom fancied sympathy for the Negro had blinded into the espousal of the abolition cause. It was now perceived that the war steed of Northern patriotism must experience a slight goad from the spur of his furious rider, in order to enable him any longer to penetrate to the front of the battle, and grapple with his rebel combatant upon the field of Southern conflict. This slight prick was essayed in the passage of the Act of Congress of July 17th, 1862, which authorized the calling out by draft of the militia of the loyal States for nine months, for the suppression of the Southern armies, and the restoration of the national authority.

But the rebellion against abolition domination, notwithstanding this, stood up in all its mighty strength and colossal magnitude. The enlisted legions of the North, from Maine to California, were sinking before the shafts of Southern resistance; and the invading armies had become so attenuated by the close of 1862 that more stringent means than had as yet been made use of must be employed if the Administration of Abraham Lincoln was to triumph over its stubborn foe. The might of Herculean despotism must be invoked to the rescue, or the flag of abolitionism must lower its folds on the field of battle. Neither the war cry of freedom for an enslaved race, nor the paeans of the victorious soul of the felon in Charlestown, marching to victory, were sufficient any longer to arouse martial ardor in the breasts of the enrolled soldiers of Northern fanaticism.

The loathsome beast of despotic innovation now reared a more hideous aspect than it had as yet presented. An act was passed in both houses of Congress ignoring all authority of the States over their own militia; and subjecting all able-bodied men of the North, between certain ages, to a merciless conscription, which found sanction neither in constitutional warrant nor in prior Anglo-Saxon history. Britain's annals were scanned in vain for a model to subject to presidential control the independent freemen of the North; and resort was necessarily had to the continental despotisms of the old world, which alone were able to supply a genuine copy. Charles J. Biddle, a member of Congress from Pennsylvania, in his speech of February 23, 1863, grouped the Conscription Bill as one of the concatenation of measures which changed the whole fabric of the Government from a Republic into a consolidated despotism. In his speech he said:

This (the Conscription Bill) is a part of a series of measures, which to my mind seem materially to alter the structure of the Government under which we live. The bill to transfer to the President, without limitation of time or place, our power over the writ of *Habeas Corpus;* the bill of indemnity which, to use the words of the Senate's Amendment, secures for all wrongs or trespasses committed by any officer of the Government, full immunity, if he pleads in the courts of justice the order of the President, and which also deprives State Courts of their jurisdiction in such cases; the bank bill, which puts the purse strings in the same hands with the sword; these bills, to my mind, couple themselves with this bill, and they seem to me, taken together, to change the whole framework of this Government; and instead of the Constitutional Government, which was originally so carefully devised for this country, they leave us a system which does not materially differ, according to any definition I can frame, from the despotism of France or Russia.

The passage of the Conscription Bill was found to be indispensable, because the abolition leaders perceived that the prosecution of the war, by means of enlisted soldiers, would surely prove a failure. Thaddeus Stevens, the coryphaeus of abolition impulse, in the House of Representatives already had declared on the floor of Congress, that no more volunteers could be had from the North; and that other methods of filling the Union armies must be adopted. Vast numbers of soldiers who had voluntarily entered the Northern armies afterwards deserted; some because they believed the Administration had forsaken the principles upon which the war was originally prosecuted; others did so infected by the corrupt influences already everywhere prevalent. . . .

The Democrats and Border-State men of both houses of Congress combatted the Conscription Bill with a zeal and ardor worthy of Charlemagne's paladins, and the knights of feudal history. But the conflict waged by these chivalric friends of their country in behalf of liberty and the Constitution, was nevertheless hopeless; yet, impelled by motives of uncalculating patriotism, they rushed within the breach and yielded themselves, sacrifices worthy of immortal glory,. Senator Bayard of Delaware, in his speech of February 28, 1863, used the following language concerning the Conscription Bill:

> From the foundation of the Government to this day, no attempt has been made in this country to pass a law of this character, by any Congress of the United States; no such bill has been introduced; no such doctrine as is involved in this bill has been contended for—that under the power to raise armies, you can raise them in any other mode than by enlistment or recruiting, or by the acceptance of volunteers. Has the power ever been attempted to be exercised by the Parliament of Great Britain, with all its omnipotence? No!

Senator Kennedy, of Maryland, in the debate on this bill, said: "As to the bill itself, I look upon it as odious and despotic. It goes further to subjugate the people of a free country than any I have ever read of in history."

Senator Saulsbury of Delaware, during the same debate, uttered the following sentiments:

I regard it as the crowning act, in a series of acts of legislation, which surrender all that is dear to the private citizen into the keeping and at the mercy of the Executive of this nation. . . . I assert, that under the law governing this administration, under the law as declared by the highest law officer of this Government, this bill not only authorizes the calling into the service of every able-bodied white man, but it authorizes the calling into the service of every able-bodied free Negro, between the ages of twenty and forty-five, in the land. I say this because the Attorney-General of the United States has expressed the opinion, in writing, that the free Negroes are citizens of the United States. . . . Sir, if the theory of this bill be the theory of your Government, if this be the power conferred upon Congress by the Constitution of the United States, tell me where is the difference between your form of Government and the most absolute and despotic form upon the face of the earth.

The Conscription Bill received the assent of President Lincoln March 3d, 1863, and contrary to the patriotic wish of the older statesmen, the power of the purse and the sword was united. The passage of the National Bank and Conscription Bills effected a complete revolution in the workings of the General Government, and though retaining the name of a Republic, no Empire in Europe now exerted a more absolute and despotic control over its citizens.

Absolutism had been reached in the passage of these two last-named bills; but to round the figure more in harmony with Asiatic despotisms, all the unconstitutional excesses that had been committed since the advent of the Republican Party to power must be condoned, and unlimited authority granted to the Federal Executive to trample in future upon civil liberty. It was not enough to satisfy the abolition appetite that the Constitution had been ignored, the reserved rights of the States overthrown, and the liberty of the citizen set aside; all these flagrant violations of right must be justified by an American Congress, intoxicated with the fumes of fanatical zeal and revolutionary incendiarism. It was a dark period in our history, when an assemblage of enthusiastic emancipationists had under deceptious colors stolen their way into the seats of representation in the National Capitol, and at length had it in their power to repudiate all the traditions of the anterior epochs of the Republic, and desecrate the holiest sanctuaries of the people.

Thaddeus Stevens, the cool, calculating demagogue, like his prototype, Cardinal Wolsey, paying hypocritical adoration at the shrines of zealous humanitarianism, on the 8th of December, 1862, brought into the lower house of Congress a bill to indemnify the President and other persons for suspending the privilege of the writ of *Habeus Corpus*, and acts done in pursuance thereof. Up to this period it would have been difficult to have discovered in the utterances of the real or pretended emancipation zealots, with a few exceptions, that anything had been done by the President and Cabinet, or by any of their numerous subordinates throughout the country, that was not in strict accordance with the Constitution and the laws of Congress heretofore enacted. . . . Mr. Stevens was far too clear in his perceptions to be deluded into the belief that any sanction could be found in the Constitution for many acts to which he himself had freely given his adhesion. In supporting the admission of West Virginia, he had declared that there was no constitutional warrant for such action; but contended that the measure was justified by the exigency of the times. On many other occasions he had expressed similar sentiments, defending his views nevertheless by political necessity, and not any authority to be found in the Federal Constitution. At the beginning of the session of this Congress, he even had the boldness to declare upon the floor of the House, that he "had grown sick of the talk about the Union as it was, and the Constitution as it is."

The bill of indemnity, as it passed the lower house of Congress, lead by Mr. Stevens, was too open a repudiation of the Constitution to receive the unqualified approval of a more cautious Senate. . . .

The bill, as submitted by the Committee of the Senate and House of Representatives, met the approbation of the majority of both these bodies; and receiving the sanction of President Lincoln March 3d, 1863, became a law. This act completed the series of measures which completely changed the character of the Government from a Confederation of States, into what history should entitle *the monarchically consolidated American Union.* With the enactment of this series, the legislative revolution was completed. The party of fanaticism had at length introduced their principles into the workings of the General Government; it next behooved them to sustain these upon the battlefield, and thus carry forward and complete the social revolution, towards which they looked with anxiety.

The purse and the sword had now been grasped in one hand, and civil liberty, the birth-right of every American freeman, was wrested from its deposit, the Constitution, and committed to the keeping of Abraham Lincoln. This Chief Magistrate, whose oath demanded obedience to the Constitution and a faithful execution of the laws, though a guilty participant in the sacrilege of robbing his country's *Magna Charta,* became by the act of his criminal compeers, the repository of the sacred emblems of civil right, which anterior ages had bequeathed. Freedom ceased to be any longer what its name signified. From that period forward every American citizen possessed only such liberty as the Federal Executive saw proper to accord him. The President had it in his power, by virtue of the act of Congress, to order the arrest and incarceration of any citizen in the broad arena of the Union; and no authority in the States or in the Federal Judiciary could withstand the dictator. His will, though feeble, was absolute, and that of the fiendish Nero and the tyrants of the French Revolution was no more. These earlier despots were able to deprive of liberty whomsoever they chose; so could the American President.

Abraham Lincoln and his guilty associates in crime were voted by the

Rump Congress entire immunity for all offences that any of them, under the guise of authority, had perpetrated, since the commencement of the rebellion, upon the persons and property of innocent and unoffending citizens; against whom no accusation could be preferred, save that they believed the abolition war policy to be unconstitutional and inimical to the principles of republics. But fortune, in her grant of imbecility, compensated for the grave error that a maddened and intoxicated people, in the midst of an appalling revolution, had committed. That beneficent goddess either had other duties for the American Union, or she wished in future to witness on the Western Continent, a chivalric combat of crown-worthy heroes; for had Napoleonic will and ambition conjoined themselves with the powers of the Federal President, the days of the great occidental republic in name, even, would have been chronicled amongst the things of the past. The name was retained, however, because fear forbade its abandonment; but governmental consolidation in its fullness had been reached. . . .

The presidential campaign of 1864 was an anomalous one in the history of the American Union. It was to be conducted during the existence of the most gigantic revolution which free government had ever experienced, since the commencement of time. The sectional party which had grasped the reins of Administration in 1860 had, as before shown, been the result of the long period of agitation which had cemented together the fanatical elements of the North, and made the ruling aggregation of this section a somewhat homogenous compound.

But the long period of turbulence and civil war which had separated the sections of the country had proved an eliminating process which had more and more strongly placed fanaticism and reason in opposition to each other. From the time when it was discovered, after the secession of the Cotton States, that the Republican leaders would not consent to settle the difficulties between the North and South by fair and honorable compromise, the reasoning classes began to enter their protests; and, although this protesting was chiefly in silence, it nevertheless had its influence in molding the aspect of the parties of the country. From that period, reflective men began to drop their connection with the Republican, and become quietly absorbed in the Democratic, Party. And from the beginning of the war, during its whole progress, this process of separation was going on, and a counter-elimination was likewise all this time taking place, which was drawing the most corrupt and selfish material from the Democratic into the so-called loyal party of the country. Fanaticism had at length become profitable; and it was not unusual to find men who had figured as conspicuous friends of peace and compromise, turn out to be the most blatant advocates of the war and Southern subjugation.

When the time approached that candidates should be selected for a chief magistrate of the United States to succeed Abraham Lincoln, the two parties of the country had become more diametrically antagonistic than had ever before been witnessed in the country. The boiling caldron of war had stirred society to its foundation; and its sedimentary dregs, that heretofore had remained quiescent, were cast to the surface and were exerting an influence not felt on former, like occasions. The enthusiastic mob, the fanatical agitators, and the intolerant clergy of the North, found themselves in the so-called Republican Party, which was bent upon crushing out all resistance to the Federal despotism reared by them; and against these were arrayed the calm, considerative classes, who could only see destruction to free government in the policy and movements of the party that sustained the war and its further prosecution.

Never in the history of the country did the people's government exhibit itself in such odious features. Its like had alone been seen during the dark and bloody epoch of the French Revolution. The preservation of republicanism had ever, to thinking men, seemed problematical; and the old Federal Union was believed to have afforded the most perfect illustration of a representative Republic which was anywhere to be found upon the globe. But all through the representative system of the American Union, a necessary substratum of intellectual and cultivated society, from the formation of the Constitution, had firmly held the helm of State; and cautiously guided it amidst the rocks and quicksands of social disorder, upon which like forms of government had been wrecked. An intelligent and polished class of society existed in the Southern States, from the peculiar race subordination of that section, which produced a succession of clear-headed statesmen, in whose estimation honor and integrity formed guiding stars. The plan of the Federal Union itself was the conception of these eminent men; and its unclouded prosperity, until 1860, was owing to the influence they exerted in the maintenance of order and the repression of corruption.

But, whilst Southern statesmen formed a Union with slavery, it remained as the task of the intelligence of New England and the North to form a more perfect Union, where men of all races should be equal, both socially and politically. Northern fanaticism, by means of the free school system, conceived this to be attainable, although in direct contravention to all anterior political philosophy. Sound reason would rather have dictated a method of instruction which would render each individual better fitted for the task and station of society for which God and nature had chosen him; for the statesman and the religious perceptor, the highest grade of moral and scholastic culture, but for him chosen to fill the humble walks of life, the plainest elements of knowledge.

Human equality was first promulgated by the Redeemer of men, in a spiritual sense, and by Thomas Jefferson, in the Declaration of Independence, as the deduction of the thought of the seventeenth and eighteenth centuries in an ethical and philosophical sense; yet contradistinguished from a natural and political sense. For no man of the keen sagacity, and intuition of the Virginia statesman would have been willing to stultify himself in the eyes of the scientific and philosophical world by asserting what his unclouded reason must have assured him was untrue; *viz.*, That all men are created equal; as he could not but see that all men are created unequal, intellectually, physically and politically. The Hyder Alis and Pontiacs of their times are born unequal to any of their subjects; and though devoid of all save nature's education, exert a political power that their innate superiority alone accords them. Could it be proven that the author of the declaration meant to teach the entire equality of men, he would forever stand in the light of reason and common sense, as the purest demagogue that ever attempted to delude mankind. Such a conclusion is not, however, to be assumed, without the clearest evidence to sustain it. Natural and political inequality obtains amongst all men, because of the original endowment of creation; and it does not disappear in a representative republican government, when it is abstractly said, that all men are born equal. . . . But for the men whose thought controls communities, eternal anarchy would reign. Political power is simply the effort of intellect directing society; and a few thinkers perform the tasks in every subdivision of government. The very superior minds control the aggregated whole of society, and the body of voters exert no more authority than the same number in the purest despotism of Asia. All the people can have is the liberty for each individual to fill up and enjoy the full measure of his being. Good government does not depend, therefore, upon the general intelligence of the masses, but upon the superior intellect, culture and virtue of the few who are by nature fitted for rulers.

The first successful effort of the abolitionized North, independent of the cultured South, to select a President, had resulted in a concession to the equalizing ideas of that section. Instead of an erudite, high-toned and honorable scholar, a tricky, jocular, village politician of mediocre capacity was chosen to fill the seat that the most eminent citizens and educated statesmen alone had heretofore graced. A boorish President was acceptable to partisans, who believed in the full equality of all men; and, although men are necessitated to qualify themselves for the ordinary avocations of life, a rail-splitter and flat-boatman was deemed equally as competent for President of the United States as the most acute logician and finished statesman. Indeed, it may be averred, as a political axiom, that modern fanaticism can neither produce nor secure the services of a statesman of Hamiltonian or Websterian calibre. This declaration finds support, when reference is made to the class of men elevated by the revolutionary party to Congress, and to other governmental trusts. Charles J. Ingersoll, a modern thinker, says: "We know, and only a great public change can account for it, that in the Revolution of 1776, a country of some three millions of people produced illustrious men; and in that of 1860 the same country, ten times as populous, did not produce one."

The unnatural, equalizing tendency of the Republican Party, having originally secured a President of ordinary ability and low tastes, and a Congress likewise of nearly the same grade, it was not to be expected that higher aspirations would guide the party in 1864 inasmuch as the whole social structure was in a condition of turbulence and revolution. But, common and revolutionary as Abraham Lincoln had exhibited himself during his Administration, he yet lacked some of the qualities that were considered at that time desirable to be possessed by the President of the United States. He did not have the lightning celerity of movement and that utter disregard of the whole spirit of the Constitution which the radicals desired. His common sense assured him that *too great haste spoils the work;* and he waited to see the currents of opinion, before too clearly disclosing his own views. The radicalism of the President was intense, in the highest degree; but he caused it to be tempered with a greater degree of caution than the extreme revolutionists desired.

In pursuance of a movement inaugurated, in the winter of 1863-64, a convention of extreme radicals, who were opposed to the renomination of Abraham Lincoln for President met at Cleveland, May 31st, 1864; and after the adoption of a platform of principles, named John C. Fremont as their candidate for the presidential chair. And in order, the more fully, to place themselves in direct opposition to the President's policy, they announced the doctrine that the reconstruction of the Southern States was a question for the consideration of Congress, rather than the Federal Executive. The extreme revolutionary character of the sentiments of the members of this Convention was also displayed in the endorsement of the principle of confiscating the lands of the rebels, regardless of law and the express words of the Constitution. In this Convention, Thaddeus Stevens, Charles Sumner, and men of their revolutionary principles, if true men, should have been found, either in person, or by letters. Being deceivers, however, they waited the assembling of another convention, which feared to avow what its real leaders intended to carry into execution.

Great numbers of the radicals, no doubt, strongly sympathized with the Cleveland Convention movement; and wished it success, but were too timid openly to commit themselves to it. They altogether doubted that it could accomplish any potent result, inasmuch as the popular current in the Republican Party seemed too strong in favor of Abraham Lincoln to be diverted from him by any effort that could be made. They surmised correctly, for the Cleveland Convention scarcely produced more than a passing ripple upon the surface. The President had a large army of subordinates who were all interested in his re-nomination; and besides, his skillful knowledge of the politician's art had enabled him to appear before the country as the man of all others who was believed to be fitted to carry his party onwards to victory. His own remark, that it is never safe to change horses in crossing a stream, served to coin an impress upon the public mind that was now craftily utilized by him.

The Republican politicians assembled at Baltimore, June 7th, 1864, to make presidential nominations for their party, and amongst these Thaddeus Stevens appeared as a delegate to the Convention. And, in order to appear consistent before the country, in view of the contemplated plan of reconstruction, which was now the kernel of radical policy, Mr. Stevens strove to the utmost of his power to exclude all delegates to the Convention from any of the rebel States. "He declared that he had never recognized Virginia as being in the Union, since she passed the Ordinance of Secession; and the applause which had greeted the delegates from those States that had spoken in the Convention to-day was to him a more dangerous element than armed rebels in the field." In spite of the commoner's protest, the delegates from Tennessee, Louisiana and Arkansas, were admitted to seats in the Convention and accredited the full privileges of members of other States.

The Republican representatives in the Baltimore Convention announced their platform as demanding the unconditional abandonment of all resistance to the Government, without any tender of compromise, and that slavery should no longer be tolerated by the Federal authorities as an institution of the country; the Emancipation Proclamation of the President, and the employment of African soldiers were also approved by the party leaders. An amendment to the Constitution was likewise recommended, so as finally to put an end to slavery in all of the States. But, although President Lincoln had made the subject of reconstruction the capital topic of his message in December, 1863, and although his plan was already scouted and derided by a large section of his party, a cowardly hypocritical silence was maintained upon this most important point. . . .

The nomination of Abraham Lincoln, as Robert Breckinridge, the temporary chairman of the Baltimore Convention substantially expressed it, was *une fait accompli,* even before the assembling of that body. It simply registered the party determination, as it had generally been arranged and understood throughout the North; inasmuch as no other candidate would be substituted who would so heartily unite all classes of Republicans in his support. Being a man of no positive ideas, he could permit his opinions to be shaped to suit the popular gale. He, therefore, admirably suited as the presidential football to be played by the revolutionists, who could propel him in whatever direction they chose. A man of fixed principles was by no means a suitable instrument of the existing emergency. Besides, Abraham Lincoln had the sobriquet of *"honest"* appended to his name, which was well calculated to catch the unthinking herd of voters.

The nomination of a candidate for Vice-President, was a matter that likewise called for shrewdness at the hands of the Republican managers in the Baltimore Convention. Three men of early democratic faith—Andrew Johnson of Tennesse, Hannibal Hamlin of Maine, and Daniel S. Dickinson of New York—were the prominent candidates for this position. The first-named of these received the endorsement of the Convention, in the face of the protest of Thaddeus Stevens, who saw in the nomination of this candidate a stab at his favorite theory of reconstruction. But the valuable services to the cause of abolitionism rendered by the Military Governor of Tennessee could not be overlooked by party manipulators, who more highly prized the ignoble surrender of life-cherished principles than the manly performance of honorable duty. . . .

The selection of rulers by universal suffrage, to govern mankind, is a republican process. It is the result of modern thought, in opposition to the principles of monarchy; and designed to bestow upon all classes of men as large an amount of liberty and power as may be compatible with moral and governmental integrity. . . .

But the Federal Union was the product of modern thought . . . under the administrations of wise rulers it was rendered the model republic of both the ancient and modern world. The extraordinary prosperity which it en-joyed under the principles of Democracy was because wisdom kept in harmony the complicated machinery of the whole system, based upon tacit, universal consent. During all this time, the turbulent, lawless and fanatical elements of society were kept in due subordination by that succession of wise and eminent statesman who stepped to the helm of Government in 1800, and held the ship steady for sixty years. But the violent rocking of the vessel began almost instantaneously to show itself with the departure of the great helmsmen, Clay, Webster and Calhoun. The false doctrine of equality had become so impressed upon the popular mind that with the retirement of these distinguished statesmen nearly every newspaper reader conceived himself as equally competent to rule the nation as the elected representative of the people. Free schools in the North had done their fancied work; they had educated a nation of statesmen; and the millennial days of freedom were yet in store for the republic.

With such thoughts, the Northern people having originally elevated Abraham Lincoln to the presidency, not because of his intellectual superiority, but because of his representing the ruling sentiments of his section; it was not to be expected that another than he or his like would be the presidential nominee of the Republican Party in 1864. Reason had been discomfited in the election of 1860, and being fully dethroned, was in ban-ishment in 1864. Popular election being the mode during pacific times, which wise men in State and Federal compacts had agreed upon for the choice of rulers, to whom the reins of power were to be entrusted, would this same method promote liberty and equity when these Constitutions were overthrown, and a period of disorder had seized the country?

Such was the condition of affairs when Lincoln and Johnson were nomi-nated at Baltimore as candidates for President and Vice-President of the United States. Republican success in 1860, under the watchwords of economy and reform, was now necessitated to defend, not the annual expenditure of seventy millions of dollars for the support of the Government, but of one thousand millions. Delightful economists and reformers in truth! The party also, that had through the thousands of utterances of its leaders proclaimed that no danger was to be apprehended from the secession of the Southern States, was now compelled to face an unsubdued rebellion of near four year duration. And the men who came into power vituperating and villifying Democratic Administrations as having been dishonestly conducted were, since their advent to place, busily engaged in rearing a pagoda of fraud, iniquity and corruption such as the civilized world had never before contemplated.

The Republican Party, although boasting itself of its Christian designs and moral purposes, was the great destroyer of principle amongst the American people. . . . Its secret, but unavowed objects, had attracted to its folds the infidel clergy and statesmen of the North whose numbers are legion and whose God is humanity. The party, from its origin, was the embodiment of conscious untruth in pretending that its only object was to prevent the extension of slavery into free territory; whereas, from its organization, it aimed at the complete extirpation of the institution, even where it had a constitutional existence. . . . During the whole war, indeed, falsehood colored the utterances of the Republican press, so as to delude the people concerning the progress and movements of the national arms. Oaths were not binding upon the consciences of the President, Cabinet Ministers, Senators or Congressmen, who subscribed to a higher law than the Constitution. Plighted faith was no longer required to be observed, according to the principles of those who sought by all means the eradication of the hated Southern institution. From the Head of the nation, therefore, to the lowest party subaltern, almost, deception and fraud were employed to further the cause for which war had been made against the South. These and other influences necessarily germinated the festering corruption and demoralization that arose all over the North in gigantic forms after the installation of the Republican Party; and which threatened to bury humanity in a night of universal gloom.

But the deluge had come; the foundations of the great deep of society were broken up, and constitutional ruin and prostration were everywhere visible. The anarchical mob of the North was ruling the nation, both in the Cabinet and upon the field. The Baltimore Convention was its selection, and the candidates its choice. Law, liberty and order were subordinated to the dictates of fanatical propagandism and revolutionary freedom. And it even militated nothing adversely to Abraham Lincoln, the favorite of the social dregs, that he had the courage at length to avow his infamous conduct in violating the Federal Contsitution. In his letter of April 6th, 1864, to Colonel Hodges, he said: "I felt that measures, otherwise unconstitutional, might become lawful by becoming indispensable to the preservation of the Constitution, through the preservation of the nation. Right or wrong, I assumed this ground, and now avow it."

Society, being at this time in a condition almost of chaotic anarchy and tumultuous disorder, public opinion was no fair index of the intelligent reflection of the reasoning classes, who must always guide the ship of Government, or ruin invariably ensues. . . . A bitter partisan press was all the time fanning the flames of hatred against the South, and urging onwards the Northern armies to finish the work of destruction in which they were engaged. The anti-war Democrats were pointed out as sympathizers with the Southern rebels, who were drenching the fields of the Republic in the best blood of its citizens, patriotically fighting in defence of the life of the nation. . . .

In this state of sentiment, there existed but little probability that the Democrats could do more than protest against the acts and policy of the Administration party. But that they should resist was in the nature of things; for do not all oppose those injuring them, if they have the power to do so? The Democratic Party perceived that war was anti-republican and suicidal to the principles of free government; and they should have been false to the instincts of humanity not to have expressed their disapprobation of a further prosecution of the war. Accordingly, on the 20th of August, 1864, the National Convention of this party assembled in Chicago, and resolved in favor of a cessation of hostilities, in order that peace and the Union might ultimately be restored by pacific remedies. And as the dictate of reason and true republican sentiment, this resolution must ever stand justified before the world and the intelligence of coming ages.

The large majority of the members of this Convention were decided peace men, and made but little concealment of their views. But a portion of the delegates viewed the platform as entirely too strong a committal in favor of peace; and to counterbalance this, they insisted upon the expediency of nominating a war Democrat as the party candidate for the Presidency. The name of General George B. McClellan was presented to the Convention, amidst great applause; and being known to be very popular with the masses of the party, he received the nomination. This candidate was, however, by no means the choice of the avowed peace men, and was accepted by them with considerable reluctance. Could the reverse of that have been expected, when the peninsular hero's participation in the illegal arrest of the Maryland Legislature was as yet unforgotten? George H. Pendleton, a peace man, was settled by this Convention as the Democratic candidate for Vice-President.

General McClellan's letter of acceptance had the effect of deadening Democratic enthusiasm in his support. The military chieftain carried his martial autocracy with him in his letter accepting the nomination; and laid down an interpretation of the platform of his party which was agreeable to himself. But his letter evinced a base truckling to the corrupted war sentiment of the North; and the party should at once have repudiated him as its nominee, and selected a true representative of Democratic principles, who could have aroused warm enthusiasm in his support. There were indeed mutterings heard; but the Democracy had become too far demoralized under the guidance of selfish leaders to be capable of bold action. There were yet Spartan bands in its ranks in abundance, but competent leaders were wanting to unite and lead them to victory, or even honorable defeat.

But even the apparent united array of the old party, that had so long borne victory upon its banners, was terrifying to the enemy. A closing up of ranks was at once ordered. Fremont and his retiring followers deemed it also prudential to return to the fold in order that fanaticism united might be able to grapple with the common foe. The campaign was short and spirited upon one side alone. Genuine enthusiasm was lacking in the breasts of the anti-war Democracy. The candidate was tarnished in the eyes of true men, having fought the battles of the wicked despotism that was overthrowing the liberties of the country.

The Republican leaders, on the contrary, were buoyant with enthusiasm in anticipation of the victory of might over right. The legions of infidelity, malice and rapine, were moving their serried columns to the battle that was to crown them victors over equity and plighted compact. The spirit of intuition appeared to the Democratic freemen of the North, and audibly whispered in their tents, before the onset began, "*I will meet thee at Phillippi.*" On November 8th, 1864, the battle was fought, and constitutionalism was prostrated upon the Western continent.

Abraham Lincoln was again elected President, carrying the electoral vote of every State considered in the Union, except three—New Jersey, Delaware and Kentucky. Over four hundred thousand of a popular majority endorsed his election. The anarchical mob-spirit of the North had again triumphed over reason and reflection; and the party, which was regardless of law and order, had anew seized the helm of Government. The exhausted youth of the South, now alone stayed the oppressor's advance. Should their resistance at length be fully overcome, the Juggernaut of Northern incendiary fanaticism would then roll its hideous figure over the prostrate form of constitutional government.

29

Southern Morale: A Patriot's View

Edward A. Pollard

In the winter of 1864-65, intelligent minds in the Confederacy became, for the first time, impressed with the idea that its victory and independence were no longer certain conclusions, and conceived a painful distrust as to the issues of the war.

General Lee, a man who used few words, and had the faculty of going directly to the point of a discussion, and putting sagacious judgments in plain phrases, once said of the conduct of the people of the Confederacy in the war, that "they were only half in earnest." But this remark, unlike most of Lee's judgments, was only half true. No one can doubt that the Confederates had been thoroughly and terribly in earnest in the first periods of the war; and if, in its later periods, they appeared to lack earnestness, the truth was they did not lack it so much as they did confidence in their rulers, and a disposition to continue the war under an Administration whose squanderings and make-shifts turned all the sacrifices of the people to naught. In the later periods of the terrible conflict through which the Confederacy had passed, its moral condition was peculiar. All confidence in the Administration at Richmond was gone; the people were heart-broken; they had been cheated too often by the highly colored prophecies of President Davis, and those boastful predictions which are unfailing characteristics of the weak mind; they saw that their sacrifices were squandered, and their most patriotic efforts misapplied; they were so far demoralized by want of confidence in their authorities, and in some instances by positive antipathy to them, that it may be said that in the last periods of the war, a majority of the people of the Confederacy actually deprecated any single success, and did not desire a victory to their arms which might give a new occasion of prolongation of the war—for having already taken it for granted as hopeless, they prayed in their hearts that it would be closed at the earliest moment. They did not desire the delay of any mere fluctuations of fortune,

EDWARD A. POLLARD, *The Last Year of the War* (New York, 1866), Ch. x.

which they were sure was to be adverse at the last. "If failure was to ensue, then the sooner the better." Such was the phrase of the vulgar judgment which everywhere in the Confederacy assailed the ears of nobler and more resolute men.

Whatever share the maladministration at Richmond may have had in producing this public demoralization, it is not to be excused entirely on this account. It involved with it much that was shameful, for which the people had themselves to blame, and to charge to the account of their own disposition to let the war lapse to its final conclusions of defeat and ruin.

For months Mr. Davis had been a president with nothing at his back but a clique of office-holders. The people had become thoroughly estranged from him. If all did not speak of him in terms of derision or hate, there were but few who named him without expressions of distrust. But although the country was thus thoroughly dissatisfied with Mr. Davis' Administration, there was not nerve enough in it, not courage enough among its public men, to overthrow his rule, or put it under a severe and effective check.

In the first months of 1865 there were introduced in Congress some partial but remarkable measures to correct the Administration. They indicated public sentiment; but they failed and utterly broke down in their execution, and left Davis the defiant and angry master of the field.

The first of these was an act of the Confederate Congress making General Lee commander-in-chief of the armies. The intention of this law was never executed. Lee was unwilling to accept practically its trust; he was unwilling, too, to break a personal friendship with the President; and so he remained in immediate command of the Army of Northern Virginia, and Davis continued in the practical control of the armies at large, without any diminution of his power or insolence.

In January, 1865, the Virginia delegation in the House of Representatives, headed by Mr. Bocock, the Speaker of the House, addressed to the President an earnest, but most respectful paper, expressing their want of confidence in the capacity and services of his cabinet, the members of which for four years had been mere figure-heads in Richmond. Mr. Davis resented the address as impertinent. Mr. Seddon, the Secretary of War, a citizen of Virginia, recognizing the censure as coming from Virginians, and therefore, as peculiarly applicable to himself, and conscious of the excessive unpopularity he had incurred in the administration of his office—an ugly little circumstance of which had recently come to light, namely, that while he had been impressing the grain of the Virginia farmers at nominal prices, he had sold his own crop of wheat to the Government at forty dollars a bushel—insisted upon resigning, and thus appeasing the public indignation against himself. Mr. Davis opposed this action of his secretary, sought to dissuade him from it; and when Mr. Seddon did resign, the President went out of his way to declare in a letter, published in the newspapers, that the event of this resignation would in no manner change the policy or course of his Administration, and thus, in words not to be mistaken, threw down his defiance to Congress and the country.

Another point which Congress made with the President was the restoration of General Joseph E. Johnston to command. For weeks in the Confederate Senate, Mr. Wigfall of Texas—a coarse, heavy man, of large brain, who under an unsentimental exterior, possessed more of the courage and fire of the orator than any other man in the South—dealt his sledge-hammer blows on the President, who, he declared, not satisfied with persecuting Johnston, was trying to make him the scapegoat for his own sins. The debate in the Johnston-Davis imbroglio was a memorable one in the dreary annals of the Confederate Congress. The fierce impatience of Mr. Wigfall more than once caused him to launch into philippics against the President, which most of the Richmond newspapers did not dare to report. The President was denounced without mercy. "He was," said Mr. Wigfall, summing up on one occasion his points of indictment, "an amalgam of malice and mediocrity."

The President did restore Johnston; but under circumstances which made it no concession to the public. To an intimate friend he remarked with grim humor, that "if the people wanted to try homœopathic treatment—*similia similibus curantur*—he would give them another dose of Johnston." He restored this commander, as he well knew, to the conduct of a campaign that was already lost; he put him in command of a broken and disorganized force that Sherman had already swept before him through two States into the forests of North Carolina; and Johnston was right when some weeks before he wrote to a private friend that he was quite sure that if the authorities of Richmond restored him to command, they were resolved not to act towards him in good faith and with proper support, but to put him in circumstances where defeat was inevitable, and thus confirm to the populace the military judgment of President Davis.

The people of the Confederacy, towards the final periods of the war, may be said to have looked with folded arms upon the sins of its Government, and to have regarded its general tendency to disaster and ruin with a sullen disposition to let matters take their own course or with weak and blank despair. These sins were not only the fruit of Mr. Davis' violent and imperious animosities; they covered the whole conduct of his Administration, and involved as much the want of capacity as that of official candor and personal impartiality. Everywhere the military establishment was falling to decay, and although the Confederacy was still full of fighting men and war material, there was nothing but the dregs of its resources at the practical command of the Government.

The most remarkable fact in the later days of the Confederacy was that while the country was really capable of fighting the war indefinitely, and accomplishing its independence, if by nothing more, yet surely by the virtue of endurance, it had in active employment but the smallest portion of its resources, and was loitering on the brink of destruction at a time when victory, *with proper efforts,* was never more surely in its grasp.

To understand this great and melancholy fact in the history of the war—that the Confederates, with an abler government and a more resolute spirit, might have accomplished their independence—we have only to review, with candor, the situation as it existed in the opening of the memorable year of 1865.

In the summer of 1864 everywhere the thought of the North was peace; not so much in the newspapers, whose office, especially with the Yankees, was rather to disguise public sentiment than to express or apply it; but in every circle of conversation, and every quarter where men dared to unmask their minds and to substitute their true convictions for the stereotypes of affectation, there was to be found a real desire for peace, which had almost ripened into a popular demand, ready to define its terms and resolved to insist upon its concession. The Chicago Convention meant peace; this and that man, least suspected of generosity to the Confederacy or of deference to truth, privately confessed the war to be a failure; even Republicans of Mr. Lincoln's school, seizing upon certain amiable expressions in the Confederate Congress of the summer of 1864, wanted to know if they might not mean some accommodation of the question of the war, and replied to them with those affectations of generosity with which the dexterous cowardice of the Yankee is always ready to cover his sense of defeat.

This disposition of the public mind in the North was easily accounted for when it was closely observed. It was clearly not the fruit of any decisive disasters to the Northern arms in the summer campaign of 1864. But that campaign had been negative. Atlanta had not fallen. All the engagements in northern Georgia had not amounted, as Johnston said, to the sum of more than one battle, and it was yet doubtful on which side to strike the average of success. Richmond was erect and defiant; and Lee's army had given new and conspicuous proofs of fortitude at Cold Harbour and Petersburg. Nowhere, then, could the enemy find any prospect of the speedy termination of the war; and though he had searched every link of the armor of the Confederacy he had been unable to plant anywhere a serious wound. It was simply because the enemy's campaign was negative, simply in prospect of a prolongation of the war that, in midsummer of 1864, the Yankee public halted in its opinions and seriously meditated a proposition of peace.

The great lesson which the South was to learn of public opinion in the North was this: that the prospect of a long war was quite as sure to obtain the success and independence of the Confederacy as the positive victories of her arms. It might not have been so in the first periods of the war, when the resolution of the enemy was fresh and patient, and the Union was then really the apple of his eye. But it was when patience had been worn threadbare by promises—when expectation had stood on tip-toe until it had ached; when the sentiment of Union had lost all its original inspiration; when "the

Union as it was" had become more and more impossible to the hopes of the intelligent, and the attempt to realize it had fallen from the resolution of a sovereign necessity to a mere preference of alternatives—that we find the enemy quite as likely to be defeated by the prospect of a prolonged war as by the dint of positive disaster, and, in fact, meditating more anxiously the question of Southern endurance than the immediate fortunes of any military campaign.

It was a great mistake to suppose that in these later years of the war the North was fighting for the Union as the *sine qua non,* the indispensable thing. That was the clack of Yankee newspapers and the drone of demagogues. But the facts were to the contrary. It was to be admitted that the North, in the development of her resources in the war, and the discovery contemporary with it of an almost fabulous wealth in her oil regions and mines, and new fields of enterprise opened along the entire slope of the Rocky Mountains, had obtained a confidence which had assured her, among other things, that, even apart from the South, she had in herself the elements of a great national existence. It was this swollen wealth—some of it the windfalls of a mysterious Providence—which had appeased much of that avarice which formed so large a share in the Northern desire for the Union. Again, as the war had progressed, it had become more and more obvious to countless intelligent persons in the North that it had wasted what was most desirable in the Union; destroyed its *esprit;* left nothing to be recovered but its shadow, and that along with such paltry recovery of a mere name, were to be taken the consequences of such despotic government as would be necessary to hold two hostilized countries under a common rule. It was thus that the sentiment of the Union had lost much of its power in the North. The first fervors of the war were scarcely now to be discovered among a people who had chosen to carry on hostilities by the mercenary hands of foreigners and Negroes, and had devised a system of substitution— a vicarious warfare—to an extent that was absolutely without parallel in the history of any modern nation.

All persons in the North, with the exception of some hundreds, professed that they preferred the Union; it was a universal desire spoken everywhere; but spoken only as a preference and desire, and no longer as a passion that insisted upon an object which it considered death and ruin to dispense with. Of all who declared for the Union, but few were ready to testify sincerely that they were for it at all hazards and consequences. Whatever might be the convenient language or the fulsome protestation of public opinion in the North, two things were certain.

First, that the North would not insist upon the Union in plain prospect of a war indefinitely prolonged.

And second, that the North would never fight the war beyond that moderate point of success on the part of the South, where she would be disposed to accommodate the enemy with certain treaty favors which might stand in lieu of the old Union, and where she would not be quite confident enough in her position to insist upon a severe independence.

It was thus that the war, on the part of the North, was limited by contingencies, which were very far short of decisive results one way or the other, and which might transpire even without any very signal successes of the Confederate arms.

What had been said of the peace movement in the North in the summer of 1864, before the fall of Atlanta, has its application to the times of which we are now writing. That movement was simply the result of a conviction, not that the South was about to accomplish a positive triumph, but that she was able to endure the war much longer than had been expected, and yet had not reached that point of confidence where she would not be likely to make valuable concessions to the North for the early and graceful acknowledgment of her independence. That acknowledgment the North was then on the eve of making under certain disguises, it is true, of party convenience, but none the less certainly because it sought decent excuse for the act. The Democratic Party was then well nigh a unit on the subject of peace. "Burn my letter," wrote a distinguished politician of New England to a Confederate then in New York; "but when you get to Richmond, hasten to President Davis, and tell him the Chicago Convention means peace, and nothing but peace." It was the military events which followed that interrupted this resolution, and showed how little there was of principle or of virtuous intention in Yankee parties; and with the fall of Atlanta, Savannah, Wilmington, and Charleston, and Sherman's campaign of magnificent distances, the Northern mind had again become inflamed with the fervor of new hopes, and clamored for unconditional war, when it thought that it was in the last stages of success.

Yet in face of this clamor it was plain enough that if the Confederates could ever regain substantially nothing more that the *status quo* of seven months ago; if they could ever present to the North the same prospect of a long war as they did then, and put before them the weary task of overcoming the fortitude of a brave people, they would have peace and independence in their grasp. It was a vulgar mistake that to accomplish our success in this war we had to retrieve all of the past and recover by arms all the separate pieces of our territory. It was to be remembered that we were fighting on the defensive, and had only to convince the enemy that we were able to protect the vital points of our country to compel him to a peace in which all was surrendered that he had overrun, and all the country that he held by the worthless title of invasion, would fall from him as by the law of gravitation.

It may be said briefly that if the Confederates could only regain the situation of the last summer, or even if they would only give a proof to the enemy that they were not at the extremity of their resources, or at the last limits of resolution—that they were able and determined to fight the war indefinitely—they had then accomplished the important and vital conditions of peace. Nor was the first impossible—to recover substantially, in all important respects, the losses of the past few months, and even add to the *status quo* of last summer new elements of advantage for us. To defeat Sherman at any stage short of Richmond would be to reopen and recover all the country he had overrun. If the enemy was left in possession of the seaports, these had but little value to us as ports of entry, and were but picket-posts in our system of defences. Sherman's campaign clearly came to naught if he could not reach Grant—nothing left of it but the brilliant zig-zag of a raid vanishing as heat lightning in the skies. The consequences of Sherman's misadventure would be obvious enough. Grant's army, without the looked-for aid from the Carolinas, was by no means certain of the capture of Richmond. It was true that Grant was within a few miles of the Confederate capital when the same time last year he was on the Rapidan. But that was a fool's measure of danger, for in each case we had the same army shielding Richmond, and whether that shield was broken ten or one hundred miles away was of no importance to the interest it covered.

There was nothing really desperate in the military situation of the Confederacy, unless to fools and cowards who drew lines on paper to show how the Yankees were at this place and at that place, and thought that this cobweb occupation of the country, where the enemy had no garrisons and no footholds, indicated the extent of Yankee conquest and gave the true measure of the remnant of the Confederacy! And yet this was too much the popular fashion of the time in estimating the military situation. Men were drawing for themselves pictures of despair out of what were, to those who thought profoundly and bravely, no more important than the passages of the hour. It is not to be disguised that the condition of the Confederacy was demoralized in the extreme, and that it was difficult to reorganize, as the patriots of 1861, men who were now exclaiming everywhere their despair, and counselling embassies of submission.*

* In March, 1865, the author printed an address in the Richmond newspapers, of which the following was the concluding portion. The occasion and spirit of this address are significant enough of what was taking place in Richmond at that time:

"I am determined to express the truth, no matter how painful to myself or unwelcome to others. In the first period of this war who was not proud of the Confederacy and its heroic figure in history! Yet now it is to be confessed that a large portion of our people have fallen below the standards of history, and hold no honorable comparison with other nations that have fought and struggled for independence. It is easy for the tongue of the demagogue to trip with flattery on the theme of the war; but when we come to the counsels of the intelligent the truth must be told. We are no longer responding to the lessons and aspirations of history. You speak of the scarcity of subsistence. But Prussia, in her wars, drained her supplies until black bread was the only thing to eat in the king's palace; and yet under Frederick, she won not only her independence, but a position among the five great powers of Europe. You speak of the scarcity of men. Yet with a force not greater than that with which we have only to hold an invaded country and maintain the defensive, Napoleon fought his splendid career, and completed a circle of victories that touched the boundaries of Europe.

"It is enough to sicken the heart with shame and vexation that now, when, of all

Briefly, if the fatal facts in the condition of the Confederacy at the time of which we write, are to be summed up, they are simply these:

1. A want of confidence in the Administration of Mr. Davis—such as was never before exhibited between a people and its rulers in a time of revolution. 2. And as main consequence of that want of confidence, when all measures to repair it had failed, a general breaking down of the public virtue, and the debasement of a people who, having lost hope in the existing order—rather than the existing disorder—and having no heart for a new experiment, or thinking it too late, descend to the condition of time-servers, and those who tamely and infamously submit to fortune.

THE FORTRESS MONROE COMMISSION

But another and last appeal was to be made to the resolution of the South.

In January, 1865, Mr. Francis P. Blair of Maryland made several visits to Richmond, which were the occasion of much speculation and curiosity in the public mind. He had gone to Richmond with Mr. Lincoln's pass; but the objects of his mission were not committed to paper. However, they were soon developed. On his return to Washington, Mr. Blair showed Mr. Lincoln a letter which President Davis had written, stating that Mr. Blair was at liberty to say to Mr. Lincoln that Mr. Davis was now, as he always had been, willing to send commissioners, if assured they would be received, or to receive any that should be sent; that he was not disposed to find obstacles in forms. He would send commissioners to confer with the Northern President with a view to the restoration of peace between the two countries, if he could be assured they would be received.

Mr. Lincoln, therefore, on the 18th day of January, addressed a note to Mr. Blair, in which, after acknowledging that he had read the note of Mr. Davis, he said that he was, and always should be, willing to receive

times, it is most important to convince the enemy of our resolution—now, when such a course, for peculiar reasons, will insure our success—there are men who not only whine on the streets about making terms with the enemy, but intrude their cowardice into the official places of the Government, and, sheltered by secret sessions and confidential conversations, roll the word "reconstruction" under the tongue. Shame upon the Congress that closed its doors that it might better consult of dishonorable things! Shame upon those leaders who should encourage the people, and yet have broken down their confidence by private conversations; and who, while putting in newspapers some cheap words of patriotism, yet in the same breath express their despair by a suspicious cant about trusting in Providence, and go off to talk submission with their intimates in a corner! Shame upon those of the people who have now no other feeling in the war than an exasperated selfishness! who are ready to sink, if they can carry down in their hands some little trash of *property!* who will give their sons to the army, but not their precious Negro slaves! who are for hurrying off embassies to the enemy to know at what price of dishonor they may purchase some paltry remnants of their possessions! Do these men ever think of the retributions of history? . . .

"The arguments of the traders and time servers . . . are not unknown to Richmond.

any agent that Mr. Davis, or any other influential person now actually resisting the authority of the Government, might send to confer informally with him, with a view to the restoration of peace to the people of "our common country."

In consequence of this notification President Davis requested Vice-President Stephens, Senator Hunter, and Judge John A. Campbell, to proceed through the lines to hold a conference with Mr. Lincoln, or such persons as he might depute to represent him. The following report, made by the Confederate commissioners, gives the official narrative of the affair:

Richmond, February 6th

To the President of the Confederate States:

SIR—Under your letter of appointment of commissioners, of the 8th, we proceeded to seek an informal conference with Abraham Lincoln, President of the United States, upon the subject mentioned in the letter. A conference was granted, and took place on the 30th, on board the steamer anchored in Hampton Roads, where we met President Lincoln and Hon. Mr. Seward, Secretary of State of the United States. It continued for several hours, and was both full and explicit. We learned from them that the message of President Lincoln to the Congress of the United States, in December last, explains clearly his sentiments as to the terms, conditions, and mode of proceeding by which peace can be secured to the people; and we were not informed that they would be modified or altered to obtain that end. We understood from him that no terms or proposals of any treaty or agreements looking to an ultimate settlement would

---

But shall we not also find in this city something of the aspirations of Cato—a determination, even if we are overcome by force, to be unconquered in spirit, and, in any and all events, to remain superior to the enemy—in honor.

"I do not speak to you, my countrymen, idle sentimentalism. I firmly believe that the great commonwealth of Virginia, and this city, which has a peculiar title to whatever there is of good and illustrious report in this war, have been recently, are yet in some measure on the verge of questions which involve an interest immeasurably greater than has yet been disclosed in this contest—that of their historical and immortal honor.

"I know—I have had opportunities of informing myself—that there are influences at work to place the State of Virginia, in certain contingencies, in communication with the public enemy, for terms of peace, which cannot be otherwise than coupled with the condition of her submission to the Federal authority. The extent of this conspiracy against the honor of Virginia has been screened by secret sessions, and been covered up by half-mouthed suggestions, and the *ifs* and *ands* of men who are not yet ready to disclose their corruption, and to spit from their lips the rottenness in their hearts. I know the fashionable arguments of these men. 'If there is to be a wreck,' say they, 'why not save what we can from it?' 'Honor,' they say, 'is a mere rhetorical laurel'; 'General Lee talks like a school-girl when he speaks of preferring to die on the battlefield to getting the best terms of submission he can'; 'Let us be done with this sentimental rubbish, and look to the care of our substantial interests.'

"My friends, this is not rubbish. The glory of history is indifferent to events; it is simply honor. The name of Virginia in this war is historically and absolutely more important to us than any other element of the contest; and the coarse time-server who would sell an immortal title of honor as a trifling sentimentalism, and who has constantly in his mouth the phrase of 'substantial interests,' is the inglorious wretch who laughs at history and grovels in the calculations of the brute.

be entertained or made by him with the authorities of the Confederate States, because that would be recognition of their existence as a separate power, which, under no circumstances, would be done; and for like reasons, that no such terms would be entertained by him from the States separately; that no extended truce or armistice, as at present advised, would be granted or allowed, without the satisfaction or assurance in advance, of the complete restoration of the authority of the constitution and laws of the United States over all places within the States of the Confederacy; that whatever consequences may follow from the re-establishment of that authority, it must be accepted; but all individuals subject to the pains and penalties under the laws of the United States, might rely upon a very liberal use of the power confided to him to remit those pains and penalties if peace be restored. During the conference, the proposed amendments to the constitution of the United States, adopted by Congress on the 31st, was brought to our notice. These amendments provide that neither slavery nor involuntary servitude, except for crime, should exist within the United States or any place within its jurisdiction, and Congress should have power to enforce the amendment by appropriate legislation. Of all the correspondence that preceded the conference herein mentioned, and leading to the same, you have heretofore been informed.

Very respectfully, your obedient servants,

A. H. STEPHENS,

R. M. T. HUNTER,

J. A. CAMPBELL.

"Those who have lived entirely in the South since the commencement of this war have little idea of the measure of honor which Virginia has obtained in it, and the consideration she has secured in the eyes of the world. One away from home, finds even in intercourse with our enemies, that the name of Virginian is an ornament to him, and that the story of this her heroic capitol—the record of Richmond—is universally accepted in two hemispheres as the most illustrious episode of the war. Honor such as this is not a piece of rhetoric or a figure of speech; it is something to be cherished under all circumstances, and to be preserved in all events.

"It is scarcely necessary to say that I regard subjugation but as the vapor of our fears. But if remote possibilities are to be regarded, I have simply to say, that in all events and extremities, all chances and catastrophes, I am for Virginia going down to history, proudly and starkly, with the title of a subjugated people—a title not inseparable from true glory, and which has often claimed the admiration of the world—rather than as a people who ever submitted, and bartered their honor for the mercy of an enemy—in our case a mercy whose *pittance* would be as a mess of pottage weighed against an immortal patrimony!

"The issue I would put before you is: No submission; no State negotiations with the enemy; no conventions for such objects, however proper for others. Let Virginia stand or fall by the fortunes of the Confederate arms, with her spotless honor in her hands.

"If Virginia accepts the virtuous and noble alternative, she saves, in all events, her honor, and by the resolution which it implies, may hope to secure a positive and glorious victory; and I, among the humblest of her citizens, will be proud to associate myself with a fate which, if not happy, at least can never be ignoble. But, if she chooses to submit, and make terms for Yankee clemency, the satisfaction will at least remain to me of not sharing in the dishonor of my native State, and of going to other parts of the world, where I may say: 'I too was a Virginian, but not of those who sold the jewels of her history for the baubles and cheats of her conquerors.'"

Of the conference Mr. Seward testified that "the Richmond party approached the discussion rather indirectly, and at no time did they make categorical demands, or tender formal stipulations or absolute refusals; nevertheless, during the conference, which lasted four hours, the several points at issue between the Government and the insurgents were distinctly raised and discussed fully, intelligently, and in an amicable spirit. What the insurgent party seemed chiefly to favor was a postponement of the question of separation upon which the war was waged, and a mutual direction of the efforts of the Government, as well as those of the insurgents, to some extraneous policy or scheme for a season, during which passions might be expected to subside, and the armies be reduced, and trade and intercourse between the people of both sections be resumed."

The proposition which looked to an armistice or truce was distinctly answered by Mr. Lincoln, who stated that he would agree to no cessation or suspension of hostilities unless on the basis of the disbandment of the Confederate forces. There were no notes of the conference. There was no attendance of clerks or secretaries; and nothing was written or read. But the result of the whole conversation, which was earnest and free, may be summarily stated to have shown that the enemy refused to enter into negotiations with the Confederate States, or any of them separately, or give to their people any other terms or guarantees than those which Congress might grant; or to permit the Southern people to have a vote on any other basis than unconditional submission to their rule, coupled with the acceptance of the recent legislation at Washington, including an amendment to the Constitution for the emancipation of all Negro slaves.

The failure of the Fortress Monroe commission was made the occasion in the South of a new attempt to rally the spirit of its people, and to infuse into the war a new element of desperate passion. The people were told that the result of the conference at Fortress Monroe showed plainly enough that every avenue to peace was closed, except such as might be carved out by the sword. It was calculated ingeniously enough that the party in the South which had so long clamored for negotiations with Washington would now abandon its visions of reconciliation and generosity, and give in their adhesion to a renewed and even desperate prosecution of the war.

These expectations were not realized. The attempt to raise the drooping spirits of the South, and to introduce, as some of the public men in Richmond fondly imagined, a new era of resolution and devotion in the war, shamefully failed. The Fortress Monroe affair produced in the Confederacy a feeble flare of excitement which was soon extinguished. A mass-meeting was called at the African church in Richmond, that the people might renew their testimony of devotion to the Confederacy. The meeting was held at high noon; all business in the city of Richmond was suspended, as if to give extraordinary solemnity to the occasion; fiery addresses were made, and tokens of enthusiasm were said in the newspapers to have been abundant. But speeches and hurrahs are cheap things. The public mind of the South made but a sickly response to what was undoubtedly, in all its circumstances, one of the most powerful appeals ever calculated to stir the heart and nerve the resolution of a people fighting for liberty; and in its relapse into the abject and timid counsels of the submissionists, exhibited a want of spirit which, it must be confessed, must ever make a painful and humiliating page in the history of the Confederacy.

Mr. Davis also spoke at the African church. He did not omit the occasion of exhorting the people. But he unfortunately fell into that style of boastful prediction and bombastic speech which was characteristic of all his public addresses; which was evidence of his weak mind; and which furnished the grave ground of accusation against him that in his public declarations he never dealt with the people in a proper spirit of candor. He declared that the military affairs of the Confederacy were in excellent condition; he hinted at great victories which were about to be accomplished; he boasted that "Sherman's march through Georgia would be his last"; he completed his rhetorical flourish with the strange prediction that before the summer solstice fell upon the country it would be the Yankees who would be asking for terms of peace and the grace of conferences in which the Confederates might make known their demands.

But in this unfortunate address of the President there was one just and remarkable sentiment. He referred to the judgment of history upon Kossuth, who had been so weak as to abandon the cause of Hungary with an army of *thirty thousand* men in the field; and spoke of the disgrace of surrender, if the Confederates should abandon their cause with an army on our side and actually in the field more numerous than those which had made the most brilliant pages in European history; an army more numerous than that with which Napoleon achieved his reputation; an army standing among its homesteads; an army in which each individual man was superior in every martial quality to each individual man in the ranks of the invader, and reared with ideas of independence, and in the habits of command!

It was very clear that the Confederacy was very far from the historical necessity of subjugation. But it was at any time near the catastrophe of a panic. If the cause was to be lost, it was to be so by weak despair; by the cowardice of suicide; by the distress of weak minds.

A measure indicative of the desperate condition of the Southern mind was that to extend the conscription to the slaves. A proposition to arm the Negroes of the South, and use them as soldiers in the Confederate Army, had been debated in the Richmond press as early as the fall of 1864. It was favored by General Lee, but variously received by the general public. There were many persons who argued that the Negro might be effectively used in this new department of service; that military experience had shown

that a soldier could be made of anything that had arms and legs; that the
United States had formerly recruited its regular army from the dregs of
humanity; that the experience of the North with the Negro had shown him
to be a serviceable soldier; and that the South could offer him superior
inducements to good service, by making him a freeman in his own home,
and could give him officers who could better understand his nature and
better prompt his good qualities, than his Yankee military taskmasters.
These views were encouraged by General Lee. Indeed, this distinguished
officer made no secret of his opinion that the military service of the slave
should be secured on the basis of general emancipation; arguing, with no
little ingenuity, that the institution of slavery had been so shaken by the
invasions and raids of the enemy, which had penetrated every portion of
the country, that its practical value had become but a small consideration
in view of the insecure tenure of the property; that it might, eventually, be
broken up if the war continued; and that, by a decree of emancipation, the
South might make a virtue of necessity, remove a cause of estrangement,
however unjust, between it and the Christian world, and possibly neutralize
that large party in the North, whose sympathy and interest in the war were
mainly employed with the Negro.

The question divided the country. The slaveholding interest, in its usual
narrow spirit—in its old character of a greedy, vulgar, insolent aristocracy—
took the alarm, and in Congress and in the newspapers, proclaimed that the
use of Negroes as soldiers was the entering wedge of Abolition; that it
would stultify the whole cause of the Confederacy; that it would give up
what they falsely imagined to be the leading object of the war—the protection of the interests of less than a quarter of a million of people who owned
slaves in the South. The Charleston *Mercury* declared that if the slaves
were armed, South Carolina could no longer have any interest in prosecuting the war.

But beyond the opposition of the slaveholders and the cotton aristocrats,
there were many intelligent men in the South who seriously doubted both
the capacity and fidelity of the Negro as a Confederate soldier. General
Lee and many of his distinguished officers were not among these.

A majority of the Confederate army were probably in favor of the experiment of Negro soldiers; and many who doubted their efficiency at the front
were persuaded that they might be made useful in other parts of the military field. General Ewell, who commanded in the Department of Henrico,
declared that the employment of the Negroes in the trenches, around
Richmond, would relieve fifteen thousand white soldiers, who might be
used on the enemy's front, and thus make an important accession to our
forces actually in the field.

The action of the Confederate Congress with reference to the military
employment of the Negro was characteristic of that body. The subject was
debated threadbare, discussed and dissected in open and secret session;

but no practical action could be obtained on the matter, but what was too late in respect of time, and absurdly small with reference to the measure of the necessities by which legislation on the subject had been invoked.

Congress took no action on the subject until at the heel of its session. A bill was passed on the 7th of March authorizing the President to ask and accept from the owners of Negro slaves as many able-bodied Negroes as he might deem expedient, to perform military service in any capacity he might direct, and providing that nothing in the act should be construed to alter the existing relation between master and slaves.

The entire results of this ridiculously small and visionary legislation, which proposed to obtain Negro soldiers from such volunteers as their masters might patriotically dedicate to the Confederate service, and was omniously silent on the subject of their freedom, were two fancy companies raised in the city of Richmond, who were allowed to give balls at the Libby, and to parade in Capitol Square, and were scarcely intended to be more than decoys to obtain sable recruits. But they served not even this purpose. The measure passed by Congress may be taken, indeed, as an indication of that vague desperation in the Confederacy which caught at straws, and had not nerve enough to make a practical and persistent effort at safety.

The Congress of the Confederate States was a weak, spasmodic body. There was no organization of opinion in it; no leaders; plenty of idle debate, capricious measures, weak recrimination, and but little of the sense and order of legislative assemblies. It went in and out of secret session almost every twenty-four hours; it was fruitful of propositions without results; and it finally adjourned on the 18th of March, after a session of four months, in which it had failed to enact any effective measure to recruit the army, to improve the finances, to mobilize the subsistence of the country, or, in fact, to serve one single important interest in the Confederacy.

30

Irreconcilably Hostile Systems

Frank H. Alfriend

It is no disparagement of the wisdom and patriotism of our forefathers, for us who have survived the wreck of the government of their creation, to ascribe its destruction to certain radical errors of principle, which escaping their penetration are revealed in the calamities which afflict their posterity. It is no ungrateful denial of their merited fame, to avail ourselves of the lights which experience has given us, while reading the philosophy of the failure of the Union, in the events which marked its career, and culminated in its downfall.

The Revolution, through whose blood-stained paths we are now treading our way to independence, is but the natural sequence, with all its coincident features of misery and desolation, of those causes whose operation began with the existence of the late Union, and have steadily increased in force and directness with each stage of our national development.

John Randolph, when a youth of sixteen, with that sagacity which so eminently distinguished his later years, clearly detected that insidious germ of consolidation which he afterwards so aptly characterized as the "poison under the wing of the Federal Constitution." But this alarming evil against which even then the forecast of Mason, and the inspired prophecy of Henry, warned their countrymen as the source of contention and strife, if not the instrument of destruction to all rights and powers of state sovereignty, was not the only cause for apprehension, nor indeed the most formidable. Later events have proven that the most powerful cause operating for the severance of the bonds of Union between North and South was far beyond the reach of legislative remedy, and far superior to the statesmanship of the wisest framers of the Federal Constitution.

We advance no new theory in this interpretation of the philosophy of this revolution, when we ascribe the necessity of separation to the irrecon-

FRANK H. ALFRIEND, "A Southern Republic and a Northern Democracy," *Southern Literary Messenger*, Vol. 35 (Richmond, March, 1863), pp. 283-290.

Alfriend, a Richmond lawyer, summed up the political philosophy which frequently found expression in Southern newspapers and journals of opinion.

cilable antithesis and utter incompatibility of the civilizations of the two sections. That cavalier element predominating in Southern civilization, and giving tone to Southern society, and character to Southern politics, had its representatives in the early days of the Union in those who opposed the surrender of the liberties of the States to a necessarily inimical, centralized power. That Puritan element which underlies the fabric of Northern civilization clearly manifested its antagonism to the other, by seeking in the very incipiency of the government, to deprive the States of all their power, and to establish with an irresponsible supremacy, a monster consolidated empire, which like that of Augustine, should have the name of Republic, but the character of an unmitigated despotism. The former, in later periods of our history, had a worthy champion in Carolina's great son, who on all occasions nobly sustained the eminence of his mother State, as the most vigilant of all the vestals in her jealousy of Federal encroachment. The latter found an early and powerful advocate in Webster, who despite that professed comprehensive patriotism, embracing equally all sections of his common country, and despite the concealed splendor of his eloquence and statesmanship, was yet an appropriate representative of New England selfishness, and descends to history as the author of the ablest and most elaborate vindication of that policy now applied to the extinguishment of liberties of a free people.

But apart from the considerations of an essential difference of origin and race, there are other evidences of widely distinct and conflicting social establishment. These conflicting elements were not only incapable of harmonious co-operation in the old Union, but have never been harmoniously blended under any system of government; and will ever stand as two irreconcilably hostile systems, until the established wisdom of the one shall secure the universal repudiation of the other.

It will not be denied that the two Confederacies, as they now confront the world, represent, approximately at least, essentially different establishments—the one a Democracy, with a redeeming feature of regulated liberty, the other, in its *social* character, eminently Patrician, and utterly opposed to a system thoroughly popular.

The Federal Constitution, the government of our common creation, from the moment of its adoption, has presented an open question, which has finally sought its solution in the arbitrament of war, as to the rightful interpretation of its design, whether Confederate or Democratic, Republican or Consolidated. Respecting its tendency in operation, there can be no doubt to its complete success as an instrument for the establishment of an unqualified Democracy, to be followed in the sequel by the most bloody of all political disorders, that which constitutes the inviting occasion for military usurpation. A correct estimate of its character will reveal the fact that the Federal Constitution received, though to an unequal extent, impressions traceable to each of the contending civilizations. The balance was unquestionably unfavorable to the South. But the evidence of the tendency to Democracy in the North, and of the presence of a counter-influence in the South, is most clearly witnessed in the widely different social characteristics and institutions of the States constituting the two sections.

We need no elaborate discussion of the boasted "Free Labor System" of Northern Society, to establish, beyond controversy, the fact of the overshadowing preponderance, there, of the extreme Democratic element. We can discover the absence of no essential feature of Radical Democracy in their accepted political philosophy. The United States now affords one of the most complete practical exemplifications, of the most extreme theories of popular privileges and license recorded in the history of the Democracy since the days of its advocacy by Syrias, the leader of the Athenian rabble, to those of "Butler, the Beast," the fitting champion of Massachusetts fanaticism. If the North be not a Democracy, then the term, in its universal use and accepted meaning throughout history, is a misnomer, and the world has yet to witness the first example of an unqualified system of popular government. In what respect is there wanting that possession of absolute power by the masses; of absolute control of all offices and elections, of the laws and institutions, in a word, of that complete investiture of popular omnipotence in the government, which are usually received as the evidence of an establishment thoroughly Democratic? Was Rome a Democracy in those fearful times of plebian ascendancy, when the wisdom and patriotism of the Senate was mute and voiceless amidst the clamor of an infuriate populace? . . . How strikingly parallel the idea advanced by Butler, in the recent ovation given in honor of the successful illustration of the most immeasurable depravity of which human nature is capable, that the "aristocracy of the South have rebelled against the poorer classes of the country.". . . General Banks, in New Orleans, repeats the order previously issued by Butler, taxing the rich for the support of the poor.

But surely neither argument nor illustration are needed here to establish the character of a complete Democracy in the United States. . . . But if further evidence be needed, it can easily be found in the State constitutions of the North—in the laws, institutions, and social habits of the people—which do not admit of a question that the North is essentially and radically Democratic in all its social and national characteristics.

It is equally undeniable that many of these pernicious features are shared by the *political* organism of the South, and it is an assertion, capable of conclusive demonstration, that from these very points of resemblance the South has most of the evil which threatens her to apprehend. In the *political* frame-work of the South, there are many features pointing to that eventual excess of Democracy, which has been the bane of all free governments. That we have escaped the innumerable evils which impend over our enemies, we are indebted not so much to those wise enactments of legislation, which are usually deemed the safe-guards of a people, as to the prudential establishment of our social structure.

We have characterized the North as socially and politically Democratic. With equal propriety, we claim for the South the acme, the dignity and the character of an Aristocracy—socially, at least, while admitting the prevalence of Democracy in our political constitution. Let us not be misunderstood in our intended use of the term Aristocracy. We use it in no sense of invidious distinction between classes of our citizens, but simply as affording an adequate embodiment of that regulated liberty beyond the control of ignorant and fanatical mobs; of that perfect order which reposes in security in that virtue, intelligence, and interested attachment, which the experience of all nations tells us are the only reliable safe-guards of freedom. We trust never to witness in the South that form of Aristocracy which suggests the consolidation of power in the hands of a privileged few, always wielded to the detriment and oppression of the majority. Never, in the sense of the Athenian tyranny, do we wish to see the South an "Aristocracy," but in that true Republican sense which creates a supremacy of those who, from education, can appreciate the blessings of liberty; who from virtue, can be entrusted with its guardianship; and those who, from the possession of property, and an interest in the maintenance of order, will be equally vigilant against popular excesses and the usurpations of tyrants.

To this proper definition of our intended use of the term "Aristocracy," as applied to the organization of Southern society, no enlightened judgment will object as involving an invidious distinction between classes of our citizens. Such is the force of our social system, imparted not only from the homogeneity of our people, but from that community of interest, and absolute mutual dependency springing from that all-pervading tie of Negro slavery, which, with the grasp of a Briaereus, extending its roots through every ramification of our system, moulds every feature, and unites every constituent member, until, as we are at present constituted, there is no possible ground upon which to erect a wall of division between separate classes and interests. In that sense, in which one is an aristocrat, inasmuch as all are interested in the security of that institution which creates the aristocracy.

The North carrying out to its legitimate conclusion the pernicious doctrine of the Declaration of Independence, that "all men are born free and equal," recognizing no distinction whatever of race, intellect, or character, witnesses in its fullest development, that never-ending conflict of classes, between the rich and the poor, those who have accumulated property, and the breadless pauper, the "codfish" element, and the idle, starving "sansculottes." And this perpetual strife between the conservative elements, property and intelligence, and the revolutionary materials, ignorance and indigence, will continue to agitate Northern society, until the bloody drama of the Parisian massacres shall be re-enacted in the streets of their cities, and a whirlwind of passion and strife shall sweep over their land, with such scenes of bloodshed and desolation as have never been rivalled save in the annals of revolutionary France.

The South, on the other hand, by a fortunate dispensation of Providence, has, in place of the turbulent factious element known at the North as the "working class," and devoted to the menial pursuits of bondsmen in all countries where slavery is tolerated, a class of population noted for its want of enterprise, intellect, or any quality which could make it a disturbing element of society, and peculiarly adapted to a condition of absolute subordination, by a characteristic docility and inability to provide for its own wants when beyond the control of the superior race.

Then in the Democracy of the North, we witness slavery no less than in the Aristocracy of the South. The difference, however, is essential. Slavery at the South embraces those who are, in all respects, the inferior of the governing class, and who, if not "conscripta gleba," are, at least, entirely subservient to the will of the governing race. Slavery at the North is a deliberate system of oppression by a class over those who are intellectually, morally, and politically their equals. At the South it is a benevolent system of tutelage by a superior over an inferior race. The difference is similar to that of the condition of Rome before and after the admission of the aliens, freedmen, and slaves, to the rolls of citizenship. The latter condition, with all its faction, tumult, and corruption, clearly pictures the present phase of Northern society, while the South, like the original "Populus Romanus," is pure and undefiled; her patrician blood uncorrupted by the degenerate current of an inferior race.

This view, which we did not design to be elaborate, will, we trust, answer its purpose, not only to indicate the "irrepressible conflict" between the social establishment of the two sections, but to demonstrate that, differing not so much in their actual political frame-work, as in their characteristic social features, the North and the South now represent, the one a social and political Democracy, the other a social Aristocracy.

It may be suggested that we are inconsistent in thus characterizing as a Democracy, a political condition which has resulted in Lincoln's despotism, a palpable and violent usurpation of tyrannical power. We see nothing inconsistent in the establishment of an usurped tyranny, following a triumph of Democracy. History teaches, that the one is the entirely legitimate, if not inevitable, sequel to the other. It is a noticeable fact, verified in the history of almost every violent despotism, that the tyrant began his usurpation with an affectation of extreme solicitude for the rights of the people. Julius Caesar, the most detestable of tyrants, and worst of men, at the very moment of marching his army into Italy, with the completion of every preparation for the possession of absolute power, protested that his mission was the restoration of the Tribunition authority, the great palladium of popular privilege. Caius Marius inaugurated his entrance into power, not only with declarations of favor to popular rights, but with numerous innovations of a popular character in the laws. Augustus began his wonderful career of usurpation with professions of profound respect for the authority of the Senate, and with adulation of the populace. Each of these tyrants was regarded by the lower classes as their peculiar champion, and each one used Democracy as a ladder to despotism. Lincoln's election was a complete triumph of Democracy. Elected by the *foreigners* and the working classes, he came into power as the avowed champion of the interests of the poor and laboring classes, which he declared to be in conflict with those of the slaveholding aristocrats of the South. Democracy triumphed, and despotism followed.

In opposition to our view, the intimate connection, as in the cause and effect, between the Democracy of the North and the failure of the Union, it has been suggested that the Puritanism, not the excessive Democracy, of that section has produced that result. This is a striking, but, we think wholly superficial explanation of a revolution, which, like all others, is based upon great principles of political philosophy which have been in constant operation through the entire history of ethnological development. Puritanism we conceive to be a mere phase of society, powerful, it is true, in the immediate influence which it has exerted, in precipitating the catastrophe of physical conflict. The difference in race is unquestionably not to be forgotten, and the antithesis of Puritan and Cavalier (using the two not strictly in a generic sense, but rather as comprehensive terms, embracing the two races; for however thoroughly Puritan the North may be, the South is certainly not all Cavalier) has certainly played a conspicuous part as an auxiliary in the contest of ethnological principles. But further than this, characterizing it as a mere phase of society, wielding a powerful auxiliary influence in a great battle of political principles, we cannot go in our estimate of the power of Puritanism in producing this revolution. The preponderating cause of controversy far superior to any mere antagonism of race has been the great question arising from the principles upon which rest the social organizations of the two sections—the North seeking by every expedient of legislative appliance to consummate an entire equality of all classes—the South maintaining the subordination of the inferior, and the ascendancy of the superior. But a question of principle should not degenerate into a mere controversy as to names. Call it Puritanism or Democracy, we care not which, we claim that excessive popular power accomplished the same results in the United States which have followed its establishment everywhere else. Consider it as we may, it is still the old Greek question of the "Few or the Many," the "King Number" of the North against the Conservative Aristocracy of the South. It was the old contest revived, of Cleon and Nicias, commenced in the Athenian Agora, and struggling on through the political battlefields of free governments in all ages.

Thus we feel that we have been guilty of no sacrilegious profanation of the "sacred name of Democracy," in characterizing the North as a most perfect ideal of popular government. We feel equally justified in ascribing to the South the character of a "Republican Aristocracy."

What then has the South to apprehend from those excessive Democratic tendencies which have prevailed at the North, when Southern society so obviously inclines to an aristocratic system? From the very plausibility of this question, and the seeming insuperability of the objection which it raises to any anti-popular re-modelling of our political organizations, the Southern patriot has most cause to tremble with anxious solicitude for the stability of our national structure.

We have acknowledged that the purely *political* systems of the two sections do not materially differ, and we have ascribed the superior excellence of the Southern system to the providential arrangement of its social organization. It is unquestionably true that these very social features have made a striking contrast in the political character of the two sections, that of the South developing a marked pre-eminence of statesmanship, and a greatly superior political intelligence among all classes of her people. Of this difference the legislative history of the Union exhibits a forcible illustration. The South ever advocates adherence to the strict letter of the Constitution, and urged, as with the fidelity due to sacred things, the rigid preservation of established institutions. The North as constantly gave expression of the feverish restlessness of Democracy, in its zealous support of Homestead bills, providing "homes for the homeless," and "lands for the landless," with numerous other expedients for the gratification of agrarian propensities. But these are results legitimately flowing from the social difference of the two sections, and offer no vindication of the political constitution of the South.

If it be true that whatever there is deserving of commendation in the political character of the South is to be ascribed to the successful development of its social character, is it not a question of vital moment as to the best and happiest method of giving security and stability to her social system? If our social system, vindicated by its successful operation up to the present moment is, as we believe, the only safe pedestal on which the Republican structure can stand, should we not jealously guard the last citadel of Republican liberty, around which the hopes of freedom will yet centre, as in its expiring struggles, the free spirit of old Rome hovered about Utica, the last refuge of the noble Cato? These questions naturally suggest another. Can we trust that social system to the operation of tendencies, which if not so dangerous as those which so successfully warred against everything like conservatism at the North, are at least, only different in degree, not in character?

There is not one feature in the political organization of the South protecting her from the vandalic inundation of agrarian Democracy which has swept away every vestige of established order and regulated liberty in the United States. If our statue books are not dishonored by the wholesale endorsation of that odious doctrine of '76, the perfect equality of all men which to the Northern mind is the "ovum Republicae," the very germ of the Republican essence; if they do make a discrimination against the African, they are equally deficient with those of the North, in provisions favorable to property and intelligence—the great bulwarks of liberty against indigence and ignorance, the favorite materials for the schemes of demagogues and tyrants. It is no refutation of this view to cite the numerous legislative enactments recognizing slavery as that basis of Southern civilization, and the universal recognition by our people of slavery as the foundation on all their hopes of national prosperity. It is folly to suppose that slavery unaided can protect the South from the tendency to Democracy in free government, and with such a powerful impetus as Democracy will derive from the extensive popular character of our political establishment. How long will slavery itself successfully combat *universal suffrage*, a *ceaseless tide of foreign emigration*, and the *uninterrupted introduction of free labor!* This is the very difficulty, upon the solution of which depends the future of the South. If we can by any expedient secure the perpetuity of slavery, then indeed we may cease to apprehend any danger from excessive Democracy, for the salvation of the one depends upon the perpetual restraint and depression of the other. How inconsistent our proffered confidence in slavery as our safe-guard against the spread of political power—when our whole political constitution, so far as it relates to the communication of political privilege, is plainly at war with the existence of the institution. We erect the foundation of our fabric, proclaim its perpetuity, and then prepare its speedy overthrow by incorporating features which must inevitably undermine it. Who can deny that such is the effect of *universal suffrage:* of the unchecked introduction of free labor? No one can deny that universal suffrage, affording a complete investiture of the privileges of citizenship to all who come among us, invites the presence of free labor. With free labor at liberty to extend itself over the land, how long will slavery stand? This is Seward's own idea, when he threatened us with the irresistible power of progressive free labor, and unless the South is now true to slavery in providing its necessary safe-guards, we shall yet witness the revival of the "irrepressible conflict" among our own people.

But how shall we avert these threatened evils? The answer is easy and satisfactory. Let us strengthen slavery by every possible appliance, regarding that institution as the very base, the corner-stone of our system, which once rudely framed, the whole superstructure will totter in the imminent peril of hopeless ruin. Let us spare nothing which in any means conflicts with slavery and the Republican aristocracy which it creates, by excluding the laboring class, who would discharge its menial duties if slavery had no existence, and who will be its competitors even with slavery firmly established. To this end we should deny all political power to all others than those who, born in the South, are enabled to appreciate the character and understand the operation of our system. We should refuse to the unlettered foreigners, who will flock to our shores to enjoy the fruits of our struggle and the wealth of our magnificent domain, that political equality with the largest property holders and best educated gentlemen of the land, of which they are now in possession.

But even this may be deemed insufficient to protect us against violent revolution. It may be said that though we deprive this dangerous "laboring class" (embracing natives as well as foreigners) of political privilege, we do not take from them that physical power which after all makes revolution successful. This danger too may be safeguarded against by depriving free labor of every encouragement to make its home among us. The *South needs no laboring class*, other than her *slaves*, making of course a proper exception in favor of those higher branches of the mechanic arts, in which many worthy Southern citizens are interested, and which are indispensable to a proper development of our physical resources. Let us have no protective tariff. With open ports, free to the commerce of the world, let us make the natives of Europe our laborers, while we preserve unimpaired among us that simplicity, virtue, and intelligence, which so eminently distinguish an agricultural people. We of the Border States are especially interested in this matter of preventing the establishment among us of those dens of corruption, the "Lowells" and "Manchesters," "sores upon the body politic," whose contagion will spread its contaminating effect, corrupting and destroying the health and vitality of our whole system. Let us not allow ourselves to be made the "great manufacturing States of the Confederacy," as some say we shall be. We must not suffer our wheat and tobacco fields to be converted without the aid of the slave, who is driven off to the rice and cotton fields of the far South. We must not allow our beautiful and picturesque villages to become immense manufacturing marts, breeding an overwhelming laboring population, with all its ignorance, vice and demoralizing influences, instead of that refinement, cultivation and morality which characterizes all *sparsely* settled agricultural and pastoral countries. If the policy which we have here advocated does not result in the exclusion from the South of those dangerous elements which have destroyed the North, its effect will certainly be to create that supremacy of property and education, which we believe absolutely indispensable for the enjoyment of true liberty. And this we confess to be the great end which our argument was designed to promote, the great *"summum bonum"* for the attainment of which Republics should strive.

We may be charged with an advocacy of "Aristocracy," a term ever odious to the ignorant and vulgar, and never omitted by the demagogue in the vilification of those who seek to place a proper restraint upon the evil passions and excesses of the people. If there be any just reproach, because of the advocacy of such an "Aristocracy," as we have indicated as proper in the South, an aristocracy of the wise and the good, then we freely accept the obloquy, and confess our title to the supposed disgrace.

We confess we see no other termination to the struggle in which we are engaged than the still higher elevation of the Patrician character of the South, that will make our success valuable to ourselves in promoting the durability of our national fabric, or to mankind, in the establishment of safe and reliable principles of free government.

The South has now within her grasp the most splendid opportunity presented in all history, of vindicating the sublime truth of Republican Government based upon regulated liberty. Her social system is complete, and she needs only such reformation of her *political* character as shall render perfect the harmony of her *Patrician society* with a *Patrician government*. The success of such a government is in perfect accord with the philosophy of history. Every nation to whom has been guaranteed a permanently free constitution is indebted for its liberal features to its educated, property-holding classes, while all the decayed Republics of history owed their downfall to the corruption and excesses of an "unbridled Democracy." How much does England owe to her noble barons for their grand achievement on "that great day at Runnymede," who forcing a tyrant to acknowledge their own rights, refused any settlement which did not guarantee equal privileges to the people. And, thus it has ever been, the two great conservatives, property and education, in the beautiful language of Bulwer, applied to the English nobility,

> Stand towers of order
> 'Twixt the red cap and the throne . . .

ever the true guardians of liberty and law. The masses are easily deceived by demagogues, but the educated class are more discerning and vigilant.

Which then will the South choose, a Democracy or an Aristocratic Republic? History proves the one an absurdity, while the other conflicts with no facts of history or principle of philosophy. A Democracy to be successful, presupposes an Utopian idea, building its hopes upon an integrity and intelligence in the mass of mankind which they have never been known to possess. A Republic, in the sense in which we have described it, gives the keeping of liberty and the preservation of law to those whom reason and experience alike indicate as its natural protectors.

31

The Test of Civilization

Atlantic Monthly

The history of the war of the Rebellion cannot be comprised in a narrative of military operations and political and financial conditions. The historian who confines himself to these omits an important part of his work. To understand the war, to obtain a correct notion of the principles on which it was waged, to appreciate the necessity even of special military movements, and to comprehend its results, especially in its effect upon the national character and ideas, a large share of attention must be given to the social conditions of the country, to the opinions, sentiments, impulses, and desires of the American people, and to the forms in which their exertions to maintain the cause which they had at heart took shape. The novel conditions of national life, which had their source in our democratic system, and which, up to the period of the war, had been but partially recognized and imperfectly appreciated even by ourselves, manifested themselves during its course in ways not less striking than unanticipated, and gave to it a character different from that of any war previously recorded in history.

Its most remarkable feature was not the enormous magnitude of the forces engaged, or the extent of the territory over which it was waged, or the strategy displayed in marches or battles, or the methods by which it was carried on; but it was what lay behind all these—it was the conduct and bearing of the people by whom and for whom the war was fought and victory won. It was most remarkable for being in every sense a popular war; and unless this fact be brought clearly into view, and its relations be plainly exhibited, there can be no true history of the time. . . .

The breaking out of the Rebellion found our people, not only ignorant of war, but unprepared for it. Domestic, civil war is a catastrophe not contemplated in our system, for which it made no provision, and against which it was indeed secure, but for the abnormal sectional division created by

Atlantic Monthly (Boston, January, 1867).

Reviewing Charles J. Stillé's *History of the United States Sanitary Commission,* the *Atlantic* found deeper meaning in the work of the humanitarians. The Sanitary Commission promoted the efficiency of soldiers, relieved the sufferings of sick and wounded, and contributed largely to victory. It was, thought the *Atlantic,* "framed and administered in entire accordance with the principles of our national life."

slavery. Freed from this extraneous element, our system is, in truth, its own safeguard against civil war. A democratic commonwealth, based on the principle of the equality of human conditions, is less exposed to civil violence and war than any other existing order of society. The Government, which was in possession of but an insignificant force to resist the attack upon it, was as unprepared as the people. The first and most absolute consideration for it was whether the people would supply it with the men and means to carry on the war. The Administration naturally faltered. There were few men in the United States who would have believed, beforehand, that such a war as that in which we have lately been engaged could be carried on for more than five years without national exhaustion and surrender of the cause. Each man knew himself, but others had other hearts, and for them he could not speak. We had a vague trust in the people; we were accustomed to rhetorical phrases about the grandeur of the nation; but when the trial of our confidence came, there was little comfort in the Fourth-of-July oratory. We had not yet learned to have faith in the public conscience and the public thought, although our whole system was founded upon the most entire faith in the ultimate prevalence of right ideas among the people. We did not yet know the full force of the principles which had been at work in the making of the nation, nor what the nation which had been moulded by them was capable of. All unawares to ourselves, the principles of democracy and equality had developed in our people the intensest and highest spirit of nationality that the world had ever known.

The instinct of the people was true to itself. The attack of the Southern oligarchy upon the national life roused instantly an enthusiasm which filled the hearts of men and women, and lifted them to the exigencies and demands of the time. The nation for the first time felt the irresistible force of its ideas, and distrusted not its own power. It went to war as to a jubilee—eager, confident, audacious, with the heedlessness of inexperience of the trials and sufferings and stern discipline of war. It had yet to learn that the stout heart alone would not suffice; but that "an army, like a serpent, went upon its belly." At this moment of ardor and recklessness the Sanitary Commission was born. Mr. Stillé in his first chapter sets forth in simple but striking terms the conditions under which our first troops set forth for the field. "To the calm observer who knew anything of history, the view of this mass of enthusiastic and undisciplined men, calling themselves soldiers, suggested sad forebodings." "We were forced to try the novel experiment of improvising the most artificial and complicated of human organizations—an effective and disciplined army, under what had hitherto been esteemed insurmountable obstacles." The military department of the Government, accustomed to the routine management of the handful of men which had formed our standing army, was suddenly called upon to provide for a force so enormous as to have taxed the resources and energies of the greatest military power. It was in vain to hope that it could at once and in a moment meet and supply all the needs of the army that had been called at a day's notice into the field. The people were going to war, and it was for the people to take care of itself. The impulse to supply the citizens who were suddenly transformed into soldiers with every aid and comfort which tender solicitude and personal sympathy could minister was "as earnest and as spontaneous and as general on the part of those who stayed at home, as that which rallied round the flag of the country the very flower of its youth." . . .

To organize this general, spontaneous outburst of patriotic zeal, to concentrate diffused efforts into proper channels, to convert the popular emotion into a steady and disciplined habit, to endeavor to infuse the popular sympathy and enthusiasm into the machinery of government; and, above all, to prevent any irregular or embarrassing interference with the work and the responsibilities of the civil and military authorities, but to act "strictly in aid of the government plans, as far as possible through government means," so as to bring the efforts of the people and of the Government into harmony for the successful prosecution of the great objects of the war—this was the original conception of the enlightened men by whom the Sanitary Commission was established, and who directed its great operations throughout the war. . . .

The Sanitary Commission owed its power and success to the fact that it never lost sight of the double nature of its duties—on the one hand, as the instrument by which the people were brought into relation with the army, to encourage, to aid, to support and take care of it; on the other hand, as the guardian of those interests of the army which were intrusted to its charge by the popular confidence. It was fortunate for it that, while authorized and recognized by the Government, it never became directly dependent upon it or responsible to it. It was a wholly popular and extra-governmental body, responsible only to the people, and dependent for its support upon them. In this respect, in view especially of the immense work which it performed supplementary to that of the Government, it possesses a peculiar interest to the student of politics as a striking example of the extra-governmental organized action of a free community, for the accomplishment of public ends which the Government is unable or incompetent to secure. This action exists in every civilized state to a greater or less degree; but it reaches its largest development in a democratic community like our own, in which the State is the people, and the Government itself simply a popular organization for the performance of certain definite functions. The test of the civilization of a community is its capacity for self-government; and this capacity finds its expression in that moral order which gives its form to the system of government, and which exhibits itself in the spontaneous and harmonious co-operation of the individuals by whom the nation is composed in the performances of works of social obligation or common concern.

The development of freedom in America is marked by the development in the faculty of association, and in the power which results from it. Our populace is accustomed, as no other has even been, to association for every public purpose; and its whole history affords frequent illustration, not only of the effect of this principle in developing nationality, but of the fact that it is one of the greatest agencies in the progress of mankind in intelligence, sympathy, and self-discipline.

The existence of the Sanitary Commission was possible only in a nation habituated to extra-governmental organization and to associate action; and its whole dependence was upon the readiness and ability of the people to concentrate diffused and individual efforts into a single channel of combined activity. As soon as information of its methods, purposes, opportunities, and needs could be spread through the country, it at once began to receive support and draw its resources from every section of the land. From Maine to Oregon it had its army of workers; and for every soldier that the Government could put into the field there was at least one worker for his support among the million laborers enlisted in aid of the Commission. The story of the vast network of co-operating agencies which stretched over the land, embracing every village, town, and city in its meshes, is one of the most delightful records of humane sympathy, generous devotion, and patriotic labor that was ever written. It would be difficult to exaggerate the value of the work thus accomplished, not merely in its direct application to the special objects of the Commission—the promotion of the health, the comfort, and the efficiency of the army, the prevention and relief of suffering, and the keeping close the relations between the people in the military service of the nation and those who remained at home engaged in the usual callings of life—but in its indirect operation in the development of national feeling and confidence, in binding the people of the remotest regions in the close cords of service for a common end, in quickening and deepening zeal for our great cause and sympathy for those who were engaged in maintaining it at the hazard of their lives. What the Sanitary Commission thus effected for the country cannot be stated in columns of figures or measured by any material standard; but great as was its manifest work of beneficence, we esteem the influence which it exerted on the spirit of the people and on the development of the nation as of still greater worth, and as productive of still higher and more permanent results.

Among these results there is not one of more importance than the part in the war which was secured through its agency for our women. And in this again its correspondence with the genius and tendency of our system was strikingly manifested. It is plain that the principle of equality embodied in our democratic civilization has already wrought a marked change in the position of woman as a member of the community. But the change already wrought is indicative of a still greater change to come. The portion of woman in the future will be far different from her portion in the past. There is at last not merely a promise, but a certainty, that society is to be perfected by the admission of woman to her full rights, and to essential equality with man; democracy, as the outgrowth of Christianity, reverencing the rights of all, and requiring the powers of all for its full development, will not remain maimed and weak through the failure to provide for the equal participation between man and woman of the burdens and the blessings of civilization.

The part which the women of America took in the recent war was proof of the virtue of the system of our democratic society. The days for the flattery of women, like the days of chivalry, have gone by; but never did women, as a portion of the community, show themselves more worthy of respect and admiration than during these years in which they bore so heavy and bitter a portion of the sacrifices, so essential a portion of the labors, which the country required from her children. The main work of the supply of the necessities of the Sanitary Commission was performed by them; and to every demand made upon them, whether for such work as only they could do or for work in which they shared with men, they showed themselves sufficient. Whatever women have done in other countries and in past times for soldiers whom they loved, or for a cause to which they were devoted, was now more than matched by what our women did. The story of the war is a story of what was done by the combined efforts of men and women; and the history of the Sanitary Commission is a record of their common zeal, devotion, and labor.

The same influences which are modifying the constitution of American society, by securing for woman her true place in the community, are directly operative in developing in the national character those humane feelings which mark the progress of Christian civilization. The principle of the equality of mankind cannot be accepted without leading to a new sense of the intimacy of the relations which bind man to man in society, and to a recognition of the broad claims of humanity. The doctrine of equality, whatever be its origin and consequences in politics, is in its nature a religious doctrine. It is simply the form by which the principle of love is embodied and expressed in politics. "Thou shalt love thy neighbor as thyself," has for its corollary the truth, that "All men are created equal;" and the nation which has adopted this principle as the corner-stone of its system finds in truth that love is the fulfilling of the law. The mutual confidence and helpfulness which are characteristic of American life, the kindliness, sympathy, and humanity which distinguish the community, are the natural and inevitable results of its politico-religious faith. Far as the practice of humane virtues may fall short and fail to fulfil the image of the life of a perfect community, there is plainly visible among us a tendency toward a completer performance of the duties of active benevolence. In this respect, the constitution of the Sanitary Commission, the objects which it held in view, and the manner in which those objects were attained, were but the expression of the human instincts and principles and of the moral sense of the people. The horrors and sufferings of war were inexpressibly grievous and repugnant to a nation that was daily growing more kind and tender-hearted. It longed to carry on war without misery; it hated to hurt even its enemies; and when it learned that war meant hurt and harm to them, and that for the sake of love it must strike and wound and kill, and that its children must suffer every agony, it strove with all its novel tenderness, not only to succor its own soldiers, but to treat even its enemies with a humanity which found little response in their natures. The contrast between the civilization of the democracy of the North and the people of the South was drawn in sharpest lines by the difference of their temper in these respects. Freedom and equality on the one side, slavery on the other, had wrought their effects on the souls of men. The barbarous atrocities committed on the bodies of our dead, the horrible cruelties of Andersonville, Millen, and Belle Isle, were the results of passions to which the disrespect of man in slavery had given birth and nurture. The men who could treat prisoners of war as our prisoners were treated at the South, were not men to invent or maintain sanitary commissions for the relief of their own soldiers. It is with no vindictive feeling that we remember the fate of those dearest to us who fell into Southern hands, as we read the account of the manner in which our enemies were treated after the great battles of the war by the hands of the ministers of Northern beneficence; but it is with devout thankfulness that our great cause—the cause of human rights—was maintained by those who honored man even in the guise of an enemy. . . .

While in these impartial and liberal ministrations of the popular beneficence the Sanitary Commission fulfilled the national sentiment of humanity, it exhibited, in the variety of its operations, the fertility of its resources, the readiness of its adaptation to changing circumstances and conditions, and in the pliability of its methods of work, still another striking feature of the national life as manfested in an educated democracy. Under our free institutions the amount and variety of the personal energies which may be called out at any moment depend only on the number and the intelligence of the people. Freedom and equality develop all resources. Each man contributes his special quota to the general sum of activity. In the unimpeded use of his faculties, he not only promotes his own well-being, but increases the power and the prosperity of the state. Mr. Mill, in speaking of America in his treatise on Representative Government, says: "No such wide diffusion of the ideas, tastes, and sentiments of educated minds has ever been seen elsewhere, or even conceived of as attainable." He does not point out the result of this fact, that nowhere else has there been displayed such mastery of circumstances by man, in readiness of invention and in the rapidity of his adaptation of means to the ends which he seeks, whether it be in the field of arts, of politics, or of society. In the associate action which is characteristic of our democracy, and by which the most rapid advance in civilization is secured, the resources of each individual are drawn upon for the production of the common end, and the infinite and complex variety of individual devices, powers, faculties, and energies is harmonized into co-operative unity. The flexibility of organized effort is secured by individual freedom and equality.

The Sanitary Commission might well be selected by the philosophic student of our system as a conspicuous example of the operation of these principles. It showed not only the capacity of a people for independent organization, but the unlimited abundance of their resources, and their unexampled skill in dealing with unexpected emergencies. Carefully conducting its operations upon general principles, and under wisely devised rules, it was bound neither by precedent nor routine, where these interfered with the best execution of its work, but accepting the lessons of experience, it adapted its measures to each new occasion, each fresh demand, and each varying need. . . . It thus became the expression of the intelligence, the moral sense, and the humane sentiment of the people. It became their great agency of beneficence. To the men who directed its affairs, and who as the ministers and representatives of the people showed themselves sufficient for the arduous duties and the weighty responsibilities imposed upon them, and proved themselves worthy to be the almoners of America, the nation owes unstinted gratitude and honor.

To the end of time the Sanitary Commission will stand in history as a worthy monument of the patriotism, the humanity, and the religion of a Christian democracy.

PART VI

THE
ECONOMIC
IMPACT

The processes of nationalization were not confined to political change or even to the development of a new, humane, national spirit which one commentator found. The true nature of the nation was to be discovered in the realm of economics—in the new national banking system, in the stimulation which came to inventive genius, in improvements in transportation and communication. There were, it is true, new adjustments to be made, and often in the transition period there was fraud, but it all added up, in the long run, to a new national outlook. It was, as one writer concluded, "schooling," and it was reflected in alterations in "the habitual working of the American mind."

There remained, indeed, in Abraham Lincoln's words in his Second Inaugural, much left to be done—to bind up the nation's wounds, and to promote justice "among ourselves and with all nations." But the new nation was firmly grounded in a new economics and a new vision of progress, both material and spiritual.

32

Financial Resources of The North

The Knickerbocker Magazine

Nothing has so astonished Europe in modern times as the magnitude of the scale on which the American Republic carries on the war for the maintenance of its own integrity. For the enormous expenditure of men and money, and the vastness of the theatre on which the military operations are conducted, there is no parallel in the history of any European nation, not excepting even France, under the *régime* of the elder Napoleon. There is no civil war to be compared with it in extent, either in ancient or modern times. It is a war commensurate with the gigantic features of the country, its vast area, bounded by two oceans; its mighty rivers, watering valleys of wonderful fertility; and its inexhaustible agricultural, mineral, manufacturing, and commercial resources. The war is commensurate, too, with the tremendous issues involved in the result: the continued existence, or the dissolution of the great American Union; the preservation of law and order, or the prevalence of anarchy and political chaos; the solution of the problem of self-government by the final triumph of democratic institutions, or by the failure of that which the founders of the Government regarded and the destinies of millions of the living human race, and of millions still unborn in both worlds.

Already a million of volunteers have been called into the field, with three hundred thousand drafted men in reserve; and an immense naval force has been improvised to operate on the sea-coast and navigable rivers of the enemy. By land and water the conflict has been carried on for eighteen months, with the most lavish expenditure for arms, of the best construction known to modern art and science; for the most improved equipments, and for all the munitions and appliances of war, of the most costly description. It is hardly necessary to say that to maintain such an army and navy, and as "an experiment," a triumph or a failure affecting the interest, the liberties,

"Financial Resources of the United States," *The Knickerbocker Magazine* (New York, October, 1862), Vol. 61, pp. 354-359.

After the Emancipation Proclamation and a change in editors, *Knickerbocker* became a stout critic of Lincoln and the administration. In the first months of the war, the widely read magazine gave cautious support to the Union cause.

to wage such a war, involves a corresponding outlay, and financial resources so immense, that no European power could attempt it without certain bankruptcy. Hence, when hostilities were fairly inaugurated, and our Government commenced in preparations upon such a gigantic scale, the great financial organs of England laughed to scorn the idea of the United States without a dollar in its treasury, and with doubtful credit in Europe, being able to carry on the struggle for any length of time. . . .

The resources of England are limited and for the most part artificial, and worn out, and her people are impoverished by accumulated taxation. Our resources are fresh and boundless, and continually growing; our people have been hitherto almost untaxed, and wealth is so diffused among them that they can bear, without feeling it very severely, an amount of taxation that would grind the British people to powder. Besides, it is not intended that the war should be a long one. The idea is that it be an expensive and short one, and such wars are the cheapest in the end. It might suit the policy of the British Empire to extend a war over many years. That would never suit the policy of the American Government, or harmonize with the interests of the American people. To enable them to cultivate the arts of peace, and to prevent future war, is one of the chief designs of the present conflict. Hence the great sacrifices which have been so cheerfully made. We admit that to carry on the contest very long upon its present scale would be to use up the resources even of the United States, and that it must be speedily brought to an end from sheer exhaustion, and this is still more true of the enemy. A long war under the circumstances is, therefore, impossible. The American mode is rapidity in everything. The jog-trot, slow-coach style of European wars does not suit the genius of our people. They are quick in perceiving the situation of affairs. Their intelligence and general education give them that advantage. Hence in the most warmly contested elections, the moment the result is known, the beaten party acquiesce with perfect good humor. In this struggle now pending, which appears to be at its crisis, if the Southern Confederacy is defeated in a decisive battle, the rebellious States will probably submit with the best grace they can. If the rebels should succeed in winning two or three more great battles, it is extremely probable that the feeling of the majority of the people of the North would soon develop itself by unmistakable symptoms, that their Southern brethren should be allowed to depart from the Union and permanently establish a separate Confederacy. We are a practical people, and will not adhere long to a theory if it does not produce the promised fruit.

Now let us examine the capabilities of the nation to meet the war-debt, consisting of a loan by act of February, 1861, of $25,000,000; Treasury Notes, six per cents, $10,000,000; Treasury Notes, $7.30 and $3.65, together with Demand-Notes, $250,000,000; Legal Tender Demand-Notes, February 25th, 1862, $150,000,000, of which $50,000,000 were to take up the Demand-Notes of July 17th, 1861. Additional Legal-Tender Notes, July 11th, 1862,

$150,000,000, of which $35,000,000 may be of lower denomination than $5; coupons or registered bonds, not exceeding $500,000,000, bearing interest at six per cent, into which the Treasury Notes are convertible; lastly, stamps as currency, $40,000,000. Though the Secretary of the Treasury is authorized to issue the foregoing securities, he does not necessarily issue them to the full amount. Accordingly, on the 29th of May last, the whole funded debt of the United States, including the loans of 1842, 1847, 1858, and 1860, was $491,446,184, at an average interest of four and thirty-five-hundredths per cent, as reported by Mr. Chase himself; and the actual debt on the 1st of July, 1862, we know to be $504,500,000; the estimated debt, July 1st, 1863, after applying the direct tax to its reductions, $626,000,000. Now what is this compared with the debt of Great Britain, which in round numbers is $4,000,000,000, and requiring each year to be paid for interest and management, $127,695,701, against $26,000,000, the probable interest of our debt, July 1st, 1863? The English debt would, therefore, be nearly seven times as great, and the interest nearly five times that of the interest of the debt of the United States, while the ability to pay would be greatly inferior. It is the mass of the people, and not the rich, who pay the taxes. Now what is the condition of a large number of the people of England? Mr. Pashley, in his work on "Pauperism," states that of the population three millions belong to "an ignorant, degraded, and pauper class"; and actually receive parish relief in the course of every year, while a still larger class are but little less ignorant, degraded, and miserable. The interest of the English debt is equal to four dollars and thirty-six cents per head; the interest of the French debt is one hundred and ten million dollars, and is three dollars and four cents per head; the interest of the American debt is one dollar and fourteen cents per head. The national debt of England will never be paid. The debt of the United States will be paid off, principal and interest, in a very few years. . . .

War and direct taxation were new to us; and it was with extreme difficulty that Congress, from fear of the unpopularity of the measure, could be induced to pass the national tax bill, which is expected to produce two hundred million dollars. Had it not been adopted, the depreciation of the paper issued by the Government would have entailed financial ruin. As it is, the depreciation is about twenty per cent; so that a five-dollar Demand-Note is only worth four dollars in gold. What would it have been had not Mr. Chase's recommendation been embodied in a law, at the last moment? The new paper currency would soon share the fate of the French assignats, and the continental money issued during the Revolutionary War. . . .

The total issue of the continental money was $362,546,822, which was a circulation far in excess of the wants of four millions of population, having at that time but little trade or commerce. The number of notes issued by Mr. Chase, for circulation among twenty millions of a trading and commercial population, does not exceed the wants of the community—and therefore it cannot be depreciated like the continental money and French assignats; but let Mr. Chase continue to issue more of these notes, year after year, by the authority of Congress, and make no provision for their redemption, and they would soon become of the same value as the continental money. But the fact of the notes being convertible into bonds, bearing six per cent interest, and the interest being payable in specie, and the other fact that a tax has been laid to pay the interest, and gradually extinguish the principal of all the war loans and liabilities of the Government, will save the present issues from much further depreciation. The direct tax will be ample to cover the ground. As for the tariff, it is not likely—owing to the great falling off in the imports—to do more than pay the ordinary expenses of the Government—say sixty million dollars per annum. And here we may observe, that the curtailment of imports is to be regarded rather as an evidence of prudent economy than of inability to purchase. Persons engaged in the dry-goods business have, no doubt, suffered by the change; but not the general community. Our exports have been immense, during the past year—particularly in breadstuffs, our control of which has compelled Europe to keep the peace to us. Corn, and not cotton, is now king. The ships bearing our commerce whiten every sea. Our agricultural and mining interests are in a most flourishing condition; and our manufactures were never more active than at present. The tariff is prohibitory of many foreign articles which formerly competed successfully with our domestic manufactures; and the enormous expenditures for the war have stimulated those branches of native industry which embrace such articles as are used by the army and navy. The effect of so large a circulation of money cannot but have a beneficial effect upon the internal trade of the country, while the burthen of repayment of the debt will be distributed over a great many years; and posterity, which has an equal interest in the objects of the war with the present generation, will have to pay a share of the expense. Hitherto, the Northern territory of the Union has been saved from the destructive ravages of war, involving great loss of property, and the interruption of the operations of agricultural trade, and every description of business. Nor is it possible that the Southern armies can ever penetrate the North, except for a brief space, beyond the border. We may, therefore, safely calculate upon immunity from future invasion.

The loss of population would be the greatest loss of all, were it not that Europe stands ready to fill up the chasm; so that at the end of the next decade—provided the war ceases before the expiration of another year— there would be no evidence of the effects of the conflict as far as the diminution of population is concerned. In 1816, the population of the United States was eight and a half millions; by the last census it was thirty-one and a half millions. During the decade between 1850 and 1860, the population increased four millions and a half, or nearly twenty per cent. Population is the wealth of nations because it supplies the labor; and the demand for labor is unbounded. Every settler from Europe not only contributes his labor, but many of the emigrants bring money with them—thus swelling the national wealth. The loss of population by the war will soon, therefore, be repaired by the continual living stream from Europe. With the South the case is different, and time would not repair the ravages of the war so rapidly, as the current of emigration from Europe is chiefly directed to the Northern States. The injurious effects of the war are scarcely perceptible as yet. Only let the struggle terminate before the first of next July, and in three or four years the country would be as prosperous and happy as ever— such is the buoyancy of the American people. . . . When the civil war broke out, the country was in the very acme of prosperity; and soon after the war shall have closed, the prosperity of the republic will rise to a higher point than it ever did before. Notwithstanding the enormous wars in which Napoleon had been engaged, he expended in the course of nine years, in public improvements, upwards of two hundred million dollars. And what were the resources of the French Empire compared with those of the United States! The area of the country is more than two thousand millions of acres— including immense tracts of the richest virgin soil in the world—inviting the ploughshare to make it productive of wealth untold. For the future of the country we have no fears. When the element of disunion, North as well as South, is crushed, the republic will spread over this vast continent like a banyan-tree; each branch will put forth its root, and each root will become a stem of the great parent-tree—*e pluribus unum*—a spectacle of growth and prosperity such as the world has never seen.

33

The Carnival of Fraud

Henry S. Olcott

Mine is the most repulsive task that any one of the writers of this series will have assigned to him. All the others have their stories to tell of the clang of arms, the marshaling of armies, the thrilling episodes of personal danger and suffering, the political vicissitudes of the mighty struggle. To me comes the duty of showing the corruption that festered beneath the surface. The eye kindles, the pulse leaps, the imagination fires with their narratives of martial deeds; but what I shall say will make the writer and reader alike deplore the baseness of human nature, which most displays itself in times of national calamity....

The initial Confederate act of war not only forced upon us the gigantic work of transforming an industrial people into soldiers, but of arming and equipping them as well. This was the harder task of the two. Men there were by the hundred thousand, ready to take the field; but, to uniform them, cloth had to be woven, leather tanned, shoes, clothing, and caps manufactured. The canvas to shelter them had to be converted from the growing crop into fabrics. To arm them, the warehouses and armories of Europe, as well as of this country, had to be ransacked. All considerations of business caution had to be subordinated to the imperious necessity for haste. It was the golden hour of patriotism, so was it equally that of greed, and, as money was poured by the million, by the frugal, into the lap of the Government, so was there a yellow Pactolus diverted by myriad streamlets into the pockets of scoundrels and robbers—official and otherwise. The public necessity was their opportunity, and they made use of it.

The rush of men to the front left the War Office no time to be nice over details; so that, as the volume of administrative business overflowed the bureau machinery for its supervision, things were, in a measure, suffered to take their course. An unhealthy tone pervaded everything; speculation was the rule, conservatism the exception. We floated, on a sea of paper, into a fool's paradise. Contractors, bloated with the profits on shoddy, rode

HENRY S. OLCOTT, "The War's Carnival of Fraud," Philadelphia Weekly *Times, Annals of the War* (Philadelphia, 1879), pp. 705 ff.

in emblazoned carriages, which, a little while before, they would have been glad to drive as hirelings; and vulgar faces and grimy fingers were made more vulgar and coarse with the glare of great diamonds. Intrigue held the key to the kitchen-stairs of the White House, shaped legislation, sat cheek to jowl with Congressmen, and seduced commissioned officers from the strict path of duty. . . . Our soldiers were given guns that would not shoot, powder that would only half explode, shoes of which the soles were filled with shavings, hats that dissolved often in a month's showers, and clothing made of old cloth, ground up and fabricated over again. . . .

In the military arsenals, the same rottenness prevailed, Here and there were to be found public servants without a moral ulcer within their breasts. But such were annoyed and hampered in the execution of duty, overridden, too, often by positive orders from superiors to receive supplies not up to army standard, and when too obstinate, were removed to posts less desirable. The army standards were themselves debased under the plea of an exigency. In the letting of contracts, a fair competition was frustrated by the transparent conspiracy of bidders, who would put in absurdly low proposals under fictitious names, and then bid themselves at the highest price that, from surreptitious information received, they knew would throw out honest competitors and secure them the contract. Their profits were calculated to come out of the delivery of inferior articles of skimped measure to government inspectors, with whom they had an understanding. Presents of horses, carriages, jewelry, wines, cigars, and friendly help toward promotion, though passing under a politer name than bribery, effected the same results as though they had not. Every artifice that rascally ingenuity could devise, and clever men and women carry out, was resorted to, to procure the brigadier's stars or the colonel's eagles for ambitious incompetents. The sacredest secrets of our Government were sold to the enemy; loud-mouthed hypocrites trafficked across the lines; the very medicines for the sick were adulterated, and dishonest gains were made out of the transportation of the wounded. Nay, so vile was the scramble for money, so debasing its influence, that our dead heroes were followed into the very grave by the plundering contractor, who cheated in the coffin that was to hold the sacred dust, and amassed fortunes by supplying rotten head-stones in defiance of accepted stipulations. What shall we call this wretched episode of national history but a Carnival of Fraud? This was the Augean stable to cleanse which the broom of authority was placed in my hands.

Of all this I knew nothing in November, 1862, when Secretary Stanton first applied, through the United States Marshal at New York, for my services. . . .

The occasion of my employment was the giving of a Delmonico dinner by a German Israelite to a distinguished company of guests. The host was one Solomon Kohnstamm, who had accumulated a fortune of over a quarter of a million in the importing business at New York, and enjoyed the reputation of a giver of good dinners and a jolly sort of fellow in general. In an evil hour he took to discounting the volunteers of recruiting officers, cheated, was suspected, in danger of arrest, and as a grand *coup* of diplomacy had spread the feast in question and bidden to it every civil and military official in the New York district who, under any contingency, might have a hand in arresting or prosecuting him criminally. I will spare the blushes of men now, as then prominently before the public eye, by not mentioning the names of Kohnstamm's guests. His frauds had come under the surveillance of the United States Marshal, and the circumstances of the dinner alarmed the authorities, who saw through the trick and feared the ends of justice might be defeated. I was, as I have said, convalescent at this time, and getting ready to return to the front at a very early date, when I received a notification that my services to examine the papers in this case of Kohnstamm were required. The Marshal told me that I would be free to leave for the army within a fortnight at farthest, and that the amount of fraud was supposed to be within twenty-five thousand dollars; in place of which my service was continued more than three years. The frauds of Kohnstamm turned out to be some three hundred thousand dollars, and the little local examination of a single case grew into a general inspection of arsenals and navy-yards as connected with the equipment and clothing of the land and naval forces.

The vouchers discounted by Kohnstamm were the bills of landlords for the lodging and board of recruits for volunteer regiments prior to their muster into the United States service. They were certified by the ranking officer of the regiment and by the company officer engaged in the recruiting. After muster the men were duly taken on the regimental rolls, and the quartermaster was then legally empowered to issue to them tents, rations, and clothing. These necessary costs of organization were at first defrayed either out of the Union Defense Committee's fund or advanced by the officers of regiments and their friends out of their private means.

Kohnstamm's crime consisted in his procuring from landlords—generally German saloon-keepers—their signature to blank vouchers, which he would have filled up by his clerks for, say, one or two thousand dollars each, and then either get unprincipled commissioned officers to append their certificates for an agreed price, or, cheaper still, forge them. By this device he drew over three hundred thousand dollars from the "Mustering and Disbursing Office" in New York, of which sum the greater proportion was in due time ascertained by me to be fraud. The examination of all these accounts was a work of time and laborious and patient research, as may be imagined. It was also necessary to proceed with the greatest prudence, for only a few days after my taking the papers in hand Secretary Stanton, acting, as soon became evident, upon erroneous reports, caused the offender to be arrested and lodged in Fort Lafayette. Kohnstamm was a Democrat, except, of course, in business matters, and a rich importer of thirty years' standing; had plenty of money, spent it liberally, and had but just given his grand dinner at Delmonico's. No wonder, then, that his arrest should have excited a bitter feeling against the War Department in the minds of people who knew nothing whatever of his offenses. There was a Democratic Governor at Albany, a Democratic Mayor at New York, a Democratic District Attorney, and Democrats on the grand jury. It came to my ears that the Secretary of War, the United States Marshal, and myself, were to be indicted for resisting the writ of *habeas corpus* under the alleged unconstitutional act of Congress suspending the same. It was an emergency demanding a bold course; so with the consent of the department, I went myself before the grand jury with my papers, and offered to answer any questions that might be asked of me. The result was a vote of commendation for what had been done, and all danger of indictment was removed. I pursued the same course with Governor Seymour and the District Attorney with equally satisfactory results, and then the trump card was played of giving the facts to the press, which was only too willing to publish them, and never subsequently, to my recollection, interfered with my official labors.

This adroit and epicurean criminal employed the best counsel at our bar, and enjoyed all the immunity from annoyance, after his release from Fort Lafayette, that one so circumstanced could expect. But that there were thorns in his bed of roses is beyond any doubt. In due time, he was held in one hundred and fifty thousand dollars bail in a civil suit, and, after a three weeks' session with me, the grand jury, under the lead of the late James W. Beekman, brought in forty-eight bills of indictment against him. Failing to get the required security, he lay two months in the House of Detention, after which his bail was reduced, and he was liberated from confinement. I found so many obstacles to getting him to trial that, finally, the Secretary caused a resolution of inquiry to be introduced in the Senate by Mr. Wilson, which settled the business. The case was peremptorily moved on, and that venerated jurist, Judge Samuel Nelson, turned a deaf ear to the excuses of counsel, and ordered the District Attorney to open for the prosecution. Out of the forty-eight indictments one had to be selected on the spur of the moment, and the court would only permit us to introduce testimony about seven others, to show the *scienter*, or guilty knowledge. Accordingly, eight cases of palpable forgery were designated, the trial proceeded (May 17th, 1864), and, on the 21st, the jury, after deliberating only twenty minutes, brought in a verdict of guilty. The court promptly sentenced him to ten years' imprisonment, at hard labor, at Sing Sing, and the rich Kohnstamm made his exit from the busy scene of his tradings and his triumphs.

So unexpected, but so welcome, was this result to the Secretary of War that, upon receiving the news, he telegraphed back a characteristic message, which, as I recall it, was as follows:

War Department, May 21st, 1864
Colonel H. S. Olcott, New York

I heartily congratulate you upon the result of to-day's trial. It is as important to the government as the winning of a battle.

EDWIN M. STANTON
Secretary of War

Since I have anticipated events somewhat, to give a connected history of the Kohnstamm case, it may as well be said here that the civil suit was duly prosecuted to a successful issue, and a large sum of money paid over to the Treasury by the trustees of the felon's estate. As a farce after the tragedy, naturally followed his pardon by President Johnson, after two years' imprisonment, upon the petition of the usual string of wealthy and influential New Yorkers, who so often give their signatures to papers of this kind without proper consideration.

In December, 1862, being in Washington, the Assistant Secretary of War handed me, for examination, a claim for above three thousand dollars, which had been collected by one D'Utassy, colonel of the Garibaldi Guard, a New York volunteer regiment, upon his affidavit that it was correct. I found it to be a total fraud, the very signatures upon the sub-vouchers being forged. The delinquent was court-martialed, convicted, and sentenced to the penitentiary. The inquiry into this and the Kohnstamm cases developed such an astonishing condition of moral obliquity among contractors and regimental officers that the Secretary of War took prompt measures to bring the guilty to punishment. Several commissioned officers were dismissed from the service, and a number, among them two officers of the regular army, were handed over to the civil authorities for prosecution. The Adjutant General also availed of my help, sending me claims filed for payment, that I might report my opinion of their validity; and various practical suggestions from me, for the reformation of abuses in local bureau management, were favorably received and acted upon. By the time that six months had elapsed, I had examined some two hundred witnesses, taken two thousand folios of testimony, and all idea of my being relieved from this unwelcome, though necessary, duty had been abandoned. The department threw upon me more and more responsibility, but, it must be confessed, accompanying it with a more than ample discretionary authority, thus affording me the highest proofs of the Secretary's satisfaction, and stimulating me to deserve its continuance. At the date of my second semi-annual report to the War Department, I had, in the preceding six months, made inspections in ten States; taken testimony in twenty-four cities and towns, beside camps and military posts; examined, with assistance, eight hundred and seventeen witnesses, written five hundred and fifty-three letters, and traveled over nineteen thousand miles. . . .

The responsible officers of the War Department were all overworked. From the Secretary down there was no exception. Each crowded at least three years' proper work into one year, and some of us four or five. It was all I could do, though working night and day, Sundays and all, and with one, two and at times three and four stenographers to help me, to keep ahead of my work. . . .

The close of the war found me with this work only half completed, and so some great culprits, military and civilian, escaped the just punishment of their offenses, to figure as noisy politicians and be looked up to as successful men of affairs! The archives of the War Department have many an ugly secret smothered in its pigeon-holes, and, heaven knows! it will not be myself who will disturb them; there is stench enough in the air without this carrion.

34

Inventive Genius

Scientific American

At the close of the year Eighteen Hundred and Sixty we congratulated our readers upon a year of unexampled national prosperity. Never before had the fields and orchards of our husbandmen yielded so profusely, or our manufacturers and merchants enjoyed a period of more profitable success. It would have afforded us intense pleasure had we been able to close our present volume in the same tones of peaceful gladness; but in thousands of workshops, factories and farms, the hammer, the saw and the plow have been laid aside for the sword, the rifle and the cannon, and our country has become one vast camp of armed men. Fierce battles have been fought, and many brave men have fallen, and now "sleep the sleep which knows no waking." Still there is much to cheer and awaken faith and hope for the future. Many philosophers believe that wars are tribulations which exert similar influences among the nations that thunder storms do upon the atmosphere. They are evils while they exist, but when the clouds are dispersed, men breathe a purer and more serene atmosphere. May this be the happy consummation of our national troubles!

Although the vast insurrection has exerted a disorganizing influence upon many manufactures and other branches of business, it is really wonderful to witness the elasticity of our people, and the facility with which they have adapted themselves to altered circumstances. Many old branches of industry have been destroyed, but new ones have sprung up, and there is now a great amount of industrial prosperity enjoyed in most of the manufacturing sections of our country.

The war has stimulated the genius of our people, and directed it to the service of our country. Sixty-two new inventions relating to engines, im-

Scientific American (December 28, 1861; June 13, 1863; December 26, 1863; December 19, 1863).

Scientific American recorded, week by week, the progress of invention and took particular pains to point out Northern superiority over the South. The editorials here illustrate the strength of the artisan tradition in America, the pride of craftsmanship, and the clear conviction that the mechanic arts were the highest accomplishments of civilization.

plements and articles of warfare, have been illustrated in our columns, with no less than one hundred and forty-seven figures. These embrace a great variety of cannon, rifles, shells, shot, tents, kits and almost all articles found in the military vocabulary. Rodman's monster cannon, Dahlgren's howitzers, De Brame's revolving cannon, Winslow's steel cannon and several others have been thus brought before the public. No man can really be intelligent in matters relating to modern warfare unless he has made himself acquainted with these inventions.

Other departments of industry have also been well represented. Our inventors have not devoted themselves exclusively to the invention of destructive implements; they have also cultivated the arts of peace. In the present volume of the *Scientific American*—extending only over six months, one hundred and sixty different subjects have been illustrated, averaging from three to four figures each. It would take up too much space to enumerate all these, but in thus summing up our yearly progress in a general way, we can safely assert that for original and well-studied efforts of genius, they equal if they do not surpass the inventions of any former year. And as the number of patents issued is a very good exponent of the progress of our country, we can point to no less than 2,919, which is equal to the number (2,910) issued in 1857—four years ago. When the defection of eleven States, and the distractions of our country are taken into consideration, it is not too much to assert that our inventors have done better last year than ever before, and that inventions are perhaps the most safe and profitable sources of investment in times of war as well as peace.

Considering the nature and extent of the tremendous struggle in which our country is engaged, we have really great reason as a people, to feel grateful, and call this a prosperous year after all. Never before have our fields yielded so bountifully. The great West is surcharged with wheat and corn, and we are in the happy condition of enjoying a surplus of the necessaries of life. In thus viewing the past, we can still say with cheerfulness, thy face, old year, has been deeply furrowed by scars and tears, but it has also been illuminated with many sunny smiles.

WAR AND INCREASING WEALTH

War is undoubtedly a condition of destruction to life and property; but it is possible that a nation may conduct a great war and, instead of becoming impoverished, may increase in both wealth and power. The condition under which war chiefly impoverishes a nation is by having it conducted within its own domain. But when a nation maintains a war upon the enemy's soil, and so manages its affairs that the annual expenses fall below the real value of its industrial products, it is evident that it must increase in wealth. The merchant who makes more than he spends increases in riches, and it is the same with a nation. An increase of national debt is no sign of increasing poverty in the people, for this debt may be a simple transfer of only a small portion of the surplus wealth of individuals to the general fund of the commonwealth—an investment in public instead of private stocks. Those who have made political economy a subject of study know well that Great Britain maintained a war with France and sometimes with nearly all the nations of the world for many years; and while the Government debt increased, the national wealth accumulated. She battled with Napoleon and clothed the armies of Russia, Spain and Prussia, and the sword was scarcely sheathed for thirty years; and yet at the end of the struggle she was vastly more wealthy than at the beginning of the contest. The first condition of this success was maintaining the war upon foreign soil, thus allowing the industrial arts—which furnish the sinews of war and the comforts of peace—to be conducted freely upon her own soil; and secondly living within her income. These facts should never be overlooked by a nation which would carry on an aggressive war successfully.

As the present war has been and is being conducted on the soil of the enemies of the Constitutional Government, industry therein has been paralyzed and the destruction of property has been prodigious. The seceded States are, therefore, necessarily becoming impoverished while the war is being continued. On the other hand, the Northern States pursue their industrial avocations in peace, and if they are "living within their income" they must be growing in wealth. Perhaps the best signs of increasing wealth in any country are new buildings—manufactories, houses, barns, ships, etc., and a decrease of common mercantile and mortgage debts. At present all these good signs may be noticed on every hand in all the loyal States, except perhaps the Border ones. In New York there are more new ships and steamers being built than at any former period within our recollection, and in almost every street many new houses are being erected. In Brooklyn the same signs of increasing wealth may be seen everywhere. In the Eastern States new factories are in the course of construction in almost every city, town and village, and in New Jersey and Pennsylvania the same signs of increasing wealth are just as plentiful. From the West also, the same cheering news comes floating on the breeze. A correspondent of the New York *Times,* signing himself "A Veteran Observer," writing from Ohio, asserts that the debts in that State were reduced $20,000,000 last year, and he is confident that the wealth of the country is increasing at the present moment at the rate of over six hundred millions per annum. We have no doubt but this intelligent observer is correct in his estimate. Never before in the history of the world has God blessed a nation with so much outward prosperity in the midst of such a chastisement as this great civil war.

Universal bankruptcy was predicted for this entire nation by the London *Times,* at the beginning of this contest, but while the Government borrows from its own people, and while they expend less than they produce, the nation cannot become bankrupt. Europeans generally are profoundly ignorant of the source of our nation's wealth and strength. The great essential of daily life to any people is food for man and beast, and in this essential no other country, with an equal population, can compare with the United States. The vast grain crops of our Western valleys and plains are of more value than mountains of gold and silver. In these consist the palpable power of the republic, and no European can appreciate the magnitude of that power without traveling extensively in America. Our educational establishments, the fine arts and manufactures in general, are sustained by the surplus of the soil. From every section the cheerful assurance comes up that the crops of the season afford promises of a most abundant harvest, thus inspiring hopes of continued material prosperity amid the havoc and sorrows of the great national conflict.

ANOTHER YEAR CLOSED

Like the weaver's shuttle speeding along in the loom, so our days and years sweep rapidly past, and thus our web of life is woven. During periods of great excitement, when mighty events crowd swiftly upon each other, the mind fails to take cognizance of the fleeting moments. We can scarcely realize the fact that another year in the life of the *Scientific American* has been measured out, and that this number completes volume nine of our new series. For about three years now our nation has been engaged in the most momentous civil war on record, and the struggle has been increasing in magnitude and importance. Originating in the unreasonable disaffection of ambitious and selfish men, it was forced upon the legal rulers and loyal people of the land, who accepted it with hesitation and sorrow in view of the affliction which would naturally attend it. But amid the grief of thousands whose homes and hearts have been made desolate, the nation has cause for being devoutly thankful at its unexpected and surprising prosperity. Civil war usually crushes out useful industry, and in every such case the people become impoverished. But every attempt to carry the conflict into the loyal States has been frustrated, and the armies of the Government have pushed back the insurgents, and have also been successful in reducing extensive territories to legal authority. Such results are very encouraging, auguring well for future success in ultimately subduing the rebellion and conquering obedience to law and order.

Amid this great war the people of the loyal States have been permitted to pursue their usual avocations in peace. No better evidence of material national prosperity can be adduced than the general and active employment of the people in useful industry, which is the true "Wealth of Nations." There has been plenty of employment for all, and the wheels of commerce have rolled on with unexampled speed and success. New sources of industry have been developed, and old branches have received a marked impetus, so that our industrial products have exceeded in quantity those of any similar period in the history of our commonwealth. Herein lies the great strength of our country, for the productive power of a nation is the true measure of its strength.

No better proof can be adduced of our progress and improvement in the industrial arts than the achievements of inventors. The number of patents issued in our country during the year closing with this number is 3,746, against 3,220 for the same period in the previous year—being an increase of no less than five hundred and twenty-six! Every department of industry has been benefitted by these improvements, and the numerous illustrations of new inventions which have appeared in the columns of the *Scientific American* afford cheering evidence of great progress made in the useful arts during the past year. A great scarcity of labor has necessitated a demand for new inventions to abridge human toil, and inventors have been more than usually successful. The demand for labor, however, is still urgent, and inventors never had a more favorable prospect for obtaining lucrative employment in devising new labor-saving mechanisms. In conclusion, we can heartily join the President in the introductory lines of his late message: "Another year of health and of sufficiently abundant harvests has passed. For this, and especially for the improved condition of our national affairs, our renewed and profoundest gratitude is due."

SOUTHERN OPINION OF MECHANICS

If there be any well-meaning but deluded mechanics among us who have advocated the cause of those now in arms against the Government, and have sought by all the means in their power to disparage the efforts of our people to subdue those who would destroy this country utterly and forever, we beg them to read the following extracts from the Richmond *Examiner*, and ponder upon the animus or spirit which prompted the paragraphs alluded to. What can be the future of any nation or country which so despises operatives of all classes? Disaffected workingmen at the north, who pine for a more intimate association with rebels, should read carefully the extracts appended. We quote:

> Even before the war the so-called "workingmen" had their candidates in our larger towns; and since the war we have seen in the very Capital of the Confederacy an appalling display of mechanic "goosery," which nearly frightened our worthy Representatives out of their propriety. Indeed, such is the arrogance of the few artisans of the South that well-meaning men, who, a few months ago, reveled in visions of the future development of the material resources of Virginia, stand aghast at the sequel of their dreams as they forsee the whole "chaos come again" of a corrupt civilisation; all the _____isms of the North, all the _____ologies of Germany, the phalansteries of the French communists, the extravaganzas of English radicals, running riot through our Southern country. Mills and manufactories on every stream and in every valley would be a poor compensation for the introduction of such a crew of the sons and daughters of Belial; and no wonder that those who cling with love, which

is often the highest reason, to the old framework of our society, shudder at the thought of a Lowell on the Appomattox, or a Manchester in the Piedmont region. And yet they see no other future for the Border States of the Confederacy. Slave labor is to be withdrawn from the northern side of the James, and the country is literally and metaphorically to go to grass. The old lords of the soil are to migrate to the far South, and Yankees and Yankeefied Southerners are to dye the rivers of Virginia with indigo and copperas, and make her skies black with the smoke of her furnaces. Then the fatal process which led to the dissolution of the old Union is to be repeated, and another fratricidal war inaugurated.

"The old framework of our society" means of course slave labor. In another part the rebel editor says:

But suppose, for the sake of argument, that after the war is over manufactures will be found to pay in the South. Even then we are not disposed to admit that our social system will necessarily undergo a radical change, and we shall be forced to import laborers from abroad, and with those laborers the germs of Red Republicanism and its kindred tares. An easier solution of the problem is found in the advanced intelligence of our slave population, who are, in some respects, not a whit behind the operatives of Lancashire. When the blacks cease to be profitable in the field we can transfer them to the workshops; and the more elaborate the fabric the more minute the subdivision of labor—the easier will be the management of the race, the less the danger from the thievish propensities of this peculiar people. Everybody knows, although everybody seems determined to blink at the disagreeable fact, that of late years all the higher order of slaves, such as domestic servants and mechanics, have been bent on the acquisition of money, which they either hoard with senseless avarice or spend with reckless profusion. Hence we have said that such slave labor as may not be profitable in agricultural or domestic servitude should be employed in those manufactures which require a variety of independent processes, rather than in the more simple handicrafts for which alone Negro operatives have been deemed fit. At all events, the capacity of the Negro race for manufacturing operations, not simply for the heavy work of the foundry and the flouring mill, but for the production of delicate fabrics of every kind, deserves a series of careful experiments at the hands of those who wish on the one hand to see our system of slavery perpetuated and developed, and on the other to prevent the rise of a mere mechanical class; which, by its license, its half education, its narrow views, its low moral standard, has endangered every form of free government, and has always proved the worst foe to social order.

Even the corrupt governments of the Old World recognize and admit the claims of labor, and encourage industry in all possible ways, but this stupid editor is of opinion that when the war is over, and if their leaders had succeeded in their attempts, they would have been able to do as they choose with white mechanics. The tone of the extracts is worthy of notice by all artisans. They have reason to thank themselves that in the society they live, respectable mechanics are as much honored and esteemed as the highest officials in the land.

35

The New National Mind

Harper's New Monthly Magazine

The nation was becoming rich to an enormous extent, and in the ten years from 1850 to 1860, the estimated cash value of farms under cultivation had gone up from $3,271,575,426 to $6,645,045,007, an increase of 103 per cent in ten years. The amount of capital invested in farm implements and machinery in 1860 was $246,118,141, being an increase of over ninety-four millions in ten years, or more than 63 per cent; while our population during that period increased only at the rate of 35.5 per cent. Something is said of the training, the practical training, of the mind of our people in thought as well as toil, by the fact that the manufacture of farm implements in 1860 amounted to $17,487,960—an increase of 160 per cent in ten years on the whole, and of 325.05 per cent in the Western States. The South concerned itself little with this enterprise and its important educational bearings. . . . and slavery could not make the South very winning to the inventors and workmen who have so thriven in the regions of liberty where labor is so much respected and in such close relations with thought and public spirit.

The war found our people busy with their immense work of agriculture, mechanism, and commerce; and bent upon money-making as never before. The great conflict did not take them from their activity, but changed its field or its motive, and put a grand national enthusiasm into the place of their industrial utilitarianism. Everywhere throughout the Free States they had been learning to put mind into material implements; and iron, brass, wood, leather, and stone were made servants of thought. Their vast mechanical force stood ready to pass from the arts of peace to the arts of war; and plows, reapers, mowers, spindles, lathes, engines, furnaces, rolling-mills, foundries, seemed to rush like living creatures to arms, at the call of our President, and to fight against the rebellion, as the stars in their courses fought against Sisera. They clothed and fed our army, made our bridges and roads, furnished swords, muskets, and cannon of unexampled excellence, and sent forth against the insurgents a navy that startled the world, and made every resource of invention and science tell in the

"New Aspects of the American Mind," *Harper's New Monthly Magazine* (New York, May, 1867), Vol. 34, pp. 795-800.

triumphs of our flag upon the sea. So it was that a new life went into the fields and work-shops, and even when the old kinds of work were done they were done with new motive, and great thought and purposes went into the day's patient toil. The industrial arts that had made our people strong, docile, and persistent, and had saved them from the braggart indolence of the insurgents who had so boasted of being owners of men and masters of their labor, now rose into heroic grandeur. Our giant servitors stood by us in time of need, while the minions of the slave lords deserted them in time of need. The American mind that had gone into mechanism did a great deal to give us the victory, and Franklin, Fulton, Erricson, and their peers and disciples, were but representatives of the intellect of the nation in its great industrial work.

I remember one day, after a good deal of depression at public disaster, visiting a large cluster of work-shops that gathered round a huge steam-engine, not far from Harper's printing-house. I went down into the basement, and there saw the giant plower lifting and dropping his ponderous shaft, and turning all those machines by his great force. The workmen in a mood of grim humor had put little flags upon his great head and arms, and the monster seemed to be alive with patriotism. The sight was most suggestive and encouraging. I could have cried for joy or sung hallelujahs to the Lord of Hosts, for all was clear then. There, and everywhere through the loyal States, was that same mighty force working for us—the Providential arm of this nineteenth century, whose mission it is to organize liberty by law and put the old tyranny under its feet.

Our people were perhaps as busy in 1860 as since, and that enormous product of the year, $18,000,000 of manufacture, shows something of what they were about. But since then their labor has taken a different turn, and breathed a different spirit. The dominant idea was then private or individual, and our people were bent upon money-getting and awake to every opportunity of bettering their fortunes under the mighty spur of equal competition that so quickens every impulse and faculty, and brings all energies into play. We are not to despise this motive, nor to say that the new patriotism made our people unmindful of private thrift. Getting a living in America is of itself an education, for it is ever opening new fields, courting ever-changing chances, and breaking up mental stagnation. But now new incentives came, and even the contractors who went for large profits could not but carry a certain enthusiasm into their schemes, and catch something of the sacred passion that cares for the flag for itself, not merely for the money that its success secures. With the people at large public spirit entered into their private business as well as their military enterprise, and the war was a popular education as well as a national drill. All the lines of industry turned toward the one centre; and at heart the whole loyal people worked or studied, marched or sailed under the brave old banner of the Union. Our Yankee utilitarianism took an ideal turn, and thrift caught fire at the flaming altar of patriotism. The women and children knit stockings and scraped lint; the men plowed and reaped, sawed and hammered, planned and built, when they did not fight for the nation.

It is an important question how far this six or seven years' schooling has told upon the habitual working of the American mind, and made of us a new and better people; and especially if it has acted upon us in the higher plane of thought. It is very clear that our affections have been brought into our patriotism as never before, and we never knew how much we could love our country until it was in peril, and not only one sheep but the whole flock seemed in danger of being lost among the deep valleys or dark mountains. . . . Consider the effect of our great armies upon the national mind in this one respect, the training of our people to look upon the whole country, alike the land and the people, in the light of their intense solicitude and personal affinities. . . . Our affections go into our historical studies, and we read of the old revolutionary times, and the old Constitutional debates as parts of our own family history, or as bearing on the pedigree and title-deeds of ourselves and our children. So we have all studied the country by heart, and are so studying it still; and we know it more and better by this recent schooling than from our whole lifetime before.

How vast must be the power of our great armies, alike by their sufferings and victories, their absence and return, their lives and deaths, to bring the nation and its history and prospects home to us all! The army rolls number 2,653,062 men in the aggregate, which, reduced to the three years' standard, number 2,129,041; and, with due allowance for re-enlistments, we have not far from two millions of men mustered into service, and most of them carrying the hearts of others with them to the war. . . . Now those millions are absorbed in the nation, and our army numbers only some 50,000 men.

We have certainly far more pathos and sentiment in our habitual temper than before, as also far more humor and courage. It cannot be that the great conflict has failed to educate our intellect to higher thinking and aspiration. Americans have always had a certain ideal as well as emotional tendency; and the great response given to such apostles of faith as Wesley and his brethren, and the strong-hold that Jonathan Edwards and his Puritan scholasticism has so long maintained over our more orthodox clergy and churches, and the wide influence of Channing and his school of Christian Humanists upon the opinion of our leading Liberals, are ample proof that we are by no means a plodding nation of utilitarians, whose god is the belly or the purse. Yet the public habit of our people has been somewhat utilitarian; and Franklin, alike in his sagacity and his narrowness, has been too much the master of our public councils. Our statutes and debates have taken it too much for granted that our Government is in the main a business partnership for the security of property and life, and that it is airy enthusiasm to speak of God and the Supreme good in Congress or Cabinets. Faith and ideas we had, but we were doubtful as to their connection with civil affairs; and that pattern of conservative Americanism, James Buchanan, seems to have thought it wholly out of place to apply the test of conscience, humanity, and religion to the slave question and the enormous pretensions of the slave power. Of course we are not to accuse Franklin of any such degradation, for he was a thorough Liberal, and strong in the free temper of the eighteenth century; but he was not a man of the nineteenth century—not a representative of its spiritual convictions, its personal independence and intuition, and its broad catholicity. We, as a people, were becoming dissatisfied with his utilitarian school of thinking, but had not carried our protest out into action.

More and more we felt the power of ideal principles, and more and more lamented the great gulf between our principles and our policy and our politicians. We believed in the supreme worth of man with Wesley, Edwards, and Channing, and we followed Webster and Clay, and even Pierce and Buchanan, who taught that those things that have been must be, and gave little if any hope of redemption. All this was changed by the war and its sequel, and mainly by the act of the enemy, that forced the issue of arms that we accepted but never originated. Our ideal thinking is now in the line of our manifest destiny, and the Declaration of Independence is incorporated into the Constitution of the nation. Liberty is now not an abstraction, but an institution; not a speculative idea, but a legal fact; not an imaginative notion, but a constructive power. Our great thinkers and sages in literature now need no expurgation at the North or the South, and we read the grand visions of the ages in the clear light of to-day. The whole horizon indeed is not clear, but the principle is undoubted; and in that principle the nation finds rest, and takes it not from man but from God— from His Eternal Word that calls us all to one Sonship; and from His Eternal Spirit that offers to all the one glorious liberty of His children.

The exclusion of certain classes from full civil liberty is nothing against the certainty of the principle, for the exclusion is only temporary, and as a punishment for treason; and as such it proves the rule of loyal privilege. The temporary exclusion of the traitorous classes is in order to secure the results of the strife, and to make universal freedom the birth-right of the whole nation. Never before was a moral principle so mightily asserted by so great a nation through such struggles and sacrifices. The fact cannot but inspire the intelligence of the people, and tell upon our popular thinking and rising literature. It is eminently proof of the mind of the many, and has not been the work of any dominant thinker. We have had no great man to lead us, no Washington, Franklin, Hamilton or Madison to guide us from the beginning, or even to tell us what was likely to happen. Our most prominent statesman, our Secretary of State, did not ride the whirlwind and direct the storm, but rather tried to ignore or prevent the uprising. Our literary and political *doctrinaires*, who urged the idea of universal liberty and called slavery barbarism, never had any great weight with the nation at large, and were very sectional in their affinities and often unheroic in their temper. The representative man of the eventful years, our martyred President, rather followed than led the nation; and saw the hand of Providence in events as they came rather than in prophetic visions that claimed authority over events in the name of God. He learned his lesson of statesmanship of God and the times; he said it to the people and the army; and then died, struck by a foul hand that wrote its own doom and the doom of its rebel crew; and raised the victim into the triumphant martyr whose name is one forever with liberty now.

We have had no great intellectual leader, and God clearly means that the nation shall be great and the mind of America shall be imperial and not depend upon any one chief who may imperil its dignity or tempt it to servility. Noble men we have had, indeed, who have helped to form the national thought—preachers, moralists, historians, journalists, poets, orators, statesmen, philosophers—but the mind of the nation is greater than them all; and refusing to follow the lead of any of them when swerving from the path of principle, it walks the way of God's Providence and is open to the call of His Spirit, true to its convictions with a calm decision, that no veering President or truckling Secretary of State, no wavering popular preacher or wily editor, can shake. May we not say that the nation has not only won more light, but deeper visions, and shown a power of *insight* more precious than the shrewd *sight* that has so long been its boast and sometimes its danger. We have been quick at inductive reasoning from facts to general rules, and have been no dull scholars in tracing natural phenomena to their cause or principle. Now our people have learned the higher wisdom of intuition and deduction, and starting from great principles in clear insight, they are deducing from their just consequence; and our national life is opening into the upper sphere of thought, and primal ideas are lighting us on to our daily work. We are not losing our old inductive prudence, but allying it with deductive wisdom; and we who have been learning to go from fact to principles are now learning, as never before, to go from principles to fact. Our popular opinion, that was before great but somewhat nebulous, has become settled and clarified, its nebula has been consolidated into a globe, and its haze has flamed into a shining start.

The American intellect has thus won and matured the two leading elements of sagacity or sound judgment, comprehensiveness and point. We have learned to look about us and see men and things as never before, and also to trace out their bearing upon the main point. So, too, we have learned to go from the main point to the subordinate particulars, and argue from the sacred idea of the nation to its proper work and manifest destiny. We have believed that the God of our fathers has called us to organize liberty in this nineteenth century, and that this is the American's mission, and ought to be his inspiration. We may not all nor generally be fully conscious of this conviction, but it is none the less real, and is constantly coming out in the thought and legislation of the country. It is not a private opinion, but a universal truth, and as such it is taking possession of our schools, legislatures, literature, and churches, and becoming the tacit principle when it is not the open assurance of the general mind, never so much so as in this spring of the year 1867, which rounds the seven years since secession dared to show its head at the Convention in Charleston, and John C. Breckinridge was set up as the predestined leader of the pro-slavery Democracy in the political campaign that was to call Abraham Lincoln to the Presidency.

When we turn to the active elements of the American mind, or take the *dynamic* view of its recent training, its aspects are quite as memorable. We are seeing the results of the heroism of their schooling as well as of its thinking. We have been all along well aware that our people were doing a great many things with a versatility and pluck unknown before even in America; and that they have learned to do them, moreover, with a certain bearing upon the great work of saving the nation, and with much help from the master motive, the public spirit or national will that has been so marvelously drawn out and exalted; but it has not been clear to us what the end would be, or how much of the war heroism would be carried into the new age of peace. What a vision of human activity opens to us in those years of conflict, that immense change of effort in our millions of workers from the arts of peace to the arts of war, and their return to the old paths of regular industry! How much the millions did who worked for the nation at home, and how much the millions did and dared and suffered who went to the field! Fancy fails to paint the picture of all the work-shops, ship-yards, foundries, those marches, camps, hospitals, forts, fleets, and fields. It is easier to tell what our people have not done than what they have done; for there is little within the power of the human will, either in its might or its mercy, that has not been done in our America within these late years. Think of the withdrawal of two millions of men from the eight millions of industrial workers for military service, and then of their return to the old ways with so much new observation, experience and incentive. We were laughed at as a people who were up to doing anything and everything, the universal Yankee nation, every man a Jack-at-all-trades, able to farm or fish, preach or plead or physic, keep store or school, and what not. Now that we can do more than ever, and have done the one thing most essential, we are not laughed at as of old, and the nations of Europe seem to think that our versatility of fingers really amounts to something that they would like to have.

The main fact in our dynamic training, however, is not that our people have done so many things in their separate crafts and spheres, but that they have done them with a common motive and in a heroic temper. The national work has come from and strengthened a great national will; and the question is, what is to become of this national will now that the occasion that stirred and formed it is over? A superficial philosophy might easily suppose that the martial spirit would cease with the war, and the heroism of the people would end with their return home and sheathing their swords and laying aside their muskets; but a deeper wisdom proves to us that the heroic will is as steadfast as the earnest intellect, and our courage perpetuates its habit as stoutly as our thinking does. The war is, we hope, for once only, but the war power is forever; and the military bill that is now the law of the land needs comparatively little actual force to carry it into execution, because the war power is known to be a fixed fact; and the transgressors will beware of waking the sleeping lion, because they know full well that he is the lion, and can easily show his teeth when provoked. Very interesting and instructive it is to study what may be called the dynamic history of nations, and trace out the evolution of heroic powers that are as enduring as dominant ideas. There are virtues, like truths, "that wake to perish never"; and such, we trust, is the destiny of that heroism that has risen in this country among our people, who were forced into civil war simply because they would not consent to extend the area of slavery. The heroic power is not a mere impulse or private volition, but a moving of the national life in its universal sphere, and is like one of those heavings of the earth from the great central fire that send up the everlasting hills, and open within them living springs that never fail to pour down their healing and refreshing and fertilizing waters. The upheaving is once, but the mountains and the streams are forever. Divine as well as human agencies move this great purpose, and all earnest patriots know that the movement is not theirs alone, and believe that God has stirred this great purpose, which is as much an inspiration as a resolve, and which rises into religious dignity, and sings in our hymns and speaks in our prayers. It possesses us more than we possess it. We feel it whenever we hear a drum beat, or a bugle sound, or a cannon roar; we see it whenever our sacred banner lifts aloft its stars upon our forts, or is borne through the streets by stout and loyal arms.

There is, of course, much of our alleged patriotism that is a human feeling, and perhaps a party passion, or local impulse, or sectional animosity; but who will say, after these years of sacrifice, that such has been the character of our national will? Must we not say that the strength of the people has been trained like its intelligence under the discipline of Providence, and that as its intelligence has learned range and point, deductive sequence as well as inductive breadth, so the public will has learned versatility, persistence, and unity, and has been trained not only to do many things for the one good cause, but to do them from the central and commanding motive, and press forward into every field of action in a brave purpose that is deductive as well as inductive, in an industry that covers all spheres, and a heroism that lifts over them all the same flag, and puts into them all the same flaming love of country. The form of the heroic purpose will change with the times; but we must not wonder that it keeps its militant temper so long as the results of the war are in peril, and the slave powers persist in assailing the first principles of our republican government, and threatening the liberty and even the life of Union citizens.

Our new idealism is not a doctrinaire speculation but a far-sighted sagacity; and asks to walk its open path with sufficient power. Its open eye demands the quick foot and the strong and ready hand. As in the Berkeleyan theory of vision, it helps sight by touch, and measures distances and judges substances by muscular action as well as nervous sense. It is clear that we are adding power to ideas as never before, and our thought is becoming dynamic as well as ideal, and muscle is allying itself with mind. We are making the dynamic estimate of men and things, and after so long and many disappointments at mere reputations and professions, we are quietly asking what men and measures will do the work needed, and coolly guiding our conduct by the result. This temper has kept our people from all rash extremes, and put them upon the path of discretion and courage. The President has not been impeached, nor has his dictation been followed; the States in rebellion have not been overrun or destroyed, nor have their rebel leaders been allowed to resume their power. A very shrewd judgment has been brought to bear upon the rash partisans of either faction, and there are no signs of our yielding to the pretensions of any dictator, whether of the White House or the Capitol. We have learned in a very costly school to discern the limitations of human characters and abilities; to use men for what they can do, without expecting them to do everything; and to admit a certain amount of imperfection without contempt or proscription. We have taken the measure of our President, his coadjutors, and his antagonists, and have not lost our temper or our principle in our likes or dislikes. We have given the President the full swing of his notions, impulses, and rhetoric, and allowed him to pass from fever heat to moderate coolness on the great questions at issue. He is evidently a calmer if not a wiser man than a year ago, and has made up his mind that he is not the only head in the nation or the Government. He has been treated in the main, and especially of late, with much dignity; and the lesson has not been lost upon his somewhat irascible nature. The people are seeing that Andrew Jackson is his model, and that he has not added any essential idea to the Old Hickory Platform; and has accepted emancipation more as a necessary circumstance than an essential principle. He has gone considerably forward, but not upward; he has advanced somewhat, but not grown much; and finds it hard to believe that the people have outgrown him, and that new days have come to the nation that call for new measures and men. Many who think his ideas of constitutional law right in themselves give him the benefit of this judgment, while they think him wholly wrong in overlooking the demands of the political situation, and not admitting the necessity of putting the rebel States upon probation until they are fitted to resume the old privileges and functions. There is no aspect of our political history more instructive and cheering than the bearing of our Congress and our people toward the Chief Magistrate, who holds the office by a calamity, and whose policy is an offense to the reason and conscience of the nation. The people have kept cool, and threatened as little as they have boasted. The conviction of possessing substantial power has given them sobriety and moderation; and they do not blow the trumpet either to keep their courage up or to tell the world that they are not afraid. . . .

The same cool sagacity that has marked our political temper and our military policy appears in our relation to the freedmen. Our people have not lost their wits in rapture for the Negro's emancipation or in disgust at his new prerogative. They take the humane and kindly, but still the sternly practical view of him, and weigh and measure him carefully. The Negro's status depends upon what he can do, and it is clear that a race that takes freedom so mildly and seeks instruction and keeps at work so signally, is a substantial power of the nation. The nearly two millions of bales of cotton of the year 1866 speak volumes for the Negroes' sobriety and industry, and should relieve the nation from all fear as to their future development under liberty, union, education, and religion.

Exactly what is to come within the next few years we do not profess to say. It is safe to say, however, that the national life will gain vigor and unity, and that the central power will demand the fullest local liberty and action compatible with the preservation of the Union; and with this reconciliation of interests, a new day of reconciled feeling and enterprise will come. Hatred too much there has been and still is; but not between those who have been most active in the contest; and our soldiers have not found it hard to give their hand to their old enemies as soon as they laid down their arms and owned one country. In time the dominant ideas and interests will pervade the ruling elements even of the seceded States; and before the year 1876, the centennial of our national life, comes round, we may hope to be one people, with one mind and heart.

When we are most disturbed by the willfulness and passion of the seceding States and their apparently stubborn determination never to assimilate with us in thought and feeling, even when they return fully to their old place in the Union, we must not forget that there is an older element than secession and slavery in their blood. Of old the leading Southerners looked forward to the extinction of slavery, and were hearty friends of the arts, sciences, and letters, that are the glory of free States. The time was when Charleston was in advance of New York in culture and taste, and Virginia excelled New England and even Massachusetts in champions of philosophical liberalism. Blood always tells, and often the grandfather reappears in the features and temperament of the grandchild. Already there are some note-worthy facts that prove the affinity of the Southern mind with our Northern education, and the desire of an important class to share our literary privileges before they are restored to their political status. The leading importer of German books in this city assures me that the largest orders for rare works of Oriental learning, especially for Sanscrit literature, are from the South, and the love for such books, which was so baffled by the war, seems now to have come out with new fervor. Many indications show that before what we call essential comforts are secured, there are Southern scholars that crave the nurture of good learning, and care more for a rare book than for a rare dish; and our soldiers agree in testifying to the remarkable taste for libraries, painting, sculpture, and artistic gardens in the Old Southern States. Of course popular education can never thrive under slave institutions, with their contempt for labor and the common lot; but the fact may be none the less real, that back of the new cotton interest that made the South cling to slavery as the corner-stone of its wealth, there was an old and generous spirit of letters and civilization that has never died out, and by the law of historical continuity must in some way revive.

I attended not long ago a most interesting meeting of the American Academy of Science in Boston, and saw the Rumford Gold Medal presented by the President, Dr. Gray, to Mr. Alvan Clarke of Cambridge for the best telescope ever yet made, the object-glass being eighteen inches in diameter —three inches larger than the diameter of the object-glass at Cambridge. The story of Mr. Clarke's labors in making his peerless lenses was most instructive and interesting. He began the work over twenty years ago with his son, as a kind of boys' play, and he naïvely said that it had been to him boys' play ever since. It was a note-worthy fact that this object-glass was ordered by a college in the State of Mississippi before the war, and was of course left on the maker's hands after the war broke out. While the slow dignitaries of Cambridge were raising the money to secure the prize, and had subscribed $4,500 for this gem, more precious in radiance than the Koh-i-noor diamond, that mountain of light, Chicago, that is becoming in public spirit the *hub* of the West, and perhaps of the whole Union, paid the $11,000 down at once, and had the lens mounted fitly into the best telescope ever known to the world. Let the South have the benefit of originating this work, and it is the first step that costs; though in this case the cost that followed came out of Northern pockets. Such facts show dispositions, and hint of a time when a true ambition will bring the Southern mind into the great fellowship of American education; and its pro-slavery metaphysics shall give place to the true philosophy of America and the nineteenth century of organized liberty and law.

The noble bequest of George Peabody is a forerunner of the good times of intellectual and moral comity between North and South. A friend who was present at the meeting in Washington for organizing the government of that benefaction says that after the business was done, the venerable Bishop of Ohio proposed that all present unite in prayer for the blessing of God upon the enterprise, and all knelt down—men of all sections, parties, and creeds—and implored the grace of Heaven upon the work. Such acts are not vain, and carry good fellowship wherever they are known, and sow the seed of future charity and wisdom.

One thing, however, is very clear, and must be stated with all distinctness. The Southern mind is fond of power, and fascinated alike by its possession and its possessors. It thought that the power of the future was with itself and its institutions; and the more thoroughly this idea is rooted out so much the better for the South and the whole nation. It is well, then, that the country has so decidedly settled the question of the supremacy of the Government; and the Military Bill will in its principal features prove more attractive to the convalescent rebel madmen than any half-way measures of conciliation. The essential point to be urged is that the nation is the sovereign power; and that power will soon become as fascinating and commanding to the Southern temper as it has been repulsive. When the Southern people come loyally under the flag, and use their great energies for the good of the country, for its wealth and peace at home, and for its honor abroad, the old fellowship will return, and all disabling and exclusive legislation will cease. Americans are a generous people, and never was such a war waged with so little vengeance on the part of the conquerors. We may have decision without bigotry; strength without cruelty; and may be assured that by the time we celebrate the jubilee of our national life in 1876 the sovereign power of the Union will be the liberty and prosperity of all the States.

PART VII

RECONSTRUCTION

The purpose of the Civil War was reconstruction. It was against the possibility of reconstruction that the Southern States seceded, it was against the reconstruction of a new nation in place of the Old Federal Union that critics protested. It was in one phase of reconstruction that new economic forces came into play, and it was only as one aspect of reconstruction that new concepts came to dominate the American mind. Throughout the war, and for a dozen years after the end of armed conflict, problems of reconstruction dominated politics, and economics, and social organization.

There was no doubt in the minds of the victors that the Northern concept of the new nation must be extended to the South. But the means of the extension were the occasion of fresh and bitter conflicts. Andrew Johnson and his Congress quarreled over political readjustments both in the national Government and in the States. There was confusion of ideas and ideals, corruption in government and in business, divided councils on the social adjustment of races in the South. The complications of reconstruction were greater than those of the war itself, and the form of the new nation would but slowly emerge from the epoch of the Civil War and its aftermath.

36

Northern Invasions

E. E. Hale

Northern invasions, when successful, advance the civilization of the world.

It would not be difficult to present from all history a mass of illustrations of this thesis well-nigh sufficient in themselves to establish it. And there is no doubt that the principles of human nature, which appear in those illustrations, can be set in such order as to prove the thesis beyond a question. The softness of Southern climate produces, in the long run, gentleness, effeminacy, and indolence, or passionate rather than persevering effort. It produces, again, the palliatives or disguises of these traits which are found in formal religions, and in institutions of caste or slavery. The rigor of Northern climate produces, on the other hand, in the long run, hardy physical constitutions among men, with determined individuality of character. It produces, therefore, freedom even to democracy in politics, protestantism even to rationalism in religion, and grim perseverance even to the bitter end in war. A certain stern morality, often amounting to asceticism, is imposed on Northern constitutions. . . . Nobody pretends, of course, that war itself does anything final in the advance of civilization. . . .

War, in itself, does nothing but plough—but immediately on the end of the war, in any locality, he who succeeds begins on the harrowing and the planting. And because God is, and directs all such affairs, it is wonderful to see how short is the June which in His world covers all such furrows as His ploughmen make with new beauty. It is to the methods of that new harvest that the President has boldly led our attention in his admirable Proclamation of Amnesty. It is to the details of it that each loyal man has to look already. . . .

The President, with courage which does him infinite honor, leads the

E. E. HALE, "Northern Invasions," *Atlantic Monthly* (Boston, February, 1864), Vol. 13, pp. 245-250.

Lincoln's Proclamation of Amnesty and Reconstruction, in December, 1863, offered to recognize State governments in the South which had been organized by ten per cent of the voters of 1860. The President's political opponents saw in the proposal a scheme for making "rotten boroughs," under Lincoln's control, in the South. Some of his supporters saw opportunities for extending both Northern culture and Northern economic organization to the area.

way to this future. His Proclamation is really a rallying-cry to all true men and women, whether they are living at the North or at the South, to take hold and work for its accomplishment. With an army posted in each of the revolted States, with more than one of them completely under national control, he considers that the time for planting has come. He is no such idealist or sentimentalist as to leave these new-made furrows, so terribly torn up in three years of war, to renew their own verdure by any mere spontanous vegetation.

Practical as the President always is, he is sublimely practical in the Proclamation. "Let us make good out of this evil as quickly as we can," he says; "let peace bring in plenty as quickly as she can." To bring this about, he promises the strong arm of the nation to protect anything which shall show itself worth protecting, in the way of social institutions of republican liberty. He does not ask, like a conqueror, for the keys of a capital. He does not ask, like a Girondist, for the vote of a majority. He knows, it is true, as all the world knows, that, if the vote of all the men of the South could ever be obtained, the majority would utterly overshadow the handful of gentry who have been lording it over white trash and black slaves together. But the President has no wish to prolong the martial law to that indefinite future when this handful of gentlemen shall let the majority of their own people pronounce upon their claims to rule them. Waiving the requisites of the theorists, and at the same time relieving himself from the necessity of employing military power a moment longer than is necessary, he announces, in advance, what will be his policy in extending protection to loyal governments formed in Rebel States. If there can be found in any State enough righteous men willing to take the oath of allegiance and to sustain the nation in its determination for emancipation—if there can be found only enough to be counted up as the tenth part of those who voted in the election of 1860, though their States should have sinned like Gomorrah, even though its name should be South Carolina, they shall be permitted to reconstruct its government, and that government shall be recognized by the Government of the nation.

It is true that this gift is vastly more than any of the Rebel States has any right to claim. . . . If the nation were contending against real and permanent enemies, in reducing to order the States of the Confederacy, or if the national feeling towards the people of those States were the bitter feeling which their leaders profess towards our people, the nation would, of course, offer no such easy terms. The nation would say, "When you threw off the Constitution, you did it for better or for worse. It guaranteed to you your State governments. You spurned the guaranty. Let it be so. Let the guaranty be withdrawn. You cannot sustain them. Let them go, then. You have destroyed them. And the nation governs you by proconsuls." But the nation has no such desire to deal harshly with these people. The nation knows that more than half of them were never regarded as people at home—that they had no more to do with the Rebellion than had the oxen with which they labored. The nation knows that of the rest of the Southern people literally only a handful professed power in the State. The nation knows, therefore, that what pretended to be a union of republics was, really, to take Gouverneur Morris's phrase, a union of republics with oligarchies—seventeen republics united to fourteen oligarchies, when this thing began. The nation knows that the fourteen will be happier, stronger, more prosperous than ever, when their people have the rights of which they are partly conscious— when they also become republics. The nation means to carry out the constitutional guaranty, and give them the republican government which under the Constitution belongs to every State in the Union. The nation looks forward to prosperous centuries, in which these States, with these people and the descendants of these people, shall be united in one nation with the republics which have been true to the nation. For all these reasons the nation has no thought of insisting on its rights as against Rebel States. It has no thunders of vengeance except for those who have led in these iniquities. For the people who have been misled it has pardon, protection, encouragement, and hope. It can afford to be generous. And at the President's hands it makes the offer which will be received.

We say this offer will be received. We know very well the difficulty with which an opinion long branded with ignominy makes head in countries where there is no press, where there is no free speech, where there are no large cities. Excepting Louisiana, the Southern States have none of these. And the "peculiar institutions" throw the control of what is called opinion more completely into the hands of a very small class of men, we might almost say a very small knot of men, than in any other oligarchy which we remember in modern history. It is in considering this very difficulty that we recognize the wisdom of the President's Proclamation. He is conscious of the difficulty, and has placed his minimum of loyal inhabitants at a very low point, that, even in the hardest cases, there may be a possibility of meeting his requisition.

It is not true, on the other hand, that he has placed his minimum so low as to involve the Government in any difficulty in sustaining the State governments which will be framed at his call. It must be remembered that this "tenth part" of righteous men will have very strong allies in every Southern State. It is confessed, on all hands, that they will be supported by all the Negroes in every State. Just in proportion to what was the strength of the planting interest is its weakness in the new order of things. Given such physical force, given the moral and physical strength which comes with national protection, and given the immense power which belongs to the wish for peace, and the "tenth part" will soon find its fraction becoming larger and more respectable by accretions at home and by emigration from other States. We shall soon learn that there is next to nobody who really favored this thing in the beginning. They will tell us that they all stood for their old State flag, and that they will be glad to stand for it in its new hands.

It will be only the first step that will cost. Everybody sees this. The President sees it. Mr. Davis sees it. He hopes nobody will take it. We hope a good many people will. The merit of the President's plan is that this step can be promptly taken. And so many are the openings by which national feeling now addresses the people of the States in revolt, and national men can call on them to express their real opinions and to act in their real interest, that we hope to see it taken in many places at the same time. . . .

Take, for instance, this magnificent Florida, our own Italy—if one can conceive of an Italy where till now men have been content to live a half-civilized life, only because the oranges grew to their hands, and there was no necessity for toil. The vote of Florida in 1860 was 14,347. So soon as in Florida one-tenth part of this number, or 1,435 men, take the oath of allegiance to the National Government, so soon, if they have the qualifications of electors under Florida law, shall we have a loyal State in Florida. It will be a Free State, offering the privileges of a Free State to the eager eyes of the North and of Europe. That valley of the St. John's, with its wealth of lumber—the even climate of the western shore—the navy-yard to be re-established at Pensacola—the commerce to be resumed at Jacksonville—the Nice which we will build up for our invalids at St. Augustine—the orange-groves which are wasting their sweetness at this moment, on the plantations and the islands—will all be so many temptations to the emigrant, as soon as work is honorable in Florida. If the people who gave 5,437 votes for Bell and 357 for Douglas cannot furnish 1,435 men to establish this new State government, we here know who can.

"Armies composed of freemen conquer for themselves, not for their leaders." This is the happy phrase of Robertson, as he describes the re-establishment of society in Europe after the great Northern invasions, which gave new life to Roman effeminacy, and new strength to Roman corruption. The phrase is perfectly true. It is as true of the armies of freemen who have been called to the South now to keep the peace as it was of the armies of freemen who were called South then by the imbecility of Roman emperors or their mutual contentions. The lumbermen from Maine and New Hampshire who have seen the virgin riches of the St. John's, like the Massachusetts volunteers who have picked out their farms in the valley of the Shenandoah or established in prospect their forges on the falls of the Potomac, or like the Illinois regiments who have been introduced to the valleys of Tennessee or of Arkansas, will furnish men enough, well skilled in political systems, to start the new republics, in regions which have never known what a true republic was till now.

To carry out the President's plan, and to give us once more working State governments in the States which have rebelled—to give them, indeed the first true republican governments they have ever known—would require for Virginia about 12,000 voters. They can be counted, we suppose, at this moment, in the counties under our military control. Indeed, the loyal State government of Virginia is at this moment organized. In North Carolina it would require 9,500 voters. The loyal North Carolina regiments are an evidence that that number of home-grown men will readily appear. In South Carolina, to give a generous estimate, we need 5,000 voters. It is the only State which we never heard any man wish to emigrate to. It is the hardest region, therefore, of any to redeem. At the worst, till the 5,000 appear, the new Georgia will be glad to govern all the country south of the Santee, and the new North Carolina what is north thereof. Georgia will need 10,000 loyal voters. There are more than that number now encamped upon her soil, willing to stay there. Of Florida we have spoken. Alabama requires 9,000. They have been hiding away from conscription; they have been fleeing into Kentucky and Ohio: they will not be unwilling to reappear when the inevitable "first step" is taken. For Mississippi we want 7,000. Mr. Reverdy Johnson has told us where they are. For Louisiana, one tenth is 5,000. More than that number voted in the elections which returned the sitting members to Congress. For Texas, the proportion is 6,200; for Arkansas, 5,400. Those States are already giving account of themselves. In Tennessee the fraction required is 14,500. And as the people of Knoxvill said, "They could do that in the mountains alone."

We have no suspicion of a want of latent Southern loyalty. But we have brought together these figures to show how inevitable is a reconstruction on the President's plan, even if Southern loyalty were as abject and timid as some men try to persuade us. These figures show us, that, if, of the million Northern men who have "prospected" the Southern country, in the march of victorious armies, only seventy-three thousand determine to take up their future lot there, and to establish there free institutions, they would be enough, without the help of one native, to establish these republican institutions in all the Rebel States. The deserted plantations, the farms offered for sale, almost for nothing, all the attractions of a softer climate, and all the just pride which makes the American fond of founding empires, are so many incentives to the undertaking of the great initiative proposed. In the cases of Virginia and Tennessee, and, as we suppose, of Louisiana, Arkansas, and Texas, the beginning has already been made at home. In Florida a recent meeting at Fernandina gave promise for a like beginning. If it do not begin there, the Emigrant Aid Company must act at once to give the beginning. There will remain the Carolinas and three of the Gulf States. The ploughing is not over there, and it is not time therefore to speak of the harvest. For the rest, we hope we have said enough to indicate to the ready and active men of the nation where their great present duty lies.

37

Beckoning Fields of Cotton

Thomas W. Knox

When General Grant encamped his army at Milliken's Ben and Young's Point, preparatory to commencing the siege of Vicksburg, many of the cotton plantations were abandoned by their owners. . . . leaving the plantations and the Negroes to the tender mercy of the invaders. In some cases the fugitives took the Negroes with them, thus leaving the plantations entirely deserted.

When the Negroes remained, and the plantations were not supplied with provisions, it became necessary for the Commissary Department to issue rations for the subsistance of the blacks. As nearly all the planters cared nothing for the Negroes they had abandoned, there was a very large number that required the attention of the Government.

On many plantations the cotton crop of 1862 was still in the field, somewhat damaged by the winter rains; but well worth gathering at the prices which then ruled the market. General Grant gave authority for the gathering of this cotton by any parties who were willing to take the contract. There was no lack of men to undertake the collection of abandoned cotton on these terms, as the enterprise could not fail to be exceedingly remunerative.

This cotton, gathered by Government authority, was, with a few exceptions, the only cotton which could be shipped to market. There were large quantities of "old" cotton—gathered and bailed in previous years—which the owners were anxious to sell, and speculators ready to buy. Numerous applications were made for shipping-permits, but nearly all were rejected. A few cases were pressed upon General Grant's attention, as deserving exception from the ordinary rule.

There was one case of two young girls, whose parents had recently died, and who were destitute of all comforts on the plantation where they lived. They had a quantity of cotton which they wished to take to Memphis, for

THOMAS W. KNOX, *Campfire and Cotton-field: Southern Adventure in Time of War* (Philadelphia, 1865), Chs. xxix, xxx, xxxvii, xlii, xlvi.

Knox, a New York *Herald* reporter in Missouri at the outbreak of the war, covered the first part of the war in Kansas. In 1863 he leased a plantation in Louisiana. His experiences and observations threw significant light on one economic aspect of reconstruction.

sale in that market. Thus provided with money, they would proceed north, and remain there till the end of the war.

A speculator became interested in these girls, and pleaded with all his eloquence for official favor in their behalf. General Grant softened his heart and gave this man a written permit to ship whatever cotton belonged to the orphans. It was understood, and so stated in the application, that the amount was between two hundred and three hundred bales. The exact number not being known, there was no quantity specified in the permit.

The speculator soon discovered that the penniless orphans could claim two thousand instead of two hundred bales, and thought it possible they would find three thousand bales and upward. . . .

Immediately, as this transaction became known, every speculator was on the *qui vive* to discover a widow or an orphan. Each plantation was visited, and the status of the owners, if any remained, became speedily known. Orphans and widows, the former in particular, were at a high premium. Never in the history of Louisiana did the children of tender years, bereft of parents, receive such attention from strangers. . . . Everywhere in that region there were men seeking "healthy" orphans for adoption. . . .

The disposition to be made of the Negro women and children in our lines was a subject of great importance. Their numbers were very large, and constantly increasing. Not a tenth of these persons could find employment in gathering abandoned cotton. Those that found such employment were only temporarily provided for. It would be a heavy burden upon the Government to support them in idleness during the entire summer. It would be manifestly wrong to send them to the already overcrowded camps at Memphis and Helena. They were upon our hands by the fortune of war, and must be cared for in some way.

The plantations which their owners had abandoned were supposed to afford the means of providing homes for the Negroes, where they could be sheltered, fed, and clothed without expense to the Government. It was proposed to lease these plantations for the term of one year, to persons who would undertake the production of a crop of cotton. Those Negroes who were unfit for military service were to be distributed on these plantations, where the lessees would furnish them all needed supplies, and pay them for their labor at certain stipulated rates. . . .

The plantations were readily taken, the prospects being excellent for enormous profits if the scheme proved successful. . . . From five to thirty thousand dollars was the estimated yearly expense of a plantation of a thousand acres. If successful, the products for a year might be set down at two hundred thousand dollars; and should cotton appreciate, the return would be still greater.

It was late in the season before the plantations were leased and the work of planting commenced. The ground was hastily plowed and the seed as hastily sown. The work was prosecuted with the design of obtaining as much as possible in a single season. In their eagerness to accumulate fortunes, the lessees frequently planted more ground than they could care for, and allowed much of it to run to waste.

Of course, it could not be expected the Rebels would favor the enterprise. They had prophesied the Negro would not work when free, and were determined to break up any effort to induce him to labor. They were not even willing to give him a fair trial. Late in June they visited the plantations at Milliken's Bend and vicinity. . . .

Similar raids were made at other points along the river, where plantations were being cultivated under the new system. At all these places the mules were stolen and the Negroes either frightened or driven away. Work was suspended until the plantations could be newly stocked and equipped. This suspension occurred at the busiest time in the season. The production of the cotton was, consequently, greatly retarded. On some plantations the weeds grew faster than the cotton, and refused to be put down. On others, the excellent progress the weeds had made, during the period of idleness, rendered the yield of the cotton-plant very small. Some of the plantations were not restocked after the raid and speedily ran to waste.

In 1863, no lessee made more than half an ordinary crop of cotton, and very few secured even this return. . . .

The majority of the lessees were unprincipled men, who undertook the enterprise solely as a speculation. They had as little regard for the rights of the Negro as the most brutal slaveholder had ever shown. Very few of them paid the Negroes for their labor, except in furnishing them small quantities of goods, for which they charged five times the value. One man, who realized a profit of eighty thousand dollars, never paid his Negroes a penny. Some of the lessees made open boast of having swindled their Negroes out of their summer wages, by taking advantage of their ignorance.

The experiment did not materially improve the condition of the Negro, save in the matter of physical treatment. As a slave, the black man received no compensation for his labor. As a free man, he received none. He was well fed, and, generally, well clothed. He received no severe punishment for non-performance of duty, as had been the case before the war. The difference between working for nothing as a slave, and working for the same wages under the Yankees, was not always perceptible to the unsophisticated Negro. . . .

Everything considered, the result of the free-labor enterprise was favorable to the pockets of the avaricious lessees, though it was not encouraging to the Negro and to the friends of justice and humanity. All who had been successful desired to renew their leases for another season. Some who were losers were willing to try again and hope for better fortune.

All the available plantations in the vicinity of Vicksburg, Milliken's Bend, and other points along that portion of the Mississippi were applied for before the beginning of the new year. Applications for these places were generally made by the former lessees or their friends. The prospects were good for a vigorous prosecution of the free-labor enterprise during 1864.

In the latter part of 1863, I passed down the Mississippi, *en route* to New Orleans. At Vicksburg I met a gentleman who had been investigating the treatment of the Negroes under the new system, and was about making a report to the proper authorities. He claimed to have proof that the agents appointed by General Thomas had not been honest in their administration of affairs.

One of these agents had taken five plantations under his control, and was proposing to retain them for another year. It was charged that he had not paid his Negroes for their labor, except in scanty supplies of clothing, for which exorbitant prices were charged. He had been successful with his plantations, but delivered very little cotton to the Government agents.

I pressed forward on my visit to New Orleans. On my return, two weeks later ,the agents of General Thomas were pushing their plans for the coming year. There was no indication of an immediate change in the management. The duties of these agents had been enlarged, and the region which they controlled extended from Lake Providence, sixty miles above Vicksburg, to the mouth of Red River, nearly two hundred miles below. . . .

There was one pleasing feature. Some of the applicants for plantations were not like the sharp-eyed speculators who had hitherto controlled the business. They seemed to be men of character, desirous of experimenting with free labor for the sake of demonstrating its feasibility when skillfully and honestly managed. They hoped and believed it would be profitable, but they were not undertaking the enterprise solely with a view to moneymaking. The number of these men was not large, but their presence, although in small force, was exceedingly encouraging. I regret to say that these men were outstripped in the struggle for good locations by their more unscrupulous competitors. Before the season was ended, the majority of the honest men abandoned the field.

During 1863, many Negroes cultivated small lots of ground on their own account. Sometimes a whole family engaged in the enterprise, a single individual having control of the matter. In other cases, two, three, or a half-dozen Negroes would unite their labor, and divide the returns. One family of four persons sold twelve bales of cotton, at two hundred dollars per bale, as the result of eight months' labor. Six Negroes who united their labor were able to sell twenty bales. The average was about one and a half or two bales to each of those persons who attempted the planting enterprise on their own account. A few made as high as four bales each, while others did not make more than a single bale. One Negro, who was quite successful in planting on his own account, proposed to take a small plantation in 1864, and employ twenty or more colored laborers. How he succeeded I was not able to ascertain.

The commissioners in charge of the freedmen gave the Negroes every encouragement to plant on their own account. In 1864 there were thirty colored lessees near Milliken's Bend, and about the same number at Helena. Ten of these persons at Helena realized $31,000 for their year's labor. Two of them planted forty acres in cotton; their expenses were about $1,200; they sold their crop for $8,000. Another leased twenty-four acres. His expenses were less than $2,000, and he sold his crop for $6,000. Another leased seventeen acres. He earned by the season's work enough to purchase a good house, and leave him a cash balance of $300. Another leased thirteen and a half acres, expended about $600 in its cultivation, and sold his crop for $4,000. . . .

The planters are bitterly opposed to the policy of dividing plantations into small parcels, and allowing them to be cultivated by freedmen. They believe in extensive tracts of land under a single management, and endeavor to make the production of cotton a business for the few rather than the many. It has always been the rule to discourage small planters. No aristocratic proprietor, if he could avoid it, would sell any portion of his estate to a man of limited means. In the hilly portions of the South, the rich men were unable to carry out their policy. Consequently, there were many who cultivated cotton on a small scale. On the lower Mississippi this was not the case.

When the Southern States are fairly "reconstructed," and the political control is placed in the hands of the ruling race, every effort will be made to maintain the old policy. Plantations of a thousand or of three thousand acres will be kept intact, unless the hardest necessity compels their division. If possible, the Negroes will not be permitted to possess or cultivate land on their own account. To allow them to hold real estate will be partially admitting their claim to humanity. No true scion of chivalry can permit such an innovation, so long as he is able to make successful opposition.

I have heard Southern men declare that a statute law should, and would, be made to prevent the Negroes holding real estate. I have no doubt of the disposition of the late Rebels in favor of such enactment, and believe they would display the greatest energy in its enforcement. It would be a labor of love on their part, as well as of duty. Its success would be an obstacle in the way of the much-dreaded "Negro equality.". . .

The suppression of the rebellion, and the restoration of peace throughout the entire South, have opened a large field for emigration. The white population of the Southern States, never as dense as that of the North, has been greatly diminished in consequence of the war. In many localities more than half the able-bodied male inhabitants have been swept away, and everywhere the loss of men is severely felt. The breaking up of the former system of labor in the cotton and sugar States will hinder the progress of agriculture for a considerable time, but there can be little doubt of its beneficial effect in the end. The desolation that was spread in the track of our armies will be apparent for many years. The South will ultimately recover from all her calamities, but she will need the energy and capital of the Northern States to assist her.

During the progress of the war, as our armies penetrated the fertile portions of the "Confederacy," many of our soldiers cast longing eyes at the prospective wealth around them. "When the war is over we will come here to live, and show these people something they never dreamed of," was a frequent remark. Men born and reared in the extreme North, were amazed at the luxuriance of Southern verdure, and wondered that the richness of the soil had not been turned to greater advantage. It is often said in New England that no man who has once visited the fertile West ever returns to make his residence in the Eastern States. Many who have explored the South, and obtained a knowledge of its resources, will be equally reluctant to dwell in the regions where their boyhood days were passed.

While the war was in progress many Northern men purchased plantations on the islands along the Southern coast, and announced their determination to remain there permanently. After the capture of New Orleans, business in that city passed into the hands of Northerners, much to the chagrin of the older inhabitants. When the disposition of our army and the topography of the country made the lower portion of Louisiana secure against Rebel raids, many plantations in that locality were purchased outright by Northern speculators. I have elsewhere shown how the cotton culture was extensively carried on by "Yankees," and that failure was not due to their inability to conduct the details of the enterprise.

Ten years ago, emigration to Kansas was highly popular. Aid Societies were organized in various localities, and the Territory was rapidly filled. Political influences had much to do with this emigration from both North and South, and many implements carried by the emigrants were not altogether agricultural in their character. The soil of Kansas was known to be fertile, and its climate excellent. The Territory presented attractions to settlers, apart from their political considerations. But in going thither the emigrants crossed a region equally fertile, and possessing superior advantages in its proximity to a market. No State in the Union could boast of greater possibilities than Missouri, yet few travelers in search of a home ventured to settle within her limits.

The reason was apparent. Missouri was a slave State, though bounded on three sides by free soil. Few Northern emigrants desired to settle in the midst of slavery. The distinction between the ruling and laboring classes was not as great as in the cotton States, but there *was* a distinction beyond dispute. Whatever his blood or complexion, the man who labored with his hands was on a level, or nearly so, with the slave. Thousands passed up the Missouri River, or crossed the northern portion of the State, to settle in the new Territory of Kansas. When political influences ceased, the result was still the same. The Hannibal and St. Joseph Railway threw its valuable lands into the market, but with little success.

With the suppression of the late Rebellion, and the abolition of slavery in Missouri, the situation is materially changed. From Illinois, Ohio, and Indiana, there is a large emigration to Missouri. . . . There will undoubtedly be a large emigration to Missouri in preference to the other Southern States, but our whole migratory element will not find accommodation in her limits. The entire South will be overrun by settlers from the North.

Long ago, *Punch* gave advice to persons about to marry. It was all comprised in the single word, "DON'T." Whoever is in haste to emigrate to the South would do well to consider, for a time, this brief but emphatic counsel. No one should think of leaving the Northern States, until he has fairly considered the advantages and disadvantages of the movement. If he departs with the expectation of finding everything to his liking, he will be greatly disappointed at the result.

There will be many difficulties to overcome. The people now residing in the late rebellious States are generally impoverished. They have little money, and, in many cases, their stock and valuables of all kinds have been swept away. Their farms are often without fences, and their farming-tools worn out, disabled, or destroyed. Their system of labor is broken up. The Negro is a slave no longer, and the transition from bondage to freedom will affect, for a time, the producing interests of the South.

Though the Rebellion is suppressed, the spirit of discontent still remains in many localities, and will retard the process of reconstruction. The teachings of slavery have made the men of the South bitterly hostile to those of the North. This hostility was carefully nurtured by the insurgent leaders during the Rebellion, and much of it still exists. In many sections of the South, efforts will be made to prevent immigration from the North through a fear that the old inhabitants will lose their political rights. . . .

This feeling extends throughout a large portion of Virginia, and exists in the other States of the South. Its intensity varies in different localities, according to the extent of the slave population in the days before the war, and the influence that the Radical men of the South have exercised. While Virginia is unwilling to receive strangers, North Carolina is manifesting a desire to fill her territory with Northern capital and men. . . . Northern capital and sinew is already on its way to that region. The great majority of the North Carolinians approve the movement, but there are many persons in the State who equal the Virginians in their hostility to innovations.

In South Carolina, few beside the Negroes will welcome the Northerner with open arms. The State that hatched the secession egg, and proclaimed herself at all times first and foremost for the perpetuation of slavery, will not exult at the change which circumstances have wrought. Her Barnwells, her McGraths, her Rhetts, and her Hamptons declared they would perish in the last ditch, rather than submit. Some of them have perished, but many still remain. Having been life-long opponents of Northern policy, Northern industry, and Northern enterprise, they will hardly change their opinions until taught by the logic of events. . . .

Until the present indignation at their defeat is passed away, many of the Southern people will not be inclined to give countenance to the employment of freed Negroes. They believe slavery is the proper condition for the Negro, and declare that any system based on free labor will prove a failure. This feeling will not be general among the Southern people, and will doubtless be removed in time.

The transition from slavery to freedom will cause some irregularities on the part of the colored race. I do not apprehend serious trouble in controlling the Negro, and believe his work will be fully available throughout the South. It is natural that he should desire a little holiday with his release from bondage. For a time many Negroes will be idle, and so will many white men who have returned from the Rebel armies. According to present indications, the African race displays far more industry than the Caucasian throughout the Southern States. Letters from the South say the Negroes are at work in some localities, but the whites are everywhere idle.

Those who go to the South for the purposes of traffic may or may not be favored with large profits. All the products of the mechanic arts are very scarce in the interior, while in the larger towns trade is generally overdone. Large stocks of goods were taken to all places accessible by water as soon as the ports were opened. The supply exceeded the demand, and many dealers suffered heavy loss. From Richmond and other points considerable quantities of goods have been reshipped to New York, or sold for less than cost. Doubtless the trade with the South will ultimately be very large, but it cannot spring up in a day. Money is needed before speculation can be active. A year or two, at the least, will be needed to fill the Southern pocket.

So much for the dark side of the picture. Emigrants are apt to listen to favorable accounts of the region whither they are bound, while they close their ears to all stories of an unfavorable character. To insure a hearing of both sides of the question under discussion, I have given the discouraging arguments in advance of all others. Already those who desire to stimulate travel to the South are relating wonderful stories of its fertility and its great advantages to settlers. No doubt they are telling much that is true, but they do not tell all the truth. Everyone has heard the statement, circulated in Ireland many years since, that America abounded in roasted pigs that ran about the streets, carrying knives and forks in their mouths, and making vocal requests to be devoured. Notwithstanding the absurdity of the story, it is reported to have received credit. . . .

Those who desire to seek their homes in the South will do well to remember that baked pigs are not likely to exist in abundance in the regions traversed by the national armies.

The hindrances I have mentioned in the way of Southern emigration are of a temporary character. The opposition of the hostile portion of the Southern people can be overcome in time. When they see there is no possible hope for them to control the national policy, when they fully realize that slavery is ended, and ended forever, when they discover that the Negro will work as a free man with advantage to his employer, they will become more amiable in disposition. Much of their present feeling arises from a hope of compelling a return to the old relation of master and slave. When this hope is completely destroyed, we shall have accomplished a great step toward reconstruction. A practical knowledge of Northern industry and enterprise will convince the people of the South, unless their hearts are thoroughly hardened, that some good can come out of Nazareth. They may never establish relations of great intimacy with their new neighbors, but their hostility will be diminished to insignificance. . . .

Formerly, the West was the only field to which emigrants could direct their steps. There was an abundance of land, and a great need of human sinew to make it lucrative. When land could be occupied by a settler and held under his pre-emption title, giving him opportunity to pay for his possession from the products of his own industry and the fertility of the soil, there was comparatively little need of capital. The operations of speculators frequently tended to retard settlement rather than to stimulate it, as they shut out large areas from cultivation or occupation, in order to hold them for an advance. In many of the Territories a dozen able-bodied men, accustomed to farm labor and willing to toil, were considered a greater acquisition than a speculator with twenty thousand dollars of hard cash. Labor was of more importance than capital.

To a certain extent this is still the case. Laboring men are greatly needed on the broad acres of the Far-Western States. No one who has not traveled in that region can appreciate the sacrifice made by Minnesota, Iowa, and Kansas, when they sent their regiments of stalwart men to the war. Every arm that carried a musket from those States was a certain integral portion of their wealth and prosperity. The great cities of the sea-board could spare a thousand men with far less loss than would accrue to any of the States I have mentioned, by the subtraction of a hundred. There is now a great demand for men to fill the vacancy caused by deaths in the field, and to occupy the extensive areas that are still uncultivated. Emigrants without capital will seek the West, where their stout arms will make them welcome and secure them comfortable homes.

In the South the situation is different. For the present there is a sufficiency of labor. Doubtless there will be a scarcity several years hence, but there is no reason to fear it immediately. Capital and direction are needed. The South is impoverished. Its money is expended, and it has no present source of revenue. There is nothing wherewith to purchase the necessary stock, supplies, and implements for prosecuting agricultural enterprise. The planters are generally helpless. Capital to supply the want must come from the rich North.

Direction is no less needed than capital. A majority of Southern men declare the Negroes will be worthless to them, now that slavery is abolished. "We have," say they, "lived among these Negroes all our days. We know them in no other light than as slaves. We command them to do what we wish, and we punish them as we see fit for disobedience. We cannot manage them in any other way."

No doubt this is the declaration of their honest belief. A Northern man can give them an answer appealing to their reason, if not to their conviction. He can say, "You are accustomed to dealing with slaves, and you doubtless tell the truth when declaring you cannot manage the Negroes under the new system. We are accustomed to dealing with freemen, and do not know how to control slaves. The Negroes being free, our knowledge of freemen will enable us to manage them without difficulty."

Everything is favorable to the man of small or large capital, who desires to emigrate to the South. In consideration of the impoverishment of the people and their distrust of the freed Negroes as laborers, lands in the best districts can be purchased very cheaply. Plantations can be bought, many of them with all the buildings and fences still remaining, though somewhat out of repair, at prices ranging from three to ten dollars an acre. A few hundred dollars will do far more toward securing a home for the settler in the South than in the West. Labor is abundant, and the laborers can be easily controlled by Northern brains. The land is already broken, and its capabilities are fully known. Capital, if judiciously invested and under proper direction, whether in large or moderate amounts, will be reasonably certain of an ample return.

38

General Sherman Negotiates Peace

Jacob Donalson Cox

To understand Sherman's negotiations with Johnston, we must recall the general's attitude toward the rebellious States and his views on the subject of slavery. Originally a conservative Whig in politics, deprecating the anti-slavery agitation, as early as 1856 he had written to his brother, "Unless people both North and South learn more moderation, we'll 'see sights' in the way of civil war. Of course the North have the strength and must prevail, though the people of the South could and would be desperate enough." In 1859 he was still urging concessions instead of insisting on the absolute right. . . . But he was also one of the clearest sighted in seeing that when slavery had appealed to the sword it would perish by the sword. In January, 1864, he expressed it tersely: "The South has made the interests of slavery the issue of the war. If they lose the war, they lose slavery." At the end of the same month, he said, "Three years ago, by a little reflection and patience, they could have had a hundred years of peace and prosperity; but they preferred war. Last year they could have saved their slaves, but now it is too late—all the powers of earth cannot restore to them their slaves any more than their dead grandfathers." And in the same letter, written to a subordinate with express authority to make it known to the Southern people within our lines, he said of certain administrative regulations: "These are well-established principles of war, and the people of the South, having appealed to war, are barred from appealing for protection to our Constitution, which they have practically and publicly defied. They have appealed to war, and must abide *its* rules and laws."

Two years later Thaddeus Stevens, as radical leader in Congress,

JACOB DONALSON COX, *Military Reminiscences of the Civil War*, 2 vols. (New York, 1900), Ch. xlix.

General Cox, Cincinnati lawyer, served on Sherman's staff, and later was in Grant's Cabinet. Sherman's agreement with Joseph E. Johnston met violent opposition in the Cabinet of Andrew Johnson, and Grant went to Greensborough to soften the blow to Sherman's pride. General Cox's story relates not only the last days of the Confederate government, but presents, as well, Lincoln's last plans for a moderate reconstruction program. The rejection of the Sherman-Johnson Convention produced, indeed, the interregnum which Sherman feared, and the disbanded Southern soldiers, wandering to their homes, wrought great damage.

enounced the same doctrine in no more trenchant terms. Sherman was explicit in regard to its scope, but he differed from Stevens in the extent to which he would go, as a matter of sound policy and statesmanship, in applying the possible penalties of war when submission was made. It is clear that he insisted there could be no resurrection for slavery, and that the freedmen must be protected in life, liberty, and property, with a true equality before the law in this protection; but he held that they were as yet unfit for political participation in the Government, much less for the assumption of political rule in the Southern States. . . .

In his feelings toward the men chiefly responsible for secession and the war, Sherman had never measured his words when expressing his condemnation and wrath. In a letter to General Robert Anderson, written only a few days before meeting Johnston in negotiation, he had spoken with deepest feeling of his satisfaction that Anderson was to raise again the flag at Fort Sumter on April 14th (the fatal day on which also Lincoln died), saying he was "glad that it falls to the lot of one so pure and noble to represent our country in a drama so solemn, so majestic, and so just." To him it looked like "a retribution decreed by Heaven itself." Reminded by this thought of those who had caused this horrid war, he exclaimed: "But the end is not yet. The brain that first conceived the thought must burst in anguish, the heart that pulsated with hellish joy must cease to beat, the hand that pulled the first laniard must be palsied, before the wicked act begun in Charleston on the 13th of April, 1861, is avenged. But 'mine, not thine, is vengeance,' saith the Lord, and we poor sinners must let Him work out the drama to its close." Such was the man who went to meet General Johnston on the 17th of April; and in considering what he then did, we must take into account the principles, the convictions, and the feelings which were part of his very nature.

Still further, we must remember that he had, less than three weeks before, a personal conference with the President at City Point, and had obtained from him personally the views he held with regard to the terms he was prepared to grant to the several rebel States as well as to the armies which might surrender, and the method by which he expected to obtain an acknowledgment of submission from some legally constituted authority, without dealing in any way with the Confederate civil government. General Sherman is conclusive authority as to what occurred at a conference which was in the nature of instructions to him from the Commander-in-Chief; and the more carefully we examine contemporaneous records, the stronger becomes the conviction that he has accurately reported what occurred at that meeting.

"Mr. Lincoln was full and frank in his conversation," says Sherman, "assuring me that in his mind he was all ready for the civil reorganization of affairs at the South as soon as the war was over; and he distinctly authorized me to assure Governor Vance and the people of North Carolina that as soon as the rebel armies laid down their arms and resumed their civil pursuits, they would at once be guaranteed all their rights as citizens of a common country; and that to avoid anarchy, the State governments then in existence, with their civil functionaries, would be recognized by him as the government *de facto* till Congress could provide others."

When the general met Mr. Graham and others, he was aware that General Weitzel at Richmond had authorized the Virginia State government to assemble, Mr. Lincoln being on the ground. The views expressed in the famous interview at City Point had taken practical shape. In correspondence with Johnston while they were awaiting action on the first convention, Sherman referred to Weitzel's action as a reason for confidence that there would be "no trouble on the score of recognizing existing State governments."

With the burden of the terrible news of Lincoln's assassination, Sherman went up to Durham Station to meet the Confederate general on the 17th of April. His grief was mingled with gloomy thoughts of the future, for it was natural that he as well as the authorities at Washington should at first think of the great crime as part of a system of desperate men to destroy both the civil and the military leaders of the country, and to disperse the armies into bands of merciless guerrillas who would try the effect of anarchy now that civilized military operations had failed. We did injustice to the South in thinking so, but it was inevitable that such should be the first impression. As soon as we mingled a little with the leading soldiers and statesmen of the South we learned better, and the period of such apprehensions was a brief one, though terrible while it lasted.

But we must here consider what were the motives and purposes which, on his part, Johnston represented, when he came from Greensborough to meet his great opponent. To understand these we must trace rapidly the course of events within his military lines. When Petersburg was taken and Richmond evacuated, Mr. Davis with the members of his Cabinet went to Danville, where he remained for a few days, protected by a small force under General H. H. Walker. Beauregard was at Greensborough, collecting detachments to resist an expedition which General Stoneman was leading through the mountains from Tennessee. Johnston was at Smithfield with the main body of his forces, watching our army at Goldsborough and preparing to retreat toward Lee as soon as the latter might escape from Grant and give a rendezvous at Danville or Greensborough. The retreat from Petersburg made a union east of Danville probably impracticable.

Grant's persistent and vigorous pursuit soon turned Lee away from the Danville road at Burkesville, pushed him toward Lynchburg, and destroyed all hope of union with Johnston. Davis had no direct communication with Lee after reaching Danville, and his position there being unsafe, after Grant had occupied Burkesville, he went to Greensborough. From Danville, on the 10th, he telegraphed Johnston that he had a report of the surrender of Lee, which there was little room to doubt. He also asked Johnston to meet him at Greensborough to confer as to future action.

In a formal conference with his advisers on the 13th (Thursday), all of the Cabinet officers except Benjamin declared themselves of Johnston's and Beauregard's opinion, that a further prosecution of the war was hopeless; that the Southern Confederacy was in fact overthrown, and that the wise thing to do was to make at once the best terms possible. Davis argued that the crisis might rouse the Southern people to new and desperate efforts, and that overtures for peace on the basis of submission were premature. The general opinion, however, was so strong against him that he reluctantly yielded, and, to make sure that he should not be committed further than he meant, he himself dictated, and Mr. Mallory, the Secretary of the Navy, wrote, the letter to Sherman, signed by Johnston, asking for an armistice between all the armies, if General Grant would consent, "the object being to permit the civil authorities to enter into the needful arrangements to terminate the existing war." The form of each sentence of the letter is significant, in view of its authorship, but most so is the plain meaning of that just quoted, to make a complete surrender upon such terms as the National Government should dictate. In like manner the opening sentence, "The results of the recent campaign in Virginia have changed the relative military condition of the belligerents," was a confession in diplomatic form of final defeat. Before sending the letter to Sherman, Johnston copied it with his own hand, in order, no doubt, to have a duplicate for his own protection, as well as to preserve secrecy.

Sherman lost not a moment in answering, first, that he had power and was willing to arrange a suspension of hostilities between the armies under their respective commands, indicating a halt on both sides on the 15th; second, that he offered as a basis the terms given Lee at Appomattox; third, interpreting Johnston's reference to "other armies" which he desired the truce to include as referring to Stoneman (whom we had heard of in Raleigh as burning railway bridges on both sides of Greensborough), he said that Stoneman was under his command, and that he would obtain from Grant a suspension of other movements from Virginia. All this was strictly within the limits of Sherman's military authority and discretion. . . .

On the 15th, Sherman had sent both to Grant and to the Secretary of War copies of Johnston's overture and his own answer. He added that he should "be careful not to complicate any points of civil policy"; that he had invited Governor Vance to return to Raleigh with the civil officers of the State, and that ex-Governor Graham, Messrs. Badger, Moore, Holden, and others all agreed "that the war is over and that the States of the South must resume their allegiance, subject to the Constitution and laws of Congress, and that the military power of the South must submit to the National arms. This great fact once admitted," he said, "all the details are easy of arrangement.". . .

On Monday (April 17th), with the burden of the knowledge of Lincoln's assassination on his mind, Sherman went up to Durham by rail, accompanied by a few officers. There he met General Kilpatrick, who furnished a cavalry company as an escort, and lead-horses to mount the party. The bearer of the flag of truce and a trumpeter were in advance, followed by part of the escort, the general and his officers came next, the little cavalcade closing with the rest of the escort in due order. They rode about five miles on the Hillsborough road, when they met General Wade Hampton advancing with a flag from the other side. The house of a Mr. Bennett, near-by, was made the place of conference. When Sherman and Johnston were alone, the dispatch announcing Mr. Lincoln's murder was shown the Confederate, and as he read it, Sherman tells us, beads of perspiration stood out on his forehead, his face showed the horror and distress he felt, and he denounced the act as a disgrace to the age. Both realized the danger that terrible results would follow if hostilities should be resumed, and both were impelled to yield whatever seemed possible to bring the war to an immediate end. In this praiseworthy spirit their discussion was carried on, Johnston saying that "the greatest possible calamity to the South had happened."

Johnston's first point was that his proposal of the 14th had been that the civil authorities should negotiate as to the terms of peace, while the armistice should continue. Sherman could not deal with the Confederate civil government or recognize it. It could only dissolve and vanish when the separate States should make their submission, and these were the only governments *de facto* with whom dealings could be had. Postponing this matter, they proceeded to the practical one—the terms that could be assured to the armies of the South and to the States.

Here they found themselves not far apart. As to the troops, nothing more liberal could be asked than the terms already given to Lee. Sherman knew of Mr. Lincoln's willingness that the State governments should continue to act, if they began by declaring the Confederacy dissolved by defeat, and the authority of the United States recognized and acknowledged. He had no knowledge of any change in the policy of the Government in this respect, and what he had said to Governor Vance's delegation was satisfactory to both negotiators.

But how as to amnesty? Here Sherman was also able to give Lincoln's own words, declaring his desire that the people in general should be assured of all their rights of life, liberty, and property, and the political rights of citizens of a common country on their complete submission. Lincoln wanted no more lives sacrificed, and would use his power to make amnesty complete. He could not control the legislative or the judicial department of the Government, but he spoke for himself as Executive. An agreement was easy here also.

What, then, as to slavery? Sherman regarded it utterly dead in the regions occupied by the Confederates at the time of the Emancipation Proclamation (Jan. 1, 1863), and Johnston frankly admitted that surrender in view of the whole situation acknowledged the end of the system which had been the great stake in the war. The Thirteenth Amendment of the Constitution, abolishing slavery, had then been accepted by twenty States, Arkansas did so three days later, and the six Northern States which had been delayed in action upon it were as certain to ratify as that a little time should roll round. It was therefore no figure of speech to say that slavery was dead: Sherman, Johnston, and Breckinridge knew it to be true. But Johnston urged that to secure the prompt and peaceful acquiescence of the whole South, it was undesirable to force upon them irritating acknowledgments even of what they tacitly admitted to themselves was true; further, that the subject was not included in the scope of a military convention. . . .

As to the disposal of the arms in the hands of the Confederate soldiers from North Carolina to Texas, both knew that little of practical moment depended on the form of the agreement. So many arms were thrown away, so many were concealed by soldiers who loved the weapons they had carried, that even in our own ranks no satisfactory collection of them could be made. But a real and present apprehension with both officers was the scattering of armed men in guerrilla bands. If the law-abiding were disarmed and those who scattered and refused to give up their weapons were at large, how could the States preserve the peace? To this point Sherman said he attached most importance. This was not an afterthought when defending his action; he wrote it to Grant in the letter transmitting the terms when they were made. The same thought was forced home on the Confederates by their experience at the time. Before the negotiations were finally concluded, bands of paroled men from Lee's army and stragglers were able to stop trains on the railroad on which Johnston's army was dependent for supplies, and it would have been intolerable to leave the country at the mercy of that class. To keep the troops of each State under discipline till they deposited the arms at State capitals, where United States garrisons would be, and where the final disposal of them would be "subject to the future action of Congress," seemed prudent and safe; and this was agreed to.

In the first day's conference it seemed clear that the generals could easily agree upon all they thought essential, except the exclusion of Mr. Davis and his chief civil officers from any part in the negotiations and making the terms of the amnesty general. An adjournment to Tuesday was had to give Johnston time to consult with General Breckinridge, the Secretary of War, and for Sherman to reflect further on the amnesty question. . . .

When the two generals met again on Tuesday, General Breckinridge was with Johnston's party, and the latter requested that he might take part in the conference; but Sherman adhered to his position that he would deal only with the military officers and objected to Breckinridge as Secretary of War. Johnston suggested that he might be present simply as a general officer, but adding that his personal relations to Mr. Davis would greatly aid in securing final approval of anything to which he assented. With this understanding he was allowed to be present. . . . [Sherman] therefore took his pen, and then and there wrote off rapidly his own expression of the points he had intended to agree to, but explicitly as a "memorandum or basis" for submission to their principals.

They were, *First*, the continuance of the armistice, terminable on short notice; *Second*, the disbanding of all the Confederate armies under parole and deposit of their arms subject to the control of the National Government; *Third*, recognition by the Executive of existing State governments; *Fourth*, re-establishment of Federal Courts; *Fifth*, guaranty for the future of general rights of person, property, and political rights "so far as the Executive can"; *Sixth*, freedom for the people from disturbance on account of the past, by "the Executive authority of the Government"; the *seventh* item was a general résumé of results aimed at. The most striking difference between this statement and that which Mr. Reagan had drawn, besides the omission of the preamble, was the express limitation of the proposed action by the powers of the National Executive, with neither promise nor suggestion as to what the courts or Congress might or might not do.

In transmitting the memorandum through General Grant, Sherman wrote that the point to which he attached most importance was "that the dispersion and disbandment of those armies is done in such a manner as to prevent their breaking up into guerrilla bands," whilst there was no restriction on our right to military occupation. As to slavery, he said, "Both generals Johnston and Breckinridge admitted that slavery was dead, and I could not insist on embracing it in such a paper, because it can be made with the States in detail." He also referred to the financial question, and the necessity of stopping war expenditures and getting the officers and men of the army home to work. Writing to Halleck as chief of staff at the same time, he referred to the same topics, expressed his belief, from all he saw and heard, that "even Mr. Davis was not privy to the diabolical plot" of assassination, but that it was "the emanation of a set of young men of the South who are very devils.". . .

A week now intervened, in which the important papers were journeying to Washington and the orders of the Government coming back. On the 20th Sherman had occasion to inform Johnston of steps he had taken to enforce the details of the truce, and as evidence that he had not mistaken Mr. Lincoln's views in regard to the State governments, he enclosed "a late paper showing that in Virginia the State authorities are acknowledged and invited to resume their lawful functions." The convention seemed therefore in harmony with the course actually pursued by the Administration at Washington, and the negotiators were justified in feeling reassured. . . .

On the 23d he sent a bundle of newspapers to Johnston and Hardee, giving the developments of the assassination plot and the hopes that the Sewards would recover. In the unofficial note accompanying them, he said: "The feeling North on this subject is more intense than anything that ever occurred before. General Ord at Richmond has recalled the permission given for the Virginia legislature, and I fear much the assassination of the President will give a bias to the popular mind which, in connection with the desire of our politicians, may thwart our purpose of recognizing 'existing local governments.' But it does seem to me there must be good sense enough left on this continent to give order and shape to the now disjointed elements of government. I believe this assassination of Mr. Lincoln will do the cause of the South more harm than any event of the war, both at home and abroad, and I doubt if the Confederate military authorities had any more complicity with it than I had. I am thus frank with you, and have asserted as much to the War Department. But I dare not say as much for Mr. Davis or some of the civil functionaries, for it seems the plot was fixed for March 4, but delayed awaiting some instructions from Richmond.". . .

The correspondence thus quoted reveals to us Sherman's thoughts from day to day, the real opinions and sentiments which he intended to embody in the convention, and his recognition of the probability that its provisions would need more explicit definition before the final acts of negotiation. It shows, too, how frank he was in warning Johnston that the terrible crime at Washington had changed the situation. It seems indisputable that this open-hearted dealing between the generals made it much easier for them to come together on the final terms, by having revealed to Johnston the motives and convictions which animated his opponent in seeking the blessing of peace as well as in applying the scourge of war.

As further evidence of what Sherman told us, his subordinates, of the terms agreed upon, I quote the entry in my diary of what I understood them to be, on the 19th, the day following the signing of the convention, after personal conversation with the general: "Johnston's army is to separate, the troops going to their several States; at the State capitals they are to surrender their arms and all public property. Part of the arms are to be left to the State governments and the rest turned over to the United States. The officers and soldiers are not to be punished by the United States Government for their part in the war, but all are left liable to private prosecutions and indictments in the courts."

39

Excluding the Rebel

Whitelaw Reid

The months of May and June were the chaotic period of the returning Rebel States. All men were overwhelmed and prostrated under the sudden stroke of a calamity which the fewest number had anticipated. Many had believed the war hopeless, but nearly all had thought their armies strong enough, and their statesmen skillful enough, to extort from the North terms that would soften away, if not conceal, the rugged features of utter defeat. They expected the necessity of a return to the Union, but they hoped to march back with flying colors, with concessions granted and inducements offered that would give them the semblance of a victory. Studious encouragement had been given from the Rebel capital to such hopes; and outside of Virginia there were scarcely a dozen men in a State who comprehended the straits to which the Confederacy was reduced in the winter of 1864-65, or were prepared for the instantaneous collapse of the spring.

The first feelings were those of baffled rage. Men who had fought four years for an idea, smarted with actual anguish under the stroke which showed their utter failure. Then followed a sense of bewilderment and helplessness. Where they were, what rights they had left, what position they occupied before the law, what claim they had to their property, what hope they had for an improvement of their condition in the future—all these were subjects of complete uncertainty.

Here was the opportunity for a statesman to grasp. I speak advisedly, and after a careful review of our whole experiences through the months of May and June, in all the leading centers of Southern influence, when I say that the National Government could at that time have prescribed no conditions for the return of the Rebel States which they would not have promptly

WHITELAW REID, *After the War: A Southern Tour, May, 1865-May 1, 1866* (New York, 1867), Chs. xxx, xxxi, xliii, xliv.

Reid, Ohio journalist, traveled south in search of economic opportunities. His report of Southern conditions and the temper of Southerners contributed to the development of the Radical program of reconstruction, and conditioned his readers to accept the leadership of Thaddeus Stevens and Charles Sumner.

accepted. They expected nothing; were prepared for the worst; would have been thankful for anything.

In North and South Carolina, Georgia, and Florida, we found this state of feeling universally prevalent. The people wanted civil government and a settlement. They asked no terms, made no conditions. They were defeated and helpless—they submitted. Would the victors be pleased to tell them what was to be done? Point out any way for a return to an established order of things, and they would walk in it. They made no hypocritical professions of new-born Unionism. They had honestly believed in the right of secession. The hatred of Yankees, which had originally aided the conspirators in starting the movement, had grown and strengthened with the war. Neither the constitutional theory nor the personal hate of their lives could be changed in a day, but both were alike impotent; and having been forced to abandon the war, they longed for the blessings which any peace on any terms might be expected to bring in its train. With unchanged faith in the constitutionality of their secession, they were ready to abandon or ignore it, at the requirement of the victors. Fully believing the debts of their Rebel Government legal and just, they were prepared to repudiate them at a hint from Washington. Filled with the hatred to the Negroes, nearly always inspired in any ruling class by the loss of accustomed power over inferiors, they nevertheless yielded to the Freedmen's Bureau, and acquiesced in the necessity for according civil rights to their slaves. They were stung by the disgrace of being guarded by Negro soldiers; but they made no complaints, for they felt that they had forfeited their right of complaint. They were shocked at the suggestion of Negro suffrage; but if the Government required it, they were ready to submit.

The whole body politic was as wax. It needed but a firm hand to apply the seal. Whatever device were chosen, the community would at once be molded to its impress. But if the plastic moment were suffered to pass—!

So we found public feeling everywhere along the Atlantic coast. So, by the common testimony of all, it was found throughout the limits of the rebellion, down to the period when the terms of the President's North Carolina proclamation came to be generally understood. On the Gulf we caught the first responsive notes given to that proclamation by the revived Southern temper. By the time we reached New Orleans the change was complete; the reaction had set in. Men now began to talk of their rights, and to argue constitutional points; as if traitors had rights, or treason were entitled to constitutional protection. They had discovered that, having laid down their arms, they were no longer Rebels, and could no longer be punished; as if the thief who is forced to abandon his booty is no longer a thief, and may laugh at penitentiaries. As Mr. Randall Hunt dextrously put it, "We withdrew our Representatives from Congress, and tried to go out of the Union. You went to war to keep us in. You have conquered; we submit, and send back our Representatives. What more do you want?" The President had lustily proclaimed treason a crime, but the Southern people took his actions in preference to his words, and were confirmed in their own view that it was but a difference of opinion on a constitutional point, in which, under the circumstances, they were ready to yield.

Not less marked was the reaction on all points connected with the Negro. He was saucy and rude; disposed to acts of violence; likely, by his stupid presumptions, to provoke a war of races, which could only end in his extermination. In all this the Freedmen's Bureau encouraged him, and thus became solely a fomenter of mischief. The presence of Negro troops tended to demoralize the whole Negro population. Negro evidence would make courts of justice a mockery. As to Negro suffrage, none but the black-hearted Abolitionists who had brought on this war, and were now doing their best to provoke a second, could dream of seriously asking the South to submit to so revolting a humiliation.

The mistake of the last four or five years had been the one against which Henry A. Wise had warned them in the beginning. They ought to have fought for their rights within the Union. That they must do now. . . .

No party ever made a graver mistake than did the one that had elected the Administration during the summer after the assassination of Mr. Lincoln and the surrender of the Rebel armies. Representatives, Senators, leading men of the party in other social stations or in private life, abandoned their new President before he was lost. Dissatisfied with the North Carolina proclamation, they made little effort to convince the President of the justice of their dissatisfaction. Whispering to one another their fears that his Southern prejudices would lead him over to the side of the returning Rebels, they made little effort to retain him. Occasionally some prominent Unionist came down to Washington to see the President, found the ante-room filled with pardon-seeking Rebels, and the city rife with the old Rebel talk, became disgusted and hurried back to the North.

All summer long the capital was filled with the late leaders in Rebel councils, or on Rebel battlefields. They filled all avenues of approach to the White House. They kept the Southern President surrounded by an atmosphere of Southern geniality, Southern prejudices, Southern aspirations. Mr. Johnson declared that treason must be humbled—they convinced him that they were humble; that traitors must be punished—they showed him how they had suffered; that only loyal men should rule—they were all loyal now.

He had been a "poor white," with all the hatred of his class to the Negroes. They showed him how the "Radicals" wanted to make the Negroes as good as the white men. As a Tennessee politician, it had been necessary for him to denounce the "Abolitionists and fanatics of the North"; to declare, in the stereotyped phrase of the stump, that he had equal hatred for the Secessionists of South Carolina and the Abolitionists of Massachusetts. They asked him if he was going to let Massachusetts Abolitionists lead him now and control his Administration, while his own native South lay repentant and bleeding at his feet. He was ambitious, proud of his elevation, but stung by the sneer that after all he was only an accidental President. They cunningly showed him how he could secure the united support of the entire South and of the great Democratic Party of the North, with which all his own early history was identified, for the next Presidency.

Such were the voices, day by day and week by week, sounding in the President's ears. He heard little else, was given time to think little else. And meanwhile the party that had elected him, simply—let him alone. The history of our politics shows no graver blunder. . . .

The capital had been full of exciting rumors for a fortnight, on the subject of the admission or rejection of the Southern Representatives and Senators; and, finally the action of the House Union Caucus had been announced; but, still the Southern aspirants hoped against hope.

At last came the decisive day. Floor and galleries, lobbies, reception-rooms, passage-ways, and all manner of approaches were crowded. The Diplomatic Gallery—so called, because diplomats are never in it—beamed with many new and many familiar faces. The Reporters' Gallery—so called, because the members of the press are always crowded out of it on important occasions—was crammed by persons who, for the nonce, represented the Daily Old Dominion and the Idaho Flagstaff of Freedom's Banner. Elsewhere the "beauty and fashion" (as also the dirt and ill manners, for are we not democratic?), of the capital looked down upon the busy floor, where members, pages, office-holders, office-seekers, and a miscellaneous crowd, swarmed over the new carpet and among the desks. Thus from ten to twelve.

Then the quick-motioned, sanguine little Clerk, with sharp rap, ends the hand-shaking, gossip, and laughter among the jovial members. A moment's hasty hustling into seats; the throng of privileged spectators settles back into a dark ledge that walls in the outer row and blockades the aisles; the confused chatter subsides into a whispered murmur, and that, in turn, dies away. . . .

Members quietly respond, the busy subordinates at the desk note responses, and everybody studies the appearance of the House. There are enough old faces to give it a familiar look, and yet there are strange changes. The Administration side has, in more senses than one, been filled too full. It has spilled over the main aisle till half the Democratic seats are occupied with its surplus, and the forlorn hope, that still flies the banner of the dead party, is crowded into the extreme left. James Brooks, however, smooth, plausible, and good-natured, sturdily keeps his seat by the main aisle. Directly in front of him, two or three desks nearer to the vacant Speaker's chair (which neither is destined to fill), sits a medium-sized, handsome man-of-the-world-looking gentleman, with English whiskers and moustache—Henry J. Raymond. "Grim old Thad.," with wig browner and better curled than ever, occupies his old seat in the center of the Administration side; and directly behind him, greeting his friends with his left hand, which the Rebels left uncrippled, is General Schenck. Toward the extreme right is Governor Boutwell in his old seat; and beside him is a small but closely knit and muscular figure, with the same closely cropped moutache and imperial as of old, the jaunty, barrel-organ-voiced General Banks, ex-Speaker, ex-Governor, etc. Next to him is a bearded, black son of Anak, with a great hole in his forehead, which looks as if a fragment of shell might once have been there—General Bidwell, one of the new members from California. Garfield is in his old place near the Clerk's desk, and just across the main aisle from him, on what used to be the Democratic side, when there was a Democratic Party, is that most nervous and irritable-seeming of all figures, the best-natured and crossest-looking man in the House, John A. Bingham. He has been absent from Congress for a term, has filled arduous posts and won high praises, and comes back, they say, to take high place on the committees.

Away across, in the midst of the Democratic desks, rises a head that might be called auburn, if the whiskers were not brick-dust red. It is a brother-in-law of the semi-rebel Governor Seymour of New York—one of the ablest Republicans of the House in old times, defeated two years ago, but sent back now, more radical than ever—Roscoe Conkling. If he had been a little better tempered, the House, in the Thirty-seventh Congress, would have placed him within the first five in the lists of its most honored and trusted members. Near him, one naturally looks to the desk of the candidate opposed to President Johnson at the late election. Alas! a West Virginia Unionist fills the seat of George H. Pendleton. Back of him is the desk of the little joker of the Ohio delegation. But the little joker played his tricks too often, and has been dismissed to a second-rate claim agency business, while another West Virginian occupies his seat in the House.

In the front row of desks on the Union side is a clumsy figure of gigantic mould. The head matches the body; and in old times (when such men as A. Lincoln were his colleagues), Long John Wentworth proved that there was a good deal in it. His immediate predecessor in the representation of Chicago, now sixth Auditor, is in the lobby.

So one's eye ranges over familiar faces or picks out noted new ones, in this House which is to administer on the effects of the great Rebellion, while the Clerk vociferates the roll.

"Samuel McKee" has just been called, and the young Kentuckian has answered; "William E. Niblack," continues the Clerk. He has skipped, on the printed roll, from Kentucky to Indiana, omitting Tennessee. From the very heart of Massachusetts' group rises the "black snake of the mountains," the long, black-haired, blackfaced, Indian-looking Horace Maynard. Every man knows and honors the voice, but it cannot be heard now. He shakes his certificate of election from Parson Brownlow and begins to speak. The sharp rap of the Clerk's gavel is followed by the curt sentence, "The Clerk declines to be interrupted during the roll-call. William E. Niblack; Michael C. Kerr"; and so the call goes steadily on. At last the member from Nevada had answered; the territorial delegates had answered; Mr. Maynard rose again. But "The Clerk cannot be interrupted while ascertaining whether a quorum is present." Then, reading from the count of the assistants, "One hundred and seventy-five members, being a quorum, have answered to their names." "Mr. Clerk," once more from Horace Maynard. "The Clerk can not recognize as entitled to the floor any gentleman whose name is not on the roll." And a buzz of approbation ran over the floor as the difficult point was thus passed.

Then, as if poor Mr. Maynard's evil genius were directing things, who should get the floor but that readiest and most unremitting of talkers on a bad side, Mr. James Brooks. Mr. Morrill had moved to proceed to the election of Speaker, but had made the mistake which at once suggested how defective he was likely to prove in the leadership of the House, to which rumor already assigned him—had forgotten to call the previous question.

Brooks never misses such an opening. He proposed to amend the motion. He thought the roll ought first to be completed. He couldn't understand why a State good enough to furnish the country a President wasn't good enough to furnish the House members. If Mr. Maynard of Tennessee was to be kicked out by the party in power, he hoped they would proceed to perform the same operation on their Tennessee President. And then he told how, in the years of the war, he had heard the eloquent voice of this persecuted and rejected Tennesseean ringing on the banks of the Hudson, on the side of an imperiled country. But he forgot to add (as his hearers did not forget to remember) how earnestly he had himself then taken— the other side! And, as if determined to stab poor Maynard as dangerously as possible, he even dragged up the Rebel Virginians ("Sandie" Stuart at their head), placed them by the loyal east Tennesseean's side and claimed for them equal rights!

Long John Wentworth made his *début* by slowly rearing aloft his ponderous hulk, and calling like a stentor, for order. The Clerk, handsomely and fairly, decided the speaker in order. Long John sank down, and Brooks improved his chance: "When the newly arrived gentleman from Illinois

becomes a little more familiar with matters in the House, he will be a little
slower in undertaking to find me out of order." Presently he essayed a tilt
against Thad. Stevens, but came out from that, as most men do, badly
beaten, with House and galleries roaring at his discomfiture. Finally, Brooks
was ready to close and sought to yield the floor to a Democrat; the Unionists
were quick enough, this time, and objected. Points of order were raised,
and old heads tried to entangle the Clerk; but he was clear as a bell, and
his rulings were prompt, sharp, and decisive. The moment a Unionist fairly
got the floor, the previous question was moved, and the contest was over.
"If Maynard had spoken," says Judge Warmouth, the delegate from the
"Territory of Louisiana," "I should have claimed the right to speak too." . . .
There remained one thing to do. The door had been shut in the Rebel
faces; it was still to be bolted. Thad. Stevens, getting the floor, sent a little
paper to the desk, with this:

> *Resolved,* By the Senate and House of Representatives in Congress assem-
> bled, That a Joint Committee of fifteen members shall be appointed, nine of
> whom shall be members of the House and six of the Senate, who shall inquire
> into the condition of the States which formed the so-called Confederate States
> of America, and report whether any of them are entitled to be represented in
> either House of Congress, with leave to report at any time, by bill or otherwise;
> and until such report shall have been made and finally acted upon by Congress,
> no member shall be received in either House from any of these said so-called
> Confederate States; and all papers relating to the representatives of the said
> States shall be referred to said Committee without debate.

This is the last straw, and the burdened opposition determine to filibuster.
They object, under the rules, to its reception. Stevens grimly moved to
suspend the rules. They demand the yeas and nays, and get them; one
hundred and twenty-nine to their beggarly thirty-five. They move to lay on
the table, and demand the yeas and nays again, with like uncomfortable
fate. Ashley wants to make a slight amendment, but members all around
shout, "No! no!" The Democrats abandon the hopeless contest for their
friends; and the resolution passes. . . .

The organization is perfect, and the bars are put up before disloyal representatives of lately rebellious States—the day's work is well done. All
thanks to the true men whose honest purpose insured its doing. And so
auspiciously opens the Thirty-ninth Congress.

December broke the earliest hope of the revived Southern temper. The
preponderating Rebel element, which reorganized the State governments
under Mr. Johnson's proclamations, first expected to take Congress by a
coup de main, organize the House through a coalition with the Northern
Democracy, and, having thus attained the mastery of the situation, repeal

the war legislation and arrange matters to suit themselves. Defeated in this by the incorruptible firmness of Mr. McPherson, the Clerk, they next hoped by Executive pressure, combined with Southern clamor, to force a speedy admission of all Representatives from the rebellious States who could take the prescribed oath. These once in, the rest was easy. They were to combine with the Northern Democracy and such weak Republicans as Executive influence could control, repeal the test oath, thus admit all the other Southern applicants, and turn over the Government to a party which, at the North, had opposed the war for the Union, and at the South had sustained the war against it.

By the 1st of January all knew that the plot had failed. A few days later, I left the capital again for the South.

40

On the State of the Country

Bill Arp

"Sweet land of Liberty, of thee I sing."

Not much *I* don't, not at this time. If there's any thing sweet about liberty in this part of the vineyard, I can't see it. The land's good enough, and I wouldn't mind hearin a hyme or two about the dirt I live on, but as for findin sugar and liberty in Georgy soil, it's all a mistake. Howsumever, I'm hopeful. I'm much calmer and sereener than I was a few months ago. I begin to feel kindly towards all people, except some. I'm now endeaverin to be a great national man. I've taken up a motto of no North, no South, no East, no West; but let me tell you, my friend, I'll bet on Dixie as long as I've got a dollar. It's no harm to run both schedules. In fact it's highly harmonious to do so. I'm a good Union reb, and my battle cry is Dixie and the Union.

But you see, my friend, we are gettin restless about some things. The war had become mighty heavy on us, and after the big collapse, we thought it was over for good. We had killed folks and killed folks until the novelty of the thing had wore off, and we were mighty nigh played out all over. Children were increasin and vittels diminishin. By a close calculashun it was perceived that we didn't kill our enemies as fast as they was imported, and about those times I thought it was a pity that some miracle of grace hadn't cut off the breed of foreigners some eighteen or twenty years ago. Then you would have seen a fair fight. General Sherman wouldn't have walked over the track and Ulysses would have killed more men than he did—*of his own side*. I have always thought that a general ought to be particular which side he was sacrifisin.

Well, if the war is over, what's the use of fillin up our towns and cities with soldiers any longer? Where's your reconstruction that the papers say is goin on so rapidly? Where's the liberty and freedom? The fact is, General Sherman and his caterpillars made such a clean sweep of every thing, I

BILL ARP, so-called, *A Side Show of the Southern Side of the War* (New York, 1867), pp. 139-146.

As reconstruction developed in the South, Bill Arp, popular humorist, saw the grim inconsistencies between the humanitarian theories and the political practices.

don't see much to reconstruct. They took so many liberties around here that there's nary liberty left. I could have reconstructed a thousand sich States before this. Any body could. There wasn't nothin to do but jest to go off and let us alone. We've got plenty of statesmen—plenty of men for governor. Joe Brown ain't dead—he's a waitin—standin at the door with his hat off. Then what's the soldiers here for—what good are they doin—who wants to see 'em any longer? Everybody is tired of the war, and we don't want to see any more signs of it. The niggers don't want 'em, and the white men don't want 'em, and as for the women—whoopee! I golly! Well, there's no use talking—when the stars fall agin maybe the women will be harmonized. That male bisness—that oath about gittin letters! They always was jealous about the males anyhow, and that order jest broke the camel's back. Well, I must confess that it was a powerful small concern. I would try to sorter smooth it over if I know'd what to say, but I don't. If they was afeered of the women why didn't they say so? If they wasn't what do they make 'em swear for? Jest to aggravate 'em? Didn't they know that the best way to harmonize a man, was to harmonize his wife first? What harm can the women do by receiving their letters oath free? They can't vote, nor they can't preach, nor hold office, nor play soldier, nor muster, nor wear breeches, nor ride straddle, nor cuss, nor chaw tobacco, nor do nothing hardly but talk and rite letters. I hearn that a valiant colonel made a woman put up her fan because it had a picture of Beauregard 'pon it. Well, she's harmonized, I reckon. Now the trouble of all sich is that after these bayonets leave here and go home, these petticoat tyrants can't come back any more. Some Georgia fool will mash the juice out of 'em, certain, and that wouldn't be neither harmonious nor healthy. Better let the women alone.

Then there is another thing I'm waitin for. Why don't they reconstruct the niggers if they are ever going to? They've give 'em a powerful site of freedom, and devilish little else. Here's the big freedmen's buro, and the little buros all over the country, and the papers are full of grand orders and special orders, and paragrafs, but I'll bet a possum that some of 'em steals my wood this winter or freezes to death. Freedman's buro? freedman's humbug I say. Jest when the corn needed plowin the worst, the buro rung the bell and tolled all the niggers to town, and the farmers lost the crops, and now the freedman is gettin cold and hungry, and wants to go back, and there ain't nuthin for 'em to go to. But freedom is a big thing. Hurraw for freedom's buro! Sweet land of liberty, of thee I don't sing! But it's all right. I'm for freedom myself. Nobody wants any more slavery. If the abolitionists had let us alone we would have fixed it up now. The buro ain't fixed it, and it ain't a goin to. It don't know any thing about it. Our people have got a heap more feelin for the poor nigger than any abolitionist. We are as poor as Job, but I'll bet a dollar we can raise more money in Rome to build a nigger church than they did in Boston. The papers say that after goin round for three weeks, the Boston Christians raised thirty-seven dollars to build a nigger church in Savannah. They are powerful on theory, but devilish scarce in practice.

But it's no use talkin. Everybody will know by waitin who's been foold. Mr. Johnson says he's gwine to experiment, that's all he can do now—it's all anybody can do. Mr. Johnson's head's level. I'm for him, and everybody ought to be for him—only he's powerful slow about some things. I ain't a-worshipping him. He never made me. I hear folks hollerin hurraw for Andy Johnson, and the papers say, Oh! he's for us, he's all right, he's our friend. Well, spose he is—hadn't he ought to be? Did you expect him to be a dog, or a black republican pup? Because he ain't a-hangin of us, is it necessary to be playin hipocrite around the foot-stool of power, and making out like he was the greatest man in the world, and we was the greatest sinners? Who's sorry? Who's repenting? Who ain't proud of our people? Who loves our enemies? Nobody but a durned sneak. I say let 'em hang and be hanged to 'em, before I'd beg 'em for grace. Whar's Socrates, whar's Cato? But if Andy holds his own, the country's safe, provided these general assemblys and sinods and bishop's conventions will keep the devil and Brownlow tied. Here's a passel of slink-hearted fellers who played tory just to dodge bullitts or save property, now a-howlin about for office—want every thing because they was for Union. They was for themselves, that's all they was for, and they ain't a-goin to git the offices neither. Mr. Johnson ain't got no more respect for 'em than I have. We want to trade 'em off. By hoky, we'll give two of 'em for one copperhead, and ax nothin to boot. Let 'em shinny on their own side, and git over among the folks who don't want us reconstructed. There's them newspaper scribblers who slip down to the edge of Dixey every twenty-four hours, and peep over at us on tip-toe. Then they run back a-puffin and blowin with a straight coat tail, and holler out, "He ain't dead—he ain't dead—look out everybody! I'm jest from thar—seen his toe move—heard him grunt—he's goin to rise agin. Don't withdraw the soljers, but send down more troops immegeately." And here's your "Harper's Weekly" a-headin all sich—a-gassin lies and slanders in every issue—makin insultin pikters in every sheet—breedin everlastin discord, and chawin bigger than ever since we got licked. Wish old Stonewall had cotched these Harpers at their ferry, and we boys had knowd they was goin to keep up this devilment so long. We'd a-made baptists of them sertin, payroll or no payroll. Hurraw for a brave soldier, I say, reb or no reb, Yank or no Yank; hurraw for a manly foe and a generous victor; hurraw for our side too, I golly, excuse me, but sich expressions will work their way out sometimes, brakes or no brakes. . . .

Well, on the whole, there's a heap of things to be thankful for. I'm thankful the war is over—that's the big thing. Then I' thankful I ain't a black republican pup. I'm thankful that Thad Stevens and Sumner and Phillips, nor none of their kin, ain't no kin to *me*. I'm thankful for the high privilege of hatin all such. I'm thankful I live in Dixey, in the State of Georgia, and our Governor's name ain't Brownlow. Poor Tennessee! I golly, didn't she catch it! Andy Johnson's pardons would do rebs much good there. They better git one from the devil if they expect it to pass. Wonder what made Providence afflict 'em with sich a cuss.

But I can't dwell on sich a subject. Its highly demoralizing and unprofitable.

> Sweet Land of Liberty, of thee
> I could not sing in Tennessee.

But then we've had a circus once more, and seen the clown play round, and that makes up for a heap of trouble. In fact, it's the best sign of rekonstruction I have yet observed.

Yours, hopin,
BILL ARP

41

A Changed Government

Henry Adams

That the Government of the United States is passing through a period of transition is one of the common-places of politics. This transition, which few persons deny, illustrates in a scientific point of view the manner in which principles are established. The generation that framed the American form of government meant it to be, not only in mechanism but in theory, a contradiction to opinions commonly accepted in Europe. The men who made the Constitution intended to make by its means an issue with antiquity; and they had a clear conception of the issue itself, and of their own purposes in raising it. These purposes were perhaps chimerical; the hopes then felt were almost certainly delusive. Yet persons who grant the probable failure of the scheme, and expect the recurrence of the great problems in government which were then thought to be solved, cannot but look with satisfaction at the history of the Federal Constitution as the most convincing and the most interesting experiment ever made in the laboratory of political science, even if it demonstrates the impossibility of success through its means.

The great object of terror and suspicion to the people of the thirteen provinces was *power;* not merely power in the hands of a president or a prince, of one assembly or of several, of many citizens or of few, but power in the abstract, wherever it existed and under whatever name it was known. . . . Supreme, irresistible authority must exist somewhere in every government—was the European political belief; and England solved her problem by intrusting it to a representative assembly to be used according to the best judgment of the nation. America, on the other hand, asserted that the principle was not true; that no such supreme power need exist in a government; that in the American Government none such should be allowed to exist, because absolute power in any form was inconsistent with

HENRY ADAMS, *Historical Essays* (New York, 1891), pp. 367-412.

Originally published in the *North American Review* (July, 1870), Adams' review of the first years of the Grant administration dealt extensively with Secretary Boutwell's financial policy, and with foreign affairs. Adams himself had spent the war years in England, where his father, Charles Francis Adams, was the American minister.

freedom, and that the new Government should start from the ideas that the public liberties depended upon denying uncontrolled authority to the political system in its parts or in its whole.

Everyone knows with what logic this theory was worked out in the mechanism of the new republic. Not only were rights reserved to the people never to be parted with, but rights of great extent were reserved to the States as a sacred deposit to be jealously guarded. Even in the central Government, the three great depositories of power were made independent of each other, checks on each other's assumption of authority, separately responsible to the people, that each might be a protection and not a danger to the public liberties. The framers of the Constitution did not indeed presume to prescribe or limit the powers a nation might exercise if its existence were at stake. They know that under such an emergency paper limitations must yield; but they still hoped that the lesson they had taught would sink so deep into the popular mind as to cause a re-establishment of the system after the emergency had passed. The hope was scarcely supported by the experience of history, but, like M. Necker in France, they were obliged to trust somewhat to the "virtues of the human heart."

The two theories of government stood face to face during three-quarters of a century. Europe still maintained that supreme power must be trusted to every government, democratic or not; and America still maintained that such a principle was inconsistent with freedom. The civil war broke out in the United States, and of course for the time obliterated the Constitution. Peace came, and with it came the moment for the settlement of this long scientific dispute. If the constitutional system restored itself, America was right, and the oldest problem in political science was successfully solved.

Everyone knows the concurrence of accidents, if anything in social sequence can be called accident, which seemed to prevent a fair working of the tendency to restoration during the four years that followed the close of actual war. Wth the year 1869 a new and peculiarly favorable change took place. Many good and true Americans then believed that the time had come, and that the old foundation on which American liberties had been planted would be fully and firmly restored. A brilliant opportunity occurred for the new Administration, not perhaps to change the ultimate result, but to delay some decades yet the demonstration of failure. The new President had unbounded popular confidence. He was tied to no party. He was under no pledges. He had the inestimable advantage of a military training, which, unlike a political training, was calculated to encourage the moral distinction between right and wrong.

No one could fail to see the mingled feelings of alarm and defiance with which senators and politicians waited President Grant's first move. Not they alone, but almost the entire public, expected to see him at once grasp with a firm hand the helm of Government, and give the vessel of state a steady and determined course. The example of President Washington

offered an obvious standard for the ambition of Grant. It was long before
the conservative class of citizens, who had no partisan prejudices, could
convince themselves that in this respect they had not perhaps overrated so
much as misconceived the character of Grant, and that they must learn to
look at him in a light unlike any they had been hitherto accustomed to
associate with him. This misconception or misunderstanding was not matter
for surprise, since even to the President's oldest and most intimate associates
his character is still in some respects a riddle, and the secret of his uniform
and extraordinary success a matter of dispute. Indeed, if he ever fell into
the mischievous habit of analyzing his own mind, he could answer his own
questions in no manner that would satisfy curiosity. Nothing could be more
interesting to any person who has been perplexed with the doubts which
President Grant's character never fails to raise in everyone who approaches
him than to have these doubts met and explained by some competent
authority—by some old associate like General Sherman, with an active
mind ever eager to grapple with puzzles; by some civil subordinate such
as a civil subordinate ought to be, quick at measuring influences and at
unravelling the tangled skein of ideas which runs through the brains of an
Administration. Yet as a rule, the reply to every inquiry comes in the form
of confessed ignorance: "We do not know why Grant is successful; we only
know that he succeeds."

Without attempting to explain so complicated an enigma, one might still
predict General Grant's probable civil career from facts open to all the
world. Grant's mind rarely acts from any habit of wide generalization. As
a rule, the ideas executed with so much energy appear to come to him one
by one, without close logical sequence; and as a person may see and calculate the effect of a drop of acid on an organic substance, so one may sometimes almost seem to see the mechanical process by which a new idea eats
its way into Grant's unconscious mind—where its action begins, and where
its force is exhausted. Hence arise both advantages and misfortunes. This
faculty for assimilation of ideas, this nature which the Germans would call
objective, under ordinary circumstances and when not used by selfish men
for corrupt purposes gives elasticity, freedom from inveterate prejudices,
and capacity for progress. It would be likely to produce a course of action
not perhaps strictly logical, or perfectly steady, or capable of standing the
sharper tests of hostile criticism, but in the main practical, sensible, and in
intention honest. When used by Jay Gould and Abel Rathbone Corbin with
the skill of New York stock-brokers for illegitimate objects, the result is the
more disastrous in proportion to the energy of execution for which the
President is remarkable.

Most persons, and especially those who had formed their ideas of the
President from his Vicksburg campaign, entertained a different notion of
his intellectual qualities. The Vicksburg campaign puzzled equally the
enemies and the friends of General Grant. General Sherman's frank expres-

sion of surprise found its way into print in the form of a sincere tribute of admiration spoken by a man conscious of having underrated his superior officer. The public, on the strength of this brilliant campaign, assumed with reason that a general capable of planning and executing a military scheme such as Napoleon might have envied must possess an aptitude for elaboration of idea and careful adaptation of means to ends such as would in civil administration produce a large and vigorous political policy. Yet no such refinement of conception was in Grant's nature; no such ambition entered his head—he neither encouraged it nor believed in its advantages. His own idea of his duties as President was openly and consistently expressed, and is best described as that of the commander of an army in time of peace. He was to watch over the faithful administration of the Government; to see that the taxes were honestly collected, that the disbursements were honestly made, that economy was strictly enforced, that the laws were everywhere obeyed, good and bad alike; and as it was the duty of every military commander to obey the civil authority without question, so it was the duty of the President to follow without hesitation the wishes of the people as expressed by Congress.

This is not the range of duties prescribed to an American President either by the Constitution or by custom, although it may be that which Congress desires and to which the system tends. The President may indeed in one respect resemble the commander of an army in peace, but in another and more essential sense he resembles the commander of a ship at sea. He must have a helm to grasp, a course to steer, a port to seek; he must sooner or later be convinced that a perpetual calm is as little to his purpose as a perpetual hurricane, and that without headway the ship can arrive nowhere. President Grant assumed at the outset that it was not his duty to steer; that his were only duties of discipline.

Under these circumstances, with a President who while disbelieving in the propriety of having a general policy must yet inevitably assume responsibility—with one too whose mind, if not imaginative or highly cultivated, was still sensible to surrounding influences—the necessity was all the greater that the gentlemen on whose advice and assistance he would be compelled to lean should be calculated to supplement his natural gifts. From him the public had not required high civil education. Rulers have always the right to command and appropriate the education and the intelligence of their people. Knowledge somewhere, either in himself or in his servants, is essential even to an American President—perhaps to him, most of all rulers; and thus, though it was a matter of comparatively little importance that the President's personal notions of civil government were crude, and his ideas of political economy those of a feudal monarch a thousand years ago, it was of the highest consequence that his advisers should supply the knowledge that he could not have been expected to possess, and should develop the ideas which his growing experience would give him. Questions of finance having assumed overruling importance, a responsibility of the most serious character would evidently rest on the Secretary of the Treasury.

The official importance of the Secretary of the Treasury can hardly be over-estimated. Not only is his political power in the exercise of patronage greater than that of any other Cabinet officer, but in matters of policy almost every proposition of foreign or domestic interest sooner or later involves financial stand-point. Hence in the English system the head of administration commonly occupies the post of premier lord of the Treasury. In the American form of government the head of the Treasury is also the post of real authority, rivalling that of the President, and almost too powerful for harmony or subordination. The Secretary's voice ought to have more weight with the President than that of any other adviser. The Secretary's financial policy ought to be the point on which each member of the Administration is united with every other. At a time like the summer of 1869, when old issues were passing away and a new condition of things was at hand, when the public was waiting to be led or kneeling to take up its master, it was more than ever important that the President should have in the Treasury a man who could command and compel respect.

Secretary Boutwell was not a person to make good the needs of the President. General Grant wanted civil education, but in return was open to new ideas, and had the capacity to learn from anyone who had the faculty to teach. Mr. Boutwell had no faculty for teaching, and little respect for knowledge that was not practical. . . .

So far as finance was concerned, Mr. Boutwell's policy might have been poorer even than it was, and yet the vigor of the country would have made it a success. The greatest responsibilities of a Secretary of the Treasury are not financial, and an administration framed upon the narrow basis of mere departmental activity must be always, except under the strongest of Presidents, an invitation to failure. The stormiest of Cabinets, the most venturesome of advisers, the boldest of political rivals for power, are likely to produce in combination a better result than that unorganized and disjointed harmony, that dead unanimity, which springs from divided responsibility. Mr. Boutwell had neither the wish nor the scope to assume the functions or to wield the power of his office; and instead of stamping upon the President and his Administration the impress of a controlling mind, he drew himself back into a corner of his own, and encouraged and set the example of isolation at a time when concentrated action was essential to the Executive.

Even in the quietest of times, and under the most despotic chief, such a departmental government is a doubtful experiment, but in the summer and autumn of 1869 it was peculiarly ill-timed. Every politician felt that the first year of the new Administration would probably fix the future character of the Government. The steady process by which power was tending to centralization in defiance of the theory of the political system; the equally steady tendency of this power to accumulate in the hands of the Legislature at the expense of the Executive and the Judiciary; the ever-increasing encroachments of the Senate, the ever-diminishing efficiency of the House; all the different parts and processes of the general movement which indicated a certain abandonment of the original theory of the American system, and a no less certain substitution of a method of government that promised to be both corrupt and inefficient—all these were either to be fixed upon the country beyond recall, or were to be met by a prompt and energetic resistance. To evade the contest was to accept the revolution. To resist with success, the President must have built up his authority upon every side until the vigor of his Administration overawed the Senate, and carried away the House by the sheer strength of popular applause. That such a result was possible no one can doubt who had occasion to see how much it was dreaded by the Washington politicians of the winter and spring of 1869, and how rapidly they resumed confidence on discovering that the President had no such schemes.

By the time Congress came together, in December, 1869, the warm hopes which illumined the election of November, 1868, had faded from the public mind. Clearly, the Administration was marked by no distinctive character. No purpose of peculiar elevation, no broad policy, no commanding dignity indicated the beginning of a new era. The old type of politician was no less powerful than under other presidents. The old type of idea was not improved by the personal changes between 1861 and 1870. The Administration was not prepared for a contest with Congress, and at the last moment it was still without a purpose, without followers, and without a head.

Under these circumstances the President's Message was sent to the Capitol. It was studied with the more curiosity because it was supposed to reflect the internal condition of the Government. Nothing could have presented a less reassuring prospect. The want of plan and unity of idea was so obvious that no one needed to be assured of the harmony of the Administration. An Administration that did not care enough for its own opinions to quarrel about them was naturally harmonious. The President and the Secretary of the Treasury were discovered expressing opinions and offering recommendations diametrically opposed to each other, apparently unconscious that under ordinary theories of government a head is required. . . .

Had it not been for the good sense of the remarks on reconstruction and foreign affairs, the President's first appearance before Congress would have hazarded the reproach of absurdity.

The result, already a foregone conclusion, became apparent when Congress took up its work. So far as initiative was concerned, the President and his Cabinet might equally well have departed separately or together to distant lands. Their recommendations were uniformly disregarded. Mr. Sumner, at the head of the Senate, rode rough-shod over their reconstruction policy, and utterly overthrew it in spite of the feeble resistance of the

House. Senator Conkling then ousted Sumner from his saddle, and headed
the Senate in an attack upon the Executive as represented by Judge Hoar,
the avowed *casus belli* being that the attorney-general's manners were
unsatisfactory to the Senate. Then Conkling attacked the Census Bill, where
he had a three-fold victory; and it would be hard to say which of the three
afforded him the keenest gratification. Single-handed he assailed Sumner,
the House, and the Executive, and routed them all in disastrous confusion.
Never was factiousness more alluring or more successful than under Conkling's lead. Then again Sumner came to the front, and obtained a splendid
triumph over the President in the struggle over San Domingo. Senator
Sherman was less vigorous and less fortunate in regard to the currency and
funding measures, but Boutwell asked so little it was difficult for Sherman
to do more than ignore him; and even in the House, Mr. Dawes, the official
spokesman of the Government, if the Government has an official spokesman, startled the country by a sudden and dashing volunteer attack on the
only point of General Grant's lines on the security of which he had prided
himself—his economy; and to this day no man understands how Dawes's
foray was neutralized or evaded, or whether he was right or wrong. . . .

On the subject of Reconstruction little need be said. The merits or
demerits of the system adopted are no longer a subject worth discussion.
The resistance to these measures rested primarily on their violation of the
letter and spirit of the Constitution as regarded the rights of States, and
the justification rested not on a denial of the violation, but in overruling
necessity. The measures were adopted with reluctance by a majority of
the people; but they have become law, and whatever harm may ultimately
come from them is beyond recall and must be left for the coming generation, to which the subject henceforth belongs, to regulate according to its
circumstances and judgment. The present generation must rest content
with knowing that so far as legal principles are involved, the process of
reconstruction has reached its limits in the legislation of 1869. The powers
originally reserved by the Constitution to the States are in future to be
held by them only on good behavior and at the sufferance of Congress; they
may be suspended or assumed by Congress; their original basis and sanction no longer exist; and if they ever offered any real protection against the
assumption of supreme and uncontrolled power by the central Government,
that protection is at an end. How far Congress will at any future day care
to press its authority, or how far the States themselves may succeed in
resisting the power of Congress, are questions which must be answered by
a reference to the general course of events. Something may be judged of
the rate of progress from the theory so energetically pressed during the
past season by Senator Sumner, that the New England system of common
schools is a part of the republican form of government as understood by

the framers of the Constitution—an idea that would have seemed to the last generation as strange as though it had been announced that the electric telegraph was an essential article of faith in the early Christian Church. Something also may be judged from the condition of New York City and the evident failure of the system of self-government in great municipalities. Something more may be guessed from the rapid progress of corruption in shaking public confidence in State legislature. Finally, something may be inferred from the enormous development of corporate power, requiring still greater political power to control it. Under any circumstances the first decisive, irrevocable step toward substituting a new form of government in the place of that on which American liberties have heretofore rested has been taken, and by it the American people must stand. . . .

Not only has the internal fabric of the Government been wrenched from its original balance until Congress has assumed authority which it was never intended to hold, but as the country grows and the pressure of business increases, the efficiency of the machine grows steadily less. New powers, new duties, new responsibilties, new burdens of every sort are incessantly crowding upon the Government at the moment when it has become unequal to managing the limited powers it is accustomed to wield. Responsibility no longer exists at Washington. Every department of the Executive says with truth that it cannot deal with the questions before it because Congress neglects legislation. If members of Congress are charged with responsibility for the neglect, they reply that the fault is not theirs; that the action of Congress is wholly in the hands of committees which constitute small, independent, executive councils; that some of these committees are arbitrary, some timid; some overpoweringly strong, some ridiculously weak; some factious, some corrupt. The House has little or no control over the course of business. The rules have become so complicated as to throw independent members entirely into the background. The amount of business has become so enormous as to choke the channels provided for it. In the Senate greater power, less confusion, and more efficiency exist; but on the other hand, more personal jealousy and factiousness. In both Houses all trace of responsibility is lost; and while the Executive fumes with impatience or resigns itself with the significant consolation that it is not to blame, that this is the people's Government and the people may accept the responsibility, the members of the lower House are equally ready with the excuse that they are not responsible for the action of senators; and senators, being responsible to no power under heaven except their party organizations, which they control, are able to obtain what legislation answers their personal objects or their individual conceptions of the public good.

Under the conditions of fifty years ago, when the United States was a child among nations, and before railways and telegraphs had concentrated the social and economical forces of the country into a power never imagined by past generations, a loose and separately responsible division of government suited the stage of national growth, and was sufficiently strong to answer the requirements of the public. All indications point to the conclusion that this system is outgrown. The Government does not govern. Congress is inefficient, and becomes every year more and more incompetent, as at present constituted, to wield the enormous powers forced upon it; while the Executive, in enjoyment of theoretical independence, is practically deprived of its necessary strength by the jealousy of the Legislature. Without responsibility, direct, incessant, and continuous, no government is practicable over forty millions of people and an entire continent; but no responsibility exists at Washington. Everyone in the least acquainted with the process of American government knows that the public business is not performed. . . . Congress rejoice at carrying a small reduction on pig-iron, or regret the omnipotence of the steel lobbyists, they turn about in their seats and create by a single stroke of special legislation a new Pacific railway—an imperishable corporation with its own territory, an empire within a republic, more powerful than a sovereign State, and inconsistent with the purity of republican institutions or with the safety of any government, whether democratic or autocratic. While one monopoly is attacked, two are created; while old and true believers in republican purity and simplicity are engaged in resisting a single corruption, they are with their own hands stimulating the growth of many more. The people require it, and even if the people were opposed, yet with the prodigious development of corporate and private wealth resistance must be vain.

Two points, distinct to outward appearance but closely connected in reality, have received the whole attention of this *Review*. The first has consisted in general evidence that the original basis of reserved powers on which the Constitution was framed has yielded and is yielding to natural pressure, and the gradual concession of power to the central Government has already gone so far as to leave little doubt that the great political problem of all ages cannot, at least in a community like that of the future America, be solved by the theory of the American Constitution. The second has depended on correlative evidence that the system of separate responsibility realized in the mechanism of the American government as a consequence of its jealous restriction of substantial powers will inevitably yield, as its foundation has yielded, to the pressure of necessity. The result is not pleasant to contemplate. It is not one which the country is prepared to accept or will be soon in a temper to discuss. It will not be announced by professional politicians, who are not fond of telling unpleasant truths. Nor is it here intended to suggest principles of reform. The discussion of so large a subject is matter for a lifetime, and will occupy generations. The American statesman or philosopher who enters upon this debate must make his appeal, not to the public opinion of a day or of a nation, however large or intelligent, but to the minds of those persons who in every age and in all countries attach their chief interest to working out the problems of human society.

42

Republican Corruption in the South

Daniel W. Vorhees

MR. SPEAKER:—The condition of many of the States of this Union excites to-day the mingled pity and indignation of the civilized world. They are the theme of sorrowful and of bitter comment wherever the channels of human intelligence penetrate. They engage the attention of all the departments of this government. Executive proclamations spread evil tidings about them, and hurl every principle of their liberties, every muniment of their safety, to the ground. Congress enacts laws against them, which utterly destroy every vestige of freedom, and forge and rivet on their helpless limbs the fetters of despotism. It also sends forth its powerful missionaries of mischief in the form of committees, backed by the money and the power of the Government, whose labors are to blacken the character and fame of their people, under the guise of official investigations and official reports. The head of the Department of Justice, the late Attorney-General— he who led his people into the war, and then returned to plague and lay waste the hearthstones of his followers—superintended in person the inquisition and the torture inflicted upon the descendants of those who fought in the battles of the Revolution. The army of the United States, in a time of profound peace, is launched like a bolt of destruction into their midst. It is engaged in seizing, without sworn charge or warrant of law, the youth, the middle-aged, and the gray-haired grandsires, in the sanctuary of American homes, and driving them like herded beasts into crowded prisons. The odious service of Claverhouse, Kirke, and Dundee, in the bloody oppressions of Scotland, which gave their names more than a hundred years ago to the everlasting execration of mankind, is being repeated hourly on American soil. And the President himself, in his recent message, prepared, as he says, in haste, as if he had affairs of greater importance to engage his

CHARLES S. VORHEES, ed., *Speeches of Daniel W. Vorhees of Indiana* (Cincinnati, 1875), pp. 382-414.

Congressman Vorhees, Democrat with a vengeance, was one of the foremost political orators of his day. His speech in the House of Representatives on March 23, 1872, "Plunder of Eleven States by the Republican Party," not only summarized the course of political reconstruction but squarely pinned the blame for corrupt governments in the South on his political opponents.

attention, yet found time to give his sanction to all this, and to add his malignant mite to the general arraignment and accusation.

Surrounded and confronted by this disastrous state of public affairs, I rise to address this House in behalf of free institutions, of impartial justice, and of the oppressed and outraged citizens, wherever his home may be planted. I shall speak by the authority of those who sent me here. To them I am beholden for all that I am, and to them alone I acknowledge myself responsible in this world for what I utter on this floor.

Sir, who has filled one-third of the boundaries of this Republic with all the curses and calamities ever recorded in the annals of the worst governments known on the pages of history? Nearly seven years ago, blessed peace, like a merciful, white-winged angel, came to the land. Who, since then, has poured upon the unresisting and helpless South the floods of disorder, corruption, bankruptcy, crime, oppression, and ruin? Every result has its distinct and specific cause in the moral and political world as well as in the mathematical realms of the physical sciences. . . .

"Ye shall know them by their fruits. Do men gather grapes of thorns or figs of thistles?"

"Even so every good tree bringeth forth good fruit; but a corrupt tree bringeth forth evil fruit."

Let this unchangeable standard of truth, established by the physical and the moral sciences, and sanctioned by the voice of Divinity, be applied to the party now in power, and to its unbridled and unrestrained dealings with the people and the States of the South. . . .

We have heard endless speech here and everywhere in regard to the fruits of the war. . . . By whose conduct and policies has every blessing of free government been scourged from the face of a country containing over twelve millions people and larger in extent than many of the foremost powers of Europe? I call upon the majority in this House to answer. Have you not had all power from the beginning of what you call reconstruction over that subject? Has there been anything wanting to your absolute authority? What has stood in the way of your wishes, your partisan plans, your lawless fanaticism?

The Constitution has been no restraint upon your actions. It has been trampled under foot, dwarfed into a dead letter, or widened and extended by fraudulent amendments, according as the unscrupulous purposes of a powerful party would be best promoted. To quote the dear and hallowed principles of that immortal instrument here now is only to excite the displeasure and the sneers of those who are bloated and overgrown with the insolence of office and a long lease of power. . . . Your own will, without let or hindrance from any quarter, has been the measure of your legislation.

The army of the United States has also been made ready and obedient to your command. It has been the irresistible instrument with which to execute your pleasure on a prostrate people.

The purse of the nation, too, has been in your grasp, as well as the sword. The tax-payers of America have toiled for you as the serfs of Russia have not for their rulers. Their streaming floods of golden tribute have been poured into your coffers with every motion of the pendulum of time. You have taken the laborer's earnings and lavished uncounted millions on your baleful schemes of government under a Southern sky.

You have likewise controlled Presidents. When one of your own election rose up and stubbornly confronted you with your own precedents and solemn committals in regard to the inviolable existence of States, and their perpetual right of representation, you sought his overthrow and ruin with a fury and a hate until then unknown in the history of legislative bodies. While you barely failed to hurl him from his place, you were completely successful in rendering him powerless to execute his policy, or to prevent you from executing yours. This House was purged in a memorable way, in order that you might have two-thirds majority with which to pass unconstitutional laws over presidential vetoes. Expulsions of members took place under the thin and flimsy guise of contested elections, until the minority here was sufficiently depleted, and you became paramount over the Executive, and absorbed all his official functions. Lawless legislation then broke loose upon him, by which he was bound hand and foot, and made as powerless as a manacled prisoner in the depths of a dungeon. Andrew Johnson no longer divided with you the responsibility of the Government; you wielded it alone. The Executive who has succeeded him submits willingly and unconditionally to whatever Congress may propose. You hold all his powers in your hands and level them against any liberty or right of the citizen which you may wish to destroy. He avows his purposes to run any career you may point out to him, with no more mind of his own than the orderly who holds his horse. I pause not now to ask how you obtained this degrading control. Whether it is the cunning of a vaulting ambition on his part, which, with a pretended humility, has been known to push aside the imperial crown in order to be a little further persuaded, or whether it springs from his ignorance, matters not for the purposes of my present argument. The great fact that you possess all the powers and control all the departments of this Government is what I demonstrate.

The federal patronage, with its immense and corrupting influences, has also come into your hands with the surrender of the Executive. The venal and the mercenary have been seduced into your support by your offices and your profligate expenditure of the public money, while the timid have been overawed by the bayonet and the cannon. Every appliance by which men have ever been subdued to tyranny has been held and used in profusion by the party now in power, from the day that the war closed on the bloody soil of Virginia until the present hour. In proof of this, let the specific details of long-continued usurpation, evil government, and maladministration be presented to the candid judgment of the country.

Sir, the absolute destruction of free institutions from the Potomac to the Rio Grande commenced with the earliest dawn of peace. Sherman received Johnston's surrender upon the precise basis on which the war had been prosecuted at every stage. He stipulated that the soldiers of the South should lay down the arms of their unequal warfare, return to their States, whose existence had not then been denied, and resume the pursuits of industry where they had left off, subject only to the destruction of slavery, which was wrought by the movements of armies, and not by proclamations. He had more than a thousand precedents in the deliberate and recorded actions of this Government for his conduct. He was sustained by both branches of Congress in innumerable ways; by four years of incessant and voluminous legislation, by the enactment of apportionment laws throughout the States whose people were in rebellion, by districting them for judicial purposes, by levying upon them direct taxes as members of the Union under the Constitution, by the constant reception of their representatives on this floor and in the Senate, by the most solemn and binding joint resolutions, and by every other mode in which this department of the Government can commit and pledge itself. He was upheld by every document also to which the name of the Executive was attached during the war—by every message, inaugural, proclamation, and order of that prolific period. The courts added their weighty sanction, from those of the lowest and feeblest jurisdiction to those of the loftiest pretensions and powers. No government in the wide-spread history of the nations of the earth was ever under voluntary and self-imposed obligations of greater force and magnitude. The word and the honor of the Republic had been plighted over and over again to its own citizens, and in the sight and hearing of the civilized world. The moment, however, that resistance ceased, and the way was opened for the long pent-up purposes of revolution, centralization, and rapine, the party in power broke with shameless haste its most sacred faith, flung aside the mask it had worn for years, admitted that its previous pretensions and promises were fraudulent, and clamored with wild ferocity against the hero of the march to the sea because he had believed they were true and sincere, and had acted on them. The terms which Sherman gave to a fallen foe had often been tendered to that foe before he fell; but they were now madly thrust aside in the hour of victory, and the general himself denounced far and wide as a traitor to his country. The hue and cry was raised against him as if he was a fleeing fugitive from justice. That memorable and disgraceful outburst cannot be covered with oblivion. It more resembled the enraged scream of a beast of prey about to be baffled out of its victim than the reasonable expression of human beings. The victim, however, was surrendered to the clutches of an inflamed and victorious party, and the work of demolition and ruin was at once commenced. From turret to foundation you tore down the governments of eleven States. You left not one stone upon another. You rent all their local laws and machinery into fragments and trampled upon their ruins. Not a vestige of their former construction remained. Their pillars, their rafters, their beams, and all their deep-laid corners, the work of a wise and devoted generation of the past, were all dragged away, and the site where they once stood left naked for the erection of new and different structures. You removed the rubbish, pushed the army into the vacant ground, established provisional governments as you would over territory just acquired by conquest from a foreign power, and clothed brigadier and major generals with extraordinary functions as governors.

This was the beginning of the present organizations—those odious and unsightly fabrics which now cumber the earth, and which stand as the open, reeking, and confessed shambles of corruption, pollution, and revolting misrule. They embrace not one single element of popular consent. They are the hideous offspring of your own unnatural and unlawful force and violence. The great body of the people of that unfortunate section had no more share in the rebuilding of their local governments than the sepoys of the East Indies have in the affairs of the British Empire. They were excluded from all participation by the most elaborate and minute schemes of legislative proscription of which history makes any record.

The first duty of the provisional governments which you established was to call conventions to frame new constitutions for these old States, and to prepare them for readmission into that Union from which you had sworn so often and so solemnly that no State could ever withdraw. These conventions were provided for by laws enacted here. The number and the quality of the delegates to them were here specified. Who should be eligible and who ineligible was your work, and not the work of the people who were to be governed. You not only said who should be elected, but you likewise determined who should elect them. You fixed the qualifications and the color of the voters. You purged the ballot-box of the intelligence and the virtue on which alone popular liberty can be safely founded, and you admitted in their stead the suffrage of the most ignorant and unqualified race now inhabiting the globe.

Mingled with this dark and turbid tide of dense ignorance came all the vices of this lower race, together with the crimes of a more powerful and a more profligate class, with pale faces, from the North, now and then receiving their worst recruits from the apostates of the same complexion in the South. . . . When these conventions met, they represented the wretched constituency which spoke them into existence, and they went to their servile tasks with the bayonet of the federal Government at their throats. They sat, in every instance, within point-blank range of shotted cannon. The delegates crept about and framed constitutions with the eyes of military governors upon them. The sword rested lightly in its scabbard, and was ready to leap forth at any moment and upon the slightest pretext to assist in devising fundamental laws for a people said to be free. The State constitutions that were thus created and thrust upon the country could not fail to partake of the depraved nature of their illegitimate origin. They sprang from the loathsome union of ignorance, vice, and despotism; and they have inherited many of the ugliest features of each one of their progenitors. The despotic principle is strongly marked in them all. It is there in obedience to the mandates of federal power, as well as in accordance with the character of the instruments who were used to fasten it upon American citizens. Proscription and ostracism are the leading elements of every State government in the South. Intellect and virtue, public and private worth, spotless character, splendid attainments, graceful culture, and the experience and wisdom of ages were all passed by under the reconstruction of violence and fraud. Those who were possessed of these traits and acquirements were pushed aside, and made to give place to the most degraded classes of mankind. The people were not allowed to select their official agents from among those who were qualified for public station, but were driven into the purlieus of ignorance and vice to choose their rulers.

In the reorganization of all the States whose present condition is matter of such sore complaint and such bitter accusations, the dominant party here, and in those States, excluded from office and deprived the people of the services of every man who, by his talents, industry, and integrity, had sufficiently acquired the confidence of his fellow-citizens before the war, to be made governor, secretary, auditor, or treasurer of state; attorney-general, judge, clerk, or reporter of the Supreme Court; superintendent of public instruction, member of either branch of Congress, or of the legislature of his state; clerk, sheriff, treasurer, auditor, or recorder of his county; judge of a probate court, whose jurisdiction follows the inevitable footsteps of death, and whose functions are those of benevolence toward the orphans and the widows of the human race; justice of the peace, or constable of his township, or notary public. . . . A more sweeping and universal exclusion from all the benefits, rights, trusts, honors, enjoyments, liberties, and control of a government was never enacted against a whole people, without respect to age or sex, in the annals of the human race. The disgraceful disabilities imposed upon the Jews for nearly eighteen hundred years by the blind and bigoted nations of the earth were never more complete or appalling. . . .

Sir, shall a people thus bereft of every attribute of self-government, be held responsible at the bar of public opinion, or at the judgment-seat of God, for the consequences which have overtaken them? . . . The stream has been defiled by the party now in power, and it rends and tears the unresisting people of the South for its own offense. This shall no longer be done without exposure and warning to the country. I call upon that party to assume its just responsibility, and not to shrink back now from the bad eminence it has attained in the conduct of Southern affairs. To it much has been given, and from it much is demanded. More than the ten talents have been intrusted to its care, and the present and future generations will exact a rigid account at its hands. But now, as the ghastly and hideous results of its control in the South appear on every square mile of that oppressed and plundered section, it starts back with horror and disclaims its own offspring, the fruits of its own unholy rapine and lust. With pale lips and affrighted mien, it ejaculates, "Thou canst not say I did it." But the deeds which it has committed are of imperishable infamy, and they will not down at its bidding, nor can all the waters of the ocean wash away their guilty stains.

Having, however, now shown where the absolute, thorough, and minute managements of every interest, right, and privilege of the Southern States and their people has been lodged during the whole process of pulling down and rebuilding their local governments, I shall proceed next to call upon the results which have followed.

Let the great State of Georgia speak first. The preparations which she underwent were prolonged, elaborate, and complete. The work of her purification was repeated at stated intervals until she was radiant and spotless in your eyes. One reconstruction did not suffice. You permitted her to stand up and start in her new career, but seeing some flaw in your own handiwork, you again destroyed and again reconstructed her State government. You clung to her throat; you battered her features out of shape and recognition, determined that your party should have undisputed possession and enjoyment of her offices, her honors, and her substance. Your success was complete. When did the armed conqueror ever fail when his foe was prostrate and unarmed? The victim in this instance was worthy of the contest by which she was handed over, bound hand and foot, to the rapacity of robbers. She was one of the immortal thirteen. Her soil had been made red and wet with the blood of the Revolution. But she contained what was far dearer to her despoilers than the relics of her fame. Her prolific and unbounded resources inflamed their desires. Nature designed Georgia for the wealthiest State in this Union. She embraces four degrees of latitude abounding with every variety of production known to the earth. Her borders contain fifty-eight thousand square miles, eleven thousand more than the State of New York, and twelve thousand more than the State of Pennsylvania. She has one hundred and thirty-seven counties. The ocean washes a hundred miles of her coast, provided with harbors for the commerce of the world. Rivers mark her surface, and irrigate her fruitful valleys from the boundaries of Tennessee and North Carolina to the borders of Florida and the waves of the Atlantic. All this vast region is stored with the richest and choicest gifts of physical creation. The corn and the cotton reward the tiller of the soil, and coal and iron, tin, copper, and lead, and even the precious metals, gold and silver, in paying quantities, await the skill and industry of the miner. This is not a picture of fancy. The statistics of her products even heighten the colors in which I have drawn it. Georgia was the fairest and most fertile field that ever excited the hungry cupidity of the political pirate and the official plunderer. She was full of those mighty substances out of which the taxes of a laboring people are always wrung by the grasping hand of licentious power. She was the most splendid quarry in all history for the vultures, the kites, and the carrion-crows that darken the air at the close of a terrible civil war, and whet their filthy beaks over the fallen; and they speedily settled down upon her in devouring flocks and droves.

Sir, let us refresh ourselves at this point with some reminiscences of the former history of Georgia, and in that way fix a basis for comparisons between her condition in the past and the present deplorable state of her affairs. When the calamities of the war broke upon the country, in 1861, she was free from debt. If she had any outstanding obligations at all, they were for merely nominal amounts. Her people felt none of the burdens of taxation. The expenses of her State government were almost wholly paid by the revenues of a railroad between Chattanooga and Atlanta, which was constructed and owned by the State. Taxes throughout all her wide-spread borders were trifles light as air. The burdens of government were easy upon her citizens. Her credit stood high wherever her name was mentioned; and, when the war closed, she was still free from indebtedness. If she had incurred any during the four years of strife, she was required by the federal Government to repudiate it upon the advent of peace. Now, look at her to-day, after six years and a half of supreme control by the Republican Party. She had been a member of this Union more than seventy years when the war came, and found that she owed no man anything. Her rulers in the olden times, doubtless, had faults in common with the imperfect race to which we belong, but larceny of the public money was not among them. You took her destiny into your hands a few brief years ago, incumbered by no liabilities, and you now present her, to the amazement and horror of the world, loaded with debts which reach the appalling sum of at least $50,000,000. A large portion of these debts are officially ascertained and stated, and the remainder are sufficiently well known to warrant the statement I make. The mind recoils, filled with wonder and indignation, in contemplating this fearful and gigantic crime. It had no parallel in the annals of all the nations and the ages of mankind until the ascendency of the Republican Party and its inauguration of State governments in the South. Now, all the seven vials of the Apocalypse have been opened on that great and beautiful, but unhappy region; and the crime against Georgia is but one of the many others of kindred magnitude inflicted by the same party on other States.

The authors of this stupendous burden, however, are not even entitled to the benefit of the full time since the incoming of peace for its creation. It was mainly the work of only about three years. In 1868—a year more fatal to the interests of the people of that State than the scourge of pestilence, war, or famine—the most venal and abandoned body of men ever known outside of the boundaries of penal colonies, State prisons, or Southern reconstruction, was chosen as the legislature of Georgia; not by the people, but by virture of the system which you enacted and put in force. It contained a large majority of your political adherents, men who vote your ticket, support your candidates, and with whom you embrace and affiliate on all political occasions. They were the leaders and the representatives of the Republican Party.

With them, too, came into office one who speedily secured a national reputation, and became a controlling power in your national councils. At one time Rufus B. Bullock dictated the legislation of Congress and the actions of the Executive in regard to the great and ancient commonwealth that was cursed by his presence. It was his potent finger that pointed out the pathway which led to your second assault upon her State government; and it was his voice and his presence in and about these halls that commanded and cheered you on to the breach. He was mentioned in many quarters as the probable candidate of his party for that exalted place now held by a distinguished citizen of my own State, the second highest in the gift of the American people. He was a successful, conspicuous, and brilliant specimen of your system. His advent into Georgia was as the agent of some express company. He had no permanent interests there. I have been reliably informed that his poll was his entire tax when he was elected governor. He neither knew nor cared for the people or their wants. He was there as an alien and a stranger spying out the possessions of a land that was at his mercy, and embracing every opportunity to seize them. He is now a fugitive from justice, a proclaimed and confessed criminal, with stolen millions in his hands. He went into the South on that wave of reconstruction which bore so many eager, hungry, and inhuman sharks in quest of prey; and, having in a few short years glutted his savage and ravenous maw, he now retires into the deep waters of the North to escape punishment on the one hand, and to enjoy the comforts of his plunder on the other.

With such a governor and such a legislature in full and perfect sympathy and harmony with each other, morally and politically, a career of villainy at once opened on the soil of Georgia, which will go down to posterity without a peer or rival in the evil and infamous administrations of the world.

The official existence of the legislature lasted two years, commencing in November of 1868. The governor was elected for a term of four years, and served three before he absconded with his guilty gains. Pirates have been known to land upon beautiful islands of the sea, and, with cutlass, dirk, and pistol, proclaim a government, pillage and murder their inhabitants, and from the shelter of their harbors sally forth on all the unarmed commerce that the winds and the waves brought near them. Bandits have been known to rule over the secluded wilds and fastnesses of mountain ranges, and, with bloody hands, extort enormous ransoms for their prisoners; but the pirate and the bandit have not been worse or blacker in their spheres than the Republican legislature and the Republican governor of whom I am speaking were in theirs.

Sir, I hold in my hand the official statistics on which I make this charge. The reports of the comptroller-general of Georgia show that for eight years, commencing with 1855 and ending with 1862, there was expended for the pay of members and officers of all her legislatures during that entire period the sum of $866,385.53. This is the record of her administration under the management of her own citizens. During the two years existence of the Republican legislature, elected in 1868, the report of the comptroller-general shows that there was expended for the pay of its members and officers the startling sum of $979,055, only a fraction less than $1,000,000. One legislature is thus discovered to have cost $112,669.47 more than the legislatures of eight previous years in the single matter of its own expenses. There has been no increase in the number of members. On the contrary, there are fewer now than under the former appointment.

In earlier times the clerk hire of the legislatures of that State did not average over $10,000 per annum. That item alone reached the sum of $125,000 for the one legislature whose conduct I am discussing; more than equal to the expenditures on that account of any ten years of the previous history of Georgia. Her general assembly consists of one hundred and seventy-five representatives and forty-four senators, making two hundred and nineteen, taking both branches together. The record discloses one hundred and four clerks in the employ of this body while the Republican Party had the ascendency there. One clerk for every two legislators is a spectacle which I commend to the consideration of the American tax-payer and voter everywhere. Who can doubt that such a body was organized for the purposes of robbery and extortion. There is another high-handed outrage, however, in connection with the payment of its members and officers which surpasses the deeds of even a professional highwayman. The children of the State did not escape. By the constitution of Georgia the poll-tax of its people is made a part of the common-school fund, and set aside as sacred to the cause of education. Two hundred and fifty thousand dollars had accrued from this source when the ill-omened legislature of 1868 convened. Before it finally adjourned this whole amount provided for the cause of learning and human progress was swept away. Not a single dollar was left. An appropriation for their own expenses placed it all in the pockets of the members, clerks, and other officials. They took this money belonging to children white and black, as pay for their own base services in the cause of universal destruction, bankruptcy, and misery. They robbed the rising generations of both races, deprived them of school-houses and seminaries, and left them to grope their own unaided way out of the realms of ignorance.

The hand of the spoliator, at times in the history of the world, has taken consecrated vessels from the altar and plundered the sanctuary of God. Even the hallowed precincts of the grave have sometimes been invaded and the coffin rifled of its contents; but human villainy has sounded no lower depth than was here fathomed, in stealing the very books of knowledge from the youth of the land.

Having given these evidences of inherent depravity, this most memorable legislature proeeded naturally to its work of more gigantic peculation, fraud, and corruption. The limits of my time on this floor will permit me to bring forward only a few of its deeds, but like the specimen ore of the mines, they will satisfy the explorer that strata, veins, lodes, and layers of rascality lie under the surface beyond. The treasurer of Georgia, in his recent report, informs the public that prior to the year 1868, and since reconstruction commenced, there were issued in State bonds, $5,912,500. He further states that he has ascertained the amount of $13,756,000 to have been issued since the year 1868, and then proceeds to say:

"Governor Bullock had other large amounts under the same act engrossed and sent him. But this office does not know what has become of them."

The treasurer has pushed his discoveries to nearly twenty millions, and then finds that large amounts of other bonds have been issued which are not registered, and which are now in unknown hands. The extent of these floating, vagrant liabilities may fairly be estimated by the character and conduct of those who created them. Let us, however, examine one transaction which will serve as a key to the whole history of that legislature. A charter was granted to construct what was to be known as the Albany and Brunswick Railroad, a distance of two hundred and forty-five miles. For this work the governor was authorized to issue the bonds of the State to the extent of $23,000 per mile, making a subsidy in money to one railroad corporation of $5,639,000. The bonds have been issued, put upon the market, the money realized from them, and their redemption will fall upon the tax-payers of the State. In the meantime the road has not been built, and the proceeds of these bonds have gone into the coffers of private individuals. This fact is not disputed; it stands confessed; and no words of mine can darken the hues of its infamy or increase the horror and indignation with which it will be regarded by the American people.

Other railroad schemes followed in rapid succession as the easiest method of plunder. The Macon and Brunswick Railroad, the South Georgia and Florida Railroad, the Cartersville and Van Wert Railroad, the Georgia Air-line Railroad, the Cherokee Railroad, the Alabama and Chattanooga Railroad, and many others, were all made the recipients of subsidies from the State, by which uncounted millions were stolen from the tax-payers. The traces of vast sums of squandered money can be found on every hand, except upon the railroad lines themselves, in whose names the work of fraud and plunder was conducted.

But while the legislature of Georgia was thus engaged in its unparalleled career of crime, the governor, in his sphere, was also busy, and by his individual deeds proclaimed to the world that a perfect harmony, not only of political faith, but of official practices, prevailed between the executive and legislative branches of the State government. He ranged in his peculations from the smallest to the greatest objects and amounts; from the petit to the grand larcenies of this new era of felonies. . . . But his exploits in connection with the State railroad will more especially be remembered by the people of Georgia. This road, as I have heretofore stated, was built by the State of Georgia nearly twenty years ago, from the city of Atlanta to Chattanooga. . . . We have seen that before the war its proceeds paid into the treasury almost defrayed the entire expenses of the State government, and in an official report, made July 1, 1867, Colonel Jones, the treasurer of the State, and who had for eight years received the earnings of this noble public work, estimated its net products for the following year at $600,000.

In February, 1870, General Bullock appointed one Foster Blodgett, recently a claimant for a seat in the United States Senate, superintendent of this road. He held that position eleven months. During the entire term of his superintendency, he paid into the State treasury only $45,000; less than the net proceeds of one month before he took the place. The repairs which the ravages of war had made necessary had been completed at a heavy expense under the administration of Governor Jenkins. The road was in good condition, and but few expenditures outside of the regular course of business were needed when Blodgett assumed his ruinous control. Its freight and travel were greater than ever before, and yet its earnings, as accounted for, were comparatively nothing. In 1867 we find it paying all expenses and yielding besides $50,000 per month. At the same rate there are $500,000 now retained in the hands of Blodgett and his accomplices. What answer can be made to this? Will anyone pretend that such a vast sum was properly expended in equipping a road already equipped, in repairing a road already repaired, in stocking a road already stocked? I find one item of expense which may, however, indicate the character of them all. Twenty-one thousand dollars were paid as lawyers' fees to partisan favorites for alleged legal services in behalf of this peaceable corporation during these disastrous eleven months of its existence. It might perhaps more properly be said that there was a division of a general plunder under the head of expenses incurred. But the work of spoliation did not stop with the close of Blodgett's management. A law was obtained from the legislature of which I have spoken, authorizing the road to be leased in the interest of Bullock and his friends. Under that law it has been leased for $25,000 per month, about one-half of its real value. One of the lessees under this most valuable contract is a member of the present Cabinet, and was so when the lease was made; and another is a distinguished Republican member of the other branch of Congress.

Sir, there was but one thing more to be done by this shameless adventurer whom your policy has made governor of Georgia against the consent of her people. He completed his record and finished his work by corrupting the channels of justice. He rendered the courts powerless to enforce the laws and punish criminals. The emissaries of convicted felons crowded his ante-chambers and trafficked with him for his pardoning power. The record shows that the verdicts of juries were thus wiped out, the doors of the prisons opened, and the guilty turned loose to prey again upon the peace of society to an extent never before known in American history. He pardoned three hundred and forty-six offenders against the law, out of four hundred and twenty-six who made application to him! His amnesty for crime was almost universal. Indeed, his zeal in behalf of those under indictment was so great that his grace and clemency was often interposed before the trial of the culprit. He granted seven pardons in advance of trial to one man in the county of Warren, who pleaded them to seven separate indictments when he was arrested and brought into court. This special object of favor is one J. C. Norris, who haunts committee-rooms and swears on all occasions to fabulous outrages and the imperfect administration of the law in the South. As a spared monument of Bullock's mercy, with manifold villainies unatoned for, he is always to be seen lurking around investigating committees, and pouring into their ears the black and concentrated malice of an apostate against a people whom he hates because he has betrayed. . . .

And now, Mr. Speaker, at this point I must take leave of the State of Georgia, her plundered treasury, her oppressed tax-payers, her railroad schemes of robbery, her squandered school funds, and her mocked, insulted, and baffled courts of justice. Other impoverished fields cry to us in piteous tones for redress, and have long cried in vain. Let us at least for a few moments hearken to the story of each one's woes, whether we are willing to enter into righteous judgment with them or not.

I turn to South Carolina, once the proud land of Marion and Sumter, now the most wretched State that the sun shines on in its course through the heavens. There is no form of ruin to which she has not fallen a prey, no curse with which she has not been baptized, no cup of humiliation and suffering her people have not drained to the dregs. I am told that disorder has reigned in some counties within her borders, and we behold martial law, worse than the lawless tyranny of the dark ages, ravaging her firesides and scattering her households. Bad governments are fruitful of such calamitous results. History has taught this lesson in every age. The wickedness of corrupt rulers breeds outbreaks among citizens. How has South Carolina been governed? The Republican Party has held undisputed sway there every hour since the overthrow of the rebellion. Her entire delegation in both branches of Congress belong to the party now in power. Her State officers and legislatures, of all colors, have been of the same political faith.

What are their works? What trophies of progress and civilization do they bring to propitiate the judgment of the world? Not one good deed adorns the polluted pages of their record. At the close of the war, the valid debt of the State amounted to $5,000,000. . . . There she stands, the result of your own handiwork, bankrupt in money, ready to plunge into the dismal gulf of repudiation, ruined in credit, her bonds hawked in the markets for sale in vain at ten cents on the dollar, her prosperity blighted at home and abroad; without peace, happiness, or hope; and all her liberties stolen as well as her material substances. There she stands, with her skeleton frame and withered death's head, admonishing all the world of the loathsome consequences of a government fashioned in hate and fanaticism, and founded upon the ignorant and vicious classes of mankind. Her sins may have been many and deep, and of the color of scarlet, yet they will become as white as wool in comparison with those that have been committed against her in the hour of her helplessness and distress.

In North Carolina, the same scenes of misrule salute us as we cross her borders. Her debt, in 1861, was $9,699,500. A debt now of $34,000,000, without the ability to pay the interest on it, $11,000,000 of her bonds besides declared to have been fraudulent and void, her people groaning beneath unbearable taxation, and despair and gloom gathering over their future, are the chief consequences which have befallen North Carolina under the policy and ascendency of the Republican Party.

Louisiana presents even a still more striking instance of scandalous and stupendous robbery. The official statistics show her to be in debt to the appalling amount of $50,540,206; all of which, except $10,099,074, has been created in the degenerate days that have overtaken her since the war. The human mind, as it ponders over these figures, recoils from the villainy which they necessarily involve.

The feeble State of Florida comes forward also with her burden of complaint. When she fell into the clutches of her new rulers she had a little debt of $221,000. Now her liabilities reach the sum of $15,763,447.54, the payment of which is utterly and totally beyond her power. She has suffered from drought and flood and worm, but the presence of Republican officials had been more damaging to her than them all combined. But I can go no further in the discussion of these terrible details. Time and space would fail me. I submit the following condensed table of figures, and I defy their successful contradiction on this floor or anywhere else:

Alabama—Debts and liabilities at the close of the war, $5,939,654.87; debts and liabilities, January 1, 1872—$38,381,967.37.

Arkansas—debts and liabilities at the close of the war, $4,036,952.87; debts and liabilities, January 1, 1872—$19,761,265.62.

Florida—Debts and liabilities at the close of the war, $221,000; debts and liabilities, January 1, 1872—$15,763,447.54.

Georgia—Debts and liabilities at the close of the war, nominal; debts and liabilities, June 1871—$50,137,500. (See statement of Mr. Augier, treasurer of Georgia.)

Louisiana—Debts and liabilities at the close of the war, $10,099,074.34; debts and liabilities, June 1, 1871—including the excess of expenditures over receipts—$50,540,206.91.

North Carolina—Debts and liabilities at the close of the war, $9,699,500; debts and liabilities, January 1, 1872—$34,887,467.85.

South Carolina—Debts and liabilities at the close of the war, $5,000,000; debts and liabilities, January 1, 1872—$39,158,914.47.

Mississippi—Debts and liabilities at the close of the war, nominal; debts and liabilities, January 1, 1871—about $2,000,000.

Tennessee—Debts and liabilities at the close of the war, $20,105,606.66; debts and liabilities, January 1, 1872—$45,688,263.46.

Texas—Debts and liabilities at the close of the war, nominal; debts and liabilities, January 1, 1872—$20,361,000.

Virginia—Debts and liabilities at the close of the war, $31,938,144.59; debts and liabilities, January 1, 1872—$45,480,542.21.

The present assessed value of the taxable property of the States on whom this vast mountain of debt has been so fraudulently and so frightfully accumulated, is considerably less than one-half what it was in 1860. It was not merely the liberation of their slaves that wrought this great change. Their system of labor was broken up, great battles were fought in all their borders, their railroads were destroyed, their towns and cities and cotton burned, and every description of property handed over to the destruction of a fierce and implacable war. They emerged from the desolating conflict fit objects for the wisdom and care of a benevolent statesmanship, rather than as the proper prey of hungry jackals, who mangle and feed upon the wounded after the battle. Their fate, however, in many respects, surpasses in infamy and in misery the worst that ever befell a conquered people.

Sir, what single benefit, what solitary blessing has been bestowed on that devastated region in return for the hundreds of millions of taxation which have been wrung from it, and the yet greater burdens which still impend over its struggling and impoverished inhabitants? . . . You look in vain from Hampton Roads to the Bay of Galveston for a single monument erected to the public good by that party which has so sternly and so corruptly governed in all that wide-spread region. No colleges, seminaries, or schools founded and endowed with the treasures that have been stolen; no lofty edifices or durable roads constructed; no massive bridges thrown across wide rivers; no parched plains irrigated and made productive; no rice-swamps ditched and redeemed for cultivation; no canals cut in order to connect the natural channels of trade and commerce; no rivers improved or harbors made more spacious and secure; none of these works of utility and patriotism relieve the monotonous desolation which unholy avarice and unrestrained oppression has stamped upon the South. She has nothing to mitigate her degradation. She has been stripped and robbed and left by the wayside. Her effects, moneys, and credits have been transported to other States and climes, to return to her no more forever. Her well-favored and fat-fleshed kine, feeding in her meadows, have been devoured. The frogs, the darkness, the lice, and the locusts left more blessings behind them in Egypt than this portion of the Republic has received from its modern rulers.

Sir, I challenge the darkest annals of the human race for a parallel to the robberies which have been perpetrated on eleven American States. . . . What right have you to expect peace and order in a land whose rulers are lawless felons? When did a bad government ever fail to produce wickedness and crime? Do you expect the people to obey the laws when their officials do not? Do you expect them to love and reverence a government whose policy has made them bankrupt and miserable? Do you wonder that they become restless, desperate, and disobedient, as they daily behold the fruit of their toil stolen in the name of their government? Are you amazed at scenes of violence, outrage, bloodshed, and cruel vengeance, when the executive of a State sets aside the entire administration of justice? Rather should you be filled with astonishment at the forbearance and moderation you have witnessed. If the foremost agents in the work of Southern ruin and destruction, since the close of the war, had been driven from that country by its plundered citizens, who now would rise up here and condemn the act? In the disorders which afflict the South, the philosophic mind beholds the inevitable results of well-known causes. Had you sown the seeds of kindness and good-will, they would long ere this have blossomed into prosperity and peace. Had you sown the seeds of honor, you would have reaped a golden harvest of contentment and obedience. Had you extended your charities and your justice to a distressed people, you would have awakened a grateful affection in return. But as you have planted in hate and nurtured in corruption, so have been the fruits which you have gathered.

43

The Disputed Election

Hugh McCulloch

The presidential election of 1876 was contested with great vigor on both sides. Rutherford B. Hayes, the nominee of the Republican Party for President, had done good service in the army, and as the candidate for governor in Ohio in 1875, had led the party to victory when financial questions were the main subjects for discussion. William A. Wheeler, the nominee for Vice-President, was a man of a high order of ability, who had acquired distinction in Congress. The ticket was a strong and popular one. Mr. Hayes was not the first choice of his party, but it was thoroughly united by his nomination. It had, however, been shorn of a good deal of its strength during General Grant's second term. It had lost the control of the House of Representatives, but it held the mastery in the Senate and retained a good deal of the prestige which it had acquired during the war. It was still confident and aggressive. The Democratic Party was especially sagacious in the selection of its candidates. Of its nominee for Vice-President, Thomas A. Hendricks, I have already spoken. Samuel J. Tilden, the nominee for President, was a man of distinguished ability in his profession. "He is," said Henry Stanbery to me, in 1864, "the ablest corporation lawyer in the United States." The consolidation of the Ohio and Pennsylvania, the Ohio and Indiana, and the Fort Wayne and Chicago railroads into the great trunk line, the Pittsburgh, Fort Wayne and Chicago, was, as far as all legal questions were involved, his work. The three roads were constructed under the laws of four States, Pennsylvania, Indiana, Ohio and Illinois, and in their consolidation many new, complicated and difficult questions were to be grasped and solved. It was the first great work of the kind that had been undertaken in the United States, and the manner in which it was accomplished placed Mr. Tilden as a railroad lawyer at the head of his profession. His distinction was not,

HUGH MCCULLOCH, *Men and Measures of Half a Century* (New York, 1888), Ch. xxvii.
    The political culmination of reconstruction came with the disputed election of 1876. The settlement, sometimes known as "the Compromise of 1877," involved the subsequent withdrawal of federal troops from the South, and the restoration of the Southern State governments to the white Democrats. Hugh McCulloch, Indiana banker, had served as Secretary of the Treasurer, and was in an excellent position to judge both men and measures.

however, limited to his superior knowledge of the laws by which corporate bodies were created and governed. His general legal learning was extensive and accurate. He was not an easy and graceful speaker, and he was rarely effective in addressing a jury; but as a legal counsellor, he had few equals and no superior in New York. He was also a man of large literary acquirement, a forcible and instructive writer, and when he entered the political arena he was leader and master. To all these qualities he united sagacity and pluck. It was by his skilful and persistent labors that a powerful ring that had for years been governing and robbing the city was exposed and broken up. Then, too, he was a worthy representative of Jeffersonian democracy—sound to the core upon all financial and economical questions according to the standards of that school. That he was thoroughly equipped for the Presidency, was not denied by his opponents. The main objections to his nomination were that, although a Union man, he had been more disposed to criticise the actions of the Government than to strengthen it by his hearty support during the war. He was rich, and the most of his large fortune had been acquired in railroad operations, in which he was an adept, and in which a large part of his gains were the losses of other people; but these drawbacks were not considered serious by the party leaders.

The tickets on both sides were highly respectable. On the whole it would have been difficult for the managers to have selected men better fitted to bring out the full Republican and Democratic strength. The comparatively few votes which were cast for the Greenback ticket, at the head of which was the venerable and honored name of Peter Cooper, were drawn about equally from the two parties.

The mention of Mr. Cooper's name reminds me of a conversation which I had with him at the dinner which was given to Bayard Taylor just before the latter's departure to enter upon the discharge of his duties as Minister Plenipotentiary at Berlin. Mr. Cooper's chair was next to mine. I knew, of course, that his opinions in regard to the general currency question were the very opposite of mine, and I desired to avoid all reference to it; but just before the dinner was over, he made some remark about the money market, which was then stringent, which fact he attributed to the scarcity of money. I therefore could not help asking him if he thought that the best interests of the country would be promoted by a further issue of Government notes. "Undoubtedly I do, sir. What is wanted now to bring back the country to a really prosperous condition is an additional issue of at least two thousand millions of legal-tender notes." Coming as this remark did from a man of excellent business capacity, I was amazed by it. How such an opinion could be entertained by such a man was to me incomprehensible.

The canvass of 1876 was, as I have said, a vigorous one. Neither money nor effort was wanting on either side. Both sides were confident, but neither was so confident as to neglect the use of all the ways and means which were considered by the keenest politicians essential to success. The result was doubtful up to the day of the election; it was doubtful after the election was over, and to this day the question, Was Tilden or Hayes duly elected? is an open one. The first reports received in New York were so decidedly in favor of the Democratic ticket, that the leading Republican journals admitted its success. The next day different reports were received, and both sides claimed the victory. In regard to the votes in all the States except South Carolina, Florida, Louisiana, and Oregon, there was no question. By the first decisions of the returning boards of these States enough votes were declared to have been given to the Democratic ticket to establish its success by a decided majority. These decisions were, however, changed, either as the result of more careful examinations of the poll-books, or the pressure of the contending parties upon the State officials, and it was soon well known that two election certificates from each of these States would be presented when the count before the two Houses would be made on the second Wednesday of February, and that the question which should be received as being the proper certificate must then, in each case, be decided. The Constitution merely required that the President of the Senate, in the presence of the Senate and House of Representatives, should open all the certificates, and that the votes should be then counted. It was silent in regard to the manner in which the votes should be counted, nor did it direct how questions which might arise in regard to the correctness of the certificates or the eligibility of the electors were to be decided.

The contents of the certificates from the States referred to were well known; and it was understood that the Republican members of Congress favored one set of certificates, the Democratic members another, and that neither would yield. The Republicans controlled the Senate, the Democrats the House, and there was no umpire. If the two Houses should meet when the votes were to be counted, it was quite certain that there would be no accord between them as to the manner in which the votes should be counted, and the certificates which should be received. The condition was critical. Anarchy might follow. There had been great excitement throughout the country from the time the first election returns were received, and this excitement was culminating as the time for counting the votes drew near. Never since the formation of the Government, not even in the darkest days of the civil war, were there such anxious forebodings among thoughtful men as prevailed for some days in January, 1877. Fortunately Congress was equal to the emergency. By a bill which went through the Senate on the 25th of January by the decisive vote of 47 to 17, and through the House the next day by the equally decisive vote of 191 to 86, and which became a law the next day by the approval of the President, a commission was created to which all questions growing out of the election returns were to be referred, and whose decisions were to be final. Anxious people breathed freely again. A danger, the extent of which could not be foreseen, which threatened the very existence of the Government, was escaped by the creation of this commission. It consisted of five senators—George F. Edmunds, Oliver P. Morton, Frederick T. Freylinghuysen, Republicans; and Allen G. Thurman and Thomas F. Bayard, Democrats; of five members of the House —Henry B. Payne, Eppa Hunter, Josiah G. Abbott, Democrats; James A. Garfield and George F. Hoar, Republicans; and of five justices of the Supreme Court, four of whom were designated in the act by the circuits to which they were assigned, to wit: Nathan Clifford and Stephen J. Field, Democrats; William Strong and Samuel F. Miller, Republicans. By the act, the four justices were to select the fifth justice to make the number fifteen. The Commission thus consisted of five Republican and five Democratic Congressmen, and two Republican and two Democratic justices. The interesting question upon which the result might turn was, which of the remaining justices would be selected to make up the complement. When the Electoral Commission Act was passed, the following were the justices of the Supreme Court: Morrison R. Waite, Chief Justice; Nathan Clifford, Noah H. Swayne, David Davis, Samuel F. Miller, Stephen J. Field, William Strong, Joseph P. Bradley and Ward Hunt. All were Republicans except Clifford and Field, who were Democrats, and Davis, who before the war was a Democrat, but who had been a warm personal friend of Mr. Lincoln, and an ardent supporter of his Administration, but an opponent of General Grant's. He was therefore regarded as being in politics an independent, and it was generally expected that he would be selected to be the fifth member of the Commission. It so happened, however, that after the act had become a law, but before any action was taken under it, he had been elected United States Senator from Illinois, and had resigned his justiceship. Justice Bradley was selected, and the Commission stood politically—eight Republicans to seven Democrats.

The judges of the Supreme Court are out of politics, and are supposed to be absolutely free from political bias and aloof from political influence, and such they undoubtedly are when acting in a judicial capacity; but the duties which these five justices were called upon to perform as members of this commission were not considered judicial. The questions to be examined and decided were questions for a proper understanding of which superior legal knowledge was not essential. It was a purely political proceeding, and everybody expected that the justices would be subject to the same influences that would be sure to control the action and votes of their associates. So strong was this expectation that many Democrats did not hesitate to say, when they heard that Justice Bradley had been made a member of the Commission, that the game was up with their party; and so it turned out. The members of the Commission had been respectively sworn that they would impartially examine and consider all questions submitted to the Commission, and a true judgment give thereon, according to the Constitution and the laws; and yet every member of it—the justices as well as the

Congressmen—acted and voted as political partisans. On every question on which the Commission was divided—and it was divided on every material question—the vote stood eight to seven. By this vote the electoral votes of Florida were counted for Hayes and Wheeler, and so were the votes of South Carolina, Louisiana, and Oregon. With the votes of these States, and the votes which it had received in the other States, in regard to whose returns there had been no disagreement between the two Houses, the Republican ticket was elected by a majority of one. The certificates from all the States had been opened by the President in the Senate, in the presence of both Houses, and only those to the receipt of which objections had been raised were referred to the Commission. On the second day of March, 1877, the counting of the votes having been concluded, Senator William M. Allison, one of the tellers on the part of the Senate, in the presence of both Houses of Congress, announced as the result of the footings, that Rutherford B. Hayes had received 185 votes for President, and William A. Wheeler 185 votes for Vice-President; that Samuel J. Tilden had received 184 votes for President, and Thomas A. Hendricks 184 votes for Vice-President, and thereupon the presiding officer of the Convention of the two Houses declared Rutherford B. Hayes to have been elected President, and William A. Wheeler Vice-President of the United States for four years from the 4th day of March, 1877.

This decision was quietly acquiesced in by the Democrats, but not without heartburnings, nor without the feeling, which continues to this day, that they had been cheated out of the Presidency. Whether the result would have been different if Justice Davis, instead of Justice Bradley, had been the fifth justice in the Commission, is a question that must always remain open. By no utterance of Mr. Davis was there ever an indication of what his action would have been, but he had a high opinion of Mr. Tilden, and his political sympathies were known by his intimate friends to have been on the side of the Democrats. Hence the prevailing opinion among the Democrats has been that if he had not been elected senator, Tilden would have been President. The decision of the Commission at an early stage of the proceedings, by a vote of eight to seven, that the Commissioners were not authorized by the Constitution and the Act to go behind the returns that had been certified to by the returning officers of the State, and that no evidence could be received to impeach their correctness, indicated very clearly what the result would be; as by the certificates of the returning board from Florida, South Carolina and Louisiana, Republicans had been elected. In the Oregon case, there were two certificates; but the only question was in regard to the eligibility of one of the Republican electors, John W. Watts, which was by the vote of eight to seven decided in his favor. If the Commission could have gone behind the returns which bore the names of the State officials, they might have discovered that those from Louisiana, South Carolina, and Florida were not true. If they could have gone further and examined into the manner in which the elections in those States had been conducted, they might have ascertained that a great number of Republican Negroes had been unlawfully prevented from voting. My own opinion at the time was, and still is, that if the distinguished Northern men who visited those States immediately after the election had stayed at home, and there had been no outside pressure upon the returning boards, their certificates would have been in favor of the Democratic electors. This opinion was confirmed by a remark of the president of the Union Telegraph Company at the annual meeting of the Union League Club of New York in 1878. In a conversation which I had with him, I happened to speak of the election of Mr. Hayes, when he interrupted me by saying: "But he was not elected." "If he was not, the examinations of your office failed to show it," I replied. "Oh, yes," he rejoined, "but that was because the examiners did not know where to look." This was not said to me in confidence. My wife was with me, and he might have been heard by others who were standing near, as he spoke in his usual tone. "Mr. Tilden," said a prominent Republican to me, a year or two ago—"Mr. Tilden was, I suppose, legally elected, but not fairly"; and this was doubtless the conclusion of a great many other Republicans.

But whatever may be thought about his election, it must be admitted that Mr. Hayes proved to be an upright, fair-minded, intelligent and conscientious President. In all respects his Administration was an improvement upon the one that preceded it. He made some unwise appointments, of which that of Major D. G. Swaim, to be Judge Advocate General in place of William McKee Dunn, was the most objectionable; but they were exceptional, and his Administration will bear a favorable comparison with those which have been most highly commended by the public. It has not received, even from the Republican press, the credit to which it was justly entitled. During the term of Mr. Hayes all branches of the public service were efficiently administered, and the country was unusually prosperous. By his political enemies, Mr. Hayes has been more violently assailed than any other President except Andrew Johnson; not, as far as I have observed, because he failed in the proper discharge of his duties as President, but because he accepted the Presidency. He has been stigmatized by leading public journals as "the fraudulent President"; but there has never been the slightest evidence that he had any agency in the alleged frauds by which his election was secured. It was not by his influence or advice that the Electoral Commission was created. By that Commission, which was created by the intelligent and patriotic action of both parties, he was declared to have been duly elected President, and he was under solemn obligations, not only to his party, but to the people without respect to party, to accept the office. In the then condition of the country, it would have been his duty to accept it even if he had doubted that he was legally elected.

My acquaintance with Mr. Hayes was limited, but I carefully observed his public career, and discovered much for which he should be commended; very little for which he should be censured. There is nothing in his record as President of which his friends should be ashamed, or which his countrymen should desire to conceal. His messages were well written; his public addresses were in good taste; his personal character was above reproach. The social and moral tone of the White House was never higher than when he was its master and his accomplished wife its mistress. If in the performance of official but social duties their temperance principles were too rigidly adhered to, the mistake was not one that lessened them in public estimation.

44

The Negro Character:
A Southern Review

General Basil W. Duke

Any attempt to describe the social conditions prevailing in Kentucky and the South before the Civil War—that epoch which, like a cataclysm, divided the old order from the new—without mention of the Negro as he was before he became a freedman, must necessarily be incomplete.

The "Negro question" as we have to deal with it to-day is altogether unlike what it was when it conduced so largely to that strife. Quite as perplexing, although, we hope, not nearly so dangerous, it is presented in a totally different aspect. Then it was a sectional issue, now it is a national problem. When the maintenance or the extension of slavery was the subject of dispute, the Negro, as an individual, a personality, was a factor hardly taken into account. The institution of slavery as it affected the interests or might shape the future of the white race—as it might operate to open territory to occupation entirely by slaveholding or by non-slaveholding populations—was almost exclusively considered in the discussion. The small minority which regarded it purely from a philanthropic point of view was eloquent and insistent but, until debate was succeeded by actual combat, was heard with little favour or patience by the other disputants.

So long as slavery existed, it was impossible to consider the racial question except in its economic phases, or as it appealed to the more benevolent instincts of humanity. The Negro might be treated humanely or cruelly, his master might be kindly and considerate or harsh and unfeeling, nevertheless, as he concerned the public and from every social and political standpoint, he was regarded simply as a chattel.

The great change wrought in this respect by the enfranchisement of the black man and his elevation to the rank of citizen and voter has also utterly

BASIL W. DUKE, *Reminiscences of General Basil W. Duke* (New York, 1911), Ch. xi.

General Duke, brother-in-law of Confederate General John Hunt Morgan, was a cavalry commander who fought with Morgan. After the war he served in the Kentucky legislature, was commonwealth attorney, and for a long time was counsel for the Louisville and Nashville Railroad. His observations on the Negro in slavery and freedom reflected clearly the post-reconstruction attitudes which became dominant in the South.

changed not only his former relations with the Southern whites, but the feeling with which the white people everywhere regarded him. He has unquestionably gained much along certain lines, but he has lost much along others. With the independent action, free choice of employers, and control of his own labour now permitted him, his condition has, of course, been greatly improved. Yet we may doubt if even the better opportunity which all this affords, and the respect which must be accorded a freeman, entirely compensates for the lack of the tolerance and indulgence which was formerly extended him. The advance made by many of the race in education and general intelligence has been extraordinary. But a much greater number have not so advanced, while they have retrograded in morality and integrity. The political rights granted the Negro have done him little benefit. Suffrage was given him suddenly and before he was in any wise prepared to judiciously or safely exercise it. With no previous training, hereditary or individual, he was entrusted with powers on the proper use of which good government depends, and was expected to use them wisely—something the Anglo-Saxon, with eight hundred years of racial experience, has scarcely yet learned to do.

The Negro's incapacity properly to perform the duties thus thrust upon him was, however, nowhere accepted as an excuse for their mal-performance. Many of those who professed themselves his friends, and perhaps desired to aid him, seemed to think that, when he had been given the ballot, ample provision had been made for his material welfare. It is not surprising that he also should have fallen into that way of thinking, and, like many white men, have reached the conclusion that the best use that could be made of a vote was to sell it. In the Southern states where, during the reconstruction period, the Negro became the dangerous tool of certain thoroughly unscrupulous white politicians, Negro suffrage wrought well-nigh irretrievable disaster. So menaced, such a people wasted little time in inquiring whether the evil inflicted on them was induced by ignorance or malice, but sought and applied remedies sharp, drastic, and decisive. The result is epitomized in one of Private John Allen's best stories.

A certain candidate, he said, told an old Negro, whose support he was soliciting, that his opponent had declared that a "nigger had no more right to vote than a mule." "Now, Uncle Lige," he asked, "what do you think of that?"

"Well, master," Uncle Lige answered, "I don't know whether a nigger ain't got no more right to vote den a mule or not. But I know he ain't got much more chanct to vote den a mule."

The "wards of the nation" had reason at one time to regret that their tutors had included politics in the curriculum adopted for their instruction; but the matter became alarming when the example so furnished was copied in localities and under circumstances where no conceivable excuse for such policy was offered, and it became the practice to "count out" white as well as black men.

But I wish to describe the Negro as I knew him *au naturel,* so to speak; as I remember him before and during the war, and antecedent to the time when freedom had transformed and politics had demoralized him.

I have little personal knowledge of the conditions of slavery as it existed in the extreme Southern States nor of the character and habits of the Negroes employed upon the larger sugar and cotton plantations. From what I have been told by those who were better informed, I am of the opinion that the servitude there was sterner and less relieved by the ameliorating features which in the Border Slave States contributed to mitigate its harshness. In the far South and on the very large plantations, where the slaves were counted by the score, the proprietors and masters were absent from their homes during a considerable part of each year; and, even when present, saw little of the slaves, leaving their care and management almost entirely to the overseers. The labour upon these plantations was also more severe, constant, and exhausting than upon the farms in the States with more temperate climates and where cereal crops were chiefly grown. Under such conditions the Negro's standard, both of intelligence and character, was necessarily lower than it was in the communities where circumstances permitted a treatment more favourable to his comfort and improvement. Furthermore, the frequent importation into that region of the more vicious Negroes from the Border States, sold to work on the plantation as a punishment for incorrigibly bad conduct, was a constant cause of demoralization to those among whom they were sent.

With all this, however, the stories told by Northern ante-bellum writers of the brutal usage of the slaves in those States were grossly exaggerated; and it may be confidently asserted that in all cases wherein they were treated with unreasonable severity the indignation of the majority of the whites of the community was emphatically and practically exhibited toward the offenders.

In Kentucky, Virginia, and Missouri, in all of which States I had ample opportunity of becoming personally and accurately acquainted with the methods by which the master managed his slaves, and how the white population felt and acted toward the black, I can conscientiously testify to the kindness and consideration which the latter almost invariably received. It must be remembered that the people of the States in which slavery existed at the date when the question of its abolition or restriction was first seriously agitated, were responsible, in far less degree, for its establishment on this continent than were those who had become their censors. They had taken little, if any, part in the "slave trade," the original introduction of the Negro into this country, and the imposition of his servile condition. A very considerable number of the Negroes held in bondage in the South were descendants of slaves brought to New England years previously, and employed in Northern and Eastern States, until their labour ceased to be so profitable there, and then sold into communities where it commanded a premium. I mention this oft-recited and well-established fact, not as an historical gibe, or in the spirit of *tu quoque* contention, but because it serves, I think, to strongly rebut the presumption of deliberate inhumanity or conscious wrong-doing on the part of the Southern slaveholder, and affords reason, therefore, for the supposition that he would have been disposed to mitigate, rather than aggravate, a condition so unfortunate.

No argument would be accepted to-day in excuse or palliation of involuntary servitude. No plea in justification of the holding in bondage of a man of any race or colour would be listened to. Yet it might be readily understood that at a time when this form of slavery—which not long before had been universally sanctioned and was not yet generally condemned—seemed to the people of certain localities to furnish the kind of labour best adapted to their wants, they should have, without scruple, employed it. But, although slave labour was greatly desired and sought by the people of the South, and was esteemed by them to be the most valuable, they at no time, as I have said, participated in or approved the slave-trade. While willing to buy and employ Negroes already in slavery, and whose manumission was impracticable, they had never countenanced the importation of the native Africans for that purpose, and were among those who most earnestly demanded the suppression of the practice.

There may seem, and be, little theoretical difference between the crime of inaugurating and that of accepting and maintaining slavery, but when the manners and the opinions of the age are considered, it is not difficult to believe that the man who erred in the latter respect might be less cruel and more humane than he who made the system, with all of its attendant evils, possible. Such, at least, was the sincere conviction of the slaveholders of the South. They honestly believed that they were guiltless, but realized their duty to make the condition of the Negro better. With rare exceptions they strove to do this. It would be palpably unjust to censure a man who commits an act not accounted wrong by the code and civilization of the age in which he lives so severely as it would be proper to visit it on the man who does the same thing after a more advanced and enlightened sentiment has branded it as a crime. In process of time, perhaps, war for any provocation—warfare between rival nations and antagonistic peoples—will come to be regarded as the direst crime that can be perpetrated against humanity. But so long as it is recognized as the *ultima ratio regum;* as it is esteemed justifiable in cases of last resort, only a visionary dreamer will hold the soldier who slays a foe in battle to be as criminal or as wicked as the homicide who takes life for personal animosity or gain. The man who does a wrong ignorantly or not in violation of the code of ethics he has been taught, is neither morally so bad nor necessarily so depraved as the man who sins consciously and in defiance of the law he knows. Even when he errs, much good may be expected of him.

A great number of the slaves held in Georgia and the Carolinas at the date of the Civil War, and a yet greater proportion of those in Virginia, Kentucky, and Tennessee, had been inherited by their owners. They and their ancestors had belonged to the same families for two, three, or more, generations. For these "family Negroes" the masters entertained not only a warm interest but real attachment, and this sentiment influenced the master's treatment of other Negroes, who bore to him no such relation.

But for other reasons, chiefly the economic one, the slaveholder was disposed to treat his Negroes considerately. If a mule valued at $150 was worth caring for, there was a similar and stronger inducement to care for a slave worth from $800 to $1,000, and some pains would be taken to keep him in good health and serviceable condition. A selfish concern, therefore, as well as a certain sentimental regard, operated to protect the Negro, in a great measure, from wanton injury or abuse. I think this was more particularly the case in the Border States where the blacks were not so numerous. No individual slaveholder in the Bluegrass region of Kentucky, in which I was reared, held at any time a considerable number of slaves, but many of the farmers there owned six, eight, or ten.

Two of my uncles, with whom I passed much of my boyhood after the death of my parents, were the largest slaveholders whom I knew in that country. Each of them had a farm of about a thousand acres, and owned sixty or eighty slaves. Knowing these Negroes as I did, during my childhood and youth, and those on the farms immediately adjoining, I became well acquainted with their peculiar characteristics, and can perfectly remember them. Subsequent observation convinced me that the darkeys who were, after a fashion, my companions at that day, were genuine types of their race. These Negroes were well cared for and kindly treated, and were unquestionably the most contented and jolliest human beings I ever saw. They were kind-hearted, docile, and, in their way, quite honest. If they occasionally appropriated articles belonging to their masters it was upon the theory that it was "all in the family," and that they were entitled to a certain share of what was produced on the farm and by their labour. Unless the offence was unusually audacious the master generally regarded the matter in the same light, and was not inclined to punish the culprit.

The cabins in the Negro quarters were rude but comfortable structures, usually built of logs, and affording substantial protection from the weather. The cottages provided for servants habitually engaged in household work, or for some who were especial favourites, often constituted, with their small but well-kept gardens, quite attractive abodes.

I am quite sure that, as an almost universal rule, the slaves were well housed, comfortably clothed, and bountifully fed. I do not remember to have ever heard one complain of short rations, and have more than once seen three or four of them eat more food at one meal than would have been furnished—at the latter part of the war—to a platoon of Confederate soldiers. Nor, so far as my observation extended, were they overtasked, or required to labour more than eight to ten hours a day. In Kentucky, and I believe it was the custom throughout the South, the "dinner horn" was blown at noon, and the Negroes, however employed, came to the "quarters" for their mid-day meal. Upon the farm on which I was raised, a big conch shell was used for the dinner signal instead of a horn. A houseboy, who was christened by his mother Peregrine Pickle—which she thought a very becoming name—was, for many years, in charge of this instrument. Punctually at twelve o'clock Perry would brace himself against the wall of the kitchen, place the shell to his lips, and send forth a sonorous summons which seemed to promise corn-bread, bacon, and cabbage to every hungry stomach in the county. Almost before the echoes died away a troop of jocund darkeys would flock in from the fields, some riding the farm horses or mules, which were also brought in to be fed, and all gabbling and guffawing, as if the quantity of victuals each would be permitted to consume depended on the volume of noise he could make.

On nearly every farm in the neighbourhood with which I was best acquainted, the Negro men were allowed to cultivate small patches of ground for their own benefit, and the Negro women raised poultry. The sale of vegetables, chickens, and eggs so produced furnished them with money for their Sunday clothes and Christmas revelry.

The Kentucky farmers killed and cured the hogs, which supplied the greater part of their meat consumed during each year, when the first real cold weather set in. "Hog-killing time" was an important event, therefore, and it was not easy to determine whether the Negroes or the small white boys most enjoyed it. Long before daybreak an immense fire of logs would be blazing near the hog-pen, on which large stones were placed. When these stones were heated red-hot they were thrown into big troughs filled with water, and as soon as the water was at boiling pitch the carcasses of the slaughtered hogs would be placed in the troughs and kept there until the hair, thoroughly scalded, could be readily scraped off. Then the carcasses would be hung up on stout cross poles and disembowelled, preparatory to being taken to the "meathouse" to be cut up into hams, chines, sides, and sausage meat. Much else, also, that was edible, did that useful animal provide. Even while the work was in progress, hogs' tails and livers were broiled on the big fire and eaten with a relish that only the small white boy and the adult darkey can experience. We were wont also on such occasions to procure our stock of "bladders," which, inflated and hung up in the garret to dry, were relied upon, in those comparatively primitive times, to produce the quantum of noise without which Christmas would have scarcely realized the bright expectations of boyhood.

But when Christmas came, all the black folk and all the small white fry fraternized in an acme of enjoyment. The frolics at the quarters usually began about midnight on Christmas Eve, and continued throughout the night and until the next evening. On Christmas morning, before the eastern sky grew gray or the stars had lost their lustre, the revels were at their height. In addition to the good things the Negroes themselves provided, a fair share of the cake and eggnog made for the white people was always supplied them, and master and overseer alike would wink at a Negro drinking some whiskey on Christmas, although they might tolerate it at no other time.

To the white boys in the "big house," who had lain awake throughout the night in anticipation of the signal, the first obstreperous burst of African mirth was an irresistible call. Strict orders were usually given us upon the previous night not to visit the quarters in the morning, but obedience to such injunctions was impossible; indeed, I think it was not really expected, for we were never reprimanded when we disobeyed, which we invariably did. Snatching up our packs of firecrackers and everything else with which we could hope to swell the clamour, we would make a bee-line for the cabins. The big logs, glowing and roaring in the wide fireplaces, threw dazzling gleams from the open doors and windows far out into the night. Dancing, shouting, screaming with laughter, men, women, and "little niggers" were wild with joy. When occasionally a big firecracker exploded among the dancers, or a bladder stamped on by sturdy feet boomed like a small piece of artillery, the women would shriek in simulated fright, and the delight of the spectators was unbounded. Thus, without cessation, the merriment—this howling paradise—was continued until the morning sun smiled upon the scene.

It has been customary to describe the Negro, when in slavery, as idle and shiftless. There has never existed a people, perhaps, which would not have been "shiftless" if maintained in a state of constant dependence; required to take no thought of the morrow, cared for like children, assured, no matter what change came to them, of food, shelter, and clothing, of all necessary provisions when in health, and of medical attention when ill.

But many of them were not idle; and those who were placed in positions of trust and quasi-responsibility were not only themselves industrious, but were very exacting of proper attention to duty on the part of others. As I have said, I knew little of the conditions obtaining on the large Southern plantations, but have often heard that the black foremen—the "drivers"— were stricter in compelling labour from those under them than were the white overseers.

That the average Negro—that much the greater number of them—vastly preferred leisure to labour is an undeniable fact. But the same thing may be said of very many, if not a majority, of every race. Many white men are indolent, although feeling an incentive to exertion which was not offered the black slave. It must be remembered, also, that the Negroes, as a race, slightly appreciated and had scarcely yet learned to work. They were re-moved only five or six generations from the savage—from the native, naked African—who deemed work the direst affliction humanity could suffer. Emancipation has opened an immense opportunity to the Negro, and I be-lieve it will ultimately be improved. Slavery undoubtedly arrested his de-velopment at a certain point, but its discipline was of incalculable racial advantage. The number of vicious Negroes among the slaves was not so large as is the criminal class of the freed blacks.

The Negro of to-day may differ from the ante-bellum darkey very slightly in his love of fun and sense of humour, but he certainly fails to give it the same quaint and ludicrous expression. An experience of the harder realities of life seems to have dulled his capacity for finding enjoyment in the things which formerly amused him, and "book-learning" has made him strained and affected where he was formerly simple and natural. There was an essentially practical flavour in the dry witticisms of the plantation darkey, a subtle recognition of human nature in his sly satire, and a real and keen, although limited, perception of individual character.

The Negro humour was most mirth-provoking when it was evidently un-conscious, and he had a more than Irish faculty for blundering that was ludicrous indeed, but sometimes conveyed his meaning more perfectly than he could have expressed it in any other form. His aptitude for making excuses, frequently unsatisfactory, but almost always ingenious, was un-rivalled. I once heard Mr. Davis tell a story that well illustrated the con-fidence with which an old-time darkey, who knew himself to be a favourite, would undertake to defend a manifest delinquency.

Mr. Davis was commenting on two curiously inconsistent reports upon the same matter, submitted to him by a certain official, and which seemed to amuse him greatly. He was reminded, he said, of how a Negro who had been his especial attendant on his Mississippi plantation was accustomed to excuse the shortcomings of which he was often found guilty. One of the duties of this servant, whose name, I believe, was Tom, had been to make the fire in his master's bedroom during cold weather. The fireplace, like all those in the old Southern mansions, was commodious and the only fuel used was wood. On some mornings Tom would bring in logs of very in-convenient length; so much so that while one end of a log was burning the other would extend out some distance on the hearth. When Tom's attention would be called to this misfit he would answer: "Marse Jeff, you oughtn't to blame me; it's dis fireplace. Dis fireplace is entirely too narrer." On the very next morning, perhaps, he would furnish logs too short to re-main in position, and they would fall between the irons. Mr. Davis would gravely point out this negligence, but Tom, with an air of injured inno-cence, would promptly respond: "Marse Jeff, dey ain't no use in blamin' me; de whole trouble is wid dis fireplace; dis fireplace is entirely too wide."

Judging by the relish with which Mr. Davis told this story, one might have been justified in believing that, much as he would have liked a properly constructed fire, he decidedly preferred Tom's attempted explanations.

I remember vividly an incident which occurred in my boyhood, when I was living in the Bluegrass country, and in which the more amusing traits of the Negro character were brought out in distinct relief. An unusually audacious and extensive raid had been made upon the watermelon patch of one of my uncles, and a brief investigation disclosed the fact that it had been planned and executed by some of the younger Negroes. The overseer, who was a rather harsh disciplinarian, wished, without further inquiry, to flog them all, but my uncle would not consent to this, and preferred to discover, if possible, who had been the most guilty and the leaders in the enterprise. A formal trial was therefore held, and all of the evidence, previously heard, recapitulated, with as much more, pro and con, as could be procured or suggested. I was then about sixteen years old, and with a cousin of the same age volunteered to act as counsel for the accused. We were each burning to acquire forensic experience and distinction, and entered into the case with great zeal. A number of footprints of different shapes and sizes had been discovered in the patch, some of shod and others of bare feet. The measurement of these tracks bore hard upon the prisoners at the bar, because closely corresponding with that of their shoes or bare feet. It became a matter, therefore, of prime importance with the defence to prove, when the measurement of a shod track fitted the shoes of one of the defendants, that he had not worn his shoes on that night; and, *per contra,* to prove that he had been shod at the time, if his bare feet resembled in conformation and dimension a measured track of that kind. It was very difficult to do this except by the testimony of the accused themselves, and, of course, no one would believe that. The most damaging evidence offered for the prosecution was that of two of the crowd, who had become, so to speak, state's witnesses, claiming that their connection with the offence was of an extremely slight and venial nature. One of them, named Toby, would have sworn away the life of his own grandmother if he could have escaped the cowhide in no other way. Upon cross-examination, while admitting that he was present when the melons were stolen, he denied all complicity in the theft. "Didn't you take one of the melons yourself?" I asked.

"No, suh, I nuvver tuk nothin' outen de patch. I nuvver went inside of de patch. De mo' I done wuz to ketch hol' of a watermelon when Dow handed it over de fence." The other informer's testimony—Sim was his name—sealed the fate of Dow, the one of all my clients I wished most to save. Sim, while positively declaring that he himself had no connection with the robbery, seemed cognizant of all Dow's movements on that occasion, from an early hour in the afternoon until late at night, and ingeniously related many apparently trivial incidents which, taken together, very strongly indicated Dow's guilt. I knew that there was bad blood between them, but when I tried to make Sim acknowledge this he swore that he loved Dow rather better than a brother. One of the tracks made by bare feet corresponded exactly with Dow's huge and ungainly hoof, and Sim swore that Dow had gone barefooted during the entire evening of the raid. At this point Dow's patience utterly gave way and he indignantly shouted, "I wish dat lyin' nigger had'er said I wuz wearin' my shoes. I'd'er proved I had 'em locked up in my chist."

A remark made by an elderly Negro, after the trial was over, summed up all the philosophy of the subject. "When watermillions is ripe," he said, "you allus gwine to find niggers close to de patch."

All who served in the Confederate army will remember that, however much the soldiers might be straitened in other respects, almost every command was, for the two first years of the war at least, well supplied with Negro servants. The Second Kentucky Cavalry, which I commanded for more than a year, was abundantly provided in this regard. The darkeys attached to this regiment were so numerous and so constantly scurrying about the country—leaving the column when it was on the march or running out of the camp—in search of food for their masters more palatable than the ordinary ration, that I was compelled finally to take measures to stop a practice which had become a nuisance. I organized the Negroes into a quasi-company and placed them under the command of a staid, reliable Negro of about fifty years of age, who, on that account, acquired the sobriquet of "Captain" Jordan, I gave Jordan instructions to keep his "command" well in hand; to allow not more than four men to leave at one time, who should be absent not more than two hours; and to observe this rule, with certain others which were indicated, both in camp and on the march. Jordan strictly obeyed the instructions given him, enforced the sternest discipline in every respect, and became, indeed, a fearful martinet. Those under him used to say, "Ef you wuz burnin' in torment dat ole man wouldn't let you leave de ranks to git a drop of water."

When the soldiers, desiring to have their Negroes go after a square meal, sought, as they often did, to have him relax the rules, he would answer grimly, "I gits my orders from de cunnel."

I remonstrated with him, on one occasion, for having punished, with what I thought undue severity, a young darkey who had been guilty of some breach of discipline. "What I gwine to do wid 'em?" he said. "Jess let 'em go long to suit deyselves?"

"Oh," I said, "report them to me and I'll have them tried by a court-martial."

"Now, cunnel," he replied with fine scorn, "what's de use of you talkin' like dat. Youse knowed niggers all yo' life. Dey doan' know nothin' 'bout no cote-marshal, and dey ain't skeered of it. But ef you warms dey hides wid a switch, dey 'preciates de 'tention."

When Bragg was retreating from Kentucky and Morgan was assisting to cover the rear of the army during the pursuit of the enemy, which was kept up for three or four days, we were constantly skirmishing during that period, and exposed at times to a brisk cannonading. Jordan's squad, on one such occasion, was drawn up on the pike, nearer to the enemy than they should have been and a smart shower of shells fell around them. The darkeys were ashen with fright, and begged piteously to be taken out of danger. But Jordan, who was as fearless as he was stern, stubbornly refused to move, because, as he said, he "hadn't no orders." I subsequently complimented him on his courage, but suggested that it would have been better if he had moved out of range.

"Dar' wan't no 'casion for it," he replied. "Dem fool niggers wuz skeered mi'ty nigh to death; but mos' of de shells 'sploded way up in de a'r. Only three of 'em 'sploded on de pike, and dey didn't bust."

I may be pardoned for thinking that the best specimen of Negro logic and irony that I can remember was one furnished by an old Negro who did so in my defence. About ten years after the close of the war I was making a canvass in Louisville for the office of commonwealth's attorney for that judicial district. My opponent was also a Democrat, but at that date the party lines were not strictly drawn and nominations were not made, and he believed, with reason, that he could carry the Negro vote against me because of my having been a Confederate soldier. Some of his more zealous and unscrupulous friends circulated a report among the Negroes that I had, during the war, cut off the ears of unoffending coloured men—had perpetrated such mutilation upon a great number of them. They were, naturally, profoundly excited and angered by such a story, which there was little difficulty, at that time, in making them believe.

To the great disgust and irritation of the others, however, one old darkey declared his disbelief of the charge and his intention to vote for me. A large deputation of coloured brethren called upon him to protest against what they deemed a flagrant sin and infidelity to his race. He listened until they finished their remonstrance, and then quietly but firmly replied.

"You niggers," he said, "is all wrong about dis. Some of de white folks has fooled you. I doan' know Gin'rul Duke pussonally, but I was raised up whar he wuz born and brung up and knowed his people mi'ty well, and dey wan't de kind of people to cut off niggers' ears. But I'll make dis bargain wid you; ef you kin show me one nigger—jess one—who's done had one ear cut off—I won't ax for bofe—den I'll agree dat Gin'rul Duke cut it off, and I'll vote agin him. But onless you fetch me dat nigger wid only one ear I ain't er gwine to b'leeve no sich tale."

The receptive nature of the Negro and his fervid, emotional temperament made him peculiarly susceptible to religious impressions, and a great number of the elderly and more respectable Negroes of both sexes professed some kind of religious belief. It would not have been easy, however to define it. There were few Presbyterians among them. The doctrines of

Calvin were not readily grasped by the African understanding, and the asceticism of such a creed was altogether distasteful. With many, of course, "getting religion" was a mere hysterical fancy, conceived under excitement, and as easily forgotten. Yet I remember some who, I believe, entertained sincere and intelligent religious convictions.

It is scarcely necessary to say that they were extremely superstitious. All ignorant people are so; and the vivid Negro imagination conjured up a host of strange myths and fears. They talked much about the Devil, not only as a personage to whose custody they might be consigned in the future life, but as one whom they might at any time encounter in this world. But witches and ghosts—"sperits," the latter were termed in Negro parlance—were the chief subjects of their superstitious faith and awe. I could never clearly comprehend the Negro's idea of witches, whether he believed them to be human beings—men or women, who had in some strange fashion, by some illicit compact, become possessed of supernatural or preternatural powers—or believed them to be creatures alien to humanity, something like the fairies of European folk-lore and the genii of Eastern story.

I am inclined to think that they entertained both such beliefs, but without attempting to distinguish between them. The younger Negroes, frequently spoke of some very aged individual of their own race as a witch, but seemed not to ascribe any undue wickedness or malevolence to the persons so stigmatized, or to think him or her gifted with unusual capacity for either good or evil.

But they believed in another kind of witch—a sort of wood-sprite—which performed strange and mischievous pranks. Horses running in pastures, partly marshy and containing brier patches, frequently appeared in the morning, splashed with mud and with curious tangles in their manes. The slow-witted, unimaginative white man supposed that the animal had been wallowing in the wet ground or wandering among the briers. But the intelligent and better-informed darkey discerned immediately that he had been ridden by a witch, and knew that the knots and tangles in his mane were "witches' stirrups."

They were not prone, however, to form or to express such opinion, when a horse which had been stabled over-night showed on the next day signs of having been hard-ridden. If any darkey, especially one who was suspected of being addicted to such practices, ventured the suggestion that the horse had been witch-ridden, the others would wag their heads and significantly remark, "I reckon dat nigger wuz de witch hisself."

I do not remember any trace of the voodoo superstition, so common in the extreme South, among the Kentucky Negroes of the ante-bellum period; but have been told that it has prevailed among them, to some extent, since the war.

The belief in ghosts, however, was universal and implicit. Every deserted house, almost every secluded and weird-looking corner of the forest or field, was supposed to be haunted by some spirit which jealously guarded its peculiar premises and resented nocturnal intrusion. This was an exceedingly disagreeable feature of the Negro superstition, and made me, when as a boy I listened to their stories, feel very uncomfortable. "Doan you nuvver let a sperit see you," they would say. "Ef he once sees you, he gwine to allus ha'nt you." Near the place where I was born two duels were fought, in each of which one of the combatants was killed. There was a difference of opinion among the darkeys as to whether these spots were haunted—or should properly be haunted—for no one had ever seen a ghost at either. One side held to the opinion that every locality where a violent death had occurred was always and necessarily haunted by the spirit of the person who had so suffered. The other side contended that the spirit appeared only when foul murder had been done; and insisted that, "No white gen'elman what was killed in a fa'ar fight would 'sturb niggers what hadn't done him no harm."

A warm, reciprocal attachment almost invariably obtained between the family Negroes and the white people, more particularly in the case of those servants who were especially trusted by their masters. So much has been written about the fidelity and devotion of the old "black mammy," that I feel that little can be said on the subject, and I will only avouch that it cannot be exaggerated. The love of these old nurses for the children committed to their care, and their unremitting attention to their wants, could not have been exceeded even by parental feeling.

The most remarkable example of this kind that I ever knew was that of the nurse in the family of my mother-in-law, Mrs. Henrietta Hunt Morgan. Bouvette, or "Aunt Betty," as we usually called her, was a woman of strong sense and extraordinary character—amiable, sweet-tempered, yet very firm upon occasions, and imbued with a truly Christian spirit. She nursed all of Mrs. Morgan's six sons, including the general. To the day of her death, they regarded her as a monitress, and repaid her care with the warmest affection. Mrs. Morgan regarded her more as friend than servant, insisted that the other servants should show her every respect and attention, and relied very much upon her advice in all household matters. When Aunt Betty died the funeral services were held in the parlours of Mrs. Morgan's home, which were placed at the service of the pastor of the coloured church to which the old servant belonged. Many of the congregation attended, but Mrs. Morgan especially requested her surviving sons and myself to act as pallbearers, and we bore the good, faithful old woman to her grave.

These old nurses, although very indulgent in some respects, were autocratic and strict in all matters wherein they thought correction necessary, and would roundly scold the young ones under their charge for any serious misconduct. They sometimes asserted this privilege even after the children they had nursed had long outgrown their care and authority. But they re-

sented such interference upon the part of others, were rather jealous sometimes of even the exercise of parental authority, and usually sought to screen
the youngsters from punishment, although it might be richly deserved. On
the contrary, the elderly male servitors who occupied responsible posts,
the gardener or carriage driver, were as a rule offensively officious and
arbitrary—at least the boys thought so—in the protection of everything
about which they could possibly claim a right to be vigilant. If a boy tres-
passed on the strawberry or raspberry patches, loafed about the stables,
threw a stone at a chicken, or chased a turkey until it took refuge in a tree,
one of these argus-eyed detectives would almost certainly discover and
report the offence, and magnify it in such a fashion that there was little
chance of the offender escaping punishment.

During much of the Civil War, even after almost the entire South had
been occupied by the invading armies, the slaves conducted themselves in
a manner and with a remarkable docility, which can scarcely be understood except by those well acquainted with the Negro character. Not only
in Kentucky and Tennessee and other territory, the greater part of which
was practically lost to the Confederacy at an early period of the struggle,
but upon the more Southern plantations where slight protection was
afforded the white people, the Negroes, with few exceptions and nearly
until the close of the war, remained at home, continued their accustomed
vocations, were tractable, and gave little trouble.

Much the greater number of those—and there was a large number of
them—who accompanied the Confederate armies, and served in various
menial capacities, were faithful, the majority of them remaining with their
masters until the final surrender. These Negroes seemed to be as thoroughly
imbued with the feeling which prevailed in the Confederate ranks as were
the soldiers themselves, and spoke with as much pride of Confederate
achievement.

Impressionable and so long as under salutary influences amiable, the Negro of that generation readily accepted the sentiment of those—especially
those above him—with whom he was associated, and just as readily recipro-
cated kindness and returned gratitude and affection for considerate treatment. He was essentially conservative, disposed to adhere to first opinions,
or rather impressions, and maintaining in some measure the respect he had
been taught for certain things and certain families, even after he ceased
to entertain any personal regard for them. But beyond all else he believed
that absolute obedience was due to power—to might, whether with or without right—and when he saw, or thought he saw, the sceptre pass from the
white people of the South, nothing seemed to him more natural or proper
than that he should transfer his allegiance to the Freedman's Bureau and
the Republican Party, which, to him, then represented the authority he so
revered.

The fierce atmosphere of the strife, the terrible apprehension felt by the white people, the unwonted privations and humiliation to which the white were subjected, and the presence of the Federal troops seemed finally to bewilder and demoralize the Negro, and when the proclamation of emancipation was issued they were like creatures deprived of reason. But the radical change in their feelings and conduct was more completely wrought by their enlistment as soldiers in the Federal army than by anything else. The simple fact that they were free, startling and attractive as it was to their imagination, might have been, at first, too abstract for their exact comprehension. But when they were clad in uniform, had guns placed in their hands, were made policemen where they had formerly been servants, and invested with, at least, apparent authority—all this was an object lesson they could perfectly understand, and which fired their blood. As a war measure their military enlistment may have been politic; in every other regard it was unwise and of vast injury. Long before the Negro had acquired the discipline of the soldier he lost that which he had been taught as a slave.

If, previously, he had been ignorant and half savage, he had at any rate, been a "gentle savage." Given the bayonet and turned loose on those he had formerly served, it would have been a marvel if all of the insolence, ferocity, and evil passion that might have been latent in his nature had not been aroused. When he returned from military service to pose as a hero among those of his own colour he became a henchman of the white "scalawags" and "carpet-baggers," who incited the agitation and strife of the reconstruction period, and, abusing the confidence of the deluded blacks, robbed the whites, and well-nigh destroyed the already devastated South.

The Southern people were unquestionably the best friends the Negro had in his years of slavery, and of all those concerned in or who profited by his servitude, they had the least to do with its imposition. They resented his violent emancipation, and the untimely conferring of a suffrage for which he was not prepared. They were bitterly indignant when he was armed and employed in an effort made, they believed, for their subjugation. Since he has become a freeman, they have sometimes been compelled, in defence of their civilization and protection of their homes, to deal with him in a manner which may not have seemed compatible with the rights of freemen, and in doing so they may sometimes have erred. But I am convinced that in the future, as in the past, the Negro will find his real and intelligent friends among the people of the South.

And it is just as well and natural that this should be so. The Southern people know his better qualities as well as his weaknesses. They know that if he has sinned, others have sinned against him; and very often the wrong has been committed in the guise of benevolence. The South is the true habitat of the Negro on this continent. He will always be needed there as an agricultural labourer, and in that capacity he has no superior. He will never find a congenial home in the North. Any hope he may entertain of "social equality" will prove as mythical there as in the land where he was recently a slave, and the people of the North will never understand him as thoroughly, nor be as lenient to his faults, as the people among whom he and his fathers were reared. The Northern white labourer will also always regard him jealously, as one who may some day became a competitor more or less formidable. In the South, among the descendants of his former masters, the old relations between the whites and the blacks, but under better conditions and all compulsions removed, may be restored; and there, I hope and believe, he will receive the best incentive and the best help to attain the highest plane to which he may be destined.

45

Forgotten

Paul Hamilton Hayne

FORGOTTEN! Can it be a few swift rounds
　　Of Time's great chariot wheels have crushed to naught
The memory of those fearful sights and sounds,
　　With speechless misery fraught—
Wherethro' we hope to gain the Hesperian height,
Where Freedom smiles in light?

Forgotten! scarce have two dim autumns veiled
　　With merciful mist those dreary burial sods,
Whose coldness (when the high-strung pulses failed,
　　Of men who strove like gods)
Wrapped in a sanguine fold of senseless dust
Dead hearts and perished trust!

Forgotten! While in far-off woodland dell,
　　By lonely mountain tarn and murmuring stream,
Bereavèd hearts with sorrowful passion swell—
　　Their lives one ghastly dream
Of hope outwearied and betrayed desire,
And anguish crowned with fire!

Forgotten! while our manhood cursed with chains,
　　And pilloried high for all the world to view,
Writhes in its fierce, intolerable pains,
　　Decked with dull wreaths of rue,
And shedding blood for tears, hands waled with scars,
Lifts to the dumb, cold stars!

MARGARET T. PRESTON, ed., *Poems of Paul Hamilton Hayne* (Boston, 1882), p. 86.
　　In 1867, the Southern poet predicted that the memory of the central epoch in American History would remain for a thousand years.

Forgotten! Can the dancer's jocund feet
  Flash o'er a charnel-vault, and maidens fair
Bend the white lustre of their eyelids sweet,
  Love-weighed, so nigh despair,
Its ice-cold breath must freeze their blushing brows,
And hush love's tremulous vows?

Forgotten! Nay: but all the songs we sing
  Hold under-burdens, wailing chords of woe;
Our lightest laughters sound with hollow ring,
  Our bright wit's freest flow,
Quavers to sudden silence of affright,
Touched by an untold blight!

Forgotten! No! we cannot all forget,
  Or, when we do, farewell to Honor's face,
To Hope's sweet tendance, Valor's unpaid debt,
  And every noblest Grace,
Which, nursed in Love, might still benignly bloom
Above a nation's tomb!

Forgotten! Tho' a thousand years should pass,
  Methinks our air will throb with memory's thrills,
A conscious grief weigh down the faltering grass,
  A pathos shroud the hills,
Waves roll lamenting, autumn sunsets yearn
For the old time's return!

BIBLIOGRAPHY

BOOKS

ADAMS, HENRY. *Historical Essays.* New York, 1891.

ARNOLD, ISAAC N. *History of Abraham Lincoln and the Overthrow of Slavery.* Chicago, 1866.

ARP, BILL. *A Side Show of the Southern Side of the War.* New York, 1867.

BENNETT, WILLIAM W. *A Narrative of the Great Revival Which Prevailed in the Southern Armies.* Philadelphia, 1877.

BENTON, THOMAS HART. *Thirty Years View . . . 1820–1850.*

COX, JACOB DONALSON. *Military Reminiscences of the Civil War.* New York, 1900.

DANA, CHARLES A. *Recollections of the Civil War.* New York, 1898.

DAVIS, JEFFERSON. *The Rise and Fall of the Confederate Government.* New York, 1881, 1958.

DUKE, BASIL W. *Reminiscences of General Basil W. Duke.* New York, 1911.

DYER, JOHN WILL. *Reminiscences; or Four Years in the Confederate Army.* Evansville, Ind., 1898.

EATON, JOHN. *Grant, Lincoln and the Freedmen: Reminiscences of the Civil War.* New York, 1907.

GRANT, ULYSSES S. *Personal Memoirs.* New York, 1885.

GREELEY, HORACE. *The American Conflict.* Chicago, 1864–1866.

HACKETT, HORATIO B. *Christian Memorials of the War.* Boston, 1864.

HARRIS, ALEXANDER. *A Review of the Political Conflict in America.* New York, 1876.

HERNDON, WILLIAM H., and WEIK, JESSE W. *Life of Lincoln.* New York, 1949.

HESSELTINE, WILLIAM B. *Three Against Lincoln.* Baton Rouge, La., 1960.

HUNT, CORNELIUS E. *The Shenandoah; or the Last Confederate Cruiser.* New York, 1867.

HUSE, CALEB. *The Supplies for the Confederacy . . . Personal Reminiscences and Unpublished History.* Boston, 1904.

JOHNSON, CHARLES BENEULYN, M.D. *Muskets and Medicine.* Philadelphia, 1917.

KNOX, THOMAS W. *Campfire and Cotton-field: Southern Adventure in Time of War.* Philadelphia, 1865.

LOGAN, JOHN A. *The Great Conspiracy: Its Origin and History.* New York, 1886.

MCCULLOCH, HUGH. *Men and Measures of Half a Century.* New York, 1888.

MOORE, FRANK. *Women of the War.* Chicago, 1867.

OLCOTT, HENRY S. "The War's Carnival of Fraud." *Times' Annals of the War.* Philadelphia, 1879.

PEPPER, GEORGE W. *Personal Recollections of Sherman's Campaigns in Georgia and the Carolinas.* Zanesville, Ohio, 1866.

POLLARD, EDWARD A. "The First Year of the War." *Southern History of the War.* New York, 1863.

—— . *The Last Year of the War.* New York, 1866.

PRESTON, MARGARET T., ed. *Poems of Paul Hamilton Hayne.* Boston, 1882.

REID, WHITELAW. *After the War: A Southern Tour, May 1865–May 1, 1866.* New York, 1867.

RUSSELL, WILLIAM H. *The Civil War in America.* Boston, 1861.

SMEDES, SUSAN DABNEY. *A Southern Planter; Social Life in the Old South.* New York, 1900.

STEPHENS, ALEXANDER H. *A Constitutional View of the Late War Between the States.* Philadelphia, 1868.

VORHEES, CHARLES S., ed., *Speeches of Daniel W. Vorhees of Indiana.* Cincinnati, 1875.

WEST, JOHN C. *Texan in Search of a Fight.* Waco, Tex., 1901.

NEWSPAPERS AND PERIODICALS

ALFRIEND, FRANK H. "A Southern Republic and a Northern Democracy," *Southern Literary Messenger,* Vol. 35. Richmond, March, 1863.

HALE, E. E. "Northern Invasions," *Atlantic Monthly,* Vol. 13. Boston, February, 1864.

MALLETT, J. W. "Work of the Ordnance Bureau," *Southern Historical Society Papers,* Vol. 37. Richmond, 1909.

Atlantic Monthly. Boston, January, 1867.

Harper's New Monthly Magazine, Vol. 34. New York, May, 1867.

New York *Herald,* September 26, 28, 1862.

Scientific American, December 28, 1861; June 13, 1863; December 19, 26, 1863.

The Crisis. Columbus, Ohio, August 26, 1863.

The Knickerbocker Magazine. New York, October, November, 1862.

The Record of News, History, and Literature. Richmond, July 30, 1863.